Scientific and Engineering Applications with Personal Computers

Scientific and Engineering Applications with Personal Computers

A SOFTWARE APPROACH WITH EXAMPLES FOR THE APPLE-, IBM-PC-, AND CP/M-BASED MICROCOMPUTER SYSTEMS

RAYMOND ANNINO
RICHARD D. DRIVER

A WILEY-INTERSCIENCE PUBLICATION
JOHN WILEY & SONS
New York • Chichester • Brisbane • Toronto • Singapore

Library of Congress Cataloging in Publication Data:

Annino, Raymond.
    Scientific and engineering applications with personal computers.
    "A Wiley-Interscience publication."

    1. Science—Data Processing.   2. Engineering—Data processing.
3. Programming (Electronic computers)   4. Microcomputers.
I. Driver, Richard D.   II. Title.

Q183.9.A56   1985   502'.8'5416   85-20275
ISBN 0−471−79978−5

Printed in the United States of America

10 9 8 7 6 5 4 3 2

I fy mhlant,
Gareth,
Ellen
a Megan
R.D.D.

Marie,
the dawn
is breaking
R.A.

Preface

As scientists and experimentalists we view a laboratory computer system as an instrument to aid us in our work—to ease the burden of data acquisition and reduction, and to enhance the quality and value of experimental data. The availability of data acquisition and control hardware interfaced to personal computers (PCs), as well as the cost effectiveness of these systems, which can be a fraction of the total instrumentation cost in an experiment, has accelerated their laboratory use. In addition, the host microcomputer can be used for such tasks as modeling or word processing.

We have used computers for years in our own research and are aware of the problems faced by the laboratory user. We have also been fortunate to participate in the recent explosive growth of PCs in science and engineering. For us at least, using PCs for data acquisition and control has made laboratory work much easier. Although a number of books are available that discuss the interfacing of PCs to the real world, there is no single book that adequately discusses the important software aspects of these systems. We feel that the strength of these systems will only be realized by fully utilizing and extending the software tools currently available.

Our purpose, therefore, in writing this book is to provide the experimentalist with a single source that introduces the important software aspects of laboratory PC usage. Although the material is primarily software oriented, some basic hardware considerations are discussed. But this is *not* an "interfacing" book. Rather, it continues where many of these interfacing books end. Our contention is that whereas it is one thing to connect hardware to perform a specific function, it is yet another to have the system do meaningful work. Resolving this latter problem is our concern here.

Finally, we recognize that, in this fast-moving computer world, specific hardware and software items quickly become obsolete. But if we tried to generalize too much, the book would lose its practical value. Hence, we tried to compromise as much as possible. We use existing software and computer products in all our examples, yet at the same time endeavoring to explain the particular solutions in terms of the limitations of the system used.

RAYMOND ANNINO
RICHARD D. DRIVER

North Smithfield, Rhode Island
Cambridge, Massachusetts
March 1986

Acknowledgments

We gratefully acknowledge the help and encouragement of many people, without whom we would have surely floundered.

The systems houses were more than cooperative. Paul Warme of Interactive Microware not only furnished us with user manuals but also reviewed the text of the ADLAB software. Likewise, Rush Slivjanovski of MIA supplied documentation and a complementary demonstration disk and reviewed the EASY-LAB software description that we wrote. Cheryl Lekstrom of Data Translation sent us all the documentation she could lay her hands on. Mike Mathison, Marketing Director of Keithley DAS, supplied us with user manuals for their IBM-based systems, and Peg Burgess loaned us her copy of their Apple-based user's manual.

The people at Cyborg were super. Rick Kramer was a tremendous help in programming the ISAAC/Apple system in assembly language. Ron Sostek, Gary Gaudet, Jeff Hookaloo, Jim Ciocolo, and Joy Dardinski were always eager to demonstrate hardware, furnish us with whatever information or documentation we needed, and do whatever else they could to help us to finish the book. The people at Madwest Software provided us their graphics package, and Southwestern Data Systems kindly provided us their assembly language library package. Jeff Bernoff of Software Arts was particularly helpful in helping us develop the TKSolver engineering model and to demonstrate the power of that software. Dick Miller of the Foxboro Company guided us through the intricacies of fluid flow and came up with a modeling exercise from his handbook that is guaranteed to challenge any programmer.

Don Nadon of National Instruments and their representatives in the Boston area, Scheinffein Associates, were very willing to help and gave us much valuable information on the GPIB bus. Bill Kemper of Hewlett-Packard provided invaluable help on the HP-IL interface. We would especially like to thank the Manx Software Company and Harry Suckow for providing us a C compiler on such short notice. Other individuals and organizations deserving our thanks are Jeff Burman of Ashton Tate, Judy Hanby of Quadram, Adam Green of Software Banc, the people at Eco-C, and Tandy Trower of Microsoft. Gerard Geggis of Computer Showcase, Norwood and Leo Wong of Computer Maintenance Service gave us invaluable help in keeping our trusty Kaypros in top form.

Without the help of an old friend and fantastic programmer, Aaron Sawyer, assembly programming would have been much more difficult—if not impossible. He also reviewed and edited the assembly language chapter. Individuals who provided invaluable hints and suggestions throughout the course of this project were Jan Pejchar, Dave Johnson, Duane Thompson, Greg Maurer, Bob Vernon, and Bob McNally.

Finally, I (RA) would like to acknowledge the patience of my wife, who, for a year and a half, watched me disappear every night into my study with my faithful Kaypro II. She not only put up with this nonsense, but she learned Perfect Writer and typed a large portion of this manuscript during the day while I was at work. I (RDD) would like to thank my family for the support and encouragement necessary to complete this project, and the Delaneys for allowing me to spread my papers across their dining room table during the most intense phase of this project.

R.A.
R.D.D.

Contents

3 FILE AND PROGRAM MANAGEMENT

7 CONFIGURED LABORATORY SYSTEMS

10 ANALYSIS OF EXPERIMENTAL DATA 326

11 ASSEMBLY LANGUAGE PROGRAMMING 365

13 THE GPIB INTERFACE 453

Scientific and Engineering Applications with Personal Computers

1

Introduction
To the System

The purpose of this introductory chapter is to provide the reader with a broad overview of microcomputer usage for data acquisition and control. It, in essence, distills the contents of the book and highlights what the authors feel are the important aspects and areas of this subject with which the laboratory scientist and engineer should be familiar. Thus, in addition to defining and summarizing the subject matter, it provides the reader with a quick view of the authors' prejudices.

The only assumption made throughout this book is that the reader has some competency with the BASIC computer language.

The authors' own experience with microcomputers has been with the Apple II Plus and the IBM-PC. To date, most applications for the personal computer system in the laboratory have been made with some version of these machines. Therefore the following discussions will be directed to both of these microcomputer systems.

1.1. INTRODUCTION TO MICROCOMPUTERS

Examples of the personal-computer-based laboratory data acquisition and control systems are the ISAAC/Apple* in Figure 1.1, and the Keithley DAS IBM-PC.† in Figure 1.2. Basically, each system contains the computer itself with its own self-contained keyboard, monitor, printer, disk drive, and the laboratory interface.

A view of the Apple II Plus with its cover removed is shown in Figure 1.3. The large circuit board (shown in detail in Figure 1.4) contains a number of integrated circuit chips arranged in orderly rows (*memory*), a microprocessor (a 6502 for the Apple and an 8088 for the IBM-PC), a power supply, and, finally, along the back panel, a row of circuit-board plugs called *slots*. Looking at the computer from the front (keyboard), we see that the slots are numbered 0 through 7 from left to right. Similar circuit-board slots are available in the IBM-PC, but, unfortunately, there are only five of them.

The slots are used to plug in the special circuit-board cards (called *controllers*) that are required to interface the various peripheral devices (Disk drive,

*Cyborg Corporation, 55 Chapel St., Newton, MA 02158.
†Keithley DAS, 349 Congress St., Boston, MA 02210.

Figure 1.1. ISAAC–Apple system for data acquisition and control. Photograph courtesy of Cyborg Corporation.

Figure 1.2. Kiethly–DAS, IBM-PC-based data acquisition and control system. Photograph courtesy of Kiethly-DAS.

Figure 1.3. View of an Apple II computer with its cover removed. also shown is an interface card to be inserted in one of the slots. Photograph courtesy of Apple Computer.

Figure 1.4.   Close-up view of the apple motherboard showing the placement of the IC chips and the row of eight slots along the top edge that accepts the interface cards. Photograph courtesy of Apple Computer.

printer, ISAAC, serial communication, IEEE, extra RAM memory, etc.) with the main computer. It is quite apparent that one can quickly run out of slots. Thus the limited number of slots available in the IBM PC has been recognized as a disadvantage and expansion modules are now available from IBM and various other manufacturers.

One of these interface cards, removed from the Apple, is shown in Figure 1.3, and the placement of the various cards in their respective slots is shown in Figure 1.5. Except for the language or RAM card, which must reside in slot 0, the other cards may, in theory, reside anywhere. In our Apple-based laboratory system, the disk controller card is in slot 6, the printer interface card is in slot 1, and the ISAAC interface card is in slot 3.

A view of the disk drive is shown alongside the computer in Figure 1.6. The

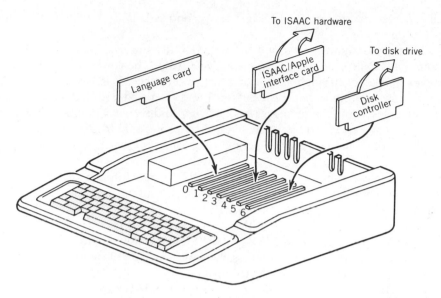

Figure 1.5. An illustration of the placement of the various interface cards in their respective slots.

Figure 1.6. Apple II Plus personal computer with dual disk drives. Photograph courtesy of Apple Computer.

disk serves as an external storage device and is a must for laboratory applications.

Memory is found as *read-only memory* (ROM) and *read-and-write memory* commonly called *random access memory* (RAM). The contents of the former never change, even when the power is turned off, whereas RAM can be altered by the user (the program resides there) and is erased with a power loss. A detailed description of memory (*memory map*) is given in Chapter 2. Memory size is usually specified by the number of bytes it can hold. A *byte* is an 8-bit chunk of data and represents one-half of a computer word. A *kilobyte* (K) is 1024 bytes.

All Apple computers contain 16K of ROM but differ in the amount of RAM that they have on the motherboard. The maximum amount of RAM that can appear on the main circuit board of the Apple is 48 kilobytes. For the older versions of the Apple, it is the main board RAM memory that is usually specified as, for example, a 24K Apple II Plus or a 48K Apple II Plus, and so on. This specification is not necessary, however, for the newer Apple IIe, which comes with 64K of RAM/ROM memory.

The IBM-PC motherboard, on the other hand, is expandable to 256 of memory. Further expansion is possible by using the slots to a maximum of 1 megabyte (M).

Some of the ROM in the Apple can be replaced by RAM, which is added to the system by means of a circuit card plugged into one of the slots. The language card for the Apple, which can only occupy slot 0, is a special type of RAM card. It contains 16K of RAM and 4K of ROM. This memory, plus the 48K of RAM that is present, exceeds by 4K the 64K directly addressable locations that can be handled by the Apple computer. This problem is handled by a memory management scheme that is discussed in greater detail in Chapter 2.

Finally, we have the *laboratory interface*, which consists of the hardware necessary to support the tasks of *data acquisition* and *instrument control*. The Cyborg designers and those from Keithley DAS decided to package all the necessary hardware separately and to connect it to the Apple by a circuit card in one of the slots. The ISAAC model shown in Figure 1.1 will accept 16 analog inputs and provide four digital to analog (D/A) outputs. The 16-bit binary/BCD input and output that is also provided can be use for anything from simple on/off switching and status sensing to high-speed data communication (see Chapters 11 and 12). Also present in the unit is a 16-bit counter coupled to an 8-channel input multiplexer and a timer.

With the systems discussed above, all connections to the experiment are made to the back panel of the ISAAC or DAS units. Alternatively, the hardware can be packaged in simple subunits and placed directly on the interface card that plugs into the Apple or IBM-PC. Connections to the experiment are then made directly to this board or to a connector from this board. An example of such an interface is shown in Figure 1.7. This is the approach

Figure 1.7. ADLAB data acquisition interface card and signal connector box. (Photograph courtesy of Interactive Microwave, Inc.).

adopted in the ADLAB,* EASYLAB,† and Data Translation‡ laboratory computer packages. Although this provides a nice, neat solution to the packaging problem, it does suffer from the obvious disadvantage that the complexity of the system is limited by the number of available slots.

1.2. GETTING STARTED WITH THE APPLE-BASED SYSTEM

There are a number of versions of both the Apple and the IBM-PC micros: Apple II, Apple II Plus, Apple IIe, IBM PC, IBM-XT, and so on. Each of these units has its own peculiar set of idiosyncrasies. As an example of getting on stream we will use the following configuration of an Apple II Plus based system.

1. 3.3 Disk operating system (DOS) (16 sectors) with either single or dual disk drives.
2. 48K of RAM on the main circuit board.
3. An Applesoft II BASIC plug-in RAM language card (A280006) with 16K of RAM/ROM.

Before turning on power, a master diskette is inserted in the disk drive. The identity of this diskette depends on the laboratory interface: With the ISAAC, a Labsoft master disk is used; with the DAS system, a Series 500 disk is used.

*Interactive Microware, Inc., P.O. Box 771, State College, PA 16801.
†MIA, RR#1, Box 137, Califon, NJ 07830.
‡Data Translation, 100 Locke Drive, Marlboro, MA 01752.

1.2.1.   Diskettes and Off-Line Storage

Diskettes are the most popular form of off-line storage for personal computers. As can be seen from Figure 1.8, a diskette consists of a circular vinyl disk enclosed in a rigid plastic envelope. The envelope protects the disk from damage during normal handling. The diskette spins freely within this envelope. Openings in the envelope provide access for the read/write head and also for the drive to enable it to grip and spin the diskette.

Information is stored on a diskette in concentric *bands* or *tracks*. Each of these tracks is divided into *sectors*. As can be seen from the detail provided in Figure 1.8. *Sector holes* are placed between sectors in the hard-sectored version of the diskette. These holes pass over the index hole as the diskette is spun, and the LED, which is aligned to shine through this index hole, provides a synchronizing signal that is used by the computer to tell the *read/write* head when to read or write information to the disk. The Apple, however, does its sector/track management electronically without using the sector holes provided. Thus, both soft-sectored and hard-sectored diskettes can be used by the system.

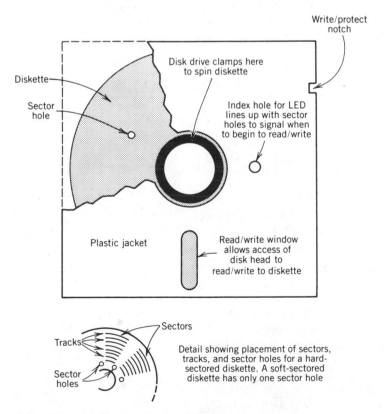

Figure 1.8.   Illustration of diskette construction.

The packing of the tracks and sectors determine how much information can be stored on a disk. So-called *double-density disks* holding 200 K or more of information on each side are quite popular these days. The Apple disk is a *single-sided single-density* type and can hold 143,360 bytes of information. The newer Apple II system contains 35 tracks with 16 sectors per track and the older system contains 13 sectors per track. This older, 13-sector version is managed by DOS 3.2, whereas the newer 16-sector diskette is managed by a DOS program labeled DOS 3.3 (more about DOS later). The IBM-PC floppy disk uses 40 tracks per disk with eight 512-byte sectors per track (compared with the 256-byte Apple track). This gives the IBM-PC formatted system 163,840 bytes of storage per disk side.

It will become obvious in the following discussion of operating systems that information stored on a diskette using one particular operating system cannot be retrieved by a program using another operating system. This also applies to DOS 3.2 and DOS 3.3, even though they are both Apple DOS. However, the Apple master disk does contain a program to convert the DOS 3.2 stored files to DOS 3.3 (e.g., see Apple II DOS Manual, p. 192).

1.2.2. The Operating System

We return now to our original thought about getting started with the Apple-based system. A master diskette is inserted and the system is powered up. When the Apple is turned on, a special program in the *Autostart ROM* takes over. Among the things that this program does is clear the screen and display "Apple II" at the top center. The program then searches to see if a disk controller card is in place (usually in slot 6). If the controller is there, the program accesses the diskette and loads the DOS into memory, runs the diskette's "HELLO" program, and then loads the language (e.g., Labsoft) on the diskette into the RAM location of the language card. The appropriate cursor is then displayed to let you know that everything is ready to go.

In contrast, when the IBM-PC is first turned on, a series of tests are automatically performed on the system, and any errors are reported immediately. The 8088 microprocessor is tested along with the internal ROM, the main memory, the video display card, the keyboard, and the floppy disk system. Read/write tests of the entire memory area are performed. Thus, a system containing a large amount of memory may take as much as one to two minutes for complete *boot-up*.

The programs performing the initial chores of getting the computer ready for a user input are part of a larger package of programs that make up the computer's *operating system* (OS). Normally, since the OS is transparent, the user pays little attention to it. However, a poor OS will quickly make itself known, since the computer, through no fault of the hardware, will appear slow, error prone, balky, and generally hard to live with. Thus, the OS is an important consideration when selecting a computer.

The computer's operating system has the important function of policing the workings of a computer system both in its hardware and its software functions. It does all the tedious unglamorous jobs necessary to make the computer work. It monitors the keyboard and branches to subroutines indicated by the keyboard entry. It also operates the display, sees that information is read and written onto disk in the proper format, and performs many other housekeeping jobs.

In addition, the OS contains routines, called *device drivers*, that allow the computer to communicate with printers and other peripherals. And, finally, the OS has a number of utility programs that make it easy for the user to complete such tasks as copying files onto disk, maintaining a directory, and so on.

As described previously for the Apple, most microcomputers today have a small portion of the OS permanently stored in ROM, with the task of booting in the rest of the OS from disk when the computer system is first powered up. The term DOS is applied to these disk-based operating systems. This process of loading DOS is called, in computer slang, "booting" or "booting DOS" or "booting the disk." The DOS is loaded into RAM, so it is lost when power is removed. Therefore it must be rebooted each time on "power up." It is a good idea to leave a diskette in the disk drive at all times, so that upon accidental "power down" and "power up" occasions, the continuous whirring, clicking, and clacking of the disk drive as the monitor program searches for DOS is avoided.

There are a number of different operating systems around, and the novice can be quickly overwhelmed by the terminology and the *buzz words* that abound. Therefore a brief tabulation and description of the important OS for microcomputers is provided in Appendix A. The OS's pertinent to this book are the Apple DOS 3.3,[*] IBM PC-DOS[†] and, MS-DOS[‡]

The Apple DOS 3.3 is an OS that is used almost exclusively on Apple-based 6502 computers or their derivatives. Its limitations are somewhat compensated for by the large amount of available software running under this system.

The MS-DOS operating system, originally developed by Microsoft for the IBM-PC under the name PC-DOS, has become the accepted standard for the 8088 16-bit processor. A large number of IBM-PC-compatible microcomputer systems using this OS have been developed recently and more are sure to follow. Note, however, that there are differences between MS-DOS and PC-DOS that can lead to an incompatibility in software from one system to another. The differences in the two operating systems will be highlighted in Chapter 3, which is concerned exclusively with filing and file management.

---

[*] APPLE DOS 3.3 is a trademark of Apple Computer.
[†] PC-DOS is a trademark of IBM.
[‡] MS-DOS is a trademark of Microsoft Corporation, 10700 Northup Way, Bellevue, WA 98004.

1.3.   OVERVIEW OF THE SYSTEM

We have thus far looked at the system as a collection of hardware, with only vague reference to its function. It might be helpful for the neophyte to review the system again in terms of functionality.

Memory

The most fundamental part of a computer system is the computer's *main memory*. Most modern memory is the semiconductor type, where a large number of bits of information can be stored in a chip no larger than a postage stamp. Information is stored in memory in binary form as a packet of on/off or hi/lo states. Each packet contains *N* of these binary states (called *bits*) coded into a *word* of information. Each of these words has an *address* associated with it, and the information contained within the word can be *fetched* or *stored* in memory by specifying the address.

As previously stated, there are two areas of RAM memory available in the Apple II Plus and, the basic system size usually mentioned when specifying a unit refers to the amount of RAM memory on the main circuit board. It is a portion of this memory that is accessible to the user for writing and running BASIC programs and storing data. The maximum size of this RAM is 48K. The rest of the system (16K) is usually found in ROM. It is important for the user to understand exactly how much of the RAM is available for program and data. A detailed discussion of memory allocation and management is given in Chapter 2.

We have already mentioned that replacing some of the Apple ROM with the RAM memory on a Language Card increases user available memory and thus provides the user with a very flexible version of the system. With such a system the appropriate language Labsoft, FORTRAN, or PASCAL which is contained on the *master* diskette can be loaded into this extra RAM memory when the system is initialized, thereby freeing some of the main board memory for programming and data storage.

Alternatively, instead of just replacing the ROM portion of memory with RAM, all of main board memory space can be duplicated on a *RAM Expansion Card*. This is the option selected by computer designers of very large programs and/or operating systems. Examples of this design are found in the Keithley DAS laboratory data acquisition system, described in Chapters 5 and 6, and Dynamic Solution's system, described in Chapters 5 and 7. Also, it is essentially the design used in the Apple IIe (slot 0 has been eliminated in this version of the Apple).

Microprocessor

The brain of a computer is called the *central processing unit* (CPU). It contains the *control logic*, which sequences the instructions held in memory; a circuit, called the *arithmetic logic unit*(ALU), which performs the arithmetic and logic operations, and a number of *registers* that are used for temporary storage. When the CPU is contained on a single chip, it is called a *microprocessor*.

The CPU understands only two states, "on" or "off." It is possible however, to describe a number of instructions by a combination of these binary states. One can imagine a bundle (or a *bus*) of wires, each of which can be "on" or "off", to be the hardware implementation for passing these binary combinations between various parts of the system. The various buses are named by the functions they perform. For example, binary-coded data are transferred on a *data bus* and the set of connections that physically connects the microprocessor to memory locations is called an *address bus*. The *control bus* carries the various synchronizing signals, such as read/write (i.e., is this read or write operation?).

Block diagrams of a microprocessor and its connections to the various buses are shown in Figures 1.9 and 1.10.

The data bus is bidirectional, that is, data can be transferred in both directions either to or from the CPU and memory or an input/output (I/O) device. In contrast, the address bus is unidirectional. Only the CPU can send address information to a unique memory location or I/O device.

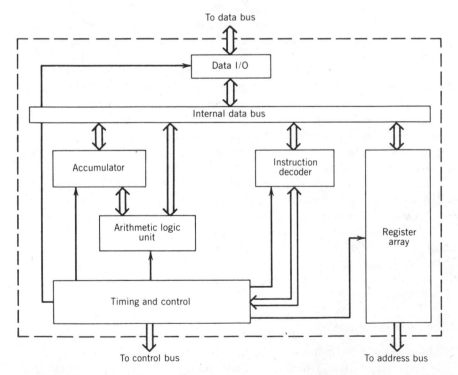

Figure 1.9. Block diagram of a typical microprocessor. From Gary Horlick, *Talanta*, **28**, 487 (1981). Courtesy of Pergamon Press.

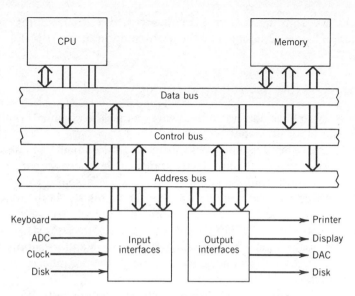

Figure 1.10. Block diagram of a microcomputer.

The I/O data bus allows the transfer of binary-coded information from external (peripheral) devices, such as a printer, monitor, tape, and disk, to and from the CPU. The particular device addressed is indicated by a *device select* code that directs the I/O information to or from the appropriate device.

Microcomputers may differ in the microprocessor they use. The Apple, for example, uses a 6502 microprocessor, whereas the IBM-PC uses an 8088. The 6502 microprocessor works on data in 8-bit chunks. Therefore, to process the usual 16-bit computer word takes more than one sequence of a fetch and store operation and consequently, the execution of an instruction requires extra time. The 8088 could, in theory, process data twice as fast since the basic processor, called the arithmetic unit, is a 16-bit register. However, the internal bus structure of the 8088 is only eight bits so the data must be passed in two chunks just as with the 6502 8-bit processor. Thus, the IBM-PC speed is reduced to that of a very fast 8-bit system.

The maximum number that can be represented by 16 bits is 65,536. This is the maximum number of 8-bit (byte) memory locations addressed by an 8-bit processor, such as the 6502. The various versions of the Apple differ in how these 65,536 (nominally, 64K) locations are organized in terms of read-only memory (ROM) and random access memory (RAM).

It should be mentioned here that since an 8-bit data-bus structure is also used with the 8088, it would appear that this system would also be limited to 64K of memory locations. How is it possible then to address over 1 Mbyte locations on the IBM-PC? The answer is found in the structure of the address buses of the two systems. The Apple uses a 16-bit address bus, whereas the IBM-PC uses a 20-bit address bus and can therefore address 1 Mbyte of memory. How the

16-bit address from the data bus is converted to a 20-bit address is further discussed in Chapter 2, along with the segmentation of the IBM-PC memory.

1.4. HARDWARE EXTENSIONS

It is necessary to have additional hardware so that the personal computer can function as a laboratory tool.

Because the computer only works in the digital domain, it is necessary to convert analog signals to digital signals. It may also be necessary to convert the digital signals of the computer back to the analog domain if one wishes to record the stored data with an analog recorder. Similarly, both analog and/or digital signals may be needed for instrument control. All of this requires additional hardware. In the not so very distant past, the user was expected to build the necessary units. This is no longer the case. Vendors supply complete hardware packages along with the software at a cost not much greater than a high-class digital recording system.

However, the particular hardware required depends both on the characteristics of the data to be collected and on the capabilities of the microcomputer employed. The user is in the best position to make decisions regarding his needs. Thus, he or she should have some knowledge of the important parameters that must be considered when selecting a particular system.

We introduce some of the important hardware considerations in the next section and discuss them in more detail in Chapter 5.

1.4.1. Analog/Digital (A/D) Conversion

There are two types of converters: *Integrating* and *Successive approximation*. The former have excellent noise immunity albeit at the expense of speed. Typically, these converters operate at 20 to 200 samples per second. The input voltage is measured by charging a capacitor over a fixed interval. The final charge on the capacitor that occurs during this fixed time interval is directly proportional to the input voltage. The time required to discharge the capacitor is also proportional to the input voltage. The analog value of this capacitor charge is therefore converted to its digital value by counting the number of clock pulses that occur when the capacitor is discharged.

The successive approximation A/D converter uses a D/A converter and a voltage comparator to determine voltage in the following manner. The most significant bit of the D/A converter is turned on, and the voltage comparator compares this voltage with the experiment. Depending on whether the D/A voltage is greater or less than the experiment, the bit is turned off or left on. The next bit is turned on, and the comparison repeated. This process of turning bits on and off continues until the D/A value exactly matches the experiment.

The successive approximation A/D converter is quite susceptible to noise. However, it is much faster than the integrating type and is therefore used in applications requiring "fast" data acquisition (200 Hz to 20 kHz data rates).

Until recently, most instrumentation application A/D converters were 12 bit. This was a compromise between price and desired resolution. Recently, 14- and 16-bit A/D converters have been reduced in price, and are now available in "laboratory interface" packages.

The 12-bit converter divides voltages into 4096 steps (the maximum value for 12 bits). If the A/D converter's input voltage range is 10 V, the value of one bit is 10 V/4096 = 2.44 mV. If your maximum signal is 10 mV, you obviously have a problem.

One solution is to amplify your signal by 1000 with an analog amplifier. Alternatively, with a 16-bit A/D converter, each bit is worth 10 V/65,536 = 0.152 mV, and you may not require any preamplifier, depending on the desired accuracy. However, if noise is of this magnitude, you must use an integrating type of A/D converter and thus sacrifice speed for accuracy.

1.4.2. Data Rate and Memory

The user must determine the necessary *sampling rate* required by the experiment and which of the A/D converters discussed earlier would be appropriate. Monitoring slowly changing temperatures may require data rates of 1 Hz or less. The usual gas chromatography analysis requires a sampling rate of no more than 20 Hz. However, some high-speed applications where the peak width may be 0.1 s will require a sampling rate of 200 Hz or more. Spectroscopy applications are varied. For spectra that are only slowly changing, the sampling rate will be determined by how fast you want to scan the optical frequency. On the other hand, transient phenomena may require rates up to 50 kHz.

Also, the type of signal processing that will be used on the data may determine the sample rate used to gather the data. For example, an accurate frequency analysis of the data by Fourier transform analysis requires that the original data be sampled at a frequency twice that of the highest-frequency component of the signal.

Finally, having determined the data rate required and the average time interval over which the experiment will be sampled, one must ascertain if there is enough memory available to handle the data. For slow data rates this is usually not a problem, because at this slow rate one can transfer each data point to mass storage, such as a diskette. For high-speed data acquisition, this is not possible, and one must have memory available on the main board for storage (this block of memory is commonly called a *buffer*) during the experiment. The data can then be transferred after the experiment.

Recently, there have appeared on the market peripheral memory boards (64K, 128K; 256K, etc.) that will plug into the various slots available on the computer's main board and emulate a disk, albeit at transfer speeds many times faster, so that for many medium-speed data acquisition experiments direct transfer to these memories solves the problem. In other cases RAM memory boards are available that can be *bank switched* by the OS to replace main board memory. A number of laboratory data acquisition systems use this technique to increase the size of their data buffer (Keithley DAS and Appligration, to name just two). Also, on many systems, data can be reduced on-the-fly, so that sample records occupy much less space. This is sometimes advertised as "compressed storage" and can generally increase by a factor of two the amount of data that can be stored. In addition, the main memory buffers can be cleared periodically by transferring the data to mass storage while another buffer is still acquiring new data.

Finally, it may be that even by eliminating any on-line processing of the data, the sample throughput demanded by the experiment is so high that it requires the full-time attention of the microprocessor. This does not leave it any time to perform control functions. In these cases it may be necessary to consider *parallel processors*. In this system the first processor is devoted to collecting and storing data, and the second processor, is used to control the experiment, process the data, and so on.

1.4.3.   Digital I/O

Digital data is data that can be represented by a series of on/off states. In contrast to analog signals it is already in a form that appears computer compatible. Unfortunately, there is little standardization in older instruments as to what voltage or current levels constitute an "on" signal and what constitutes an "off." Some circuitry using TTL (transitor-transistor logic), where 3.5 Vdc represents "on" or a bit value of 1, may be required to match the instrument to the computer.

Data transfers through the digital I/O are usually *asynchronous*. The sender sends data whenever it has data to send, if the receiver is ready to accept it. In general, the procedure involves the instrument (sender) sending the computer (receiver) a signal asking if it is ready to receive data. It waits for the computer to reply with a "yes" signal and then sends the data. The software needed to coordinate this process is called *handshaking software*, and any special lines to carry the signals may be called *handshaking lines*.

1.4.4.   Parallel IEEE-488 Standard Interface

The *GPIB* interface (IEEE-488 standard specification) fully defines the digital I/O parallel interface between the computer and the instrument. It specifies the 16-wire cable physical link between the two, the connectors, the handshaking process, all voltages, and the method of data transfer.

Instrument and computer should have plug-in compatibility if both have specified GPIB interfaces. However, there is no specification on the organization of the data that is transmitted. The GPIB interface is discussed in great detail in Chapter 13.

1.4.5.   Serial ASCII Interface

The bit code for alphanumeric characters has been defined by the American Standard Committee for Information Interchange (ASCII) and is reproduced in Appendix I. Each character is represented by eight data bits plus a start bit and a stop bit.

ASCII information can be sent serially or in parallel form. Eight of the 16 IEEE-488 lines discussed previously are designated as data lines and are for the parallel transmission of ASCII data.

An instrument with an ASCII serial transmission port (called an RS-232 link) will send the ASCII alphanumeric characters serially as the appropriate coded bit-strings. The transmission can be coded either as current or voltage variations.

The two-wire RS-232 current loop provides 20 mA for a bit value of 1. A bit value of 0 is signified by a current of 0 to 4mA. The principal advantage to this mode of transmission is that it is relatively noise free and permits one to isolate the computer from the instrument (up to 1000 ft), which may be necessary if the instrument is in a hostile environment. Handshaking lines are not provided, however, and synchronization of signal transmission and receiving must be provided by software on both devices.

The voltage mode of serial transmission is designated RS-232C. This is an Electronic Industries Association standard for representing data, in which the "1" state of the bit is represented by any voltage more negative than -3 Vdc with respect to ground, and the "0" state is represented by any voltage more positive than $+3$ Vdc with respect to ground. A 25-pin connector with handshaking and modem control lines is specified, and the utilization of each pin is defined. However, *manufacturer's sometimes change these assignments to utilize their own options.* The user must be careful that the output signal on an instrument listed as "RS-232C compatible" is available on standard connector-pin assignments.

A problem with the RS-232C system is that of noise pickup by the transmission cable. The maximum distance the two devices may be separated is limited to about 50 feet. Even so, because of the number of lines available for handshaking, and so on, RS-232C is a popular interface and is discussed further in Chapter 12.

1.5. LANGUAGES AND LANGUAGE EXTENSIONS

The sequence of instructions executed by the computer is called a *program*. Since the microprocessor can only understand binary coded information, which is difficult to write, most programs are usually written in a higher-level language. A program residing in the computer (called the *interpreter*) translates this high-level language to its machine language equivalent.

There are a multitude of computer languages available for some of the more popular microcomputers being used in scientific and engineering applications. Their relative merits and disadvantages are functions of the tasks to be performed rather than the language itself. To complicate things further, there are usually a number of versions of the same language for each computer system, each varying in its interpretation of the language standards. A list and brief description of the more popular computer languages that have been used in laboratory applications is given in Appendix B.

In reality, for laboratory applications, the user's choice of language will be limited by the language extensions supplied by the vendor for a particular computer language and computer system. Since an overwhelming majority of laboratory applications made with personal computers has been with some version of the Apple or IBM-PC, the languages of concern are Applesoft BASIC and BASICA. Applesoft[*] is a general-purpose BASIC used only on Apple computers. The language was developed by Microsoft[†] and has many features in common with Microsoft BASIC, but it is much simpler and takes up only 8K of memory. It runs under DOS 3.3 and was written in a form that allows it to be easily extended.

In common with Applesoft, BASICA[‡] is also a general-purpose, simple-to-use BASIC. It was written by Microsoft for IBM, but it is also featured in a stripped down form on other personal computers under the name Microsoft BASIC. It is probably the most popular version of BASIC on the market today. Versions of this language run under PC-DOS, MS-DOS, and CP/M and require 32K of memory.

Actually the IBM-PC comes with three versions of BASIC. *Casette BASIC* is the simplest and is contained in a 40K-byte ROM. *Disk BASIC* is an extension to this Cassette BASIC and adds the options of disk I/O, access to a date and time-of-day clock, and communications support, using a standard RS232C port. It is called by typing BASIC from the DOS prompt. An additional extension to BASIC is called *advanced BASIC* or BASICA. It is called up by typing BASICA from the DOS prompt. BASICA adds some advanced graphics commands, event trapping, and so on, to disk BASIC.

As indicated previously the microprocessor understands only machine language. Since this is a difficult and time-consuming language in which to program, so-called high-level languages like BASIC have been developed to make it easier for the user to program the computer. However, this necessitates that another program be available, an interpreter, to translate the BASIC back to machine code for the microprocessor. This works very nicely, but it takes time; that is, BASIC instructions are executed much slower than machine language instructions because of this need for translation.

To speed things up, short machine language or assembly language programs can be written to accomplish specific chores when time of execution is important. These programs can be called from a BASIC program much like subroutines. Chapter 11 is devoted to creating data acquisition programs in assembly language and illustrating their use with CALLs from a BASIC program.

---

[*] Applesoft is a trademark of Apple Computer, Inc., Cupertino, CA.
[†] Microsoft, 10800 N.E. 8th, Suite 819, Bellevue, WA 98004.
[‡] BASICA is a trademark of the IBM Corporation.

This is exactly what has been done by the various vendors who are offering the laboratory microcomputer packages. They have written machine language routines that are important to laboratory applications of the computer, and they have incorporated them into the BASIC language of the particular microcomputer they are using. With Cyborg's ISAAC system, booting Labsoft also loads the machine language routines that Cyborg has written into specific memory location. These machines language routines are called from BASIC-like high-level languages, such as Labsoft (Cyborg Corporation), QUICK I/O (Interactive Microware, Inc.), EASYLAB (Mia Corporation), or Soft500 (Data Acquisition Systems, Inc.).

For example, using LABSOFT to acquire data from an analog input to Channel 5 at the rate of one point every millisecond (ms) and store them in an array called A%, one writes only one line of code:

```
&@AIN, (AV) = A%, (C#) = 5, (RT) = 1
```

The data acquisition continues until the array is filled with the number of points specified in a previous dimension statement (e.g., DIM A% (100).

In EASYLAB the same job would be accomplished by the statement

```
Collect 5, A%,1
```

Language extensions are discussed in greater detail in Chapter 6. An in-depth treatment of the programming involved to give the user the flexibility provided by these language extensions is given in Chapter 11. An assembly language program is developed to sum 15 data points at maximum computer speed, store the sum in the proper array location, wait for a timer to signal the start of a new data burst, and repeat the process for as many times as the user has indicated. This routine is called from a BASIC program written in Applesoft and, when the task is completed, returns to Applesoft and user control.

Although BASIC, used with callable machine language programs, may suffice for most data acquisition and control problems, it may be more efficient to use one of the compiled languages for complex data manipulation. We prefer C for this purpose for the following reasons:

1. It is a structured language with an extensive library that facilitates modular programming.
2. It has a standardized code that makes it quite mobile; that is, it has been used on everything from a DEC VAX to an Apple IIe.

We have therefore included a section in Chapter 4 on programming in C.

1.6.   DATA HANDLING

Another aspect of effective computer utilization can be broadly categorized under the heading of *data handling*. There are two important areas for consideration under this title. One of these might be entitled *data management*; the other, *data reduction and presentation.*

One of the problems of computer use is the generation of large amounts of data. If one is not careful in planning how to manage this data, it will be lost. There is nothing so frustrating as knowing that you've done the experiment, but you can't recall where or under what name you filed it. Various aspects of data management are treated under File and Program Management (Chapter 3). The topic of data reduction and presentation is treated in Chapters 8 and 10 and, to some extent, in Chapter 7. The relative importance of each of the above topics will vary with the application, but data handling is an important aspect of efficient computer utilization for any laboratory data acquisition and control problem.

In the following chapters all of the topics reviewed in this introductory chapter will be discussed in greater detail and expanded to cover what we feel are important aspects of computer utilization in the laboratory.

2

Critical Areas of BASIC Programming For a PC

We are presuming in this book that the reader has some familiarity with BASIC and has done some programming. However, if the reader's experience parallels ours, most of the programming has been done on large, time-shared systems. Hence, there are some programming areas, such as those relating to direct access of memory and communication with peripheral devices, that may be as unfamiliar to him as they were to us.

This chapter will serve as an introduction to these topics, many of which will be treated in greater detail in subsequent chapters. To begin we:

1. Point out the differences in the principal dialects of BASIC in which we are interested: namely, BASICA and Applesoft.

We then

2. Introduce the reader to the memory-access commands PEEK and POKE.
3. Introduce the DOS and the DOS instruction set.
4. Discuss in depth memory allocation and usage on both the Apple and the IBM-PC microcomputers.

Finally, we

5. Discuss the use of the ampersand, &, as a method for building an extension to Applesoft.

2.1. BASICA VS APPLESOFT

The BASIC languages on the IBM and Apple computer systems are very different in their capabilities and, hence, their usefulness in scientific and engineering applications. Although a detailed description of these languages is not within the province of this book, some of the major differences between the two forms of BASIC will be highlighted here.

BASICA is an extended form of Microsoft BASIC and is available on most microcomputers. Some of the major differences between IBM BASICA and Applesoft are shown in Table 2.1. Both languages were developed by Micro-soft[*] and have many aspects in common. These have not been included in the table, nor is every aspect of the differences between these two languages discussed; the table should be self-explanatory. Further details on both may be found in the literature.

Each variable of BASICA can have up to 40 characters, as opposed to 2 for Applesoft. This makes program debugging and maintenance much more straightforward. The variable designations are extremely flexible in BASICA, since every variable may be defined explicitly at the beginning of a program. The option of using double precision variables insures the ultimate accuracy of the calculations.

The BASICA interpreter contains a number of modular and structured aspects that make program development extremely efficient. In particular, program modules may be easily moved in and out of program memory as overlays. This is described in one of the sections on program management. In that section modular programming is discussed for both BASIC dialects. In Chapter 4 the power of structured programming and the creation of a modular programming environment using Applesoft will be reviewed.

The file-handling capability of BASICA makes it an exceptionally powerful environment for laboratory data acquisition and control. This aspect of Apple-soft and BASICA is later treated in detail.

The serial communications capability of BASICA is contained in a specific subset of communications statements that integrate the interface into the software environment of BASIC. This aspect of BASICA is further discussed in Chapter 12.

2.2.   ADVANCED BASIC COMMANDS

The foregoing discussion is not meant to replace the documentation available from the vendors of the Apple and IBM-PC, which is really quite readable. This is all the more remarkable for the IBM documentation which, in the past, has been all but undecipherable. Instead we will highlight those commands that are especially important to the subject area of this book.

As mentioned in Chapter 1, the IBM-PC has a 20-bit address bus. However, the 8088 uses 16-bit addressirg. How does the system directly address a 1 M-space when 16 bits can access only 64 K? The designers accomplish this by segmenting memory into maximum segment sizes of 64 K. The program-mer must then specify the segment he/she is addressing, because the same

---

*Microsoft, 10800 N.E. 8th, Suite 819, Bellevue, WA 98004.

Table 2.1. Comparing BASICA [IBM] and Applesoft

Description	BASICA	Applesoft
VARIABLES		
Number characters	40 bytes	2 bytes
Integer	DEFINT or A%	A%
Real { single	DEFSNG or A! (4 bytes)	A (5 bytes)
{ double	DEFDBL or A# (8 bytes)	n.a.
Array base	OPTION BASE 1 or 0	0 only
Modular Programming Aspects		
Assemby	CALL varname (var list)	&name,vars
	DEF USR<n>=<int exprsn>	n.a.
Chaining programs	CHAIN statement	CHAIN machine prog.
Passing variables	COMMON variable list	n.a.
Structured Flow		
	IF. . . THEN. . . ELSE	IF THEN
	WHILE. . . WEND	n.a.
Data File Handling		
Sequential	OPEN <mode>,#n,	PRINT D$;"OPEN fname"
or random	<filename>,[<reclen>]	PRINT D$;"WRITE fname"
	multi open files n	single file
Field defn.	FIELD #n,. . .	n.a.
Input/output	PRINT #n, INPUT #n	PRINT only
Graphics Statements		
Circle	CIRCLE (x,y),r	n.a.
Line	LINE(x1,y1)−(x2,y2)	HPLOT x1,y1 TO x2,y2
Fill in area	PAINT(x,y), . . .	n.a.
Communications		
Serial comm.	OPEN "COMM options"	PR#n. . . PRINT Z$;". . .
Multiple inputs	ON COMM(n). .	n.a.
Output data	OUT m,n:byte m to port n	PR#n. . .PRINT. . .
Memory Management		
Memory segment	DEF SEG mem. segment	n.a.
Clear variables	CLEAR. [,[n]][m]	CLEAR
Erase arrays	ERASE arraynames	n.a.
Mem. location	VARPTR<variable name>	n.a.
Utility Commands		
Line numbering	AUTO number, increment	n.a.
Merging code	MERGE	n.a.

address will access a different physical location in memory, depending on the segment addressed.

With some language extensions, such as DAS's Soft500, memory management is taken care of internally and need not concern the user. In other cases, such as with Data Translation's PCLAB, segmentation is a necessary step in programming.

Memory segmentation is discussed in further detail in Section 2.4.2, which is concerned with memory mapping the IBM-PC.

2.2.1.   DEF SEG

The statement DEF SEG appears in BASICA only, and is used to facilitate addressing greater than 65,536 locations. This statement defines a "segment" of storage. Subsequent statements like PEEK, POKE, BLOAD, BSAVE, and CALL define the actual physical address of its operation as an offset to the boundary address of this segment.

```
DEF SEG[=address]
```

where: address is in the range 0 to 65,535. If address is omitted, the segment is set to BASIC's data segment. If address is given in decimals, the actual address of the segment boundary will be 16 times the value specified. If address is given in hexadecimal, add 0 to find the actual address.

For example, the line of code

```
10 DEF SEG=&H1700
```

defines a segment of memory starting at hexadecimal location 17000 (92K)

2.2.2.   POKE and PEEK Commands

Applesoft BASIC

The PEEK command is part of the utility command package that allows us to look at the contents of a particular memory location. PRINT PEEK ADR1 returns the contents (in decimal) of the byte at the decimal address given by ADR1. This extremely useful command allows the programmer to keep track of things during the development of the program. For example, questions such as How much memory is my program taking? Do I have enough room for my data? and so on. can easily be answered by addressing the proper memory location with a PEEK command. Specific examples will be given later in the chapter.

The POKE command allows one to place a number in a specific memory location. POKE ADR1, DEC stores an 8-bit quantity, the binary equivalent of the decimal value given by DEC, into the location whose address is given (in decimal) by ADR1. This command is used to pass data from a BASIC program directly into memory. Its use will be demonstrated in greater detail in Chapter 11.

BASICA

The PEEK and POKE commands have equivalent meanings in Microsoft BASIC, except that the ADR1 variable specifies an offset from the boundary address of the segment specified by the last DEF SEG statement. The actual address of the location poked or peeked is found by adding the offset to the segment boundary address. For example, the lines of code

```
10 DEF SEG=&H1700
20 POKE 0,200
```

would place 200 in the hexadecimal location 17000. The allowed values of the offset (ADR1) are 0 to 65,535.

2.2.3. The CALL Command

The CALL instruction appears both in Applesoft BASIC and BASICA. They both accomplish the same thing, but the BASICA CALL instruction is somewhat more powerful. However, utility programs are available to expand the Applesoft CALL instruction to the power of BASICA's CALL. The reader is referred to Chapter 11 for details of such a utility program, which allows parameters to be passed to the machine language program.

Applesoft BASIC

```
CALL aexpr
```

Causes the execution of a machine language program whose starting address is specified by aexpr

BASICA

```
CALL, numvar[variable list]
```

where: numvar is the name of a numeric variable.Its value, when added to the address set by DEF SEG gives the address for the starting point of the machine language routine.
variable list contains the variables, separated by commas, that are passed as arguments.
Examples of the use of both of these CALL statements may be found in the Chapters on language extension and assembly language programming.

2.2.4. The CLEAR Command

Applesoft BASIC

The CLEAR command [no parameters], when executed, zeros all variables, arrays, and strings, and resets pointers and stacks. CLEAR does not erase the program currently in memory.

BASICA

In addition to the previously described operation in Applesoft, the CLEAR instruction in BASICA contains parameters.

$$CLEAR[,[n][,m]]$$

where: n is a byte count that sets the maximum workspace for BASIC (program, data, and interpreter workspace). It might be compared in this sense with the HIMEM instruction in Applesoft that sets the highest address that BASIC can access.

m sets aside stack space for BASIC. It should be specified if you use many FOR. . .NEXT loops or nested GOSUBs.

For example, the instruction

$$10\ CLEAR\ ,\&H8000$$

restricts the BASIC workspace to 32K and leaves 4K of free space for the storage of subroutines. The change in memory space allocation before and after the execution of this command is shown in Table 2.2.

Table 2.2. The Reallocation of Memory after CLEAR

89K ————————		89K ———————————	
	BASIC program and Data (60K)		FREE (4K)
		85K ———————————	
			BASIC program and Data (56K)
29K ————————		29K ———————————	
	Interpreter Work area		Interpreter Work area
25K ————————		25K ———————————	
	BASICA		BASICA
12K ————————		12K ———————————	
	DOS		DOS

(a) Normal space allocation (b) After execution of CLEAR ,&HF000

2.3. INTRODUCTION TO DOS

As indicated in Chapter 1, besides the System monitor program, which is part of the OS, there may be another program available to control and manage disk operations. The OS is then usually renamed as a disk operation system (DOS). As the name implies this additional program is present only with a disk-based system such as we are using. In the IBM-PC, DOS is loaded from the diskette into a lower memory area ($0600 to $3600), whereas in the Apple it is usually loaded into the highest RAM memory address ($BFFF to $9D00). However, it is possible to move this program to auxiliary memory. For example, the *Saturn* memory expansion* card for the Apple comes with a routine called MOVEDOS that relocates DOS on the card. This frees 10K of memory on the motherboard for program use.

2.3.1. DOS Instructions

There are a number of simple commands that allow the user to access the DOS program for the execution of disk-related tasks. Even though these commands *look* like BASIC commands, they are not, and they do not always follow the same rules. For example, multiple DOS commands cannot be strung on the same line separated by colons. The DOS commands are usually executed from the immediate mode—that is, entering a DOS instruction from the keyboard and striking <RETURN>. However, *some*, but not all, DOS commands can be incorporated in a BASIC program (see next section) and their execution *deferred* until the program is run and that particular instruction is encountered by the interpreter.

Although the specific identifiers for DOS commands and the syntax may differ from system to system, they are all related to disk transfer and can be easily recognized. For example, to see what files are stored on a diskette from Apple DOS 3.3, one types CATALOG and then <RETURN>. With a CP/M operating system the same command is labeled DIR for directory (a not surprising abbreviation). To *transfer* files from one diskette in Drive A to another in Drive B and rename the file at the same time, one uses

          PIP B:NEWFILE1=A:OLDFILE1

from CP/M and

          COPY A:OLDFILE1 B:NEWFILE1

from IBM-PC-DOS.

As will be discussed later in the chapter, the Apple uses a memory-mapped architecture in which specific addresses in the memory space may be assigned

---

*Registered trademark, Titan Technologies, Inc. (formerly Saturn Systems, Inc.), P.O. Box 8050, Ann Arbor, MI 48104.

to certain pieces of hardware or I/O equipment and accessed from BASIC. In contrast, the IBM software can only interact with its hardware through a part of DOS called the *BIOS* (basic input/output system). All calls to BIOS are executed as 8088 *software interrupts*. BASIC also uses many of these interrupts to interact with the rest of the machine. By using interrupts as "hooks" to routines stored high in memory, the user can add new devices to the system and easily change the behavior of existing ones by writing new routines in user memory and then changing the "pointers" to access the new code. In the same way the user can modify BIOS by placing the appropriate commands into an AUTOEXEC.BAT file (e.g. see Chapter 6.2.6).

If the AUTOEXEC.BAT file is stored on the disk used to start the system, it is automatically executed after the boot. The .BAT file statements are executed sequentially as if they had been typed in from the keyboard in a manner similar to a CP/M .SUB file or an Apple II DOS 3.3 EXEC file. (See Chapter 4 for further discussion of command strings from an EXEC file.)

2.3.2.   Execution of DOS Commands From Within a Program

Quite often it is useful to execute DOS commands from within a BASIC program. For example, you may wish to store your experimental data as a file on the disk after or during the data acquisition. You can execute many DOS commands from inside a BASIC program by preceding it with a PRINT CHR$(4). The most important (to us, anyhow) of the DOS commands are those for "writing" to disk and "reading" from disk.

Filing is an important aspect of scientific programming and is treated separately in Chapter 3. We use this section only to introduce the details of the mechanics of filing to the reader.

The simple routine in Program 2.1 for saving an array of data to disk in a sequential file illustrates the use of DOS from within a BASIC program:

```
          Program 2.1.  Save Data to Disk              (Applesoft)
3000   REM SAVE DATA TO DISK
3010   D$ = CHR$ (4):REM CHR$(4) IS THE ASCII
       CHARACTER FOR CONTRL-D WHICH MUST PRECEDE EVERY DOS COMMAND
3020   INPUT "ENTER NAME OF DATA FILE";F$
3030   PRINT D$;"OPEN";F$
3040   PRINT D$;"WRITE";F$
3050   FOR I = 0 to N%:PRINT A%(I)
3060   NEXT
3070   PRINT D$;"CLOSE";F$
```

Line 3030 is the first DOS command (D$ has been set equal to CHR$(4) by line 3010). Line 3020 allows the user to name the file as a string that is identified internally as F$. The file is then opened, and the array A%(I) is "written" to the disk by lines 3050 and 3060. At the completion of this task the file is "closed" by line 3070.

You can read data from the disk in a similar manner by using only the READ command. Program 2.2 demonstrates this option and the use of the POKE and ONERR GOTO commands.

Program 2.2.   Read Data from Disk   (Applesoft)

```
2050  REM APPLE'S ERROR PATCH
2060  POKE 768,104: POKE 769,168: POKE 770,104: POKE 771,166
2070  POKE 772,223: POKE 773,154: POKE 774,72: POKE 775,152
2080  POKE 776,72: POKE 777,96
2090  :
2100  D$=CHR$(4):G$=CHR$(7): DIM H%(1000): TEXT:HOME
2110  INPUT "ENTER NAME OF DATA FILE";F$
2120  ONERR GOTO 2220
2130  PRINT D$;"VERIFY";F$
2140  PRINT D$;"OPEN";F$
2150  PRINT D$;"READ";F$
2160  FOR I=0 to 999
2170  INPUT " ";H%(I)
2180  NEXT:POKE 216,0
2190  PRINT D$; "CLOSE";F$
2200  RETURN
2210  REM ERROR HANDLER
2220  POKE 216,0:CALL 768:REM ERROR PATCH
2230  J = PEEK(222)
2240  IF J = 5 THEN IEND = I-1: RETURN
2250  IF J = 6 THEN PRINT: PRINT G$;"NO FILE BY THAT NAME":PRINT
2260  GO TO 2110
```

This is an interesting and instructive example. In the first place, we don't know how many data points are in the file, but there are less than 1000. Thus, we dimension H% to 1000, and we try to read 1000 points off the disk (lines 2150–2180). We have a problem though, and that is, as soon as we try to read a data point beyond the last point in the file, the DOS program will generate and END OF DATA error message and stop execution of the program. To avoid this interruption, we use the ONERR GOTO command. This sets a flag causing an unconditional jump to the line number named (2220) whenever an error message is generated. At line 2220 the error flag is cleared so that normal error messages will be printed; that is, we negate the ONERR GOTO instruction for program lines that follow. We do this by loading a 0 into decimal location 216 (POKE 216,0), which is the location of the error flag.

The program is then directed to location 768 (CALL 768). If you examine line numbers 2050 to 2070, you will see that we have poked numbers into locations 768 to 777. These numbers form a machine language routine starting at location 768 that is to be used in error-handling routines. It clears up some ONERR GOTO problems with PRINT and ? OUT OF MEMORY error messages.*

---

*NO! Don't try to memorize this code. Look it up when you need it in *Applesoft II, BASIC Programming Reference Manual* (Apple Computer, Inc., Cupertino, CA 95014) p. 136.

After control is transferred to location 768, the succeeding code in locations 768 to 777 is executed sequentially, and then control is returned to the next instruction—that is, line 2230.

Notice that we have two possible error messages to check. The VERIFY instruction will generate a FILE NOT FOUND error if the file named, F$, is not found on the disk. Each error will cause a unique number to be placed in location 222. If we peek at this location and set its contents equal to J, we can test J to see which error was encountered. An END OF DATA generates a 5, and FILE NOT FOUND generates a 6.

Line 2240 tests for EOD and determines how many data point, there were in the file by setting IEND equal to I−1 and then returns from whence it was called.

If J = 6, a FILE NOT FOUND message is printed along with a ring of the Apple bell (G$), and execution is returned to the input statement, asking the user to try another file name.

Similarly, by including the VERIFY command in Program 2.1, we could have built into the program, protection against overwriting files of the same name.

Program 2.3.   Save Data and Protect Files   (Applesoft)

```
3000  REM SAVE DATA TO DISK BUT PROTECT EXISTING FILES
3010  D$=CHR$(4):G$=CHR$(7):REM  CHR$(4)=CTRL D AND
3011  REM CHR$(7)=APPLE BELL
3015  INPUT "ENTER THE NAME OF DATA FILE"; F$
3020  ONERR GOTO 3080
3025  K=1
3030  PRINT D$;"VERIFY";F$
3035  PRINT G$;"FILE BY THAT NAME ALREADY EXISTS"
3040  INPUT "HIT RETURN TO CONTINUE";A$:  GOTO 3015
3045  K=0
3050  PRINT D$;"OPEN";F$
3055  PRINT D$;"WRITE";F$
3060  FOR I=0 TO N%:PRINT A%(I)
3065  NEXT:POKE 216,0
3070  PRINT D$;"CLOSE";F$
3075  RETURN
3080  POKE 216,0
3085  CALL 768
3090  J=PEEK(222): IF J=6 AND K=1 GOTO 3045
3095  PRINT G$;"DISK ERROR"
3100  INPUT "HIT RETURN TO CONTINUE";A$:GOTO 3015
```

Admittedly, we have used the VERIFY command in a somewhat confusing way to protect our files, so let's go through this portion of the program.

If a file of the same name *does* exist line 3030 *does not* generate an error message and the next two lines, 3035 and 3040, are executed to bring you back to line 3015, so that you can enter another name for the file.

If a file named F$ *does not* exist, an error message is generated and the program continues at line 3080, 3085, and finally 3090. In line 3090, we determine that the error was generated by line 3050 (since K = 1 and not 0) and we therefore ignore it by returning to line 3045 to continue the execution of the program.

In some language extensions filing is simplified because filing commands are included as part of the language extension routines. For example, with EASY-LAB only one line is required to store on disk the data array, A%, obtained in Dick Driver's laboratory on October 31, 1983, which we have named Experiment A1.

```
10 PRINT D$ "EXPERIMENT A1,DICK DRIVER LABORATORY 10/31/83,A%"
```

2.4. INTRODUCTION TO THE MEMORY MAP

For the reader whose programming experience is primarily with large systems, the question of available memory probably never comes up. In our experience, programs quickly grow in size as the user becomes familiar with the system and its capabilities. Personal computers like the Apple do not have unlimited memory. It is important, therefore, to understand how the RAM memory is arranged in order to make maximum use of it. A memory map for the reader's system can provide this information.

In addition, the reader should be familiar with the two basic *memory management* schemes employed by the Apple and the IBM-PC. *Bank switching* is easy to visualize as a hardware solution to the memory problem. The same 64K addresses are routed to different memory chips, depending on which bank of memory is switched in at that particular moment. This is the method used with the Apple. Examples of this scheme will be given using a language card or a Saturn memory expansion card as the additional physical memory, over and above that present on the motherboard, that is bank switched at the appropriate time.

Since the IBM-PC has a 20-bit address bus (whereas the Apple has a 16-bit address bus), all of the 1 M memory locations can be simultaneously attached to this bus. However, the 8088 can only produce 64K unique addresses, since it uses a 16-bit data structure to pass information. A scheme is used that fences memory into segments within which the 8088 can address up to 64K of address space. The software implementation of this scheme is the DEF SEG command previously discussed under the heading BASICA.

2.4.1. Review of the Numbering System

Before proceeding to a discussion of the memory map, it might be helpful to review some details of computer language and the hexadecimal numbering system.

Recall that a computer recognizes only two states, "on" and "off." This is the origin of the *binary system* used in machine language. The 6502 microprocessor only understands instructions coded in blocks of eight binary bits—0 to 255 (decimal). Each block of eight bits is called a *byte*. Entering binary coded instructions is tedious, but most computers can accept a shorthand representation of binary—that is the *hexadecimal number system*. Four binary digits [maximum value = 15 (decimal)] can be represented by one hex digit [maximum value = 15 (decimal)]. Thus one byte (eight bit) instruction can be represented by two hex digits.

Some further confusion may be created in the user's mind because decimal and hexadecimal notation are both used when describing memory maps in the literature. Both numbering systems are used in programming. When accessing memory locations from BASIC (the PEEK and POKE commands), the decimal designation is used, whereas hexadecimal addressing is used when programming in *assembly* language. The relationship between the two is illustrated below. See Appendix G for a complete description.

The decimal system contains the symbols 0,1,2,3,4,5,6,7,8,9. All numbers are expressed as some multiples of the power of 10. The least significant figure is given as a multiple of 10^0, the next significant as a multiple of 10^1, and so on. Thus, for a number with five significant figures [starting with the most significant (MSB) and ending with the least significant (LSB)], we have

$$(MSB)\ (X * 10^4) + (Y * 10^3) + (Z * 10^2) + (U * 10^1) + (V * 10^0)\ (LSB):$$
$$\text{for example, if } X = 2,\ Y = 3,\ Z = 5,\ U = 2,\ V = 6,$$

The number is

$$
\begin{aligned}
2 * 10^4 &= 20000 \\
3 * 10^3 &= 3000 \\
5 * 10^2 &= 500 \\
2 * 10^1 &= 20 \\
6 * 10^0 &= 6 \\
\hline
&\ \ 23,526
\end{aligned}
$$

In the hexadecimal system the base is 16, not 10. How do we write this? What do we use for 10, 11, 12, and so on? In the decimal or base 10 number system, $12 = (1*10^1) + 2$ and $10 = (1*10^1) + 0$. However, in the hexadecimal system we use letters to designate 10, 11, 12, 13, 14, and 15: that is, 1,2,3,4,5,6,7,8,9,A,B,C,D,E,F. A 15 in the decimal system is F in the hexadecimal system.*

What is the decimal value of the hexadecimal number 300?

$$(3 * 16^2) + (0 * 16^1) + (0 * 16^0) = 4096\ (decimal)$$

With the IBM-PC, to distinguish hexadecimal nomenclature from its decimal equivalent, we use & H and with the Apple we use $ before the number: for example,

$$\$FF = (15 X 16) + 15 = 255\ (decimal)$$

*Throughout we use the accepted computer language symbol, *, to indicate a multiplication.

2.4.2. IBM-PC Memory Map

As mentioned previously, the traditional 8-bit microprocessors, such as the 6502, access memory by using a 16-bit address word on a 16-bit address bus. The maximum number of unique addresses with a 16-bit word is 65,536 or 64K.

With the 8088 in the IBM-PC, we still use a 16-bit word, but the total memory that can be addressed is increased to 1024K (1 M) through a scheme called *memory segmentation*.

Each segment may contain up to 64K of data; thus, within the segment, standard 16-bit addressing can be used. The real memory locations are addressed, however, with a 20-bit address word (2^{20} = 1,048,576).

The DEF SEG statement specifies the 16-byte boundary of the segment within the 1-M address space. The segments need not contain the maximum 64K of data.

How is the 20-bit real address formed from the 16-bit segment address? In effect, the 8088 microprocessor selects the segment code specified by DEF SEG, multiplies it by 16, and adds it to the offset value specified by the instruction following DEF SEG to obtain a 20-bit physical address that is actually used to access memory.

For example, suppose we have the following:

```
10   DEF SEG 10000
20   POKE 200,10
```

The address into which the value 10 is POKED would be calculated as ((10,000)*16)+200=160,200.

A memory map of the IBM-PC is shown in Table 2.3. Normally, disk BASIC and BASICA require, respectively, 32K and 48K of memory. However, as mentioned previously, they are both written as extensions to cassette BASIC, which is contained in a 40K ROM. Only the extensions are loaded into RAM at $3700 to $5700. It is this extension that uses 8K of RAM and together with cassette BASIC forms the disk BASIC language. An additional 5K of RAM is required for BASICA.

Notice that the maximum space that can be accessed by interpretive BASIC is 64K. Compiled BASIC, on the other hand, can link to the total megabyte address space. The implication of the preceding statement is that the user has only 64K of memory in which to write the program and store the data. What good is 1 Mbyte of memory if you can't use it. This can be a problem if the language extension does not provide for it. Actually, as previously mentioned, memory management is a part of language extensions such as Soft500 and array dimensions are not limited to 64K (although, as mentioned earlier, your program is limited to 64K).

2.4.3. Apple II Memory Map for the Apple II Plus

Think of memory as a book of 256 pages with 256 memory locations on each page. This is a total of 256 × 256 = 65,536 locations, which is the maximum

Table 2.3. IBM-PC Memory Map for DOS and BASIC

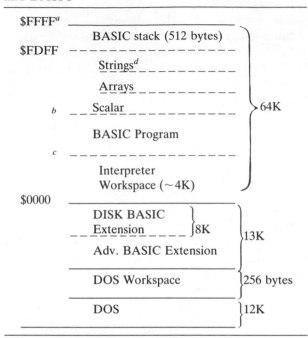

^{a} All addresses are given within the 64K-byte BASIC data segment.
^{b} The address for the end of the BASIC program is found at $30 and $31 (low byte, high byte).
^{c} The address for the beginning of the BASIC program is found at $358 and $359.
^{d} Strings build downward from high memory. Arrays build upward from the end of scalar space.

number that can be addressed by the 6502 microprocessor. *Each page* can be addressed by two Hex digits, and *each location* on a page can be addressed by two hex digits.

Let us now map out the memory for the Apple system with 48K of RAM and a language card in place along with the usual 16K ROM (see Table 2.4).

Notice the address area $D000 to $FFFF in which the language card resides. In terms of physical layout there is actually *28K of memory* available (12K in ROM on the main circuit board and 16K in RAM/ROM on the language card) that must be accessed by *only 12K of address space*. This is going to take some memory management, because 28K of memory must share 12K of address area.

With the Apple II Plus system the Applesoft interpreter program exists on the main circuit board in ROM in the address area $D000 to $F7FF. When the Apple disk is used for booting, integer BASIC is loaded into the RAM on the language card in the same address space. When the Labsoft disk is booted,

Table 2.4.   Apple Memory Map

Page		Memory Address		Location	
				Motherboard	**Language Card**
Decimal	*Hex*	*Decimal*	*Hex*		
0	$00	0−255	$0000−$00FF		
1	$01	256−511	$0100−$01FF	RAM	
2	$02	512−767	$0200−$02FF	(48K)	
3	$03	768−1023	$0300−$03F		
...					
...					
190	$BE	48640−48895	$BE00−$BEFF		
191	$BF	48896−49151	$BF00−$BFFF		
192	$C0	49152−49407	$C000−$C0FF		
...				I/O	
...				(2K)	
...					
199	$C7	50944−51199	$C700−$C7FF		
200	$C8	51200−51455	$C800−$C8FF		
...				I/O ROM	
...				(2K)	
...	$CF	52992−53247	$CF00−$CFFF		
208	$D0	53248−53503	$D000−$D0FF		First and second 4K
...	...			ROM	RAM bank
...	...			(4K)	
	$DF	57088−57343	$DF00−$DFFF		
244	$E0	57344−57599	$E0000−$E0FF		
...				ROM	(RAM)
247	$F7	62232−62487	$E700−$F7FF		(6K)
248	$F8	63488−63743	$F800−$F8FF		
...				ROM	(ROM)
255	$FF	65281−65536	$FF00−$FFFF		(2 K)

Labsoft, rather than integer BASIC, occupies this address space on the language card.

The problem of deciding which physical space will be accessed by a command to a specific address in the aforementioned area is solved automatically by the operating system during program execution.

In versions of the Apple prior to the IIe, the Apple designers did not make it easy for the user to change or influence memory management of the RAM card. It is possible to do so, however, and those readers who wish to study the procedure in greater detail are referred to some excellent articles on the subject.*

Briefly, whether the language card or the main circuit board will be acessed is determined by addressing a software switch in the $C000 area of memory.

The area of memory bounded by addresses $C000 to $CFFF is a specialized one reserved for I/O functions associated with the Apple slots. In many cases these locations do not behave at all like ordinary memory locations. Reading or Writing to these particular locations will activate their specialized function. This technique of treating external devices just like memory locations is often called *memory-mapped I/O*. It is a much simpler management system than that of the register-based architecture of the 8088, where all data handling and manipulation must be passed through a working register.

A read from a location controlling a flip-flop switch will flip the switch to its opposite state. Two position switches can also be set to each of two states by reading or writing from one of two addresses associated with that switch.

For example, the switch that places the display in text mode can be activated by poking (writing) or peeking (reading) the address 49233 ($C051). POKE 49233,0 switches the display to the text mode, whereas POKE 49232,0 switches it back to the graphics mode.

Referring to our memory management problem with the language card, we use the soft switches $C080, $C081, $C082, and $C083 when switching back and forth between main memory and the language card with Bank 2 active. $C088, $C089, $C08A, and $C08B are used when Bank 1 is to be active.

Banks 1 and 2 refer to a specific set of memory chips on the language card. Actually the language card contains 16K of memory. However, there is only 12K of address space available. Hence, two 4K segments (called Bank 1 and Bank 2) of the language card memory are made to share the same address space, $D000 to $DFFF. The segment that owns the address space is again determined by the set of soft switches accessed.

The Saturn 64K memory card performs similarly to the auxiliary 80-column card for the Apple IIe discussed later. It should not be confused with the 16K and 32K language cards, although all of them only work in slot #0. The operation of the language cards, as we have just seen, involves bank switching only the upper 12K of memory. The Saturn card, on the other hand, comes with utility subroutines (RAMEXPAND), accessible from Applesoft BASIC, that permit virtual overlays of the lower 48K of memory on the expansion board. Arrays, subroutines, and parts of programs can be saved and loaded rapidly. This program works under DOS, which must be moved from its original memory location to the second 16K bank of the 64K or 128K RAM board prior to invoking RAMEXPAND.

In addition, the Saturn card can be used as a pseudodisk. In this mode of

---

*A series of articles appeared under the heading *"Memory Management and Utilization"* in *Call-A.P.P.L.E.,* In Depth #3, All About DOS, Val J. Golding, Ed. Also see *"Switchcraft: Memory Management"* by Coleman Logan in *Call-A.P.P.L.E.,* pp. 9−11, March 1983.

operation all disk commands access this card rather than the diskette. The data transfer rates to this pseudodisk are in the range of 50,000 to 70,000 bytes per second. This can greatly speed up the execution of large, modular-type programs, which must load from disk the various portions of the program as they are needed. Similarly, an increase in speed is realized when using operating systems, such as CP/M, that require a great number of disk accesses.

A further discussion of the $C000 to $CFFF area of memory will be found in Chapter 11, where another practical example of its functions will be demonstrated.

The problem of user control of memory management has been avoided in the IIe version of the Apple, and the overall memory design has been simplified. The entire 64K address space is replicated on the auxiliary 80-column card (slot 0 has been eliminated). This avoids switching blocks of auxiliary memory into a fixed address range. Soft switches enable either main or auxiliary memories in various address ranges (see Table 2.5).

Moreover, two special routines are provided for the user: AUXMOVE and XFER. AUXMOVE is used to copy data from main memory to auxiliary

Table 2.5. Apple IIe Memory Map

MAIN		AUX
BFFF		
24K		32K
$6000 − − −	⟵⟶	
8K HGR		
page 2		
$4000 − − −		
8K HGR	⟵⟶	8K HGR
page 1		page 1
$2000 − − −		
5K		6K
$C00 − − − −		
Text/Low-resolution page 2	⟵⟶	
$800 − − −		
Text/Low Resolution page 1	⟵⟶	Text/Low Resolution page 1
$400 − − −		
0.5 K	⟵⟶	0.5 K
$200 − − −		
STACK		STACK
$FF − − − −	⟵⟶	
Page Zero		Page Zero

memory or vice versa. XFER is used to jump between programs in main memory and auxiliary memory.

Referring to our memory map, Table 2.4, notice that the first two digits (one byte) of the hexadecimal address indicate the *page number*, and the last two digits (one byte) designate the *memory location* on that page. The 6502 uses two bytes to form the address of each memory location: the page and the location on that page.

Thus, two locations are required to store a complete address. A peek at the higher-order location returns the decimal equivalent of the page number. This page number multiplied by 256 yields the absolute address of the first entry on that page. A peek at the next lower memory location yields the decimal equivalent to the absolute address on that particular page (0 to 255).

One peeks at two locations to get a complete address. For example, the decimal address of the location containing the *pointer* to the end of numeric storage in use is 109 to 110. To find the address at which numeric storage ended, one would type

$$\text{PRINT PEEK(110)*256+PEEK(109)}$$

2.4.4.   RAM Organization

User programs and data are stored in RAM memory. Certain areas of RAM, however, are reserved for system functions. It is important that the user be thoroughly familiar with the organization of RAM to be able to efficiently utilize all the available space.

A map of Apple II Plus RAM is shown in Table 2.6 as a useful reference to the following discussion.

The highest RAM address is $9BFF. When DOS is booted, 10,752 ($2A00) bytes of memory are used to hold DOS and the three disk file buffers of 595 bytes each. This pushes the highest memory location available to the user down to $9600 (38400). The contents of Applesoft program strings are stored starting at this HIMEM location on down toward low memory locations.

Some language extension programs are stored below DOS. For example, Labsoft can be used *without a language card*. In this case it is loaded below $9600 (38400), thereby decreasing by 8K the area available to the user as HIMEM is pushed down to $7000.

2.4.5.   HIMEM

The current address of HIMEM is stored at memory locations 116 and 115. Type PRINT PEEK(116)*256 + PEEK(115) to see this address.

2.4.6.   The Beginning and End of the BASIC Program

The lowest RAM memory available for a user-written BASIC program is 2048 ($0800), and this is where the BASIC program begins. The address of LOMEM

Table 2.6. Apple II Plus RAM Memory Map

$BFFF(49151)————	Highest RAM address ——————
	3 disk file buffers and
	booted DOS
$9600(38400)————	HIMEM —————————————
	BASIC strings[a]
$6000(24576) ————————————————————	
	High-resolution graphics
	page 2[b]
$4000(16384) ————————————————————	
	High-resolution graphics
	page 1[c]
$2000(8192) ————————————————————	
	BASIC variables
	BASIC program lines[d]
$0800(2048) ———— LOMEM —————————	
	Text and low-resolution
	graphics
$0400(1024) —— —————————————————	
	Labsoft reserved area
$0380 ——————————————————————	
	Apple patch area
$0300 ——————————————————————	
	Apple monitor program
	area
$0000	

[a]Strings start at HIMEM and build downward.
[b]The execution of the program command HGR2 clears this area.
[c]HGR clears this area.
[d]BASIC program lines start at $0800 regardless of where LOMEM is set. Variables are stored from LOMEM up.

is pushed up toward HIMEM by the BASIC program. However, LOMEM can be set to a higher address by a statement in your BASIC program. For very large programs it is necessary to keep track of where you are in memory as you develop your program. To find the address of the end of your program, irrespective of where LOMEM is set, type PRINT PEEK(176)*256+PEEK (175). When <RETURN> is pressed, the address of the end of your program will appear on the monitor.

2.4.7. Storage of Simple Variables

Storage of simple variable pointers and data starts at LOMEM and builds toward HIMEM. If you have not set LOMEM to some other address, the variables will be stored from the end of your program up toward HIMEM. To see the address for the beginning of simple variable space (which is LOMEM), type PRINT PEEK(106)*256+PEEK(105) and then <RETURN>.

2.4.8. Array Space and the End of Numeric Storage

Array space starts at the end of variable space. To see the beginning of array space, type PRINT PEEK(108)*256+PEEK(107). The end of numeric storage is found by typing PRINT(110)*256+PEEK(109).

2.4.9. String Storage

The pointer to the beginning of string storage is found at $6F to $70. To see the address of the beginning of string storage, type PRINT PEEK(112)*256+ PEEK(111). Strings are stored between this location and HIMEM. The storage of strings, however, starts at HIMEM and builds downward toward LOMEM. Thus, this address varies with the number of strings defined. Also, when the contents of strings are changed during the course of a program, Applesoft does not erase the value of the old definition from storage; it just stores the new one. Therefore, it is quite possible for these old string values to gradually fill this space and overwrite the high-resolution page buffers (more about this problem in the next section). To avoid this, use a statement of the form X=FRE(0) periodically within your program. This will force Applesoft to "houseclean" and get rid of the old string characters. Also, typing, at any time, PRINT FRE(0) and then <RETURN> will return the amount of memory (in bytes) below string storage space and the top or end of numeric storage.

2.4.10. Screen Buffers

The areas denoted as graphics storage areas require some explanation. Ask yourself the question, "How does text or graphics appear in its proper place on the monitor screen?" The answer is found in the memory map. Each display position on the screen is associated with a particular memory location. For example, when a screen full of text is displayed, it is really a reflection of the contents of memory locations on pages 4, 5, 6, and 7 (decimal address 1024 to 2047).

Note that your program begins at $0800 (decimal 2048). Suppose you had a set of instructions such as

```
10 HOME
20 PRINT "ARE YOU ITALIAN?"
30 END
```

These instructions would be found starting at location 2048 and on up into memory. When this program is run, the instruction HOME clears the contents of pages 4, 5, 6, and 7, and the ASCII codes for the words "ARE YOU ITALIAN?" are placed in locations starting at 1024 on up. These same codes are sent to the video driver chip, which in turn directs the characters to be reproduced on the screen.

The Hi-Res graphics areas $2000 to $4000 and $4000 to $6000 provide a display on a 280 × 192 grid (53,760 individual dots). The command HGR clears the high-resolution screen and leaves four lines of text at the bottom with a graphics grid of 280 x-positions wide and 160 y-positions high.

Similarly, HGR2 (locations $4000 to $6000) clears the screen, leaves no text space, and gives you a graphics grid of 280 × 192.

Again, let us remember that the display is a reflection of the contents of memory in these specified areas. There is no magic gate, however, to keep this memory area separated from the other areas. It is possible, therefore, to overwrite into the screen buffer.

Examination of the RAM memory map reveals this potential difficulty. Unfortunately, the Apple designers chose to locate the two screen storage areas (Hi-Res 1 and Hi-Res 2) between LOMEM and HIMEM. Two separate problems are apparent. One is related to program length, and the other is concerned with large data arrays. Fortunately, one can set the location of HIMEM and LOMEM with a simple BASIC statement. Thus, it is possible to force the program and data into certain areas.

For example, if your program is small, but you have large data arrays, include in your program the statement LOMEM:16384. Data will be stored between LOMEM 16384 and HIMEM 38400, which gives you 22K bytes of storage. You cannot use Hi-Res 2 screen, but you *can* use Hi-Res 1 if you limit your program to 6K (start at 2048 and end at 8192). Remember, you can determine the address of the end of your program by typing PRINT PEEK (176)*256+PEEK(175).

Similarly, setting LOMEM at 24577 and writing over the screen 1 area (2048 to 16384) gives you 14K for your program, the use of Hi-Res 2, and 13.8K (24577 to 38400) for your data, other variables, and strings.

Again, recall that one can always determine the number of bytes left for data storage between HIMEM and LOMEM by typing PRINT FRE(0).

Finally, for programs larger than 8K there are utility programs available that allow one to utilize all of the Apple memory*. One of these was furnished to us with our ISAAC system. It slices the program and puts one portion in memory between 2048 and 8192, skips the area 8192 to 16384 (so that you can use Hi-Res screen 1), and puts the rest of the program starting at 16384 and extending up toward HIMEM.

No such gyrations are required with BASICA on the IBM-PC. Note that the memory map indicates a clean 64K space for the BASIC program. This is possible because the color/graphics monitor adapter card has its own 16K bytes of on-board memory. It can display two kinds of text (25 rows of 40 characters or 25 rows of 80 characters) and two kinds of graphics: medium resolution (200 rows of 320 pixels each, which is comparable to the Apple computer's high-resolution mode) and high-resolution (200 rows of 640 pixels each).

Since the above referenced graphics card has 16 K bytes of memory and the two text pages take only 2K and 4K-bytes, respectively, you can store up to four 80-column pages or eight 40-column pages at once. Furthermore, through

---

*See, for example, M.J. Parrott, in *Creative Computing*, 312 (December 1982).

the very flexible SCREEN instruction, a page can be displayed independently of the page being written at the time.

One final comment regarding the Apple RAM map, and specifically page 3, is in order. The beginning locations on this page are used by many programmers for small machine language programs. It also contains a number of important monitor and DOS vectors. In our system a portion is reserved for Labsoft, which also utilizes space to give important jump vectors. There may be problems when invoking some Apple commands (such as CHAIN) that utilize this page, since initializing Labsoft may scramble page 3.

2.4.11. Soft500 Memory Management

Apple II Plus and Apple IIe

Soft500 is a copyrighted name for the Keithley DAS Data acquisition system that will be discussed in greater detail in subsequent chapters. Of interest in this chapter is the memory management scheme used by DAS for both the Apple- and the IBM-PC- based systems. In view of the rather limited memory of PC-based systems, this is an important aspect of evaluating a system for a particular task.

Because the Series 500 system is modular and expandable, as discussed in Chapter 2, there are a number of possible hardware and memory configurations. The user must run a CONFIGURE program supplied on the Soft500 disk to supply the Soft500 software with a description of the size and location of all memory expansion cards installed in the user's particular system.

Once this information has been supplied, memory allocation is managed solely by the software and is transparent to the user.

The memory maps shown in Tables 2.7 and 2.8 for the Apple II Plus-based system provide information as to how much memory is available for programming and data storage.

Note that Soft500 is indeed a very large system occupying a total of 75K (21K in main memory and 54K on the Saturn card). Also, the emphasis in memory allocation has been made to data storage. Program area is only 6K, unless one chooses to write over the graphics area, which increases this space to a total of 14K. In most cases programs dealing with data acquisition and control will be much smaller than the allocated space, and then some of this area can be allocated for data storage (through specific software commands MEMVAIL and SAVEMEM). A total of five additional Saturn cards can be managed, allowing a total of 640K of data storage.

IBM-PC

Soft500 memory management for the IBM-PC controls 1 M byte of memory. It provides space for large, data arrays, and it frees the 64K of BASICA programming space for programs.

As with the Apple system, a CONFIGURE program is first run so that the

Table 2.7. Soft500 Apple Memory Map

Apple Memory		Saturn Memory Expansion
Apple ROM	12K	
I/O ROM	2K	Free Memory
		data storage
DOS	11K	up to 74K
Soft500		
System	21K	
Applesoft graphics		
or Soft500 program		
storage		Soft500 system
	8K	
Free memory		
Soft500 program		54K
storage	6K	
Applesoft BASIC		
interpreter	2K	

Table 2.8. Soft500 Memory Map for the IBM-PC

DOS	35K
BASICA interpreter	10K
BASICA programming space	64K
SOFT500 system	96K
Free memory for data storage, and so on. Incorporated in Soft500 memory management system	483K
Series 500 I/O map and IBM graphics	64K
Free memory	192K
IBM ROM	64K

user can specify the system. The minimum IBM-based memory space required with a SOFT500 system is 128K in addition to the original 64K that comes with every IBM-PC.

2.5.   THE USE OF AMPERSAND, &, IN APPLESOFT

Finally, we cannot leave a specialized programming chapter without discussing the ubiquitous ampersand, &, of Applesoft. This is a handy tool left by the Apple designers to allow for expansion of the language, and it is used by many of the laboratory language extensions.

When the Applesoft interpreter encounters the ampersand character, it jumps to locations $3F5 to $3F7. The number 20 (this is the code for the machine instruction JUMP) is stored at $3F5, and the address for the JUMP is stored at $3F6 to $3F7 (low byte−high byte). Thus, if one writes a machine language program and stores it at some convenient location, and if the entry point address to this program is stored in locations $3F6 to $3F7, control would pass to the machine language program whenever the & was encountered during the execution of an Applesoft instruction.

The above explanation describes a rather limited use of the ampersand. The technique is far more useful if the ampersand can pass control to a number of alternative routines, and if the arguments to be used in the routine can be passed at the same time. For example, the BASIC statement

$$\&"DATIN",A,X,Y$$

calls the routine DATIN and at the same time passes the values of the variables *A*, *X*, and *Y* that must be used in the routine.

In this case the address stored at $3F6 to $3F7 points to a utility program that evaluates the string name DATIN as a pointer to the address where the program DATIN is stored. In addition, the values of *A*, *X*, and *Y* are loaded by the utility or "interface" program into the A, X, and Y registers to be used by DATIN when control is finally passed to it.

There are a number of "specialty" programs in the literature that utilize the Applesoft interpreter's own subroutines to accomplish the required evaluation of the ampersand statement to pass control to the right program. The reader is referred to Chapter 11 for a brief discussion of the technique in the section concerned with extending the Applesoft CALL instruction to include passing parameters.

It is the authors' opinion that since many of the commercially available language extensions use the ampersand convention to call their own routines, it is safer for the user to access his own routines through some version of the CALL statement. In this way user machine language programs may be incorporated in any programs the user may write using the language extension, and the routines will not interfere with each other.

However, for the readers who wish to add utility programs to their own unique Applesoft programs, we suggest they first investigate what is commercially available before attempting to write their own ampersand utilities. For example, there are libraries of ampersand-called utilities available for sophisticated manipulation of arrays—from searching and sorting to matrix inversion, transposition, and so on. These can be easily appended to your existing Applesoft program.*

The Routine Machine is used to append the ampersand utilities found in *&ARRAY* and *AMPERSOFT PROGRAM LIBRARY* available from Southwestern Data Systems, 10761-E Woodside Ave., Santee, CA 92071.

As we have indicated previously, software development is the most time-consuming aspect of computer usage and is not an efficient utilization of your time as a scientist or an engineer. If what you require is commercially available, buy it. You will be much further ahead both in the quality of the final program and the time spent in getting there.

3

File and Program Management

In this chapter we expand our discussions of advanced programming concepts begun in Chapter 2 to include some of the standard filing procedures used in BASIC. To begin, we briefly review the different information storage media which are available on microcomputers. We then follow this with a detailed description of various filing methods. In particular, we discuss the methods that are used from within the BASIC environment for both the Apple and IBM personal computers for data and program storage. Problems encountered in scientific and engineering problems provide a logical basis to the subject of data structures, which is considered later in this chapter. Finally, we briefly review the vast subject of database management as it may be used by the scientist or engineer.

3.1. MASS STORAGE

A list of the typical data storage media used on microcomputers is shown in Table 3.1 To date the 5 ¼-in disk drive has been the accepted medium on most microcomputers for the permanent storage of programs and data. Recently the availability of low-cost mass-storage devices, such as hard disks, with much more information storage capacity has changed the preferred mass-storage configuration of microcomputer systems to a single floppy drive and a single hard-disk drive. The newer microcomputer systems, such as the IBM-XT, are configured with a 10-Mb hard disk already included.

An ideal laboratory microcomputer configuration from the mass-storage standpoint is shown in Figure 3.1. A large-capacity, hard-disk drive provides central storage. The 5 ¼-in disk drive offers the flexibility necessary for program and data transfer external to the computer system. Finally, the cassette tape drive offers the possibility of hard disk data backup at a low cost. These are often used to automatically backup a hard-disk once a day.

The addition of an alternative data storage system to an existing computer system is greatly simplified if the (DOS) is capable of controlling the peripheral. PC-DOS 2.0, for example, is capable of supporting a hard disk on the IBM-PC, whereas DOS 3.3 for the Apple IIe does not. The newer PRODOS

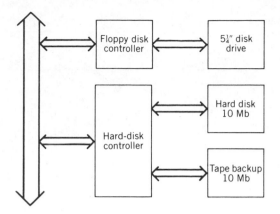

Figure 3.1.   Ideal mass-storage configuration for a laboratory computer system. (Reprinted from *Popular Computing* May 1984 "How a hard disc works," by David Powell, Illustration by Valerie Lewis.

operating system on the Apple will, however, support the addition of a hard disk.

The bubble-memory device is capable of being used as an alternative to disk drives for permanent data storage. It is the only nonmechanical storage media that competes in density with the floppy disk drives, but as yet the capacity of these devices is not high enough to provide a viable alternative for the larger hard disks. This storage media is extremely reliable, with mean time between failures quoted at around 40 years. Storing information on such systems is appreciably slower than with the volatile memory disk emulator devices but much faster than with mechanical drives.

The final method of mass storage listed in Table 3.1, the *RAM disk emulator*, is not a permanent medium of information storage. It may be used effectively as a dynamic storage media during fast data acquisition. Battery backup can extend the reliability of the method over short time periods. We include it here for completeness.

Up to this point we have been discussing mass-storage requirements on a single microcomputer system. In many laboratory situations it will be much more cost effective to network a number of systems to a single, high-capacity, mass-storage device such as a 100 M hard disk. Such a system might be configured as in Figure 3.2. Each microcomputer may retain a floppy drive and also a medium-storage bubble memory for fast short-term data storage during the daily acquisition of data in the laboratory. The network link would allow a longer-term storage of large databases. A cutaway diagram of a typical large-capacity, Winchester disk drive is shown in Figure 3.3. The multiple-disk design allows storage capacities of as much as 400 M to be achieved within the package size of a standard 5 ¼-in drive.

Table 3.1. Mass-Storage Configurations for Microcomputers

Storage Type	Dimension	Storage Capacity	Average Read Time
Floppy Disks			
Apple (SSDD)[a]	5¼	147 K	200 ms
IBM(DSDD)[b]	5¼	360 K	
Others	5¼	100−800 K	
Hard Disks			
Apple ProFILE		5 M	
IBM-XT		10 M	
Winchester	5¼" removable	10−15 M	30−80 ms
Winchester	8" Fixed	100−150 M	
Magnetic Tape (hard disk backup)			
Cassette tape	450 ft	10 M	10 M in 4 min
Bubble Memory			
INTEL 7110-4		512 K	20 Ms
Ram Disk Emulators			
Synetix RAM card		147 K	5 Ms

[a]SSDD—single-sided double density
[b]DSDD—double-sided double density

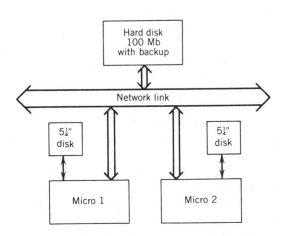

Figure 3.2. Networked mass-storage configuration.

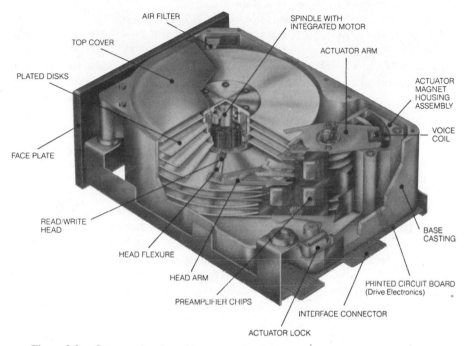

Figure 3.3. Cutaway drawing of large-capacity Winchester drive with multiple disks. Reprinted from *Popular Computing*, May 1984.

3.2. DATA FILING IN APPLESOFT

In this section we restrict ourselves to discussing the standard methods of data storage using an Apple computer's floppy disk drives. The standard Apple configuration allows for three different methods of storing data on a floppy disk. These are:

1. Sequential text files.
2. Random access text files.
3. Binary files.

The first two methods use text files in which alphanumeric characters are written on the disk in ASCII code character by character. The third method uses binary files in which the contents (or image) of a region of the Apple computer's memory that contains data may be saved directly on the disk.

Before going on to describe any of these methods in detail, it is instructive to compare the filing times for an array of identical data points under the three filing techniques. To insure a fair comparison, we have calculated the array of points from the trigonometric SIN(X) function. We have not attempted to restrict the number of significant digits.

For the random access (RDM) file we chose a *record* length of 14 in order to safely store any generated real number on the Apple computer. The storage times and resulting file lengths for various numbers of data points are shown in Table 3.2. These were all executed under DOS 3.3. All methods of filing show a sizable overhead of approximately 5 s, which reflects the time that DOS 3.3 takes to get the floppy disk going. The sequential and random access methods of filing are equivalent in almost all respects as far as data filing is concerned. With 1000 points, for example, the filing time is approximately 25% longer for the RDM case, and the disk space used is approximately the same, an indication that our field length was well chosen. The binary filing method is seen to be extremely fast by about a factor of six, and the data takes up one-third of the disk space.

There is a distinct advantage in using binary files for the storage of data when the data is numerical and stored in a data array. The other filing methods have other equally important advantages in applications, where, for example, there are mixed data types being stored that include string characters.

It is in data retrieval that the fixed field length of the random access data unit becomes a distinct advantage. Records may be retrieved directly in the case of a random access file, whereas with sequential files one must start at the beginning of the file and search until the required data is found. The data retrieval time in a sequential file therefore depends on the position of the data in the file. For random access files the time will be fairly constant and independent of the record position in the file.

In binary file data retrieval the whole data file must be read back into memory. The procedure, therefore, takes up valuable data space. However, this penalty may be acceptable if speed of retrieval is important. For example, one can read 1000 points in from a binary file in less time than it takes to read 100 points from a sequential file.

Table 3.2. Comparison of Filing Times and File-Lengths for Apple Filing Methods under DOS 3.3

Number Data Points	Sequential Time sec.	Sequential Storage recs.	Random Time sec.	Random Storage recs.	Binary Time sec.	Binary Storage recs.
1	6.1	2	5.7	2	4.3	2
10	6.5	2	6.5	2	4.5	2
100	11.8	8	14.7	8	4.5	3
1000	63	62	89	64	9.5	21
2000	116	122	170	128	15.3	41

3.2.1. Sequential Text Files

A typical program for sequential text file storage is shown in Figure 3.4. In this section we are programming within Applesoft BASIC. The standard method of communicating with the DOS from within Applesoft is by means of the CTRL-D character. In the sample program in the figure we store NN elements of the array A(..) in the file SQTL.FILE. The WRITE command in this example instructs the DOS to send the contents of all PRINT statements to the disk until a CLOSE DOS command is encountered. To add data to an already existing file, the APPEND command must be used.

```
10  DIM A(1000)
15  D$=CHR$(4)  :REM CTRL-D
20  INPUT "ENTER NUMBER OF ELEMENTS TO BE STORED";NN
 .
 .
 .
1000  REM SEQUENTIAL TEXT FILE STORAGE
1010  PRINT D$;"OPEN SQTL.FILE"
1020  PRINT D$;"DELETE SQTL.FILE"
1030  PRINT D$;"OPEN SQTL.FILE"
1040  PRINT D$;"WRITE SQTL.FILE"
1050  FOR I = 1 TO NN
1060  PRINT A(I)
1070  NEXT I
1080  PRINT D$;"CLOSE SQTL.FILE"
```

Figure 3.4. Storing data in a sequential file.
Language: Applesoft.

The opening and subsequent deletion of the file is a standard technique that guards against a file already existing with the same name. If the file does not exist, then the blank file that has been momentarily created will be deleted. The net effect is to produce an empty file at the second opening. If a file of the same name already exists, an error message to that effect is generated. After this bookkeeping, the file is set up for writing with line 1040, and the array A(I) is copied onto the disk. When all the data have been written, the file is closed with line 1080.

There are many alternative forms of coding the Applesoft-DOS hybrid commands, all of which are essentially a variation of line 1010. The file names, control characters, and so on, may be explicitly listed or specified in the PRINT statements as variables. An alternative form of line 1010 is

```
 1005  INPUT "WHAT IS THE FILE NAME?  ";FL$
*1010  PRINT CHR$(4)"OPEN";FL$
```

*The semicolon after the DOS PRINT command is optional and may be omitted.

where FL$ is the file name variable, and CHRS(4) is the ASCII code for CTRL-D.

Real numbers in Applesoft take up 5 bytes of memory location, *integers* take 2 bytes. When data is printed to the disk by means of the disk memory buffer, the numbers are converted into the *ASCII representation of each digit*. Thus, a number such as

$$-0.53278905E-05$$

takes 16 bytes on the disk, as opposed to the original five in memory, including the single <CR>, to separate the number from the next one.

One extremely important consideration, given the restricted storage space available on the standard Apple II disk format, is to try and keep a balance between maximizing valuable information and minimizing storage of meaningless numbers. For example, the input of an A/D converter rated at 12 bits provides a number to the computer memory from the A/D buffer in the range of 0 to 4095 representing 0 to 10 V. If the raw numbers are to be converted to their corresponding voltages before being stored on the disk, the converted numbers will invariably reflect the number of significant bits that are available on the machine.

The smallest voltage of significance read on a 12-bit A/D converter spanning 0 to 10 V is 0.024 V. Thus, voltage numbers may be converted easily in Applesoft to numbers containing the required significant digits by including the instruction

```
1060 PRINT INT (A(I)*1000+0.5)/1000
```

in the program, where the INT function converts a real number into the next lowest integer. Since Applesoft real-to-integer conversion is always a truncation process, we add 0.5 to round off to the nearest significant digit. Since integers in Applesoft cannot be greater than 32,767, this method cannot be used for the whole real-number space, but it is suitable for data that represent voltages in the typical ranges encountered in laboratory situations.

The command & "ROUND" in the &ARRAY* language extension utility package may be used to round an entire array to any number of decimal places.

```
100 PC = 2
110 & "ROUND" ,A(0) TO PC
```

This simple instruction rounds the entire array A(..), which should have been dimensioned prior to this point in the program to two significant figures. This may be done immediately prior to storing an array in a sequential text file in order to best utilize valuable disk space.

The recommended method for writing data to the disk file is with a <CR> (carriage return) following each number or string. The <CR> is automatically

---

* &ARRAY is a trademark of Southwestern Data Systems, 10761 Woodside Avenue, Suite E, Santee, CA 92071.

included if the PRINT statements are placed on different lines. It is not permissible to write data to the disk by using the statement

```
1060 PRINT A(0),A(1),A(2), ...
```

Commas do not have the same effect in PRINT statements in Applesoft when writing to the disk as they do when writing to the screen monitor. If one attempts to write to the disk with the above PRINT statement, the commas will be ignored, and the numbers will be concatenated in one long string.

If one requires a delimiter other than a <CR> to be placed between the numbers, one of the lines in Figure 3.5 may be substituted for program line 1060.

```
comma delimiter(,)
  1060 PRINT A(I);",";
slash delimiter (/)
  1060 PRINT A(I);"/";
spaces delimiter (   )
  1060 PRINT A(I);"  ";
or
  1060 PRINT A(I);CHR$(34)CHR$(32)CHR$(34);
```

Figure 3.5.   Using different data delimiters.
Language: Applesoft.

These program lines all use the standard Applesoft technique of using a semicolon (;) to suppress a <CR> at the end of the PRINT statement. Note that a single character may be replaced by its ASCII code, as shown by the last example in Figure 3.5, where CHR$(34) and " are completely equivalent. Note that a <CR> should be made before closing the file.

We have, until now, restricted our discussion to filing numerical data. *String* data can also be written into text files. In this case the text buffer does not have to make a conversion because the data is already in the form required for disk storage.

Reading sequentially filed data follows closely the method used for *writing* data. If the data in the data file is in numerical form, it may be read back directly into the variable array by using the INPUT statement (see Figure 3.6).

```
5000 REM READ SEQUENTIAL DATA
5020 PRINT D$;"OPEN SQTL.FILE"
5030 PRINT D$;"READ SQTL.FILE"
5040 FOR I = 1 to NN
5050 INPUT A(I)
5060 NEXT I
5070 PRINT D$;"CLOSE SQTL.FILE"
```

Figure 3.6.   Reading a sequential file.
Language: Applesoft.

If alphanumeric string data is being read with a variable A$(I), the INPUT statement will only read data into a string variable until it encounters a <CR>, a comma, or a semicolon. If the string is too long the buffer will be filled. In the event that there are characters in a text file that may cause problems, it may be wise to read one character at a time from the buffer and test the data (see Figure 3.7).

```
10  DIM A$(1000)
20  ONERR GOTO 5290
     .
5200  REM READ IN DATA ONE CHARACTER AT A TIME
5220  PRINT D$;"OPEN SQTL.FILE"
5230  PRINT D$;"READ SQTL.FILE"
5235  FOR I=1 TO 1000:A$(I)=" ":NEXT I
5240  I = 1
5250  GET T$
5260  IF T$=CHR$(13) THEN I=I+1;GOTO 5280
5270  A$(I)=A$(I)+T$
5280  GOTO 5250
5290  PRINT D$;"CLOSE SQTL.FILE"
```

Figure 3.7. Reading data from a sequential file character by character.
Language: Applesoft.

This program reads in one character at a time and tests for the delimiting character CHR$(13). If there is no match, the character is added to the string element being assembled. Once a delimiting character is found, the array counter is incremented by one and a new string array element begun. Note that the GET instruction in line 5250 is used to enter data into the computer one character at a time from the open file and not from the keyboard, as is usually the case. At the end of file when an error is encountered the file is automatically closed.

3.2.2. Text File Subroutine Language Extensions

The writing and reading of large data arrays to and from the disk by using sequential text files is a slow process in Applesoft. A matrix language extension package* for Applesoft is available that has a number of utility commands, allowing one to write an entire array of data to the disk with a single command. Filing time is much shorter with this utility program than with the standard method. Here we only mention the two of the subroutines or "quasi-instructions" used for data storage.

The single instruction

```
& "ARRAY", "W", F$, E, A(100) TO A(1000)
```

*Southwestern Data Systems, 10761 Woodside Avenue, Suite E, Santee, CA 92071.

opens a file with the name stored in variable F$; the "W" option specifies that this is a new file being opened, and E is an error-return variable. The instruction allows for only part of an array to be stored, which, for our example, is the range of elements 100 to 1000. The instruction leaves the newly created file open after completion, a convenience when writing multiple arrays or other data in sequence.

A program appending an array of data to an already open file is shown in Figure 3.8. This simple program demonstrates how standard DOS and &ARRAY commands may be intermixed.*

```
100 REM  DATA WRITE
110 PRINT D$;"OPEN ";F$
120 PRINT D$;"WRITE ";F$
130 PRINT "DATA TITLE"
140 PRINT PM%  :REM PRINT DATA PARAMETERS HEADER MATERIAL
.
.    store background information
.
200 & "ARRAY WRITE", "C", E$, E, B(0,0) TO B(2,100)
210 PRINT D$; "CLOSE";F$
```

Figure 3.8.   File writing with the &ARRAY commands.
Language: Applesoft + &ARRAY.

Down to line 200 this program is standard DOS-Applesoft syntax. At line 200 we append the two-dimensional array B(.,.) to the system parameters and then close the file. The "C" parameter indicates that we are writing data to an already opened file.

Reading the data from the file by using the & "ARRAY READ" command is equally simple. For the file created in Figure 3.8 we would require the program in Figure 3.9 to retrieve the data from the file;

```
400 REM  DATA READ
410 DIM HD$(20),B(2,200)
415 NH% = 10: NA% = 303
420 & "ARRAY READ", "R", F$, NH%,E,HD$(0)
430 & "ARRAY READ", "M", F$, NH%, NA%, E,B(0,0)
```

Figure 3.9.   Retrieving data with the &"ARRAY READ" command.
Language: Applesoft + &ARRAY

---

*These utility commands, however, cannot be used with language extension packages that also use the & convention unless they can be converted to CALL statements. More information on this can be found in Chapter 11.

The array READ command is different from the WRITE command in that it does not open the file in the conventional DOS sense. Each array READ command accesses the file at its beginning, so that, in this case, combined DOS and &ARRAY commands do not work together in a predictable fashion. For that reason the second & "ARRAY READ" command uses the "M" option to indicate that it requires data from the middle of the file, must skip the first NH% records, and then read in the next NA% into the two-dimensional array dimensioned earlier.

3.2.3.   Random Access Text Files

Random access files (RDM) represent a very clean way to store data, but they do require that forethought be given to the form that the data will take. As in the case of sequential files, a careful analysis of the significance of the data to be stored can often lead to a dramatic increase in the efficiency of data storage.

The layout of data bytes written on a random access data file is shown in Figure 3.10a. A random access file consists of a number of *records* of equal numbers of bytes. The length of this record is specified by the user when creating the random access file. In this case we show a record of 16 bytes. The records are numbered consecutively, starting with 0. Each data field representing a number normally fills a field terminated by a <CR>.

A typical program for filing data in a random access file is given in Figure 3.11. As described for a sequential file, the first OPEN and DELETE statements clear the disk of any previously written file with the same name. From here on the format is somewhat different. The OPEN command for a random access file must contain a *length* parameter. In fact, it is this parameter, shown in line 2030, that signifies that we are opening a random access file. In this particular case we are opening a file with record lengths of 14 bytes. These must be long enough to store the number and the terminating <CR> (which

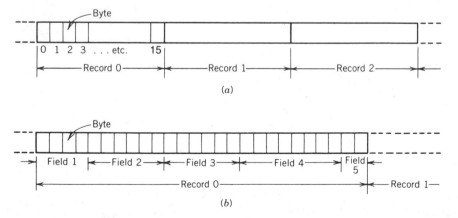

Figure 3.10.   Layout of data bytes in random access BASIC file: (*a*), for Applesoft random file; (*b*), for IBM BASICA random file.

requires 1 byte). A DOS command must be sent out for each data record being written into the file. The WRITE command is included in the FOR... NEXT loop in this case, and the record parameter R is set by the value of I and is incremented by 1 each time the program passes through the loop.

```
10  DIM A(1000)
15  D$=CHR$(4)
20  INPUT "ENTER NUMBER OF ELEMENTS TO BE STORED ";NN
    .
    .
    .
2000  REM RANDOM ACCESS TEXT FILE STORAGE
2010  PRINT D$;"OPEN RDM.FILE"
2020  PRINT D$;"DELETE RDM. FILE"
2030  PRINT D$;"OPEN RDM. FILE, L14"
2040  FOR I  =  1 TO NN
2050  PRINT D$;"WRITE RDM.FILE, R";I
2060  PRINT A(I)
2070  NEXT I
2080  PRINT D$;"CLOSE RDM.FILE"
```

Figure 3.11.   Storing data in a random file.
               Language: Applesoft.

The <CR> terminating each field is sent automatically at the termination of the PRINT line unless, as described in the previous section, a semicolon terminator is used. An additional parameter, B (byte), may be used to write multiple fields into a single record. The B parameter specifies the record byte where the number begins. The default is zero. The program in Figure 3.12 would write 10 integers of maximum length 7 bytes each, including the terminating <CR>, into a single record. This might be a preferable method of storing data from two-dimensional arrays in which one dimension of the array is represented by the field within a record and the other dimension is represented by the records themselves.

```
2030  PRINT D$;"OPEN RDM.FILE, L70"
2040  FOR I  =  1 TO NN
2050  FOR J  =  1 TO 10
2060  K  =  7 * (J-1)
2070  PRINT D$; "WRITE RDM.FILE ,R"I",B"K
2080  PRINT A%(I,J)
2090  NEXT J
2100  NEXT I
2110  PRINT D$;" "CLOSE RDM.FILE"
```

Figure 3.12.   Storing data in a random file byte by byte.
               Language: Applesoft.

What has been said about efficient data packing in the case of sequential files is equally true for the random access files with the important additional advantage that the <CR> delimiting terminators can be superfluous since we have an independent method of identifying the beginning of each number. Thus, if necessary, we could eliminate these delimiting <CR> markers and execute a further data compression, but only if we are confident of our knowledge of the data format.

We have considered at some length the mechanisms for filing data in random access files. The strength of using this filing technique is the speed with which a single record may be read. Random access files are extremely well suited for database mangement, where data must be read from the disk file at a reasonable rate. The two program lines below may be used to read a single field starting at byte 7 within the record stored in variable "RC%" into a variable A1.

```
2500  PRINT D$; "READ RDM.FILE, R"RC%", B7"
2510  INPUT A1
```

3.2.4.   Binary File Text Storage

The final filing technique that we wish to discuss for the Apple computer is that of *binary files* for storing numerical data. These files represent a memory dump of the locations in computer memory where an array of data is stored. Unlike the other filing methods, it is not possible to access individual records from the file once it is stored. The complete file must be read back into RAM if the data is needed. The comparison of filing times and storage volume presented at the beginning of this chapter is clearly convincing evidence of the usefulness of these files for data storage.

A method of storing an array of data in a binary data file is shown in the sample program in Figure 3.13. The program was written to store the first NN elements of an array A(1000). In general, NN will be equal to 1000. Two numbers are needed as parameters in the binary filing command the exact *length of the array in bytes*, and the *address of the first element of the array*. For a real array each element takes up 5 bytes of memory. Because the zero element A(0) is permissible in Applesoft, there are 5005 bytes in a 1000-element array, and to store all elements up to NN we need to store the first $5*(NN+1)$ bytes of memory, starting at the location of the first element. This number is entered by using the parameter P1 in our example.

Program lines 3040 to 3060 contain the coding necessary to obtain the address of the first array element; this may then be entered as the parameter P2 in the BSAVE command in line 3070.

```
10  DIM A(1000)
15  D$=CHR$(4)   :REM CTRL-D
20  INPUT "ENTER NUMBER OF ELEMENTS TO BE STORED ";NN
    .
    .
```

```
3000  REM BINARY FILE STORAGE
3010  REM P1   LENGTH OF ARRAY IN BYTES TO BE STORED
3020  REM P2   START ADDRESS OF FIRST ARRAY ELEMENT
3030  P1 = (NN + 1)*5
3040  A(0) = A(0)
3050  POKE 60,PEEK(131): POKE 61,PEEK(132)
3060  P2 = PEEK(60) + PEEK(61) * 256
3070  PRINT D$;"BSAVE BNR.FILE,A"P2",L"P1


Alternative forms of line 3070
3070  PRINT D$;"BSAVE ";FL$",A"P2",L"P1
where FL$ is the filename
3070  PRINT CHR$(4)"BSAVE "FL$",A"P2",L500"
```

Figure 3.13.   Storing data in a binary file.
Language: Applesoft.

Locations 131,132 (decimal) contain the address (pointer) of the most recently used variable in any executing program. Line 3040 sets this pointer to the location of A(0) by executing the statement A(0)=A(0). Line 3050 stores (pokes) this address at 60,61 (decimal), and line 3060 sets the address equal to P2.

Multidimensional arrays may be stored just as easily by using a similar technique. We show in Figure 3.14 the changes that must be made in our storage program to accommodate this. A two-dimensional array with 65 by 21 elements is being stored. The location of the beginning of the array is found in the same way as for a one-dimensional array.

```
10  DIM(64,20)
    .
    .
    .
3030  P1 = (64 + 1) * (20 + 1) + 5
3040  A(0,0) = A(0,0)
```

Figure 3.14.   Two-dimensional binary file storage.
Language: Applesoft.

The discussion so far has been for real arrays that take up 5 bytes per element. Integer arrays take only 2 bytes. Lines 3030 to 3040 will be rewritten as

```
3030  P1 = (NN + 1) * 2
3040  A%(0) = A%(0)
```

The potential saving in disk space if data can be stored in integer arrays is quite dramatic, and it is worth spending some time investing the range and accuracy of data to see whether it is suitable for binary storage.

The program steps to retrieve binary data from disk files are very similar to those for storage and even simpler to implement. The only parameter we need to specify in binary retrieval is the start address of the array specified by the A parameter, as shown in Figure 3.15.

```
3500  REM BINARY DATA READ
3505  A(0) = A(0)
3510  POKE 60,PEEK(131): POKE 61,PEEK(132)
3520  P2 = PEEK(60) + PEEK(61)*256
3530  PRINT D$;"BLOAD BNR.FILE,A"P2
```

Figure 3.15.   Binary data file reading.
Language: Applesoft.

The DOS system puts data into the Apple memory in adjacent memory locations, starting at the initial address and continuing until all the data has been transferred. If the array in which the data is to be stored was not dimensioned large enough, the data coming from the disk will overwrite memory locations used by other variables. One method of guaranteeing that we have sufficient information on the length and nature of the array to reproduce the data storage conditions is to include that information as part of the file name.

3.2.5.   File Naming

We have alluded a number of times in our earlier discussions to the necessity for a well-thought-out system of file naming. Applesoft file names may be up to 30 characters in length and may include all alphanumeric characters but the comma. We will use the period to delimit different descriptive fields, which may be configured almost like a database, to describe the stored data. An example of a file name for binary file storage of 1024-point spectrum is

$$\text{SPECT.8/26/83.B(1024);1}$$

where the first field describes the data type stored in the file; next is the date, followed by a field that indicates that a real binary array of dimension 1024 is stored in the file. A binary integer array could be indicated by B%(1024), and so on. The last number in the file name, delimited by a semicolon, might be a counter, which could be used to distinguish different spectra taken on the same day. In summary, the following is information that one might include in a file name to ease the burden of data retrieval:

1.   A descriptive field.
2.   The date of filing.

3. The type of data file.
4. The dimension of the array needed to retrieve the data.
5. An extension (and subextension) to distinguish data filed on the same day.
6. Any extenders needed by the writing program (e.g., VISIPLOT requires a .VP at the end of the filename).

3.2.6. Data Compression

Finally, a brief note on *data compression* techniques, which, when used in combination with some of the filing methods discussed, may help to increase dramatically the amount of data that can be filed on the disks. Data compression essentially concerns finding a transform that allows information to be stored in a much smaller disk space without loss of significance.

Sometimes a study of the nature of the data being produced in a particular application or experiment may lead us to new ways of storing the data more efficiently. For example, we might consider the results of a counter experiment. In this case the counter is counting events such as photons or nuclear events where Poisson statistics hold. In most photon-counting experiments the range of data is always positive and does not normally exceed 1,000,000 counts per second (it is usually much less).

From our viewpoint the importance of Poisson statistics is that the statistical variation in the data from one count cycle to the next will scale as the square root of the mean number of counts. Thus, if the mean count over many time periods falls around 100 counts per second, the root mean square variation will be the square root of 100 or $\pm$ 10%. On the other hand, if we count 10,000 counts per second on average, the variation should drop to $\pm 1\%$ if no other source of variation, such as light source fluctuation, is present.

For counts up to 32,767 we could store the counting result directly in an integer binary file (each number only takes 2 bytes of data storage. What of numbers in the range 32,768 to 1,000,000? One possible solution is to rescale these numbers by dividing by -100. A number like 32,768 can be specified with any confidence only, approximatley, to the nearest ± 200 (181 is the square root of 32,768) counts, whereas for 1,000,000 the variation is ± 1000 counts. These two numbers can thus be stored as -328 and $-10,000$, respectively, without affecting the fundamental accuracy of the data. The negative sign on the number is used to indicate which numbers have been rescaled.

It should be obvious that a simple rescaling such as this leads to an increase in data storage by a factor of 2.5 over that possible for real binary numbers. Much more compression may be possible by using other, more advanced, data compression methods.*

---

*T. Berger, *Rate Distortion Theory; A Mathematical Basis for Data Compression* (Prentice-Hall, Englewood Cliffs, N.J., 1974).

3.3.   DATA FILING UNDER BASICA ON THE IBM-PC

The I/O capabilities of BASICA/MBASIC are extremely powerful when compared to many other versions of BASIC, especially Applesoft. As with Applesoft, it is possible to store data in three types of files: sequential, random, and binary. In this discussion we concentrate on only the first two.

Central to the sequential and random methods are the OPEN and CLOSE commands of BASICA/MBASIC. These have the syntax shown in Figure 3.16.

```
OPEN <mode>,[#]<file number>,<filename>, [<record length>]
CLOSE [#]<file number>[,[#],<file number.......>]
```

Figure 3.16   Syntax of IBM file storage and retrieval commands.
Language: BASICA/MBASIC.

There are three modes: namely, "O" for sequential output, "I" for sequential input, and "R" for random I/O. The file number(s) creates a buffer for the file named by the file name. A powerful feature of BASICA/MBASIC is that a number of files may be open at any one time, and the particular file buffer selected for I/O is done with the INPUT#, GET#, and PRINT# statements, depending on the context.

In BASICA there is an alternative syntactical form for the OPEN command that is somewhat more flexible and easier to read than the form of Figure 3.16—namely;

```
OPEN <filename> [FOR<mode2>] AS [#] <filenumber>
```

where mode2 stands for OUTPUT, INPUT, or APPEND, where necessary, and the other parameters have the same meanings as before.

3.3.1.   Sequential Data Files under BASICA/MBASIC

Sequential files are very easy to create by using the above commands. The simplest way to demonstrate the method of file management is with an example. The program segment in Figure 3.17 is used to file the contents of two arrays of data, WAVELENGTH(..) and INTENSITY(..), with corresponding elements of the two arrays on the same line and separated by a comma. Headers are placed at the beginning and end of the data, and this data file is in a form suitable for transfer to a mainframe computer in a format compatible with the TEL-A-GRAF graphics package.*

*TEL-A-GRAF is a trademark of ISSCO Corporation.

```
1000 REM ------------- Filing Subroutine-----------
1005 REM Externals FNAME $, NPTS, WAVELENTH(),INTENSITY()
1010  OPEN,"O",#1,FL$          :REM open file for output
1020  PRINT #1,"INPUT DATA." :REM add file header
1025  WRITE #1,SERIES$          :REM series name with quotes
1030  FOR I = 1 TO NPTS
1040   PRINT #1 USING "####.#,";WAVELENGTH(I);
1050   PRINT #1 USING "#.####^^^^";INTENSITY(I)
1060  NEXT I
1070  PRINT "END OF DATA."   :REM end of data string
1080  CLOSE #1
1090 RETURN
```

Figure 3.17. Storing data in sequential files under BASICA/MBASIC
             Language: BASICA/MBASIC.

The OPEN command creates a buffer (#1) for data transfer to the file named in the variable FL\$. If any file with the same name is already present on the disk, it will be destroyed by this command. The 'PRINT #' commands are used to transfer data to the buffer file, and the 'PRINT # USING' command formats the data in the form in which we wish it to be stored. The '####.#,' format prints a number to the buffer in real form followed by a comma, whereas the '#.####^^^^' produces a number in scientific notation. A semicolon at the end of line 1040 suppresses the <CR> and produces the following data on the disk. The WRITE # command writes the contents of the string variable surrounded by quotes.

```
INPUT DATA.
"SPECTRUM 1"
   .
   .
   .
3234.5 , 5.3245E+04
END OF DATA.
```

In BASICA line 1010 could also be written

```
1010   OPEN FNAME$ FOR OUTPUT AS #1
```

which is much easier to read.

Data may be appended to a sequential text file in BASICA by using the statement.

```
OPEN FNAME$ FOR APPEND AS #1
```

The other form of OPEN that is used in both BASICA and MBASIC does not have a specific parameter for append. The more complicated form of Figure 3.18 must be used in this case. A dummy file for writing is first opened with "I." The file to be appended for reading is then opened with "O." The contents of this file are then read into the dummy file, followed by the new data to be appended to that file. Finally, the dummy file is closed, the first file destroyed, and the dummy file renamed with the original file name. The program demonstrates some advanced aspects of BASICA/MBASIC, such as the simultaneous use of two open files.

```
2000 REM-----Appending Data To A File
2010 ON ERROR GOTO 2200  :REM if no file create one
2020 OPEN,"I",#1,FL$:REM only executed if a file exists
2030 OPEN,"O",#2,"DUMMY"
2040 LINE INPUT#1,L$
2050 IF L$ = "END OF DATA." GOTO 2080
2060 PRINT#2,L$
2070 GOTO 2040
2080 CLOSE #1: KILL FNAME$
2090 REM---------- Add New Data Here
2100 WRITE #2,SERIES$
2110 FOR I = 1 TO NPTS
2120   PRINT #2, USING "####.#,";WAVELENGTH(I);
2130   PRINT #2, USING "#.####^^^^";INTENSITY(I)
2140 NEXT I
2150 PRINT #2, "END OF DATA."
2160 CLOSE #2
2170 NAME "DUMMY" AS FL$
2180 RETURN
2200  IF ERR=53 AND ERL = 2020 THEN OPEN "O",#2,
      "DUMMY": PRINT #2,"INPUT DATA.":  RESUME 2090
2210 END
```

Figure 3.18.   Appending data to an MBASIC sequential file.
Language: BASICA/MBASIC

If no previous file exists with the name contained in FL$, an error message is normally generated, and the program would stop executing at this point. However, line 2010 will instead force a jump to line 2200 where a check is made to ascertain that file existence error (ERR 53) has occurred and that the program has reached there from line 2020 (ERL), after which the dummy file is opened and the header is put at the beginning. If there is no error at line 2020 then lines 2030 to 2080 will be executed to transfer the existing data from the old file.

The action of this subroutine is equivalent to the preceding example for the case when no previous file exists. If, on the other hand, a previous file does exist, the new data will be effectively appended to the existing data, with INPUT DATA. and END OF DATA. appearing at the beginning and the end of the file, respectively. Each series of data will be preceded by its series name in quotes.

3.3.2. Random Data Files under BASICA/MBASIC

Data is stored in random files on the IBM-PC in a data compressed mode using a packed binary format. This is comparable to storage in sequential files in standard ASCII format. The individual units of the random files are the records. Each record is in turn divided into a number of fields that identify the different quantities being stored as we show in Figure 3.10b.

We give in Figure 3.19 a short example for writing data into a random access file. The example is of the type often found in scientific applications in which we might wish to keep an independent record of the sequential data files contained on a disk in a single "library" or "data base" file for that disk. Data-bases in particular are almost always created with random files.

Let us specify that each sequential spectrum file from our previous example is given a unique identification number code, CODE%, with which that data can always be found. To each of these sequentially numbered files we delegate a single record in our random "library" file that contains the minimum information to indicate the contents of the corresponding spectrum file.

The minimum information that we require is specified in Table 3.3:

The information will be written to the random library file from within the same program that creates the spectrum data file itself. The variables listed on the left in Table 3.3 contain the information that we want to store in a single random file record. For each piece of information, we must specify a string-variable field label F1$ to F5$ by which the data is referenced in the random access buffer and the corresponding length is delegated to it in the buffer.

The program subroutine in Figure 3.19 demonstrates the method of adding a record to a random file 'SPECTRUM.CAT', where we have added our own extension CAT to indicate that it is a catalog of information.

```
3000  REM  ADD DATA TO RANDOM FILE SUBROUTINE
3005  REM EXTERNAL  WAVELENGTH( ), NPTS, NSERIES%, SPECIES$ ,CODE%
3010  OPEN "R" ,#3 ,"SPECTRUM.CAT" ,26
3020  FIELD #3 ,4 AS F1$ ,6 AS F2$ ,6 AS F3$ ,8 AS F4$ ,2 AS F5$
3030  LSET F1$  = MKS$(NPTS)
3040  LSET F2$  = MKS$ (WAVELENGTH(1))
3050  LSET F3$  = MKS$ (WAVELENGHT(NPTS))
3060  LSET F4$  = SPECIES$
3070  LSET F5$  = MKI(NSERIES%)
3080  PUT #3 ,CODE%
3090  CLOSE #3
3095  RETURN
```

Figure 3.19. Random file storage routine under BASICA/MBASIC.

Table 3.3.   Configuration of Spectrum Data Record

Variable	Field	Length (bytes)	Description
NPTS	F1$	4	number of points in spectrum
WAVELENGTH(1)	F2$	6	starting wavelength
WAVELENGTH(NPTS)	F3$	6	end wavelength
SPECIES$	F4$	8	name of species scanned
NSERIES%	F5$	2	number of data series in file
TOTAL LENGTH		26 bytes	

After opening the random access file as file number 3, the user must do some preparatory work to set up the data fields with the FIELD statement prior to any data filing. Data must be moved from the computer memory to the random buffer with the LSET (or RSET) statements: LSET left-justifies the data in the buffer variable, and RSET right justifies. Variable conversions MKS$, MKI$ are required to convert the data being moved to the buffer into data strings. Data is moved to the disk from the random access buffer with the PUT statement.

Data is read from a random-access file in a very similar manner. A GET statement is used instead of PUT. (Note that GET in Applesoft has an entirely different meaning.) Substituting lines 3030 to 3080 in Figure 3.20 with the following code returns the values to the proper variables.

```
3030 GET #3,CODE%
3040 NPTS = CVS(F1$)
  .
3070 SERIES$ = F4$
3080 NSERIES% = CVI(F5$)
```

Figure 3.20.   Retrieving data from a random file under BASICA/MBASIC.

When moving data from a buffer variable to a standard BASICA/MBASIC variable, you may place the buffer variables directly on the right side of the equivalence statement so long as the correct mode conversions—CVS (string to single precision) and CVI (string to integer)—are made.

3.4.   PROGRAM MANGEMENT UNDER APPLESOFT

To make programming in Applesoft BASIC easier, we must be able to create a flexible programming environment in which programs may be effectively managed. The concept of modular program design figures strongly in this regard.

We discuss in Chapter 4 the subject of writing modular programs. For this to be done effectively there must be a method of *chaining* programs in a way that does not restrict one to the size of the computer's memory. In program development, for example, we may wish the coding perfected for one laboratory task to be transferable to other applications. Both of these aspects of program management are dealt with in this section.

3.4.1. Chaining Programs Together

Because of the lack of sufficient memory, in many programming situations in Applesoft it is not desirable to have the whole program code in computer memory at one time. At other times it may be necessary to operate on the same data set with a number of related programs that cannot simultaneously fit into memory. In these cases it is convenient to carry out some form of program chaining.

The simplest method of program chaining is to run one program within another program by using the CTRL-D character to signal DOS commands within Applesoft. Let us say that we are running a data acquisition program and have created an array of data, A(NN). Now we wish to operate on this data with a smoothing program "SMOOTH.BAS". We could use the lines of code given in Figure 3.21.

```
        .
        .
975 A(0) = NN  :  REM STORE NUMBER OF POINTS
    .  set up parameters P1, P2 here
980 PRINT D$; "BSAVE TEMP.DAT, A"P1",L"P2
985 PRINT D$; "RUN SMOOTH.BAS"
990 END
```

Figure 3.21. Passing data to and running a program from within an executing program.

The important point here is that we save the array of data in a temporary file, TEMP.DAT, that includes the parameter NN describing the number of data points. This method is described in Figure 3.13. Other important parameters might be passed in this temporary file as well as the data itself. Once line 985 is executed, the computer's memory is cleared and the new program, SMOOTH.BAS, is loaded into memory and run. SMOOTH.BAS must read the data in as one of its first tasks. The concept of modularity can be extended by always returning to a menu program after the completion of any other program in the system. In this way a complex series of tasks can be executed within a single programming environment with minimal operator effort.

Due to the relative slowness of disk access, it may not always be desirable to store data on the disk as an intermediate step. The data may not be as straightforward as a single data array, and there may be string data involved that would have to be stored in sequential files—a much more time-consuming prospect. In these circumstances we may use the CHAIN program included on the Apple DOS 3.3 system master disk. The CHAIN program must be transferred to the disk that contains the programs to be chained. The simple two-line program shown in Figure 3.22 is sufficient to perform the program transfer and, this time, leave the whole variable list in the system's memory untouched.

```
10  D$=CHR$(4)
950  REM RUN SMOOTHING PROGRAM
955  PRINT D$;"BLOAD CHAIN, A520"
960  CALL 520"SMOOTH.BAS"
```

Figure 3.22.   Chaining to a program from within an executing program.
Language: Applesoft.

A large number of programs that share a common variable list may be run sequentially in a single programming environment. A complete explanation of this procedure can be found in the Apple DOS 3.3 manual.

3.4.2.   The EXEC Command

The EXEC command is one of the most powerful aspects of the Apple computer's DOS 3.3 command language. With a little imagination it can be used creatively as a convenient tool for modular programming. The EXEC command operates on text files. The file becomes the substitute path for input data to the Apple computer; the keyboard is disconnected from further contribution. What effect the contents of the text file have on the Apple depends on the state of the Apple and the contents of the text file. The EXEC commands has three uses.

1.   Provide input data for an executing program.
2.   Operate as a command file.
3.   Aid in concatenating program segments.

Let us first create a text file with the following contents. The file may be produced by using a word processor or by writing a simple BASIC program to carry out the task.

```
2000  REM PROG TO TEST EXEC
2010  A = 3.1415: B = 4
2020  PRINT SIN(A/B)
2030  PRINT "END"
```

This is a simple Applesoft program to calculate the sine of $\pi/4$. Remember, of course, that Applesoft program files are not text files, and any attempt to *run* this file directly as an Applesoft program will be unsuccessful. However, if we type the following sequence at the keyboard, we can see what is going on:

```
NEW
EXEC TEST.TXT
RUN
```

We clear the memory with NEW. The next immediate execution command causes the contents of the text file to be transferred into the computer's core exactly as if it were being typed at the keyboard. Because there are line numbers in front, it treats the contents of the file as deferred execution program commands. When the end of the file is encountered, control returns to the keyboard and allows us to run the program. Everything looks like the LOAD command for Applesoft program files. The difference is only evident if we had not typed NEW, in which case, the *new program lines* would have been *added to the existing program lines* in memory. The other difference would have been evident if we had not included the program line numbers 2000 to 2030. In that case the lines being "EXECed" from the text file would have been treated as immediate execution commands, and the calculation would have been immediately carried out. The program lines would not be residing in memory at the end of the *immediate execution* session.

3.4.3. Dissecting and Concatenating Programs

The previous discussion regarding the transfer of an Applesoft program from a text file into the computer's memory, although illuminating, does not provide an especially convenient environment in which to develop programs. If a program has to be changed in the text file and then transferred to the memory with the EXEC command each time a correction is made, program development will be quite tedious. We need a method of transferring the finished program or part of a program into a text file after it has been developed, so that it can be later concatenated with another section of completed code. In this way a library of program modules can be developed.

A simple program to store any program lines between 62000 and 62052 in a text file is shown in Figure 3.23.

```
62000  REM  TEXT FILE STORAGE
62002  D$ = CHR$(4); REM CTRL-D
62003  INPUT "ENTER TEXT FILE NAME ";F$
62004  PRINT D4;"OPEN ";F$
62006  PRINT D$;"WRITE ";F$
62008  POKE 33,30
62010  LIST 62000,62052
62050  PRINT D$;"CLOSE ";F$
62052  END
```

Figure 3.23. Storing program segments in a text file.
Language: Applesoft.

This section of code can be typed in at the end of a large program. Line 62010 and any other LIST commands are changed by the user in order to list the line numbers the user wants to save as an EXEC file. The program is then run with the command RUN 62000. If the program is run with the LIST command shown, it will save itself (lines 62000 to 62052) into a text file. This is convenient, since it can be included at the end of any program that must be wholly or partially saved in a text file. Note that the line numbers specified in the LIST commands cannot be entered as variables, as is the case with most numbers that occur in an Applesoft program. A final word on program development is related to the use of the EXEC command in a dynamic mode from within a program. This is another method upon which to build modular programs. By first deleting a number of lines that have already been executed and using the EXEC command to enter a new sequence of program lines, we can accommodate a much larger program than would normally be possible. A sample of code demonstrating this procedure is

```
10  RUN THIS PART OF THE PROGRAM FIRST
     .
     .
2550  DEL 10,2499
2555  PRINT D$;"EXEC PROGRAM.2"
     .
     .
```

This method may be used to produce a menu-driven text save program. This depends on being able to EXEC in a portion of a program after program execution has begun. The program variables are not cleared by the EXEC command, which makes this technique possible. One must be careful not to refer to a line number that has been destroyed in a GOTO or GOSUB command, or a program error will occur.

3.4.4. Command Files

The contents of a text file may be used as a *command* stream. This provides an alternative method for the entry of DOS commands, Applesoft commands, and program input data. For the contents of the text file to be treated as a command file, line numbers are not used. As shown previously, this insures that each line of the command file is treated exactly as if it were an immediate execution command typed in at the keyboard. However, if an executing program encouteres an INPUT instruction, each line of the command file will be used as input data. A number of programs may be run in turn from the command file. This is a very powerful aspect of the EXEC command file and will be illustrated later.

For illustrative purposes let us assume that we have an experiment to perform that requires three large programs to accomplish the various tasks of data taking, data evaluation, and graphing. Normally one would have to wait until the first data acquisition portion of the experiment is completed, load the data evaluation program, run it, and finally run the plotting program.

The following command file contains the necessary input data for these three programs. It is the same command stream that would normally be typed in when these various programs are loaded and then executed from the keyboard.

```
Contents of the Command file
    RUN DATA.TAKING.PROG
    3050,3200
    0.02
    Y
    RUN DATA. EVALUATION.PROG
    125
    RUN GRAPHING.PROG
```

This is a very convenient method for running programs in sequence without operator assistance. In particular, it is a convenient way of running the same program many times with different data. Care must be taken that there are no EXEC commands in any of the programs being run, or the command EXEC file will be closed as soon as new EXEC file is opened.

3.5. PROGRAM MANAGEMENT WITH BASICA

The vocabulary of BASICA is much more conducive to good program mangement practices than is Applesoft. There are statements included in the language that allow the passing of data from one program to another as they are run in sequence.

3.5.1. Chaining Programs in BASICA

The dynamic chaining of programs is straight forward from within BASICA by using combinations of the CHAIN, COMMON, and MERGE statements. The program segment below appends a smoothing routine at the end of another executing program.

```
975 REM  CHAIN TO SMOOTHING PROGRAM
980 COMMON NN,A()
985 CHAIN "SMOOTH.BAS"
```

The COMMON statement is followed by the list of variables to be passed to the new program. The parentheses after A denote that a complete array of data is being transferred. The existing program in memory is replaced by the new program. If we wished to transfer all the variables currently in existence to the new program, we would have to specify the ALL option and leave out the COMMON statement:thus

```
985 CHAIN "SMOOTH.BAS",12000,ALL
```

where in this case we are instructing the new program to start executing at line 12000, and we are passing it all the variables.

The MERGE option allows the existing program to be kept in memory while merging in a new program segment. This is extremely powerful if, for example, we have a number of possible operations that we wish to carry out on some data as part of a data-taking program. We would leave the main data-taking routine in memory permanently and call in the data-massaging subroutines into memory as we needed them. We would always use the same group of line numbers for the data-massaging routines.

```
985 CHAIN MERGE"SMOOTH.BAS",12000,DELETE 12000-12999
```

In this case all variables are preserved in the transfer, and the merged program that should have been written to begin at line number 12000 is executed. This is the nearest routine that BASICA has to named subroutines.

3.6.   DATA FILE STRUCTURES

The structural organization of data storage within data files is a complex subject with critical consequences for subsequent retrieval in data analysis. There are many well-written commercially available programming packages, such as VISITREND/VISIPLOT, LOTUS 123 or dBASEII, each with their own unique data file structure. What we wish to discuss in this section are the various options available for file structure organization. We propose the creation of a single unified programming environment in which data may be easily moved back and forth between user-written programs and commercially written software. An example of such a programming environment is shown in Figure 3.24. The environment is an example of a modular programming structure.

We first describe a number of file structures in common use. Some of the more flexible, commercially available programs allow for a number of different file formats. Programs such as VISIPLOT/VISITREND* or TKSolver† allow for data input files in the program's primary file format and also in a more flexible, but far less volume-efficient, form by using the data interchange format, (DIF), which allows data exchange with other programming packages.

---

*VISITREND/VISIPLOT is a trademark of VISICORP Corporation, 2895 Zanker Road, San Jose, CA 95184.
†TKSolver is a trademark of Software Arts, 27 Mica Lane, Wellesley, ME 02181.

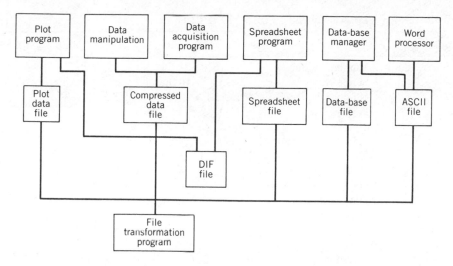

Figure 3.24. Unified file structure programming environment.

In contrast, some programming packages, such as dBASEII* allow for data input from correctly formatted text files. In this section we describe three of the data structures most commonly used. We describe the data structure used for normal data storage for the VISIPLOT/VISITREND package as well as the alternative filing method using the DIF format. Finally, we discuss the simplest method of data interchange for the dBASEII database management program.

3.6.1. The VISIPLOT/VISITREND Data Structure

The VISIPLOT/VISITREND programming package is a prompt-driven environment for data display and data analysis. Although originally developed for financial planning, it is extremely well suited for all forms of data plotting. Data can be stored or retrieved by using either the DIF format or the internal VISIPLOT format to be described here. Both use sequential text files.

Data is stored in the VISIPLOT format in the form of data series. A data series is a collection of numbers relating to the same measured parameter. A VISIPLOT file may contain one or more data series. All data pertaining to a single data series are stored in a single block in the file, followed by the next series, and so on, as shown in Table 3.4. If we were, for example, storing the wavelengths and intensity information for a spectrum, the data would be stored as two data series with the wavelength information in one block, followed by the intensity wavelength in the next block.

The first field in a VISIPLOT—compatible file is an integer indicating how

*dBASEII is a trademark of Ashton-Tate, 9929 West Jefferson Boulevard, Culver City, CA 90230.

Table 3.4.   The configuration of a VISIPLOT File

Series#	Description	Limits	Sample Data
file header	Number of Series	1–16	2
	╱ – Series Name	String 1–16 characters	WAVELENGTH
	┆ Number data points	1–250	101
Series	┆ Periodicity	1–99	1
1	┆ Start Year	0–2499	1
header	┆ Start Period	1–99	1
	┆ End Year	0–2499	101
	╲ _ End period	1–99	1
	╱ ⁻ Data point 1		305.00
Series	┆ Data point 2		305.01
1	┆ Data point 3		305.02
data	┆ .		.
	┆ .		.
	╲ _Data point 101		315.00
	╱ ⁻Series Name	String 1–16 characters	INTENSITY
	┆ Number data points	1–250	101
Series	┆ Periodicity	1–99	1
2	┆ Start Year	0–2499	1
header	┆ Start Period	1–99	1
	┆ End Year	0–2499	101
	╲ _ End period	1–99	1
	╱ ⁻ Data point 1		10891
Series	┆ Data point 2		11986
2	┆ Data point 3		13045
data	┆ .		.
	┆ .		.
	╲ – Data point 101		8765

many data series are to follow in the file. The information for a single data series is divided into a number of fields of variable field lengths. Each field is terminated by a <CR>, <LF>. The first seven fields for each data series contain header information, and the remaining fields contain the series data, as shown in Table 3.4.

At first glance the data format in this file is somewhat baffling. One must remember that, because the format was first developed for financial planning, each series is naturally assumed to be measured at equal time intervals. The periodicity information in the header section of each series thus represents the number base of the time axis units (12 divisions for yearly units, 60 for minutes, etc.).

Unless one is specifically interested in plotting data against time, it is much easier to set the periodicity to unity and treat the array field as an array index integer. The results of doing this are shown for our sample data in the right-hand column of Figure 3.25. Here we have two data series, each of which

```
5    REM****************** VISIPLOT FORMAT PROGRAM ******************
10    DIM H(120),P(120)      :REM DIMENSION ARRAYS FOR DATA SERIES
20    N=1                    :REM DEFINE LOOP PARAMETER
100   D$=CHR$(4)             :REM DEFINE CTRL-D FOR DOS COMMANDS
110   ON ERR GO TO 300       :REM SET UP ERROR PATCH
120   PRINT D$;"CATALOG,D2"  :REM CATALOG FOR USER CONVENIENCE
140   INPUT "ENTER FILENAME";F$        :REM ORIGINAL DATA FILE
150   INPUT "ENTER H SERIES NAME";SH$  :REM DEFINE SERIES NAMES
155   INPUT "ENTER P SERIES NAME":SP$
160   PRINT D$;"OPEN";F$     :REM OPEN FILE FOR READING
180   PRINT D$;"READ";F$
200    INPUT H(N)            :REM DATA INPUT LOOP
210    INPUT P(N)
220    N=N+1
230    GO TO 200             :REM END OF DATA INPUT LOOP
300 & ERRPTCH                :REM ERROR PATCH AFTER END OF FILE
320 PRINT D$;"CLOSE";F$      :REM CLOSE INPUT FILE
330 N=N-1 : PRINT N
400 REM--------------- REFILE DATA IN VISIPLOT FORMAT
420 PRINT:INPUT "ENTER OUTPUT FILENAME";F$ :REM DEFINE OUTPUT FILENA
ME
440 F$=F$ + ".VIS"           :REM TAG ON .VIS EXTENSION
460 PRINT D$;"OPEN";F$        :REM OPEN FILE FOR WRITING
480 PRINT D$;"WRITE";F$
500 PRINT "2"                 :REM THERE ARE TWO DATA SERIES
510 PRINT SH$ :REM SERIES 1 HEADER;        NAME OF FIRST SERIES
520 PRINT N                   :REM        NUMBER POINTS
530 PRINT "1"                 :REM        PERIODICITY
540 PRINT "1"                 :REM        START YEAR
550 PRINT "1"                 :REM        START PERIOD
560 PRINT N                   :REM        END YEAR
570 PRINT "1"                 :REM        END PERIOD
580 FOR I=1 TO N: PRINT H(I): NEXT I: REM ACTUAL DATA SERIES
600 PRINT SP$ :REM SERIES 2 HEADER  etc.
610 PRINT N
620 PRINT "1"
630 PRINT "1"                  | same as above
640 PRINT "1"
650 PRINT N
660 PRINT "1"
670 FOR I=1 TO N: PRINT P(I): NEXT I
700 PRINT D$; "CLOSE";F$       :REM CLOSE VISIPLOT FILE
710 REM************** END VISIPLOT PROGRAM *********************
```

Figure 3.25. Program to reformat data for VISIPLOT.
Language: Applesoft and Labsoft.

contains 101 numbers that may be labeled by the array indices (Year!), 1,...,
101. Thus, we have set the periodicity to unity, so that the start and end
periodicities are also unity. For example, if we set the *start year* to 1, the *end
year* must turn out to be 101. Notice that the first field in the file had to be set to
2 to indicate that two series reside in the file. Note also that since there is a
one-to-one correspondence between the data in these two series, the header
information must be indentical for both, apart from the names of the series.

For data series that we wish to plot against each other (scatter plot) rather
than against time, there are constraints on the header information. First, of
course, the periodicities of both series must be the same; and, second, only the
data points with equal array indices (Year) may be plotted against each other.
In cases where data from two series are only partially overlapping in the array
indices, the plotting program looks at the start year and end years of each series
and only plots the overlapping data in terms of (x,y) data pairs. For example, if
we had a third spectrum "intensity" data series to add to our existing file, with
the spectrum information taken from 310.00 to 315.00 nm in increments of 0.01
nm, we would have only 51 points in the data series with a starting index of 50
and an end index of 101, as shown below

```
INTENSITY2
51
1
50
1
101
1
12973
  .
  .
```

Since the VISIPLOT format is stored in a text file, it is a rather trivial exercise
to create a data file in the correct format from any user-written program that
may later be read in by VISIPLOT.

The program of Figure 3.25 reads into memory two sets of data, H(N)
and P(N), from the diskette that have been stored in data pairs and reformats
it for VISIPLOT as it is written back to diskette. The final output produced
by VISIPLOT with this reformated data is shown on the right of Table 3.4.

Note that the error patch technique demonstrated in Program 2.2 of
Chapter 2 could be used instead of the Labsoft command &ERRPTCH of
line 300.

3.6.2.   The Data Interchange Format

The *data interchange format* (DIF)* has been developed to store and interchange data between a wide range of sources—from plotting programs to

---

*DIF is a trademark of Software Arts, DIF Clearinghouse, P.O. Box 527, Cambridge, MA 02139.

spreadsheets. To accommodate the widely different requirements that these programs may have for data storage, especially when attempting to transfer data between them, the DIF format must not only be able to accommodate the numerical data itself, but it must communicate added information about the form and quality of the data.

The DIF* format is based on the representation of data in two-dimensional tables. To illustrate the nomenclature of the DIF format, we consider the data shown in Figure 3.26, which represent three parallel data series. These could have been created by a spreadsheet program such as VISICALC, or they could represent the results of a laboratory experiment. The column headings and table title must be considered an integral part of the data to be stored in the DIF file and must be accommodated in the format.

The DIF format formalizes the storage of data with respect to rows and columns of data. A naming convention has been established to replace the more familiar row and column labelings; we talk of *tuples* and *vectors*. It makes very little difference whether the rows (columns) are defined as tuples or vectors, but, once defined, the DIF format stores data sequentially with respect to tuples. For convenience in our particular example, we define the rows in Figure 3.26 to be the tuples and the columns to be the vectors.

A DIF file is made up of two sections: a header section containing descriptive information on the table, including the dimensions of the tuples and vectors; and a data section containing the actual numerical (or string) values. The header section groups lines in combinations of threes. Thus, three lines are required to uniquely define a single item. The data section groups lines in sets of twos.

The DIF header format requires that each item be described by three lines containing four fields exactly following the form below.

Line 1	*Tuple*
Line 2	*Vector Number, Value*
Line 3	*String*

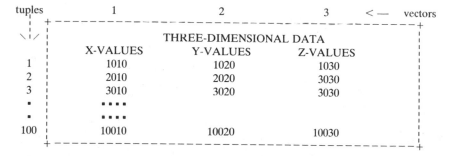

tuples	1	2	3	< — vectors
	X-VALUES	THREE-DIMENSIONAL DATA Y-VALUES	Z-VALUES	
1	1010	1020	1030	
2	2010	2020	3030	
3	3010	3020	3030	
.	. . . .			
.	. . . .			
100	10010	10020	10030	

Figure 3.26. A Sample Data Table.

---

*"*DIF: A format for data exchange between applications programs," Byte* (November 1981).

The topic must be a single one of the key words listed below.

Topic Key Words
TABLE
VECTORS
TUPLES
LABEL
DATA

Each one of these key words requires specific numerical values to be placed in some of the fields depending on the key word. The complete set of topic key words with their required numerical values is shown in Table 3.5.

The first item in the file must be the TABLE label, followed by one of the VECTORS, TUPLES, and LABEL labels in any order. The VECTORS and TUPLES declare the dimensions of the vectors and tuples. The DIF format requires that all the tuples and vectors be of equal dimensions. The final header entry, before any numerical data is encountered in the file, must be the DATA declaration.

Referring to our table of data in Figure 3.26, we have a set of 3 vectors and 100 tuples. Each vector has a specific header label. The resulting DIF header file section is shown in Figure 3.27. The header section can be deciphered by referring to the declaration formats in Table 3.5 and our data table in terms of tuples and vectors in Figure 3.26

Table 3.5. Topic Identifiers in the DIF Format

TABLE	VECTORS
0, Version #	0, count
"Title"	" "
TUPLES	LABEL
0, count	vector #, line # n
" "	"label 1"
	"label 2"
	.
	"label n"
DATA	
0,0	
" "	

```
TABLE
0,1
"THREE-DIMENSIONAL DATA"
VECTORS
0,3
" "
TUPLES
0,100
" "
LABEL
1,1
"X-VALUES"
LABEL
2,1
"Y-VALUES"
LABEL
3,1
"Z-VALUES"
DATA
0,0
" "
```

Figure 3.27. A sample file header for the DIF format.

The numerical data takes on a different format than the header section. This time each unit of information entered requires three fields spread over two lines with the format

```
type indicator, number value
string value
```

The DIF format using this nomenclature is flexible enough to deal with both numeric and string data. The type indicator can take on one of the three values shown below.

Type Indicator	Interpretation
-1	*boundary delimiter*
0	*numerical data*
1	*string data*

Let us first consider the significance of the boundary delimiter. We indicated earlier that data is stored in tuples. In our particular example of 100 data point, this means that the data will be packed in 100 groups of threes. At the beginning of each grouping (tuple) there must be a tuple boundary delimiter with entry

$$-1,0$$
$$\texttt{BOT}$$

where BOT stands for beginning of tuple. The other boundary delimiter defined for the DIF format must occur at the end of the DIF file with entry

$$-1,0$$
$$\texttt{EOD}$$

where EOD stands for end of data.

Now the numerical entry values must correspond to the form

$$\textit{0,numerical value}$$
$$\textit{data definition (string value)}$$

The numerical value field in this format contains the actual data to be stored. This is the only field in the DIF format where non integer numerical values are admissible. The data for most applications may be in real or scientific notation, although this, in the end, depends on whether the reading program can recognize scientific notation. Each data field in the DIF format must be accompanied by a corresponding data definition, which is transferred in the string-value field. The possible settings of the string value for numerical data are shown in Table 3.6.

Turning our attention once again to Figure 3.27, we see that the logic of data entry should now make some sense. We show the resulting data file format in Table 3.7 with comments where necessary. The tuples have been marked out for convenience. Each tuple is headed by the BOT flag, and the file is finally closed with the EOD flag. All data in this example have the V string definition, designating that the numeric field contains a valid numeric value.

Table 3.6.   Numerical DIF Data Format Definitions

String Value	Interpretation
V	Indicates a valid numeric value
NA	Indicates that the numeric value is not available and value set to 0
ERROR	The number in the file is the result of an invalid calculation
TRUE	The data is a logical value with numerical value 1
FALSE	The data is a logical value with numerical value 0

Table 3.7.   A Sample Data Section for
a DIF Format File

−1,0	beginning of first tuple
BOT	
0,1010	first vector
V	
0,1020	second vector
V	
0,1030	third vector
V	
−1,0	beginning of second tuple
BOT	
0,2010	first vector
V	
0,2020	second vector
V	
0,2030	third vector
V	
.	
.	last tuple
.	
0,10030	third vector
V	
−1,0	
EOD	end of data

For future reference, even though the format is not used in this particular
example, a string data value would be entered as

$$1,0$$
$$EXAMPLE\ STRING$$

The data in this case should be entered without quotation marks unless a null
string is to be stored. In that case double quotation marks with no space in
between ("") must be entered into the file.

3.6.3.   A File Structure for Experimental Data

Although each experimental configuration brings with it unique requirements
for data storage, one soon finds certain features always present that may be
exploited to guarantee a flexible and universal file structure. We can conveniently divide the information to be filed into the following categories, although
not necessarily in the order given:

Documentation of experimental procedure
Equipment parameter settings

Fixed experimental parameters
Primary data series

The *primary data series* will consist of a single independent variable together with one or more series of dependent variables. The *fixed experimental* parameters are those parameters kept fixed throughout given experimental run, but which may vary from experiment to experiment. The other items are evident.

We shall describe a method of data storage that meets our criteria for flexibility. The method borrows some of the organizational ideas used for the DIF format. All data connected with a single experimental run are stored in a single text file. We have found that the flexibility in data storage does not so much have to be applied to the storage of primary data as it does to the other three categories of data described above.

As is the case for the DIF format, the file will be divided into two major divisions: the first contains the header material; the second, the data. The header contains the comments, the fixed parameter values, and the equipment settings.

Each header item is described by a minimum of three lines containing four or more fields in the following format.

```
Topic
Number of lines n, Value
String 1
String 2
      .
String n
```

The *topic* category contains one of a number of possible topic identifiers describing the nature of the appended data. The fields are so organized that the second and third fields are always numerical data, and all other are string data. Below is a list of the header topic categories used on experimental data.

DATE
TIME
EQUIPMENT
PARAMETERS
COMMENT
DATA

In all of these header categories, the second field indicates the number of string lines of data that are to follow. The *value* field may be any real or integer number. All string fields must be surrounded by quotes. The topic field is not surrounded by quotes.

A detailed description of the fields related to each of these categories is shown in Table 3.8. In the first three categories the value field must be set to

Table 3.8.   Proposed Field Definitions
for Experimental Data File

TITLE	COMMENT
n,0	n,0
title string 1	*comment string 1*
title string 2	*comment string 1*
.	.
.	.
title string n	*comment string n*

DATA	TIME
1,0	1,0
date string	*time string*

EQUIPMENT	PARAMETER
n, Set value	*n, measured value*
equipment name	*parameter name*
setting name	*parameter units*
units	*comment 1*
.	.
.	.
comment (n−3)	*comment (n−2)*

zero, and the date and time must be written as strings in the fourth or subsequent fields. The format allows for comments either to be added at the end of any one of these descriptors or in a separate comment descriptor.

As an example of some of these descriptor topic categories, we give a short header in Figure 3.28.

```
TITLE
1,0
"THIS IS A SAMPLE HEADER"
COMMENT
1,0
"WITH A COMMENT INCLUDED"
EQUIPMENT
3,1
"DIGITAL VOLTMETER"
"VOLTAGE RANGE"
"KILOVOLTS"
PARAMETERS
2,355.2
"TEMPERATURE"
"DEGREES KELVIN"
```

Figure 3.28.   Data entry for typical experimental file.

Of course, there may be many descriptors entered, all with the same topic category.

We now turn our attention to the organization of the data series themselves. Again, we want to allow maximum flexibility while making the file structure as simple as possible. We have introduced the DATA series header previously. The data section must be headed by the following lines, which correspond to the same format as the header section.

```
DATA
Number of Series n, Number of points in each series
Series 1 title
Series 2 title
       .
Series n title
```

As in the DIF format, we must constrain the file construction so that each series has the same length (number of points). We end the file with the unit

```
DATA
-1,0
EOD
```

The data series are listed immediately after the DATA header. Each series (dependent variables $y,z,...,w$) is assumed to be a function of some independent variable x. The first three fields of the data are the start, end, and increment values of x. The following fields contain the data series with the corresponding $y,z,...,w$ points collected next to each other.

```
start x
end x
increment x
y0
z0
 .
w0
y1
z1
 .

 .
yn
zn
 .
wn
```

In the case where the data represents scatter data points, the x variable has no meaning other than as array indices, and start x may be set to 0, end x to the number of points, and increment x to 1. Otherwise the x variable might be *wavelength* in the case of a spectrum or *time* if we were representing the data from a chromatograph.

The data section corresponding to our example is shown in Figure 3.29, where the object of the experiment was to measure and store data corresponding, in this case, to a spectrum.

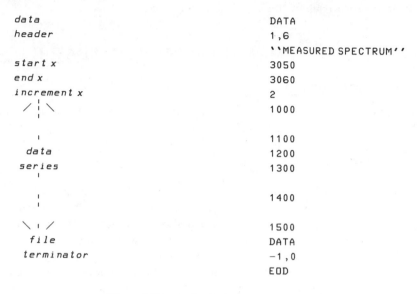

Figure 3.29. A simple data file format.

This format follows from what we have already discussed. Note that we have an independent check on at least the number of data points stored in the file. The following equality must hold.

$$number\ points\ in\ series\ =\ 1\ +\ (end\ x-start\ x)\ /\ increment\ x$$

and the total number of data points must equal this number times the number of data series.

Our discussion so far has been concentrated on a single file solution to data storage, where all the information connected with a single experimental run is stored in one file. We could extend the format described here to allow large arrays of data to be stored in binary files. A pointer field could be included in the topic categories to indicate that the data series should be retrieved from there and not the main text file. In cases where we are sure that our experimental configuration will not change and no subsequent modifications in terms of the number or type of data parameters will be necessary, we could use a random access file or a database file to store the header material. This would speed up data retrieval. Database management, described in the next section, is a procedure for managing large amounts of data. Applying some of the file-management ideas discussed here, we could store the primary data series in a compressed mode as a binary file. Each floppy disk would contain a single library file containing all the parameters related to each of the data files on the disk. A database library disk would be created containing the accumulated information for each of the individual data disks.

3.7.   DATABASE MANAGEMENT WITH dBASEII

3.7.1.   Introduction

The subject of database management is much too large to be adequately covered in a single section. Instead, we give a brief overview of database techniques for research applications. We recommend that the reader supplement the material in this section with some of the excellent literature on the subject.[*,†]

A database is a collection, possibly an especially large collection, of information that, in its most efficient form, is restricted to a single subject or category. For example, we might create a database on "books about chromatography" or a catalog of information related to data taken in the laboratory (an electronic notebook). Database management programs are used to organize and categorize such data in a way that allows fast access to it at a later time. Typically, under optimum conditions, one should be able to access a single piece of information from the database in 2 s or less.

Database managers come in many different forms. One of the most advanced is dBASEII, a relational database that may be adapted to countless tasks in science and engineering. It is a command-driven system (as opposed to menu driven) with a comprehensive vocabulary of commands that can be strung together in sequence just as in a programming language. dBASEII can be used either in an immediate execution mode during an interactive session or from a command file in a deferred mode in which a series of commands may be executed sequentially. The dBASEII programming language is structured. This allows very readable code to be written for advanced applications. The structured flow aspects of the language can only be used in the deferred command mode.

There are a number of areas of research where the use of a program such as dBASEII can be immensely useful—namely:

1.   Creating and cataloging a database of scientific references to journal articles.
2.   Keeping an electronic notebook related to the acquisition and storage of scientific data.

*A.B. Green, *dBASEII User's Guide* (Prentice-Hall, Englewood Cliffs, N.J., 1983).
†A.B. Green, *Advanced dBASEII User's Guide* (Prentice-Hall, Englewood Cliffs, N.J., 1984).

3. Cataloging information related to a particular scientific discipline such as a database of the properties of complex molecules in chemistry or of drugs in medicine.
4. Cataloging research notes and ideas.

Each of these tasks brings its own particular requirements. However, most cataloging tasks have enough in common to benefit from the use of a universal tool, such as dBASEII or some other database manager, rather than trying to create a dedicated program.

3.7.2. Records and Fields

Central to any database management program is the structure of the data both within the computer's memory during the running of the database manager program and in its permanent storage on disk. Data in a database is sectioned into equal memory units called *records*, which may loosely be considered the electronic equivalent to the file card. Each record is divided into a number of *fields*. The fields are the different categories of data to be filled with data for each record.

The concept of data types is important to this discussion. Data types are of central importance both in database management and in structured languages and will be considered again in some detail in Chapter 4. dBASEII has three data types, *character*, *numerical*, and *logical*. Many of the structured languages, such as PASCAL, have many more types, but three are sufficient for most applications in database management.

To create a database, one must define in the initialization stage, the names, data types, and widths of each field to be filled with data. To illustrate the creation and operation of a database, we take as an example a database *template* of scientific interest—namely, a database for storing and cataloging the titles and references of journal articles. An illustration of the database structure is shown in Figure 3.30. Each record in the database in represented by a different row. The various fields are represented by the different columns.

Fields→	Field 1	Field 2	Field 3	F4	F5	F6	Field 7
	Names	Title	Journal	Vol	Pg	Yr	Keywords
	C40	C40	C20	C5	N5	N4	C30

Records							
0001							
0002							
0003							
•							
etc.							

Figure 3.30. Illustration of a database structure.

We use only the character and numerical data fields in this example. The input in Figure 3.31 is all that is necessary to create the database template for our journal articles example. The example assumes that we are already in the dBASEII environment.

```
· CREATE
ENTER FILENAME: b:exmpl
ENTER RECORD STRUCTURE
AS FOLLOWS
FIELD NAME, TYPE, WIDTH, DECIMAL
0001  Names, c, 40
0002  Title, c, 40
0003  Journal, c, 20
0004  Volume, c, 5
0005  Page, n, 5
0006  Year, n, 4
0007  Keywords, c, 30
```

Figure 3.31.   Entry necessary to create database.
Language: dBASEII keyboard entry commands.

In this example, italics are used to denote the words generated by the program; regular type denotes the information to be entered by the user. The Names field is specified to be 20 characters wide, and so on, and we specify the Page and Year fields to be numerical. The resulting template created by dBASE, which needs to be filled in for each new record entered into the database, is shown in Figure 3.32.

Once the data fields have been specified in this way, data may be entered into the database one record at a time, starting with record number one. The user of dBASEII has a comprehensive series of commands available that may be used to enter data, edit, and manage the files connected with a given database.

3.7.3.   Working with Records

If we have created a large database of journal references, then dBASEII contains a comprehensive series of commands designed to search and manipu-

```
Names:
         ------------------------------------------
Title:
         ------------------------------------------
Journal:                          Volume:      Page:
         --------------------       -----        -----
Year:            Keywords:
         ----             --------------------------------
```

Figure 3.32.   A database template for journal references.

late the information in the records. The database can either be searched interactively, where the operator enters one command at a time at the console, or, as we describe at the end of this section, a command file may be written resembling in many ways a conventional computer language program but operating on the data fields of the database.

In our just-created database we could search through all the records and list on the console only those articles that were published between 1979 and 1982: thus,

```
USE b:Exmpl
LIST FOR Year >='1979' AND Year <='1982'
```

Often one is not interested in the complete contents of a particular field. For example, we may wish to search for a single author in the Names field, which might normally contain multiple authors. The command $ is particularly useful in this regard. The command shown below instructs dBASEII to search the Names field and list only the records that contain Annino as an Author.

```
LIST FOR 'Annino' $ Names
```

Quite complex searches can be executed by using logical or relational operators. The following instruction searches and lists only those articles published by Annino in the years 1979 to 1982.

```
LIST FOR 'Annino' $ Names .AND. (Year <='1981' .AND. Year >='1979')
```

Note that the relational operators do not necessarily have to operate on numerical data. It is perfectly logical to compare the first character of one word to the first character of another word and conclude that one word is less than another, based on the relationship of these characters in the alphabet.

We list, in Table 3.9, the complete set of relational and logical operators which may be used to operate on the contents of database fields.

Table 3.9. Some dBASEII Operators

Relational Operators	Logical Operators
< : less than	( ) : parentheses for grouping
= : equals	.NOT. : Boolean not
<= : less than or equals	.OR. : Boolean or
> : greater than	$: substring logical operator
<> : not equals	.AND. : Boolean and
>= : greater than or equls	

3.7.4. The dBASEII File System

The dBASEII program recognizes six main file structures, each labeled with a different file extension, as shown in Figure 3.33. The most important file containing all the field initialization and data for a particular database is the .DBF file. It contains the information necessary to recreate the field divisions, followed by the data content of each record in turn.

The .DBF file is not directly accessible with a word processor. However, the dBASEII program can read data from a standard text (.TXT extension) file created by a word processor, some other database manager, or a spreadsheet program. The following command lines are used to append data from a text file named B:TEMP.TXT to a standard dBASEII file named B:EXMPL.DBF.

```
USE b:Exmpl
APPEND FROM b:temp.txt SDF
```

The first line selects the main database file for editing. The next line appends the text file, Temp.txt, that has been written in the standard text format, SDF, to the existing database. The standard format requires a <CR>, <LF> after each line of text. Other text formats can be accommodated, making dBASEII a most flexible environment for data storage.

The .CMD files play an important role in the mechanics of using dBASEII. The strength of dBASEII or, for that matter, most relational database managers is the way in which the information stored in the records and fields can be searched and compared with each other. We might, for example, wish to search all records between numbers 200 and 400, pick out all papers published between 1979 and 1984, and list the authors in alphabetical order by first author together with the titles of the papers. Such a task is relatively straightforward if programmed from within a command file.

The .NDX file of dBASEII is to collect information related to the operation of the INDEX command. This command produces a relational index of one or more of the field contents of all the records. For example, we might wish to create an index of the journals in which the articles in our database were published. This is a time-consuming operation, since each record has to be searched through in turn. An index file contains the result of such an index

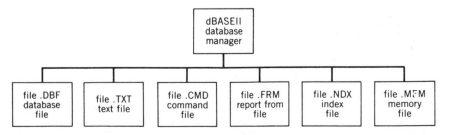

Figure 3.33. The dBASEII file structure.

operation in the form of pointers to the various records. The following command would be used to create such an index.

```
USE b:Exmpl
INDEX ON Journal TO b:Jrnls
```

This command will produce the index in a file called b:Jrnl.ndx of the ordered set of records for the Journal field.

The last two file categories are used for more advanced operations of dBASEII. The .MEM files are used to store the contents of certain computations, constants, and variables during a save operation when a database is being manipulated. Finally, the .FRM file contains information related to the production of reports on a particular database that has been saved.

The power of dBASEII can be appreciated by examining the number of commands that it has available for working with complete files of data. We list the complete sets of commands for database creation and file manipulation in Table 3.10, together with an explanation of the role that the commands play in database management.

3.7.5. The dBASEII Command File

The full power of dBASEII is only realized when using the command files for database management. The dBASEII command language provides for

Table 3.10. File Related Commands in dBASEII

File Creation Commands

* CREATE	- create new structured database files
* MODIFY	- alter existing database structures
* REPORT	- create a report form file
* SAVE	- copy memory variables to disk
* INDEX	- create an index file
* REINDEX	- realign an old index file
* JOIN	- creates a new joined database
* TOTAL	- output a database of totalled records

File Manipulation Commands

* APPEND	- appends SDF format files to database in memory
* COPY	- copy databases to SDF format files
* DELETE	- delete files
* DO	- specifies command file containing procedure
* RENAME	- renames a file
* SELECT	- switches between USE files
* SORT	- creates a copy of a database sorted on one of fields
* USE	- specifies database file to be worked on

operator-assisted inputs from the keyboard. This allows for general solutions to be programmed in the command files without compromising programming speed at points where the BASIC software calls for decisions.

There are four fundamental programming structures for program flow in the dBASEII command language that are shown in Table 3.11.

The dBASEII program interpreter executes the commands in the command file sequentially unless one of the other three program structures is used. The IF...ENDIF structure allows decision/choice to be directly carried out in the command files, and the DO WHILE...ENDDO is a structured primitive for looping under some specified condition.

The simple command file shown in Figure 3.3. uses the first three structured procedures to search between the years 1979 and 1982 for a publication by Annino that possibly appeared in the Journal of Analytical Chemistry. If it is not found there, a search is conducted for papers by this author appearing in other journals.

```
USE b:Exmpl
DO WHILE .NOT. EOF
  IF Year >='1979' .AND. Year <='1982'
    IF Names $ 'Annino' .AND. Journal='Anal. Chem.'
      ? Title,Names,Year
    ELSE
       IF Names $ 'Annino'
         ? 'Paper in other Journal'
       ENDIF
    ENDIF
  ENDIF
ENDO
```

Figure 3.34.   A dBASEII command file.
Language: dBASEII command file commands.

Procedures or subroutines play an important part in most computer language structures. Procedures are programmed in dBASEII by creating a separate command file containing the procedure operation. Up to 16 command files may be open at any one time, allowing the execution of some fairly

Table 3.11.   Programming Flow Structures in dBASEII

Sequential flow	default
Choice/Decision flow structure	IF(condition)...ELSE...ENDIF
Repetition flow structure	DO WHILE(condition)...ENDO
Procedure utilization	DO filename

complex tasks. The DO filename command is used to invoke a procedure as in
the example below.

```
USE b: Exmpl
DO WHILE .NOT. EOF
  IF Year > '1976'
      DO After76
  ELSE
      DO Pre76
  ENDIF
ENDO
```

Here we have two procedures: one in file After 76.cmd, the other in Pre76.
cmd. Such a program might be used if we wished to sort data into two
databases: one containing articles published before 1976, and the other after
1976.

This concludes our discussion of dBASE II.

4

Modular and Structured Programming

4.1. INTRODUCTION

We discuss two related topics—*modular* and *structured* programming, where modularity can be considered to be a subset of the structured programming concept. The use of modular programming design techniques can aid in program development even with a nonstructured language such as BASIC. Truly structured programming, on the other hand, can only be satisfactorily accomplished by using one of the many structured languages available on personal computer systems.

4.1.1. What is Structured Programming?

A number of concepts set structured programming languages apart from nonstructured languages—namely:

1. A completely modular programming structure.
2. Procedures called by name.
3. An advanced set of program flow primitives.
4. Availability of structured data types.
5. The ability to define new data types.
6. A language syntax and command structure that makes program development self-documenting.

Not all of these criteria are exclusively the domain of the so-called structured programming languages. Many of the concepts are now being incorporated into conventional languages such as FORTRAN and BASIC.

A flow diagram of a computer program written in a nonstructured language is shown in Figure 4.1a. The flow within a program may be quite complex, and, in general, a modification to the program at one point will likely produce changes to the flow within the program at other points and may make debugging very difficult.

If, on the other hand, a modular approach to program development is used, the number of interconnections for program flow is drastically reduced, as

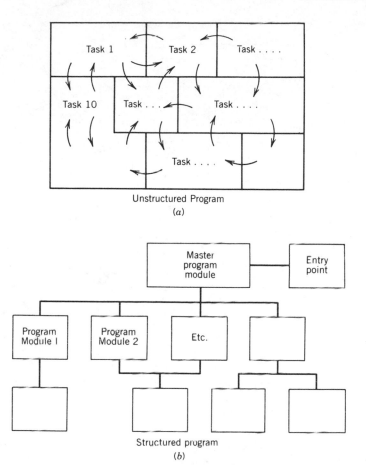

Figure 4.1.   Diagram of program flow structure. (*a*) Computer program written in an unstructured fashion. (*b*) Computer program written in a structured fashion.

shown by Figure 4.1*b*. The complexity of program development is dramatically reduced by dividing the programming task into smaller and smaller semi-independent modules or procedures. Interactions or *correlations* between the modules are kept to a minimum by program design and the structure of the programming language. Of course, repeated division of a programming task into increasingly trivial procedures will eventually reach the point of diminishing returns, where the complexity of the program begins to increase.

4.1.2.   Computer Languages in This Book

We concentrate most of our attention on a single *interpreted* language and a single *compiled* language. BASIC is by far the most widely used interpreted language and has become firmly entrenched as the language medium of data

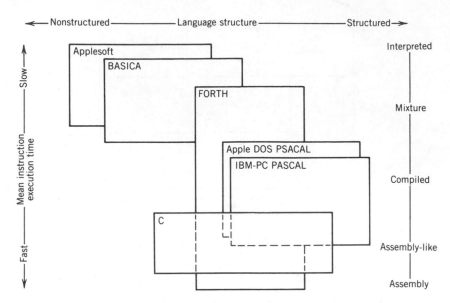

Figure 4.2.   A schematic representation comparing popular computer languages structure and execution speed.

acquisition and control on small computers. Clearly, the development of convenient laboratory language *extensions* for many BASIC interpreters has been an important factor in this regard. The compiled language that we use is called C. This language is fast becoming one of the most popular on micro-computers. We use it in programming examples where both calculation speed and a modular structure are required.

A diagram showing the qualitative relationship of these and other languages to each other is shown in Figure 4.2. The abscissa measures the language structure, and the ordinate indicates the language speed in performing calcu-lations. The language structure, compiler speed, and processor speed are all important parameters in the comparison of these languages.

In situations requiring sophisticated data reduction, one has a choice of coding the programs in *assembly* language or using a higher-level compiled language such as PASCAL, FORTRAN, C, or FORTH. We describe some of the ways in which assembly language can be used in Chapter 11. Here we discuss using the C language for writing data reduction routines. At the end of the chapter we briefly discuss the FORTH language.

4.2.   MODULAR PROGRAM DEVELOPMENT IN THE LABORATORY

4.2.1.   Layout and Definition

The basics of modular programming involve an initial description of the problem from a global viewpoint, followed by a synthesis of the solution from smaller detailed program units. A good, but by no means unique, approach to a modular-designed structured program is to observe the following procedure.

1. Write a program definition.
2. Break the problem down into its major procedures.
3. Configure the algorithms.
4. Code and debug the algorithms separately.
5. Test the completed program.
6. Document the program.

Many of us give the first and last points on this list the least attention, resulting in unfortunate consequences for program development and maintenance. The first step in *top-down* program design concerns the writing of a well-thought-out *program definition* (sometimes called problem definition). This is where we delineate just what we expect the program to do.

The features needed to make a program of much wider generality may absorb the greatest part of the time needed for program development. Common sense argues against overgeneralizing the program definition unless, by doing so, we open up the possibility of being able to use previously written software.

We list below what we consider to be some of the important points to be included in a program definition. The list has been compiled for program development in laboratory situations.

PROGRAM DEFINITION BREAKDOWN

1. Brief descriptive title, date, and so on.
2. Special hardware specifications.
   a. Computer specifications—hardware, storage, display.
   b. Laboratory equipment specifications.
   c. Interfacing information.
   d. Timing constraints.
3. Special software specifications.
   a. Programming language.
   b. Interface communications software.
   c. Already written software to be utilized.
4. Input specifications.
   a. Command, parameters, and data input definitions.
   b. Origin of the parameters.
   c. Valid range of the parameters.
   d. End of input signal.
5. Output specifications.
   a. What data is to be produced.
   b. Format of the data.

    c. Output data storage.

    d. Data display.

    e. Documentation, labeling, headings.

6. Processing and control specifications.

    a. Major tasks to be performed.

    b. Important time order constraint.

    c. Special conditions and constraints arising from program definition.

    d. Recovery action.

    e. Role of the operator in program control.

This is an exhaustive list, much of which will not change from program to program.

Let us now write a program definition. We consider the problem of *interfacing* an emission spectrometer consisting of a monochromator, detector, and control and detector electronics to an Apple computer. The system will be used to study the emission spectrum of a light source. A block diagram of the data acquisition layout is shown in Figure 4.3. We need not concern ourselves with the detailed nature of the equipment at this point.

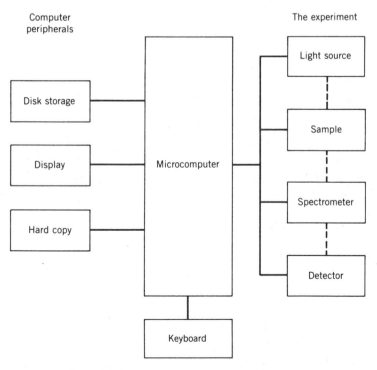

Figure 4.3.   Block layout of data acquisition system.

PROGRAM DEFINITION

Title:

Emission Spectrometer Program   Version 1   1/1/85

Hardware:

Apple II computer 64K

RS232 card to control light source

ISAAC 91A to control monochromator

GPIB card to interface to the detector electronics

Software:

Applesoft BASIC

Labsoft language extension

Input Data:

The start wavelenth, end wavelength, wavelength increment of the monochromator scan

The light source wavelength must be typed in by the operator at the keyboard

The operator will be asked to choose a file name for the data to be stored

Output Data:

A plot of the emission spectrum versus intensity will be produced on the monitor

A file containing the intensity spectrum will be stored on the disk

The file will contain the date and time together with experimental parameters

An option of displaying baseline corrected data

Recall option for previous emission spectra on same graph and ratioing the spectra

A hard copy of the data will also be available on request

Processing:

At each spectral wavelength the intensity will be measured and the data transmitted over the GPIB bus to the computer

At each monochromator wavelength setting, the detector and electronics will be checked to be sure they are not overranged

All graphs will be scaled automatically. At the end of each cycle more instructions will be obtained by returning to an operator input mode.

Armed with this program definition we can write a system level flowchart complete with a decision regarding the major divisions of the problem into its primary modules.

4.2.2. Modular Program Design

The division of a programming task into modules is a somewhat subjective exercise. Each programmer brings to it his or her own particular flavor, and no two programmers will produce exactly the same set of procedures and program divisions. In any problem, however, there are natural divisions that can be used to one's advantage. This is particularly true for laboratory data acquisition and control tasks where the same modules may be used to oversee different pieces of scientific equipment. In the context of this section the term *module* is a generic term that may refer to a procedure, program function, or any other program division that you may wish to define.

A simple set of rules for what should be expected of each module is listed below:

1. Module boundaries should be chosen so that separate modules perform minimally connected tasks.
2. Modules should be addressed by a single descriptive name.
3. The boundaries of a module should be well defined.
4. A module, in general, should call a number of other modules in a hierarchical structure.
5. A single module may be capable of performing more than one task. These tasks should have a great deal of commonality with each other and share primitives.
6. Each module should be accessed by a single entrance point and a single exit point.
7. When a module is exited, control should return to the next statement in the calling module.
8. If possible, the *goto* statement should not be used to transfer control within a module.
9. It should be possible to test each module of the program separately.
10. If a module is absent from a program, it should still be possible to run the program.

In general, we have found it best never to include *input* and *output* statements in modules whose function is not primarily concerned with I/O. Such tasks are best defined separately in another module. This allows far greater flexibility in tailoring procedures for use in different programs and minimizes the number of points within a program that involve the operator.

Let us return to the simple problem for which we wrote the program definition in the last section. As we have mentioned, I/O tasks will be handled by separate procedures. We define the following modules in this problem.

Module	Description	Module Name
Module 1	Main Control Module	*main_controller*
Module 2	Data Storage Module	*data_storage*
Module 3	Spectrometer Control Module	*spectrometer_control*
Module 4	Detector Module	*detector_read*
Module 5	Data Display Module	*data_display*
Module 6	Menu Module	*menu*
Module 7	Data Manipulation Module	*data_massage*
Module 8	Light Source Control	*source_control*

The interrelationship between modules at the systems level is best presented in the form of a *system level flowchart*. Such a flowchart for our example is shown in Figure 4.4.

We have chosen to center the systems level algorithm about the *controller* module. This, and the *menu* module, should be the only ones that need changing if we want to totally reconfigure the experiment or to add further options to the list of experiments. The menu module is the main point of contact with the user. We will find that configuring the system in this way makes it a relatively simple matter to expand the program merely by including more options in the system menu.

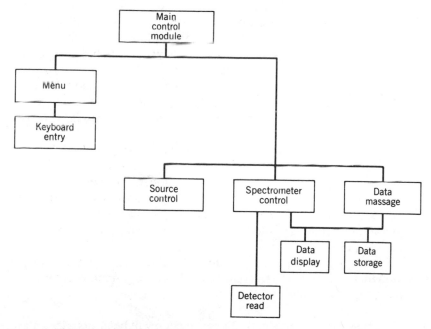

Figure 4.4.   System level flowchart for experimental program flow.

Once we have defined the main modules of the program and configured the system level flowchart, we can write *algorithms* to accomplish the tasks in each of these modules. This is best done using the nomenclature of structured programming. Before pursuing this subject any further, however, we describe one method to modularize programs using an unstructured language such as BASIC.

4.3.   MODULAR PROGRAMMING IN APPLESOFT

Here we outline some guidelines that we have found convenient for modular programming in Applesoft. Modular programming can only be used with BASIC in a restricted sense, given the underlying structure of the language. Most of the concepts developed here may be applied to any of the BASIC dialects. We discuss the use of modular programming in BASICA/MBASIC in Chapter 9.

4.3.1.   Dividing up the Program

Applesoft BASIC has a number of syntactical features that make modular programming particularly challenging. First, procedures can only be accessed by line numbers, not by name. Second, only two characters may be used for variable names; the first must be an alphabet character; the second may be a character or a number. Third, there are no local variable designations in Applesoft. Thus, all variables are global, and this fact, coupled with the limited choice of variable names, restricts the configuration of program modules. These facts make program documentation somewhat difficult compared to more advanced programming languages.

We will not treat every subroutine in a large Applesoft program as a separate module. Even though the subroutines may be separate procedures in the sense that they each perform different tasks, we reserve the term *module* in Applesoft for a larger division of the program. These Applesoft modules will be equivalent to the system level procedures shown in the system level flowchart.

A graphical representation of the program structure is shown in Figure 4.5. Each module is divided into an *initialization* section, a *program* section and, a *data* section. Although all these sections could be included in the main body of each module, we have decided to separate them and place all the initialization statements at the beginning of the program. This is an important consideration in a long program.

We offer the following set of guidelines for line numbering and variable designation that will allow you to create a modular programming environment within the syntax of Applesoft.

1. *Line designation.*   A thousand lines of code will be arbitrarily set aside for each module, starting on a round number. Thus module 1 starts at line number 1000, module 2 at 2000, and so on.

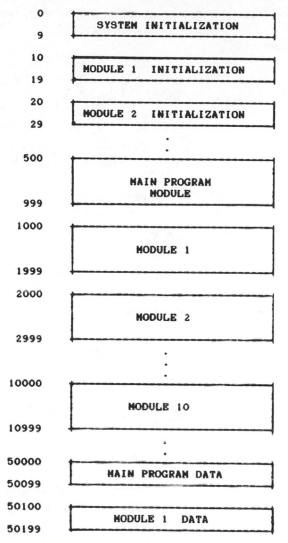

Figure 4.5. Modular program structure in Applesoft BASIC.

2. *Control module.* The line numbers from 500 to 999 are reserved for the *control module*. This is a very short program consisting only of global parameters and calls to the main program modules.

3. *Global variables.* Variables containing two alphabet characters are reserved as *global* variables. Examples are AB, XY, and so on. Global variables are recognized by every module and are the only way that data is communicated from one module to another.

4. *Local variables.*   Variables containing an alphabet character and a number are designated *local* variables. Examples are A1, B2,...,Z0. Remember that the first character cannot be a number.

5. *Variable designation.*   We arbitrarily designate local variables for each module by the number of the second character. Thus, module 1 has the local variables A1, B1, C1,..., Z1, module 2, A2,..., Z2, and module 10, A0,..., Z0. Using this system, we can have a maximum of 11 modules, including the control module 0 in the program, each with 26 *real,integer*, and *string* variables.

6. *System initialization.*   Line numbers between 0 and 9 are kept for system initialization. Identical coding is included with each program module stored on file.

7. *Module initialization.*   We use line numbers between 10 and 499 to set up all module initialization statements, such as DIM and READ, that are used only once. The initialization for module 1 is numbered from 10 to 19, module 2 between 20 and 29, and so on. The main control module is initialized between 300 and 499.

8. *DATA statements.*   We designate line numbers above 50000 for DATA statements. DATA statements corresponding to module 1 run from 50100 to 50199, module 2 data from 50200 to 50299, and so on. The control module data is set between 50000 and 50099.

9. *Module options.*   Each module is, in general, able to execute one of a series of related tasks. The various options within a module are accessed by means of option flags. No matter what option is chosen, the module is entered at a single point—namely, 1000 for module 1, 2000 for module 2, and so on. When we adopt this convention, nothing of the module's internal structure need be known to the calling routine. We can change a single module without having to change the other modules.

If you want to create more modules you could assign the variables starting with A to module 1—thus, A1, A2,..., A0; those starting with B to module 2, and so on. In this way you could have a maximum of 26 modules, each with 10 real, integer, and string variables.

We purposely have not, up to this point, mentioned anything about the internal structure of the individual modules. The essence of modular programming is that very little information is necessary to use a program module. The information outlined here is the most you need to know about any of the modules in the system.

4.3.2.   Program Flags

One of the most important aspects of modular programming in BASIC is to keep the program modules from becoming knotted or intertwined in their respective internal structures. To meet this requirement, we need a way of communicating *branching decisions* from one module to another.

We have found that *program flags* are a particularly valuable way of passing control information without having to access the primary subroutines of the modules by their beginning line numbers. We use these program flags to control a number of other important tasks, namely, to indicate whether a module has been called during program execution, and to indicate if a particular module is present in the program.

Referring to Figure 4.5, we see that lines 0 to 9 contain all of the system level information. Identical copies of these lines are stored with each module when they are filed on disk. In this area we dimension a two-dimensional array $F\%(10, 5)$. This array, taking up just over 100 bytes in Applesoft, contains all the program flags necessary for the complete control of the program. The first index of this array refers to the corresponding module of the same number in the system. Thus $F\%(2, J)$, where J can lie in the range 0 to 5, are the six modular flags for module 2. The meanings of the second array index for any module K are shown in Figure 4.6.

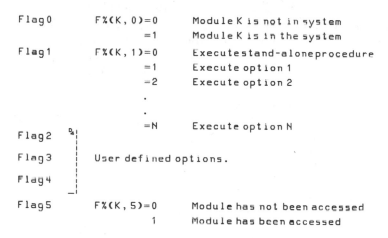

```
Flag0       F%(K,0)=0    Module K is not in system
                 =1      Module K is in the system
Flag1       F%(K,1)=0    Execute stand-alone procedure
                 =1      Execute option 1
                 =2      Execute option 2
                  .
                  .
                 =N      Execute option N
Flag2
Flag3            User defined options.
Flag4
Flag5       F%(K,5)=0    Module has not been accessed
                  1      Module has been accessed
```

Figure 4.6. Program flags for module K.
Language: Applesoft.

The first flag is used to indicate the presence or absence of module K in the system. Remember, we dimension the array $F\%(\ )$ in the system level initialization section, and this array should always be present no matter what module or modules are present in the system. The coding of module K, beginning at line K000 will contain, the statement $F\%(K, 0)=1$. If, however, module K is *not* present, then by default the element $F\%(K, 0)$ will equal zero, since all variables are cleared at run time. Thus, if we were to call a module, module 5, say, and execute option 3 of that module with the calling instruction

```
F%(5,1)=3:IF F%(5,0)=1 THEN GOSUB 5000
```

we would only jump to module 5 if it were in the system. This may or may not be a valuable facility, depending on the complexity of the task and the tradeoff between facile debugging and the increase in execution-time overhead as a result of the added IF...THEN statement.

We have already introduced the second module flag $F\%(5, 1)$ in the above example to call a particular option within module 5. Before we call up a particular module it is imperative that we satisfy all global variables required by the module and the option being addressed. Thus, we may need to write

```
F%(5,1)=3:NM%=A1%:AA=B1:GOSUB 5000
```

Again, we are calling module 5 to execute option 3. However, we are also setting the global variables NM% and AA equal to A1% and B1, respectively. Since these local variables are only recognized by module 1 (by our convention), we can only execute this line of code from within module 1.

We have reserved the flags $F\%(K, 2),..., F\%(K, 4)$ for other options that we may wish to specify in addition to those in the main option table. For example, if we had an output module with which to print different texts, we might use the element $F\%(K, 2)$ to denote the printer style, and so on.

We have designated a value of zero for the option choice element—namely, $F\%(K, 1)=0$—to indicate that a special default procedure is to be executed from within the module. This might be a subroutine that executes a stand-alone procedure to test the internal structure of the module.

Finally, the last flag, $F\%(K, 5)$, will also default to zero unless it is set to some other nonzero value during program execution. This may be done when the module is exited for the first time. On subsequent calls to the module, this flag may be tested, and time-consuming setup procedures, which need be executed only once, may be skipped.

4.3.3. The Module Structure

We now consider a possible plan for the internal structure of the individual modules in the program. A block diagram of a module structure that we have found to work quite well is shown in Figure 4.7. We show the module structure for some arbitrary module, n. An identical system initialization code is placed at the beginning of each module, so that these lines of code are always in the system regardless of the number of modules we are using. All other lines of code enclosed in any of the blocks on this figure are unique to that particular module.

Some of the lines of code that are important in creating our modular structure and system facilities for module 8 are presented in Figure 4.8. In the system initialization area, we have included the dimension statement for the flag array $F\%(\ )$ in line 5. Lines 80 to 89 are used for module initialization, such as DIMension and data READ statements. Also, this is the place where the element $F\%(8, 0)$ is set to a nonzero value to indicate that module 8 is in the system.

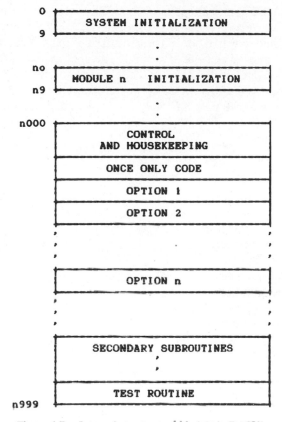

Figure 4.7. Internal structure of Module in BASIC.

Global array variables should always be dimensioned within the control module initialization area (lines 300 to 499), even though they may be used by other modules in the system. The first 50 line numbers (in this case 8000 to 8050) will contain the branching instructions for the different options available in the module being addressed as well as any housekeeping or overhead tasks for the option being run. The next 50 lines (8050 to 8099) contain procedures that need be executed only once when the program is run.

The first IF statement in line 8005 of Figure 4.8 tests to see whether the module has been executed before. If it has, the program will skip to the next statement; if not, the "once-only" code starting at line 8050 will be executed before going to line 8010, where the program branches to one of the different options given by the flag $F\%(8, 1)$. In the event that $F\%(8, 1)$ is zero, none of these options will be executed, and control will pass to the stand-alone procedure starting at line 8950. This section contains a default procedure to test the module by calling the other module procedures.

The program is so configured that after completing the option procedure, program control is returned to the module control procedure and then exits module 8 at line 8049 to the calling procedure. The only exception to this will be if the stand-alone (test) procedure is excecuted.

We have partially satisfied one of the central rules of modular programming, that modules be entered and exited at single entrance and exit points. A major feature of this scheme is that lines of code can be added at these points to monitor the progress of program execution, since we know with certainty that the program flow must pass through these points often during program execution.

```
   0 REM********** SYSTEM INITIALIZATION **************
   1
   .
   .
   5 DIM F%(10,5)
   .
   .
  80 REM****** MODULE 8  INITIALIZATION****************
  81 F%(8,0)=1
  82 DIM......
  83 FOR A5=1 TO .. :READ.... :NEXT A1
   .
   .
   .
8000 REM**** MODULE 8  name(global variables)*********
8005   IF F%(8,5)=0 THEN GOSUB 8050
8010   ON F%(8,1) GOSUB 8100,8200, ..........
8015   IF F%(8,1)=0 THEN GOTO 8950
   .
   .
   .
8045   F%(8,5)=1
8049   RETURN :REM---------END OF MODULE HEADER -------
8050   REM----------------ONCE ONLY CODE ------------
   .
   .
8099   RETURN :REM-------- END OF ONCE ONLY CODE -------
8100 REM---- OPTION 1    "NAME(GLOBAL VARIABLES)" ----
   .
8199 RETURN :REM --------- END OF OPTION 1 ------------
8200 REM---- OPTION 2    "NAME(GLOBAL VARIABLES)" ----
   .
   .
8950 REM----- STAND-ALONE PROCEDURE ----------------
   .
   .
8990 END :REM ------END OF STAND-ALONE PROCEDURE ----
8999 REM********* END OF MODULE 8 *****************
```

Figure 4.8.   Applesoft module configuration.
Language: Applesoft.

4.3.4. Bookkeeping

An extremely important aspect of programming is careful documentation. We have mentioned earlier that one of the strengths of the structured programming languages is that their structure makes them self-documenting. In the case of Applesoft or other BASIC derivatives, especially those that are only allowed two letters for the variable name, it is not possible to make every variable name reflect the meaning of the variable.

Many programmers who are forced to use Applesoft attempt to give even such a short variable name some meaning. We have chosen a different approach when writing modular programming code. This necessitates careful record keeping of the meaning of each variable. A list such as that in Table 4.1, which contains all the information on the local variables, global variables, and the various options resident in the program module, has been found to be quite helpful in this respect.

There is another simple mechanism that may be used in Applesoft to document the program with descriptive variable names. Applesoft only recognizes the first two characters of a variable name together with the variable type extension. Any characters that are placed in between are ignored by the interpreter. Thus, in the following list the three variables on the left, which might be used in an Applesoft program, will only be recognized as the variables listed on the right.

Table 4.1.   Variable Listing and Module Documentation
Language: Applesoft

Variable List					
Local Variables					
	"*Module Number*"			"*Module Name*"	
	Real		Integer		String
A	"description"	A%	"description"	A$	"description"
B	"	B%	"	B$	"
C	"	C%	"	C$	"
.	"	.	"	.	"
.	"	.	"	.	"
Z	"	Z%	"	Z$	"
Global Variables					

"listing of global variables"

Option List

      option 1   "description"
      option 2   .
          .   .
      option n   .

Program	Program Variable	Interpreter Recognition
Integer	M2WAVELENGTH%	M2%
Real	A5INTENSITY	A5
String	X9FILENAME$	X9$

4.3.5.   Modular Programming using Program Files

We have assumed up to now that although program modules might be developed separately, they would all have to simultaneously reside in memory during program execution. This need not be the case. It is possible, as we have discussed in Chapter 3, to chain Applesoft programs off the disk by using the EXEC or CHAIN commands and, at the same time, to not erase existing variables. Some of the modular initialization commands that were introduced in the previous sections will have to be configured a little differently, but that is all that must be done.

Sometimes, due to insufficient memory during program chaining, one may have to release space taken up by large arrays that have become redundant or to pass the contents of an existing array to another array to be used by the new program segment. Applesoft does not have the benefit of the COMMON statement found in BASICA, but there are utility programs available that will extend Applesoft to satisfy this requirement.

The program segment in Figure 4.9 illustrates the use of a number of these array utilities to destroy, rename, or redimension some arrays prior to loading a new module from disk.

```
200  REM  INITIALIZING AND EXECUTING A NEW MODULE
210  DEL 8000-8999
220  & "ARRAY DELETE", W8(0), X8$(0), Y8(0):REM DESTROY ARRAYS
230  & "ARRAY REDIM", V8(1000):REM REDIMENSION ARRAY
250  & "ARRAY RENAME", Z8(0), S8(0):REM RENAME ARRAY
260  PRINT D$;"EXEC MODULE8.BAS,D1"
270  GOSUB 8000:  REM GO TO SUBROUTINE EXECED IN
```

Figure 4.9.   Modular disk-based programming.
Language: Applesoft + &ARRAY.

4.4.   MODULAR PROGRAMMING IN BASICA

We have already discussed (see Chapter 3) the procedures provided in BASICA for writing modular code. The discussion of modular programming in the last section also applies to BASICA. In particular, the guidelines regarding line numbering are directly applicable to the BASIC language.

Since variables may contain up to 40 characters in BASICA, it is much easier to write readable code. Also the probability of using the same variable twice in two different modules is far less likely to happen. It is quite simple to extend the concept of global and local variables in BASICA. Because a period may be included in a variable name, a different extension to each local variable may be added, as shown below, to prevent accidental conflicts in names.

Global	WAVENUMBER
Module 1	WAVELENGTH.1
Module 2	INTENSITY.2

.

.

.

and so on

We use modular programming techniques for BASICA in Chapter 9 in the development of mathematical data analysis routines that may be used on experimental or model data. We present a slightly different approach to the problem of writing modular code than has been presented here.

4.5. STRUCTURED PROGRAMMING

Structured programming concepts are used in this book in two contexts. The first illustrates the development of algorithms without regard to the actual language in which the procedure will be coded. The second demonstrates the use of one of these structured languages, namely C, for coding procedures requiring greater execution speed.

4.5.1. Creating Structured Algorithms

It is sometimes convenient to write in simple English the logic of an idea to be programmed before actually beginning the coding. The structured languages contain enough common logic so that a simple algorithmic language may be created based loosely on their syntax. The statements will be shown in italic type. All specific statements, on the other, hand will be in regular type. The type convention for each particular language will be adhered to; for example, lowercase for C.

Our algorithms will conform to the convention in Figure 4.10, which with certain minor variations is universal for all structured languages.

```
procedure name (argument list)
Declarations
begin
Algorithm Statements
end
```

Figure 4.10. Structured program structure.
Language: Algorithmic.

The *declarations* section declares the important data types. The *statements* section contains the logical series of statements making up the algorithm.

As an example, we show in Figure 4.11 a simple algorithmic procedure for calculating the sums of the squares on *Npts* numbers $\{x_i\}$. Note that we have attempted to make variable names self-explanatory. However, since spaces are not allowed by the syntax of the language, a "_" has been substituted for a space. Thus, sum of the squares becomes sum_sq. Also, arrows are used instead of equal signs. For example, to set the sum of the squares equal to zero, we write sum ← 0.

```
procedure sum_sq(array x, Npts)
double precision  array x, sum
integer Npts
begin
    sum ← 0
    for (i is 1 to Npts) do
       sum ← sum + 2 x_i
    end_for
    return sum as answer
end
```

Figure 4.11. Sample structured program.
Language: Algorithmic.

This algorithm is easily converted into C or even BASIC.

The declaration section of a structured program depends on the data types possessed by the language. Similarly, the statement section depends on the flow and control branching statements available in the language in which the algorithm is to be coded.

4.5.2. Structured Flow and Control Primitives

It is instructive to review the statements available in the structured languages for flow and control purposes. A list of the most common, structured, flow control statements that appear in one form or another in structured languages is given in Figure 4.12.

A] CONDITIONAL BRANCHING

```
if [condition] then do              if [condition] then do
    statements                          statements 1
end_if                              else do
                                        statements 2
                                    end_if


if [condition 1] then do            case (variable)
    statements 1                        value 1:  statement 1
else if [condition 2] then do           value 2:  statement 2
    statements 2                        value....
```

else....
.
.
else if [condition n] then do
    statements N
end_if

value N: statement N
end_case

B] UNCONDITIONAL BRANCHING

goto

C] ITERATIVE PRIMITIVES

for (range & step) do
    statements
end_for

repeat
    statements
until [condition]

while [condition] do
    statements
end_while

do
    statements
while [condition]

Figure 4.12. Structured flow and control statements.
Language: Algorithmic.

The control statements in this list represent an ideal set of commands for a structured language, and not all of them will be available for every structured language. These statements simplify programming when there are repetitive tasks or branching alternatives to be programmed. One important point to note as we use these commands is that, even if we use multiple lines of code for these commands, they should be considered as a single, logical programming structure.

The list of branching primitives is divided, for illustrative purposes, into three classes of commands: *conditional*, *unconditional*, and *iterative*. Some programmers are adamant that one should never use the unconditional branching *goto* statement in a structured programming environment. One is almost forced to use the command when programming in an unstructured language that does not contain the full complement of conditional branching commands.

The combination of these structured flow statements can become highly complex in a real program. This is especially true when using the logical operators *and* and *or*; in some structured languages, *nand* and *nor* are used in the logical conditions. To illustrate, let us configure an algorithm (see Figure 4.13) to execute one of three procedures depending on the values of k and i in a logical condition.

Since it is usually possible to nest these statements so that there are branches within branches, we can program extremely complex sets of alternatives within a compact section of code. The use of indented code makes the program flow much easier to understand. We have used this facility extensively throughout this book.

The final conditional command in Figure 4.12 is the *case* command structure, which is used, for example, when the variable or the result of an expres-

```
being
  if [ i < 100 and k > 200 ] then
      execute procedure 1
  else if [ i >= 100 and i < 200 and k > 200 ] then
      execute procedure 2
  else if [ i >= 200 ] then
      repeat
          execute procedure 3
      until [no more data]
  end_if
end
```

Figure 4.13.   An example of use of structured flow and control primitives. Language: Algorithmic.

sion may have several possibilities and we wish to make some other variables dependent on the state of the variable. The switch command in C and the CASE command in PASCAL have this structure.

The final section of Figure 4.12 lists the *iterative* primitives, which are used in situations where a section of code must be executed a known number of times. The examples should largely explain the structure of these commands. The *for...next* loop occurs in almost all computer languages in one form or another. In FORTRAN, for example, the language syntax is slightly different (DO...CONTINUE) but logically completely equivalent to the FOR... NEXT in BASIC.

The other command forms in the figure only occur in structured languages. The difference between the *repeat...until* and the *while...end* loops is that the *while* loop is tested at the beginning of execution, so that if the logical operation is found to be false the first time it is encountered, the loop will never be executed; whereas in the *repeat...until* case, the loop will be executed at least once before it is tested. The *do...while* loop is also executed at least once, but in this case the condition must be true for the loop to continue, whereas in the *repeat...until* case the loop is repeated while the condition is false.

4.5.3.   Structured Data Types

The various data types available in a structured language, as much as modularity or structured flow, make the language a powerful media for programming complex algorithms. Every computer language has some elementary data types, such as *real, integer*, or *character* types. The following is a list of some of the structured data types found in computer languages such as PASCAL, MODULA-2, and, to a lesser extent, C.

Arrays
Records
Pointers

Enumeration

Subrange

Sets

Files

The *array* is a structured data type familiar to anyone with an elementary knowledge of programming. In languages such as BASIC or FORTRAN each element of an array must be of the same elementary data type whether real, integer, or string. The concept of the array in the structured programming languages is much more powerful. The elements of an array can themselves be made up of more complex structured data types, such as records, and may even be arrays themselves, as we will later show.

The *record* (called a data structure in C) is an example of a complex data type. It is made up of a number of *fields*, each of which may be made up of elementary or structured data types. We have already introduced the concept of a record during the discussion of random access files in BASICA in Chapter 3.

As an illustration of the potential use of these structured data types, let us consider the overall process of data management and documentation in the laboratory. In a nonstructured language without structured data types, such a task can quickly become unmanageable as the quantity and type of data increase. For example, consider the spectrometer system introduced at the beginning of this chapter. The primary data consisting usually of an array of spectrum intensities and corresponding wavelengths is quite easy to handle. However, real experiments include a time and date stamp as well as various instrument settings and other miscellaneous documentation.

For our experiment we will create a record template called *spectrum_scan* where the different data fields will contain all the important data necessary to characterize a single spectrum scan data set. One scheme for a *spectrum_scan* record is shown in Table. 4.2. The complete database (data structure) will consist of an entire array of similar records. Each record will contain the information collected in a single experimental scan. The breakdown of a single record is shown in Table 4.2. The record is broken up into eight different fields, five of which are themselves records and are further divided into fields. In this table are shown the lengths and data types of the elementary fields together with a sample data record.

A more detailed breakdown of the records is shown in Figure 4.14, which shows the further breakdown of the record fields into more elementary data types. Examining, for example, the *date* record we see that the *year* and the *day* fields are both integers. The *month*, on the other hand, is a character field. The *time* field is also a record made up of three integer fields. The time record could have been divided into a three-dimensional integer array, but then we would have lost the field label and would have had to work with, and interpret, array subscripts. Another field in this example is laser_param (laser parameters), which describes some of the basic information on the laser light source. The

Table 4.2.   Record and Field Structure Example

Record Name	Field Name	Field Type	Dimension	Sample Contents
spectrum_scan	title	character array	[20]	OH fluorescence
	date	record	–	see below
	time	record	–	"
	wavelengths	record	–	"
	#_points	integer	–	751
	intensity	real array	[1000]	1.5e4,.....
	sample_param	record	–	see below
	laser_param	record	–	"
date	year	integer	–	1984
	month	character array	[3]	Jan
	day	integer	–	6
time	hour	integer	–	21
	minute	integer	–	10
	second	integer	–	23
wavelengths	start	real	–	3050.
	end	real	–	3200.
	increment	real	–	0.2
sample_params	temperature	real	–	685
	pressure	real	–	1
	gas	character array	[10]	helium
	power	real	–	5.5
laser_param	wavelength	real	–	3130.03
	energy	real	–	10
	dye	character array	[12]	
	crystal	character array	[12]	
	divergence	real	–	2.5
	feedback	boolean	–	true (yes)

Boolean data type for the *feedback* field is used to indicate whether the laser was operating in a feedback mode: a simple yes/no question.

Each member of the structure is referenced by means of a structure tree as in

```
spectrum_scan.date.month
```

The higher structured languages such as PASCAL and MODULA-2 have an advanced language structure that allows arrays and records to be treated as a single unit. The *set* may be used in these languages for that purpose. At the lower end of the scale such operations in a language like C can only be managed with library functions.

The *enumeration or set subrange* or data types, which again are only available in the higher-level languages, allow one to limit the possible outcomes of a particular operation, but they rely on the program structure to keep track of the contents of a data field. In our example in Figure 4.14, using the set data type, we could have restricted the month field to the following twelve possibilities.

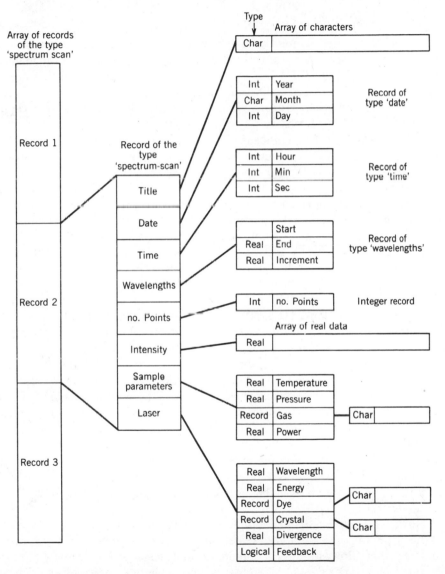

Figure 4.14. The structure of a data record configured to store experimental data from the Spectrometer experiment of figure 4.3.

```
month  =  (jan,feb,mar,apr,may...dec)
```

Similarly, a subrange data type allows us to keep track of the range of numerical data, not just its type. Finally, the *pointer* data classification is both the most difficult to understand and the most powerful to use. We discuss the particular advantages of pointer arithmetic in the next section, when we consider the C language.

4.5.4.   Structured Languages

We have mentioned a number of times the similarities that underlie the structured languages. There are also vast differences amongst these languages. The languages C and MODULA-2 are interesting to compare since they are at different ends of the spectrum insofar as many of their structured features are concerned. Both languages are available for the IBM-PC and the Apple Micro computers in various forms.

A list of some of the significant features of the two languages is shown in Table 4.3. The modular aspect of MODULA-2 is highly advanced. Library modules may be created that resemble "black boxes" having a greater level of autonomy than the corresponding procedures in PASCAL or the functions in C. Many of the features, such as a modular structure that can check for data type mismatches in parameter passing between modules, are new to computer language. Arguments in C are not checked for type mismatch by the compiler.

Both languages have extensive structured flow elements that make the task of coding structured algorithms straightforward. The subject of data types is one of the areas in which the two languages are very different. The elementary data types show clearly that C is very much a language for number and character manipulation. In terms of structured data types, on the other hand, C lacks the various complex structured features that would allow for the manipulation of arrays and records containing a mixture of data types.

Both languages have a library extendable structure. This feature creates an environment in which the features of each particular machine may be accommodated without compromising the integrity of the core language. All I/O features in C and MODULA-2 are handled by library functions, which makes the languages mobile—that is, easy to move from one computer to another. MODULA-2 has features that allow it to be used almost at the machine language level. These same features are extensive in C. Machine language programming may be required for communication with a peripheral for which no packaged software is available or in cases where the existing software must be modified.

However, referring to our list of desirable features in a structured language at the beginning of this chapter, we see that C is somewhat deficient. It is not a language that allows for easy documentation. The syntax is extremely terse, a feature which is considered a liability by some. There is, however, an almost mathematical elegance to the language, which allows huge amount of information to be compressed into a short space.

Table 4.3. Some Important Aspects of C and MODULA-2

Description	MODULA-2	C
Modular aspects	module procedure	function
Module arguments	type checked between models	not typed checked between modules
Structured flow elements	extensive	extensive
Elementary data types	integers real boolean char bitset	unsigned int,short long float double char
Structured types	array enumeration subrange set record pointer procedure	array struc record pointer function
Type	const	#define 'UPPER CASE'
Declarations	var	'lower case'
Extendable aspects	library	library
Array dimensions	extendable by pointers	extendable by pointers
Interfacing to other languages	yes	yes
I/O	library procedure	library function
Low-level support	controlled but limited	extensive
Syntax, e.g.	well documented begin...end	terse {......}
Linking modules	automatically linked when called	Use linker
Type checking	extensive	Limited

Either or both of these languages are suitable for use in any programming activity related to data acquisition, control, or data manipulation in situations where the speed obtained with a compiled language is required. MODULA-2 is the newer of the two languages and has not yet become widely used in this context, but it has many of the features that are desirable in such applications. The C language, due to its low-level support features, is already used extensively for software interfacing development. The language is also highly suitable for coding algorithms of mathematical functions in a readable fashion. Throughout the rest of this book we restrict our discussions of compiled languages to C.

4.6. PROGRAMMING IN C

This section introduces the reader to the C language. The following discussion is not meant to be comprehensive or to act as a teaching guide. We merely highlight those aspects of the language that we feel make it an important language for the future in technical applications.

The C language has thus far been used primarily by professional programmers. One appealing aspect of the language from the standpoint of the professional is its tremendous range. On the one hand, it is a high-level structured language in which complex algorithms may be easily coded. On the other hand, it has many low-level capabilities that allow it to rival assembly language. However, whereas assembly language is closely tied to a particular machine, the C language is quite portable. Much of the software development work regarding data acquisition systems by computer peripheral manufacturers is being carried out in C. We use C almost exclusively in this book as a high-level language for efficiently coding mathematical or data reduction procedures.

4.6.1. The C Language Syntax

The modules of a C program are referred to as *functions*. These functions have the characteristic of both the procedures and functions of PASCAL. Each function corresponds to the general structure in Figure 4.15.

```
#include"librarydeclarationfiles"
#define "preprocess macros"
global declarations

<type> "function_name" (arguments)
argument declarations
{
        declarations;
        statements;
}
```

Figure 4.15.   The language structure of C.

Note that braces{...} are used in place of the BEGIN...END statements of some of the other structured languages. C is based on a library structure. The language has a number of standard libraries that are discussed in the following sections. These libraries may be supplemented with user-defined libraries for special applications. When any library is being used, the functions contained in it must be specifically declared at the beginning of a function. The #include command may be used to append files such as common library-header declaration files at the beginning of the function file.

The #define preprocessor macro construction at the beginning of a function allows a string of characters to be labeled with a symbolic name. Before the compiler starts to compile, these character strings are substituted into the code where the symbolic name has been used in the program. For example, we can have the definition

```
#define      PI      3.1415926
```

Capital letters are always used for these defined symbols to distinguish them from true variables in the program.

Global variable declarations may be made at the beginning of a file containing a number of C functions. These will be recognized by all the functions in the file but not by any functions contained in other files. Functions and variables may also be declared as external to the file, which allows the compiler to proceed. The functions will be brought together during the *linker* stage.

The data type declared before the function name is only used in cases where the function is returning a single number. This is directly analogous to the function form of PASCAL. For example, the declaration

```
double bessel(n,x)   /*   function name          */
double x;            /*   argument declarations*/
int n;
{
        .
}
```

creates a double precision function, bessel ( ), with arguments n,x, where x is also a double precision number and n is an integer. The function bessel(n, x) takes on many of the characteristics of a variable and may be used by name in a program as follows:

```
y = 2 * (n-1) * bessel (n-1,x) / x - bessel (n-2,x)
```

Functions that return more than a single value are written on the declaration line without the type declaration as follows:

```
fft_prm(nu,pxreal,pximag) /* function name */
```

where the function fft_prm ( ) is a more complex operation that returns a whole array of data using pointer arithmetic, as we discuss later.

An example of a simple C program to calculate the sinc function, used for smoothing and interpolation in many aspects of data filtering, is shown in Figure 4.16.*

```
#include "libc.h"          /* standard C library header file       */
#include "math.h"          /* mathematical library header file     */
#define PI 3.1415926       /* define preprocessing macros          */
#define SMALL 1.0E-15
#define ONE 1

double sinc(x)             /* function name                        */
double x;                  /* function argument declarations       */
{
  double sin( ),abs( );

  if (abs(x) <= SMALL) return (ONE);
  else return sin (PI * x)/(PI * x);
}
```

Figure 4.16. C program for calculation of sinc function.

This is an example of a function call that returns a single number, the value of sinc(x). The *if...then* structure is used to eliminate the case where the equation is not valid—that is, when $x=0$, where the denominator will blow up. The sinc function is mathematically defined as unity as $x=0$. The two functions abs(x) and sin(x) are declared explicitly; they are contained in our mathematical function library, compiled separately, and added at the linker stage. They could have been declared in the libary header file libc.lib.

A number of syntactical features of C are unique to the language and lead to a very economically coded program. However, the compression or brevity occurs at the expense of easy translation by the uninitiated. A list of some of these features is shown in Table 4.4. with common alternatives for writing the instructions that conform more closely to the syntax used in other languages.

4.6.2. Creating a Running C Program

Compiled languages are somewhat more difficult for novice programmers to understand than are interpreted languages. The transformation from the text code to a running program takes many more steps for a compiled program than for an equivalent interpreted program. As the program gets more complex, however, the advantage of increased run speed in the compiled program and the ease of its development, especially in a structured language, becomes apparent.

*R.N. Bracewell, *The Fourier Transform and its Applications* (McGraw-Hill, New York, 1978.)

Table 4.4. Unique Syntactical Features of C

C Feature	Explanation	Alternative
Increment/Decrement		
i++	increment by 1 after test	i=i+1
++i	increment by 1 before test	
i−−	decrement by 1 after test	i=i−1
−−i	decrement by 1 before test	
y op= x	operate x on y and store in y	y = y op x
y += x	add x to y and store in y	y = y + x
y *= x	multiply x and y and store in y	y = y * x
x % y	remainder of x divided by y	
ARRAYS		
*(y+k)	one-dimensional array	y[k]
*(x+i)[j]	two-dimensional array	x[i][j]
LOGICAL		
==	logical equals to	
&&	logical *.AND.*	
¦¦	logical *.OR.*	
>=	logical greater or equals to	
<=	logical less than or equal to	
!=	logical *.NOT.* equal to	
STRUCTURED DATA		
pr −> set	(pr is a pointer) points to a particular member in the structure set	
member. set	defines member of set	

It is instructive to discuss the steps that must be taken to convert source code (program language statements) into a working program. We use as an example the sequence used with the Aztec* version of the C language. Although the steps may differ in detail from other versions of C or other languages, the main aspects remain very much the same.

Source code is usually prepared in an ASCII text file with an editor or word processor. The complete conversion sequence from the text source file file.c. to the final executable file is shown in Figure 4.17. The first step is to compile the source code into relocatable assembly language code that is stored in the file file.asm. The assembly code at this point must be relocatable to allow program modules which have been compiled separately to be merged at the final linker stage. The next phase of the "compilation" process involves operating on the assembly code with the assembler to produce the file file.o. In some language systems the compiler and assembler operations are combined into a single

---

The Aztec C86 Manual, Copyright by Manx Software Systems, P.O. Box 55, Shrewsbury, NJ 07701.

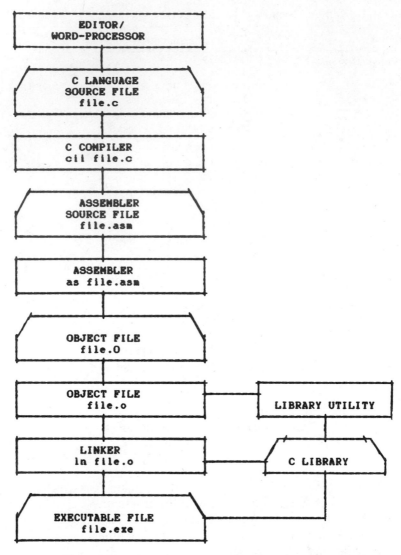

Figure 4.17. The steps in creating an executable file in C.

operation. The functions, once they have been transformed into assembly code in this way, may be placed in a function library for ease of linking.

The final stage before one has an executable program involves the linker operation. The linker operation combines separately compiled modules and also some of the standard functions needed by the programs. These functions are contained in a series of function libraries that are described in the next subsection. The executable file file.exe is a binary file that must reside in an absolute address in program memory. The program is run by typing in the root of the program name, that is, file.

4.6.3. Creating a C Library

The C language, like many structured languages, has the concept of extensibility built into its structure. The language, as implemented on most microcomputers, comes with a library of standard functions that, for most compilers, tends to follow closely those published by Kernighan and Ritchie.* We restrict our attention to the mathematical and scientific library routines found in these standard C libraries. They are listed in Table 4.5.

Most C libraries include an extensive number of buffered and unbuffered I/O routines. Unbuffered operations move data in and out of the computer one byte at a time. Buffered operations, on the other hand, use a common, though not universal, buffer size of 512 bytes. Many compilers provide interfaces to the OS being implemented on the computer. Programs interfaced to OS functions are machine dependent and should be avoided if portability is desired.

Most C compilers allow for the creation of new function libraries. This flexibility makes it quite easy to *link* the library functions to user-written programs. For example, for the Aztec C compiler the mathematical routines are contained in the library file math.lib. Our numerical function routines, discussed in Chapter 9, are contained in the library file numrcl. lib and can easily be combined with the any program.

4.6.4. Pointers and Arrays

The subject of pointers is complex but extremely important in C. It is responsible for some of the strange-looking code written in the language. We restrict

Table 4.5. Typical Mathematical and Scientific C Library

acos(x)	inverse cosine of x (arccos x)
asin(x)	inverse sin of x
atan(x)	inverse tangent of x
atan2(x,y)	arctangent of x divided by y
cos(x)	cosine of x
cosh(x)	hyperbolic cosine of x
cotan(x)	cotangent of x
exp(x)	exponential function of x
log(x)	natural logarithm of x
log10(x)	logarithm to base 10 of x
pow(x,y)	raise x to yth power
random()	random number in range $0-1$
sin(x)	sine of x
sinh (x)	hyperboli sine function

---

*B.W. Kernighan and D.M. Ritchie, *The C Programming Language* (Prentice Hall, Englewood Cliffs, N.J., 1978).

our attention in this section to the procedure for passing data to and from C functions used in numerical analysis.

Data may be passed through the arguments of a function in a number of ways. Let us consider the library function fft_prm ( ). C deals with argument passing differently than most other high-level languages. In C the numerical values of the arguments are passed through the stack, not, as in other languages, the location (address) where the data is stored. Thus, we may use and change arguments within a function without changing its value in the stack array. This is very useful for creating functions that are truly isolated and that will not affect the calling routines. As a corollary, data, especially the contents of large arrays, cannot be easily modified by a function and then passed back through the argument, as in FORTRAN or PASCAL. Also, when passing large data arrays, a new array must be set up within the calling function which mirrors the contents of the array in the called routine.

```
fft_prm(nu,xreal, ximag)
int nu;
double xreal[1024],ximag[1024];
{
        .
        .
}
```

In this example we pass two single-dimensioned arrays as well as an integer, nu, to the function fft_prm ( ). But since in this function the arrays are changed and the data needs to be passed back to the calling routine, this form of data passing is inadequate.

The alternative to passing the data is to use *pointers* and deal with the contents of specified memory addresses rather than the values of the numbers themselves. Let us consider a variable x. We can define a pointer px that must be defined as a char variable. The address of x may be put in px thus by:

```
double x;
char px;
px=&x
```

where the & operator obtains the address of x, and we put it into the pointer variable px. It is common practice to begin pointer variables with the letter p. It is inconvenient to deal with both the variable and its pointer. Another operator, *, when used with the pointer, refers to the contents of the location indicated by the pointer. For example, if we write

```
z = *px
```

we replace the contents of z with the contents of the location pointed to by px.

So far there is very little in the properties of the pointers to get excited about. Their strength becomes apparent when they are used in array arithmetic, especially across function boundaries. Consider an array, y, of one dimension containing n points that we must pass to, and receive, from a function. The C instruction

$$py=\&y;$$

places in the pointer variable py the position of the zeroth element, y[0], of the array. Once the pointer has been defined, the C syntax allows us to write the pointer to the kth element as py+k (yes, a mixture of a pointer and an integer) and the contents of the element k as *(py+k) as we show in Figure 4.18a.

If we wish to pass arguments, we need only write the following declaration at the beginning of the function:

```
fft_prm(nu,pxreal, pximag)
int nu;
double *pxreal,*pximag;
{
double y
       .
       .
y=*(pxreal+k)
       .
}
```

Here we expect that the second and third arguments in the function call will be pointers. The compiler must be told the initialization condition—in this case double precision—of the contents of the array elements. There is no need to initialize pxreal itself since the compiler can deduce from the declaration *pxreal that pxreal is a pointer. The initialization condition gives sufficient information to fix the location of any element of the array with respect to the location of the first element (8 bytes double, 4 bytes single, etc.). Using pointer arithmetic we do not need to reserve a specific area of program memory for the array in the called function fft_prm ( ).

The calling sequence in the main routine is usually written as

```
main ( )
{
    int nu;
    double xreal[50],ximag[50];
          .
          .
    fft_prm(nu,&xreal,&ximag);
          .
          .
}
```

where all we pass to the function is the pointer to the first element of the array. It is up to us to synchronize the data types in the main and library functions, or else the data will have no meaning.

Two-dimensional arrays pose more problems than the single-dimensioned ones. For such arrays it is necessary to specify the rightmost dimension and to have a correspondence in that dimension with the calling function and the function being called. The elements of a two-dimensional array such as a[j][k] may be addressed by (*(pa+j))[k]. The action of the pointer and the subscripts is shown in Figure 4.18b. Arrays in C are stored so that the subscripts to the right are stored in neighboring locations (of 8 bytes for double). The next subscript to the left is then incremented, and so on. In our case we have defined an a[NA][10] array. We can use the pointer for j, and thus we only have to dimension k. The program below illustrates the initialization sequence:

```
mtrx_sln(n,pa,px,pb)
double (*(pa))[10], *px,*pb;
int n;
{
  .
  .
  .
  z=(*(pa+j))[k];
  .
  .
  .
}
```

Not only may arrays be accessed as pointers, but it is also possible to do the same for functions themselves. For example, we consider the C function for integrating any analytical expression defined by another C function. This is done with the function intgl_f ( ), where the declaration at the beginning of the function will be written

```
double intgl_f(npts,a,b,f)
int npts;
double a,b,(*f)();
```

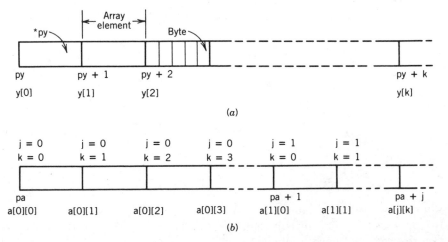

Figure 4.18. Relationship between arrays and pointers in C. (*a*) Single-dimensional array y[k]. (*b*) Two-dimensional array a[j][k].

The function f is pointed to in the calling program merely by using its name. Thus, the integral of the function sinc(x) between 0 and 1 would simply be

$$y = \text{intgl\_f(npts=101,a=0,b=1,sinc)}$$

where we are carrying out the integral using 101 points. Note the compression of code possible by the argument format.

4.6.5. Function Recursion

One of the most powerful features of the structured languages, particularly for technical applications, is *recursion*. It is possible for a C function to call itself from within the body of that function. This feature may be used, in particular, with mathematical functions that may be generated by recursive formulae. Two functions with these properties, namely, the Bessel and gamma functions, are discussed in Chapter 9. The Bessel function of order $n+1$, for example, may be generated from the known values at n and n-1 for the same x value thus by:

$$J_{n+1}(x) = 2nJ_n(x)/x - J_{n-1}(x)$$

Once we know the Bessel functions of orders 0 and 1, all others follow.

The C program structure to take advantage of the recursive properties of the C language is shown in Figure 4.19. The full listing of the program is shown in Appendix D.

```
double bessel (n,x)
double x;
int n;
{
    double y;
        .
        .
    if(n==0){
        /* zero order polynomial calculation */
    }
    else if(n==1){
        /* first order polynomial calculation */
    }
    else if(n>=2){
        y=2*(n-1)*bessel(n-1,x)/x - bessel (n-2,x);
        return y;
    }
}
```

Figure 4.19. The recursive structure of the Bessel function in C.

The compact and elegant nature of this code is readily seen by comparing the length of code needed to carry out the same calculation in BASIC. It should be noted that the speed of calculation using recursion may not be any less than with code written without recursion, and the total amount of space taken up by the program may also be comparable in the two cases, since a considerable amount of stack space may be needed for the intermediate calculations. Its major advantage then is in helping to produce readable code that follows closely the sense of functions being programmed.

4.6.6.   Advanced Programming Example in C

A more complex programming task is the evaluation of the Fourier transform of a function with a real and imaginary component. We defer an explanation of the Fourier method until Chapter 10. The program in Figure 4.20 is presented here as an illustration of the syntax of the C language.

Of prime importance is the technique of pointer arithmetic, described earlier, which is used extensively in this programming example. The addresses of the beginnings of each of the arrays (real and imaginary components of the functions) are passed to the function. In this way the values of array arguments passed to the function may be changed by directing the storage of data within the function to specific locations in the computer's memory.

```
/*                 FAST FOURIER TRANSFORM FUNCTION
 *
 *    The function calculates the fft of a complex function with
 *    real part xreal[] and imaginary part ximag[]. The real and
 *    imaginary parts of the fourier transform are returned in
 *    the same arrays.
 *    The algorithm is explained in detail elsewhere.*
 */
fft_prm(nu,pxreal,pximag)    /*    primitive FFT calculation */
int nu;
double *pximag, *pxreal;
{
    double treal,timag,p,arg,c,s;
    int n,n2,nu1,i,l,k;
    int pwr2(), bitrev();

    n=pwr2(nu);
    n2 = n / 2;
    nu1 = nu-1;
    k = 0;
    for (1 = 1; 1< = nu; 1++)
    {
        do {
        for (i = 1; i<=n2 ; i++)
        {
            p = bitrev(k/pwr2(nu1),nu);
            arg = 2 * PI * p / n;
            c = cos(arg);
            s = sin(arg);
            treal = *(pxreal+k+n2) * c + *(pximag+k+n2) * s;
            timag = *(pximag+k+n2) * c - *(pxreal+k+n2) * s;
```

```
         *(pxreal+k+n2) = *(pxreal+k) - treal;
         *(pximag+k+n2) = *(pximag+k) - timag;
         *(pxreal+k) += treal;
         *(pximag+k) += timag;
         k=k+1;
      }
      k=k + n2;
   } while(k <n-1);
   k=0;
   nu1 = nu1-1;
   n2 = n2/2;
}
for (k=0;k<=n-1;k++) {
   i=bitrev(k,nu);
   if (i>k) {
      treal = *(pxreal+k);
      timag = *(pximag+k);
      *(pxreal+k) = *(pxreal+i);
      *(pximag+k) = *(pximag+i);
      *(pxreal+i) = treal;
      *(pximag+i) = timag;
   }
}
}
```

Figure 4.20. The fft function.
Language: C.

The example shows the value of the structured layout in program writing. The layout has been used throughout this chapter, but only when one views a large program does its benefit become apparent. Each level of imbedded program structure is placed successively to the right of the listing. The fft function consists essentially of two series of imbedded loop structures. The first series of loops contains two for ( ) {...} loops and a single do{...}while. Within this loop structure is a series of matrix-element operations that look very different from their PASCAL counterparts in the PASCAL-version listing of this program in Brigham.* The one-to-one correspondence between the two program versions should be completely understandable from the discussion of pointer arithmetic carried out earlier.

4.7. FORTH

The languages that we have considered so far can be classified loosely as conventional languages, since they are, to a certain extent, linear descendents of FORTRAN or ALGOL language philosophies. FORTH[†] is one of the new

*E.O. Brigham, *The Fast Fourier Transform* (Prentice-Hall, Englewood Cliffs, N.J., 1974).
[†] FORTH is a trademark of Forth, Inc., 2309 Pacific Coast Highway, Hermosa Beach, CA 90254.

so-called "fourth-generation" languages that is structured in a radically different way from previous languages. It was originally developed for real-time data acquisition and control. It is gaining in popularity in the field of robotics as well as in process control applications and is available for most microcomputers. Surprisingly, however, there has been little support for the language from the manufacturers of personal-computer-based data acquisition and control systems.

4.7.1.   FORTH Overview*

FORTH is a modular language consisting of a set of predefined commands called *words* that are contained in a *dictionary*. Each word performs a specific task. Complex tasks can be performed by combining words to form a *program* that, in turn, can be defined as a new word and stored in the dictionary.

A number of FORTH language dialects are available, the most recent of which is called FORTH-83. If you purchase a FORTH-83 system, the dictionary will contain a FORTH-83 required word set. Other FORTH dialects are available, such as FORTH-79, FORTH-77, fig-FORTH, and poly-FORTH, and the dictionaries conform to the standard of that dialect.

The power of FORTH is the ability to link the basic words together, define this program as a new word, and then compile and store this word in the dictionary. The user thus defines and stores new words germane to his specific needs. Complex programs are easily built by using these newly defined words, each of which has been debugged during its development and is also compiled before its inclusion in the dictionary.

The elements of a FORTH program, then, are words from the dictionary (*stacked* one upon the other). The program is started by calling the first word. After its execution, the FORTH interpreter proceeds to the next word in the stack and continues executing the program, one word at a time.

Virtually all FORTH operations involve the stack. A *stack* is an area of computer memory in which information is temporarily kept. It is called a stack because the way data is stored and retrieved from this area can be likened to stacking items on top of each other. Similarly, the second data item is placed on top of the first, the third on top of the second, and so on. This type of stack is usually called a "last in, first out" or LIFO stack because the last number in is the first number out. For example, if you type the numbers 123 and then press the return key, the numbers 123 will be pushed onto the top of a stack. If you follow this with 456 and then return, the 456 will be pushed onto the top of the stack (with 123 stored below it).

Arithmetic operations are performed only on numbers on the stack. Thus, to perform the addition 1 + 2 requires that we first put the numbers on the stack. As before, we can type 1 and return and then 2 and return. If we follow this with a +, which is the word for addition, the 2 will be added to the 1 and the

---

*Leo J. Scanlon, *FORTH Programming* (Howard Sams, Indianapolis, 1982).

answer, 3, will be left on top of the stack. We can describe the procedure by writing

1
2
+

Actually we could have performed the entire operation in one line by typing 1 2 + and then return.

This operator-last notation is called *reverse Polish notation* (RPN) and is common to all stack-oriented machines, such as, for example, Hewlett-Packard's line of programmable calculators.

The advantages of a stack orientation are many. The stack architecture of FORTH reduces the overhead cost of linking subroutines to a minimum, an important consideration since the whole language is built around compiled subroutine calls. The stack also encourages modular programming, which can be easily debugged. Each module (i.e., word) has only one entry point and one exit point. Communication with the outside world occurs only through the stack, thus eliminating unprogrammed side effects on other modules, variables, and so on.

FORTH is an interactive language. All FORTH words can be executed as commands from the keyboard and will behave exactly the same as when they are later compiled. Thus, testing and debugging of new words is immediate.

FORTH debugging seldom requires examining any code except the single definition being tested. Also, unlike most other high-level languages, FORTH allows easy *machine access*. All memory and I/O can be addressed. Except for direct access to machine-specific registers (such as the A, X, and Y registers of the Apple 6502), FORTH can do anything machine language can do. In addition, FORTH usually runs fast enough so that assembly language routines are not necessary.

If full machine speed is required, a FORTH OS usually includes an assembler. The routines created by the assembler have FORTH names and behave exactly like FORTH definitions. Thus, an application can be written entirely in high level code, using FORTH words, and if more speed is required, certain parts can be converted to assembly code with no changes being required anywhere else.

Finally, FORTH code is extremely *transportable* between machines. Substantial programs have been moved between 6502-based and 8080 microcomputers and a PDP-11, with little or no change in the code.

To summarize, FORTH is truly a fourth-generation language, self-contained with editor and assembler. It is not only a language but also an operating system. Developed for the minimum configuration of micros and minis, it runs rapidly in a minimum of memory. The back-linked dictionary allows for the modular construction of a task-related vocabulary that is user friendly and can be easily expanded to encompass new problems.

5

Data Acquisition Control Hardware

5.1. INTRODUCTION

The growth of personal computer plug-in and add-on hardware has been phenomenally rapid. Up-to-date reviews of current products are periodically published in a number of technical magazines.* It is not possible, therefore, for this chapter to reflect an up-to-date review of what is available in this fast-moving marketplace.

Instead, we confine ourselves to providing the reader with a general view of the hardware required for laboratory applications, together with some representative examples of commercially available PC-based laboratory systems.

It wasn't so very long ago[†,‡] that discussions of laboratory interface hardware required explanations of AND gates, NAND gates, data latches, shift registers, counters, clocks, and so on. These circuits are still important components of the interface, but they have become integrated into packages and are transparent to the user. Less detailed knowledge of these circuits is required by the user, since it is no longer necessary to assemble individual components, build the interface, and code the device-driver software.

Several completely assembled laboratory packages using a personal computer, such as the Apple or IBM-PC, as the host are available. It is the ready availability of this hardware, along with the user-friendly software packages designed specifically for laboratory applications, that have contributed strongly to the explosive growth of personal-computer usage in laboratory situations.

Still, there are certain aspects of the hardware that should be understood by the user, since they impact on the appropriateness of the system for the user's particular laboratory problems.

---

* See, for instance, *Electronic Design New*, March 8, 1984, pp. 133–170, September 6, 1984, pp. 55–70, November 15, 1984, pp. 53–67, April 4, 1985, pp. 159–197.
† S.P. Perone and D.O. Jones, *Digital Computers in Scientific Instrumentation* (McGraw-Hill, New York, 1973).
‡ G. Lauer and R. A. Osteryoung, in *Anal. Chem.* **40**, 30A (1968).

5.2.   REVIEW OF HARDWARE REQUIREMENTS

5.2.1.   Signal Conditioning

In these discussions the presumption is made that the interface to the experiment is at the output of the appropriate instrumentation for the measurement of the desired experimental quantity. The output of the instrument will be an analog or a digital voltage, a frequency, and so on.

This output signal will have to be converted and/or conditioned before it is presented to the interface.* The most common output is a low-level (millivolt), analog recorder output. The A/D converter range, on the other hand, is usually 0 to 10 V. To utilize the full-scale capabilities of the A/D converter, we must first amplify the instrument's output signal. Whether one elects to amplify at the computer interface or at the instrument output depends on how far removed the interface is from the instrument.

Some data acquisition hardware contains a preamplifier on board that is programmable with software. This is the case with the Keithley-DAS system discussed in this chapter. Others do not, and it is up to the user to furnish the preamplifier. Alternatively, switch-selectable gains are available on most units, but this option is not as convenient as the one with software-selectable programmable gain amplifiers (PGA).

If the computer interface and experimental setup are separated by any distance, it is best to amplify the low-level signal first, before transmission. Amplifiers for this purpose are available from a number of suppliers.[†,‡]

The specifications for this amplifier again depend on the application. In general, one looks for a high, open-loop gain ($\sim 10^8$), low-drift amplifier ($V_{offset}=0.2$ μV/°C; $I_{offset}=1$ pA/°C), with a high, common-mode rejection ratio (CMRR >120 dB, 0 to 50 Hz with 1000-Ω source unbalance). If speed is critical, check the specified *slew rate*. This can range from 30 to 300 V per μs. If noise is a critical issue, look for amplifiers with noise specs of less than 1 μV rms. For frequency response, check the gain bandwidth, which should be greater than 100 MHz.

5.2.2.   Transmission Cabling

The two choices for connecting the instrument to the computer interface are illustrated in Figure 5.1. The major advantage of the single-ended wiring is that only one input terminal is required. However, it requires two ground connections—one at the instrument, and one at the interface. Unfortunately,

---

* The interface to which we refer appears between the conditioned signal and the computer bus.
† Analog Devices, Inc., Norwood, MA 02062; Burr Brown Research Corporation, 6730 S. Tucson Blvd., Tucson, AZ 85706; Harris Semiconductor, P.O. Box 883, Melbourne, FL 32901.
‡ Data Translation, 100 Locke Drive, Marlboro, MA 01752, is a good source of packaged signal-conditioning hardware.

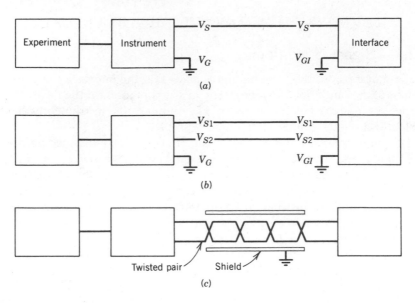

Figure 5.1.   Single-ended and differential wiring choices for connecting instrument and computer. (*a*) Single-ended. (*b*) Differential. (*c*) Twisted pair. From J.G. Liscouski, *Anal. Chem.*, **54**, 849A (1982). Courtesy of Analytical Chemistry.

ground potentials are never the same (unless both connections are made to the same point). Thus, the voltage difference, $V_S-V_{GI}=V_I$, measured at the interface is not the same as the voltage difference V_S-V_G produced by the instrument. Not only is the accuracy of the transmitted value in question, but V_G and V_{GI} *will neither remain constant nor in phase* over the specified bandwidth of the measurement, thereby superimposing a noise component on the signal. Data collection rates over single-ended wiring are limited to less than line frequency—that is, 50 to 60 samples per second.

With two-wire or differential wiring, however, we have $V_I=V_{S1}-V_{GI}-[V_{S2}-V_{GI}]=V_{S1}-V_{S2}$, which eliminates the source of the noise component discussed above. How well this works depends on the *common-mode rejection characteristics* of the differential amplifiers. Theoretically, even if $S1$ and $S2$ are 100 V, the output of the differential amplifier should be zero, since there is no voltage difference between them. Common-mode (CM) error will produce a signal at the output of the amplifier even though the input signal $V_{S1}-V_{S2}$ is zero. The commonly used figure of merit for how well an amplifier performs in terms of rejecting common-mode voltages is the *common-mode rejection ratio* (CMRR). It is an important specification for the user to check. It is defined as the ratio of the differential-signal voltage gain to the apparent gain due to a common-mode signal:

$$CMRR = A/A_{cm}$$

When A_{cm} is zero, CMRR is infinity. Although this CMRR is not practically achievable, one selects as high a CMRR as possible. It should be 10^4 or better. Expressed as dB, this value of the CMRR is

$$dB \ = \ 20 \ * \ Log \ CMRR \ = \ 20 \ * \ 4 \ = \ 80$$

A note of caution: the common-mode rejection capabilities of a given amplifier usually vary with the voltage level and the frequency of the input signal. Be sure the specs indicate under what conditions the CMRR was measured.

In addition to using differential inputs you can eliminate magnetically induced noise by twisting the pair of wires, and by using a grounded shielded cable, you can eliminate electrostatic noise.

The big disadvantage of differential wiring is that it reduces the number of inputs to the interface by one-half. The specification to the interface will read, for example, 16 single-ended input or 8 differential. The shielded, twisted-pair differential cabling will, however, handle any reasonable noise condition. Further noise suppression will require filtering and/or signal-averaging techniques.

Some manufacturers have minimized the transmission problem by incorporating in the interface enough intelligence to carry on the data acquisition and control of the experiment independently of the host computer. In this approach a CPU, RAM, ROM, and an A/D converter to ASCII code are compactly packaged for location close to the experiment. The host computer can then be placed some distance away without any undue difficulty, since the raw data is first converted to an ASCII-coded digital representation by the peripheral device before it is transmitted to the host. Two examples of such systems (the ISAAC 2000 and the 760,860 Series of intelligent interfaces) are considered later in the chapter.

5.2.3. Filtering

Some form of hardware-based filtering is always required between the instrument and the interface. Filters are used to remove those components of the signal, called *noise*, which are unrelated to the experimental measured quantity. For example, 60-Hz-signal interference is quite common in the laboratory.

In its various forms, however, the *filter can be the limiting factor in the performance of a system*. Improper use of filters can lead to considerable distortion in the signal waveform. Accordingly, filter behavior is a matter of some importance to the experimentalist.

Filters are circuits containing reactive and resistive components, such as capacitors, inductors, and resistors. Such circuits are classified as *passive* filters. This is in contrast to *active* filters, which also contain *operational amplifiers* as an integral part of the circuit. Further classification occurs depending on the range of unattenuated signal frequencies passing the filter. Thus, we have *low-pass, high-pass, bandpass,* and *notch* filters.

A simple low-pass filter is shown in Figure 5.2, along with its response to a step-voltage function. Note that the output voltage does not respond instantaneously to the input voltage. The value of e_{out} is given by

$$e_{out} = e_{in} [1 - exp(-t/RC)]   (5.2-1)$$

The product RC (where R is in ohms and C is in farads), called the *time constant*, τ, has the dimension of seconds. It is characteristic of the network and commonly used to describe the behavior of RC filters.

The solution of equation (5.2−1) for the step function demonstrates that the output voltage reaches 63.2% of its final value after RC seconds. Similarly, the time between 10% and 90% of the final value of e_{out} is 2.3RC.

The response of low-pass and high-pass filters to a square wave is shown in Figure 5.3. A closer look at the relationship between the distortion and the time constant of the filter is shown in the same figure. For a low-pass filter, minimum distortion occurs when the time constant is very small compared to the period of the pulse; for a high-pass filter the opposite is true.

All well and good in a qualitative sense, but what one really requires is some quantitative guidelines to select a filter that will minimally distort one's signal waveform and still act as a filter.

All time-varying signals can be broken down into a set of signals of various frequencies and amplitudes, which, when added together, will recreate the

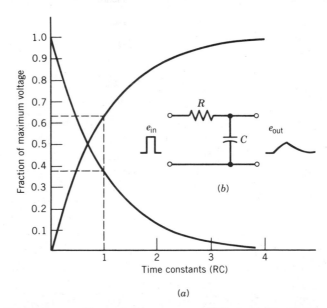

(a)

Figure 5.2.   Passive low-pass filter and response curves. (*a*) Output voltage across a capacitor in a simple RC circuit in response to a step change in input voltage. (*b*) Low-pass filter circuit and response to a square input voltage pulse.

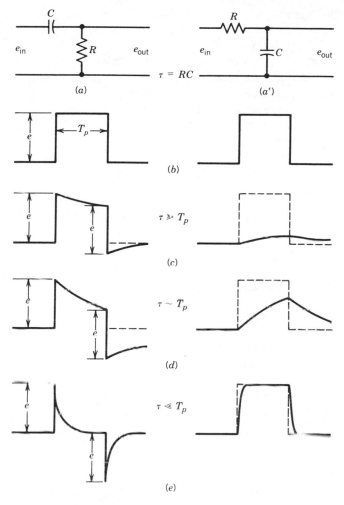

Figure 5.3. Output waveforms from High-pass, a, and low-pass, a', filters as a function of time constant of filter and period, T_p, of input pulse. (b) Input waveforms. (c, d, e) Output waveforms. (c) time constant much greater than the period of input. (d) Time constant on the same order as the period. (e) Time constant much smaller than the period.

original signal. Once we know the frequency spectrum of our signal, we can construct a filter to pass only these frequencies and attenuate all others. This process for the analysis of the frequency composition of a waveform is called Fourier analysis. The procedure produces a frequency-domain representation of the original time-domain signal. Some pictorial examples of Fourier transform pairs are shown in Figure 5.4. Fourier analysis is an important and quite useful technique, and we often refer to it in this book.

As an example of how one might use this information to design a filter, let us look at a Gaussian waveform that is similar to the signal you might wish to transmit if you were running a chromatograph.

The Fourier transform of a Gaussian is also a Gaussian. This transform is plotted in Figure 5.4 as the amplitude density vs. frequency (radians per second). To exactly reconstruct our original time-domain signal, we would have to transmit all these frequencies and *end up with no filter.* We must compromise. Let us say we accept the distortion in the time-domain waveform by filtering all frequencies whose amplitude is 0.01% of the main component. We merely solve the equation for the frequency when $F(\omega)$ is set equal to $0.0001\tau\sqrt{2\pi}$. Suppose the original chromatographic peak has a peak width at the inflection point of 1.0 (i.e., 2-s-wide peak measured at the base):

$$\tau = .5 \text{ s and } 1/\tau = 2 \text{ radians per second}$$

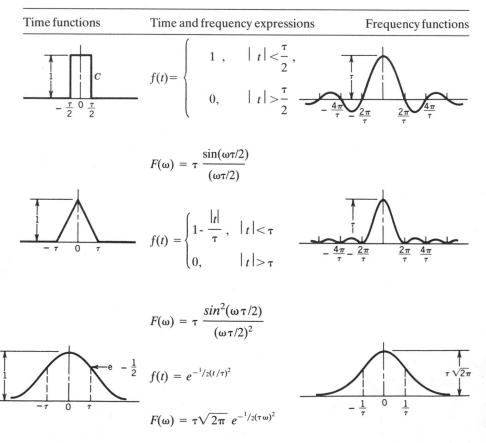

Time functions	Time and frequency expressions	Frequency functions

$$f(t)=\begin{cases} 1, & |t|<\dfrac{\tau}{2}, \\ 0, & |t|>\dfrac{\tau}{2} \end{cases}$$

$$F(\omega) = \tau\,\frac{\sin(\omega\tau/2)}{(\omega\tau/2)}$$

$$f(t) =\begin{cases} 1-\dfrac{|t|}{\tau}, & |t|<\tau \\ 0, & |t|>\tau \end{cases}$$

$$F(\omega) = \tau\,\frac{\sin^2(\omega\tau/2)}{(\omega\tau/2)^2}$$

$$f(t) = e^{-^1/_2(t/\tau)^2}$$

$$F(\omega) = \tau\sqrt{2\pi}\; e^{-^1/_2(\tau\omega)^2}$$

Figure 5.4. Time-domain waveforms and their Fourier transforms in the frequency domain.

Solving the equation for the frequency when the amplitude of the Fourier frequency spectrum has decreased to .0001 of its original value, we have

$$\omega = 8.6 \text{ radians per second}$$
$$\text{and, since } \omega = 2\pi f,$$
$$f = 1.37 \text{ Hz}$$

Now that we have established the maximum frequency that the filter must pass to insure minimum distortion of the waveform, how do we relate this to the common filter specifications quoted by the manufacturer or designer?

The frequency response of a filter is usually characterized with a *Bode* plot, examples of which are shown in Figure 5.5a. The curve has qualitatively the

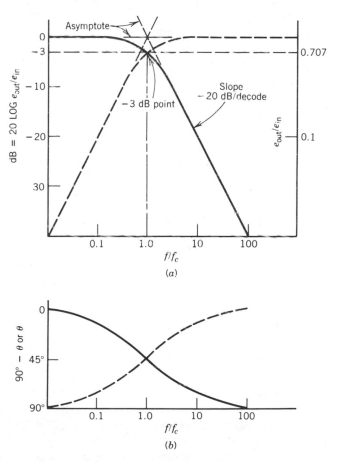

Figure 5.5. Frequency response and phase relationships for high- and low-pass filters. (*a*) Bode plots for high- and low- ——Pass filters. (*b*) Phase relationship of output to input waveform for high- (---) and low- (——) pass filters.

same slope for a given class of filters. It consists of a segment with zero slope, joined to a segment with a slope of 20 dB per decade. The intersection at frequency f_c corresponds to the reciprocal of the filter time constant, τ. This frequency is called the cutoff frequency of the filter. The abscissa of the plot shown in Figure 5.5 is given in terms of the ratio of frequency to this cutoff frequency. Thus, the intersection of the segments occurs when this ratio is 1.

In addition to frequency attenuation, filters can cause considerable *phase shifts* between input and output signals. At the so-called half-power frequency, the voltage has been reduced to 71% of its original value, -3.0 db. More importantly, the phase shift is already 45° [see Figure 5.5b].

To answer our original question, one selects a filter whose half-power frequency or-3-db point occurs at or above the highest-frequency component of the signal one wishes to transmit. In the previous example, we should select a filter with a -3-db point of 1.4 H.

A particularly versatile filter is the *state variable* filter. Several manufacturers,* offer these filters in integrated circuit form, and only a few external components are required to adapt them to one's specific application. Outputs are available to provide low-pass, high-pass, or bandpass filtering.

Finally, it should be noted that the simple filters just considered have relatively gentle *rolloffs* (20 dB per decade change in frequency). This may not be adequate for some purposes. Another class of filters, called active filters, are available, which have been designed to produce much sharper *cutoffs*. A second-order filter rolls off at 40 dB per decade, a third-order rolls off at 60 dB per decade, and so on. Filters as high as sixth-order (sometimes called a "Brick wall" for obvious reasons) are possible.

5.2.4.   Serial-Parallel Transmission

Digital data is usually transmitted either serially, by an RS-232 link or in parallel, according to the IEEE-488 standard. These interfaces are considered separately in Chapters 12 and 13. We only add here some comments regarding hardware used for serial transmission.

There are two types of circuits used for the serial transmission of data. One is based on current flow, and the other on voltage.

The current-transmission system illustrated in Figure 5.6a is based on a 20 mA current flow in a closed loop between instrument and interface. The 20 mA is generated at the active (instrument) controller. Thus, if this option is not available as an instrument output, you must provide a circuit to translate your instruments' output to 20 mA—a fairly trivial project in most circumstances. [Add to your specs for amplifier selection the ability to generate 20 mA through the load (cable and interface) that you are using.] In addition, an *optical isolator* [shown in Figure 5.6] can be inserted in the 20-mA loop to prevent the computer and instrument from trying to communicate on the same line. If it is

---

* National Semiconductors, 2900 Semiconductor Drive, Santa Clara, CA 95051; Inc., 10900 N. Tantau Ave, Cupertino, CA 95014; Burr/Brown, loc. cit.

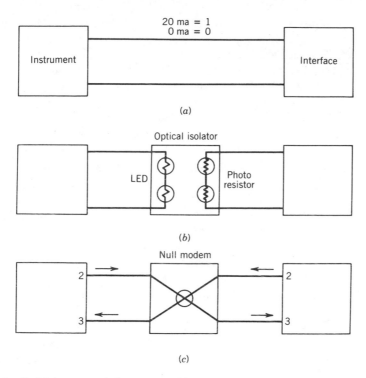

Figure 5.6. Serial data transmission systems. (*a*) current transmission. (*b*) Current transmission with isolation. (*c*) Voltage transmission. From J.G. Liscouski, *Anal. Chem*, **54**, 849A(1982). Courtesy of Am. Chem. Society.

desirable for the computer to send control signals to the instrument, another separate line can be used together with another optical isolator to assure one-way communication.

For any long distances (up to 1000 ft) between instrument and computer interface, 20 mA is, by far, the most popular method of reliably transmitting data. Extra lines must be provided, however, for handshaking. In lieu of handshaking, synchronization of sender and receiver must be provided by software at each device.

The voltage serial-transmission loop, called RS-232C, on the other hand, is quite susceptible to noise, and transmission is limited to 50 ft or less. A "1" state is represented by any voltage more negative than −3 Vdc with respect to ground (w.r.t.), and the "O" state by any voltage greater than +3 Vdc w.r.t. ground. Even though this transmission system is quite susceptible to noise, it is quite popular. This is due to the fact that the RS-232C standard defines the utilization of the 25-pin output connector. However, as mentioned previously, many manufacturers change these assignments to accommodate their own options. Thus, to avoid costly and aggravating surprises the researcher should carefully check pin assignments. (See Chapter 12 for further details with regard to these connections.)

The RS232C standard defines pin 2 of the 25-pin connector as the "transmit" pin and pin 3 as the "receive" pin. In order to link (with standard cable) two devices having RS232C plugs, a "null modem" is used (see Figure 5.6C). This avoids the problem of each device trying to communicate with the other on the same line.

The IEEE 488 parallel-transmission system is the most complicated of those discussed thus far, but it provides speed and handshaking for the complex problem. Many vendors are supplying this option as an output. It requires a special interface and software at the computer end. This interface is discussed in great detail in Chapter 13.

5.2.5. Sampling Rate

Before proceeding to a discussion of A/D conversion hardware, we briefly consider the question of deciding what sampling rate should be used to accurately reproduce our analog signal.

We know intuitively that samples taken at closely spaced intervals (high sampling rate) more accurately represent the signal than samples taken at larger intervals. But again, we don't have the luxury of infinite memory, so we must decide on some finite sampling rate.

The Nyquist Sampling Theorem states that if a band-limited dc signal is sampled at twice the highest frequency component in the signal, the sampled data will accurately represent the original signal. Thus, if we decided to sample every t seconds, the signal must not have any frequency component greater than $\frac{1}{2}t$. This critical sampling frequency is called the *Nyquist frequency*.

Recalling our recent discussion of Fourier analysis, we know that many of the waveforms shown in Figure 5.4 have frequencies from dc to very high. Obviously, we must compromise. If we band-limit these signals with a filter giving minimal distortion, we can safely sample at rates of two times the filter bandpass. For our previous 2-s Gaussian peak with a low-pass filter of 1.4 Hz at −3 db, a sampling rate of 4 samples per second. should more than satisfy this criteria. This gives a total of eight points across the whole peak. Actually, if you do the Fourier analysis, you find, surprisingly, that you only need six points to get 0.01% accuracy in the reconstruction of a Gaussian. In practice, since chromatographic peaks are seldom pure Gaussian and contain higher frequency components than predicted, a sampling rate of twice their calculated value is often used.

We have listed in Table 5.1 the errors expected between the original waveform of two commonly encountered peak shapes and the one regenerated from the experimental points with a curve-fitting program and no prior knowledge of the peak shape.

Table 5.1. Number of Samples for Common Peak Shapes*

Max Error	Samples per Full Width at half Height	
(% of peak ht.)	Lorentzian	Gaussian
10	1.8	1.5
1	3.6	2.2
0.1	4.8	2.6
0.01	6.3	3.0
0.001	8.3	3.3

* Malmstadt et al., Electronics for Scientists, (Benjamin/Cummings, Reading, MA).

5.2.6.   Analog-to-Digital Converters

The next piece of important hardware to consider is the analog-to-digital converter (ADC). There are basically two different types of converters, each of which has particular advantages.

The dual-slope integrating ADC shown in Figure 5.7 is a popular converter for relatively slow data rates (<50 samples per second) because of its high noise immunity. For this reason it is well suited for problems requiring 16-bit conversion accuracy.

Its operation is quite simple in concept. At the beginning of the conversion, the system is autozeroed (offset voltage, cancelled), and then the circuit is connected to the signal for a fixed period of time (a given number of clock cycles). During this time the signal voltage charges a capacitor, held in the feedback loop of an operational amplifier, at a rate proportional to the signal voltage. At the end of the fixed time period, the capacitor is discharged to zero at a constant rate. The number of clock cycles measured between start of discharge and when the capacitor is fully discharged is proportional to the input voltage. These steps are illustrated in Figure 5.8.

For very fast data rates, some form of the successive approximation ADC illustrated in Figure 5.9 is used. A conversion begins with a start pulse that sets the most significant bit, MSB, of each register to 1 (register contents now 1000...0 and 100...0). This value is converted by the digital-to-analog converter (DAC) to $V_{compare}$. If $V_{compare} < V_{in}$ the 1, is retained in the MSB register and the next significant bit is set to 1 and similarly tested. If at any time $V_{compare} > V_{in}$, the logic programmer resets the bit being tested to zero, and the shift register shifts a 1 into the next significant bit of the storage register. Each bit is tested in succession until finally, the LSB is encountered. An *end of conversion* (EOC) pulse is then generated signifying that the conversion sequence is complete.

The above procedure requires one clock cycle per bit of conversion. Thus, with a 10-MHz clock, a 12-bit conversion theoretically requires only 1.2 μs.

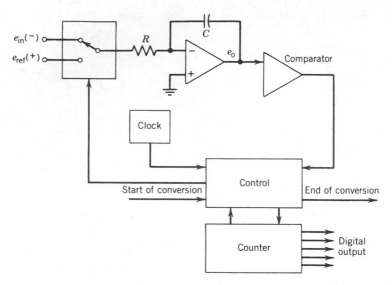

Figure 5.7. Schematic representation of a typical dual-slope ADC. From Sargent and Shoemaker, *Interfacing Microcomputers to the Real World*. Courtesy of Addison-Wesley Publishing Co.

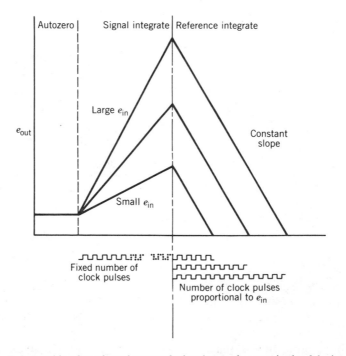

Figure 5.8. Relationship of number of output clock pulses to the magnitude of the input voltage. From Malmstadt, Enke, and Crouch, *Electronics and Instrumentation for Scientists*. Courtesy of the Benjamin/Cummings Publishing Co.

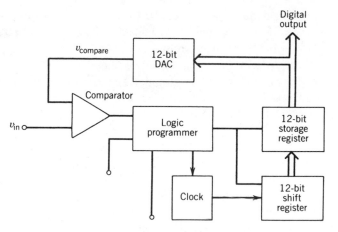

Figure 5.9. Schematic representation of a successive approximation ADC. From Malmstadt, Enke, and Crouch, *Electronics and Instrumentation for Scientists*. Courtesy of Benjamin Cummings Publishing Co.

Commonly, these converters are available with conversion times of 4 to 30 μs. for a 12-bit conversion, and the newer so-called *flash converters* are even faster (9 to 15 ns).

The successive approximation ADCs tend to be noisy. The input voltage must be constant during the comparison. This is accomplished with a sample and hold circuit that holds an instantaneous snapshot of the signal (be it a noise spike or whatever) during the comparison. Thus, adequate filtering is critically important with this ADC, whereas with the integrating type some filtering is already built into the method.

5.2.7. Important Specs

In the remainder of this chapter we review a representative sample of commercially available hardware. This is by no means a comprehensive list and is not meant to be a recommendation of any particular system.

In perusing these specs keep in mind that the hardware must perform functions specific to your particular laboratory tasks. In general, the packages will include the following:

1. *Digital I/O.* Digital I/O is necessary to control those devices which have only two states: *on* and *off*. These would include such things as relays, solenoids, on/off switches, and so on. It is also required to send or read digital information to or from external devices. At least 8 (preferably 16) lines of digital I/O should be available to send or receive computer words in a parallel fashion.

2. *Analog I/O.* Some systems will accept only digital inputs, and the vendor expects the user to convert the analog signal to digital. We feel that the

selection of any data acquisition and control system that does not provide A/D conversion is a serious mistake that will come back to haunt you later. All of the systems reviewed in this chapter contain A/D conversion.

3. The *A/D conversion time* is an important specification for the user, since it specifies how fast one can take analog data. A word of caution here: Most systems use only one ADC with a multiple poisition solid-state switch (called a *multiplexer* or MUX) to share this converter with all the channels. Thus, the data rate will therefore depend on the number of channels sampled. Channel acquisition time is also an important specification for the user to check.

4. *Hardware Drivers.*   Usually the signal transmitted from the computer is low power. Thus, it may not be able to initiate the assigned task. For example, suppose you wished to switch a solenoid that drew 50 mA in its operation. The computer signal would have to activate another device that could supply the required power, and it, in turn, would activate the solenoid. These devices are commonly called *drivers*.

All of the hardware described herein meet the first three requirements, but not all of them satisfy the fourth. Whether this requirement is of critical importance will depend on the task; thus, it is a judgment only the user can make.

5.3.   KEITHLEY DAS SERIES 500 DATA ACQUISITION SYSTEM

The DAS Series 500 measurement and control system includes both hardware and software compatible with both the IBM-PC and Apple II product families. For an IBM-PC, shown in Figure 5.10, a minimum of 128K of memory is required in addition to the main circuit 64K normally provided. A color/graphics video card is also needed along with a 320K floppy disk drive.

With the Apple II Plus or Apple IIe as the host computer, at least 64K of additional RAM (Saturn† memory expansion cards) is required along with at least one 143K floppy disk drive, video monitor, and controller. The Series 500 system hardware is separately packaged, and it is connected to the host computer by means of an interface card in one of the slots.

The Series 500 cabinet, shown in Figure 5.11 with its cover removed, contains a power supply and a motherboard containing 10 slots. The various analog input, analog output, digital input, and digital output modules are separately packaged on circuit boards that plug into these slots. You can therefore configure your system to the minimum required for your job.

---

*Keithley DAS, 349 Congress St., Boston, MA 02210.
† Registered trademark of Titan Technologies, Inc. (formerly Saturn Systems), P.O. Box 8050, Ann Arbor, MI 48104.

Figure 5.10. Keithley DAS data acquisition and control system. Photograph courtesy of Keithley DAS.

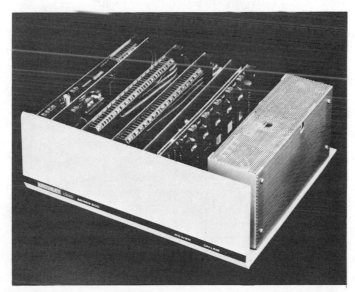

Figure 5.11. Series 500 interface hardware cabinet with its cover removed. Photograph courtesy of Keithley DAS.

The architecture of the Series 500 system is quite straightforward and is depicted in Figure 5.12. Every analog signal is processed in three stages. In the first stage, signal conditioning takes place on the circuit board module to which the signal is connected. The conditioned signal is then passed to the special module in slot 1 where it is further conditioned before it is passed to the A/D conversion module in slot 2.

Each module contains a local multiplexer to select which of the 2 channels is being sampled (channel select command). This signal is passed to the slot-1 module along a bus. Now it is necessary for the slot-1 module to select the bus wires (connected to slots) from which it will accept a signal. It does this by reading a slot select command. The slot-1 module then applies the user-specified gain and offset to this signal before passing it on to the A/D conversion module.

Both single-ended and truly differential signals are accepted by the system. In the differential mode, signals are measured as the difference between positive and negative inputs. In the single-ended mode, signals are measured between the positive input and ground.

The following modules are available:

Analog Input Modules

1. *Analog Input Module (AIM1).* The AIM1 is the heart of the A/D conversion subsystem and is always installed in slot 1. This master card provides global conditioning for all other analog modules and also hosts the first 16 channels of analog input, complete with local signal conditioning. The global-conditioning circuitry provides software programmable gain for each channel. The 16 single-ended local channels which are available on this card can be configured as eight differential ones by on-card switches. The high grade instrumentation amplifier on this card with switch selectable gain factors of ×1,

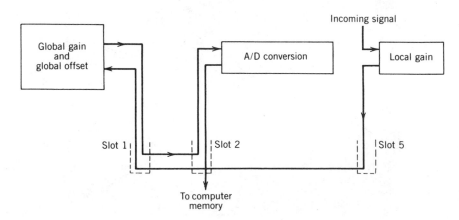

Figure 5.12. Schematic illustration of Series 500 architecture from User's Manual. Courtesy of Keithley DAS.

×10 and ×100 furnishes the local gain for these local channels (in addition to the global gain that is available)

2. *High-level Input Module (AIM2).* This module accommodates 32 additional channels of input signals with an amplitude of 1 V or more.

3. *Low-level Input Module (AIM3).* Signals with an amplitude less than 1 V are accommodated by this module. The 16 channels of differential input are designed to accept low-level signals such as those from thermocouples. Cold-junction compensation is included.

4. *Isolated High-level Input Module (AIM4).* This module is recommended for signal levels of 50 mV to 5 V full scale. Four channels of fully isolated high-level input with a separate amplifier for each channel are provided that will tolerate common-mode voltages up to 1000 V.

5. *Isolated Low-level Input Module (AIM5).* The AIMS accommodates four channels of isolated low-level input and tolerates common-mode voltages to 1000 V. It is recommended for signals in the range of 5 to 100 mV. Cold-junction circuitry is included on the card for the measurement of thermocouples.

6. *RTD and Strain-Gauge Input Module (AIM6).* Appropriate excitation, amplification, and bridge detection are available on this card to acommodate signals from platinum resistance temperature detector (RTD's), strain gauges, and semiconductor temperature sensors on four channels.

A/D Modules

1. *A/D Module (ADM1).* The ADM1 is a high-speed, successive approximation 12-bit ADC with a conversion time of 25 μs and an acquisition time of 5 μs.

2. *High-resolution A/D Module (ADM2).* ADM2 is a a 14-bit ADC. The conversion speed is 35 μs with an acquisition time of 4 μs.

Analog Output Modules

1. *(AOM1) Analog Output Module.* Up to five channels of analog output (12-bit D/A conversion accuracy) are provided on this board.

2. *AOM2.* This module provides two channels of analog output with a 16-bit D/A conversion accuracy.

3. *Current-Loop Output Module (AOM3).* The AOM3 provides four channels of 4-to-20-mA current output.

Digital I/O Modules

1. *Digital Input Module (DIM1).* Sixteen channels of optically isolated, high-speed digital input, with resistor programmable range are accommodated by this module. All inputs are TTL compatible.

2. *Digital Output Module (DOM1).* The DOM1 provides 16 channels of

digital output. These are TTL compatible but can be configured over a range of voltages.

Power Control Modules

1. *Ac Power Control Module (PCM1).*   Four channels of 120 Vac output control.

2. *Ac/dc Power Control and Sensing Module (PCM2).*   This is a direct interface to solid-state relay subsystems. Each of the 16 channels can be programmed as input or output.

Pulse-Counting Module

1. *PIM1 Pulse-Counting Module.*   The PIM1 provides 10 channels of high-speed pulse and frequency counting through five simultaneous 16-bit counters.

The DAS500 hardware anticipates many requirements of the laboratory scientist that the scientists previously had to satisfy themselves. A case in point is the availability of the power control modules that satisfy the hardware driver requirements discussed previously. These modules are necessary if heavy inductive loads like motors, lamps, solenoids, and so on, are to be turned on and off by computer command.

For documentation, two comprehensive volumes are provided, documenting both software and hardware. These user manuals contain tutorial as well as technical information.

Each system is also supplied with a 5¼-in floppy disk labeled "Soft500 Version 1.0." This contains copies of the Soft500 software, the BASIC language for the particular host computer used, and its DOS. This diskette, or a copy of it, is used to boot the system.

5.4.   ISAAC INTEGRATED SYSTEM FOR AUTOMATED ACQUISITION AND CONTROL*

Cyborg Corporation makes three models of their data acquisition and control system. The ISAAC 91A pictured in Figure 1.1 was Cyborg's original entry into the market. It comes fully configured to perform the various tasks required of a computer interface for laboratory applications and is furnished with two volumes of documentation that describe both software and hardware. In addition, a user's manual provides a quick review of the software and some example programs and exercises to aid the user in getting "on line" quickly.

All ISAAC A's require an Apple II Plus or Apple IIe microcomputer with a total of 64K of memory on the main circuit board and at least one disk drive (143 K storage). A language card is also recommended to increase the memory

---

* Cyborg Corporation, 55 Chapel Street, Newton, MA 02158.

size available for programming and data acquisition. The addition of a printer requires another interface card (controller) in one of the main board slots. RS-232C and IEEE-488 cards may be required for some, but certainly not all, applications. The purchase of these cards may be postponed.

The authors recommend purchasing the Synetix* solid-state disk emulator, which comes in 147K and 294K sizes and is plugged into one of the Apple slots. The data transfer rates to this solid-state disk are in the range of 50,000 to 70,000 bytes per second, and this additional memory is recommended for acquiring large amounts of data. The procedure for booting Labsoft is slightly different when using this card. The system is first booted using the Synetix booting disk. After running the Synetix configuration program, the Synetix disk is removed and replaced by a Labsoft master disk. Running the HELLO program from this disk then loads Labsoft into the system.

Input/output connections to experiments are made to the distribution panel on the back of the ISAAC unit by screw connections (see Figure 5.13). The panel itself connects to the main circuit board by pin edge connectors on the other side of the board. It is therefore easily removable from the ISAAC and may be left wired to the experiment while the ISAAC is moved to another job.

The ISAAC is connected to the Apple by means of an interface card that plugs into one of the Apple main board slots (usually slot 3).

The main ISAAC 91A circuit board contains the analog I/O systems. The analog input system consists of 16 channels of single-ended or 8 channels of differential input with a resolution of 12 bits and a channel acquisition time of 100 μs (not including a 25-μs A/D conversion time).

Figure 5.13. View of the back panel of an ISAAC 91A. Courtesy of Cyborg Corp.

---

* Synetix Micro Products, 15120 N.E. 95th St., Redmond, WA 98052.

The analog output system consists of four 12-bit D/A converters with (switch-selectable only) output voltage ranges of 12.5 V, 15 V, 0 to 10 V (at 1 mA).

The binary input system consists of 16 bits of TTl-level binary input and STROBE and CLEAR TO SEND handshaking lines. Signals are accepted in the form of bits, bytes, or words.

A corresponding 16 bits of binary output is available (TTL level) with STROBE and CLEAR to SEND handshaking lines.

The Schmitt trigger system converts varying analog signals to binary. Thresholds can be set with front-panel potentiometers. Input voltages above (or below, if you prefer) the threshold voltage present binary signals to the system.

A counter system (16 bit) that can be read by software (&Counterin command) is also available.

The timer/real-time clock is not located on the ISAAC main circuit board but on the interface card that connects ISAAC to the Apple. It allows timing from 1 ms to 16 s and is software resettable.

Located on the ISAAC main circuit board are eight slots that will accept any Apple prototyping card. This allows expansion of the system. For example, an analog input signal of 0 to 1 mV could not be handled by ISAAC's analog input system. It must be amplified. This may be done externally at the source. Certainly, this procedure is recommended if the ISAAC is well separated from the signal source. Alternatively, when close-coupled, the preamp circuit could be built on one of the Apple prototyping boards and plugged into one of the expansion slots. Each of the slots is addressable from Labsoft through the &RDEV and &WRDEV commands.

Some time after the introduction of the 91A, Cyborg followed with a smaller modular system (Model 41A) that could be configured as desired. This unit comes with a 16-bit counter, real-time clock, programmable timer and a 4-slot expansion case for the I/O modules. The modules are (1) a 16-channel, 12-bit ADC, (2) a 4-channel, 12-bit DAC, and (3) a 16-binary-output, 16-binary-input module with handshaking. Except for the two extra expansion slots and the four programmable Schmitt triggers available on the 91A, the fully configured 41A and 91A are equivalent.

The ISAAC 21A is a small, low-cost system featuring two built-in analog input channels plus one expansion slot. As is the case with the other equipment discussed here, all of the hardware is built to the same specifications. Low cost is achieved at the expense of flexibility, not performance.

Specs for the ISAAC expansion modules for the 41A and 21A are listed below.

I-100 ADC
Input: 16-channel single-ended or 8 differential
Resolution: 12-bit binary
Conversion time: 25 µs

Channel acquisition time: 100 μs

Handshaking: CONVERT OUT, CONVERT ENABLE IN

I-110 DAC

Output: 4 channels

Resolution: 12-bit binary

Output current: 5 mA

Settling time: 5 μs

I-120 Binary I/O Module

Input port: 16-bit TTL

Input communication: STROBE, HOLD, CLEAR TO SEND

Output port: 16-bit TTL

Output communication: STROBE, GATE, CLEAR TO SEND

Output fan-out: 12 TTL or 50 LS TTL loads

Communication fan-out: 4 TTL or 20 LS TTL loads

I-130 preamp Control Module (with/Cold-Junction Compensation)

Input channels: 1 differential

Resolution: 12-bit binary

Input impedance: 90 kΩ

Conversion time: 25 μs

Handshaking: CONVERT OUT, CONVERT ENABLE IN

Cold-junction compensation

I-140A (For Thermocouple Inputs)

Input channels: 4

Input range: 10 mV, 100 mV

Input isolation: 1000 Vdc (750 Vac)

Reference-junction temperature sensor: 2N2222

Accuracy: 100 mV; .35% of FS: 10 mV; .8% of FS

Common-mode rejection: 120 dB

Signal settling time: 400 ms

Channel select time: 4 ms

I-140B (General-Purpose Medium-Level Input)

Input range: 50 mV, 100 mV, 1 V, 5 V

Other specs same as I-140A

I-140C (Strain-Gauge/RTD Input)

Input channels: 4

Input range (strain gauge): 30 or 100 mV; (RTD): 25 to 175 Ω or 0 to 350 Ω

Accuracy: 1%

Common-mode rejection: 80 dB at 60 Hz (strain gauge)

Strain-Gauge excitation current: 0.4 mA (3-lead compensation)

I-150 16-Bit A/D Module

Input channels: 2

Resolution: 16 bit

Input impedance: 10 MΩ (filter off)

Differential nonlinearity: 0.003% of full scale

Conversion time: 60 μs

Channel acquisition time: 50 ms

Common-mode rejection: 75 dB

Handshaking: CONVERT OUT, CONVERT ENABLE IN

I-160 16-Channel Relay MUX

Input channels: 16 (differential/single ended)

Max. contact rating: 5 W resistive

Max. switched voltage: 150 Vac

Max. switched current: 250 mA

Max. scan rate: 300 channels per second

Contact resistance: 0.2 Ω

Relay thermal EMF: 10 μV

I-180 2-Channel, Low-Level A/D Module

Input channels: 2

Resolution: 12 bit

Conversion time: 35 μs

Differential nonlinearity .025% of full scale

Channel acquisition time: 50 μs

Common-mode rejection: 75 dB

Switch selectable gains of ×1, ×10, ×100, ×1000

5.4.1.   ISAAC—IBM-PC Systems

The previously discussed 91 and 41 hardware is now also available for the IBM-PC under the names of ISAAC 91I and ISAAC 41I; they are shown in Figure 5.14. In addition to the features described for the 91A, the 91I is compatible with all of Cyborg's I Series of expansion hardware.

5.4.2.   ISAAC 2000

The ISAAC 2000 (see Figure 5.15) data acquisition and control system is different in concept from other PC-based systems available to date. This includes the ISAAC 91A. The latter system, as explained earlier, was basically a hardware package in support of Cyborg's language extension software, which was integrated into the Applesoft language.

In contrast, the ISAAC 2000 has its own microprocessor—the 68000. This is an extremely powerful state-of-the-art 16-bit microprocessor with 32-bit

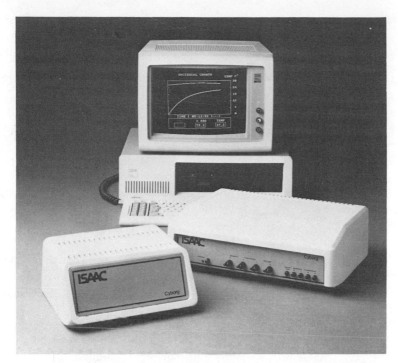

Figure 5.14. ISAAC 41I and 91-I. Courtesy of Cyborg Corp.

Figure 5.15. ISAAC 2000. Courtesy of Cyborg Corp.

registers. Also on board are four ROMs containing the ISAAC command language, 128 K of RAM, I/O interface modules, ADC modules, DAC modules, and two types of system expansion slots. The C-slots are used for memory expansion (up to 2 M) and high-speed A/D conversion, and the I-slots are used for general I/O (less than 10 kHz) system expansion.

The ISAAC command instructions can be likened to the & machine language routines of Labsoft I, which were resident in the Apple language card or in main memory—just below DOS. However, in this case the ISAAC command instruction set is not in the host computer but resides in ROM on the ISAAC 2000 board. It is accessed by a higher-level language called Labsoft II.

The ISAAC 2000 then is programmed by a host computer like the IBM-PC or -XT using Labsoft II, which is loaded into the IBM-PC and accessed from BASICA.

Two processors are available: the host computer's and the ISAAC's own 68000. Parallel processing is therefore available and a true background/foreground system is possible if the appropriate OS were available. Unfortunately, at the time of this writing, this is not the case. Even so, the advantages of parallel processing are still available. Once initiated, the ISAAC 2000 proceeds on its task independently of what is going on in the host computer.

The ISAAC 2000 is thus an intelligent peripheral, capable of data storage and manipulation, timing, and I/O control, independent of the host computer. In fact, a number of ISAAC 2000 system (up to 14) can be configured to a single host computer.

The power of this system is enormous and puts it in a class by itself. Detailed hardware specifications for this system are given below.

ISAAC 2000 Specifications

CPU:	68000 (8 MHz)
Storage:	128K RAM, 32K EPROM, PROM-configurable address mapping.
Communications:	One (1) IEEE-488 port, configurable as a talker or a listener Two (2) RS-232C ports (one DCE, one DTEO). Both ports support either hardware handshaking or XON/XOFF protocols. Programmable baud rates (110 to 19,200 baud). Each port may be configured as a 20-mA optically isolated current-loop interface.
Power Supply:	70-W switching type, supplying 6 A at 5 V, 1.5 A at 15 V.
Timer:	24-bit timer

C-Series Modules

C-100 High-Speed A/D Module

Input channels: 4

Input ranges: 5 mV, 10mV, 0 to 10 mV, 50 mV, 100 mV, 0 to 100 mV, .5 V, 1 V, 0 to 1 V, 5 V, 10 V, 0 to 10 v.

Resolution: 12-bit binary

Differential nonlinearity: .025% of full scale

Conversion time: 5 μs

Common-mode rejection: 70 dB from dc to 60 Hz (with 1-kΩ source impedance imbalance)

Handshaking: CONVERT OUT, CONVERT ENABLE IN

C-200 Memory Expansion Module

-Adds 256 K of buffer RAM at a DIP switch-selectable location (any 128K boundary).

In addition, the ISAAC 2000 accepts all of the I-Series modules previously described.

5.5. INTELLIGENT INTERFACES FOR LABORATORY DATA HANDLING

The previously discussed ISAAC 2000 concept was preceded in the marketplace by the 760 and 860 Series of intelligent interfaces manufactured by Nelson Analytical.* Originally interfaced only to Hewlett-Packard computers, they soon became available for the IBM-PC when this microcomputer appeared on the market.

A block diagram of the interface is shown in Figure 5.16. Two analog inputs are provided with a 20-bit conversion efficiency and a 10^6 dynamic range with .1% linearity. Input voltage ranges of −5 mV to 1 V, 2 V, 10 V, are provided at a sampling speed of 20 points per second or lower.

As can be seen from the block diagram, the interface contains its own CPU (a Z80), RAM, and ROM and is linked to the host computer by an IEEE-488 (760 Series) or RS-232 (860 Series) link. Thus, the interface combines the A/D conversion function with programmability, local buffer storage of raw data during a run (up to 20K data points), local data reduction, local control and status sensing through external event switches, and raw or processed data transfer to the host computer by preformatted IEEE-488 or RS-232C protocol.

---

* Nelson Analytical, 10061 Bubb Road, Cupertino, CA 95014.

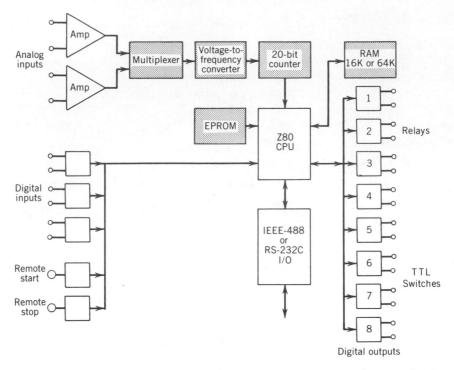

Figure 5.16. Block diagram of Nelson Analytical's intelligent interface. Courtesy of Nelson Analytical.

The entire instruction set for data acquisition and storage can be part of a host program written in BASIC, PASCAL, or FORTRAN on the host computer that is downloaded to the interface. Once the interface has started into this internal program, it does not use the connecting bus to the host computer. Thus, the host is free to perform other tasks that do not necessarily have to involve the same program currently residing in memory. A new program can be loaded from disk, and in this sense the system emulates a multitasking one but without the advantages inherent in a shared or segmented memory management scheme available with some operating systems.

Although some simple data processing can be programmed into the interface (such as digital filtering switch closures at certain points in the analysis, etc.), the complex data manipulation is done post-run, on the host, after data transfer from the interface. In the case of chromatography applications (see Chapter 7), the peak detection algorithm is stored in the EPROM. Data is stored during the run and processed post-run by a comprehensive program residing in the host.

5.6. PCDAX*

Data Translation produces a number of microcomputer analog I/O products, systems boards, and modules. They have marketed a product called PCDAX that is a data acquisition and control subsystem for personal computers, such as the DEC Rainbow 100 and the IBM-PC. Also available are subsystems for the Apple II Plus and IIe, but these are strictly for data acquisition. The product line includes an enclosure with an interface to the host computer, data acquisition boards, screw terminal panels, and software subroutine packages. Comprehensive user manuals are included with each package.

This discussion will be limited to Data Translation's I/O board for the IBM-PC and Apple II microcomputers. Figures 5.17 and 5.18 summarize the features of both boards.

5.6.1. Analog and digital I/O for IBM-PC and APPLE II

Two plug-in boards for the IBM-PC are available from Data Translation, the DT-2805 and DT-2801, which differ only in the number of analog and digital I/O channels that are supported. This IBM-PC subsystem is supported by a software library of subroutines, described in the next chapter.

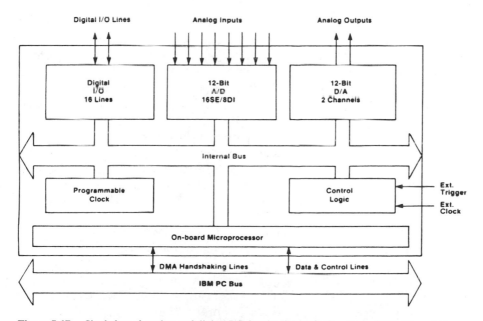

Figure 5.17. Single board analog and digital I/O for the IBM-PC. Courtesy of Data Translation.

* Data Translation, 1002 Locke Dr., Marlboro, MA 01752.

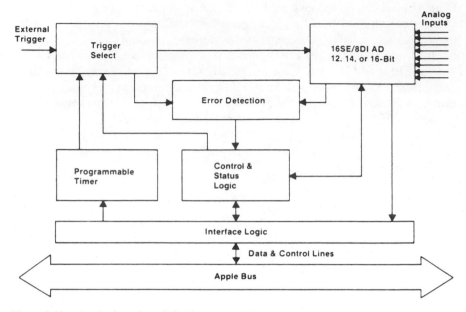

Figure 5.18.   Analog input boards for the Apple II microcomputer. Courtesy of Data Translation.

The DT-2805 is the lower-priced module. It features eight channels of differential 12-bit or 16-bit A/D conversion with software-selectable gains of 1, 10, 100, or 500, with input ranges of 20 mV full scale to 10 V. Also included are two DACs with 12-bit resolution, 16 lines of digital I/O, and an on-board programmable clock. Data rates up to 13.7 kHz are typical (compared with a 22-kHz maximum data rate for the 2801).

Several operating modes are available, including direct memory access (DMA) and programmed I/O data transfers. The I/O functions may be initiated by either hardware or software. A programmable clock can be used for timing A/D and D/A operations. Intervals can be set in 2.5-μs increments. All of these attributes are summarized in Figures 5.17 and 5.18 taken from the manufacturer's literature.

Also available is a screw terminal panel (DT-707) with an integral cable for connecting the user analog and digital signals to the board.

The DT-2832 and DT-2834 plug-in boards for the Apple II, II Plus, and IIe microcomputers differ from the IBM boards in that they only support analog input and are thus only useful for data acquisition. Also, these Apple boards are not supported by the PCLAB macro library. The user must write his own routines for the various data acquisition and control tasks. The unique features of the boards' analog I/O can be initiated from the language residing in the Apple (BASIC, PASCAL, Machine) by addressing the appropriate registers on the interface card.

5.7. ADLAB DATA ACQUISITION SYSTEM*

Perhaps the simplest and least expensive configuration for data acquisition and control with the Apple is available from Interactive Microware, Inc. (see Figure 5.19). Besides the 64K Apple II Plus or Apple IIe with a single disk drive, monitor, and printer, all that is required is an ADLAB interface card that plugs into one of the Apple slots.

This ADLAB interface card, shown in Figure 1.7, will accept a single-channel analog input or produce a single-channel output. It contains a 12-bit ADC, a 12-bit DAC, an 8-bit parallel digital input, an 8-bit parallel digital output, a 32-bit real-time clock/timer, and two 16-bit auxiliary timers. The jumper-selectable input ranges are 4 V, 2 V, 1 V, and 0.5 V. Maximum sampling speed with this card is 20 samples per second.

The software QUICK I/O supports more than one board if a larger number of analog and digital channels are required for the experiment. Recall, however, that there are only eight slots available in the Apple and at least three of them may be in use with a disk drive, printer, and extra RAM.

The software also supports the fast A/D card made by Interactive Structures, Inc.,[†] which allows data acquisition at rates up to 33KHz. Various other signal-interface hardware supported by ADLAB software are available. These units are listed below.

ADA-BYTE 32-Bit Digital I/O Multiplexer

Provides 32 bits of digital I/O, requiring only a single ADLAB interface card

Each of four groups of 8 bits may be individually specified as inputs or outputs under software control

Figure 5.19. ADLAB data acquisition system. Courtesy of Interactive Microware.

* Interactive Microware, Inc., P.O. Box 771, State College, PA 16801.
† Interactive Structures, Inc., 146 Montgomery Ave., Bala Cynwyd, PA 19004.

Each group of 8 bits has its own strobe signal (a positive pulse) for output handshaking. Input data tracks the input signal as long as a latch handshaking line is held high; when this line goes low, the inputs are latched. All four latching signals are connected to an interrupt flag that may be either polled from your program or enabled for interrupts

A manual with sample programs illustrating binary or BCD I/O is included in the package

ADA-MUX 8-channel Multiplexer

A total of eight units (64 channels) can be used

A mV-level solid-state sensor for thermocouple cold-junction compensation can be installed

Also available is a solid-state temperature sensor (type LM-334)

ADA-AMP Instrumentation Amplifier

Range: 500 μV to 10 V

Switch-selectable gains: 0.1, 1.0, 10, 100

Additional variable gain: 1 to 10 (to give overall gain adjustment of 0.1 to 1000)

Common-mode rejection: 70 to 100 dB

Input impedance: 8 MΩ

Software programmable gain/attenuation option: factors of 2, 4, 8, 16, 64, 128, 512, 1024 are selected by ADLAB's digital output bits 4 and 7

Optional multiplexer selects one of eight differential channels under control of bits 0 to 3 of ADLAB's digital output.

Multiplexing can be expanded to accommodate an additional eight differential inputs.

5.8.   EASYLAB*

The EASYLAB package includes a *clock/calendar* card and a 16-channel analog connector panel with 48K of RAM, one disk drive, and a display monitor. In addition, the following hardware, mounted on an Apple interface card is supported:

Interactive Structures, Inc.

146 Montgomery Ave., Bala Cynwyd, Pa. 19004
    A113.... 16-channel analog input system
    A003.... 2-channel analog output system
    D109.... 32-line digital I/O with timers

---

* MIA, RR#1, Box 137, Califon, NJ 07830.

California Computer Systems
7710A.... asynchronous serial interface card
D.C.Hayes
Micromodem II

5.9. APPLIGRATION HARDWARE*

Dynamic Solutions Corporation does not manufacture any hardware. Their Appligration data acquisition software is supported by two hardware packages they have put together using commercially available hardware. These are summarized below.

DYSC IS A/D Converter Subsystem
modified Interactive Structures A113 ADC
DYSC signal distribution cabinet
modified California Computer Systems 7440A precision timer card
64K RAM memory add-on card (expandable to 128K)
DYSC Cyborg Data Acquisition and Control Subsystem
91A ISAAC and 911 ISSAC
modified CCS 7440A card
64K RAM card (expandable to 128K)

Maximum single-channel data rates for the IS-based subsystem is 20 kHz, and 10 kHz for the ISAAC-based system.

*Dynamic Solutions Corporation, 61 South Lake Ave., Suite 309, Pasadena, CA 91101.

6

Laboratory Language Software

6.1. Introduction

Speaking for the experimentalist, most of us regard computer-controlled data acquisition and control hardware as merely another instrument—a tool—and programming as a necessary evil. If an experiment can be set up and run in a shorter time than it takes to set up and program the computerized system, chances are that we would run the experiment without the computer. Given that we express the feelings of a majority of scientists and engineers, it is imperative that a system be chosen whose primary language is as "friendly" as possible. This will assure the most efficient use of the system and avoid the embarrassment of having to explain to the local manager just why the computer is sitting in the corner not being used.

Thus, before acquiring a new system, it is well worth the effort to spend some time carefully scrutinizing both the language and the application software that can run on it. To aid the reader in this regard, we review in this chapter some representative samples of commercially available laboratory language extensions. We have selected examples to illustrate a whole spectrum of more or less user-friendly packages in order to provide the reader with sufficient information to make a choice suitable to his or her requirements.

However, before we embark on a discussion of *laboratory languages*, let us take an overall look at some of the requirements of such software, as we perceive them. As might be surmised from our introductory comments regarding programming, we have a strong prejudice toward the use of a *high-level* language. This chapter is devoted entirely to this class of software, created as an extension or appendage of the BASIC language. In Chapter 11 we describe the use of *assembly* language for tasks where speed is a critical requirement and no appropriate high-level software drivers are available. We have already described, in Chapter 4, the use of languages such as C and FORTH. These two languages are excellent choices for many advanced applications and a starting point for advanced laboratory language development. Finally, in Chapter 7 we discuss some menu driven application packages.

The strength of a particular laboratory language extension depends, in part, on the features of the parent language and also on the OS that manages the host computer. Minimally, the OS should include

Provision for convenient storage and retrieval of raw and processed data files as well as program modules

The ability to conveniently communicate with I/O devices and to easily add new I/O devices to the system

Support for generating, assembling, and debugging assembly language code and facilities for accessing these programs from a high-level language

Similarly, the parent language should provide an environment for

Modularity (for ease of program development)
Expandability
Standardized code
Interface drivers for standard languages
Interpreter and compiler modes
Descriptive syntax
Immediate and deferred mode of execution

These are certainly desirable features for any computer language. However, in view of the particularly complex tasks encountered in data acquisition and control, they are of critical importance to laboratory languages and laboratory language extensions.

One feature of these laboratory language attributes that should be emphasized is the ability to run the software in either an interpreter or immediate execution mode. This is quite useful for debugging. Once the program has been debugged, however, it may be desirable to increase the speed of execution by first compiling the program before running it.

Finally, the following is a list of minimum features that a laboratory language should make accessible to the user through high-level software drivers:

Interface Input Commands
Analog input
Digital input
Counter input
Trigger input
Interface Output Commands
Analog output
Digital output
Trigger output
Data Display
Graph series data
Graph (x,y) data

Each of these features is either fully or partially implemented in the language extensions reviewed in this chapter. Therefore, in the interests of brevity, we will not reproduce the entire instruction set for each of the language extensions.

We begin our discussion with a very easy to learn but powerful language extension that, when combined with the hardware described in Chapter 5, allows the user to get on stream quickly with a minimum of effort. Our descriptions will serve only to give the reader the flavor of the language and some appreciation of its strengths and weaknesses. Further details can be obtained directly from the vendor or, better yet, from another user who has worked with that particular language extension.

6.2.   LABSOFT I*

Labsoft I is a language extension to Applesoft Basic. It was developed by the Cyborg Corporation for its data acquisition and control system, called ISAAC, which is used in combination with the Apple series of microcomputers.

As with some other language extensions discussed herein, it uses the & character to alert the Apple computer's BASIC interpreter of its presence and to direct the program to the proper location for the execution of the command. If you recall, the use of the & character of Applesoft to extend the language was discussed at the end of Chapter 2. This character then must precede all Labsoft commands.

Many of the Labsoft instructions contain a number of parameters, some of which are optional. These parameters are the link between the Apple computer and the ISAAC interface. The Labsoft commands are, however, treated in exactly the same way as the standard Applesoft instructions as long as Labsoft has been booted into the system. *They may be placed at any point within a standard Applesoft program, and placing more than one instruction on a line is permissible as long as they are separated by colons in the standard manner.*

The execution of BASIC and Labsoft instructions occurs in what could be called a "single ground" environment. Each instruction is executed in sequence, and another instruction is not begun until the previous one has been completed. An alternative and popular architecture is the "background/foreground" one in which instructions can be called to be executed no matter where they are located in the program. If at the time of the request some other part of the program is being executed, it will be interrupted until the particular prioritized instruction has been executed—after which control will be returned to the interrupted task. For this reason this type of software design is often referred to as "interrupt driven." In theory it provides a more efficient use of computer time than the "single mode." However, as we later note, its use is limited by the microprocessor cycle time and the required data acquisition speed.

* Cyborg Corp., 55 Chapel St., Newton, MA 02158.

Labsoft for the Apple resides in a single ground environment, whereas Labsoft I for the IBM-PC can be run in either mode in certain cases.

The syntax of a typical Labsoft instruction is shown in equation (6.2-1). The instruction name has been generalized as '& inst'; parm1, parm2,..., parmN are the Labsoft parameters, and var1, var2,...,varM are standard Applesoft constants or variables.

& inst,(parm1)=var1,(parm2)=var2,...,_(parmN) (6.2-1)

Some of the parameters are compulsory, but others need only be included if values different from the default must be specified. Most of the parameters must be made equivalent to an Applesoft constant or variable, but a few stand alone.

More importantly, from this user's point of view, the fact that the parameters are explicitly defined in the language, and therefore *do not have to appear in any particular order* in a Labsoft instruction, contributes to the simple elegance of this language extension.

In addition, a powerful feature shared by the Labsoft instruction set, and most other language extensions, and Applesoft is that instructions is executed from within a program if the instruction is preceded by a line number, or if no line number is present, the instruction is immediately executed. This is a feature of major importance when you are setting up an experiment, since it allows you to step through the data acquisition algorithm one instruction at a time. *This flexibility alone can justify the use of an interpretive language over a compiled one.*

6.2.1. Analog I/O

An example of a typical Labsoft instruction is that for reading the voltage from one of the ISAAC's analog inputs. The ISAAC system, as described in Chapter 5, has sixteen 12-bit single-ended or eight differential analog inputs. By executing the instruction

& AIN, (TV) = X, (C#) = 5, (CV) = Y, (PR)

the voltage is read (&AIN) from analog input channel 5 [(C#)=5]. The value of the voltage reading is returned in variable X and is simultaneously printed on the screen [(PR)]. The value of the voltage is also compared to the contents of variable Y [(CV) = Y]. The result of this comparison can be used in subsequent areas of the program.

Similarly, if one wished to obtain an average value of the analog voltage appearing at channel 5, one could execute a line like

&ASUM,(TV) = A%, (RT) = 1,(C#) = 5, (SW) = 10

which would sum 10 values [(SW)=10] from channel 5 at a rate of one every millisecond [(RT)=1]. Following this line with a simple Applesoft instruction such as

$$B\%=A\%/10$$

would place the average value of these 10 readings in the variable B%.

As mentioned previously, the Labsoft language for the Apple has *no interrupt capabilities*—a potential failing of the language for tasks requiring both accurate timing of one job and parallel execution of another. In Chapter 11 we discuss a method of controlling the ISAAC interface by using interrupt-driven software.

Since Labsoft I does not reside within an interrupt-driven architecture, timing data I/O routines is a potential problem. The speed of execution of each Labsoft instruction is limited by the speed of the BASIC interpreter. The designers therefore created special blocks of machine-coded programs in which accurate timing is available. These are the so-called *matrix commands*. They are preceded by @ and when invoked can acquire a whole array of data at an accurately timed rate of sampling. For example,

$$\&@AIN,(AV)=AN,(RT)=1,(C\#)=3$$

fills the array AN with data from channel 3 at a rate of one data point per millisecond. The number of data points collected depends on the dimension of AN.

The TV parameter is used when inputting data, the DV when outputting data. For example, the instruction

$$\&AOUT,(DV)=Y,(C\#)=4$$

outputs the value contained in Y to channel 4.

The above discussion of the analog I/O commands has been restricted to a single input channel of data. The matrix commands in Labsoft can support the collection of up to 16 channels of analog data simultaneously. Since the sampling interval is still restricted to 1.035 ms per point, there will be a corresponding decrease in the rate of data collection for a single channel when more than one channel of data is being collected. This restriction is not unique to Labsoft. All data acquisition systems have similar disclaimers to the sampling rate that is advertised.

The programming example below was written to simultaneously collect analog data from input channels 1,3,5,6,7. In such a case a two-dimensional array, C(J, I), is used, where the J index represents the different channel numbers and the I indexes the data value.

```
10 INPUT "ENTER NUMBER OF POINTS TO BE COLLECTED ";N
15 N=N-1
10 DIM C(4,N)
```

```
30 INPUT "ENTER RATE OF COLLECTION ";RR
40 & ANAFMT=1,3,5,6,7
50 &@AIN, (AV)=C, (RT)=RR
60 GOSUB 1000:REM STORE DATA IN BINARY ARRAY
70 END
```

The &ANAFMT command is used to format the order in which the input channels are selected. A pointer moves down this list for each subsequent reading and wraps around to the first channel and starts again once the list has been serviced. The first index of the array is dimensioned to the exact number of channels being sampled. Failure to observe this rule will cause strobing between bins and channel storage locations. The first index of a two-dimensional array in Applesoft is the one that represents storage locations that are next to each other in memory. The layout of data storage for the above example is shown below.

INDEX J →	0	1	2	3	4
INDEX I					
0	ch0(0)	ch1(0)	ch2(0)	ch3(0)	ch4(0)
1	ch0(1)	ch1(1)	ch2(1)	.....	
2	ch0(2)				
3	ch0(3)				
.	.				
.	.				
.	.				
N	ch0(N)....				

The relationship of this layout to the program should be obvious. We have used the notation ch0(i) to represent the channel 0 bin reading, i, and so on. Data is acquired in order, so that the first row is filled, then the second, third, and so on, until the last index i location is reached—that is, the array is filled. Alternatively, the number of channel sweeps can be specified by including an SW parameter in line #50. Of course, the number used here must be less than the i dimension of the array.

Similarly, the matrix version of the summing command can also be used on a number of channels. Let us use the same five channels as the matrix &@AIN example above, but now instead of storing successive sweeps of the input lines in different elements of a two-dimensional array, we put the summed values of the inputs from different channels in different bins of a one-dimensional array; thus

```
10 DIM CC(4)
20 INPUT "ENTER RATE AT WHICH DATA IS SUMMED ";RR
30 INPUT "ENTER NUMER OF SWEEPS TO BE SUMMED ";NN
40 &ANAFMT = 1,3,5,6,7
```

```
50 &@ASUM, (AV)=CC, (RT)=RR, (SW)=NN
60 GOSUB 2000:REM STORE RESULTS
70 END
```

The array contains only five elements [DIM CC(4), that is, 0 to 4] corresponding to the number of channels to be sampled. Channel 1 will be swept NN times, and the sum will be stored as element 0 of the array. Similarly, the data obtained by summing the values obtained from each channel will be stored in the appropriate element of the array.

INDEX J →	0	1	2	3	4
SWEEP					
⫶		present contents of array elements			
＼⫶／	+	+	+	+	+
0	ch0(0)	ch1(0)	ch2(0)	ch3(0)	ch4(0)
	+	+	+	+	+
1	ch0(1)	ch1(1)	ch2(1)	ch3(1)	ch4(1)
	+	+	+	+	+
	.	.	.	.	.
	.	.	.	.	.
	.	.	.	.	.
	+	+	+	+	+
NN	ch0(NN)	ch1(NN)	ch2(NN)	ch3(NN)	ch4(NN)

Unfortunately, it is not possible to use this command to carry out digital filtering under any of the timed data acquisition commands. To do this even in the case of a single channel, you must successively sum a predefined number of sweeps from the analog input in question into a single array bin and then move on to the next bin. This is impossible from within Labsoft.

6.2.2.   Binary I/O

The 16 binary input lines (numbered 0 to 15) may be read in a single &BIN command, and the status of the lines returned in a single variable selected by the target variable. For example, the instruction

$$\&BIN,(TV)=BB$$

will return to the variable BB the decimal equivalent of the binary number obtained by reading the status of the 16 binary lines. This number will lie in the range 0 to 65,535.* You can also mask the raw values with an AND or EXCLUSIVE OR mask. An example of this parameter's use is given in the section on triggering.

   The *matrix binary commands* are an obvious extension of the single reading command. A series of handshaking lines on the ISAAC interface may be used to police the flow of binary data in or out of the interface, or the system may be allowed to run at its own pace under the control of the (RT) variable. An interesting example illustrating the flexibility available with these commands is shown below. The binary output lines are used to send a TTL 500-Hz pulse train out from one of the bits. Let us say that we wish to send the train out from bit 3 on the binary interface. What we must do then is to send the numbers 4 and 0 to the interface. The following simple program will suffice.

```
10  DIM DD(1)
20  DD(0)=0  :  DD(1)=4
30  &@BOUT, (AV)=DD, (RT)=1, (SW)=1000
40  END
```

This program sends a 500-Hz TTL pulse train out from bit 3 on binary output port 2 for a period of 2 s, as shown in Figure 6.1. Using this technique a much more complicated bit pattern may be sent out on the binary lines depending on the numbers one places in the array elements and, the dimension of the array.

Figure 6.1. A 500 Hz TTL pulse train.

The other binary commands follow closely the operation of the commands discussed above. BPOLL waits for one of the binary input lines to be set and then returns the number of the set line. It is a convenient way of monitoring a number of binary input lines and executing some action based on the lines that went high. The BCDIN command, in particular, is very useful. It converts the 16-bit binary input to a 4-digit decimal value based on the assumption that the 16-bit number is a binary coded representation. Similarly, BCDOUT converts a 4-digit number into a 16-bit binary coded output. (See Chapter 12 for a further discussion of the BCD interface.)

6.2.3. The Counter and Timer Commands

A total of eight counter channels, representing the multiplexed capability of the system from eight input ports into a single counter, are available on the ISAAC 91. All input channels will accept TTL frequency data up to 10 MHz; a single channel (7) will accept non-TTL signals with a resulting drop in bandwidth down to 3 MHz. Reading the counters depends on the frequency range involved: Three methods are available; two of these involve counting for fixed time periods of 1 ms and 1 s, respectively. The following example illustrates the

* If your binary numbering facility is rusty, review Section 2.4.1. See also Appendix G.

matrix version of these commands. Three high-frequency signals are sampled in a strobed fashion for 1 ms each, and a two-dimensional array is filled with the data.

```
10 DIM CR(2,1000)
20 &CNTFMT=0,2,4
30 &@FINH, (AV)=CR, (RT)=0, (SW)=200
40 GOSUB 2000: REM STORE ARRAY
50 END
```

The &CNTFMT specifies the channels from which the counter data will be collected. The data from the &@FINH are returned as an exact frequency number. Successive readings of channel 0 will be stored in array element CR(0, I), channel 2 data in CR(1, I), and channel 4 data in CR(2, I).

The third method of using the counter for low-frequency situations, where 1 may be too short a time period or when we may wish to trigger the counter by completing a specified event, is to explicitly start and stop the counter with the provided commands. The command &CLRCOUNTER clears the counter, and it then begins to count the events that appear at its input until the &COUNTERIN, (TV)=..., command is executed. The execution time overhead of the Applesoft−Labsoft interpreter may be eliminated by using the &LOOK FOR command, which is discussed in a following section. The value of the count is returned in the specified target variable.

The timer command is relatively straightforward and closely follows the philosophy of the counter described above. As delivered, the ISAAC system contains a 16-bit timer that can measure time intervals in the range 0 to 16,383 ms or 0 to 16.383 s. The timer is cleared with &CLRTIMER and subsequently read with &TIMERIN, (TV)=... Two things need to be remembered about the ISAAC's timer; the first is that the timer is used and cleared by the matrix command, so if timing is required while these commands are being used, which invariably is the case, then an external clock or oscillator must be connected to the counter input.* The second characteristic of the timer is that once the maximum value 16,383 is reached the timer starts counting from zero again. It is possible to use the timer in combination with the real-time clock to accurately time events much longer than 16 s.

The real-time clock, which has a battery backup to make it usable over extended time periods, is extremely convenient to stamp files and other sources of data with the time and date of filing. The time measurement that returns the hour, minute, and second at which the clock is read has a resolution of 1 s.

6.2.4. Triggering

The response time of the Labsoft commands is determined by the time that the Applesoft and Labsoft interpreters take to properly process the command.

---

*See Fig. 11.10 for a very simple but accurate oscillator that we have used many times.

Although this may be adequate for most purposes, there are cases, such as when a transient event is expected, when having to make an Applesoft calculation can delay the start of data collection by tens of milliseconds. A powerful triggering command is available in Labsoft to allow the initiation of a transient event to immediately trigger another Labsoft command. This is the important

```
&LOOK FOR labsoft command1, (TH)=var:labsoft command 2
```

where Labsoft commands 1 and 2 are valid Labsoft input or output commands. The important threshold variable parameter (TH) is used exclusively on this command and represents the programmed threshold that, if exceeded, immediately starts executing the next command. The & must be omitted from command 1 but included in command 2, and this whole line is interpreted by the interpreter at one time, after which the system sits there until the threshold is exceeded.

As an example of this command, let us consider that we are ready to acquire analog data from channel 5 once a TTL high is sensed on bit 6 of the binary input. This is a familiar example for anyone who has triggered an oscilloscope externally with a TTL pulse. The binary input command to do this has been discussed earlier. In this case, however, we will not require the (CV) parameter. The entire operation is quite simply accomplished with the program

```
10 DIM XX(1000)
20 &LOOK FOR BIN,(TV)=Y,(AM)=64,(TH)=64 : &@AIN,(AV)=XX,(C#)=5
30 END
```

where the binary input bit 6 is continuously monitored by masking it with an AND mask on which only bit 6 is high. The masking operation is a convenient way of unscrambling the status of specific bits on the binary bus. A mask of 64, (AM)=64, will AND the binary number 1000000 with the binary number appearing on the binary lines. Only if bit 6 is also high will 64 appear as the result of this operation. The AND operation with all other lines will yield only 0 regardless of their state. Thus, only when ANDed binary signal becomes equal to the threshold set by the parameter TH is the analog array completely filled with data at the free-running sampling rate of the system.

6.2.5. The Graphics Capability of Labsoft

The thirteen or so graphics commands available to Labsoft combined with the graphics parameters allow much of the data acquired on the ISAAC interface to be immediately displayed on one or both of the Hi-Res screens of the Apple computer. All graphing is displayed in equal x-axis increments of the array bin numbers and up to 16 channels of data may be simultaneously displayed in color on a single pass of the graphing operation.

The single extended example below is sufficient to demonstrate many of the important features of the graphics package. We are using the (GA) parameter to directly graph, in several colors, analog data acquired from a number of channels. The data is then manipulated in an Applesoft FOR...NEXT loop, after which it is plotted on the other Apple high-resolution page. Finally, we are able to flip back and forth from one screen to the other and compare this data with a single touch of the keyboard.

```
10  DIM C(3,200),D(1,200)
100 REM GRAPHING ROUTINE
110 HGR: &FULLSCREEN: &SCROLLSET
120 HCOLOR=7: &OUTLINE
130 &PLTFMT=1,2,3,5 :REM COLORS ARE GREEN,BLUE, WHITE, ORANGE
140 &ANAFMT=1,3,5,6
150 &@AIN, (AV)=C, (SW)=200, (RT)=0, (GA)
200 REM  DATA REDUCTION AND PLOTTING
220 HGR2:&FULLSCREEN:&SCROLLSET
220 &HCOLOR=7:&OUTLINE
230 &PLTFMT=6,7 :REM COLORS PURPLE,WHITE
240 FOR I=0 TO 200
250 X1=(C(1,I)-C(0,I) )/(C(1,I)+C(0,I) )
260 X2=(C(3,I)-C(2,I) )/(C(3,I)+C(2,I) )
270 &NXTPLT=X1 * 127
280 &NXTPLT=X2 * 127
290 NEXT I
300 REM DISPLAY ALTERNATIVE GRAPHS
310 GET A$
320 &HIRES1
330 GET A$
340 &HIRES2
350 GOTO 310
360 END
```

A number of subtle graphing techniques are illustrated here. The four channels of acquired data are directly displayed on the graph on Hi-Res page 1. The colors of these curves are determined by the &PLTFMT command. We then switch to Hi-Res page 2 and generate two curves from the four channels of data that were acquired. The massaged data can only lie in the range 0 to 1. The range of the *y*-axis data on a Labsoft graph can only lie in the range 0 to 127; thus the data must be rescaled before it is plotted. Finally, the program sits in an infinite loop switching back and forth between pages 1 and 2 every time a character on the keyboard is pressed.

6.2.6.   Labsoft I for the IBM-PC

The Labsoft commands used with the IBM-PC are basically the same as those of the Applesoft analog. Although the IBM-PC version of Labsoft lacks the elegant simplicity of its Applesoft counterpart, it contains some additional power that makes it a worthy competitor.

The addition of an option argument to some of the commands in which one can run in a so-called asynchronous mode is particularly noteworthy and addresses one of the weaknesses of Labsoft on the Apple. This mode can be used with only one of the ISAAC peripherals (analog I/O, binary I/O) at a time. It places their particular command in an interrupt driven environment and thus creates a foreground/background mode of operation. Thus analog data can be sampled at accurately timed intervals in the background, while editing or executing in the foreground.

To turn this system into a real-time data acquisition and control system would require another I/O board (like the DAC board from IBM) that resides at a different address. This would allow one to continuously examine data as it was acquired, make a decision on the basis of the data, put out a control signal to initiate the proper control action, and still maintain an accurate sampling interval.

Another convenient feature of this system is its ability to format the data so that it can be read by Lotus. This is an extremely powerful spreadsheet and allows the user to easily perform numerical analysis on his data, generate reports, and so forth.

We will briefly consider the syntax of this Labsoft version and its implementation on the IBM-PC.

Since an equivalent ampersand jump option is not available in BASICA, the Labsoft language cannot be readily incorporated, as it was into Applesoft. Instead, Labsoft is accessed with CALL statements from BASICA.

First, it is necessary to extend the operating system to recognize and access the ISAAC interface card and the ISAAC hardware. This is accomplished by the configuration procedure already provided by PC-DOS 2.0 by using the device drivers and software links provided by Cyborg. Thus, when the system is booted, DOS looks for a special file, CONFIG SYS. In the present case this file contains one command:

DEVICE= LSDVR.COM

The file LSDVR.COM contains the Labsoft device driver, and, when the configuration command is executed, it is loaded as a device driver.

One additional "link" is required, which will tell BASICA where to find the device driver when it encounters a Labsoft command during the execution of a program. This link is contained in a file called LSHDR.BAS. The contents of this file must be merged with your program before you can run it. Lines 1 to 100 are reserved for this so-called "header" file. It is appended to your program by typing

MERGE"LSHDR"

followed by a carriage return.

The syntax and the power of the language can be illustrated by examining an analog command to read multiple samples of analog voltage from a single channel.

CALL AINM (CHANNEL%, COUNT, RATE, TARGET%(I%), OPT$)

CHANNEL% is an integer variable selecting the channel to read. COUNT is an integer variable that specifies how many times to read the channel at RATE samples per second and store the values in the integer array TARGET%(I%), beginning at the element specified by I%.

The OPT$ parameter can specify any or all of the six standard analog input options: *unit, device, control, execution mode, storage,* and the *INTSOFF flag.* These input parameters impart a great deal of power and flexibility to this version of Labsoft. A *unit* refers to everything that is connected to the PC through a single ISAAC or IBM data acquisition and control adaptor card. A *device* is an actual input or output module (as, for example, an analog input device) attached to the particular unit. The *storage* option provides the user with the ability to select any of the following storage options: normal 2-byte integer array storage, sum the input values as they come in (for later averaging), store each value at the same location—overwriting the previous value stored there, sum into the same location, or, finally, do not store the value at all because you are only using it for triggering purposes.

The *control* parameter is used with specialized ISAAC cards that interface to strain gauges, RTDs, thermocouples, and other low-level signals; the *INTSOFF* flag, if present, turns off any interrupts except those at the same level as the ISAAC unit.

The *execution mode* parameter is a very powerful one. It selects the common, single-execution mode for Labsoft, where a Labsoft function must be completed before control is returned to the calling program, or an asynchronous execution mode, which is essentially a background/foreground mode of operation. While in this execution mode, control is returned to the calling program immediately after the completion of a Labsoft task but not necessarily the Labsoft command. The foreground or "calling" program is interrupted and made to return to the Labsoft command everytime the Labsoft command must be executed. This mode of operation is not well suited to high-performance operation, but it can be used effectively when low-speed data collection is being performed. At high-speed I/O the timing accuracy of the Labsoft command is lost because the servicing request must wait for the completion of an executing BASIC instruction before it can interrupt. However, provisions for monitoring the accuracy of this asynchronous operation are provided in a STATUS variable.

All of the above parameters must be explicitly defined before one calls AINM. However, default values for all of the optional analog input parameters are specified by the user during the installation of the ISAAC system and need not be reentered. In this case a "null" value is entered for the value of the OPT$ parameter. The following program* will be used to illustrate these aforementioned aspects of the language. This program will read multiple analog values from channel 1 of the ISSAC 91-I.

*ISAAC The Labsoft Users Guide 91-I (Courtesy of Cyborg Corporation).

```
110 'SET UP AINM PARAMETERS
120 CHAN%=1              'SPECIFY CHANNEL
130 NUMSAMP=100          'NUMBER OF SAMPLES TO TAKE
140 RT=20                '20 SAMPLES PER SEC
150 OPT$=" "             'NULL OPTIONAL STRING
160 DIM RAW%(99)         'DIMENSION ARRAY FOR RAWDATA
170 '
180 ' SET UP SETSTAT PARAMETER
190 ST%=0
200 CALL SETSTAT (ST%)  'SET UP STATUS
210 '
220 'SET UP SCREEN FORMAT
230 KEY OFF
240 WIDTH 80
250 CLS
260 LOCATE 3,25:  PRINT "---MULTIPLE ANALOG INPUT---"
270 LOCATE 4,25:  PRINT "          EXAMPLE          "
280 LOCATE 8,23:  PRINT "INPUTTING FROM CHANNEL 1    "; CHAN%;. . . . "
290 '
300 CALL AINM (CHAN%,NUMSAMP,RT,RAW%(0), OPT$)
310 IF STAT% <> 0 THEN PRINT "EXECUTION ERROR #"; ST%:END
320 '
330 FOR I=0 TO 99
340 '
350 LOCATE 8,23:PRINT "CHANNEL #";CHAN%; "RAW INPUT VALUE=";
360 PRINT USING "####"; RAW%(I)
370 '
380 VOLTS=RAW%(I)/409.6-5
390 LOCATE 10,23:PRINT "VOLTAGE AT CHANNEL #"; CHAN%;"=";
400 PRINT USING "##.##";VOLTS
410 '
420 NEXT I
430 'RERUN THE PROGRAM?
440 LOCATE 23,20:INPUT "WOULD YOU LIKE TO RERUN THE PROGRAM AGAIN (Y/N)";ANS$
450 IF ANS$="N" THEN CLS:END
460 IF ANS$="Y" THEN GO TO 220 ELSE BEEP:  GO TO 440
```

Lines 120 to 160 initialize the AINM parameters: Channel 1 is identified, and a total of 100 samples is specified at a rate of 20 samples per second. In line 150 the OPT$ parameter is set to null—that is, nothing different from the value of these parameters set in the installation program is selected.

Line 160 dimensions an array of 100 integers, and line 190 declares "ST%" to be the integer variable in which the status and error codes are to be stored. Line 200 calls SETSTAT.

Lines 230 to 280 set up the screen format and then line 300 calls AINM. Line 340 checks the status variable for any execution errors. If STAT% is not 0, an error message will be printed on the screen.

Lines 350 to 420 create the loop to print the 100 analog input values on the screen. Lines 350 to 360 print the raw input values. Line 380 converts the raw values to voltages, and lines 390 to 400 print these voltage values on the screen.

Lines 440 to 460 allow the user to repeat the program.

6.3.   SOFT500*

6.3.1.   Soft500 for the IBM-PC

The next language extension that we review is called Soft500 and was written by Keithley DAS to support their data acquisition and control hardware. There are two versions of this package: one for the IBM-PC, and one for the Apple. We discuss the IBM-PC version first.

This language, as you will see, is quite versatile but not quite as easy to learn as Labsoft for the Apple. Both versions of Soft500 provide a foreground/background architecture when run in the interrupt-driven mode. This is a powerful mode of operation, since potentially it allows the program to proceed to other tasks without sacrificing accurate timing or the ability to respond to specific inputs when they occur.

The Soft500 assembly language routines occupy 32K of the 96K memory space in which the Soft500 system resides. They are accessed from BASIC with the familiar CALL statement discussed in Chapter 2. As with Labsoft for the IBM, the Soft500 CALL statements must be used with certain parameters written in a required sequence. The parameters are used to pass information from the BASIC "calling" program to the (Soft500) machine program. Those readers who have already read Chapter 11 can appreciate the problem of passing information between a BASIC program and an assembly language routine. To illustrate, let us examine a Soft500 command to acquire analog data.

```
10 CALL ANIN' (Array%",100,0,,"Chan1,Chan2,Chan3",20)
```

The analog in command, ANIN, on execution creates an array for the storage of data that is given the name specified by the user; that is, Array %, dimensioned for 100 values to be taken from channel 1, 100 values from channel 2, and 100 values from channel 3.

The number 20 in the parameter list specifies the sampling interval on each of the channels in terms of the number of interrupts. In this case a sample will be taken on every 20th interrupt. The rate at which the interrupts occur is set by a parameter in the system command called INTON (interrupts on), which would have preceded the ANIN command in the program.

The depth of the array (100 in the above case) is limited only by the amount of available memory.

As mentioned previously, one of the most powerful features of Soft500 is its

*Keithley DAS, 349 Congress St., Boston, MA 02210.

foreground/background processing. This allows the Series500 system to manage apparent simultaneous execution of many independent tasks at machine language speeds. It is essentially a multitasking process controlled from a single program. Programs written in Soft500 can operate on two levels: foregrounad and background. The *foreground* level is the BASIC controlling program, and the *background* level is executed by certain Soft500 commands, which, when encountered, set up a sequence of actions that proceed independently of what is going on in the foreground.

It is *important to distinguish a true foreground/background architecture* such as this and the basically *single-ground structure of language extensions such as Labsoft I*. In the Applesoft version of the latter language, the BASIC program is halted until the execution of the particular Labsoft routine called is complete. With the former language, when a Soft500 command is encountered, the program pauses briefly while communicating with the background to begin execution of the Soft500 command, but it then resumes—that is, it goes on to the next line of the program and continues executing tasks.

Thus, foreground/background provides considerable flexibility, because while data acquisition and control tasks are being executed in the background, the foreground program can proceed to perform analysis on this data and mediate other background tasks.

The foreground/background environment is created by Soft500 with a CALL INTON command. This initiates a hardware-generated interrupt environment. The interrupts are signals generated by the Series 500 interval timer at specified intervals. Each time an interrupt occurs, the microprocessor stops what it is doing and looks at a list of tasks previously designated by a Soft500 command. Each task is checked to see if it requires handling at this time, and the appropriate action is taken. When everything has been taken care of, control is returned to the same point at which interruption occurred.

Strict timing of critical data acquisition and control tasks is maintained by this method of scheduling various tasks. At the same time, program efficiency is maximized because the time left between sampling is available for use by the foreground.

Again a word of caution. The amount of time that one has to complete foreground tasks depends on the time restraints put on the background task. For example, the fastest data rate with ANIN on the Apple is 2 ms per sample. The execution of this command in the interrupt-driven mode takes 1.486 ms (74% of the total time between samples). The execution of the average BASIC command is going to take several milliseconds. *Thus, the foreground work is not going to get very far before it is interrupted again.* Although, foreground/background operation is not expected to be a viable alternative except at fairly slow data rates, whether you are using the Apple or the IBM-PC, it is expected to be much more efficient on the faster IBM-AT.

In addition to direct foreground/background direct communication, there are certain Soft500 commands that allow background sequences to be initiated independently of the foreground. For example, the Soft500 command

SCHMITRIG allows the background to react directly with real-time events, such as a threshold value on an analog channel. When this threshold value is exceeded, some other user-selected Soft500 routine would be executed.

In common with most other language extensions, the machine language routines, once they are called, proceed automatically to completion and do not require the attention of the BASIC or foreground programs. In fact, in most cases, it is not possible to monitor the progress of these routines from the foreground.

In contrast, Soft500 does provide a way of checking on the progress of background tasks. The STATUS command can be used to determine whether a background task is executing, waiting for a trigger, or finished.

Finally, Soft500 commands can be executed in a single-ground mode. This may be necessary when the execution of the Soft500 command requires the full-time attention of the Microprocessor, as, for example, with the very high-speed data acquisition rate provided by ANINQ (analog input quick).

Disk access is another example when it might be preferable to suspend the background mode. In general, this would be the case if it were necessary to perform disk access faster than 10 ms and if the foreground/background ratio of running time were less than 50%.

6.3.2.   Programming with Soft500

Some examples using Soft500 commands to produce a program are provided next.

Program 6.2.   Analog Data Acquisition from Two Channels with Real Time Graphing of the Data (BASICA)

```
 10 Call INIT
 20 Call IONAME' ("CHO",1,0,12,2,191)
 30 Call IONAME' ("CH1",1,1,12)
 40 Call INTON' (50, "MIL")
 50 Call ANIN' ("DATA1%",100.,"CHO,CH1",2,-1, "demo")
 60 Screen 1
 70 Line (7,9)-(312,168),3,B
 80 Locate 24,1:PRINT"2 Channel Analog Input";
 90 Locate 25,1:PRINT"100 Millisecond Intervals";
100 Call GRAPHRT' ("demo","1,2","1,2", "SCROLL",0,5000.)
110 Call INTOFF
120 END
```

Line 20 creates a name for the first channel (CH0), which is located on an "analog input module" plugged into slot 1 of the Series 500. The next parameter in the list identifies the channel number as 0, the accuracy as 12 bit, and the gain as 2; the offset parameter of 191 corresponds to 5 V_{offset}. ($V_{offset}=$ [OFF% + 20.079/255] − 10.079.)

Similarly, line 30 names the second channel in slot 1 as "CH1" and identifies it as channel 1 with a gain of 1 and a 12-bit accuracy. The offset parameter, which is optional, is left out, so it assumes a default value of 128, which is an offset of zero.

The interrupts are turned on at a rate of 50 ms by line 40.

ANIN creates an array named "DATA1%" large enough to accept 100 values each from CH0 and CH1. Data acquisition proceeds at two times the interrupt period of 50 ms. The ANIN command cycles indefinitely (CY% = -1), and the values are plotted by the routine called "demo." The screen is prepared by the next lines and labeled by lines 80 and 90. The GRAPHRT command is then executed.

The data from channels 1 and 2 are plotted in colors 1 = green and 2 = red, respectively. The display is set to the "SCROLL" mode, which means that the window will be scrolled to the left as new data is plotted on the right. The y-axis is set to accept values from 0 to 5000. Finally, after graphing is complete, the interrupts are turned off.

Program 6.3. takes 10,000 samples from two stations at the fastest data rate possible and stores them on disk. Station 1 data is stored on disk drive A and Station 2 data on drive B. Arrays are deleted after saving to retain memory space. The program executes five cycles of sampling once every 30 minutes.

Program 6.3.* (BASICA)

```
10 CALL INIT
20 CALL IONAME' ("station 1",1,0,12):REM Names the #0 channel in slot
   1 as station 1 and selects a 12-bit A/D conversion accuracy. The de-
   fault values of gain (1) and offset (0) are also selected.
30 CALL IONAME' ("Station 2",1,1,12,5,128):REM similarly channel 1
   in slot 1 is named station 2. A 12-bit conversion accuracy is specified
   with a gain of 5 and an offset of 0 V.
40 FOR I=1 TO 10
50 IF (IMOD2) = 0 GOTO 70:REM IF I is even, GOTO 70
60 GOTO 90
70 ARN$ = "Station 1%":ION$ = "Station 1"
80 GOTO 100
90 ARN$ = "Station 2%":ION$ = "Station 2"
100 CALL ANINQ' (ARN$,10,000., ION$,0):REM Depending on the value of I,
    10,000 samples will be obtained at the fastest rate possible from
    station 1 and then from station 2 and stored in arrays named Station 1%,
    and Station 2%, respectively.
110 READ lab$, fil$ : REM This is a BASIC statement that assigns to lab$
    and fil$ the strings found at DATA statements.
120 CALL ARLAB' (ARN$,LAB$) : REM Labels the array ARN$ with the label
    LAB$, which will be saved with the array.
130 CALL ARSAVE' (ARN$,FIL$) : REM Saves the array ARN$ to disk and names
    the file the particular string that has been assigned to Fil$ at this
    time in the cycle.
```

---

* Courtesy of Keithley DAS.

```
140 CALL ARDEL'(ARN$) : REM Delete the data array, since we have now
    saved it to disk.
150 IF ( (IMOD2) = 1) GOTO 190
140 CLS
150 PRINT I/2; "Sample(s) from each station;"
160 IF (I = 10) GOTO 190
170 PRINT;PRINT, "Pausing 30 minutes"
180 CALL PAUSE' (30,"Min")
190 NEXT I
200 PRINT "Program Terminated"
210 END
220 DATA "Station 1,Sample 1", "ST1.1.ARY","Station 1,Sample 1",
        "ST2.1.ARY"
230 DATA "Station 1,Sample 2","ST1.2.ARY","Station2,Sample2",
        "ST2.2.ARY"
240 DATA "Station 1,Sample 3", "ST1.3.ARY","Station3,Sample3",
        "ST2.3.ARY"
250 DATA "Station 1,Sample 4","ST1.4.ARY","Station2,Sample4",
        "ST2.4.ARY"
260 DATA "Station 1,Sample5","ST1.5.ARY","Station 2, Sample5",
        "ST2.5.ARY"
```

6.3.3.   Soft500 for the Apple II Plus and IIe

Soft500 is also available as an extension of Applesoft BASIC. It provides a
foreground/background architecture, array management, memory management disk access and storage, and a library of I/O commands accessible
directly from BASIC.

As with other Apple language extensions, the Soft500 commands can be
imbedded in an Applesoft program. The instruction set is basically a duplicate
of the one just illustrated for the IBM-based system, except that each instruction is prefixed with the ubiquitous & character rather than the CALL
command.

The structure of the Apple and IBM language extensions are quite similar to
each other with the parameters to be passed imbedded in the command *in a
specific order*. For example, the syntax for the analog sampling command
ANIN is

```
&ANIN(SA$,SN,BI%[,CY%][,TM$],N1$[,N2$......N25$])
```

where

> SA$ is the name of the array created by ANIN to hold the data
>
> SN is the number of data samples to be taken
>
> BI% is an integer that, when multiplied by the previously set interrupt rate,
> will give the sampling interval
>
> CY% indicates how many times ANIN should be cycled

TM$ is a parameter that enables a trigger to start the operation

N1$ to N25$ are the names of the channels to be sampled

Again, the requirement of including the parameters in a required sequence may have simplified the programming for the designers of the system, but it does not make it easy for the user.

A sample program and some explanatory notes are shown in Program 6.4. These were taken from the Soft500 user's manual. The program demonstrates the use of ANIN to take 1000 samples of analog data from each of two channels on an analog input module, AIM1. Channel 0 is named "BOILER" and Channel 1 is given the name "PIPE". The data is then graphed in real time with the GRAPHRT command.

Program 6.4.* Analog Data Acquisition

```
90   REM INITIALIZE THE SYSTEM AND NAME TWO CHANNELS
100  &"INIT
110  BOILER$="BOILER"
120  SLOT%=1:  CHANNEL%=0:  RES%=12
130  &"NAME(BOILER$,SLOT%,CHANNEL%,RES%)
140  PIPE$="PIPE":  CHANNEL%=1
150  &"NAME(PIPE$,SLOT%,CHANNEL%,RES%)

155  REM SET UP ANIN IN THE BACKGROUND
160  SN=1000:  BI%=2
170  &"ANIN(SA$,SN,BI%,BOILER$,PIPE$)
180  PRINT "TO BEGIN SAMPLING PRESS ANY KEY"
190  GET ANS$

195  REM ENABLE INTERRUPTS; BEGIN SAMPLING
200  RT%=10
210  &"INTENABLE(RT%)

215  REM GRAPH THE INPUT FROM BOTH CHANNELS IN REAL TIME
220  MIN=0:  MAX=4095:  CP$="Y"
230  &"GRAPHRT (BOILER$,MIN,MAX,CP$,PIPE$,MIN,MAX,CP$)
```

*Courtesy of Keithley DAS.

The two channels on the AIM1 module plugged into slot 1 of the Series 500 baseboard are named in lines 110 to 150. Channel 0 in slot 1 is named Boiler$, and channel 1 in slot 1 is named PIPE$. These string-variable names will be used in the ANIN parameter list to designate the channels to be sampled. Both channels are designated as having 12-bit resolution (RES%=12). Thus, the hardware must include an ADM1 module for 12-bit conversion.

The next set of instructions, 160 to 190, sets up the ANIN instruction to be performed in the background. The sample number, SN, is given the value of

1000. Therefore, ANIN will sample each channel 1000 times. The sampling rate is set by BI%. A background interval (BI%) of 2 specifies that a sample is to be taken every second interrupt interval. Jumping ahead to line 200 where the interrupt rate, RT%, is set to 10 ms, we note that a value of 2 for BI% means that sampling will occur every 20 ms. The ANIN instruction is defined in line 170. However, since the interrupts have not yet been set up, execution will not begin until they are enabled by line 210.

Line 220 sets the maximum and minimum values of the graph to the maximum and minimum values of the A/D conversion (0 to 4095). The GRAPHRT command in line 230 graphs the values obtained from channels BOILER$ and PIPE$ by using the maximum and minimum values specified by the previous instruction.

6.4.   QUICK I/O

Interactive Microware, Inc. provides a number of software packages ranging from general-purpose graphics routines, such as Scientific Plotter, VISI-CHART, Curve Fitter, and so forth, to the menu-driven Chromatochart. The latter package is a sophisticated data acquisition, display, storage, and output program for chromatography applications. In addition, they offer a language extension to Applesoft called QUICK I/O. The syntax of this language is quite terse and may discourage the novice. However, it is quite easy to learn, and although not as broadly based as Labsoft or Soft500, it is a powerful language extension in its own right. As with other language extensions, machine language routines for data acquisition and control link the ADLAB hardware and other peripheral devices to the user's BASIC program. It occupies only 2.25K of memory and is usually loaded below DOS into the address area $8D00 through $95FF. There is no reason, however, why it could not be loaded on the language card. In fact, since it only occupies 2.25K, both it and DOS could be relocated on the language card, thus increasing the user memory area by 12K.

6.4.1.   QUICK I/O Commands

QUICK I/O commands are quite short and are preceded by the familiar ampersand (&), which causes a jump to page 3 ($03F5 to $03F7) where the QUICK I/O address pointer is stored. The first letter of each command selects the type of device: T for the timer or clock, D for digital, S for serial, P for parallel, and A for analog. The next letter designates an input, I, or output, O, command. The last letter selects a channel by using a number, a variable name, or an expression that represents the channel number.

We give a few examples:

&PIO;   parallel input on channel 0

*Interactive Microware, Inc., P.O. Box 771, State College, PA 16801.

&DO2;   digital output on channel 2
&TOX;   timer output on channel X
            X would have to have been defined earlier
            to be a number for this command to be valid

The values for input or output are placed in a variable or an array called D%. These must be defined in the first, or initialization, statements of the program. These statements are

```
10 HIMEM:36095
20 D% = 0
30 DIM C%(5), Q%(5), D% (desired size)
40 PRINT CHR$(4); "BRUN QUICK I/O"
```

The first instruction protects QUICK I/O from being overwritten. The subsequent instructions (20, 30) define the variable D% and dimension the array D% (C% and Q% are not used, but must be included for future expansion). Line 40 asks DOS to load and run the binary file QUICK I/O.

Any QUICK I/O command may be followed by a comma and a number, variable name, or expression that represents the element number in the array D%. For example, the command &AO1,5 will output, on channel 1, the analog value found at D%(5).

Analog/Digital Conversion

The example in Program 6.5 illustrates QUICK I/O programming for the collection of 100 points at the rate of 10 points per second from channel 0.

Program 6.5. Data Acquisition with QUICK I/O (Applesoft)

```
20 &TI1             :REM Get the time from timer 1
30 T=D%             :REM Save the value of time as T
40 &AI0             :REM Start A/D conversion. Get analog
                         value from channel 0
50 For N = 1 to 100 :REM Set up the loop to get 100
                         data points
60 T = T -.1        :REM Set value of T to 0.1 s less than
                         it was
70 &TI1             :REM Read the timer again
80 If D%>T Go to 70 :REM If 0.1 second has not elapsed,
                         read the timer again
90 &AI0,N           :REM Get an analog value from channel
                         0 and store it in D%(N).START
                         the conversion
100 Next N          :REM Loop back to 50
```

Timer 1 addressed by line 20 counts down continuously at 10 counts per second regardless of whether or not you set it. We could have first set it to any value by placing a value in D% and then issuing the command &TO1.

Since timer 1 is a countdown timer, it will read a smaller number as time elapses. Thus, line 60 sets the next time for sampling to occur at 0.1 s less than the original time.

The A/D conversion takes 50 ms (0.05 s). Thus, the analog value immediately returned to D% by line 40 is inaccurate. However, by the time line 90 is executed, 0.1 (100 ms) has elapsed.

The conversion process initiated by line 40 is now complete. A new request for conversion (line 90) returns to D% the current value of the conversion started by line 40 (erasing, in the process, the original incorrect value stored in D%).

Notice also that line 90 directs the A/D value into element N of D%. Thus, the first loop value is stored at D%(1), the second loop value at D%(2) and so on.

As indicated above, QUICK I/O requires the user to write a timing loop in BASIC to make sure that requests for A/D conversion do not occur at intervals smaller than 50 ms. This may be an advantage at times, since during this 50-ms interim, the program may go on to perform a number of other tasks while waiting for the A/D value. However, the accuracy of the sampling interval may suffer.

It is possible to have the program execution halted automatically while it waits for the correct A/D value. This is accomplished by including a POKE 36359,1 command in the program. For example, Program 6.6 gets 200 points at 50 ms per point, scales each for the monitor, and plots each one as it is obtained. At the completion of this task, the program waits for the user to strike any key. The monitor screen then reverts to the text mode.

Program 6.6.   Timed Data Acquisition in QUICK I/O (Applesoft)

```
 10  &AIO              :REM Ask for a conversion
 20  POKE 36259,1      :REM Set conversion done mode
 30  HGR               :REM Initialize high-resolution graphics
 40  FOR N=0 TO 199    :REM Loop 200 times
 50  &AIO              :REM Get analog value from channel 0
 60  Y=96-D%/21.5      :REM Scale it for the monitor screen
 70  HPLOT N,Y         :REM Plot a point
 80  NEXT              :REM Get another point
 90  IF PEEK (49152) <128 Go to 90   :REM Press any key to
                                          continue
100  TEXT              :REM Revert to text mode
```

Parallel and Digital I/O

Although there is an overlap in function, a distinction is made between *Digital I/O* and *Parallel I/O*. The former refers to single bit, and the latter to groups of eight bits. This simplifies programming for tasks involving single-bit on/off states, such as turning switches on and off, and reading switch states.

A single ADLAB board contains digital bits 0 to 7, which are also designated as parallel channel 0. A second board containing digital bits 8 to 15 could be used as parallel I/O channel 1, and so on.

Parallel operation means simultaneous input or output of eight bits of information. To read this information into D% from, say, channel 1 (bits 8 to 15) requires the command &PI1. Similarly, one can output a value to a specific channel (e.g., channel 2, bits 16 to 24) by placing the value (0 to 255) in D% and typing &PO2. For example,

```
D% = 7;Seven decimal converted to binary is 00000111
&PO1  ;Sets bits 8,9,10 and clears bits 11,12,13,14,15
```

The ADLAB board can also provide handshaking signals. As the reader will see in the following chapter, these handshaking signals help synchronize the computer and the instrument with respect to data transfer.

In order to activate this option, the user must write a 1 into location 36257—that is, POKE 36257,1. Writing a zero to the same location will *disable the handshaking*. There are several modes of handshaking available. You must poke the desired mode value into location $49212+256*N$, where N is the slot for the ADLAB card.

In order to fully exploit the potential of the ADLAB system, you may have to communicate with the system at the assembly language level. The reader is referred to Chapter 11 for some examples of this ADLAB option.

Interactive Microware, Inc. also provides modified versions of their QUICK I/O and VISICHART software to support the fast A/D interface card (AI13) manufacturered by Interactive Structures, Inc. A single-channel sampling rate from 771 to 18,267 samples per second is available with this card. Alternatively, ADLAB timer, interrupt-driven routines can be used to select sampling rates from 31 to 9651 samples per second.

```
&FA CHANNEL, GAIN, START, LENGTH, DELAY
```

With one line the user selects the fast A/D command, &FA, on a certain channel at one of four possible amplifier GAINS, 0 to 5 V, 0 to 1 V, 0 to 5 V, or 0 to 0.1 V. Also, within this line of code one specifies the number of samples, LENGTH, of data to obtain and to store in the array D%, starting at the array element given by START. Finally, the argument DELAY selects the mode of sampling. If DELAY = -2, free-running, *burst sampling* is performed by using a *software timing loop*. DELAY = -1 selects the ADLAB timer, interrupt-driven mode of sampling (rates up to 9.6 kHz).

6.5. EASYLAB*

In contrast to the other Applesoft extensions we have discussed, EASYLAB does not use the Applesoft & jump routine. Rather, it is integrated into the

* MIA, Box 137, Califon, NJ 07830.

Apple DOS 3.3* and supports the laboratory interface hardware made by Interactive Structures, Inc. The data acquisition routines are interrupt driven at data rates up to 10 kHz.

Although we have not had any experience with this language, it has the easy-to-learn structure so necessary for the novice. In addition, its instruction set appears to be as powerful as any of the others that we have discussed here. For example, the EASYLAB command to read an analog channel is COLLECT. There are a number of powerful arguments that can be used with this command. In addition to the usual sampling interval, channel number, array size, and so on, found with most other language extensions, there are optional parameters specifying that compressed data storage be used, that a moving average be performed on the incoming data before it is stored (digital filtering by boxcar averaging), and that the COLLECT instruction wait for a RESUME command before starting. It is quite simple to program a data collection to begin, COLLECT; to stop, SUSPEND; and resume, RESUME; and keep time, TIME.

Under data management the addition of "description" as an argument to STORE is a useful aspect and eliminates a lot of programming on the user's part when storing data.

Finally, the inclusion of DATA communication commands simplifies what is usually a problem area for the user.

6.5.1.   Programming with EASYLAB

The EASYLAB commands may be executed in the immediate mode or in the deferred mode. In the former case all that is required is for the user to enter the command through the keyboard and then strike <RETURN> for its execution. For example, if one enters

TRANSMIT A%, D, E

and follows this with a <RETURN>, the following will occur:

The whole data array A% will be transmitted, starting with the array element A%(0)

The data will be converted into ASCII decimal digits (D)

Each element will be terminated by a carriage return

A character echo (E) will be used to detect any transmission error

Because EASYLAB is an extension of DOS, however, the execution of EASYLAB statements in a deferred mode requires the same preparation as for

---

* An interesting consequence of this approach is that this language extension can probably be used in conjunction with other & utilities, such as The Routine Machine and &Array, Southewestern Data Systems, 10761 E Woodside Ave., Santee, CA 92071.

the execution of any DOS command. Thus, in the deferred mode the same statement would read

$$10 \ PRINT \ CHR\$(4) \ "TRANSMIT \ A\%,D,E"$$

where CHR$(4) is the ASCII character for CTRL-D.

Program 6.7, reproduced from the EASYLAB user's manual, illustrates a number of options available with the COLLECT command.

Program 6.7. Demonstration of EASYLAB COLLECT Command (Applesoft)

```
10                                   : REM THIS A DEMONSTRATION OF
                                     : THE COLLECT COMMAND IN THE
                                     : DEFERRED MODE
20  DIM P1%(210)                     : REM DIMENSION ALL ARRAYS
30  DIM P2%(210)
40  DIM T%(210)
50  DIM F1%(30),F2%(30)
55  D$=CHR$(4)                       : REM SET D$ EQUAL TO CTRL-D
80  PRINT D$"COLLECT 1,P1%,1000,G5,P,W"
90  PRINT D$"COLLECT 4,P2%,1000,G3,P,W"
100 PRINT D$"COLLECT 5,T%,1000,G8,P,W"
110 REM
120 PRINT D$"RESUME 1"               : REM START DATA ACQUISITION ON 1
130 PRINT D$"RESUME 4"               : REM START ACQUISITION ON CHANNEL 4
140 PRINT D$"RESUME T%"              : REM START DATA ACQUISITION TO
                                     : FILL ARRAY T%
150 REM
160 PRINT D$"COLLECT 8,F1%,10000,G8,W"
170 PRINT D$"COLLECT 9,F2%,10000,G8,W"
180 PRINT D$"RESUME"
```

The first few statements dimension the arrays. Line 55 sets up D$ as CTRL-D. Henceforth, anytime a PRINT D$ is encountered the DOS will execute the statement which follows.

The first COLLECT command sets up data acquisition from Channel 1 into data array P1% at a rate of 1000 ms per point using a gain setting of 5—that is, 1 V. The data is to be plotted in real time. The COLLECT command is not to be executed until a RESUME command is encountered (W = wait for RESUME). The first COLLECT command has the following defaults:

Single ended input (no D parameter)

No moving average (no Aa parameter)

No compressed storage (no Cc parameter)

The next two COLLECT commands differ only in the channel to be sampled, the gain to be used, and the array in which to store the data. Statements 120 to 140 start the data collection from channels 1,4, and 5.

The next commands set up data acquisition from channels 8 and 9 at 1 sample per 10 s. Statement 190 starts the acquisition. Note that channels 1, 4, and 5 are started first, and then 8 and 9 are started while 1, 4 and 5 are still running.

If we wished to plot the data from channels 1 and 4, we could follow these commands with

```
195  PRINT D$ AXES
200  PRINT D$"EPLOT P1%,C5"    :REM PLOT P1% IN ORANGE
210  PRINT D$"EPLOT P2%,C6"    :REM PLOT P2% IN BLUE
```

To store the data we would follow with

```
220  PRINT D$"STORE NAME OF EXPERIMENT 1,P1%"
230  PRINT D$"STORE NAME OF EXPERIMENT 2,P2%"
220  PRINT D$"STORE NAME OF EXPERIMENT 3,T%"
```

Lines 220 to 240 store the data in arrays P1%, P2%, and T% on a disk under the file names NAME OF EXPERIMENT 1, NAME OF EXPERIMENT 2, NAME OF EXPERIMENT 3.

To transmit the data filed in the array F1% to a mainframe computer, one would add

```
240  PRINT D$"TRANSMIT T1%,D,E"
```

which transmits the data in array T1% to the central computer in decimal format (D) and specifies that the character echo (E) be used to detect and correct transmission errors.

6.6.   PCLAB*

PCLAB is a real-time software package designed by Data Translation to support up to four of their DT-2801 series of analog and digital I/O boards that plug into the IBM-PC. In terms of its overall structure, this software package is cruder than the one offered by Keithley DAS and requires a little more computer know-how of the user. For those who wish to spend the effort though, it does offer a library of powerful subroutines and access to a direct memory access (DMA) mode of operation that is not available on the other systems discussed in this chapter. DMA is an alternative and much faster way of accessing memory than the usual register mode of data transfer. Thus, much faster data acquisition rates can be used with this system than with any of the others discussed here.

* Data Translation, 100 Locke Drive, Marlboro, MA 01752.

PCLAB is essentially a library of macro routines that the user accesses from BASIC by the familiar CALL instruction. It can be used with the BASICA interpreter or compiler. The former language is the one normally supplied with the IBM-PC.

The user loads PCLAB into the system from a Data Translation diskette, using the DEF SEG statement of IBM, BASICA to control the starting address of PCLAB. The DEF SEG instruction designates a 20-bit address using a 16-bit number. The actual address is determined by BASIC internally by taking the 16-bit number and multiplying by 16. For example, DEF SEG = 10 yields an address of 160.

PCLAB occupies 4 K bytes of memory; its load address depends on the memory available. To place it in the top 4 K of a 64 K system, one would include the statements

```
10 DEF SEG = 3840
20 BLOAD "PCLAB",0
```

The first statement defines the address to load PCLAB. This will be at 60 K bytes. 60 K bytes is equal to 60 * 1024 = 61,440 bytes. This is the address to load PCLAB. Since the DEF SEG = X command designates an address 16 ×, we must use 3840 for X (since 3840 × 16 = 61,440).

Similarly, for a 128K system, the address designation statement would read DEF SEG = 7936.

As mentioned previously, all PCLAB routines are accessed from BASIC's CALL statement. Each PCLAB routine is referenced by an entry point number (related to the specific address of the routine). The CALL statement has the general form

```
CALL NUMVAR[(variable[,variable]...)]
```

where "NUMVAR" is the numeric variable assigned as the entry point for that particular PCLAB routine, and "variable's" are the arguments belonging to each PCLAB command. For example,

```
INPUT.ADC.VALUE%(CHANNEL%,GAIN%,ANALOG.VALUE%)
```

is a valid PCLAB instruction. INPUT. ADC. VALUE% is a routine that performs a single A/D conversion on input channel, CHANNEL%, at a gain of GAIN%. It returns the result to ANALOG. VALUE%.

In this example, the arguments are "CHANNEL% (an integer that selects the input channel), GAIN% (an integer that selects the gain by which the channel input voltage is amplified before conversion) and ANALOG. VALUE%, which is the value corresponding to the input voltage measured at the input channel upon execution of the command.

Program 6.8 illustrates the use of this command.

Program 6.8.* Single A/D Conversion (BASICA)

```
10 CLEAR,14,000              'This is similar to Applesoft's HIMEM
                             statement. It restricts BASIC from
                             the top of memory (assuming a 64K
                             system)
20 DEF SEG=3840              'specifies where to load PCLAB
30 BLOAD "PCLAB",0           'Load PCLAB
40 ANALOG.VALUE%=0           'Set the value held at this memory
                             location to zero
50 INPUT.ADC.VALUE%=3        'This is the entry point (address) for
                             this routine
60 HIGH,V#=+10               'Highest voltage value in the range
70 LOW,V#=-10                'Lowest voltage value in the range
80 RANGE#=HIGH,V#-LOW,V#
90 LSB#=RANGE#/4096          'Defines  the  least  significant  bit  of
                             the input voltage in terms of the
                             defined range and the 12-bit resolu-
                             tion of the ADC
100 INPUT"ENTER   the   AD   channel"; Channel%  'Asks   the   user
                             to input the input channel number
110 INPUT"ENTER     the     desired     gain    (1,2,4,8,10,100,500)";
                             GAIN%

120 'Asks the user to input desired gain
130 ' to be applied to the input signal

140 SCALED,LSB#/GAIN%                    'Scale the LSB according to
                                         ' user inputed gain

160 SCALED,LOW#=LOW,V%/GAIN%                'Scale the LOW voltage input
140 CALL INPUT.ADC.VALUE%(CHANNEL%,GAIN,ANALOG.VALUE%)
```

Finally, after all arguments have been defined as well as the entry point for ADC. VALUE, we call the PCLAB routine to perform its function—that is, get an analog value from CHANNEL% and store it at ANALOG.VALUE%

The PCLAB package contains a variety of BASIC callable routines that may be categorized as follows:

A/D input conversions routines

D/A output conversions routines

Digital I/O routines

Control of on-board clock routines

System configuration and error processor routines

These routines can be further subdivided in terms of whether they operate in a

---

* Courtesy of Data Translation.

single mode—that is, a single event is accomplished when they are run or, a block mode, where multiple conversions take place.

Single operation is used for a single A/D, D/A, or digital I/O conversion. It is always triggered (either by a software trigger or a hardware trigger). With a hardware trigger, conversion or data transfer occur within 20 μs after an electrical high-to-low transition.

The block commands can be further subdivided, depending on whether the data transfer occurs in programmed I/O or DMA modes.

The standard block operation performs data conversion each time an interval or external clock pulse occurs. The user specifies the number of data conversions, the input channels, and gain settings.

The continuous block operation is similar to the standard, except that the data acquisition continues until the command is halted by a STOP command.

As mentioned earlier, the transfer of data directly to memory without the intervention of the microprocessor is called *direct memory access* (DMA), and it is a much faster method than the normal mode of operation. It requires a specialized circuit designed to take over the memory bus and transfer data directly into memory at the full speed of the memory. This circuit is called a DMA machine and is available on the Data Translation card.

The use of the block operation with DMA is identical to the standard mode or the continuous mode, depending on the command.

6.6.1. DT/Notebook

As mentioned in Chapter 5, Labtech Notebook supports the 2801 series boards, and Data Translation markets this same software under the name DT/Notebook.

The DT/Notebook is menu driven and is by far the least painful and most efficient method for the novice to get on line quickly. It does not sacrifice any of the performance potential of the DT 2810 series of data acquisition boards and allows sampling rates to 20,000 samples/s while continuously streaming the data to disk at 400 samples/s. The conditions that define the current data run are displayed on the screen and can be easily modified by the user.

Both open-loop and closed-loop (both PID and on/off) control algorithms can be implemented.

Sophisticated curve fitting functions are available as are FFT routines for digital signal processing. In addition, the Notebook can be interfaced to Lotus 1-2-3 for added flexibility in data reduction and analysis.

6.7. LABSOFT II ON THE IBM-PC*

6.7.1. Introduction

We have saved the discussion of Labsoft II until last because this language is fundamentally different from any of the others reviewed in this chapter. In the

* Cyborg Corp., Newton, MA 02158.

first place, Labsoft II is not the name of a language extension. It is the name given by its creators to an integrated software package for data acquisition and control using the ISAAC 2000 in combination with the IBM-PC. As discussed in the last chapter, ISAAC 2000 has its own microprocessor, ROM, and RAM. In fact, all it lacks to be a full-fledged operating microcomputing system is an OS of its own. Thus, it is not too surprising to see that the implementation of data acquisition and control software is quite different in this system than on the Apple and IBM-based ISAAC.

As discussed in Chapter 2, BASICA does not have a provision for extension as does Applesoft. Rather than design a foreground/background architecture and utilize CALLs, as with the ISAAC 91-I, the designers decided to create a system that is closer in concept to that of parallel processing than it is to background/foreground.

The potential power of this system, especially if Cyborg develops an OS, is tremendous. However, as will become obvious, it has been purchased at a price—the friendliness of the original Labsoft.

6.7.2. Overview of the Labsoft II Package

There are three aspects of the Labsoft II package on the IBM-PC that should be highlighted:

1. A set of instructions, called the ISAAC 2000 command language, comes with the system and resides in ROM on the ISAAC 2000 board. The instructions bear a more than passing resemblance to Labsoft I. These instructions are used to control the interface.

2. Communicating with the command language set requires another language, called ISAACOMM. The use of a communication language structure such as this makes the task of communicating with the ISAAC 2000 independent of the communications medium used. In this case ISAACOMM is loaded into the IBM-PC.

3. Also available are various miscellaneous Labsoft II utility routines, such as graphics.

The last two aspects of the software package are only available for the IBM-PC and IBM-XT. Communication with ISAAC 2000 is by means of the RS-232 port. However, this is transparent to the user because the ISAACOMM communications language takes care of the necessary protocol.

An example of how the ISAAC command language (ICL) is used in combination with ISAACOMM is illustrated below.

```
100 INUM% = 1 'DEFINE ISAAC DEVICE
110 CMD$ = "ANIN 2,5"
120 CALL WRITESTRING%( INUM% , CMD$ )
130 CALL READNUM%( INUM% , A% )
```

Here a string variable CMD$ is created containing a single ISAAC command language instruction called ANIN, which when executed will collect a single analog sample from channel 5 of device 2. This instruction is downloaded to the ISAAC in line 120 using an ISAACOMM call for transferring string data to the ISAAC. The instruction will be executed from the ISAAC hardware package when the program is run, and the data will be temporarily stored in an ISAAC buffer. It is transferred to the IBM-PC with the READNUM% call, and the data are placed into the variable A%.

A number of deviations from Labsoft I are evident from this instruction. In Labsoft I the *names of each parameter are explicitly written*, and they may appear in any order in the instruction. In contrast, here, as with CALL instructions, the *order* in which the parameters appear is all important. *All parameters must be explicitly referenced, and default values are not allowed.* Finally, the data collected by any instruction ends up in the ISAAC 2000s buffer memory, and one must specifically command a data transfer operation to get the data to the IBM.

If one is using the ISAAC 2000 with a host computer other than the IBM, then one must control it by downloading ISAAC command language instructions through one of the standard interfaces such as the RS-232. In this case the responsibility is on the user to configure the communications correctly.

6.7.3. ISAACOMM Communications Software

The Labsoft II software package has been configured for maximum flexibility. The ISAACOMM communications package allows the software on the IBM-PC to be independent of the path of communication, apart from the value of the single parameter INUM% introduced above.

The range of values of INUM% with the corresponding address communications paths are shown in Table 6.1. The ISAACOMM software can support up to 15 individual ISAAC devices on a single GPIB bus. On the other hand, if the RS-232 interface is used only two ISAACS may be addressed by using the two IBM serial communications buffers. Two different communications protocols may be used, the less common CTS/DTR being preferred.

Table 6.1. The Communications Addresses

INUM%	ISAAC Id. Number
0–14	ISAAC GPIB primary address
15	Not used
16	COM1 : standard RS-232 handshaking
17	COM2 : standard RS-232 hankshaking
18	COM1 : special CTS/DTR* handshaking
19	COM2 : special CTS/DTR handshaking

*CTS :=CLEAR TO SEND ; DTR := DATA TERMINAL READY

The complete set of calls in ISAACOMM is shown in Table 6.2. These six are sufficient for all communications with the ISAAC 2000 in the variety of hardware configurations described earlier.

The call WRITESTRING% is used to send all of the ISAAC command language instructions and commands as well as any data required by the ISAAC 2000. Most data to be moved from the ISAAC to the IBM-PC are in integer BASIC form and may be moved one number at a time with the call READNUM%. The READSTRING% call is used for any status words that are communicated by the ISAAC. The BREAK% call is used to interrupt ISAACs program execution. This interrupt can be used with both the GPIB and RS-232 configurations but with slightly different results.

The most flexible aspect of the ISAAC 2000 interface is the ability to move data from the ISAAC to the IBM-PC in a high-speed binary dump mode. This is a function supported by the particular GPIB interface recommended for use on the IBM-PC. Two binary dump calls are provided, BDUMP% and BDUMPCS%. The latter, which takes more time to complete, is checked for transmission errors and should be used when the overhead is acceptable.

6.7.4.   The ISAAC Command Language

The 68000 processor, the 128K of RAM, and the 32K of ROM make the ISAAC 2000 a formidable machine in its own right. The ICL is contained in the 32K of ROM. Consequently, the system may be operated in a distributed processing environment. When large arrays of data are being acquired, the host computer is free to be used for other tasks. What is not possible at the present time is for the ISAAC 2000 to be involved in decision making or branching. This capability would make the ISAAC 2000 a much more powerful system. At the moment, decisions can only be made in the IBM-PC, thus slowing down the execution of complex tasks.

The syntax of a typical ICL instruction or command has the form

```
insr <prm_val1,prm_val2,....>
```

Table 6.2.   The ISAACOMM Call Routines

CALL WRITESTRING%(INUM%,string_variable)	
	send command or data string to ISAAC
CALL READSTRING%(INUM%,string_variable)	
	read data string from ISAAC
CALL READNUM%(INUM%,integer_variable)	read data from ISAAC
CALL BREAK(INUM%)	interrupt ISAAC execution
CALL BDUM%(INUM%,array(0))	DMA dump of data from ISAAC
CALL BDUMPCS%(INUM%,array(0))	DMA dump with variable count

where insr is the name of the ICL instruction, and the parameter values prm_val1, prm_val2, and so on, follow the instruction name. Unlike the Labsoft I language syntax, the ICL parameters are *mandatory* and must be kept in the specified order.

As mentioned previously, the ICL instruction set may be likened to the Labsoft I language extension. For example, the analog input instructions look superficially like a copy of the Labsoft I analog input commands. Further examination, however, will demonstrate that Labsoft II is much more powerful. The matrix commands in Labsoft I are replaced by the multiple and block instructions (e.g., MABL is a multiple analog block input instruction). The multiple instructions are the ones used to strobe different analog channels in a real-time fashion. The block instructions are used, among other things, for the acquisition of analog data in a boxcar fashion, where data smoothing may be carried out during the acquisition of data.

Space does not allow us to pursue all of the subtleties of the analog input software of the ISAAC 2000. What we will do is present a simple example of a data acquisition program with simple digital filtering. If all the setup commands have already been communicated to the ISAAC, the following program performs a boxcar average of a defined number of points, NBOX%, with TME% microseconds between the raw data points to be averaged.

Program 6.9. Data Acquisition with Digital Filtering

```
200  INPUT "ENTER NUMBER OF POINTS IN BOXCAR AVERAGE ";NBOX%
210  INPUT "ENTER TIME SLOT IN MICROSECONDS "; TME%
220  RATE%=TME%/20
230  CALL WRITESTRING%(INUM%,"DEFI")
240  CMD$ = "BOXCAR:ZERO;UNDE;8;BIUU 2;MABL 2, 10,12, 1000," +
                  STR$(RATE%) + "," + STR$(NBOX%)
250  CALL WRITESTRING%(INUM%,CMD$)
260  CALL WRITESTRING% (INUM%, "BOXCAR")
  .

  .
500  DIM VOLT%(1000)
505  NRM$ = "NORM" + STR$(NBOX%)
510  CALL WRITESTRING%(INUM%, NRM$)
520  CALL BDUMP%(INUM%,VOLT%(0))
530  GOSUB 2000 ' DATA DISPLAY AND STORAGE
```

This example illustrates a number of the finer points of ISAAC programming. For instance, we demonstrate in line 240 how to string ICL instructions and define a new macro command called BOXCAR. Once the definition has been downloaded (lines 250 and 260) and compiled by the ISAAC processor, it may be called up by name at any time from the IBM-PC.

Unfortunately, as a language becomes more and more flexible it loses its original friendliness. Line 240 is now all but undecipherable for the novice. It's really not that bad, but it requires the user to put in some time studying the language. The sequence of instructions making up BOXCAR includes an instruction to set bit 3 high of the binary output line (BIOU 2). This might be used as a trigger in the experiment. The multiple analog block, MABL, samples data from the analog inputs 10 to 12. One thousand averaged points will be stored. The user choice of sampling rate (RATE%=TME%/20) and number of points to be averaged (NBOX%) are incorporated by concatenating the string CMD$.

The MABL instruction forms 4-byte-long words. These have to be reduced into 2-byte words before being transmitted to the host computer. The instruction NORM does this by dividing by the number of points and placing the results in normal 2-byte words in the buffer NRM$. Finally, this data is transmited to the IBM-PC and dumped into the array called VOLT%.

7

Configured
Laboratory
Systems

Thus far, discussions have been limited to a rather general treatment of laboratory acquisition software and hardware. In subsequent chapters a more focused view of these subjects is undertaken.

In this chapter some particular examples are given of laboratory instrumentation controlled and automated by personal computers equipped with laboratory interfaces. In addition, some commercially available menu- and macro-driven software for the personal computer in laboratory applications is reviewed. In contrast to the general-purpose laboratory language extensions, the menu-driven system requires no programming on the user's part. For certain well-defined situations these systems are well worth the investment because of the time and labor savings in software development (*which always costs much more than originally estimated*). Many of the companies that furnish these complete systems also sell specific data handling routines as separate packages. It is well worth investigating these options and purchasing as many of them as possible.

7.1. DESIGNING A COMPUTER-CONTROLLED CHROMATOGRAPHIC ANALYSIS SYSTEM

Let us illustrate some of the considerations that go into designing a computer-automated instrument by using a typical gas chromatographic problem that might be encountered in a process control application.

Gas chromatography is a physical method of separation whereby the sample gas is injected into an inert carrier, such as helium or nitrogen, that carries it into a system of columns for the purpose of separating (in time) each component of the sample. Usually two columns connected in series are used (see Figure 7.1). The purpose of the first column is to preferentially hold up all components of the sample that may damage the second column. These are usually components such as water, acid gases (e.g., SO_2, NO_x, H_S), and high boilers that might never elute from column 2. After all of the sample except the aforementioned components have passed through column 1, the flow is reversed in this first column while retaining the same forward flow in the second column. The unwanted components are thus "stripped" from the sample and

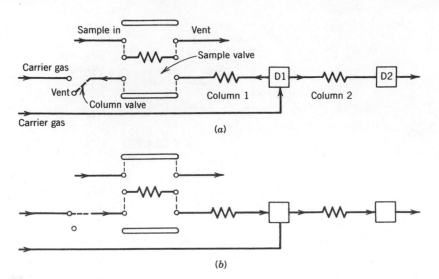

Figure 7.1. Schematic representation of gas chromatographic circuits obtained in the two positions of the sample backflush valve. (*a*) Backflush position of the valve. (*b*) Foreflush/sample inject position.

"vented" while the rest of the sample is being separated on column 2. The separated components of the sample are passed through a detector, and their concentration is determined from the detector response (peak height or peak area) curve, previously determined by calibration with known standards.

7.1.1. Hardware Requirements

The hardware required for this instrument is quite straightforward (at least in concept anyway). It includes:

1. A sample injection valve.
2. A column switching valve so as to switch flows and backflush column 1
3. A crude intercolumn detector to tell us when the desired components have exited column 1.
4. A sensitive analytical detector to record the relative amounts of sample components as they elute from Column 2.

All of this hardware and its placement with respect to the data acquisition and control hardware are depicted schematically in Figure 7.2

Additional hardware, however, may be required to automate the system. The power to drive the valves can be readily obtained from available high-pressure air. The power to drive the solenoid actuators is another matter. An unbuffered TTL signal will not suffice. Therefore hardware "drivers" are required that, when activated by the TTL signal, will furnish enough current to

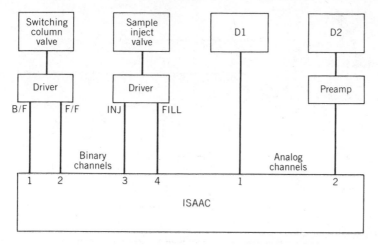

Figure 7.2. Schematic of hardware placement. D1 = Intercolumn detector, D2 = analytical detector.

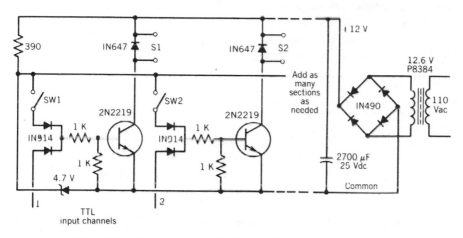

Figure 7.3. Schematic of the 12-V solenoid driver utilized in this work.

"drive" the solenoids. If the computer interface contains "power modules" (as some do), these drivers can be eliminated. Figure 7.3 shows the details of a solenoid driver that we have used.

One may also require a real-time clock for timing various parts of the operation. (See Figure 11.10 for the clock we use.)

Finally, the detector signals are traditionally in the millivolt range (for display on millivolt recorders). Thus, to utilize the full range of the 12-bit ADC (0 to 5V, 0 to 10 V) may require additional amplification of the detector signal. However, with low noise levels it may be possible to use a 16-bit ADC

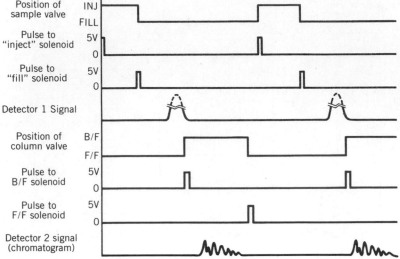

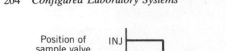

Figure 7.4. A timing diagram showing the relative time position of the various aspects of the problem.

directly. (As mentioned in Chapter 5, instrumentation amplifiers are available from a number of suppliers.)

7.1.2. Software Requirements

From a software point of view a timing or logic diagram might be helpful to focus attention on critical aspects of the analysis cycle. This is provided in Figure 7.4. Note particularly that the valves latch in each position and require separate solenoids to drive them to these positions. Also, the signal from detector 1 will usually be large enough so as not to require further amplification.

The analysis cycle can be summarized in flowchart form in order to reduce the amount of work in planning the final program coding.

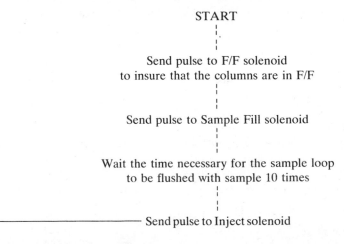

START

Send pulse to F/F solenoid
to insure that the columns are in F/F

Send pulse to Sample Fill solenoid

Wait the time necessary for the sample loop
to be flushed with sample 10 times

Send pulse to Inject solenoid

(Continued)

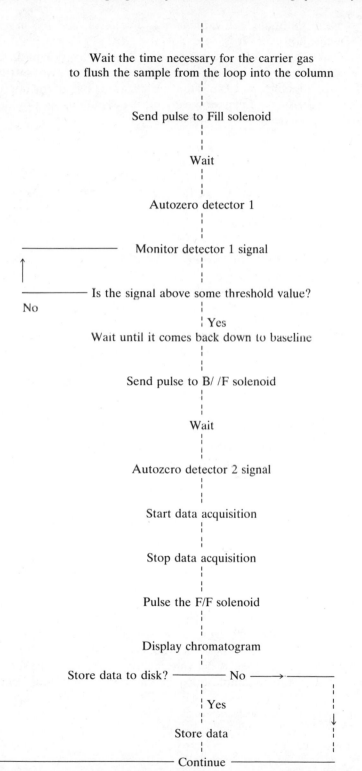

Wait the time necessary for the carrier gas
to flush the sample from the loop into the column

Send pulse to Fill solenoid

Wait

Autozero detector 1

Monitor detector 1 signal

Is the signal above some threshold value?

No

Yes
Wait until it comes back down to baseline

Send pulse to B/ /F solenoid

Wait

Autozero detector 2 signal

Start data acquisition

Stop data acquisition

Pulse the F/F solenoid

Display chromatogram

Store data to disk? ——— No

Yes

Store data

Continue

The flowchart is, in the main, self-explanatory. The term *autozero* may be unfamiliar to some, however. It is an expression denoting a procedure for adjusting an elevated baseline back down to zero. It may be accomplished in hardware, by adjusting an offset voltage until the signal reads zero, or (provided that the amplifiers are not saturated) in software, by subtracting the baseline value from the signal. Let us now examine programming the flowchart for the ISAAC/Apple system using Labsoft I.

7.1.3.   Program Development Using Labsoft I

We refer to the binary and analog channels as numbered in Figure 7.2. To activate the F/F solenoid, we must send a TTL signal on channel 2 to the driver. Assuming in this case that it takes 1 second for the valve slider to reach its new position, we must hold channel 2 high for 1 s. The code would look like this:

```
Language: Labsoft
100 &BOUT,(DV)=4
110 &PAUSE=1
120 &BOUT,(DV)=0
```

If this looks confusing, you should review the Labsoft language discussed in Chapter 6. Remember that the binary outputs and inputs must be considered as an ensemble describing a binary word. If we specify, as we have above, that a decimal 4 be sent out on the binary channels, it is translated as binary 00000100 to be sent out on eight channels. If we label the channels from left to right starting with 7, we have 7, 6, 5, 4, 3, 2, 1, 0. Thus, we can see that a binary 4 puts channel 2 high. Line 120 is required to bring channel 2 back to zero.

With some fluidic-type sampling valves, a very narrow pulse is required (1 to 50 ms).[*][†] The above code cannot supply this narrow pulse. It is necessary to use the matrix form of the BOUT command shown below.

```
Language: Labsoft
100 DIM A%(1):A%(0)=4:A%(1)=0
110 &@ BOUT, (AV)=A%,(RT)=10
```

A two-element array is dimensioned in the first line, and the value of each element [A%(0) and A%(1)] is set by the subsequent statements. The execution of the next line takes 10 ms. [(RT)=10]. The binary word for BOUT is found in the first element of the array A%. This value (binary 4) is held for 10 ms before the next element of the array is accessed to produce a binary zero [(A%(1)=0)]. Thus a 10-ms TTL pulse is produced on binary channel 2.

Returning to our problem, we next activate channel 4 for 1 s to make sure the sample inject valve is in the fill sample loop position. If the sample loop volume

---

[*] R. Annino, and J. Leone, J. Chromatogra. Sci. **20**, 19(1982).
[†] G. Gaspar, P. Arpino, and G. Guiochon, Ibid **15**, 256(1977).

is 1 ml and the sample flow rate is 1 ml per second, we wait 10 s to make sure we have a representative sample. A 1 s pulse on binary channel 3 makes the sample injection.

```
           Language: Labsoft
  130 &BOUT,(DV)=16:&PAUSE=1:&BOUT,(DV)=0
  140 &PAUSE=10
  150 &BOUT,(DV)=8:&PAUSE=1:&BOUT, (DV)=0
```

In many cases, if the pressures of the sample and carrier gas at the head of the column are not the same, a pertubation appears on the detector signal. To avoid confusion with this signal and the one we are looking for, we wait 5s before monitoring detector 1. After the pause we can start looking for a large peak, which will signal the emergence of the desired components from column 1. We can do this with the &LOOK FOR command. Thus, we have

```
           Language: Labsoft
160 &PAUSE-5
170 &ASUM,(TV)=X,(C#)-1,(SW)=10,(RT)=5:BL=X/10
180 ST=BL+200
190 &LOOK FOR AIN,(TV)-Y, (C#)=1,(RT)=10,(TH)=ST:&BEEP
200 &AIN,(TV)=Y,(C#)=1
210 IF Y>BL+10 GO TO 200
220 &BOUT,(DV)=2:&PAUSE=1:&BOUT,(DV)=0
```

Line 170 is used to establish a baseline, BL. Ten samples [(SW)=10] are obtained from channel 1 at the rate of 5 ms per sample. The average value (X/10) is then calculated to be the baseline. Next, a threshold is set (ST = BL + 200). A valid signal is assumed to be present only if this threshold is exceeded.

In line 190 a new analog value, Y, is obtained from channel 1 every 10 ms and compared to ST. When Y exceeds ST, a BEEP signals that the peak has emerged and that we are now looking for it to return to baseline (lines 200 and 210). When the detector signal decreases to below BL + 10, the B/F solenoid is activated (line 220).

Presumably we know something about the analysis time in column 2. There is no point in taking data when nothing is happening. We can pause for this time. We must decide how fast to take the data from detector 2. The optimum data rate will vary with the peak width. Twenty points per peak are certainly quite adequate to accurately describe its peak shape. However, if we are going to use a simple summation of our digital slices to find the peak area, we may want more than 20.

Suppose we decide to sample every 50 ms (20 points per second) over a 3-minute period. This gives us a total of 3600 points per chromatogram. To store the data in integer form requires 7200 bytes (18,000 bytes if we store it as real numbers). To make sure we have enough room for both the data and future program expansion, we include the statement LOMEM:16384 early in our program. This allows 22 K-bytes for data storage, 6K for the program, and the use of the first high-resolution screen (HGR1) for plotting. Also, we must dimension the array B% [DIM B%(3600)]:

```
          Language: Labsoft
230  &@AIN,(AV)=B%,(C#)=2,(RT)=50
240  &BOUT,(DV)=4:&PAUSE=1:&BOUT(DV)=0
```

The execution of line 230 initiates the collection of 3600 data samples from analog channel 2 at a rate of 50 ms per sample. At the end of this time the column valve is again returned to the F/F position (line 240).

If it is desirable to present a plot of the data on the monitor, we might follow the above code with

```
          Language: Labsoft
250  FOR N=0 TO 3600
260  IF B%(N)>MX THEN MX=B%(N)
270  IF B%(N)<MN THEN MN=B%(N)
280  NEXT
```

to find the minimum and the maximum data values, and then follow this with

```
          Language: Labsoft
290  HOME:HGR:HCOLOR=1:&ALTSET:&OUTLINE:&BUZZ
300  FOR N=0 TO 3600
310  N=N+9
320  &NXTPLT=(B%(N)-MN)/(MX-MN))*120
330  NEXT
```

to plot the data.

Although up to 530 equally spaced points can be plotted on the two grids (265 points per grid), in our case only 360 points will be plotted (see line 310). The plot will remain on the screen until the next cycle, when line 290 will again set up the screen for a new plot. To provide a more visually striking display of the chromatogram, such as that shown in Figure 7.5 (with filled-in peaks rather than a line plot), follow line 290 with

```
295  PLT=PEEK(966)+PEEK(967)*256
296  POKE PLT,2
```

To store all the original 3600 points of raw data on diskette, you should use the following program lines after those above.

```
          Language: Applesoft/Labsoft
340  D$=CHR$(4)
350  PRINT D$;"OPEN";F$
```

```
360  PRINT D$;"WRITE";F$
370  FOR N=0 TO 3600
380  PRINT B%(N)
390  NEXT
400  PRINTD$;"CLOSE";F$
```

If the analysis cycle is to be continuously repeated, you need a way to automatically change the file name after it is named in the initial run by responding to an instruction such as

```
10  INPUT"ENTER THE NAME OF THE DATA FILE";Q$
```

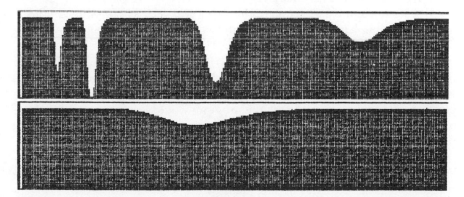

Figure 7.5. Chromatograms showing the Separation of methane, ethane, propane, propylene, and isobutane on a 3-ft alumina column. (*A*) Chromatogram display obtained using the program lines 295, 296. Baseline set to 0 V and a detector signal polarity arranged to generate a positive signal. Acquisition time = 66.74 s and sampling interval = 125 ms. (*B*) Same as (*A*), except that the baseline was set to 5 V and the detector signal polarity arranged to generate a negative signal. Acquisition time = 69.3 s and sampling interval = 100 ms.

Also, to store 3600 integer points requires 7200 bytes of storage space. An Apple diskette has a capacity of 143 K-bytes, so only 20 or so runs can be stored. Thus, you may decide to store only some of the runs. To accommodate this option, you might include the following program lines as setup options.

```
                    Language: Applesoft/Labsoft
20  INPUT"ENTER THE NO. OF CYCLES TO SKIP BETWN FILES";S
- - - - -

- - - - -

142 CTR=CTR+1:N$=STR$(CTR)
144 F$=Q$
146 F$=F$+N$
148 FOR N=1 TO S
- - - - -

- - - - -

335 NEXT
- - - - -

- - - - -

410 GOTO 142
```

Notice here that a FOR/NEXT loop (lines 148 to 335) of S cycles is completed before storing a run on disk. After filing the data the counter, CTR, is advanced and the string value of this number is added to the file name F$ after reinitializing it to the original user-entered name Q$. Thus, the file names are Q$1, Q$2, Q$3, and so on.

It should be noted here that our purpose in this discussion is to provide the reader with some idea of the fairly simple programming aspects of computer interfacing with one of the commercially available language extensions, such as Labsoft. Thus, there are a number of details we have neglected to include in this discussion. For example, all of the variables, such as sampling rate, total number of samples collected, time intervals, and so on, could have been programmed as user inputs by using INPUT statements early in the program, or the whole program could have been written as a menu-driven one if other people were to use it. It is more likely that the program would have been written using the Exec files we have created for data acquisition, data storage, plotting, and so on, in which case the program would have included a number of GOSUB commands, which would have directed the program flow to the proper line numbers for the desired routine.

In addition, we have not considered data manipulation and report generation. The fundamentals of these subjects, which may be of interest to those readers concerned with developing their own routines, are discussed in Chapters 3, 8, and 9. However, in the majority of cases it is more efficient (from both time and money points of view) to purchase software for these purposes. In order to familiarize the reader with what this software might contain as routines and what is commercially available from a number of suppliers, some typical offerings are discussed later in this chapter.

Before we leave the chromatographic problem, it might be instructive from a computer-software-architecture point of view to complicate our problem a little more. One fundamental parameter that assumes much more importance in chromatography than other instrumental methods, such as optical spectroscopy, is *time*. It is intimately involved in compound identification and quantitative analysis. Provisions for accurate timing have been made in all the data acquisitions systems with which the authors are familiar. A problem emerges, however, when a system is to be used for *both* data acquisition and control. Not all commercially available systems can satisfy the multitasking requirement of some control problems.

For example, the chromatographic problem was made quite straightforward by providing an intercolumn detector. In most cases this detector is not present. Backflushing may be timed from the moment of injection, which is no big deal, provided that there is no other task requiring the microprocessor's full-time attention. Although this is an easy alternative for the programmer, it forces tighter instrument specifications with regard to the control of such things as flow, temperature, and column loading. A much better solution is to monitor the analytical detector at the end of column 2. The time to backflush can be related to the appearance of specific peaks in the analysis. A fundamental problem becomes immediately apparent when one tries to write a program to continuously apply the appropriate operation on the signal in order to determine when to go into B/F and, at the same time, maintain an accurate data acquisition rate.

The answer to this problem is found in a system based on a clock-interrupt architecture or that uses parallel processors. The latter alternative may be the only acceptable one if the data acquisition rate is very high. For example, as indicated earlier, even though the Keithley DAS/Apple system is interrupt driven, there isn't much time available for the completion of foreground tasks if you are gathering data in the background at the rate of 2 ms per point. For reasonable data rates, however, a system such as this is able to function quite well as a multitasking system to solve our dilemma.

7.2. AN APPLE-CONTROLLED SPECTROMETER SYSTEM

In this second, somewhat more complex, example the design and implementation of a custom-assembled, experimental, fluorescence spectrometer system controlled with an Apple II plus or IIe is described. The hardware and software aspects of the spectrometer are designed to be as flexible as possible to facilitate later modifications as equipment technology and user needs change. Although the discussion is directed to fluorescence spectroscopy, much of the hardware and software is suitable for absorption or emission spectrometry with a minimum number of modifications.

7.2.1.   Background Material

Some substances that absorb visible or UV light emit part of the absorbed energy as electromagnetic radiation at longer wavelengths. This is illustrated in Figure 7.6. This emission process is called *fluorescence* or *phosphorescence*, depending on the mechanism of the return from the excited state to the ground state. The science dealing with the study of these phenomena is called *fluorescence spectroscopy*.

A typical fluorescence spectrometer, such as that shown in Figure 7.7, consists of a tunable light source, a sample chamber, a monochromator, and two detectors. One of these detectors monitors the variations in the light source intensity by monitoring the fluorescence at a fixed wavelength. The other detector, in combination with the tunable monochromator, is used to record the wavelength dependence of the fluorescent radiation—that is, the spectrum. An alternative measurement configuration preferred in some circumstances is to have one of the detectors monitor the incident radiation source intensity before it enters on the sample cell.

Fluorescence spectroscopy generally involves measuring weak signals and requires sensitive detection methods. For continuous (CW)* laser-exciting radiation, the preferred method of detection is photon counting. Pulsed laser sources require the outputs of the detectors to be gated and integrated with a *boxcar averager*. The integrated signal obtained with these sources can be used in experiments designed to study the time dependence of the fluorescent radiation. Still another approach involves a pulsed light source combined with a photon counter to measure radiative lifetimes by the time-delay method. It is advantageous to create a modular hardware and software environment where light sources and detection schemes can be substituted without having to totally rewrite the driving software with each new configuration.

There are a number of fluorescence characteristics of the sample that we may want to measure. The following are usually, but not exclusively, the most important:

1.   The wavelength dependence of the fluorescent spectrum under fixed laser wavelength and fixed sample conditions.

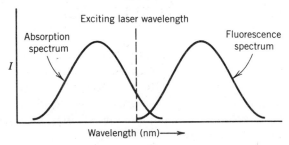

Figure 7.6.   Absorption and fluorescence spectra for a typical organic fluorescent dye molecule.

*CW is the standard notation for a Continuous Working light source.

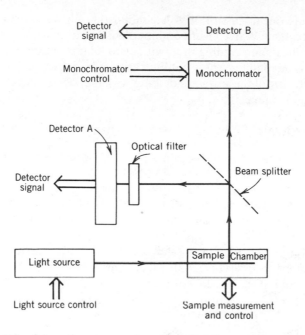

Figure 7.7. Schematic representation of a typical fluorescence spectrometer.

2. The variation of the fluorescence produced at a fixed wavelength with changing excitation wavelength.
3. The variation of the fluorescent radiation with time under pulsed excitation. This is a measure of the radiative lifetime of the sample molecules.
4. The variation in the spectrum or lifetime of the fluorescence under changing sample conditions.

A brief list of light sources and detection systems that you might want to substitute into such a system is given

EXCITATION LIGHT SOURCES
  a. High-pressure mercury light source (CW) and tunable monochromator
  b. Fixed-wavelength CW laser
  c. Wavelength tunable CW dye laser
  d. Pulsed xenon lamp and tunable monochromator
  e. Nitrogen-pumped pulsed dye laser
DETECTION SCHEMES
  a. Electrometer DC current measurement
  b. Electrometer and phase detection
  c. Photon-counting detection
  d. Boxcar-averaging detection

We concentrate our discussion in this chapter on only a single configuration based on a tunable CW dye laser combined with a photon-counting detection method, with the understanding that, with a modular program design, much of the software is adaptable to new configurations. In this regard we should not have to rewrite any of the software dealing with monochromator control if we change the light source.

7.2.2. Hardware Overview of a Photon-Counting System

A block diagram of the major components needed to assemble a photon-counting fluorescence spectrometer is shown in Figure 7.8. The host computer is an Apple IIe. The particular interfacing characteristics of the equipment used in this laboratory as well as the identities of the various connections between the equipment and the computer interface card or the ISAAC are summarized in Table 7.1.

The various fluorescence spectrometer components are connected to the Apple by three interface cards placed in the expansion slots of the Apple bus. The detector electronics are interfaced to the Apple through the GPIB interface card (see Chapter 13). The tunable laser light source is interfaced to the Apple through an RS-232 (see Chapter 12) serial interface card. The remaining elements of the equipment are connected to the ISAAC data interface, which in turn is connected to the Apple through its own interface card.

Interfacing a monochromator to a computer may or may not be a trivial task, depending on the particular model available. Many of the newer monochromators come with a "black box" controller. Thus, much of the intelligence has

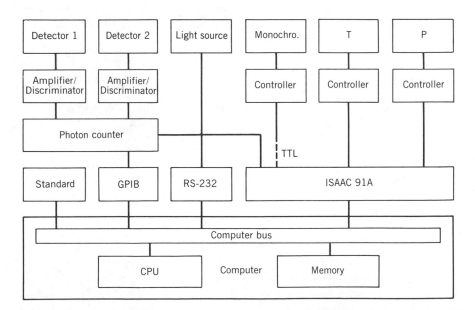

Figure 7.8. Block diagram of the major components of a fluorescence spectrometer.

Table 7.1. Interfacing Characteristics

Equipment end Interface	Computer end Interface
Monochromator Controlled by TTL Levels	
pin 1; +5 V computer control, 0 V no control	ISAAC binary out #0
pin 2; +5 V scan up in wavelength, 0 V down	" " 1
pin 3; 1 TTL pulse $\longrightarrow$ 0.0002 nm/TTL step	" " 2
Laser System Controlled through RS-232 Interface	
RS-232 DCE interface; 7+1+EVEN	Apple Super Serial Card configured as DTE.
Photon-Counter Controlled through GPIB Interface and TTL levels from ISAAC	
GPIB interface, set to primary address	Apple GPIB card.
Counter trigger; 0$\longrightarrow$5 V trigger	ISAAC binary out #4
Counter gate; 0 V counting, +5 V finished	ISAAC binary in #0
Additional measurements and Control through ISAAC Interface	
Temperature/thermocouple	ISAAC analog in #0
Pressure	" " #1
Light attenuator servo	ISAAC analog out #0
Calibration source; +5 V on, 0 V off	ISAAC binary out #3
Laser power meter 1 V/mW	ISAAC analog in #4
Secondary Measurements	
Detector cooling alarm; TTL 5 V low flow	ISAAC binary in #?
Laser cooling alarm; TTL 5 V low	" " #3
Photomultiplier HV supply monitor 1 V/kV	ISAAC analog in #4

already been built into the system by the vendor. In other instances, provision has been made for "primitive" computer control. The only task performed by the controller in this case is to transform the TTL pulse train from the computer into the correct pulse train necessary to control the phases on the monochromator stepping-motor. A single pulse sent to the controller drives the monochromator by a small wavelength increment. In such cases it is up to the programmer to keep track of the wavelength setting. This is the case discussed here.

Most laser light sources have provision for computer control, whether through a serial interface, a GPIB interface, or some more primitive control mechanism, such as a voltage input to drive the laser wavelength over a restricted range. The task of controlling a laser, or any other instrument for that matter, through the RS-232 port is dealt with in Chapter 12, where we detail the steps necessary to interface a nitrogen dye laser to an Apple computer.

The detection method used in our experiment is extremely efficient in monitoring fluorescent radiation at very low levels. The primary detector, monitoring the output of the monochromator, is a thermoelectrically cooled photomultiplier tube. Photomultiplier tubes designed for photon counting are cooled to reduce the dark count (shot noise) of thermally produced photoelectrons in the detector to below 12 cps (counts per second) in some cases. The individual charge pulses coming from the detector as a result of the photons incident on the photocathode are amplified and then pulse shaped by an amplifier/discriminator circuit for input to the gated counter. Typical amplifier/discriminator and counter circuitry have bandwidths of 100 MHz and can detect light signal levels over a dynamic range of at least five orders of magnitude (10 to 1,000,000 cps). The counter gate time on many photon-counter systems may be varied from 1 ms to 100 s, depending on the signal level and signal-to-noise ratio required.

The gating sequence of the counter is worth some discussion. Many photon counters can be used in the so-called dual-counter mode. In this mode the counter is gated to count the input count sequence in channel B until a preset number of counts is received in channel A. If channel A is a reference channel, this can be an extremely efficient method of ratioing two signals or, alternatively, of normalizing the B (monochromator) signal for variations in the light source intensity. The result of the count is returned to the Apple system along the GPIB interface. By monitoring the gate time of the counter with an ISAAC TTL binary input channel, we can obtain the individual counts in channels A and B.

A typical experimental sequence involves scanning the laser wavelength in discrete steps, with the detector counter being gated for a specified time period to obtain the integrated intensity at that wavelength. An example of this sequence is shown in Figure 7.9. First the monochromator is stepped to the

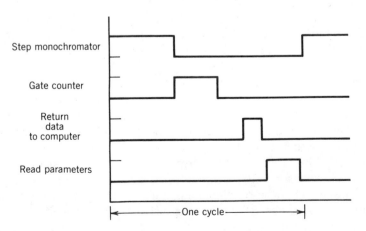

Figure 7.9.   The timing sequence for a counter experiment.

desired wavelength. Next, the counter is gated for the specified time period, and the resulting count is then communicated over the GPIB interface to the Apple. Following this, the other experimental parameters are measured. The cycle is repeated until the complete fluorescence spectrum has been acquired.

In addition to its primary role of data acquisition and experimental control, the Apple computer is used in a secondary, but equally important, role to monitor the health of some of the peripheral pieces of equipment not specifically shown in Figure 7.8. This becomes a very important secondary task if the equipment is going to be left unattended for long periods of time. Such secondary jobs may range from monitoring the flow rate of the cooling water in the photomultiplier cooler, to recording the state of the high-voltage equipment powering the photomultiplier. Many modern pieces of equipment provide a diagnostic, such as an analog or digital alarm output, for such monitoring.

7.2.3. The Software Modular Structure

The software modules shown in Figure 7.10 have been designed in a top-down manner with each major component of the experiment being controlled by a separate software module. For example, one module controls the mono-chromator, and another controls the detector and returns the value of the signal count. This approach makes it easier to replace any component of the experiment without having to rewrite the complete software package.

We have already discussed the structure of the BASIC modular software

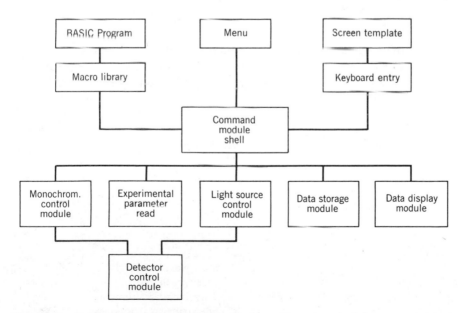

Figure 7.10. Software system diagram illustrating alternative entry methods into command module shell.

environment in Chapter 4. The monochromator control module, for example, can execute one of the two options listed in Table 7.2.

The most straightforward method for controlling the flow of the experiment is menu control, which allows the operator to execute a series of experiments in real time. The menu tree is shown in Figure 7.11. One begins at the topmost general menu to select the major categories and works down to more and more detailed menus. The major disadvantage of menu-driven software is that each task must normally be completed before the next task is entered by the operator.

7.2.4.   Macro-Driven Software

The other method of operator control is through an environment of macro commands that may be entered at the keyboard. A list of representative macro commands for our spectrometer system is shown in Table 7.3. A whole series of small program shells that carry out these commands can be written. They can be arranged by the user in the particular sequence necessary to accomplish a complex task. The management of these sequences in the order programmed is made possible through the command shell in which they reside.

These macro commands provide quite a powerful environment in which to program complex experiments. For example, the following two lines will initialize the experimental parameters in order to scan a spectrum between 600 and 800nm.

```
SETPR 600,350,10,350
MSCAN 600,800,.2,FLUOR1.DAT
```

With the first commands, the monochromator is set to 600 nm, the laser to 350 nm, and the sample pressure and temperature to 10 atmospheres (atm) and 350 K, respectively. When the second line of the program is executed, a scan is made between 600 and 800 nm, and the results are stored in the file FLUOR1.

Table 7.2.   Monochromator Control Module

Option	Variable	Description
1		Set monochromator wavelength option
	WS	Set monochromator wavelength
2		Scan spectrum option
	WS	Start wavelength
	WE	End wavelength
	WI	Wavelength increment
	FL$	File name to store data

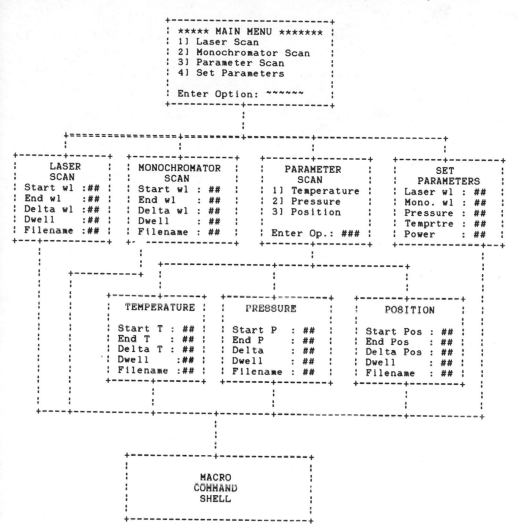

Figure 7.11. The menu tree for an Apple-controlled spectrometer system software.

DAT. These macro commands bear a more than a passing resemblance to the FORTH language syntax.

The use of macro commands necessitates that software be available to read and translate these commands into an operational sequence. We describe a simple method of doing this. A sequence of up to 20 commands from the list in Table 7.3 may be entered, followed by the command EXECUTE, which initializies the execution of the complete series. Figure 7.12 is a simple BASIC program to carry out this task.

Table 7.3. Spectrometer Macro Commands

Macro Command	Parameters	Description
MSCAN	WS,WE,WI,filename	Scan spectrum with monochromator
LSCAN	LS,LE,LI,filename	Scan spectrum with laser
PEXPT	PS,PE,PI,filename	Intensity variation with pressure
TEXPT	TS,TE,TI,filename	Intensity variation with temperature
SETPR	WL,LL,PL,TL	Set experimental parameters simultaneously
MSET	WS	Set wavelength WS on monochromator
LSET	ON,LL,PW	Set laser wavelength LL, power PW on laser
PSET	PL	Set pressure PL on sample
TSET	TL	Set temperature TL on sample
MINC	WI	Increment monochromator wavelength by WI
LINC	LI	Increment laser by LI
PINC	PI	Increment pressure by PI
TINC	TI	Increment temperature by TI
MCAL	WC	Calibrate monochromator against line WC
LCAL	LC	Calibrate laser against line at LC
END		End experiment

To use the program the user simply enters four parameters for each command. For commands that require fewer parameters, anything may be entered. We allow a provision in the software to loop through the command sequence up to NN times by means of a number entered at the beginning of the sequence. A numerical extension is placed at the end of each file name defined in the loop and incremented with each pass of the loop.

7.2.5. Labsoft Implementation of Software

As previously mentioned, there are three channels in which the Apple computer communicates with the outside world. Two of these interfaces, RS-232 and GPIB, are the subject of later chapters and are not considered at this time. The discussion is restricted to the third I/O path, the ISAAC interface as programmed through Labsoft.

Implementing the macro command *Scan Monochromator Spectrum* requires the construction of a number of small programs, each of which can be called by its macro name. For example, the programming necessary to implement the macro command MSCAN is given in Figure 7.13. The monochromator in this case is controlled from the ISAAC interface, and the binary pin assignments are given in Table 7.1. The program controls the wavelength scan from an initial value of WS to a final wavelength of WE with a scan increment of WI units.

```
20 REM ************ INITIALIZATION FOR MODULE 2 ********************
25 DIM CD$(20,4)
   .
   .
   .
1000 REM *********** MAIN ROUTINE *******************
1010 GOSUB 2000 : REM ENTER MACRO COMMANDS
1020 FOR J = 1 TO NN
1030   FOR I = 0 TO NP
1040     IF CD$(I,0) = "MSET" THEN WL=VAL(CD$(I,1)) :
                                              F%(6,1)=1 : GOSUB 6000
1050     IF CD$(I,0) = "MSCAN" THEN WS=VAL(CD$(I,1)) :
                                              WE=VAL(CD$(I,2))
         : WI=VAL(CD$(I,3) ) : FL$ = CD$(I,4) + STR$(I)
                     : F%(6,1) = 2 : GOSUB 6000
1060     .

1890     IF CD$(I,0)=........
1900   NEXT I
1910 NEXT J
1920 END : REM END OF MAIN PROGRAM **********************************
2000 REM ********** MACRO COMMAND ENTER MODULE ***********************
2010 HOME : TEXT : VTAB 6 : HTAB 4
2020 PRINT "ENTER COMMANDS AND PARAMETERS IN FOLLOWING SEQUENCE"
2030 VTAB 8 : INPUT "ENTER NUMBER OF TIMES TO EXECUTE ";NN
2040 VTAB 10 : PRINT "COMMAND" :PRINT "PRM1 , PRM2, PRM 3, PRM 4"
2050 FOR I = 0 TO 20
2060   INPUT CD$(I,0)                          :REM ENTER COMMAND
2070   IF CD$(I,0)="EXECUTE"THEN I=20 : NP = I-1 : GOTO 2090
2080   INPUT CD$(I,1),CD$(I,2), CD$(I,3),CD$(I,4):REM ENTER PARAMETERS
2090 NEXT I
2095 REM ********** END OF MACRO ENTER SEQUENCE *****************
```

Figure 7.12. The macro-driven software program.

The first action of the option 2 subroutine is to set the start wavelength of the scan by calling option 1. The number of wavelength increments and the number of TTL steps necessary to increment the monochromator by WI are then calculated in lines 6120 to 6130. The array C2%( ) used to control the binary outputs bus of the ISAAC must be initialized. Referring to Table 7.1, we see that there are three pins on the monochromator to be attached to three binary channels on the ISAAC. Let us presume that pins 1, 2, 3 on the monochromator are hooked to channels 0, 1, 2 of the ISAAC. The bit pattens corresponding to the four possible states of the binary output interface on the ISAAC are shown in Table 7.4.

The wavelength step control is set with bit 2 of the binary output. The *off* phase of the pulse is set by putting this bit to zero and substituting the appropriate

```
    60 DIM C2%(1)          :REM array containing bit pattern for
                           :REM binary out
         .
         .
         .
  6000 REM ********************** SPECTRUM SCAN OPTION *********************
  6010   ON F%(6,1) GOSUB 6500,6100
  6020 RETURN
  6100 REM ----------------------OPTION 2 -------------------
  6110   GOSUB 6500                       :REM set start wavelenth to WS
  6115   F%(9,1) = 1 : GOSUB 9000         :REM initialize parameter array
  6120   NP%=INT ((WE-WS+0.0001)/WI)      : REM calculate number points in
                                               spectrum
  6130   C4% = 200 * WI                   :REM calculate TTL pulses per
                                               wavelength step
  6140   IF WE>WS THEN C2%(0)=3:C2%(1)=7 :REM set bits for scanning up
  6150   IF WE<WS THEN C2%(0)=1:C2%(1)=5 :REM set bits for scanning down
  6160   FOR I=0 TO NP%                   :REM begin scanning loop
  6170   GOSUB 8000                       :REM read detector counter
  6180   F%(9,1)=2:GOSUB 9000             :REM read other experimental parameters
  6190   &@BOUT,(AV)=C2%,(RT)=5,(SW)=C4%  :REM send pulse train to monochromator
  6200   NEXT I                           :REM end of scanning loop
  6205   F%(9,1) = 3:GOSUB 9000           :REM average parameters
  6210 RETURN : REM -------------- END OF OPTION 2 ------------------
  6500 REM ----------------- OPTION 1 -----------------------
  6510
         .
         .
  6600 RETURN : REM ---------- END OF OPTION 1 ------------------
```

Figure 7.13.   Program to implement monochromator control
Language: Applesoft+Labsoft.

Table 7.4.   Pin Designation and Bit Pattern for Monochromator Control

Pin Designation	Pin Assignment bit → 0 1 2	Decimal
computer on, scan up, pulse off	1 1 0	3
computer on, scan up, pulse on	1 1 1	7
computer on, scan down, pulse off	1 0 0	1
computer on, scan down, pulse on	1 0 1	5

decimal value into array element $C2\%(0)$. The *on* part of the pulse represents a decimal value of 4 that must be added to the zero element of the array in each case to give the array element $C2\%(1)$. The binary output is controlled with &BOUT from the array $C2\%$. The first element of the array is sent out on the binary bus for 5 ms [(RT)=5], followed by the next element of the array, $C2\%(1)=0$, which is sent for the next 5 ms. The pulses are repeated $C4\%$ times to step the monochromator the specified number of nanometers given by WI (see line 6015). The detector is read with the detector read routine in the subroutine module at line 8000 at the beginning of each increment cycle. This is followed by a check of the other experimental parameters, which are read from the module at line 9000.

The photon counter/timer is usually set in the preset count mode as discussed earlier, and by measuring the time period for the count to take place we can obtain separately the individual counts in both channels. Even though the photon counter/timer is controlled on the GPIB bus, we can trigger it just as easily by using the TTL output of the binary-out lines of the ISAAC, with the advantage that we can make a more accurate measure of the count period. Doing this allows us to monitor the counting time with the ISAAC's internal timer.

The counter/timer provides a busy gate that goes low when the device is counting and returns to high when the count is completed. It is relatively trivial to monitor this gate with one of the ISAAC's binary input lines, as is demonstrated in the program segment reproduced below. The major problem in trying to do this in Applesoft is the error introduced by the slow speed of the Apple's BASIC interpreter. We can effectively eliminate this error by using the Labsoft &LOOK FOR command both in the triggering and the subsequent response to the counter stop signal.

```
&LOOK FOR BOUT,(DV)=16:  &CLRTIMER
&LOOK FOR BIN,(TV)=G6,(AM)=32,(TH)=32:&TIMERIN,(TV)-G2
```

The &LOOK FOR command couples two Labsoft commands so that they occur almost simultaneoulsy (within microseconds). The first instruction starts the counter and also sets the ISAAC timer going. The second instruction waits until bit 5 goes high, signifying that the counter has completed its cycle. The timer is immediately read, and the value is returned in the variable G2.

Over the course of a given experiment it is necessary to vary a single experimental parameter while keeping all other parameters as constant as possible. We might wish to average some of these parameters to obtain the best value for each of them over the course of experiment. Thus, in the above program, we make a call to subroutine 9000 to contribute more data to the average each time we loop through the data-taking loop. The seven parameters are accumulated into the 7-element array GP( ) with the Labsoft command &@ASUM.

The subroutine in Figure 7.14 has all the code necessary to initialize, accumulate, and compute the average values of the parameters.

As we have described before, the parameter $F\%(9,1)$ selects the different options of the module. The first subroutine at line 9100 is called on to initialize the data collection. The second option at line 9200 is called each time that the experimental parameters need to be accumulated into the sum. The third option may be called when the final average needs to be calculated.

7.3. COMMERCIALLY AVAILABLE DATA HANDLING SOFTWARE

There are a number of readily available menu-driven data acquisition packages, and new ones appear quite regularly. It is not our purpose to review them

```
9000 REM **********ACCUMULATE EXPERIMENTAL PARAMETERS *******
9005  ON F%(9,1) GOSUB 9100,9200,9300
9010 RETURN
9100 REM ----------- setup
9105  DIM GP(6)                    :REM  array for averaged parameters
9110  &ANAFMT = 1,2,4,6,8,9,11 :REM  channels that are measuring
9115  N%=0                         :REM  number of passes parameter
9120 RETURN
9200 REM ------------- Accumulate into total
9205  &@ASUM, (AV) = GP, (RT) = 1, ( W) = 1
9210 N%=N% + 1
9230 RETURN
9300 REM---------- Find average value
9305  FOR I=0 TO 6 : GP(I) = GP(I)/(N%+1) : NEXT I
9310 RETURN
9315 REM *************************************************************
```

Figure 7.14.   Program to initialize, accumulate, and average Parameters.
Language   Applesoft/Labsoft.

all. Instead, we limit ourselves to a few for the Apple or IBM-PC host computers using the laboratory interface hardware discussed in Chapter 5.

It is interesting that all of the so-called "turnkey" systems that are available are very similar in design. They differ from software previously offered by minicomputer vendors in that they recognize the need for the user to make adjustments and final decisions regarding data treatment. The user's experience provides him with a better perspective regarding the proper data handling than the software developer. Thus, all the menus allow the user to review and modify decisions made by software such as (in chromatography) baselines, peak cutoffs, peak exclusion or inclusions, and so on.

In contrast to these application-oriented turnkey systems, we will also look at two software packages that are somewhat different in concept. This software attempts to satisfy the user requirements for a general, flexible, easy to use programming environment by integrating the data acquisition and control functions with the data handling.

7.3.1.   Chromatochart and Other IMI Software*

Chromatochart is Interactive Microware's chromatography package. With this software, Interactive Microware can offer a complete turnkey chromatography system based on the ADLAB hardware reviewed in Chapter 5. In addition, extra RAM memory is supported (up to 128K RAM card) for the storage of raw data.

Data acquisition, display, storage, and output routines are menu driven. A view of the main menu is shown in Figure 7.15.

---

*Interactive Microware, Inc., P.O. Box 771, State College, PA 16801-0771.

MAIN MENU OPTIONS:
1. DEFINE METHOD
2. DEFINE GRADIENT
3. COLLECT SAMPLES
4. CALCULATE BASELINE
5. BASELINE REVIEW
6. INTEGRATE PEAKS
7. COMPARE TO STANDARDS
8. DISK AND RAM UTILITIES
9. EXIT TO BASIC
   YOUR CHOICE(1:9)?

Figure 7.15. Main menu entries for Chromatochart.

The user starts by *defining a method*. This definition includes such items as sampling rate, integration parameters, memory allocation, names of disk files, and so on. A *binary gradient* profile may be entered by either the keyboard or, graphically, with the cursor. The collect sample option is the entry to Chromatochart's real-time data collection system. A maximum of four channels (requiring four ADLAB cards installed in the Apple slots) can be handled. Each channel can operate independently with its own independent method, and the results displayed continuously on the monitor while simultaneously producing a hard copy on an Epson MX printer.

To conserve space Chromatochart uses a data compression algorithm that compresses the data, so that, on average, only 1 byte of memory is required to store each data point. Even so, the full 12-bit accuracy of each point is maintained. In common with other products, raw data is stored in RAM extended memory cards.

Data analysis is conducted after data collection, since better decisions can be made regarding the analysis parameters after viewing all of the data. Also, it is possible to reanalyze the data after changing certain parameters—features not available with real-time data analysis systems.

Noise is filtered with the Savitsky–Golay* least square smoothing technique to minimize peak degradation (see Chapter 10). Similarly, peak maxima are found by fitting a least square quadratic curve to five points about the peak maxima.

Reports showing chromatograms with annotations of peak height, width, and area presented next to each peak are available. Alternatively, a printed report showing retention time, type of peak integration, width, skew, height, area, and area% can be obtained. Finally, a third type of report is available that uses a "standards" file to compute actual concentration of each component.

Interactive Microware offers a number of other general-purpose software packages, of which some are listed below.

---

* A. Savitsky and M. J. E. Golay, *Anal. Chem.*, **36**, 1627 (1964).

VIDICHART.   A complete set of options for manipulating and displaying raw data. Numerical operations allow one to add, subtract, multiply, or divide all members of a data set with a constant or another data set. One can also integrate, differentiate, or compute the moving average of a data set.

CURVE FITTER.   Allows user to select from the available routines the most appropriate curve-fitting method for the data. Available methods include scaling, transformations, averaging, smoothing, interpolation (polynomial, cubic spline, or Stineman), and least squares fitting (polynomial, geometric, or exponential).

SCIENTIFIC PLOTTER.   Plots data inputted from keyboard or disk.

D/S FILE CONVERT.   Links Scientific Plotter with VISICALC.

STRIPCHARTER.   Software for display and output of lab data. It plots from one to four curves as a continuous chart of any length on the monitor and/or Epson printer.

LAB DATA MANAGER.   A general-purpose software package for data acqusition, storage, display, and output of lab data. It incorporates many of the features of the separate programs described above in one unified package. These include the computational facilities of VIDICHART, the data acquisition features of VIDISAMPLER, the extended memory management features of VISDIMEMORY, and the charting capabilities of STRIP-CHARTER.

7.3.2.   Appligration*

Dynamic Solutions Corporation, a software engineering firm, offers a laboratory data acquisition package called *Appligration*. This software was originally designed for the Apple, but it is now also available for the IBM-PC. The heart of this system is a very powerful and flexible software library of routines, such as sampling, integration, filtering, peak analysis, and so on, that are common to all laboratory analysis. This library is quite large, and all of it will not fit into the Apple Computer's memory at the same time. Therefore, segments are loaded into memory as needed by an "executive" program that loads the appropriate routine from the "program" disk in the "program" drive when menu selection is made.

On the Apple-based system, the DYSC Appligration works only with a Saturn memory expansion card. This is not to be confused with a 16K language card, although they only work in slot 0. The Saturn card, if purchased directly from its supplier, comes with two routines of interest to this discussion.

MOVEDOS.   This routine relocates DOS into the second 16K bank of the Saturn card (thus freeing 10K of RAM on the mother board).

RAMEXPAND.   This is a set of utility routines accessible from Applesoft

*Dynamic Solutions Corporations, 61 South Lake Avenue, Suite 309, Pasadena, CA 91101.

that permit virtual overlays between program memory (48K) and memory on the expansion board. Arrays, subroutines, parts of programs, and data can be saved and loaded from expansion memory at speeds comparable to speeds to and from main memory.

DYSC uses the first routine to relocate DOS into the Saturn card and uses the second to store large arrays of data.

The software is designed along three levels of sophistication. For the inexperienced user, a menu-driven system is available using routines grouped within DYSC control blocks. These are supplied with default parameters that allow the user to just "load" and "go."

Another level allows the user to modify these DYSC control blocks with Applesoft programs written by DYSC to prompt the user regarding the modifications.

Finally, for the experienced user, DYSC provides access to all of their routines through the & call from Applesoft. Thus, the user can tailor his or her program using DYSC routines at the appropriate places.

DYSC software supports a number of hardware configurations, such as Keithley DAS/Apple, Cyborg ISAAC/Apple, and Interactive Structures fast A/D board. The specific configurations of this hardware have already been discussed in Chapter 5 and will not be repeated here.

The rate at which data can be sampled varies with the hardware. If the Interactive Structures AI13 A/D converter is used, data rates as high as 20 kHz can be achieved, whereas with the ISAAC hardware, 10 kHz is the maximum sampling rate.

With a 64K RAM card, 20.5K data points can be stored. This can be increased to 53.3K data-point storage by using a 128K RAM card. Once stored, the data can be displayed on a video monitor with the axis labeled. The data displayed can be scrolled backward or forward in time. The software also allows for both expanded and compressed modes of operation. Thus the analyst can "blow up" portions of data to look for small peaks or reveal some previously hidden details of peak shape. Again, it should be remembered that you can only "blow up" your data to the maximum allowed by your dynamic range. Thus, regardless of the software a 16-bit ADC will produce more information than a 12-bit one.

Sophisticated data analysis routines are available to "Smooth" (using the convolution procedures reviewed in Chapter 8), "detect and integrate" peaks, to "add," "subtract," "multiply" and "divide" waveforms, to calculate "derivatives" of waveforms, to "pack" data buffers, and to manipulate, review, and overlay" data buffers.

Several dot matrix printers are supported (Epson MX-80/100, Epson FX-80, PRO/WRITER 8510, NEC 8023A), featuring an axis labeled with a compressed or expanded time scale and peaks that can be shaded or outlined. For chromatographic analysis the baseline, peak identities, and peak retention times are also printed out.

Although the Appligration system can be used directly in a variety of applications, some specific turnkey packages are available. These include chromatography, spectroscopy, and colorimetry. Each application package contains a user's manual and software containing specific methods setup, reporting, and application programs.

The above packages are constructed from standard Appligration modules that can be purchased separately. The technical manual that comes with the module provides detailed information on the Appligration 6502 assembly language routines, such as entry points, data buffer storage format, and parameter definition. The software modules include:

1. Real-time sampling/video strip chart.
2. Fixed- and variable-period integration.
3. Peak detection and baseline correction.
4. Data compression.
5. Timed digital switch outputs.
6. Signal averaging.
7. DYSC data analysis utilities.
8. FFT transform analysis.

7.3.3.   Model 2600 Chromatography Software for IBM-PC*

This software package supports the Model 760 and Model 860 series of intelligent data acquisition peripherals described in Chapter 5. It is a menu-driven system specifically designed for chromatography applications. The programs available from the main system menu include:

METGEN.   This is a *methods generation* program that allows the operator to create a method for data handling. The parameters involved in data aquisition, data handling and calculation, and report generation are established here. The final method can be stored on disk and recalled if the same method is to be used again.

ACQUIRE.   This program handles data acquisition and processing. It downloads the appropriate data acquisition and processing instructions from the METGEN program to the intelligent peripheral. Also present in this program are options to recall stored data from disk and subject it to "simulated data acquisition," to redetect peaks and reintegrate the data, and to replot data at settings different from those originally used.

COMPARE.   This program allows the operator to recall up to eight stored chromatograms for graphic comparison (with prior rescaling if desired) on

*Nelson Analytical, 10061 Bubb Rd., Cupertino, CA 95014.

the CRT and printer/plotter. This is useful when visual inspection of different runs is desired.

RATDIFF.   Plots ratios and differences of two chromatograms after vertical and horizontal rescaling for normalization.

AUTOCAL.   Allows the generation of calibration factors that are stored as part of the method. It automatically updates calibration files from calibration runs. It can do this either by *averaging* the new data with the old or by *replacing* the old data with new data.

The term *programmable*, which has been used in advertising this product, is somewhat misleading. It is only programmable in the sense that one can build ones own methods. One must however stay within the menu-provided options. Some timed events can be initiated from the peripheral. Auto samplers, valves, and so on, can be programmed by using the four relays or TTL switches. Runs can be autostarted, data collected, reported, stored, another run started, and so forth. However, in contrast to the other systems discussed in this chapter, no high-level development language is available for this product. Thus, this system cannot be programmed to respond to the logic of a user program written in a high-level language. For the user who does not require this flexibility, the 2600 chromatography software appears to offer almost instant on-stream capability.

7.3.4.   ASYST*

ASYST is an integrated programming package that combines the tasks of data acquisition, data analysis, numerical analysis, and data presentation. The ASYST software package, developed in FORTH for the IBM-PC, consists of three libraries of FORTH macro commands accessible from a high-level language providing an extremely powerful programming environment for the laboratory user. Thus, in addition to acquiring data, the user has the sophisticated software to manipulate and present it.

The ASYST programming environment is unique in that it was the first laboratory programming package that claimed to be *independent of the data acquisition hardware.* The 3-module package requires an IBM-PC or IBM-XT running DOS 1.1 or 2.0, 320K of RAM, an 8087 coprocessor, and the IBM color graphics boards. The data acquisition module currently interfaces ASYST directly to Data Translation's hardware and to systems from Tecmar and Keithley DAS. Presumably, more drivers will be added in the future to accommodate most of the hardware around today.

The graphics/statistics module provides graphics, basic statistics, and math functions. The graphics portion supports displays on the CRT, plotters or dot matrix printers, and features automatic plotting, array editing, and multiple

---

* ASYST is a copyright of Adaptable Software, Inc. and is distributed by Macmillan Software, Inc., Macmillan Publishing Company, 866 Third Ave., New York, N.Y. 10022.

graphics windows. The data analysis module supports FFT, polynomials, vectors, matrices and simultaneous equations, interpolation and fitting routines, data differentiation, integration, and smoothing.

7.3.5.   Labtech Notebook*

Another example of the integrated data acquisition, control., and analysis software packages for personal computers is Labtech Notebook. This software runs on the IBM-PC, PC compatibles, and other personal computers. It supports data acquisition hardware from Acrosystems, Data Translation, Metra-byte, Taurus Computer Products, Burr Brown, and National Instruments.[†] This hardware support list is currently being expanded to include all the hardware mentioned in this book and more.

The Labtech Notebook is *menu driven* and requires no computer skills on the part of the operator. The following features are offered.

Real-time data acquisition, speed limited only by the hardware

Option for continuous data storage to disk (at up to a rate of 400 Hz)

Real-time process control, open or closed loop

Real-time graphic display of data

Programming option under MAGIC/L, which allows user to automate his menu-constructed programs. Commands available under this option are:

- Branching and control
- I/O
- Looping
- Notebook defined functions (to start runs, etc.)
- DOS commands (which can be used to execute DOS programs)
- Arithmetic functions

Automatically interfaces to spreadsheet programs'such as Lotus 1-2-3 or Symphony for added utility such as:

- Data manipulation, reduction, and analysis
- Statistics
- Database management and file manipulation
- Publication-quality graphics

---

*Laboratory Technologies Corporation, 328 Broadway, Cambridge, MA 02139.
[†] Acrosystems, 66 Cherry Hill, Beverly, MA 01915; Data Translation, 100 Locke Drive, Marlboro, MA 01752; Metra Byte Corporation, 254 Tosca Drive, Stoughton, MA 02072; Taurus Computer Products, 1755 Woodward Drive, Ottawa, Ontario, Canada K2C OP9; Burr Brown, 1691 W. Grant Road, Suite 1026, Tucson, AZ 85745; National Instruments, 12109 Technology Boulevard, Austin, TX 78727.

Advanced curve-fitting routine fits math models to experimental data
- Models may have up to 10 parameters
- Uses 8087 coprocessor for greater speed and accuracy
- Performs error analysis for quality of fit

On-line HELP facility

Overall, Labtech Notebook appears to be a very powerful software package and merits serious consideration by researchers who are either thinking of purchasing or who already have purchased a data acquisition and control system.

As mentioned at the beginning of this discussion, much of the software offered by the different companies is similar in design. Except for the just-discussed ASYST and Labtech Notebook packages, however, much of it supports only specific hardware. The reader will have to obtain specific details of the software package offered by that vendor in order to select the particular software that best applies to his or her situation.

8

Computer
Graphics

The greater part of this chapter concentrates on computer graphical techniques relevant to scientific or engineering problems. We begin by briefly discussing some general concepts, without referring to any particular computer system, and we go on to discuss the graphical systems of the Apple and IBM-PC computers. In Section 8.4 we cover one of the more advanced techniques of computer graphics—namely, the representation of three-dimensional space on a two-dimensional computer screen. This subject is of special interest for data graphing and the graphical display of computer modeling results. We will briefly discuss the techniques available for higher-resolution, hard-copy graphics on dot-matrix plotters and X-Y recorders.

An area of computer graphics not specifically addressed, but which is a natural extension of much that we discuss, is computer-aided design (CAD). In its more general form, CAD/CAM (computer-aided design/computer-aided machining) uses all the techniques of graphics and computer interfacing discussed in this book.

8.1. INTRODUCTION TO GRAPHICS

The ability to represent data in graphical form is of prime importance in a laboratory computer system. The Apple and IBM computers are somewhat limited in their graphical resolution when compared to some other dedicated laboratory systems. However, this weakness is more than compensated by cost and software availability.

There are a number of methods available on personal computers for the graphical representation of data. The most obvious is direct graphical representation on a computer console. Screen graphics on most 8- and 16-bit machines is somewhat limited (typically 320 × 200 or less), but many systems have the advantage of color display, which may be used very effectively for some applications. If higher-resolution graphics are required, distributed processing graphical units are now available, containing their own storage memory and separate processor capability.

A hard copy of screen graphics screen dump may be made on a dot-matrix printer, but the advantage of color is often lost. If higher resolution is required, the full resolution of the dot-matrix printer (typically 120 × 72 dots per inch) can be utilized. However, the software to carry out such graphing is not universal. Also, the time to make a graph is relatively long, and, finally, there is no interactive capability available. If the computer has a data interface that includes DACs, graphing onto an *X-Y* plotter can be done with excellent resolution, provided that sufficiently sensitive DACs are used (typically 12 bits allow a 4096 × 4096 resolution). Alternatively, some plotters may be communicated with through a GPIB or RS-232 interface.

A comparison of the graphical characteristics of the Apple and IBM computers under a number of options is shown in Table 8.1. For data graphical display the high-resolution graphics options on either of the systems are necessary. We also include for comparison the characteristics of a typical high-resolution advanced graphics system.

8.1.1.   Display Technology

Two types of display monitor systems are in common usage on personal computers. The simplest is the *composite* video system used on many low-cost

Table 8.1.   Graphics on the Apple and IBM

Graphics Mode	Resolution	Colors
	Pixels horiz. × vert. × #	
APPLE II		
Text	80 × 29 × 2	2
Low Resolution	40 × 48 × 2	16
High Resolution	280 × 192 × 2	8
Double Resolution(IIe)	560 × 192 × 1	
Apple graphics memory	16K	
Graphics software	Applesoft commands	
IBM-PC		
Text	80 × 25 × 4	16
Low Resolution	160 × 100	16
Medium Resolution	320 × 200	4
High Resolution	640 × 200	2
IBM-PC graphics memory	16K	
Graphics software	BASICA commands	
VECTORSCAN GRAPHICS SYSTEM		
High Resolution	512 × 512	16
VectorScan memory	128K	
Program RAM	4K	
Interpreter ROM	8K	
Graphics software	Macro commands (language binding requirements)	

graphics systems. This is an extension of the monochrome display system, where the monitor contains only a single electron gun. This is used to excite all three primary colors on the monitor screen. The phosphor pixels for red, green, and blue occupy slightly different positions on the screen: RGBRGBRGB.... These positions can be related to a time in the video raster scan across the monitor screen, and thus each pixel can be activated at a certain time during this scan. The time variation of the video signal addresses the differently colored pixels on the monitor. It should be apparent that a composite color monitor must operate at a bandwidth at least three times (typically 50 MHz) that of a monochrome monitor for the same pixel density. There is also a limit to the resolution that may be realized with these systems, given that the picture must be refreshed at least 30 times per second to prevent video flicker. The input to the composite monitor is a single signal line and a corresponding grounding line, as we show in Figure 8.1a.

The more advanced color graphics systems use RGBI (red-green-blue-intensity) monitors. Instead of the single line to carry the video signal, there are nine lines carrying the separate color signals and the intensity information, as shown in Figure 8.1 b. RGBI monitors contain three cathode guns, one for each of the primary colors. A shadow mask on the screen, shown in Figure 8.2, allows each gun to excite phosphor pixels of only one color. RGBI monitors are more expensive than composite video systems, but the parallel nature of the devices makes them more suitable for high-resolution systems. Because the

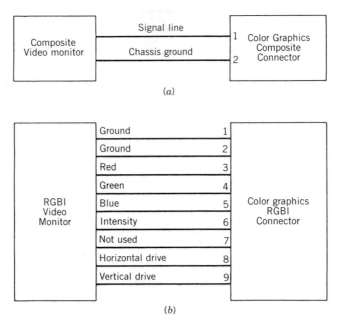

(a)

(b)

Figure 8.1.   Line designation for monitor systems. (a) The composite video monitor system. (b) The RGBI monitor system.

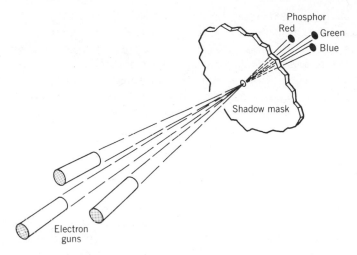

Figure 8.2. The electron gun and shadow mask configuration of an RGBI monitor system.

image must be refreshed every 1/30th of a second, a bandwidth of at least 33 MHz is required for a 1024 × 1024 display.

Present software drivers on most microcomputer graphical systems are extremely machine dependent. Within the next decade it is likely that display technology, especially in terms of solid-state display devices, will advance greatly. Resolution combined with increased display bandwidth will be increased as a result of the use of the new technology. In order to fully utilize these capabilities, software manufacturers must produce future graphics software that is independent of present-day display technology and not tied to a particular computer system or current pixel density.

8.1.2. Memory Requirements

Computer graphics relies heavily on computer memory resources. For a black-and-white graphics system a single memory bit can control the operation of a single screen pixel. When color and color shading are introduced, much more memory is required. If we assume that each pixel may be addressed with the full range of colors and each color may be taken through a range of intensities, then the minimum number of memory bytes that must be dedicated to the graphics system of the computer is

$$n_h n_v r (s+1)/8 \text{ bytes}$$

where there are r memory bits for each pixel to represent color and s bits to represent intensity. The screen is divided into a total of n_h pixels horizontally and n_v vertically. In this color system there will therefore be 2^r possible colors and 2^s possible intensities. For example, in its highest-resolution mode, the

IBM-PC has 640×200 pixels, only two possible colors ($r=1$), and no intensity variation on the colors possible ($s=0$), giving 16 K of memory requirements.

The capabilities of the software drivers for graphics systems vary greatly with the system and the language used. There are advantages to being able to create screen graphics from within an interpreted language such as BASIC. However, if one builds a graphical representation from a series of macro graphics commands, the execution will be quite slow.

8.1.3.   Advanced Graphics Systems

The internal graphical systems of most personal computer systems, controlled as they are from the main processor and sharing memory storage with the rest of the computer system, do not come anywhere near to fulfilling the graphical requirements of data acquisition systems. Such graphically based systems are usually slow, and this fact, combined with complete utilization of much of what is available in color display technology, leads to disappointingly inadequate graphics. The availability of low-cost memory and the move towards distributed processing will lead in the future to truly advanced graphics systems becoming available on many personal computers.

The configuration of a typical distributed graphics system is shown in Figure 8.3. We show a system in which the business of graphics operations is handled in a dedicated graphics unit containing its own dedicated processor and separate graphics memory. Communication between the main computer and the graphics unit is along a computer bus or a communications output port, such as an RS-232 link, depending on the system. The plotting instructions will be sent along the communications link by means of macro commands to be described later.

An example of a general graphics system capable of being utilized on any microcomputer system, such as the Apple or IBM, but with a higher resolution

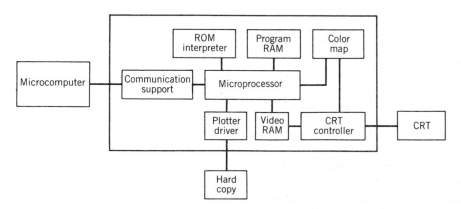

Figure 8.3.   Schematic diagram of the major components of a distributed graphics system.

than either of these systems, is the VectorScan VS512* system from Applied Data Systems. The system is typical of the new generation of dedicated graphics systems that combine improved characteristics with reasonable cost. An on-board interpreter is used to translate the graphics instructions sent along the interface from the host computer. On-board program RAM is provided to store program and graphics instructions. Some of the graphics instructions should address the problems of communications between the microcomputer and the graphics unit. The video RAM requirements are dependent on the resolution and the color requirements, as we discuss later.

The communications between the main computer and the graphics hardware shown in Figure 8.3 can occur by using one of the graphics standards being developed by the computer industry. Because of their advanced features, two standards of particular interest are the GKX** system developed in Germany and the NAPLPS[†] standard recently accepted as an ANSI standard. Both of these software systems have been developed to be independent of the graphics system being used. In this way the same set of instructions within the communications graphics language should produce essentially the same image on two different graphics systems, conforming to the graphics standards independent of the screen resolution and the color capabilities of the systems.

We focus on some of the features of the NAPLPS system in order to demonstrate the advantages of such a graphics protocol.*** We restrict the discussion to the use of the NAPLPS graphics protocol as bound to the C language in the form of C functions. The C functions presented in Table 8.2 represent a small subset of the NAPLPS graphics features available in the protocol.

Table 8.2 contains a number of geometrical graphics primitives such as point ( ), line ( ), polygon ( ), and so on. There is also a primitive for drawing an arc of a circle and an ability to make smooth spline fits through a set of data points. The write_naplps( ) command is the instruction used to carry out communications between the host computer and the dedicated graphics system for NAPLPS-compatible instructions recognized by the graphics unit but not specifically included in this table. All the other graphics primitives have the communications protocol included as an integral part of their structure, and the communications link is transparent to the programmer. The shift_in( ) and shift_out ( ) commands are used to designate the presently activated character set as a standard ASCII set or an alternative, possibly user-defined, character set.

---

*VectorScan is a trademark of Applied Data Systems, Inc., 9811 Mallard Drive, Suite 213, Laurel, MD 20708.

**The GKX system is being reviewed by ANSI committee X3H3 for possible inclusion as a graphics standard.

†The NAPLPS Standard - X3.110, American National Standards Institute, 1430 Broadway, New York, NY 10018.

***"An Introduction to NAPLS"; *Microsystems*, **5**, No. 7 (July 1984).

Table 8.2.   NAPLPS Graphics Protocol C Functions
Language: NAPLPS functions in C

point (relative, visible)	:	Draw a point.
line (set, relative)	:	Draw a line.
polygon (set, fill)	:	Draw a polygon.
rectangle (set, fill)	:	Draw a rectangle.
arc (set, fill)	:	Draw an arc, circle, spline fit.
select_color (color_mode, color 1, color 2)	:	Select foreground/background color.
set_color (red, green, blue):		Sets color palette for current color slot.
write_naplps(out_str)	:	Output string of bytes to graphics unit.
coord_convert (x, y, naplps_coord_str)	:	Convert integer coordinates to NAPLPS string.
init_dec()	:	Reset screen and stop all macro operations
shift_ein()	:	Character set is standard ASCII.
nsr(row, column)	:	Performs a nonselective reset.
shift_out()	:	Character set is alternative set.

8.2.   GRAPHICS ON THE APPLE

8.2.1.   Memory Requirements

The standard Apple computer comes with full graphics capability. The Apple text and graphics storage areas are found at different locations in the computer's memory. Table 8.3 shows the address locations for the text/graphics screens on the Apple II Plus.

The text pages may be used interchangeably for text or low-resolution (Lo-Res) graphics. In practice, the second text page is almost never used, since it is not possible to write text information directly to the area. More memory is available in the text page area than is used by the text buffer. These locations may therefore be used as scratch memory. The Lo-Res screen graphics mode is not of practical consideration within the context of this book.

The high-resolution (Hi-Res) graphics pages are located in the middle of program (and storage) memory. The Apple computer has two high-resolution graphic pages each filling 8 K of the computer's memory, as discussed in Chapter 2. The memory location may be used interchangeably for either graphics or program requirements with the LOMEM and HIMEM commands. On the Apple IIe the two Hi-Res memory locations may be combined to give an extended resolution of 560 × 192.

There is a great deal of confusion surrounding the color and resolution capability of the Apple II. The organization of memory in the high-resolution graphics pages is somewhat convoluted concerning the relationship of screen colors and pixel positions in relation to memory locations. Normally in the

Table 8.3. Memory Locations for the Screen Displays on the Apple

Screen	Page	Begins Address	Ends Address	Resolution	
Text/Lo-Res	Primary	1024	2047	Text	40 × 24
				Lo-Res	40 × 48
	Secondary	2048	3071	not normally used	
Hi-Res	Primary	8192	16383	280 × 192	
	Secondary	16384	24575	280 × 192	

Hi-Res mode, the Apple can display 53,760 pixels in a matrix 280 pixels wide by 192 pixels high. Each pixel represents one bit from the screen buffer. Seven of the eight bits of a byte are displayed on the screen. Thus, a 280-pixel-wide line requires 40 bytes. The remaining bit of each byte is used to select the color of the seven pixels controlled by that byte. The essential thing to remember is that these seven adjacent pixels have an extremely limited color combination with respect to each other.

On the black and white monitor, the pixels whose corresponding bits are *on* always appear white. With a color monitor, however, when a bit is *on* the color depends on the *location of the pixel on the screen*.

The following rules hold:

1. Pixels in even columns must be black, violet, or blue.
2. Pixels in odd columns must be black, green, or red.
3. Each byte must be either a violet-green or a blue-red byte. You cannot mix green and blue, green and red, violet and blue, or violet and red in the same byte.
4. Colored pixels side by side appear white.

We illustrate the effect of such a color system by examining the memory–pixel relationship for the first two bytes of graphics screen buffer memory, as shown in Figure 8.4. The first seven bits of each byte have a one-to-one correspondence with the seven adjacent horizontal pixels on the computer screen. Screen memory bytes 8192 and 8193 control the on/off pattern of the first 14 horizontal pixels in the upper left corner of the Apple Hi-Res screen (screen 1). Pixels 0 $\longrightarrow$ 6 are controlled by bits 1 to 7 of byte 8192, and the bits in byte 8193 control pixels 7 $\longrightarrow$ 13.

With bit 8 turned off and bit 1 on, we get a violet pixel at location 0. With bit 1 off and bit 2 on, we get a green pixel in location 1 as long as bit 8 stays off. With both bits 1 and 2 on, we get two white pixels. By switching bit 8 on and repeating this sequence, we get the blue, red, and white sequence shown in Figure 8.4. It is not possible to plot a green or red pixel in position 0 or a violet or blue pixel in position 1. We recommend that you select the HCOLOR combinations 0 $\longrightarrow$ 3 or 4 $\longrightarrow$ 7 and do not mix them.

Memory byte		8192								8193							
Relative graphics byte		0								1							
Bit		1	2	3	4	5	6	7	8	1	2	3	4	5	6	7	8
Screen pixel		0	1	2	3	4	5	6		7	8	9	10	11	12	13	
Color	H COLOR																
Black	0	0	0						0								
Violet	1	1	0						0								
Green	2	0	1						0								
White	3	1	1						0								
Black	4	0	0						1								
Blue	5	1	0						1								
Red	6	0	1						1								
White	7	1	1						1								

Figure 8.4. The memory organization of the first two bits of high-resolution program memory for high-resolution page 1 storage on the Apple computer. The first seven bits of each byte control an adjacent seven bits on the screen. The eighth bit controls color as shown by the different bit patterns listed vertically.

The final aspect of memory mapping the graphics system concerns the relationship between the memory bytes and the screen position. The information to control the graphics along a single row of graphics screen is contained in adjoining blocks of 40 bytes. Vertically the memory division is more complex. Here the rows are divided into blocks of eight. There is a 1024 memory jump between the memory location of each line. The beginning memory location of the second vertical block of eight is 40 bytes removed from the beginning of the first block, and so on. Thus bit 1 of byte 8192 corresponds to the (x,y) position $(0,0)$, byte 8232 to $(0,8)$, and byte 9216 to $(0,1)$.

Often one needs to work back form a particular screen position to a specific memory location. The following algorithm may be used to calculate the byte and bits that control the pixel at a particular screen location (x,y) where, of course, x takes the range $0 \longrightarrow 279$ and y the range $0 \longrightarrow 191$.

$$mem\_byte(x,y) = mem\_zro(y) + x \ div \ 7 \ byte$$

where

$$mem\_zro(y) = 8192 + 40 \ y \ div \ 8 + 1024 \ rdr(y \ div \ 8)$$

Similarly, the memory bit in the above-calculated byte is

$$mem\_bit(x,y) = rdr(x \ div \ 7)$$

In these formulae, *div* stands for integer division of two numbers, and *rdr* is the remainder of the division. The eighth bit of the byte *mem_byte(x,y)* is the color of the specified pixel (x,y).

8.2.2. Graphics Software on the Apple II

All of the commands required for plotting data in Applesoft BASIC are shown in Table 8.4. The screen setup commands HGR and HGR2 clear the screens when they are executed. Returning to the text screen with the TEXT command leaves the screen buffer contents intact while clearing the monitor screen. To switch back to the Hi-Res mode without clearing the buffer (as HGR will do), type POKE − 16304,0.

The configuration of a typical computer screen is shown in Figure 8.5. This example is for the Apple II Plus in the conventional high-resolution graphics mode. The screen origin is in the top left-hand corner of the screen. We label the coordinates of such a system the $\{H,V\}$ coordinate system, and data is plotted with respect to some other origin system, which we refer to as the $[X,Y]$ system.

In the case where the X-H-axes and the Y-V-axes are parallel to each other, the relationship between the two systems is straightforward. Let us specify that we have a set of (x,y) points and that we wish to plot the data between the x maximum, X_M, and minimum X_N, and the y maximum, Y_M, and minimum, Y_N. We specify the screen coordinates H_M, H_N, V_M, V_N that correspond to the corner points, as shown in Figure 8.5.

The position on the screen of any $[X,Y]$ point is then $\{H,V\}$, where

$$H = ((H_M - H_N) * X + (H_N * X_M - H_M * X_N))/(X_M - X_N)$$
$$V = ((V_M - V_N) * Y + (V_N * Y_M - V_M * Y_N))/(Y_M - Y_N)$$

The simple program in Figure 8.6 *a* may be used to plot a set of *x-y* data that are stored in two arrays, $X(\ )$ and $Y(\ )$, where the index of the array identifies

Table 8.4. Graphics Commands in Applesoft and BASICA

	APPLE	IBM-PC
High-resolution screen setup	HGR HGR2 TEXT	SCREEN [mode] [,[burst] [,[apage][,[vpage]]]
Point plot	HPLOT X, Y	PRESET (x,y) PSET (x, y), color
Line plot	HPLOT X1, Y1 TO X2,Y2	LINE (x1, y1)−(x2, y2)
Circle	none	CIRCLE(x,y), r
Color	HCOLOR = n	COLOR background, palette
Color fill-in	none	PAINT(x,y), paint, boundary
Relative coordinates	none	STEP(dx,dy)

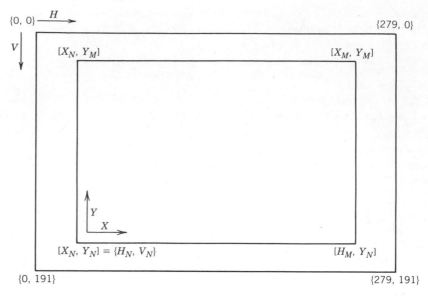

Figure 8.5. The high-resolution screen and coordinate definitions of the screen coordinates {H, V} and the graphical coordinates [X, Y] for a simple (x,y) graph.

```
1000 REM--------------- PLOTTING DATA --------------------
1010 REM EXTERNAL X( ), Y( ), NP, XM, XN, YM, YN
1020 HN = 14: HM = 264: VN = 169: VM = 19
1030 REM---------- DRAW AXES
1035 HGR2          :REM PLOTTING ON HIRES SCREEN 2
1040 HPLOT HN,VN TO HN,VM: HPLOT HN,VM, TO HM,VM
1050 HPLOT HM,VN TO HM,VN: HPLOT HM,VN TO HN,VN
1060 REM---------- PLOT POINTS
1070 FOR I = 1 TO NP        :REM DATA PLOTTING LOOP
1080   IF X(I) < XN OR X(I) > XM THEN GOTO 1130
1090   IF Y(I) < YN OR Y(I) > YM THEM GOTO 1130
1100   H = ( ( HM - HN ) * X(I) + ( HN * XM - HM * XN ) )/( XM - XN )
1110   V = ( ( VM - VN ) * Y(I) + ( VN * YM - VM * YN ) )/( YM - YN )
1120   HPLOT H-2,V TO H+2, V: HPLOT H,V-2 TO H,V+2
1130 NEXT I
1140 END :REM---------------END OF PLOTTING ROUTINE
```

Figure 8.6a. Simple graphical plotting program.
Language: Applesoft.

242

paired points and *NP* is the number of points to be plotted. Let us take the points {14,19}, {14,169}, {264,19}, and {264,169} as the corners of our plotting area. The first thing that the program does is put a box around the plotting area in lines 1040, 1050.

The assumption is made that the plotting limits are not necessarily wide enough to encompass all the data. Lines 1080 to 1090 check for out-of-range data and skip over any such points. Line 1120 puts a cross centered at {*H*, *V*} corresponding to [*X(I)*, *Y(I)*].

This graph represents a scatter plot where each (*x*, *y*) point has no correlation to any other point in the series. If, on the other hand, we were dealing with a spectral series where there is a correlation among the *x*-axis values of the data, we might wish to connect adjoining points in the series. The program in Figure 8.6*b* does this. The lines up to 1110 would remain the same.

To turn this into an acceptable graph for permanent recording, we would have to place scales and titles directly on the screen. Applesoft BASIC does not have a command to do this. However, there is a great deal of commerical and public-domain software available that does allow one to place characters on the high-resolution screens. Also, many of the program packages that come with the data interfaces contain utilities to do this labeling.

For example, under the Labsoft language extension provided with the ISAAC interface, the program element in Figure 8.7 would place a title and axes labels on the screen as well as the date, which is obtained from the ISAAC calendar clock.

We have restricted our discussion of graphics on the Apple to working from within the Applesoft language. For the type of plotting that is usually required in data presentation, we have found the Applesoft commands in Table 8.4 to be sufficient for most requirements. Fast plotting and the inclusion of text on the graphs are the primary exceptions to this rule. If speed is required in plotting, it may be necessary to utilize assembly language programs and to use some of the more involved graphing functions in Applesoft, such as XDRAW.

```
1070 FOR I = 1 TO NP
1080 IF X(I).
       .
       .
       .
1120     IF I = 1 OR I = NP THEN GOTO 114
1130     HPLOT H,V TO HL,VL
1140     HL = H : VL = V
1150 NEXT I
```

Figure 8.6b.

```
2000  REM--------------- LABEL AXES
2010   &LABEL = "GRAPH TITLE" AT 100,10
2020   &DATE TO DD,MM,YY
2030   DT$ = CHR$(MM)+":"+CHR$(DD)+":"+CHR$(YY)
2040   &LABEL = DT$ AT 200,50
2050   &LABEL = "X-AXIS LABEL" AT 75,180:
             &LABEL = "X UNITS" AT 150,180
2060   YL$ = "Y-AXIS LABEL": L% = LEN(YL$)
2070   FOR J = 1 TO L%
2080      &LABEL = MID$(YL$,J,1) AT 10,(50 + * J)
2090   NEXT J
2100  RETURN : REM -------- END OF AXES LABEL ROUTINE
```

Figure 8.7. Graph labeling. Language: Applesoft + Labsoft.

8.2.3.   Applesoft Graphics Language Extensions

Most commercially available plotting software is configured for the Apple in a stand-alone mode. There are exceptions, however, in which graphics extension commands are appended to Applesoft using the & language extension character. Typical of such plotting software packages available for the Apple are the AMPERGRAPH* and &CHART[†] packages.

The AMPERGRAPH package is an extremely simple-to-use BASIC language extension utility for carrying out plots on the high-resolution screens. A list of the Applesoft language extension statements available with AMPERGRAPH is given in Table 8.5.

Illustrated in this table are the graphics utilities for screen setup, point and curve plotting, graph labeling, and obtaining a hard copy on a dot-matrix printer. The beauty of using a graphics utility such as AMPERGRAPH is that global units rather than screen units, as in Applesoft, are used for plotting. In this way once the screen setup commands have been executed and the boundaries defined, we can work in the natural units of the data, and all the correct scalings are carried out as part of the software utilities.

An example of a program to carry out approximately the same plotting procedure as we have described in Figure 8.6 is shown in Figure 8.8.

8.2.4.   Creating a Hard Copy

Once a graph has been created on the high-resolution screen, a permanent record can be made either on a dot-matrix printer or on a storage disk. The exact method of obtaining a printout of the Hi-Res screen depends on the

---

*AMPERGRAPH and the related graphics dump program AMPERDUMP are available from Madwest Software, 121 N. Allen Street, Madison, WI 53705.

†Available from Southwestern Data Systems, 10761 Woodside Avenue, Suite E, P.O. Box 582–1, Santee, CA 92071.

Table 8.5. The AMPERGRAPH−Applesoft Graphics Statements
Language: AMPERGRAPH (Applesoft Extension)

Screen Setup:

&LIMIT, Xmin, Xmax, Ymin, Ymax
where all X, Y lie in range $0 \longrightarrow 1$

−may be used to plot on small area of screen.

&SCALE Xmin, Xmax, Ymin, Ymax	−sets limits of data to be plotted
& LOG X ; & LOG Y	−specifies the x or y-axis is to be logarithmic
&AXES	−draw axes in scaled units
&FRAME	−draws frame around graph
&GRID Xi (ntercept), Yi, Xt(ick), Yt	−draws a grid on the graph separated by Xtick, etc.

Point Plotting:

&CROSS X,Y	
&OPEN/CLOSE SQUARE X,Y	−plots relevant symbol at X, Y
&OPEN/CLOSE CIRCLE X,Y	−places an error bar on last plotted point
&ERROR BARS Xerror, Yerror	

Curve Plotting

&DRAW, X,Y	−draws a line from last point plotted to X, Y
&PENUP	−used to start new line

Graph Labeling:

&LABEL AXES

−labels axes; the strings for x any labels
must have been stored in variables LX$, LY$

&LABEL,X,Y ; &CENTER LABEL, X,Y ; &V LABEL, X,Y
&CENTER V LABEL, X,Y

−these are further labeling commands

Hard Copy:

& * DUMP

−used with further separate graphics dump utilities.

*AMPERGRAPH and the related graphics dump program AMPERDUMP are available from Madwest Software, 121 N. Allen stree, Madison, WI 53705

'Available from Southwestern Data Systems, 10761 Woodside Avenue, Suite E, P.O. Box 582−1, Santee, CA 92071.

```
1000 REM------------------- PLOTTING ROUTINE
1010  &SCALE, XN,XM,YN,YM
1020  LX$ = "X-LABEL (UNITS)":LY$ = "Y-LABEL (UNITS)"
1030  &LABEL AXES, 10,10
1040  FOR I = 1 TO NP
1050     &CLOSED SQUARE, X(I),Y(I)
1060  NEXT I
1070  &FRAME:LABEL$ = "GRAPH TITLE": &LABEL, 30,200
1080 RETURN : REM ------------ END OF PLOTTING ROUTINE
```

Figure 8.8.   Data plotting using AMPERGRAPH.
Language: Applesoft + AMPERGRAPH.

printer and the interfacing hardware used. The Apple computer does not come with a printer interface port. Many interface cards are available; a popular combination on the Apple is to use an Epson FX-80* or related format printers with a Graftrax character generator installed in combination with a Grappler interface.‡

The simple program in Figure 8.9 is all that is needed to dump out the two Hi-Res screens onto such a printer.

```
2200 PRINT CHR$(4);"PR#3"  :REM PRINTER IN SLOT 3
2210 PRINT CHR$(9);"G"     :REM COMMAND TO GRAPPLER
2220 PRINT CHR$(9);"G2"
```

Figure 8.9.   Graphics dump on MX-80 printer.
Language: Applesoft.

The first command accesses the printer port. The character ctrl-I (ASCII code 9) precedes any command that is sent to the grappler interface. The commands G and G2 are used to dump the Hi-Res pages 1 and 2 onto the Printer. Many other peripheral manufacturers have settled on this protocol as a dot-matrix printer standard.

8.2.5.   Storing Graphical Images on Disk

To save a Hi-Res screen image to disk requires a binary save of the area of memory where the screen is stored. The program in Figure 8.10 saves the two Hi-Res screen images to disk 2. It is not necessary for the images to be displayed on the console for this to take place.

The A parameter specifies the starting location in memory of the region to be stored, and the L parameter is the length of the memory region to be stored. All these are nice round numbers in hex, their decimal equivalents being much more difficult to remember. The BLOAD for retrieving the images operation does not for obvious reasons require a length parameter.

---

*Epson America, Inc., 3415 Kashiwa Street, Torrance, CA 90505.
‡Orange Micro, Inc., 3150 E. La Palma, Suite G, Anaheim, CA 92806.

```
3000 REM SAVE BOTH SCREENS TO DISK
3010 D$ = CHR$(4)
3020 PRINT D$;"BSAVE SCREEN1.PIX,A$2000,L$2000,D2"
3030 PRINT D$;"BSAVE SCREEN2.PIX,A$4000,L$2000,D2"
3040 RETURN
4000 REM  RETRIEVING SCREENS FROM DISK
4010 PRINT D$;"BLOAD SCREEN1.PIX,A$2000,D2"
4020 PRINT D$;"BLOAD SCREEN2.PIX,A$4000,D2"
4030 RETURN
```

Figure 8.10.　Saving and retrieving graphics screen images on disk.
Language: Applesoft.

The availability of two Hi-Res screens is a major advantage of using the Apple in laboratory applications. One may plot data on the two different screens and flip back and forth between the two Hi-Res screens and the text screen during program execution. The software to accomplish this without destroying the contents of the Hi-Res screens, which occurs when the HGR and HGR2 commands are used, is not available in Applesoft. It is necessary to *poke* specific locations in the Apple memory, as described in the Applesoft manual.*

As an example of using this technique, we give in Figure 8.11 a method of retrieving graphs from disk where we observe one screen while the other screen is being loaded. We assume that we have loaded the names of the files containing the data into an array FL$( ) and that there are at least NF% files stored on disk.

```
5000 REM---------- GRAPH DISPLAY
5010   D$ = CHR$(4): I = 0
5020   HGR      :REM HIRES SCREEN 1
5030   PRINT D$;"BLOAD ";FL$(I);",A2000,D2"
5040   I = I + 1
5050   PRINT D$;"BLOAD ";FL$(I):",A4000,D2"
5060   GET A$: PRINT:POKE -16300,0: I = I + 1:
5070   PRINT D$;"BLOAD ";FL$(I);", A2000,D2
5080   GET A$ : PRINT: POKE -16299,0: I = I + 1
5090   IF I <=NF% THEN GOTO 5040
5100 Return : REM ------ END OF GRAPH DISPLAY
```

Figure 8.11.　Graphical display sequence.
Language: Applesoft.

The first screen image is loaded directly on the screen being viewed, followed by the loading of Hi-Res screen 2 buffer in the background. The POKE on line 5060 switches from page 2 to 1. The screens are only switched when the GET A$ command is executed, that is, when the keyboard is pressed. The PRINT statement following GET has an important function. After a GET statement is executed, DOS *is disconnected* and is only connected with the next PRINT statement. If we did not include this dummy PRINT, the DOS command in line 5070 would not be recognized.

8.3.   GRAPHICS ON THE IBM-PC

8.3.1.   Hardware Memory Requirements on the IBM

Two different display adapters are available for the IBM-PC. In the event that the IBM is to be operated in character display mode only, an IBM *monochrome display adapter* (MDA) is available. For full graphics capability on the IBM an IBM *color/graphics display adapter* (CDA) is required. Use of the graphics adapter is supported by the BASICA interpreter. The software aspects of the graphical system are described in the next subsection. The CDA adapter is capable of carrying out all the functions available on the MDA.

The MDA system contains 4 K of static RAM memory used as a display buffer. An 8-K ROM, character-generator, memory module contains sufficient data for 256-bit mapped characters on a 9 × 14 character box. Each character on an 80 × 26 display matrix is identified with 2 bytes in the display buffer. A single 8-bit byte in the display buffer can uniquely define any of the 256 characters. A second byte, identified with each character (the odd bytes), is called the *attribute* byte; it controls display attributes such as blinking and reverse video.

The standard characters set on the IBM is worthy of mention. The standard ASCII character set (0 to 127) may be represented by seven bits only. The additional 128 characters available (no parity checking) with the use of the eighth bit represent some useful characters for technical work. These include a limited Greek character set and the standard mathematical symbols, such as integral and square root operators.

A list of the different display modes that may be obtained with a CDA adapter was given in Table 8.1. The IBM color graphics monitor adapter is versatile. It contains 16 K of on-board RAM display that may be utilized for all text or graphics requirements as a memory buffer. The text mode is similar in all but its detailed characteristics to those available on the MDA. The character generator of the CDA contains three complete character sets, each with 256 members. Normally each character is plotted on an 8 × 8 matrix. The memory display contains sufficient memory to store the information for four complete text memory screens (80 × 25 display). The division of 2 bytes, an odd and an even, that control a single arbitrary display character in the text mode is shown at the top of Figure 8.12. The attribute byte contains the information to control

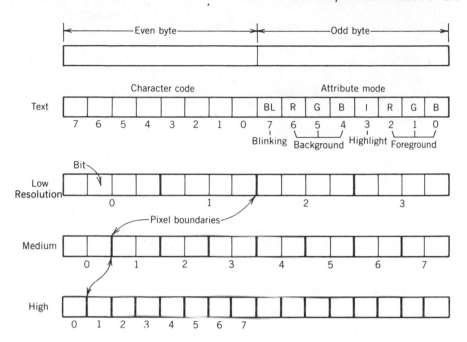

Figure 8.12. The organization of program memory for the IBM graphics (or text) page for different screen resolution. Adjacent screen pixels correspond to adjacent units of memory.

the characteristics of the display for each character defined by the ASCII (8-bit) code in the character byte.

With the IBM, three graphical modes are possible, providing low, medium, or high resolution. Each of these modes requires 16 K of display buffer memory, with the usage being a tradeoff between spatial resolution and color. The IBM is assumed to be driving an RGBI color monitor, although a composite monitor output is available on the CDA graphics card. Each pixel on the graphics screen may be set for the full range of colors available on the particular graphics mode being implemented, which makes the task of graphics programming much easier than on the Apple.

The correspondence between memory location and screen location is straightforward on the IBM. The division of the same two bytes, which we have already discussed in terms of text mode, is shown in Figure 8.12 for the three graphics modes. The low-, medium-, and high-resolution screens take, respectively, 4, 2, and 1 bits of data storage. Thus, a single byte holds the information for 2, 4, or 8 pixels, depending on the mode setting. The full color palette of 16 colors is available in the low-resolution mode. Even with the high-resolution mode (nominally black and white), the two colors may be chosen from the full range of color palette. This allows the color contrast to be chosen based on the particular task being performed.

The registers with the following addresses are used by the color graphics mode. The *color-select* register contains the information on the color selected from the color palette.

Register	Address (hex)
Color-select	3D9
Mode-select	3D8
Graphics status	3DA

The *mode-select* register contains miscellaneous information related to two-color operation and other graphical operations. The *status* register, among other things, sets attributes related to the use of a light pen, which represents one of the advanced uses of interactive graphics not specifically dealt with in this book, but which may have a profound impact on future use of microcomputers in the laboratory if the software to support such techniques is developed.

8.3.2.   Graphics Software on the IBM

We restrict our discussion to the graphical capabilities of the IBM from within the BASICA language. We have listed some of the major BASICA graphical commands in Table 8.4, where they are compared to the nearest equivalent commands in Applesoft. BASICA has a more advanced graphics command structure than Applesoft. In particular, BASICA has a specific command for drawing a circle; coordinates may be specified in relative units, and for many instructions the color may be specified as an optional parameter. There is also a color fill-in capability that allows the color within a specified boundary to be set. None of these capabilities are available in Applesoft.

The techniques of graphical programming from within BASICA follows closely what can be done on the Apple computer, taking into account the more advanced instruction set. We give in Figure 8.13 a simple program that is used to plot a graph of the Bessel function $J_0(x)$, which is one of the mathematical library programs described in Chapter 9. All that is required to utilize this library routine is the knowledge that it must be entered at line 11,300; the variables X and JN% must be specified for each call. The variable JN% specifies the order of the Bessel function, which for this example is zero. The value of the function is returned by the subroutine in the variable Y for each call. We plot the function over the X-range 0 to 20 with a Y-range of -1 to $+1$ and an X-step of 0.05.

The frame of the graph is defined by the corners (50,20), (50,180), (600,20), (600,180), leaving the rest of the screen for axis labeling.

The results of this calculation are shown in Figure 8.14. This may be compared with the plot of the same function carried out directly on a dot-matrix printer in Figure 9.4. By redefining HMAX, HMIN, and so on, this program can be easily adapted to other computers, such as the Apple Mackintosh or any MS-DOS computer with enhanced graphics capabilities, running extended

```
1000 ' plotting data
1020 HMIN=50:HMAX=600:VMIN=20: VMAX=180 ' define box
1030 SCREEN 2: CLS 'set screen mode 2 and clear screen
1040 PSET (HMIN,VMIN), 1: LINE -(HMAX,VMIN),1 ' define box
1050 LINE -(HMAX,VMAX),1: LINE -(HMIN,VMAX),1 : LINE -(HMIN,VMIN),

1060 '                        plot data
1070 JN% = 0 : X = 0 : GOSUB 11300 ' calculate first point
1080 PSET (X,Y)        ' set start position
1090 FOR X = 0 TO 20 STEP 0.05    ' loop for data plotting
1100 JN% = 0: GOSUB 11300      ' calculate Jo(x)
1110 LINE -(X,Y),1        ' plot straight line to
1120 NEXT X      '   next point
1130 END
```

Figure 8.13. A BASICA program for screen plotting a Bessel function.
Language: BASICA.

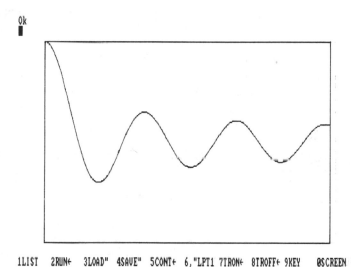

Ok

1LIST 2RUN◄ 3LOAD" 4SAVE" 5CONT◄ 6,"LPT1 7TRON◄ 8TROFF◄ 9KEY   0SCREEN

Figure 8.14. The Bessel function plot; the result of executing in program of Figure 8.13.

MBASIC. We further discuss graphics plotting on the IBM in the next section with an example of three-dimensional plotting.

8.3.3. VISIPLOT on the IBM

As an example of one of the more well-written plotting programs that have been developed for microcomputers, we discuss the VISIPLOT graphing program from Visicorp.* Although there are more advanced graphics programs

*VISIPLOT is a trademark of Visicorp, 2895 Zanker Road, San Jose, CA 95184.

now on the market, VISIPLOT possesses many of the essential features of these advanced graphics systems and will be discussed as an example. VISI-PLOT is a menu-driven program system that, together with its sister program VISITREND, creates a programming environment in which numerical data may be manipulated and graphed interactively. The programs support the DIF file format as well as their own internal data storage format. The DIF format allows data to be interchanged with other software packages, including VISI-CALC. A discussion of both of these may be found in Chapter 3, where the subject of data filing is reviewed.

As we discussed in some detail in Chapter 3, the default plotting of the VISIPLOT package assumes that the data is being plotted against time. The data must be organized into individual series with a defined periodicity. Scatter-plots (X-Y plots) in which one series may be plotted against another may also be graphed. This may only be carried out if the series have overlapping time sequences and identical periodicities.

The menu display organization of VISIPLOT is creative in its use of display resources. The program has a number of separate menus that are used to set the separate attributes of the graph being plotted. The menu in current use may be displayed at the bottom of the IBM computer screen as the graph is being created. The menus are set up in a hierarchical structure. At the higher end of the hierarchy is the choice of graphical types, such as *line* (time series) plots or *x-y* plots. Below these are various levels of menus involved with choosing the detailed aspects of data plotting. In using the menu program structure, one drops down naturally through each level of menu hierarchy. Many of the plotting options have default values, so that it is possible to create a graph quickly with little work and then change more detailed aspects in further iterations of the plotting operation. In particular, automatic scaling of both axes is made if no limits are specified.

8.4.   THREE-DIMENSIONAL GRAPHICS

We now extend our discussion of graphics to consider the presentation of data in three-dimensional projections on a two-dimensional computer screen. There are many places in which such graphics techniques are of major value in highlighting patterns not readily apparent from conventional two-dimensional screen plots. We present the absolute minimum information necessary to carry out coordinate transformations on microcomputers. Those who wish to pursue the subject in more depth should consult some references specifically written on the subject.*

*I.O. Angell, *A practical Introduction to Computer Graphics* (Halstead Press, 1981).

We begin with an example of a transformation sufficient to carry out a three-dimensional screen projection. We then discuss the formalism in more detail, giving the reader sufficient information to carry out more complex transforms.

We discuss two aspects of three-dimensional data projections. The first is a simple rotation of the axes and the resulting projection onto a single plane representing the computer screen. The second is the representation of perspective in the three-dimensional projection on the computer screen.

8.4.1. A Recipe

Since we are more interested in the final answer than the more formal aspects of three-dimensional transformations, we begin by giving one of the recipes for the general three-dimensional projection of an image onto a computer screen. Referring to Figure 8.15, we have an object that is initially described with respect to (w.r.t.) a set of orthogonal axes (x, y, z). We wish to view the object from a distance h from the origin with spherical coordinates (h, θ, ϕ), w.r.t. the original axis origin, and project the object onto a screen at a distance D from the eye. Each point P on the object projects onto the screen at point P'' and has screen coordinates $(x,''(P''), y''(P''))$. The coordinates merely have to scale the projected screen coordinates to the actual screen size.

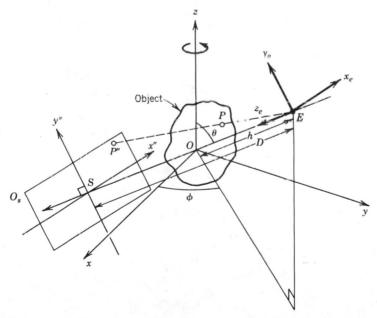

Figure 8.15. The general spatial configuration showing the relationship between object, observer, and screen in the three-dimensional projection of an object onto a computer screen.

The formulae

$$X''(P'') = D\, x_e/z_e \text{ and } y''(P'') = D\, y_e/z_e$$

completely define the transformation, where (x_e, y_e, z_e) are the coordinates of the original point P w.r.t. the set of axes centered at the eye position. We show that

$$x_e = x \cos(\phi) + y \sin(\phi)$$
$$y_e = x \cos(\theta) \cos(\phi) - y \cos(\theta) \sin(\phi) + z \sin(\theta)$$
$$z_e = x \sin(\theta) \cos(\phi) - y \cos(\theta) \sin(\phi) - z \cos(\theta) + h$$

The formulae represent a transformation in which the z-axis of the three-dimensional image is in the same plane as the y-axis (vertical axis) of the screen. The result of carrying out a three-dimensional transformation of the functions $\text{sinc}(x,y) = \sin(x)\sin(y)/xy$ in the positive (x,y) quadrant is shown in Figure 8.16. We used the values $\theta = 70$, $\phi = 135$, $h = 100$, and $D = 200$. The transformation presented here is restricted in that it only describes projections that

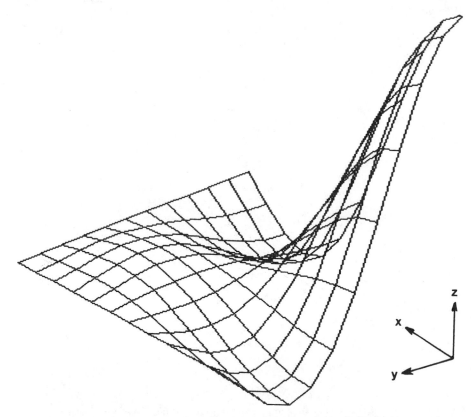

Figure 8.16. Three-dimensional projection of the function $\text{sinc}(x,y)$, for positive x and y.

keep the z-axis in a vertical plane. There follow the transformations that make any coordinate projection possible.

8.4.2. Transforming Coordinates

There are two opposite approaches taken in the literature to the transformation of coordinates in three-dimensional computer graphics. Some studies keep fixed the objects being viewed and transform the axes providing the frame of reference. Others keep the axes fixed and transform the body. Although these transformations are just the opposite of each other, they do lead to some sign differences in the intermediate transform equations that have to be kept in mind. At all times in this section we will keep the *objects fixed and transform the coordinate systems*.

For example, consider the transformation in Figure 8.17 where a point *P* has coordinates (x, y, z) in a coordinate system with origin *O*. If we rotate the coordinate system by an angle ϕ about the z-axis and keep *P* fixed, the point will have coordinates (x', y', z') in the new coordinate system. Note that the sense of the rotation is clockwise, viewed along the axis of rotation (the z-axis in this case) looking away from the origin. In the language of vectors the rotation is described by the cross product of the two unit vectors describing the old and new x-axes by x∧x.

The transformation in Figure 8.18 may be written

$$x' = x \cos(\phi) + y \sin(\phi)$$

$$y' = -x \sin(\phi) + y \cos(\phi)$$

$$z' = z$$

Any coordinate transformation in three-dimensional space may be described by 4 × 4 matrix transformations.[*] Origin translation, rotation, reflection, and scaling may all be described by such a technique. The transformation described above may be alternatively written in matrix form.

$$
\begin{vmatrix} x' \\ y' \\ z' \\ 1 \end{vmatrix} = \begin{vmatrix} \cos(\phi) & \sin(\phi) & 0 & 0 \\ -\sin(\phi) & \cos(\phi) & 0 & 0 \\ 0 & 0 & 1 & 0 \\ 0 & 0 & 0 & 1 \end{vmatrix} \begin{vmatrix} x \\ y \\ z \\ 1 \end{vmatrix}
$$

where the coordinates of the point *P* are changed from (x, y, z) to (x', y', z) by this transformation.

*Angell, loc. cit.

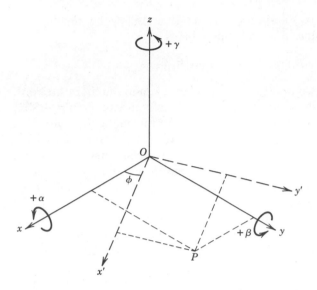

Figure 8.17. A diagram showing the simple "rotation about the z-axis" primitive in a three-dimensional transformation.

A set of transformation matrices that is sufficient to accomplish everything required for computer graphics is shown in Figure 8.18. We use some of them in the next subsection to accomplish more complex three-dimensional transformations by successive operations of these basic transforms. We use the angle α, β and γ from Figure 8.17 to describe the rotations about x, y and z.

Note that one of the greatest sources of confusion in three-dimensional transformations concerns the correct sign of the angles. The directions of positive sign for α, β, and γ are shown in Figure 8.17. Note that in each case the positive sign represents the clockwise turn of a corkscrew pointing along the positive axis direction. Be aware that different published material on the subject users different sign conventions.

8.4.3. Complex Transformations Without Perspective

In this subsection we discuss how complex transformations may be described by a number of primitive transformations detailed above. We assume for the moment that the origin is fixed and only angular changes take place in space. A view of the three-dimensional space being transformed is shown in Figure 8.19. We wish to transform the space to a new set of coordinates (x', y', z'). If we imagine the computer screen to be in the (x', y') plane, then we are interested in the projection of the space onto this plane.

The transformation of the coordinates can be accomplished in a number of

(A) Rotation Matrices

$$R_x(\alpha) = \begin{vmatrix} 1 & 0 & 0 & 0 \\ 0 & \cos(\alpha) & \sin(\alpha) & 0 \\ 0 & -\sin(\alpha) & \cos(\alpha) & 0 \\ 0 & 0 & 0 & 1 \end{vmatrix} \quad R_y(\beta) = \begin{vmatrix} \cos(\beta) & 0 & -\sin(\beta) & 0 \\ 0 & 1 & 0 & 0 \\ \sin(\beta) & 0 & \cos(\beta) & 0 \\ 0 & 0 & 0 & 1 \end{vmatrix}$$

$$R_z(\gamma) = \begin{vmatrix} \cos(\gamma) & \sin(\gamma) & 0 & 0 \\ -\sin(\gamma) & \cos(\gamma) & 0 & 0 \\ 0 & 0 & 1 & 0 \\ 0 & 0 & 0 & 1 \end{vmatrix}$$

where

$R_x(\alpha)$ = rotation of α about x-axis
$R_y(\beta)$ = rotation of β about y-axis
$R_z(\gamma)$ = rotation of γ about z-axis

(B) Translation of Axes
$T(h, k, l)$: Move origin to $(+h, +k, +l)$

$$\begin{vmatrix} 1 & 0 & 0 & -h \\ 0 & 1 & 0 & -k \\ 0 & 0 & 1 & 1 \\ 0 & 0 & 0 & 1 \end{vmatrix}$$

(C) Scaling
$S(A, B, C)$: Scale x by A, y by B, z by C

$$\begin{vmatrix} A & 0 & 0 & 0 \\ 0 & B & 0 & 0 \\ 0 & 0 & C & 0 \\ 0 & 0 & 0 & 1 \end{vmatrix}$$

(D) Reflection in a Plane

$$R_f(r(x), r(y), r(z)) = \begin{vmatrix} r(x) & 0 & 0 & 0 \\ 0 & r(y) & 0 & 0 \\ 0 & 0 & r(z) & 0 \\ 0 & 0 & 0 & 1 \end{vmatrix}$$

where

$r(x)$ = mirror x-axis through y-z plane
$r(y)$ = mirror y-axis through x-z plane
$r(z)$ = mirror y-axis through x-y plane
$r(x)$ = +1 no reflection
     = −1 reflection, etc.

Figure 8.18. Coordinate transformation primitives.

different ways. Possibly the simplest transformation that leads to that in Figure 8.19 is the following.

1. Rotate the original coordinate system clockwise by $90-\phi$ about the z-axis.
2. Rotate the coordinate system by θ about the new x-axis x'.
3. Reflect each of the new x, y, and z axes—that is, $x \longrightarrow -x$, and so on.

By this transformation we have created a new left-handed coordinate system from the original right-handed one. The complete transformation may be written as

$$
\begin{vmatrix} x' \\ y' \\ z' \\ 1 \end{vmatrix} = R_f(-1,\,-1,\,-1)R_x(-\theta)R_z(\phi\,-\,90) \begin{vmatrix} x \\ y \\ z \\ 1 \end{vmatrix}
$$

The matrices used in this transform may be found in Figure 8.19. An important point to reemphasize is that clockwise angles are positive and counterclockwise angles are negative, adhering to our earlier defintions of the sign conventions. The resulting transformation equation may be written

$$
\begin{vmatrix} x' \\ y' \\ z' \\ 1 \end{vmatrix} = \begin{vmatrix} -\sin(\phi) & \cos(\phi) & 0 & 0 \\ -\cos(\phi)\sin(\theta) & -\cos(\theta)\sin(\phi) & \sin(\theta) & 0 \\ -\sin(\theta)\cos(\phi) & -\sin(\theta)\sin(\phi) & -\cos(\theta) & 0 \\ 0 & 0 & 0 & 1 \end{vmatrix} \begin{vmatrix} x \\ y \\ z \\ 1 \end{vmatrix}
$$

Since there is no translation of the origin in this case, we could equally well have worked with a (3 × 3)-dimensional matrix, but since we introduce translation in the next subsection we keep the four dimensional matrices.

Quite often we may be working in units that do not match the screen coordinates. Referring to Figure 8.19, assume that we have ended up with a coordinate system (x', y') centered in the middle of the screen. To work in screen coordinates, we must be able to scale the x- and y-axes to match the span of the screen, move the origin to the top left-hand corner of the screen, and, finally, reflect the y-axis as shown, since the top left-hand corner of a computer screen is usually taken as the origin. All these operations could be carried out by using matrix transformations, but little would be gained. It is best to calculate the complete (x', y') data set for all points to be graphed and to scale it to fit just within the screen boundaries than it is to specify an a priori set of

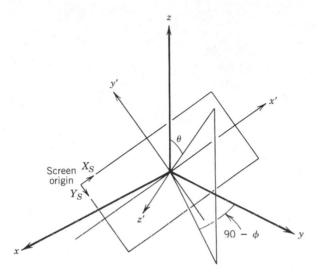

Figure 8.19. A three-dimensional coordinate transformation with the origin fixed.

scaling values and to deal with complex screen clipping problems that arise if some points lie off the screen.

Note that the observer has no role in this transformation method. The z' coordinate of each point is irrelevant, since we consider only the orthogonal (right-angle) projection of each point onto the (x', y') plane. This method is adequate for many tasks of data display, but there are times when a systematic method of accounting for the position of the observer can be illuminating.

8.4.4. Projections with Perspective

So far we have considered the operations of coordinate transformation without a transformation of the origin and without a clear view of the role of the observer in the graphical representation. The viewing point of the observer must now be defined more clearly. In human perception the point of observation is literally the center of the universe. All light rays must converge on that point. In computer graphics the observer is viewing the image on a computer screen. Thus the relative position of eye, object, and screen is important in the screen graphical representation.

Referring to Figure 8.15, let us consider that we have an object at a point O in some fixed orientation w.r.t. some set of axes (x, y, z). We wish to view the object from a point E at the eye and onto the screen located at point S. The first step in calculating the projected image involves a set of rotations and a reflection at the fixed point O. This gives us the object coordinates w.r.t. the new set of coordinates (x', y', z'), as discussed in the last subsection. To move the origin to E, we need to translate the origin along the new z'-axis by a distance of $-h$ to obtain the position of the points w.r.t.. the eye coordinates (x_e, y_e, z_e). These are all linear transformations.

$$
\begin{vmatrix} x_e \\ y_e \\ z' \\ 1 \end{vmatrix} = T(0, 0, -h) R_f(-1, -1, -1) R_x(-\theta) R_z(\phi - 90) \begin{vmatrix} x \\ y \\ z \\ 1 \end{vmatrix}
$$

Finally comes the projection of all points on the object onto the computer screen plane. This transformation is nonlinear. Any point P on the object with coordinates (x_e, y_e, z_e) must project onto the screen at point P'', as shown in Figure 8.20, where, by similar triangles, we must have

$$
X''(P'') = D \, x_e / z_e, \qquad y''(P'') = D \, y_e / z_e
$$

The final step in the transformation requires that we scale the global screen coordinates to the local screen coordinates centered in the upper left-hand corner of the screen O_s.

To avoid the problem of clipping, which is discussed in the next subsection, we may scale the resulting projected image to just fit on the screen. If the maximum and minimum x'' and y'' points w.r.t. the origin S are x''_{max}, x''_{min},

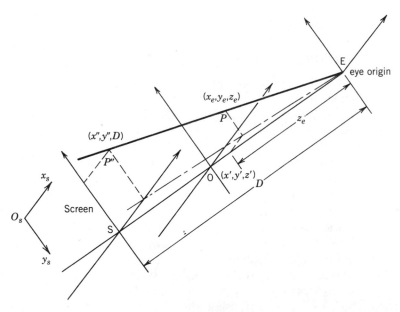

Figure 8.20.   The coordinates related to the generation of perspective on a computer screen. A point (x_e, y_e, z_e) w.r.t the eye origin point ends up at (x', y', D) on the screen.

y''_{max}, y''_{min}, then, if X_M, Y_M are the coordinates of bottom right-hand corner w.r.t. the new origin, we may write

$$x_s(P'') = X_M (x''(P'') - x''_{min})/(x''_{max}-x''_{min})$$
$$y_s(P'') = Y_M (y''(P'') - y''_{max})/(y''_{min}-y''_{max})$$

which guarantees that the complete projected image fills the screen.

8.4.5. Clipping

A problem that becomes apparent when you begin to work with computer graphics is that of *clipping*. The computer screen is a window on the graphics world. Points are calculated, often from a complex formula, and it is not always possible to guarantee that all the points lie within the screen boundary. Different computer graphics packages have different ways of dealing with off-screen points. On the Apple computer, for example, attempting to plot an off-screen point with the BASIC plotting package will generate a program error. On the IBM-PC, on the other hand, the point will be placed at the nearest boundary point to the real point. This can lead to gross distortions in a plotted image if one end of a straight line lies off the screen. This problem is illustrated in Figure 8.21. The screen is defined by the boundary *PQRS*. The line 11 will have its endpoint 1 outside the screen. On many graphical systems the line will actually be drawn as 1'2.

Some simple tests have been developed to test for the onset of clipping on a line segment. One of the simplest ways is described by referring to Figure 8.21. The diagram shows the plane containing the computer screen. The screen is at the center of the picture, bounded by the points *OPQR*. We define two

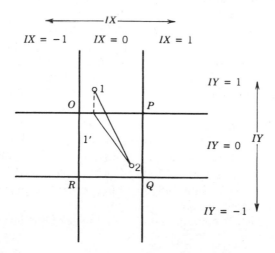

Figure 8.21. The definitions of the clipping parameters *IX* and *IY* w.r.t. the computer screen bounded by *OPQR*.

parameters *IX* and *IY* that completely define the relationship of any point to the screen boundaries. Let us consider a line segment 12. These two points have parameters $IX(1)$, $IY(1)$ for point 1, and $IX(2)$, $IY(2)$ for point 2. For a given point *IX* may take the values $-1, 0$, or $+1$, depending on its relationship to the left and right vertical boundaries of the screen. The same holds true for the *y*-axis in the vertical direction. The following test may be applied to the complete set of *IX*, *IY* parameters.

1. If $IX(1) = IX(2) \neq 0$ or $IY(1) = IY(2) \neq 0$, then the whole line segment is completely outside the screen, and the line may be discarded.
2. If all $IX(k) = 0$ for $k=1, 2$, then the line is completely inside the screen, and the line may be plotted directly.
3. If neither of these is true, then the line may clip a screen boundary, and further work is necessary to find the boundary point.

The whole subject of clipping is related to the topic of *covering*, where instead of keeping the line segments within the rectangle and throwing away the outside portions of the lines, we keep the outside portions and reject the inside lines. This is used in cases in which a portion of the screen is to be overwritten by another pattern.

8.4.6.   An IBM Programming Example

We end this section on three-dimensional graphics by returning to the example described earlier for the three-dimensional plotting of the sinc(x,y)* function. The example will be carried out by using BASICA plotting commands on the IBM computer. To avoid the complications of clipping, we store the screen (x,y) data points in a large array and scale the points so that the complete projected image will just fit on the screen.

The program syntax in Figure 8.22 has been chosen to be as near to the variables discussed in the text of this chapter as possible. The projected data to be plotted is stored in two two-dimensional arrays: XPP( ), corresponding to the projected points $x''(P'')$ (the horizontal screen data); and YPP ( ), corresponding to $y''(P'')$ (for the vertical data). The complete set of equations has already been described at the beginning of this section. Two-dimensional arrays are used for convenience in setting up the plotting grid lines parallel to the original *x*- and *y*-axes. The data is scaled to the screen dimensions by means of the functions XS(I, J) and YS(I, J), defined immediately prior to plotting. The data is plotted between lines 1300 and 1420 by plotting the lines parallel to both original *x*- and *y*-axes separately, forming a grid. The final plotted data has already been presented in Figure 8.16.

The graph in Figure 8.16 contains a projected image of the function sinc(x,y) in

---

*For the properties of sinc(x,y) see, for example, J.D. Gaskill, *Linear Systems, Fourier Transforms and Optics* (Wiley, New York, 1978).

```
1000 REM--------------- three-dimensional plot ---------------
1010 DIM XPP(15,15),YPP(15,15)        :REM array to store data
1020 XM = 600 : YM = 200              :REM define screen boundaries
1030 PI = 3.1415926 : N=15
1040 TH = 70 : PHI = 135 : H = 100    :Y = 200:REM define parameters
1050 REM----------------- three-dimensional transform parameters
1060 THRD = TH*PI/180 : PHIRD = PHI*PI/180    :REM transfer to radians
1070 A11=-SIN(PHIRD) : A12 = COS(PHIRD)
1080 A21=-COS(THRD)*COS(PHIRD):A22=-COS(THRD)*SIN(PHIRD):A23=SIN(THRD)
1090 A31=-SIN(THRD)*COS(PHIRD):A32=-SIN(THRD)*SIN(PHIRD):A33=-COS(THRD):A34=H
1100 REM----------------------- define functions
1110 DEF FNXE(X,Y)=A11*X+A12*Y              :REM define xe,ye,ze
1120 DEF FNYE(X,Y,Z)=A21*X+A22*Y+A23*Z
1130 DEF FNZE(X,Y,Z)=A31*X+A32*Y+A33*Z+A34
1140 DEF FNSINC(X,Y)=SIN(X)*SIN(Y)/(X*Y)
1150 REM------------------------- calculate points
1160 XMAX=-1.0E10:XMIN=1.0E10:YMAX=-1.0E10:YMIN=1.0E10
1170 FOR I = 1 TO N
1180   FOR J = 1 TO N
1190     X = 2*PI*I/N : Y = 2*PI*J/N
1200     XPP(I,J) = D * FNXE(X,Y) / FNZE(X,Y,Z)  :REM calculate x"(P")
1210     YPP(I,J) = D * FNYE(X,Y,Z) / FNZE(X,Y,Z):REM calculate y"(P")
1220 REM------------- ----------------- find max and min
1230     IF XMIN < XPP(I,J) THEN XMIN=XPP(I,J)  :REM xmin, xmax, ymin, ymax
1240     IF XMAX > XPP(I,J) THEN XMAX=XPP(I,J)
1250     IF YMIN < XPP(I,J) THEN YMIN=XPP(I,J)
1260     IF YMAX > XPP(I,J) THEN YMAX=XPP(I,J)
1270   NEXT J
1280 NEXT I
1290 REM--------- --------- ----- plot data
1300 DEF FNXS(I,J)=XM * (XPP(I,J)-XMIN)/(XMAX-XMIN): REM calculate xs,ys
1310 DEF FNYS(I,J)=YM * (YPP(I,J)-YMAX)/(YMIN-YMAX)
1320 SCREEN 2 : CLS : KEY OFF: REM define screen and clear
1330 FOR I= 1 TO N
1340   FOR J= 1 TO N    :REM plot lines parallel to x-axis
1350     LINE -FNXS(I,J), FNYS(I,J)
1360   NEXT J
1370 NEXT I
1380 FOR I=1 TO N        :REM plot lines parallel to y-axis
1390   FOR J= 1 TO N
1400     LINE -FNXS(J,I), FNYS(J,I)
1410   NEXT J
1420 NEXT I
1430 END  :REM  --------------------------- --------------
```

Figure 8.22. Three-dimensional plotting of sinc(x, y).

the positive (x, y) quadrant viewed from a distance of 100 units from the origin with the screen placed a further 100 units past the origin. The angles are $\theta = 70°$, $\phi = 135°$.

8.5.   HARD COPY GRAPHICS

At times the graphical resolution provided by screen graphics is not sufficient to satisfy the requirements for data presentation. It is possible to obtain much higher resolution on a hard copy device, such as a dot-matrix printer, than can be obtained by dumping an image on a computer screen. Alternatively, if analog and digital outputs are available, then a chart recorder or X-Y recorder may be utilized. Some of these devices have multiple inputs controlling different color pens that may be used effectively to plot multiple data curves.

8.5.1. Dot-Matrix Printer Graphics

The Epson series of dot-matrix printers (MX-80, FX-80, RX-80) have become established as a defacto standard for text and graphical presentation in combination with personal-computer-based systems. A large number of other manufacturers use the Epson-like, dot-matrix-printer, command protocol for controlling type and graphics operations. The preferred method of communications between computer and printer is by a Centronics parallel interface, which is described in Chapter 12. Many of the newer dot-matrix printers on the market come with multiple font styles, allowing Greek and mathematical symbols to be printed. The ability to download custom-designed character sets and the ability to control pin-sequence firing on the printer matrix head allow high-resolution graphics. We restrict our discussion to this latter topic and concentrate on describing the use of the printer for high-resolution graphics under the control of an MBASIC/BASICA program.

Programming dot-matrix graphics can become as complex as any programming task. Underlying this apparent complexity, however, are some extremely simple concepts. In using the printer for graphics, we have to decide whether to first calculate and fill the computer memory with the graph pixel image and then print the contents of this buffer, or, alternatively, to use the printer in a recorder or a continuous mode. In this approach the graph or picture is calculated for a band across the picture and that section printed before going on to the next section. The choice really depends on the application. For any three-dimensional graphs the first approach is almost mandatory. For the use of the dot-matrix printer in chart-recorder or X-Y recorder mode, where the function being plotted is single valued, the latter approach is acceptable and also much easier to represent from within a BASIC program.

We describe the use of the printer in a mode resembling a chart-recorder or an X-Y type system with the understanding that the printer operates in a completely digital mode. We chose a configuration where the *x*-axis of our graph runs the length of the paper, and the *y*-axis runs across, as we show in Figure 8.23.

All Epson-compatible printers may be placed in a number of graphics modes that differ in the dot density that may be placed in a horizontal line across the paper. A list of these mode is shown in Table 8.6 together with the various dot densities and the command sequences that must be entered to utilize each mode. We also show the maximum values of the parameters n1 and n2 that can be used.

As we can see, the dot-matrix printer is capable of realizing an extremely high printer resolution but only at the expense of plotting speed. In the

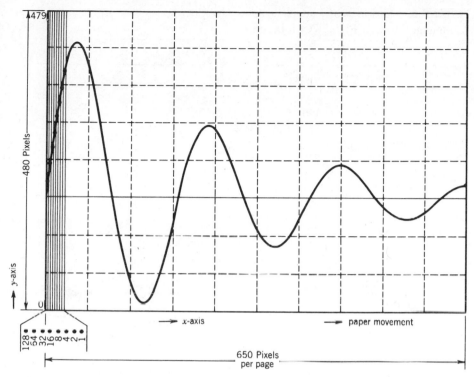

Figure 8.23. The layout of graphic pixels for graphing on an Epson MX-80 (or compatible) printer.

standard plotting configuration a single sweep of the dot-matrix printer head across the page prints eight rows of dots. A single data byte controls a single row eight dots long, as we show in Figure 8.23. If for example we were firing bits 3 and 5, which correspond to the decimal number

$$0 \times 2^7 + 0 \times 2^6 + 1 \times 2^5 + 0 \times 2^4 + 1 \times 2^3 + 0 \times 2^2 + 0 \times 2^1 + 0 \times 2^0 = 40$$

This would be output in a BASIC program by the command CHR$(40).

Data transfer between computer and printer is executed in data blocks that cannot exceed 256 bytes. Before the computer can send this information it must send one of the control sequences shown in Table 8.6 to tell the printer how many bytes to expect. The parameter N2 is the number of complete blocks, and N1 is the remainder. Thus, if the command sequence

```
CHR$(27) + "*" + CHR$(M) + CH$(N1) + CHR$(N2)
```

is sent, then the printer will assume that the next

$$N = 256 * N2 + N1$$

Table 8.6.   Epson Dot-Matrix Graphics Modes
Language: Epson Printer Commands

MODE	¦– – –DOTS– – – –¦		CODE	MAX	
m	Inch	Total		n1	n2
Single density:					
0	60	480	\<ESC\>+"K"+n1+n2 \<ESC\>+"*"+m+n1+n2	224	1
Double density, low speed:					
1	120	960	\<ESC\>+"L"+n1+n2 \<ESC\>+"*"+m+n1+n2	192	3
Double density, high speed:					
2	120	960	\<ESC\>+"Y"+n1+n2 \<ESC\>+"*"+m+n1+n2	192	3
Quadruple density:					
3	240	1920	\<ESC\>+"Z"+n1+n2 \<ESC\>+"*"+m+n1+n2	128	7
QX–10 density:					
4	80	640	\<ESC\>+"*"+m+n1+n2	128	2
One-to-one density:					
5	72	576	\<ESC\>+"*"+m+n1+n2	64	2
DEC screen density:					
6	90	720	\<ESC\>+"*"+m+n1+n2	208	2

bytes are data. It is necessary to transmit information about data bytes prior to sending the data to avoid confusion as to what is data and what is not. For example, a byte corresponding to decimal 27 could be interpreted as an \<ESC\> command and not the bit pattern 00011011 if a designation were not previously specified.

For a given mode there is a maximum value of N that can be transmitted. This sets obvious limits on N1 and N2. These maximum values are shown in Table 8.6. It must be emphasized that values of N1 and N2 corresponding to and N less than maximum are perfectly in order. The short BASICA program below sends a series of 240 data bytes (N2 = 0, N1 = 240).

```
              Language  BASICA/MBASIC
100  REM plot ============= halfway across paper
110  LPRINT CHR$(27) + "*" + CHR$(0) + CHR$(240) + CHR$(0);
120  FOR I=1 TO 240: LPRINT CHR$(40);: NEXT I
130  END
```

The program essentially draws a giant "=" sign halfway across the paper. If we change N1 to 224, N2 to 1, and the limit on I to 480, the same line is drawn entirely across the paper.

The plotting program shown in Figure 8.24 is essentially an extension of the approach discussed above. In this program we make a plot on a grid of 480 ×

```
100                                    ' main calling program
110 DEFINT I-M                         ' initialize parameters
120 DEFDBL A-H,O-Z
130 READ XMIN, XMAX, YMIN, YMAX        ' enter program parameters
140 READ NXDIV, NYDIV, JYEMPH, NLONG
150 READ TITLE$, XLABEL$,YLABEL$       ' enter labels
160 DATA 0,20,-1,1
170 DATA 10,10,5,650
180 DATA "The Function exp (-x/8)sin(x)", "x-value", "y-value"
200 DEF FNF(X)=EXP(-X/8)*SIN(X)        'define function
210 GOSUB 1000                         ' call plotting routine
220 END                                ' end main calling routine
1000 ' **************************** PLOTTING ROUTINE ***************
1010 DIM LNE(480), JXDIV(10),JYDIV(10) ' dimension plotting arrays
1020                                    ' calculate grid positions
1030 FOR J=0 TO NYDIV:JYDIV(J)=J*479/NYDIV:NEXT J
1040 FOR J=0 TO NXDIV:JXDIV(J)=J*(NLONG-1)/NXDIV+1:NEXT J
1050 LPRINT CHR$(27)+"-"+CHR$(1);      ' set underline mode
1055                                    ' print title and labels
1060 LPRINT CHR$(27)+"W"+CHR$(1)+CHR$(27)+"G";:LPRINT " "TITLE$" ";
1070 LPRINT CHR$(10)+CHR$(10);
1080 LPRINT CHR$(27)+"-"+CHR$(0);      ' turn off underline
1090 LPRINT "    X-AXIS TITLE        ";XLABEL$:LPRINT CHR$(10);
1100 LPRINT "    Y-AXIS TITLE        ";YLABEL$
1110 LPRINT CHR$(27)+"W"+CHR$(0);      ' turn off double width
1120 LPRINT CHR$(27)+"A"+CHR$(8);      ' define spacing of lines
1130 DELTAX=(XMAX-XMIN)/NLONG          ' calculate dx for single dot
1140 JX=0:JY=0
1150 FOR K=1 TO 480:LNE(K)=3:NEXT K    ' plot y-axis box
1160 GOSUB 1460                        ' call plotting subroutine
1170 FOR I=1 TO NLONG STEP 8           ' beginning of plotting loop
1180 FOR K=1 TO 480:LNE(K)=0:NEXT K    ' empty array
1190 FOR J=0 TO 7                      ' begin calculation for
1200 IJ=I+J                            ' single strip(8 bits).
1210 IF IF<>JXDIV(JX) THEN GOTO 1260   ' grid or no grid line
1220                                    ' a grid line
1230 FOR K=1 TO 480 STEP 4: LNE(K)=LNE(K)+2^(7-J):NEXT K
1240 JX=JX+1
1250 GOTO 1340
1260                                    ' not a grid line
1270 X=XMIN+(I+J)*DELTAX               ' calculate x
1280 Y=FNF(X)                          ' calculate f(x)
1290 IF Y<=YMIN THEN Y=YMIN            ' test end points
1300 IF Y>=YMAX THEN Y=YMAX
1310 JY=(Y-YMIN)*479/(YMAX-YMIN)+1     ' calculate y-axis dot
1320 LNE(JY)=LNE(JY)+2^(7-J)           ' set dot on
1330 LNE(JY-1)=LNE(JY-1)+2^(7-J)       ' set adjacent dot
1340 NEXT J                            ' end calc. for single strip
1350 FOR JY=1 TO NYDIV-1               ' add in x-grid lines
1360 LNE(JYDIV(JY))=7
1370 NEXT JY
1380 LNE(1)=255:LNE(2)=255:LNE(JYDIV(NYDIV))=255:
                                LNE(JYDIV(NYDIV)/1)=255
1390 LNE(JYDIV(JYEMPH) )=255           ' add in box lines
1400 GOSUB 1460                        ' plot strip
1410 NEXT I                            ' go on to next strip
```

Figure 8.24. *(continued)*

```
1420 FOR K=1 TO 480:LNE(K)=3:NEXT K      ' end of box
1430 LNE(1)=255:LNE(2)=255:LNE(479)=255:LNE(480=255
1440 GOSUB 1460                          ' plot end of box
1450 RETURN   ' return to calling routine after completing plot
1460 ' subroutine to send out single line of information to printer
1470 LPRINT CHR$(27)+"*"+CHR$(0)+CHR$(225)+CHR$(1);
                                          ' switch in graphics
1480 FOR K=1 TO 480:LPRINT CHR$(LNE(K) ); :NEXT K
                                          ' send out data for line
1490 LPRINT CHR$(13);                     ' send out CR
1500 RETURN
1510
'*****************************************************************
```

Figure 8.24.   The dot-matrix plotting and calling programs.
Language: BASICA/MBASIC.

650 graphical bits. This would require a memory storage of 39 K if the complete image were stored in memory. As it is, we calculate the dot pattern for a single 8-bit-deep band across the paper in mode 0 and 480 bytes long. We store the data in an integer array requiring only 1 K.

Lines 100 to 220 are the initializing program for the plotting program proper that starts at line 1000. The function to be graphed is defined as a BASICA function at line 200. The title and axes labels are printed in double width letters at the beginning of the graph. The program is extensively commented to aid the user in interpreting it. The resulting graph is shown in Figure 8.25.

The plotting program starting at line 1000 is set up as a program module, a concept expanded in the next chapter. The only information required to run the program is the list of parameters in. Table 8.7.

This program may be easily modified to plot experimental data from an array or a functional form not definable in a single line that may be set up by a function call to a subroutine.

Commercial plotting packages are available for plotting high-resolution graphics on dot-matrix printers. An example is the Dataplotter software from Lark Software,* which was developed for scientific data plotting.

8.5.2.   Graphics on an X-Y Recorder

The other direct hard copy graphical method we consider is the presentation of data on an X-Y recorder. We assume that the user has available a standard laboratory X-Y recorder and that the computer has some means of outputting binary and analog signals under software control. We describe a sample system using an Apple II computer in combination with an ISAAC 91A interface. The only constraint that we place on an X-Y recorder is that there be a provision for externally generated pen lift activated with a TTL level.

*Dataplotter is a trademark of Lark Software, 7 Cedar Road, Caldwell, NJ 07006.

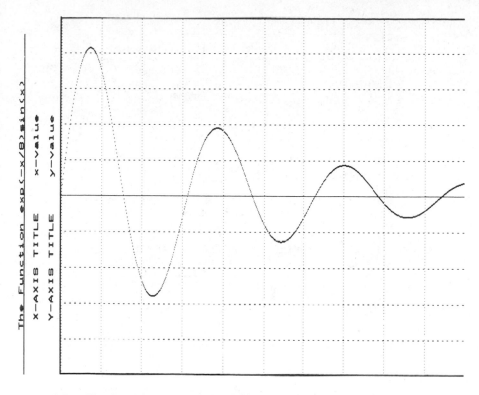

Figure 8.25. The plot of the Bessel function $J_0(x)$ generated with the BASICA program listed in Figure 8.24.

Table 8.7. The Calling Parameter List for the Plotting Program

Calling Variable	Description	Program Value
XMAX,XMIN	Maximum and minimum x-values	10,0
YMAX,YMIN	Maximum and minimum y-values	1,−1
FNF(X)	Defined BASICA function to be plotted	see listing
NLONG	Total number of bits along x-axis	650
NXDIV,NYDIV	Number of grid lines along x, y-axes $0 \longrightarrow$ NXDIV; outer lines emphasized.	10,10
JYDIV	Emphasize JYDIV grid line on y-axis	5
TITLE\$	String containing title	see listing
XLABEL\$,YLABEL\$	String containing x,y-labels	see listing

Table 8.8.   The X-Y Driver Configuration

ISAAC	Range	Digital	X–Y Recorder	Range
Analog out #0	0–10 V	0–4095	X–axis input	0–10 V
" " #1	"	"	Y–axis input	"
Binary out #0	TTL	0 or 1	pen lift	TTL
			0–pen down	
			1–pen up	

```
100 REM X-Y PLOTTER PROGRAM, MAIN ROUTINE
105 DIMENSION S(1)
110 READ XN, XM, YN, YM          :REM READ IN MAX. AND MIN. X, Y
120 DATA 0,10,-1,1               :REM AND SCALING FACTORS
130 INPUT "ENTER SCALING FACTORS FOR X, Y"; SX, SY
140 INPUT "NUMBER OF POINTS AT WHICH FUNCTION TO BE CALCULATED ";NP
150 DEF FNF(X)=EXP(-X/8)*SIN(X) :REM DEFINE FUNCTION TO BE GRAPHED
160 GOSUB 1000                   :REM CALL PLOTTING ROUTINE
170 END                          :REM END OF CALLING PROGRAM
1000 REM****************** X-Y PLOTTING ROUTINE ****************
1010 REM      GENERATE BOX
1020 &BOUT,(DV)=0:               :REM PLACE PEN AT (0,0)
1030 &AOUT,(DV)=0, (C#)=0        :   &AOUT,(DV)=0,(C#)=1
1040 &AOUT,(DV)=4095*SY,(C#)=1   :   &AOUT,(DV)=4095*SX,(C#)=0
1050 &AOUT,(DV)=0     ,(C#)=1    : &AOUT,(DV)=0     ,(C#)=0
1060 &AOUT,(DV)=2049*SY,(C#)=1   : &AOUT,(DV)=4095*SX,(C#)=0
1070 &BOUT,(DV)=0
1080 REM      START DATA PLOTTING
1090 NS = 4095/NP : NN=4095*SX   :REM STEP INCREMENT IN DX
1100 FOR I= 0 TO NN STEP NS      :REM BEGINNING OF PLOTTING LOOP
1110 &AOUT,(DV)=I*SX,(C#)=0      :REM MOVE ON TO NEXT X,Y
1120 &AOUT,(DV)=(2049+FNF(X)*4095)*SX,(C#)=1
1130 &BOUT,(DV)=1                :REM PLACE PEN DOWN
1140 NEXT I                      :REM GO ON TO NEXT POINT
1150 RETURN                      :REM END OF PLOTTING SUBROUTINE
1160 REM*****************************************************
```

Figure 8.26.   An Applesoft plotting program for X-Y recorder.
Language: Applesoft + Labsoft.

Table 8.8 shows the important hardware wiring connections between the ISAAC interface and the X-Y recorder.

The X-Y recorder is configured so that a full-scale voltage output on the ISAAC analog out for both the *x*- and *y*-axes spans the X-Y recorder full-scale range.

An Applesoft program to generate an almost identical plot to that made with the dot-matrix printer (Figure 8.25) is shown in Figure 8.26. As in the printer programming example, we divide the program into a main driver and a library-type subroutine that can be used with little modification with other data. Provision for scaling the *x*- and *y*-axes independently is by prompting the user for *X* and *Y* scaling parameters, which must be numbers in the range 0 to 1.

The plotting subroutine may be divided into two sections. The first represents drawing a box around the graph and placing a line down the central axis, both scaled to the correct X and Y scaling factors. The second part involves graphing the data. Note that if the step increment in x is too large, a staircase effect may be seen in the resulting graph.

A grid may be placed on the graph if necessary. The following simple program can be used to place a single dotted line along the x-axis at the present y-position.

```
                  Language: Applesoft + Labsoft
1200  FOR J=0 TO NP STEP NS
1210  &AOUT,(DV)=NP, (C#)=0       :  &BOUT,(DV)=1
1230  &AOUT,(DC)=NP+NS/2, (C#)=0  :  &BOUT,(DC)=0
1250  NEXT J
```

In this program NS and NP have the same values as determined in the plotting program of Figure 8.26, and this program segment can easily be incorporated as a subroutine in the main program. Finally, as the user's requirements become more demanding, at some point one may wish to incorporate text in the graphical display. Doing this for the complete ASCII character set will be extremely slow if one generates the graphical primitives from software on the microcomputer. Recently, X-Y recorders such as the HP 7940 have become available that may be communicated to along a standard interface, such as the GPIB, and that contain enough built-in intelligence to plot data and text under macrographics commands.

9

Numerical Analysis and Modeling

9.1. INTRODUCTION

Numerical analysis involves procedures used to numerically solve mathematical equations on a computer. In many cases where analytical solutions may not be possible, a standard numerical method may be used to provide a solution. Some of the fundamentals discussed here provide a basis for the techniques used in the next chapter for the treatment of experimental data where experimental noise is present. The discussion centers on the use of a series of library functions written in BASIC or C that have been developed to carry out some of the important operations needed in numerical analysis. We also treat the subject of numerical-model solving with a discussion of a commercially available programming package called TKSolver, which provides a software environment for computer data modeling.

We take a "black-box" approach to the subject—that is, we provide library modules and the minimum amount of information necessary to allow the reader to begin using these numerical techniques. Where necessary we give references to the background information so the reader can become familiar with the algorithms and approximations underlying the BASICA and C programs and gain a knowledge of their fundamental limitations.

9.1.1. The Numerical Analysis Program Library

The library programs described in this chapter have been coded in two computer languages. We use Microsoft BASIC (MBASIC; BASICA on the IBM-PC) as an interpreted language and C as our compiled language. A complete catalog of the library programs is given in Table 9.1. The modular library structure is an inherent part of the C language. For MBASIC, however, such a configuration requires somewhat more thought and organization, as we will shortly describe.

Both the BASIC and C languages are highly portable. Microsoft BASIC is available on a large number of microcomputer systems, both of the 8- and 16-bit variety. On the IBM-PC the BASICA language is an extended version of MBASIC, and all programs in this chapter, apart from the graphics programs

Table 9.1. A Numerical Function Library

Description	MBASIC			C	
	File	Starting Line	Option #	File	Function
Mathematical Modules					
(a) Error Function	ERF.LIB	11000	—	ERF.C	erf( )
(b) Gamma Function	GAMMA.LIB	11100	—	GAMMA.C	gamma( )
(c) Bessel Functions	BESSEL.LIB	11300	—	BESSEL.C	bessel( )
(d) Voigt Function	VOIGT.LIB	11500	—	VOIGT.C	voigt( )
Numerical Integration					
	INTGL.LIB			INTGL.C	
(a) Integration of analytically known function using Newton Coates method		12000	1		intgl_f( )
(b) Gauss-Legendre integration			2		intgl_gl( )
Numerical Differentiation					
	DIFFRN.LIB			DIFFRN.C	
Differentiation of analytically known function.		12500	—		diff_f( )
Spline Operations					
	SPLINE.LIB			SPLINE.C	
(a) Parameter determination		13000	1		spline_prm( )
(b) Interpolated value			2		spline_y( )
Matrix Operations					
	MATRIX.LIB			MATRIX.C	
(a) Create upper triangle matrix		14000	1		mtrx_tri( )
(b) Solve matrix equation Ax=b			2		mtrx_sln( )
(c) Calculate inverse matrix			3		mtrx_inv( )
Roots of Equations					
	ROOT.LIB			ROOT.C	
(a) Secant method		15000	1		root_sec( )
(b) Decker-Brent Method			2		root_dbr( )
Solution of Differential Equations					
	DIFFEQ.LIB			DIFFEQ.C	
(a) Predictor-Corrector, 1 equation		16000	1		deqn_pc1( )
(b) Predictor-Corrector, 2 equation			2		deqn_pc2( )
Utility Functions					
Random noise generator	NOISE.LIB	11600	—		noise( )

in Section 9.5, will run with no modifications under BASICA. They will also run on most CP/M systems under MBASIC. On the Apple computer however, one needs a CP/M card and the MBASIC interpreter to run these programs.

9.1.2. Creating a Numerical Function Library in BASIC

To create a library of program modules in BASICA, we use a variation on the modular programming techniques discussed in Chapter 4. The advanced fea-

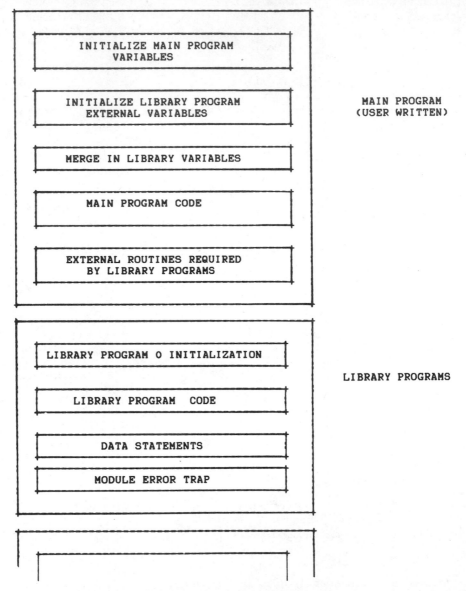

Figure 9.1. Program structure of BASICA/MBASIC modular programming environment showing internal structure of main program and a single library module.

tures of BASICA/MBASIC allow the code connected with a single module to be restricted to neighboring line numbers. Reference should be made to Figure 9.1, where the structure of the modular program environment is shown in detail. The user is responsible for the coding of the main program and the initialization of the external (global) variables used by the library routines. Modules may be moved in and out of memory as needed. Each module contains at least four sections: initialization, program, error trap, and data statement. If there are a number of options in a module, then these come after the initialization section, followed by any common subroutines that may be used by more than one module.

The BASICA/MBASIC coding that insures a modular structure is shown in Figure 9.2. In many of the modules that have been programmed in this book, a lengthy initialization from data statements is required. However, it is not expedient to carry out this initialization each time the function module is used. The code in Figure 9.2 eliminates this initialization after the first time the module is called.

```
11000******************** LIBRARY MODULE ***************************
11006 ON ERROR GOTO 11400          :REM set error vectors
11008 DIM BSL.E(6,6),ABC.E(10,2)   :REM dimension internal variables
11010 RESTORE 11502                 :REM set read point vector
11012 READ ....... etc.            :REM module data input
 .
 .
11016 ON OP% GOSUB ..... etc.      :REM option branch
11...
 .
 .                main body of program
 .
 .
 '
11400 REM------------------ERROR TRAP-------------------------
11402 IF (ERR=10) AND (ERL=11008) THEN RESUME 11016
11404 PRINT "ERROR # "ERR" IN BESSEL FUNCTION MODULE AT LINE "ERL
11500 REM------------------- DATA STATEMENTS -----------------
11502 DATA ...... etc.
 .
11510 END
11512 REM****************** END OF LIBRARY MODULE ************
```

Figure 9.2. The Structure of a library module in BASICA/MBASIC.
Language: BASICA/MBASIC.

The configuration allows all the code connected with a particular module to be localized in a single group of line numbers. The first time that the module is called the initialization section will be executed. This includes setting the error trap vector (line 11006) and dimensioning the array BSL.E and ABC.E (line 11008). Any subsequent calls to the module will generate an error (code = 10) if an attempt is made to dimension the same array. This will cause a jump to the error trap routine at line 11400. The RESUME instruction at line 11402 causes a program jump back to the main program flow at line 11016.

One other aspect of this program shell is worth mentioning. The RESTORE instruction at line 11010 sets the READ instruction immediately following to begin reading from the DATA statements at line 11502. If this instruction were not placed there, when the READ instruction was encountered the interpreter would have looked for the next DATA statements to be read from the beginning of the program. This might be in a module with lower line numbers that had not yet been executed. The RESTORE command uniquely pairs the READ and DATA statements so that no such confusion can occur.

The variables dimensioned in line 11008 are local variables and are identified for this module with the .E extension, which will only be used on this particular module. This makes the integrity of each module much easier to protect. Only global variables that are used by the main program or that are passed between the modules are used without an extension. The naming convention guarantees that function calls to library routines from within a loop of the main program will not lead to program interference. This could happen very easily if, for example, the variables I, J, K, M, N were used for loop indices in both the main and library programs. Modules may be erased from memory by deleting the line numbers and using the DELETE instruction to remove all arrays.

9.1.3. The Limitations of Numerical Analysis on Microcomputers

It must be recognized at the outset that there are fundamental limitations to the use of numerical analysis with microcomputers. "Number crunching" is usually extremely demanding on a computer system's resources, especially if one is working with double precision arithmetic on an 8- or 16-bit computer system. Two criteria are important in carrying out a particular task on a microcomputer: the speed at which the procedure is carried out, and the accuracy of the calculated results. These criteria are functions of the computer system, the programming language, and the algorithm used.

For example, the time taken to calculate a 1024 point fast Fourier transform on an IBM computer can vary by a factor of 100, depending on whether the language used supports the 8087 math coprocessor. Benchmark programs are available in the literature* that may be used to compare different compilers and different computer systems. For example, the solution of a matrix equation has been discussed by Vandergraft,* who shows that the number of calculations to invert a 10×10 matrix can vary by a factor of almost 1000, depending on the approach taken for its solution. The algorithm used in this book is an efficient approach to the problem.

A classical algorithm that should always be used in calculating an n-degree polynomial is Horner's method of factorization.

```
Horner's Algorithm
Language: Algorithmic
y ← a_n
for k is n-1 to 0
    y ← y * x + a_k
end_for
```

*See, for example, *Dr. Dobbs Journal*.

This is sometimes written

$$y \leftarrow \langle\langle \ldots \langle\langle a_n *x + a_{n-1}\rangle *x + a_{n-2}\rangle *x \ldots + a_1 \rangle *x + a_0 \rangle$$

Horner's Algorithm is normally 2 to 3 times faster than the alternative of raising the numbers to powers and adding and has smaller rounding errors, the significance of which is discussed later.

Many efficient algorithms use the fact that integer arithmetic is much faster than real or double precision arithmetic. An example of a program that makes full use of this fact is the routine for finding an upper triangular matrix, which will be described later. The algorithm is configured to switch array indices in preference to array contents to increase execution speed.

The accuracy of a particular calculation depends on a number of competing factors. If we assume that no experimental error is identified with a particular data set, two general categories of error become significant: *rounding* errors and *truncation* errors. Rounding errors are the result of the finite resources of the calculating machine. The rounding errors of a calculation may be improved by increasing the precision of calculation of the program. This usually entails carrying out the calculation in double precision arithmetic. The following is a list of the *significant figures* carried in different languages. Care must be made in precisely identifying this. In BASICA, for example, all trigonometric quantities are calculated in single precision even under double precision arithmetic.

Precision	Language	Bits	Significant figures	Designation	Definition
single	BASICA	32	7	1.0E+4 or 10000!	DEFSGL
double	"	64	16	1.0D+4 or 10000#	DEFDBL
single	Applesoft	40	9	1.0E+4 or 10000	default
single	C	32	7	1.0e+4	real variable
double	"	64	16	1.0d+4	double variable

Truncation errors can occur when using approximations in a calculation. We will have an opportunity to study the effects of such errors in detail when we discuss numerical differentiation and integration in the next section. Approximating an integral, for example, by a weighted sum of points at equal spacings can lead to significant truncation errors. As expected, increasing the number of points by decreasing the value of the increment between them leads to an increase in accuracy. On a computer with a finite arithmetic capability, however, we will reach a point where the rounding errors will become significant, thereby cancelling the increase in accuracy gained by the above procedure.

---

*J.S. Vandergraft, Introduction to Numerical Computing, (Academic Press, 1983).

9.1.4.   Commercially Available Program Libraries

In the previous subsections we have discussed some of the work necessary to create one's own mathematical function library for numerical analysis. An alternative is to use a commercially available library of functions written in a suitable computer language. There are many such libraries available. It is important in advanced applications to select software not only by availability on a particular computer or operating system but by the comprehensiveness and scope of the documentation. The user should be privy to the algorithms and approximations that were used to create the source code, and the documentation should reference, where necessary, the source of these algorithms. If possible, the user should also have available the source code for reference and possible modification. A well-written library of software functions should have sufficient error diagnostics to allow the user to track the point at which a particular program fails to provide the correct result. A well-written library program should provide not only the correct answer for a particular input but also return a measure of the accuracy of the calculation, as given by the probable error in the result compared to that obtained by solving the mathematical equation.

An important library of functions written in FORTRAN available for PC-DOS (and MS-DOS) and CP/M computers is the NAG PC50 Fortran library from Numerical Algorithms Group, Inc.* This is a particularly important library of routines, since it is a subset of the NAG library available for mainframe computers, such as the DEC VAX and PRIME series. The original library contains over 500 routines. The PC50 library contains the 50 most widely used of these routines written in FORTRAN. The programs in this library fall into the categories below, which represent some of the major categories of numerical analysis.

> ### The NAG PC-50 Library
> Zero of polynomials
> Roots of one or more transcendental equations
> Quadrature (Integration)
> Ordinary differential equations
> Minimizing or maximizing a function
> Eigenvalues and eigenvectors
> Simultaneous linear equations
> Simple calculations of Statistical Data
> Random number generators
> Linear programming
> Approximations of special functions
> Utilities

*The Numerical Algorithms Group, Inc., 1131 Warren Avenue, Downers Grove, IL 60515.

The NAG routines have been adapted for microcomputers using the Microsoft* version of FORTRAN. The linker used by the Microsoft series of languages allows compiled subroutines to be linked to languages other than FORTRAN. Specifically BASICA, C, and PASCAL are supported in this way. This allows a great deal of flexibility in problem solving, where a combination of library routines from libraries such as NAG may be interfaced with user-written functions in other languages.

A program library of a quite different source is the ASYST programming package from Macmillan Software.† Written as a series of FORTH-like library functions, the data analysis Library of ASYST contains a large collection of mathematical operations usable in numerical analysis an experimental data reduction. The library is loosely divided into the following categories.

The ASYST Library
Polynomial operations
Vectors and matrices
Eigenvalues and eigenvectors
Least squares approximations
Data manipulation
Fourier transforms

The operations available in the ASYST library parallel many of those presented in Chapters 9 and 10. The ASYST software package also contains a complete data acquisition and data presentation library, which makes it a powerful programming environment for laboratory work. The special nature of FORTH allows both interpreted and compiled routines to be used in combination, allowing flexibility and execution speed to be traded off against each other.

Program libraries in BASIC are also available. A particularly well-documented series of scientific subroutines has been written by Ruckdeschel.* Library subroutines are given in a number of dialects of BASIC, including Microsoft BASIC (MBASIC).

9.2. GENERATING MATHEMATICAL FUNCTIONS

To illustrate what can be done even with small microcomputer systems, we have chosen four mathematical functions often used in science and engineering: the error function, the gamma function, the Bessel function, and the Voigt function. The first three are of general interest throughout science, and the fourth is usually restricted to problems in atomic and molecular spectroscopy.

---

*Microsoft FORTRAN is a trademark of Microsoft, Inc.

†ASYST is distributed by Macmillan Software, the Macmillan Publishing Co., New York.

*F.R. Ruckdeschel, *BASIC Scientific Subroutines*, Vols. I, II (Byte/McGraw-Hill Books, Peterborough, N.H. 1981).

The integral or differential equations defining each function are shown in Table 9.2. None of them have a general analytical solution. A detailed discussion concerned with generating some of these functions in PASCAL is given by Miller,[*] who discusses the use of direct integration or iterative expansion techniques to obtain the functions. We outline here an alternative approach utilizing well-tested, finite-series-expansion, rational approximation available for these functions.

The error, gamma, and Bessel functions can be expressed[*] over part of their range by a polynomial expansion. The coefficients of the polynomial as well as a measure of the error of the approximations over their specified range are also given in the references. The error estimate allows one to assess the effects of using the functions in a complex calculation.

The approximation of the Voigt function is somewhat different from the others. In this case the basic functions are not polynomials but asymmetric Lorentzian curves.[†] The expansion is less accurate than the other functions but possesses the degree of accuracy required for many calculations using this function.

Listings of the library programs for each of these functions in BASICA and C are given in the Appendixes. The I/O parameter list is given in Table 9.3. This table contains all the information that is needed by the user to run the programs.

The results of generating each function over a finite range are shown in Figures 9.3($a-d$). The error function is the most straightforward, being a monotonically increasing function with a limit of 1 as x approaches infinity.

The Gamma function is also defined over all x but is a more complicated function. The function integral approximation shown in Table 9.2. is only valid in the range between 0 and 1. However, over the rest of the x range a simple recursion relationship may be used to bring the function within range.

$$\Gamma(x + 1) = x \Gamma(x)$$

The Bessel function $J_n(x)$ is a series of curves of different integer orders n. The programs may be used to calculate the function for any positive order n. Approximations for the zero and first-order Bessel functions were obtained from the literature. For all other n the recursion relationship

$$J_{n+1} = 2nJ_n/x - J_{n-1}$$

is sufficient to extend the function to all other values of n.

[*]A.R. Miller, PASCAL *Programs for Scientists and Engineers* (Sybex Inc., CA, 1981).

[*]M. Abramowitz and I.E. Stegun, *Handbook of Mathematical Functions with Formulas, Graphs and Mathematical Tables*, 9th ed. (Dover, N.Y. 1972).

[†]P. Martin and J. Puerta, in *Applied Optics* **20**, 3923 (1981).

Table 9.2. The Mathematical Definitions and Standard Approximations Used to Generate the Functions Numerically

Function	Equation	Approximation	Range	Error $\lvert\epsilon\rvert$
Error function $\mathrm{erf}(x)$	$\dfrac{2}{\sqrt{\pi}}\displaystyle\int_0^\infty e^{-t^2}\,dt$	$= 1 - \left\{\displaystyle\sum_{n=1}^{6} a_n t^n\right\} e^{-x^2}$ where $t = \dfrac{1}{1+px}$	$0 \leq x \leq \infty$	$\leq 1.5 \times 10^{-7}$
Gamma function $\Gamma(x+1)$	$\displaystyle\int_0^\infty t^x e^{-t}\,dt$	$= \displaystyle\sum_{n=0}^{8} b_n x^n$	$0 \leq x \leq 1$	$\leq 3 \times 10^{-7}$
Bessel function $J_0(x)$ $J_1(x)$	$x^2\dfrac{d^2\omega}{dx^2} + x\dfrac{d\omega}{dx} + (x^2 - \nu^2)\omega = 0$ $\nu = 0$ $\omega(x) = J_0(x)$ $\nu = 1$ $J_1(x)$ $= n$ $J_n(x)$	$J_0(x) = \displaystyle\sum_{k=0}^{6} a_k \left(\dfrac{x}{3}\right)^{2k}$ $J_0(x) = x^{-1/2} f_0\cos\theta_0$ where $f_0 = \displaystyle\sum_{k=0}^{6} a_k'\left(\dfrac{3}{x}\right)^k$ $d_0 = x - \displaystyle\sum_{k=0}^{6} b_k\left(\dfrac{3}{x}\right)^k$	$-3 \leq x \leq 3$ $3 \leq x \leq \infty$	$\leq 5 \times 10^{-8}$ $\leq 1.6 \times 10^{-8}$
Voigt profile $V(d, p)$	$\dfrac{p}{\pi}\displaystyle\int_{-\infty}^{\infty}\dfrac{e^{-y^2}\,dy}{p^2 + (d-y)^2}$	$= \displaystyle\sum_{k=1}^{4}\dfrac{\gamma_k(p - \alpha_k) + \delta_k(d - \beta_k)}{(p - \alpha_k)^2 + (d - \beta_k)^2}$	$0 \leq \phi \leq \infty$ $0 \leq d \leq \infty$	$\leq 1.5 \times 10^{-3}$

Table 9.3. Parameter List for Mathematical Functions

FUNCTION	START	MBASIC/BASICA CALLING VARIABLES	RETURN VARIABLE	C FUNCTION
Error function	11000	X	ERF	erf(x)
Gamma function	11100	X	GAMMA	gamma(x)
Bessel function	11300	X,JN%	BESSEL	bessel(n,x)
Voigt function	11500	P,D	VOIGT	voigt(p,d)

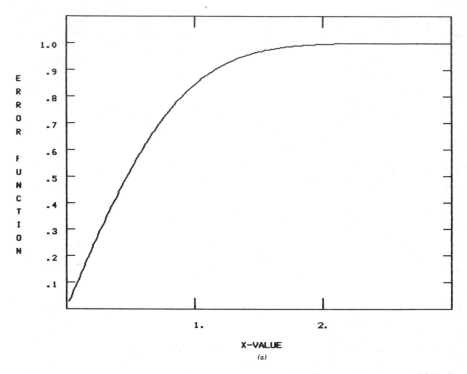

(a)

Figure 9.3. Graphs of generated mathematical functions. (a) The error function erf (x) in the range $0 < x < 3$. (b) The gamma function Γ in the range $-4 < x < 4$. (c) The Bessel functions $J_0(x)$, $J_1(x)$ in the range $0 < x < 20$. (d) The Voigt function $V(p,d)$ for $p = 0.1$ and 1.0 with d in the range $-5 < d < 5$.

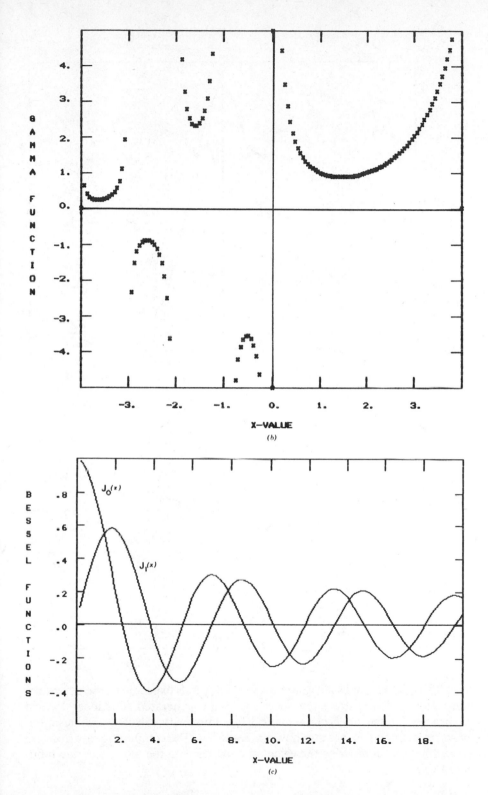

(b)

(c)

283

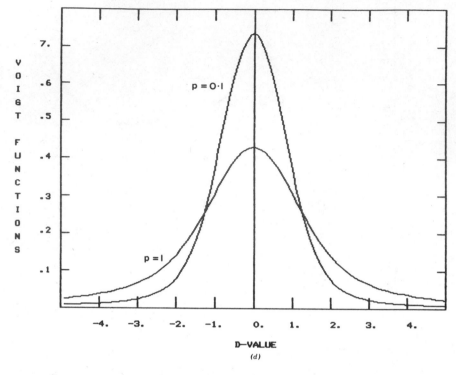

Figure 9.3d. (*Continued*)

Table 9.4. Test of Accuracy for the Mathematical Functions

FUNCTION	FUNCTION RESULT		ERRORS	
	Calculated	Tables	Calculated	Quoted*
erf(0.5)	0.52050001	0.52049987	2.5E−7	2E−7
erf(1.5)	0.96610526	0.96610514	1.2E−7	"
gamma(1/2)	1.77245399	1.77245385	7.9E−8	3E−7
gamma(1/4)	3.62561071	3.62560991	2.2E−7	"
bessel(0,2)	0.22389196	0.22389078	5.0E−6	5E−8
bessel(1,2)	0.57672482	0.57672481	1.1E−8	"

Although the graphs illustrate the general trends expected of the functions, they do not demonstrate the accuracy of the generated functions. Typical accuracies for the three mathematical functions with calculated values compared to tabulated values are shown in Table 9.4. The computational errors are determined by comparing the calculated values with the more accurate tabulated values.

The simple program in Figure 9.4 is used to fill an array B( ) with values of the first-order Bessel function at equally incremented intervals of x from 0 to 20.

This is the program used to generate the data plotted in Figure 9.3c. Similar programs may be written for the other functions.

```
5     DEFINT I-N : DEFDBL A-H,O-Z          :REM initialize variables
10    REM-------------------- calculate bessel(n,x)
90        CHAIN MERGE"B:BESSEL.LIB",100  :REM bring in bessel mod.
100       DIM B(240)                       :REM array for data
110       JN% = 1                          :REM first order bessel
120       FOR I = 0 TO 200                 :REM begin loop
125          X = 0.1# * I                  :REM calculate x
130          GOSUB 11300                   :REM calculate bessel(1,x)
140          B(I) = BESSEL                 :REM place data in array
145          PRINT X,BESSEL                :REM list data on screen
150       NEXT I                           :REM end of loop
160       GOSUB 2000                       :REM file data
900   END                                  :REM end of main routine
2000  REM----------------- file data
2010      REM etc. ........
  .
2050  RETURN
```

Figure 9.4. The Calling Program to generate the Bessel Function over the x Range 0 to 20. Language: BASICA/MBASIC.

9.3.   NUMERICAL DIFFERENTIATION AND INTEGRATION

9.3.1. Differentiation

Numerical differentiation is a deceptively simple operation, but if not handled correctly it can lead to large numerical errors in a model calculation. An excellent discussion of the limits of numerical differentiation and the approximations used has been provided by Vandergraft.* This should be consulted if further background is required on some of the techniques discussed in this chapter. We consider three methods of numerical differentiation, all of which may be easily implemented on microcomputers. In this section we describe the central difference approximation. Later we describe the calculation of the differential of a data series by the spline interpolation method. In the next chapter we describe a way of determining the differential of noisy data by using the Savitsky–Golay smoothing technique.

*J.S. Vandergraft, *Introduction to Numerical Computing* (Academic Press, N.Y., 1983).

The most widely technique for numerical differentiation is the simple *central difference approximation*, which gives the gradient of $f(x)$ at a point x:

$$f'(x) = D(h) = \frac{f(x + h) - f(x - h)}{2h} + O(h^2)$$

This approximation is equivalent to fitting a quadratic curve to the three points $f(x + h)$, $f(x)$, and $f(x - h)$ and taking its derivative. In this case the error in this approximation will be of the order of h^2.

Higher-order approximations to the differential involve fitting higher-order polynomials to more and more of the data points. The third-order approximation, again in the central model, may be written.[*]

$$f'(x) = D(h) = \frac{f(x - 2h) - 8f(x - h) + 8f(x + h) - f(x + 2h)}{12h} + O(h^4)$$

Although mathematically this approximation is a more accurate representation of the derivative, it is also more susceptible to data noise and rounding errors on the machine. The I/O parameter list for the differentiation library module is shown in Table. 9.5.

All numerical-difference differentiation approximations involve subtracting nearly identical numbers from each other. Therefore small errors in these numbers lead to very large errors in the difference. Thus, in the case of experimental data, the techniques mentioned in this section should never be

Table 9.5. Parameter List for Differentiation Module

OPTION	MBASIC VARIABLES Calling	MBASIC VARIABLES Return	DESCRIPTION	C variable
1			Differentiation of Known Function	
		BASIC Call	GOSUB 12500	
		C Call	diff_f(ndegree,mode,h,x,fn)	
	f(X)		Function to be differentiated in subroutine at 10500 for BASICA. Name of function in C.	fn( )
	NDEGREE		Degree of central difference appn. 1 and 3 supported in library	ndegree
	MODE		=1 ; standard approximation 2 : extrapolation to the limit	mode
	H		Increment used in differentiation.	h
	X		x-value at which gradient calculated.	x
		DERIVX	Calculated derivative.	diff_f( )

[*]J.R. Rice, *Numerical Methods, Software and Analysis* (McGraw-Hill, N.Y. 1983).

used without first smoothing the data. Further discussion of this subject is left until Chapter 10.

For differentiating an analytical function one would expect that by decreasing the value of the increment h in the central difference formulae shown above, we would more closely approximate the differential. In reality, however, on any computer system with a limited arithmetic capability, we will, in the end, reach a point where rounding errors will decrease the accuracy of the calculation. For each function that we wish to numerically differentiate there is an optimum point reached where the combination of rounding and truncation errors are a minimum.

We illustrate this problem with the results of numerically calculating the differential for the function $y = 13/(x^4 + 3x^3 + 9)$ for different values of the parameter h. From elementary calculus one can verify that this function has a gradient of -1 at x=1. The errors incurred by carrying out this calculation numerically are shown in Table 9.6. The two columns labelled diff should be compared for the first- and third-order calculations. As will be seen, the third-order calculation is much more accurate by significant orders of magnitude over most of the data range, and at $h=0.0001$ we reach the fundamental arithmetic accuracy of the machine, after which the rounding errors begin to accumulate.

Also shown in this table is data obtained for the gradient by using a simple technique called *extrapolation to the limit*.* This involves numerically calculating the differential as before, but at two spacings, h and $h/2$, in a region where the rounding errors of the computer are still negligible. The appropriate polynomial function approximation with zero gradient is then applied at h=0 to obtain the extrapolated value of the differential in the limit as h $\rightarrow$ 0. The following are the extrapolated polynomial functions for the two most recurring error terms in numerical calculations:

$$(1) \text{ Error term } O(h^2): \quad D_1(h) = \frac{1}{3} [4 \ D(h/2) - D(h)]$$

$$(2) \text{ Error term } O(h^4): \quad D_2(h) = \frac{1}{15} [16 \ D(h/2) - D(h)]$$

Table 9.6. Errors in the Calculation Using Different Differentiation Techniques

	First Order		Third Order	
h	diff	ETL	diff	ETL
0.1	7.6e$-$3	2.3e$-$4	2.3e$-$4	2.1e$-$5
0.01	7.7e$-$5	2.4e$-$8	2.4e$-$8	2.2e$-$11
0.001	7.7e$-$7	2.4e$-$12	2.4e$-$12	1.7e$-$14
0.0001	7.7e$-$9	$-$2.9e$-$14	$-$5.4e$-$15	$-$4.6e$-$15
0.00001	7.7e$-$11	$-$5.4e$-$13	3.9e$-$13	3.9e$-$13
0.000001	1.3e$-$11	1.5e$-$11	1.2e$-$11	1.2e$-$11

*Vandergraft, loc. cit.

The first of these formulas to obtain the ETL (extrapolated to the limit) value is applicable for the first-order approximation, whereas the second should be used in the third-order case.

The program in Figure 9.5*a* can be used to check the operation of the library differentiation module in BASIC. The program calculates the third-order approximation to the gradient both in the standard approximation and with the ETL method. The function must be placed at the subroutine at 10500. The parameter h must be entered at the keyboard by the operator.

```
10   DEFINT I-N : DEFDBL A-H,O-Z      :REM initialize variables
20   REM---------------------- integration test
90      CHAIN MERGE"B:DIFFRN.LIB",100    :REM bring in mod.
100     X=1#:INPUT "ENTER NDEGREE% AND H ",NDEGREE%,H
110     MODE% = 1 : GOSUB 12500
120     PRINT "THIRD ORDER RESULT ";DERIVX,RR
130     MODE% = 2 : GOSUB 12500
140     PRINT THIRD ORDER ETL ",DERIVX,RR
150     GOTO 100
160 END
10500 REM-------------------- function to be differentiated
10520   Y = 13# / (X * X * X * ( X + 3# ) + 9# )
10530 RETURN
```

Figure 9.5*a*.   Main BASIC program to test differential module.
Language: BASICA/MBASIC

The C program is configured with the same parameter list. The nature of the C language allows one to imbed the function directly on the right-hand side of an arithmetic expression or directly in a printf( ) statement as is shown in the simple example in Figure 9.5 *b*.

```
#include "libc.h"
#include "math.h"
#include "b:numrcl.h"
/*          differentiation function testing    */
main(){
  double h=0.01,x=1.0,f();
  int ndegree, mode;
  printf("first order gradient = %14.8e\n",diff_f(ndegree=1,mode=1,h,x,f));
  printf("first order etl      = %14.8e\n",diff_f(ndegree=1,mode=2,h,x,f));
  printf("third order gradient = %14.8e\n",diff_f(ndegree=3,mode=1,h,x,f));
  printf("third order etl      = %14.8e\n",diff_f(ndegree=3,mode=2,h,x,f));
}
/*          function to be differentiated            */
double f(x)
double x;
{
  return (13/(x*x*x*(x+3)+9));
}
```

Figure 9.5*b*.   Main C program to test differential function.
Language: C.

Here fn( ) is the name of the function to be differentiated, which is passed to diff_f( ) as a pointer, as discussed in Chapter 4. This feature allows the flexibility of differentiating a number of defined functions within the same main program.

9.3.2. Integration

Integration is another important area of mathematical modeling, and numerical analysis, as applied to integration, has been the subject of much study. The integral to be evaluated is usually written

$$I = \int_a^b f(x)\ dx$$

where the integrand may be known analytically or only at a discrete number of points. The present library routines are given for analytically known functions only. The software may be easily adapted to the case of data arrays.

There are literally hundreds of numerical integration approximations and algorithms available, depending on the form of the data and the behavior of the integrand. The following is a list of some of the methods used for numerical integration. The methods are listed loosely in increasing order of complexity.

Commonly Used Numerical Integration Techniques

Newton–Coates Methods
Trapezoidal integration
Simpson integration
Adaptive integration

Gaussian Quadrature
Gauss–Legendre integration
Gauss–Laguerre integration
Gauss–Hermite integration
Gauss–Chebyshev integration

The Newton–Coates methods are adequate for most applications when the integrands are well behaved. Gaussian methods* are an important class of

---

*Vandergraft, loc. cit.

numerical integration methods that should be considered in situations where the form of the integrand is known and when the function posseses irregularities or the limits of integration must be taken to infinity.

The general form of a Newton−Coates approximation is

$$I_n = \sum_{k=0}^{n} c_k f(x_k)$$

The *trapezoidal* and *Simpson* integral approximations are given in Table 9.7. The trapezoidal procedure approximates the area between two points as a trapezoid. The Simpson rule is the next highest approximation where a quadratic curve interpolation is assumed. Thus, the trapezoidal approximation will integrate the area bounded by a straight line exactly, and the Simpson approximation will do the same for a quadratic polynomial. Shown in Figure 9.6. is a simple algorithm for carrying out Simpson integration. In both approximations the x-axis is divided up into n elements or $n+1$ data points.

The numerical parameters lists for the BASIC and C integral program library modules are shown in Table 9.8. Both the trapezoidal and Simpson approximations are supported through the nform parameter. The main programs follow closely the structure already discussed above for the differentiation library module. Some interesting results are obtained with these approximations, and they are illustrated in Table 9.9 for the integral of sin (x) between 0 and π using various numbers of points. The theoretical value of the integral is exactly 2. We list the deviations of the results from the analytical value in Table 9.9. The

Table 9.7.   Integration Approximations
                Language: Algorithmic

---

trapezoidal Approximation
$I_n = \frac{h}{2} [f(a) + h[f(a+h) + f(a+2h) + \cdots$
$$\cdots + f(a+(n-1)h)] + \frac{h}{2} f(b)$$
  where the x-axis is divided into n elements of equal
                        increments (n+1 data points) and $h = \dfrac{b-a}{n}$

Simpson Approximation
  Let n = 2m so that n must be even
$I_n = \frac{h}{3} [f(a) + 4f(a+h) + 2f(a+2h) + \cdots$
$\qquad \cdots + 2f(a+(2n-2)h) + 4f(a+(2m-1)h + f(b))]$
  where the x-axis is divided into n elements of equal
                        increments (2m+1 data points) and $h = \dfrac{b-a}{2m}$

```
procedure simpson(a,b,n)
real a,b  integer n
begin
  integer m,j,k  real I,h,f(x)

  if n is odd print warning and end procedure
  m← n / 2
  h← (b-a) / 2m
  I← f(b) - f(a)
  for j is 1 to m
    for k is 1 to 2
      I← I + 2kf(a + [2j + k - 3]h)
    end_for
  end_for
  I← h I/3
end_procedure
```

Figure 9.6.   Algorithm for the Simpson approximation.
Language: Algorithmic.

Table 9.8.   Parameter List for Integration Library Module

OPTION	MBASIC VARIABLES Calling	Return	Description	C variable
1			Integral of Known Analytical Function	
		BASIC Call	NINTGL%=1 : GOSUB 12000	
		C Call	intgl_f(n,nform,mode,a,b,fcn)	
	N		Number of elements to be used in integration (even for Simpson).	n
	NFORM		=1 Trapezoidal integral calculation 2 Simpson integral calculation.	nform
	MODE		=1 Standard calculation. 2 Extrapolation to the limit calcln.	mode
	f(X)		Function to be integrated in BASICA. coded in subroutine at 10200. Name of C function to be integrated.	fcn( )
	A		Lower limit of integration.	a
	B		Upper limit of integration.	b
		AINTGL	Value of integral.	intgl_f()
2			Gauss−Legendre Integration	
		Basic Call	NINTGL%=2 : GOSUB 12000	
		C Call	intgl_gl(a,b,fcn)	
	A,B			a,b
	f(X)		These have the same meanings	fcn( )
		AINTGL	as above	intgl_gl()

Table 9.9.   Errors in the Calculation Using Different Integration Techniques

| | STANDARD APPROXIMATIONS | | EXTRAPOLATION TO LIMIT | |
N	Trapezoidal	Simpson	Trapezoidal	Simpson
2	−0.2146	0.04719	2.279e−03	−8.321e−06
4	−0.0519	2.279e−03	1.346e−04	−2.005e−08
8	−0.0128	1.346e−04	8.399e−06	9.086e−08
16	−3.214e−03	8.399e−06	6.101e−07	7.779e−08
32	−8.032e−04	6.101e−07	1.110e−07	8.268e−08
64	−2.007e−04	1.110e−07	8.446e−08	7.998e−08
128	−5.011e−05	8.445e−08	8.026e−08	7.939e−08
256	−1.246e−05	8.026e−08	7.945e−08	8.164e−08
512	−3.057e−06	7.945e−08	8.150e−08	8.198e−08

calculation is carried out in BASICA with the trigonometric function determined to single precision, and all other calculations carried out in double precision. The results shown here indicate that for the standard integration technique the Simpson method is vastly superior. For the sin (x) function the 512-point trapezoidal routine gives an answer that is only marginally better than a 16-point Simpson calculation. The second series of columns in this table list the results of the integration of sin(x) by using the technique of extrapolation to the limit. The trapezoidal approximation has an error term that has an $O(h^2)$ dependence, whereas the Simpson approximation is $O(h^4)$. The formulae that must be used for these calculations have been given in the discussion on differentiation.

A dramatic improvement is seen in the accuracy of these calculations for the same number of points, and we see that a 512-point trapezoidal calculation only does marginally better than a 2-point ETL Simpson calculation. Actually, of course, the number of points in each calculation is $N+1$, where N is the number listed in the columns. Also a 32-point ETL calculation, for example, makes the calculation of the integral at a 32- and a 64-point mesh. It should also be noted that the columns for the extrapolated trapezoidal and the standard Simpson approximations are identical but shifted by a factor of two with respect to the numbers of points used in the calculation. That is, a 16-point Simpson calculation gives the same result as an 8-point ETL trapezoid result as long as the rounding errors are insignificant.

Higher-order Newton−Coates integration approximations are available. Surprisingly, however, such methods, which are based on higher-degree polynomials, may be less accurate than a simple Simpson calculation. This occurs because of the oscillations that may appear in the higher-order terms of the polynomial. These oscillations serve to magnify small errors in the data. For these reasons the simple techniques discussed above are the most acceptable methods of numerical integration especially when experimental data must be integrated.

We hope this section has demonstrated clearly the competing roles that the algorithms and approximations and the arithmetic capability of the computer hold in determining the ultimate accuracy of a particular computational task.

9.3.3. The Gauss−Legendre Method

The Gaussian quadrature methods of integration represent an advanced approach to numerical integration that should be considered in cases of more complicated functions where the integrand may be ill behaved. The method is also much faster than the Newton−Coates method for the same accuracy. The Gauss−Legendre method consists of representing the integral by a sum over a set of normalized functions. One of the simplest applications is using the Legendre* orthogonal functions $P_n(x)$, where n is the degree of the Lengendre function.

$$\int_a^b f(x) \; dx \; = \; \sum_{j=1}^n A_j f(x_j)$$

A unique set of parameters (A_j, x_j) may be determined for each integrand and set of integration limits. A comprehensive discussion of these methods may be found in the literature.*

Our library of numerical analysis programs contains a single Gaussian quadrature method. A 3-point Gaussian−Legendre quadrature has the following summation parameters (A_j, x_j):

$$A_1 = \frac{5c}{9} \qquad x_1 = d - cz$$

$$A_2 = \frac{8c}{9} \qquad x_2 = d$$

$$A_3 = \frac{5c}{9} \qquad x_3 = d + cz$$

where $c = (b - a)/2$, $d = (b + a)/2$, and $z = \sqrt{0.6}$.

This method is exact for integrals of all polynomial integrands up to degree 5. For other functions it may not be as accurate, but it does offer an extremely quick way of determining an approximate value of any integral. For example, the value of the integral of $\sin(x)$ between 0 and π comes out to within 6.4e−04 of the correct answer.

---

*See, for example, M. Abramowitz and I.A., Stegun, loc. cit.

*A.H. Stroud, and D. Secrest, *Gaussian Quadrature Formulas*. (Prentice-Hall, Englewood Cliffs, N.J., 1966).

9.4.　SPLINE INTERPOLATION

In modeling or data analysis one is often confronted with a series of data points, possibly at nonregular intervals, that are not coincident with the ordinate at which the value of the function is desired. For example, in all branches of science and engineering, tables of important quantities are published that must be interpolated to obtain relevant numbers. *Spline* interpolation is an important technique for carrying out interpolation in a methodical manner with the greatest possible accuracy. Although the spline technique is heavy on the use of computer resources, the added confidence that one has in the resulting data, as compared to the simpler polynomial interpolation techniques used in the past, is well worth the extra effort.

We consider here the *cubic spline* interpolation technique. This involves fitting a series of cubic curves to the data over the range of the data points. Unlike polynomial interpolation, which involves fitting the same curve over the whole data range, a series of polynomials are found for the region between the points. The theory and detailed properties of these functions may be found in a number of references.* Their properties manifest themselves in some simple ways that are extremely easy to understand qualitatively.

Refer to Figure 9.7, where we show a data series of N points that might represent our complete knowledge of a function $f(x)$ at the discrete ordinates $x_1, x_2, ..., x_N$, where, in general, the separation between the x values cannot be assumed to be a constant. We can attempt to recreate the value of $f(x)$ anywhere in the discrete range $a < x < b$ with a spline interpolation function $s(x)$. The points x_k for $k = 1,..., N$, are called the *knots* of $s(x)$.

The cubic spline function we are concerned with approximates each region between the knots by the cubic functions below for all values of x in the range between a and b.

$$s(x) = A_{0k} + A_{1k}(x-x_k) + A_{2k}(x-x_k)^2 + A_{3k}(x-x_k)^3$$

The constants $A_{0k}, A_{1k}, A_{2k}, A_{3k}$ are different for each region $x_k \leqslant x \leqslant x_{k+1}$, and each constant is an involved function of the complete data set, not just those bounding the region of interest.

The cubic constants may be shown to be related[†] to the first and second derivatives of $s(x)$, $s'(x_k)$ and $s''(x_k)$, at the knots by

$$A_{0k} = f(x_k) \qquad A_{1k} = s'(x_k)$$

$$A_{2k} = \frac{s''(x_k)}{2} \qquad A_{3k} = \frac{\{s''(x_{k+1}) - s''(x_k)\}}{6h_k}$$

where $h_k = x_{k+1} - x_k$.

*Rice, loc. cit.

†Vandergraft, loc. cit.

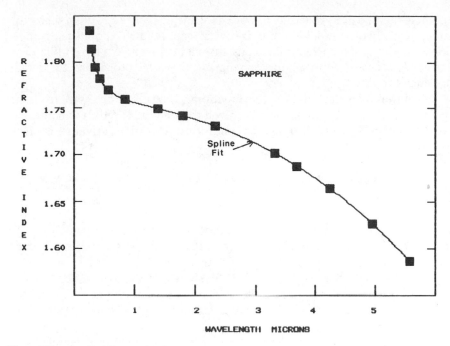

Figure 9.7. A spline fit exercise for the refractive index of sapphire. The squares are the experimentally known values taken from the Handbook of Mathematical functions. The curve is the spline fitted points.

Certain constraints are necessary to guarantee that the spline function determined from the data has a unique solution. The following is a standard set of constraints that is often used in spline interpolation and is the one utilized in the algorithm illustrated in this book:

1. The spline function $s(x)$ passes through the knots.
2. The first derivative of the spline is continuous across the knots.
3. The second derivative is continuous across the knots.
4. The second derivative is constrained to be zero at a and b.

The last point is somewhat arbitrary but gives two extra conditions that guarantee a unique solution to the spline function. There are other end conditions sometimes used.

Given a set of data, the first step in the solution of a cubic spline interpolation is the calculation of the first and second derivatives at the knots. Then the values of the cubic constants may be determined quite easily from the equations above. These constants need only be determined once for a given data set and may then be used generally to find the value of *s(x)* at any point along the curve. This involves finding the next lowest knot for the *x*-point being interpolated, so that the correct cubic constants can be used. We have utilized an extremely efficient algorithm for carrying out this whole procedure, the details of which are discussed by Vandergraft.*

The differential $s'(x)$ of the spline function *s(x)* at *x* may be shown from the theory of splines to approximate rather well the true differential of an interpolated function $f'(x)$ over a range of conditions. The first derivative is given simply by

$$s'(x) = \frac{s'(x_k) + s''(x_k)(x-x_k) + (s''(x_{k+1}) - s''(x_k))(x-x_k)^2}{2h_k}$$

Again, the value of the next lowest knot to the specified *x*-value must be determined for each value of *x*. The derivative must be determined at each value of *x* in order to select the correct series of cubic constants.

Further differentiation of this curve will show that the second derivative is approximated by a straight line between the knots, and that at the knots, the slope of the third derivative function undergoes a sudden change. This is illustrated for a real set of data below.

The parameter list for the spline interpolation program library module listed in the Appendixes is shown in Table 9.10. Option 1 in BASIC (spline_prm( ) in C) must be run once for each data set to determine the spline parameters. There after, option 2 may be run as many times as necessary to give the interpolated *y*-value for a specified *x*-value.

To demonstrate the characteristics of a spline fit for a real set of data, we use the cubic spline program in the Appendix written in MBASIC/BASICA to interpolate between the set of points given in Table 9.11. The data represent the refractive index of sapphire over an extended wavelength region. The data is taken from the *Handbook of Optics.*[†] We also list in this table the values of the first and second derivatives at the knots.

The BASIC program in Figure 9.8 is used to call the spline fit program module, initialize the system by calculating the spline parameters, prompt the user for an *x*-value, and print the calculated interpolated value and the first derivative.

To illustrate the accuracy of the spline fit, we selected a minimum number of points from the literature for inclusion in the spline fit. The spline program was then used to obtain a set of interpolated values of the refractive index at wavelengths for which the refractive index was also reported in the literature. A comparison of the results of this interpolation and the reported values are shown in Table 9.12.

*Vandergraft loc. cit.

[†]W.G. Driscoll and W. Vaughan, editors, *Handbook of Optics* (McGraw-Hill, N.Y. 1978).

Table 9.10. Parameter List of Spline Interpolation Module

OPTION	MBASIC VARIABLES		DESCRIPTION	C variable
	Calling	Return		
1			Calculate Spline Parameters	
		BASIC Call	NSPLINE%=1:GOSUB 13000	
		C Call	spline_prm(npts,&x,&f)	
	NPTS		Number of data points (knots)	npts
	XARRAY()		x−values of data points	x[]
	YARRAY()		y−values of data points	f[]
2			Interpolated y-Value (and Derivatives) at Specified x	
			Option 1 must be run first	
	BASIC Call		NSPLINE%=2:GOSUB 13000	
	C Call		spline_y(npts,xval,&x,&f,&dx,&ddx)	
	XVAL		x-value at which interpolated value to be calculated.	xval
	SPLDRV		=0 no derivatives BASIC only. =1 calculate derivative.	
		S	Calculated interpolated value.	spline_y()
		SDERIV	Calculated first derivative.	dx
		SCNDRV	Calculated second derivative.	ddx

Table 9.11. Refractive Index of Sapphire (Synthetic) for the Ordinary Ray

Wavelength Microns	k	Knots $s(x_k)$	First Derivative $s'(x_k)$	Second Derivative $s''(x_k)$
0.26520	1	1.83365	−0.58447	0.0000e+00
0.30215	2	1.81351	−0.46624	6.3994e+00
0.365015	3	1.79358	−0.21975	1.4423e+00
0.435834	4	1.78120	−0.13600	9.2299e−01
0.579066	5	1.76871	−0.055706	1.9818e−01
0.852120	6	1.75885	−0.023975	3.4236e−02
1.39506	7	1.74888	−0.016433	−6.4530e−03
1.81307	8	1.74144	−0.019182	−6.6985e−03
2.32542	9	1.73057	−0.023569	−1.0428e−02
3.33033	10	1.70140	−0.034705	−1.1737e−02
3.7067	11	1.68746	−0.039495	−1.3713e−02
4.2553	12	1.66371	−0.047125	−1.4105e−02
4.9540	13	1.62320	−0.059946	−2.2596e−02
5.577	14	1.58638	−0.066985	0.0000e+00

Table 9.12.   Comparison of Interpolated and Actual Values for Sapphire Refractive Index

Wavelength Microns	Interpolated Value	Actual Value	Difference $(n_i - n_a)*1e5$
0.28936	1.81994	1.81949	45
0.404656	1.78593	1.78582	11
1.01398	1.75537	1.75547	−10
1.52952	1.74661	1.74660	1

The full interpolated curve is shown in Figure 9.7 together with the original data points (knots). The first and second derivatives are shown in Figure 9.9. Note especially that the second derivative has a linear dependence in the regions between the knots, and that this derivative is clearly peaked in the region of 0.5 microns and is extremely steep at wavelengths below this. We find, as we would expect, that the error in the spline fit from what is anticipated is highest in this region and decreases as the curve becomes more gently varying.

```
5    DEFINT I-N : DEFDBL A-H,O-Z
10   REM--------------------------- SPLINE TEST PROGRAM
90       CHAIN MERGE"B:SPLINE.LIB",100 :REM merge in library program
100      DIM XARRAY(50),YARRAY(50)     :REM array for original data
105      READ NPTS                     :REM number of data points
110      FOR J=1 TO NPTS : READ XARRAY(J),YARRAY(J) : NEXT J
                                       :REM read data series
120      NSPLINE%=1 : GOSUB 13000      :REM calculate Spline parameters
200   REM------------------- new interpolated value
202      INPUT "ENTER X VALUE ";XVAL   :REM new x-value
205      SPLDRV% =1                    :REM calculate derivatives
210      NSPLINE% = 2 : GOSUB 13000    :REM run Spline for new x
220      PRINT XVAL,S,SDERIV,SCNDRV
230   GOTO 200                         :REM infinite loop
900  END
910  DATA 14                           :REM original data
920  DATA 0.26520,1.83365,0.30215,1.81351,0.365015,1.79358,0.435834,1.78120
930  DATA 0.579066,1.76871,0.852120,1.75885,1.39506,1.74888,1.81307,1.74144
940  DATA 2.32542,1.73057,3.33033,1.70140,3.7067,1.68746,4.2553,1.66371
950  DATA 4.9540,1.62320,5.577,1.58630
990  END
```

Figure 9.8.   The spline test program Language: BASICA/MBASIC

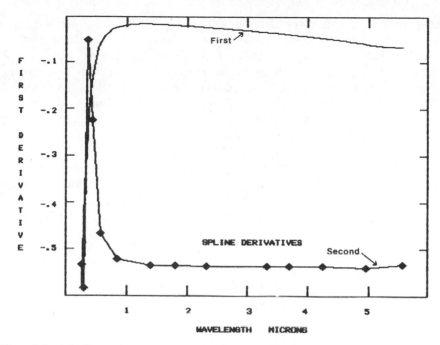

Figure 9.9. The first and second derivatives determined by spline interpolation for the sapphire refractive index.

9.5. NUMERICAL ROOTS OF EQUATIONS

Often it is necessary to backsolve a complex, analytically known function represented by $y = f(x)$ to find the value of x at which a specified value of y occurs. Such a problem may be reduced to the specific task of finding the root(s) of the equation, $F(x) = 0$. For example, imagine that we have a complicated function such as

$$y = \frac{2 + 3\cos(x)}{3 + \exp(-x)\sin(x)}$$

and we need to find the value of x for which $y=1$. Thus, we need to solve the equation

$$\frac{2 + 3\cos(x)}{3 + \exp(-x)\sin(x)} - 1 = 0$$

Since such an equation cannot be solved explicitly, it is convenient to use a numerical method of solution. The roots of this equation in the region between 0 and 10 are at 1.1254, 5.05008, and 7.51396. It is left as an exercise for the reader to demonstrate this with either of the library programs described here.

Our library of functions contains two programs that will solve such an equation. The first is a modified Newton method of solution known as the *secant* method. The operator must provide the program with two starting points, x_0 and x_1, and a means of calculating the function. The second method of solution is based on the *Decker-Brent* method of finding the roots of an equation. In this case it is necessary that we have prior information about the function—in particular, that it has a root between our starting points x_0 and x_1.

It is often advantageous in numerical analysis to have programs based on two entirely different algorithms with which to solve a problem. Invariably there will be conditions in which one or the other of these algorithms breaks down under a specific set of conditions. The I/O parameter list for the root-finding library module is shown in Table 9.13 for the secant and Decker-Brent algorithms.

Table 9.13. Parameter List for Roots of Equation Determination

OPTION	MBASIC VARIABLES		DESCRIPTION	C variable
	Calling	Return		
1			Secant Method of Finding the Root of an Equation	
		BASIC Call	NROOT%=1:GOSUB 1500	
		C Call	root_sec(x0,x1,fcn)	
	X0		⎱ The Algorithm requires two	x0
	X1		⎰ initial values of x to start.	x1
	Y=f(X)		Subroutine containing function to be used in root finding routine at line 10500 in BASIC.	
			Function name in C.	fcn
		X1	A root $f(x_1) = 0$.	root_sec()
2			Decker-Brent Method of Finding the Root of an Equation	
		BASIC Call	NROOT%=2:GOSUB 1500	
		C Call	root_dbr(x0,x1,fcn)	
			The I/O Parameter List is Identical to the Above.	
			Must have f(X1) and f(X2) of different sign	
		X1	A root $f(x1) = 0$.	root_dbr()
			Default Convergence Parameters for Options 1 and 2 in BASIC and C Programs These do not have to be entered, but they may be changed	
	NMAX = 50		Maximum number of allowed iterations	
	EPSILON1 = 0.00001		Convergence condition $\lvert x_1 - x_2 \rvert < \varepsilon_1 \lvert x_2 \rvert$	
	EPSILON2 = 0.00001		Convergence condition $\lvert f(x_2) \rvert < \varepsilon_2$	

As an example of the use of these functions, we use the two algorithms mentioned above, the BASICA and C listing of which is given in the Appendixes, to find *x*-values at which the Bessel function changes sign. The simple BASIC program in Figure 9.10 is used to call each method of solution in turn. The results are shown below.

The short demonstration program of Figure 9.10 may be used to find the roots of the Bessel function of zero order. The program may be easily adapted to Bessel functions of other orders.

```
10      DEFINT I-N : DEFDBL A-H,O-Z
90      REM----------------------- root finding test
100        CHAIN MERGE"B:ROOT.LIB",110         :REM merge in library
110        CHAIN MERGE"B:BESSEL.LIB",120       :REM  functions
120        INPUT "ENTER TWO INITIAL GUESSES ";X0,X1
125                                            :REM initial guesses
130              INPUT "ENTER OPTION ";NROOT%  :REM option
140              GOSUB 15000                   :REM call library mod.
150              PRINT "SOLUTION = ",X1        :REM screen display
160        GOTO 120                            :REM repeat loop
10500 REM--------------------- function calculation
10520      JN%=0 : GOSUB 11300                 :REM calc. bessel(U,x)
10530      Y = BESSEL                          :REM return y to root
10540 RETURN
```

Figure 9.10.   BASICA program to find roots of Bessel functions.
Language: BASICA/MBASIC.

The main routine first merges the two library modules, and in line 120 we enter the two initial guesses manually. At this point we might, for example, enter 2.3 and 2.5 by inspection of the Bessel function graph in Figure 9.3c. The secant method is chosen with NROOT% equal to 1 in line 130, where the root-finding module is called. The module in turn expects to find the function $y=f(x)$ in a subroutine at 11500. The root-finding routine places a value in the variable *x* (which is what the function subroutine expects) and expects to find the corresponding *y*-value at that point. In this instance we use this subroutine as a transfer point to the Bessel function at 11300. This routine also recognizes the global variable *x* but returns the value for the Bessel function at the given *x* in the variable BESSEL. It is necessary in line 11520 to return the data in the correct variable *y* to the root-finding subroutine.

The second option for finding the function roots by using the Decker–Brent method algorithm may be employed by simply writing NROOT%=2 in line 130. The program may be easily adapted to finding the x-value for which the Bessel function equals a certain value other than zero. For example, we might wish to know the *x*-value at which $J_0(x)=2$. This is easily accomplished by writing Y=BESSEL-2# in line 11520, where the algorithm will converge on one of the *x*-values for which this is true. In this example we did not change the values of NMAX, EPSILON1, and EPSILON2.

A table of the roots determined by using the library module and the program of Figure 9.10 is shown in Table 9.14. Both algorithms gave the same answer to

Table 9.14.   Roots of Bessel Functions

	Zero Order	First Order	Second Order
1st zero	2.40483	3.83170	5.13562
2nd zero	5.52008	7.01559	8.41724
3rd zero	8.65373	10.17348	11.61980
4th zero	11.79153	13.32369	14.79595
5th zero	14.93092	16.47061	17.95982

within the quoted accuracy. If you compare these numbers to the actual values given in the literature,* you will note a slight error in the last decimal place. Greater accuracy could be obtained by changing the values of EPSILON from the default values used here. However, one must always take into account the ultimate accuracy of the Bessel function algorithms.

9.6.   MATRIX ANALYSIS

Matrix analysis is a valuable tool for many of the techniques used in numerical analysis, especially in some of the data fitting operations to be described later. It is convenient aid in solving sets of linear, simultaneous equations. We will be dealing with only a limited aspect of matrix arithmetic in this book. We are concerned with solving linear, square-matrix, first-order equations.

A typical set of simultaneous equations has the form:

$$a_{11}x_1 + a_{12}x_2 + a_{13}x_3 + \cdots + a_{1N}x_N = b_1$$

$$a_{21}x_1 + a_{22}x_2 + a_{23}x_3 + \cdots + a_{2N}x_N = b_2$$

$$a_{31}x_1 + \cdots$$

$$\cdots$$

$$a_{N1}x_1 + a_{N2}x_2 + a_{N3}x_3 + \cdots + a_{NN}x_N = b_N$$

where $a_{11}, a_{12},..., a_{NN}, b_1, b_2,...,b_N$ are known, and we wish to solve for the unknowns $x_1, x_x2,...,x_N$. There are N equations and N unknowns. This series of equations may be written in matrix form as

$$
\begin{vmatrix}
a_{11} & a_{12} & a_{13} & \cdots & a_{1N} \\
a_{21} & a_{22} & a_{23} & \cdots & a_{2N} \\
a_{31} & a_{32} & a_{33} & \cdots & a_{3N} \\
\cdots \\
a_{N1} & a_{N2} & a_{N3} & \cdots & a_{NN}
\end{vmatrix}
\begin{vmatrix}
x_1 \\ x_2 \\ x_3 \\ . \\ x_N
\end{vmatrix}
\begin{vmatrix}
b_1 \\ b_2 \\ b_3 \\ . \\ b_N
\end{vmatrix}
$$

which is sometimes written in the compressed matrix form

$$Ax = b$$

*Abramowitz and Stegun, loc. cit.

where x and b are $1 \times N$ column matrices, and A is the $N \times N$ square matrix.

The technique of Gaussian elimination described by Vandergraft* is used to solve this equation. This method is extremely efficient for solving the equation when methods of solution fail. The solution may be thought of as finding the inverse matrix A^{-1}, so that the solution is written

$$x = A^{-1}b$$

The Gauss elimination algorithm finds the solution directly without solving for the inverse explicitly. An option in the matrix library allows the inverse to be calculated explicitly if desired. Central to the working of the Gauss elimination technique is reducing the matrix equations to an upper triangular form. Consider, for example, the special matrix

$$\begin{vmatrix} u_{11} & u_{12} & u_{13} & \cdots & +u_{1N} \\ 0 & u_{22} & u_{23} & \cdots & +u_{2N} \\ 0 & 0 & u_{33} & \cdots & +u_{3N} \\ & \cdot \cdot \cdot & & & \\ 0 & 0 & 0 & 0 & \cdots & +u_{NN} \end{vmatrix} \begin{vmatrix} x_1 \\ x_2 \\ x_3 \\ \cdot \\ x_N \end{vmatrix} = \begin{vmatrix} b_1 \\ b_2 \\ b_3 \\ \cdot \\ b_N \end{vmatrix}$$

The solution of such of such a set of equations is trivial, because starting at the bottom we may successively solve each line explicitly and use the x-values already found to solve for the one remaining unknown in the next equation up. The solution of the bottom equation is simply

$$x_N = \frac{b_N}{u_{NN}}$$

Using this value of x_N in the next equation up, we may solve for x_{N-1}:

$$x_{N-1} = \frac{b_{N-1} - u_{N-1,N}x_N}{u_{N-1,N-1}}$$

The process may be repeated up the matrix to the first equation, where the only unknown should be x_1; this may be found using the values of all the other solved x's in this first equation.

A description of the method used to produce the upper triangular matrix is beyond the scope of this book. We use the algorithm discussed in detail in Vandergraft's book with certain minor differences to accommodate the languages used for the program. The Gauss elimination algorithm utilizes the fact that each term in a set of simultaneous equations may be multiplied by a constant; any term may be replaced by the sum of that term and any other term in the equation set; and, finally, the equations may be interchanged vertically. Using these facts, we may successively eliminate terms in the equations on the

---

*Vandergraft, loc. cit.

left-hand side of the matrix and end up with a completely upper triangular matrix.

An added feature that makes the algorithm more reliable numerically and increases the accuracy of the calculations in certain restrictive circumstances is the technique of *partial pivoting*. The Gauss elimination algorithm breaks down when one of the diagonal elements a_{kk} of the original matrix is zero, and even when the diagonal elements are small but nonzero the calculation may end up with large errors. The partial pivoting technique interchanges rows of the matrix to keep the diagonal elements of the upper triangular matrix as large as possible.

The determinant of a matrix is expressed simply as the product of the diagonal elements of the related upper triangular matrix times a sign multiplier.

$$\det(A) \; = \; (-1)^r u_{11} u_{22} \cdots u_{NN}$$

The r power is the number of row interchanges that have to be traversed to turn the original matrix A into an upper triangular matrix U. We can check the value of the determinant as an indicator of whether or not the matrix A is singular. In the event that it is, no inverse will exist for the matrix, and the matrix equation will be insoluble.

The I/O variable list together with the call sequence for the BASIC and C programs is shown in Table 9.15. The first option that forms the upper triangular matrix [mtrx_tri( ) in C] must be explicitly called before any other option. As many matrix equations $Ax=b$ as necessary may be solved by using option 2 for the same initial square matrix but for different column matrices, without having to re-solve the upper triangular matrix. Finally, the third option [mtrx_inv( )] allows us to calculate the inverse matrix explicitly.

The C program listed in Figure 9.11 is used to create the upper triangular matrix for the 4 × 4 square matrix in the equation below and to solve for the column matrix x, given the matrix b on the rhs of this matrix equation.

$$
\begin{vmatrix}
3 & 2 & -1 & 2 \\
2 & 2 & 3 & 2 \\
-6 & -2 & 4 & -3 \\
-3 & -6 & -3 & -1
\end{vmatrix}
\begin{vmatrix}
? \\
? \\
? \\
?
\end{vmatrix}
=
\begin{vmatrix}
6 \\
9 \\
-7 \\
-13
\end{vmatrix}
$$

The program prints out the solution matrix x as shown below.

```
column matrix solution
      x(1) = 1
      x(2) = 1
      x(3) = 1
      x(4) = 1
```

Table 9.15.   Parameter List for the Matrix Programming Module

OPTION	MBASIC VARIABLES Calling	Return	Description	C Variable
1.			Solve the Matrix Equation $Ax = b$ for x	
		BASIC Call	NMATRIX%=2:GOSUB 14000	
		C Call	mtrx_sln(m, newa,&a,&x,&b,&det)	
	MDEGREE		Degree of the matrix.	m
	SMTRX(,)		Contains the matrix A for NEWA=1	a[][NTWO]
			upper triangular matrix otherwise.	
	NEWA		= 1 signifies new A matrix.	
	BCLM()		The column matrix b in $Ax = b$.	b[]
		DET	The determinant of the matrix A.	det
		XCLM()	The column matrix solution x in	↑
			$Ax = b$	x[]
2.			Explicit calculation of Upper Triangular Matrix	
		BASIC Call	NMATRIX%=1:GOSUB 14000	
		C Call	mtrx_tri(m,&a,&det)	
			called automatically from option 1 (mtrx_sln) for NEWA = 1	
	MDEGREE		Degree of matrix.	m
		DET	The determinant of the matrix.	det
	SMTRX(,)	SMTRX(,)	matrix A in → upper triangle out.	a[][NTWO]
3.			Calculate the Inverse Matrix	
		BASIC Call	NMATRIX%=3:GOSUB 14000	
		C Call	mtrx_inv(n,&a,&inv)	
	NMTRX		Degree of the Matrix.	m
	SMTRX(,)		The upper triangular matrix	a[][NTWO]
			calculated by running option 1.	
		INV(,)	Inverse matrix returned.	inv[][NTWO]

This solution may be easily checked by multiplying the matrices A and x to verify the resulting matrix b. The program goes on to find the inverse matrix, which is also listed below.

inverse matrix solution

−1.5185	0.3333...	−0.7407	−0.1481
0.7962	−0.3333...	0.3518	−0.1296
−0.6296	0.3333...	−0.1851	0.0370
1.6666	0.0	0.6666	0.3333

The weakness of numerical methods is evident in this solution. Clearly, there is an obvious rational matrix solution to the inverse matrix that gets lost in the numerical division of the numbers.

Finally, one word of caution about array dimensions. Even though we are using pointer arithmetic in the library programs, as discussed in Chapter 4, in the case of two-dimensional arrays we have to explicitly set one of the dimensions. In our matrix library program the two-dimensional arrays must be set as a[][NTWO], where NTWO is specified in the header file b:numrcl.h. Thus, in the calling program the arrays of the column dimensions must agree. It is easiest to specify this dimension in the same way as in the library program, but if the value of NTWO in the header file ever gets changed the complete library should be recompiled for safety. The other dimension of the array NA may be specified to optimize the use of space.

```
/*                     Matrix Test Program                        */
#include "libc.h"
#include "math.h"
#include "b:numrcl.h"

#define    NA    10

main(){
     int i,k,j,n,newa;
     double b[NA],x[NA],a[NA][NTWO],inv[NA][NTWO],det,y;
     FILE *fp,*fopen();
/*          READ in data from file    tstmtrx.dat   */
     if((fp=fopen("b:tstmtrx.dat","r"))==NULL)    /*  open file          */
               printf("cannot open file\n");      /*  test for  null     */
     fscanf(fp,"%d",&n);                          /*  matrix degree      */
     for(j=1;j<=n;j++){
          for (k=1;k<=n;k++){
               fscanf(fp,"%f",&y);
               a[j][k]=y;                         /*  matrix    A        */
          }
          fscanf(fp,"%f",b+j);                    /*  matrix    b        */
     fclose(fp);                                  /*  close file         */
     for(j=1;j<=n;j++){
          for(k=1;k<n;k++)printf("%10.6e   ",a[j][k]);
          printf("%10.6e\n",b[j]);
     }
/*               Solve the equation    Ax = b                     */
     newa=1;                                      /*  new matrix  A      */
     mtrx_sln(n,newa,&a,&x,&b,&det);              /* solve new matrix equation */
     printf("value of determinant = %10.6e\n\n",det);
     printf("column matrix solution x[]\n");      /*  print solution x   */
     for(j=1;j<=n;j++)printf("x(%d) = %10.6f\n",j,*(x+j));
/*     Find Inverse Matrix explicitally                           */
     mtrx_inv(n,&a,&inv);                         /*  solve  A-1         */
     printf("\n\ninverse matrix solution\n\n");
     for(j=1;j<=n;j++){                           /*  print out Inverse  */
          for(k=1;k<n;k++)printf("%10.6f   ",inv[j][k]);
          printf("\n");
     }
}
```

Figure 9.11. Main C program to solve matrix equations.
Language: C.

9.7. SOLVING DIFFERENTIAL EQUATIONS NUMERICALLY

We now move on to a more advanced area of numerical analysis—solving differential equations. Although a numerical solution to a differential equation may not be as intellectually satisfying as an analytical one, once the method of numerical solution is available, solutions to a large class of differential equations may be found relatively easily.

The simplest class of differential equations for which a numerical solution can be found is the first-order system

$$\frac{dy}{dx} = f(x,y)$$

This equation has the general solution

$$y(x) = y(a) + \int_a^x f(x',y)\ dx'$$

In the general case, where y can appear on both sides of this equation, the solution can be difficult. There are many numerical solution methods for such differential equations. One of the most accurate and general is the *Adams predictor corrector* method.

Predictor corrector methods consist of using two formulae in combination to obtain the most accurate possible approximation to the solution of the differential equation. One of the fomulae is explicit, the other implicit. The explicit (predictor) formula shown below makes a first attempt at obtaining the value of the solution of the equation at its $(k + 1)$st position, corresponding to x_{k+1} when the solution is known at k and $k-1$.

$$y^P_{k+1} = y_k + h_2\ [3\ f(x_k,y_k) - f(x_{k-1},y_{k-1})]$$

It may be shown that a better approximation to the solution at $k+1$ may be obtained by substituting this value of y into the corrector formula below:

$$y^c_{k+1} = y_k + h_2\ [f(x_{k+1},y^P_{k+1}) + f(x_k,y_k)]$$

The predictor corrector formulae are preferred over less sophisticated methods, since the difference $y^p - y^c$ is an indicator of the magnitude of the error accumulated during a numerical solution exercise.

To obtain a proper numerical solution to a differential equation, we need a boundary value for y to be specified at the beginning of the solution. There is also the question of how to initiate the numerical solution, since at $k=1$ we have no $k-1$ value to put into the above equations. The most popular method, and the one that is utilized in our library programs, is to use the Newton–Raphson method, which is an explicit equation to obtain this first point. The above equations can be used for all subsequent points in the solution.

Having the computational tools to solve only a first-order differential equation is somewhat limiting if we wish to build up a library of routines to solve truly representative physical or engineering problems. Second order differential equations occur often in modeling calculations.

In numerical analysis the most straightforward method of solving second-order equations is to reduce them to a series of coupled first-order equations:

$$\frac{dy}{dx} = f(x, y, z) \qquad \frac{dz}{dx} = g(x, y, z)$$

The solution of such first-order coupled equations is a direct generalization of the predictor corrector methods already discussed, where now we have three variables in each of the functions on the right-hand side instead of two. We need boundary condition values now for y and z as a starting point of the solution.

The I/O list for the numerical function library module for solving differential equation is shown in Table 9.16. The programs for solving a single and a dual set of single-order differential equations are listed in the Appendixes. Examples and a further discussion of both of these techniques are given later.

As a simple example, let us consider the first-order differential equation

$$\frac{dy}{dx} - xy = x^3$$

which we wish to solve between $x=0$ and $x=2$ with the boundary condition $y=0$ at $x=0$. This equation is soluble analytically*, as substituting the following in the differential equation will show.

$$y(x) = -2 - x^2 + \exp\left(\frac{x2}{2}\right)$$

To find the solution $y(x)$ numerically using the first-order library routine (option 1), we rewrite the equation as

$$\frac{dy}{dx} = xy + x^3 = f(x)$$

The program in Figure 9.12 may be used in combination with the library routine to give the solution.

A graph of the numerical solution is shown in Figure 9.13. Also shown at regular intervals on this figure are the exact solution points from the true analytical solution represented as shaded triangles.

*R. Becket and J. Hurt, *Numerical Calculations and Algorithms* (McGraw-Hill, New York, 1967).

Table 9.16. Parameter List for Differential Equation Module

OPTION	MBASIC VARIABLES Calling	MBASIC VARIABLES Return	DESCRIPTION	C variable
1			Predictor Corrector Solution of Single First-Order DE	
		BASIC Call	NDIFFEQ%=1:GOSUB 15000	
		C Call	diff_pc1(f,a,b,n,eta,&x,&y,&e)	
	F=f(X,Y)		Function f( ) in equation $dy/dx=f(x,y)f(x,y)$ *BASIC: Function subroutine at 10500* *C : Function passed by pointer*	
	A		*Initial* x-value of solution.	a
	B		Final x-value of solution.	b
	NDIV		There are ndiv+1 solution points in the array elements $0 \rightarrow$ ndiv.	n
	ETA		Boundary condition *y(a)*.	eta
		XARRAY()	Solution x-values array.	x[]
		YARRAY()	Solution y-values array.	y[]
		ERROR()	Error estimate at each x.	e[]
2			Predictor Corrector Solution of two First-Order Equations	
		BASIC Call	NDIFFEQ%=2:GOSUB 15000	
		C Call	diff_pc(f,g,a,b,n,eta,psi,&x,&y,&z)	
	F=f(X,Y,Z)		Function f in equation $dy/dx = f(x, y, z)$	f(x,y,z)
	G=g(X,Y,Z)		Function g in equation $dz/dx = g(x, y, z)$	g(x,y,z)
	A,B,NDIV		Same as above	a,b,n
	ETA		Boundary condition *y* at *x=a*	eta
	PSI		Boundary condition $z = dy/dx$ at *x=a*	psi
		XARRAY()	Same as option 1	x[]
		YARRAY()	" "	y[]
		ZARRAY()	Solution z-value array	z[]

```
10 DEFDBL A-H,O-Z : DEFINT I-N        :REM initialize system
20 REM------------------------ First order DE test
90      CHAIN MERGE"B:DIFFEQ.LIB",100  :REM merge library module
100     DIM XARRAY(500),YARRAY(500),ZARRAY(500),ERRORY(500)
110     A = 0# : B = 2#                :REM set x limits
120     ETA = 0#                       :REM boundary condition on y
130     NDIV = 200                     :REM ndiv+1 solution points
140     NDIFFEQ% = 1 : GOSUB 16000     :REM call library routine
150     PRINT "SOLUTION OF DIFFERENTIAL EQUATION"
160     FOR I=0 TO NDIV                :REM screen display of data
170         PRINT I,XARRAY(I),YARRAY(I)
180     NEXT I
170 END
10900 REM-------------------- Function Subroutine
10910      F = X * ( Y + X * X )       :REM function dy/dx = f(x,y)
10930 RETURN
```

Figure 9.12. BASICA program to solve first-order DE.

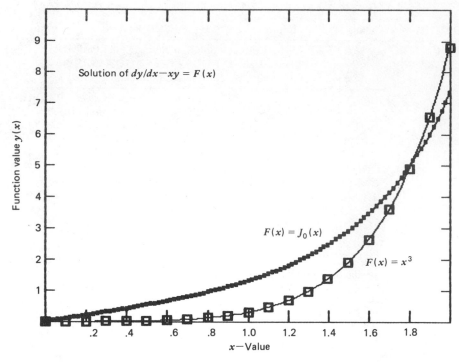

Figure 9.13. Graphical solution representation to the first-order differential equation $dy/dx - xy = F(x)$.

It is possible to choose any form for the function $f(x, y)$. As an example let us substitute the zero-order Bessel function of the first kind for the x^3 term in the above equation:

$$\frac{dy}{dx} - xy = J_0(x)$$

The solution of this equation is also shown in Figure 9.13. It is left as an exercise to the reader to come up with the program to carry out this solution.

To illustrate the use of numerical analysis techniques for the solution of second-order differential equation, we consider the Schroedinger wave equation for a harmonic oscillator. The wave equation may be written in dimensionless form as

$$\frac{d^2y}{dx^2} - (x^2 - E_{vib})y = 0$$

where $|y(x)|^2 \, dx$ is the probability of finding a particle with total energy E_{vib} at a position x within a finite element dx. The equation defines the quantum solution of a vibrating system of two atoms separated by an equilibrium distance $x+x_0$. The particles are bound together by a perfect, spring-type force having a force constant k, and the equilibrium separation distance of the atoms is x_0. It may be shown that a physically acceptable solution to this equation only occurs when the vibrational energy E_{vib} takes on the discrete values*

$$E_{vib} = 2\left(v+\frac{1}{2}\right)$$

where the vibrational quantum number v can only take on integer values $v=0$, 1, 2, ...

We may rewrite the equations as

$$\frac{dz}{dx} = x^2-2\left(v+\frac{1}{2}\right) = g(x), \quad \text{and} \quad \frac{dy}{dx} = z = f(z)$$

The major difficulty in numerically solving such a set of equations centers on the correct choice of boundary conditions. For a second-order equation it is necessary to specify the value of y and dy/dx (or z) at the starting point of the solution. In such a situation additional information about the system is used to arrive at reasonable values of the boundary conditions and, thus, an acceptable solution.

In the problem being considered here we use symmetry considerations about the starting point $x=0$. The wave function $y(x)$ can only have one or other of the following characteristics about the symmetry point $x=0$:

1. Symmetric solution: $dy(0)/dx = 0$ and $y(0)\neq 0$
2. Asymmetric solution: $y(0) = 0$ and $dy(0)/dx\neq 0$.

We have no prior knowledge to allow us to choose between these two possibilities and to set a value for the nonzero boundary condition in either case. But again we have prior knowledge that will allow us to find a unique solution. First we know that since $|y(x)|^2$ represents a probability density, then as $x \rightarrow \infty$ $y \rightarrow 0$. Only one of the two solutions for a particular vibrational level will satisfy this condition on $y(x)$. Second, the integrated probability density over all x may be normalized to unity. We will choose an arbitrary value for the nonzero boundary condition and, from the integrated density, scale the points and the boundary condition to yield the correct wave function $y(x)$.

A C program to find the solution of these coupled equations is shown in Figure 9.14. The functions $f(x, y, z)$ and $g(x, y, z)$ are represented by C functions, which are listed as part of this program. The names of these functions are passed to the library program as pointers through the function

*K.J. Johnson, *Numerical Methods in Chemistry* (Marcel Dekker, New York, 1980).

```
/*          Second-Order Differential Equation Test        *
 *              Solution of Schrodinger equation           *
 *                   for Harmonic Oscillator              */

#include "libc.h"
#include "math.h"
#include "b:numrcl.h"

#define NP 300

static double energy;

main(){
      double x[300],y[300],z[300];
      double a,b,eta,psi,f(),g();
      int i, ndiv,nprnt;
/*                      enter parameters                  */

      printf("enter energy value\n");
      scanf("%f",&energy);
      printf("enter x boundary values a and b\n");
      scanf("%f %f",&a,&b);
      printf("enter boundary conditions eta and psi\n");
      scanf("%f %f",&eta,&psi);
      printf("divide the solution into ndiv steps\n");
      scanf("%d",&ndiv);
/*           solve second-order differential equation      *
 *                  and print data on screen              */
      diff_pc2(f,g,a,b,ndiv,eta,psi,&x,&y,&z,nprnt=1);
}
/*      these are the f and g functions                    *
 *      where dy/dx = f(x,y,z)      dz/dx = g(x,y,z)        *
 *      There must be the three arguments x, y, z         */

double f(x, y, z)
double x, y, z;
{
  return (z);
}

double g(x, y, z)
double x, y, z;
{
  return (x*x-energy)*y;
}
```

Figure 9.14.   C program for the solution of a second-order DE.

arguments. The main program has been written so that most of the important parameters in the solution may be input at the keyboard through the C function scanf( ). All parameters other than x, y, z must be passed to the functions x and g as global variables.

Assuming that we had no prior knowledge as to the values of the eigenvalues (energy solutions), we could attempt to find them by trial and error, using this program. The result of doing this is shown in Figure 9.15. Here we demonstrate a number of solution attempts around the lowest acceptable energy solution corresponding to the $v=0$ solution (i.e., an *energy* value of 1). The graphs show that only the even solution is acceptable, and that as we change the energy by $+dE$ the solutions blow up in the tail at $x=|4|$. The odd symmetry solution is totally nonphysical.

The numerical solutions to the equation do not exactly coincide with the exact eigenvalues obtained from the analytical solution—namely, unity in this case. The discrepancy is a function of the number of points used in the solution, as shown in Table 9.17.

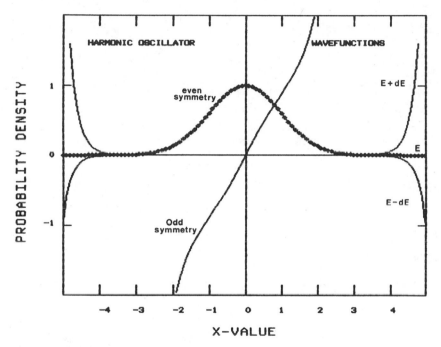

Figure 9.15. Convergent and nonconvergent solutions to lowest energy ($v = 0$) harmonic oscillator eigenfunction. Only the even symmetry solution $E_{vib} = 1$ converges at high $|x|$.

Table 9.17. Numerically Determined Eigenvalues for Different Solution Meshes

Solution Points	Eigenvalue
40	1.0011623
80	1.0003073
160	1.0000777

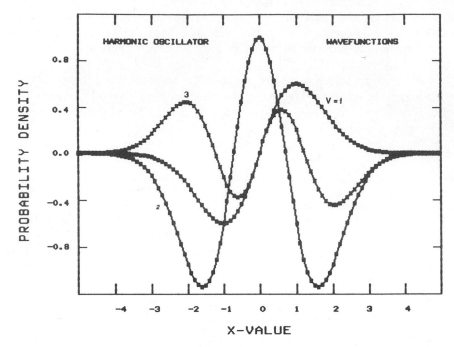

Figure 9.16. Numerically determined eigenfunction for $v = 1, 2, 3$ harmonic oscillator solutions.

The result of solving for a number of vibrational quantum numbers v is shown in Figure 9.16. The wave-function solutions for $v=1, 2, 3$ are shown on this figure as continuous lines. Also shown on this figure are the analytical solutions based on Hermite polynomials,* shown as squares and triangles.

9.8.   SIMULATING DATA NOISE

To test some of the programming methods to be discussed in Chapter 10, we must be able to simulate data sets that have random errors superimposed on a known functional dependence. The BASICA/MBASIC random number generator RND may be used for such an operation. For the C language the function ran( ) may be used. The uniform probability distributions obtained with these functions do not represent the majority of real-life situations.

Most computer-language, random number generators produce random numbers with a uniform probability distribution in the range 0 to 1. In the language of probability theory of BASICA/MBASIC or C random number generators produce random deviates from a uniform distribution on the inter-

---

*L.I. Schiff, *Quantum Mechanics* (McGraw-Hill, New York, 1968).

val (0, 1). Real data noise, on the other hand, follows one of a number of statistical distributions. The most common one found in practice, called the
normal distribution, is represented by a Gaussian error probability function
about a given mean.

We use an algorithm from the *Handbook of Mathematical Functions** for
producing a normal probability noise distribution on a data array set. The I/O
lists for the BASIC and C routines are given in Table 9.18. The routines take in
an array YARRAY(I) of data points, with each number having a corresponding variance.

Three different forms of the variance are provided in the data input specified
by the parameter MODE. A single variance may be specified for the complete
data array inputted in the zero-variable element SIGMALL. Alternatively,
individual variances may be specified for each data point by the array
SIGMA(1)...SIGMA(NPTS) and specified by the user in the calling routine.
Finally, a third option allows a Poisson distribution to be specified, where the
variances are determined from the data array itself.

Table 9.18.   Parameter List for Data Noise Generator

MBASIC VARIABLES

Calling	Return	DESCRIPTION	variable
Generates Random Noise with a Normal Distribution on an Array of Data			
	BASIC Call	GOSUB 12800	
	C Call	noise(npts,mode,&yarray,&sigma)	
NPTS		Number of points in data set.	n
YARRAY()		The data array YARRAY(1)... YARRAY(NPTS).	yarray[]
MODE		mode=0; variance SIGMALL for entire set	mode
		mode=1; individual variances SIGMA(I).	
		=2; Poisson SIGMA(I) = SQR(YARRAY(I)) auto- matically calculated.	
SIGMALL		Single variance for array, used in mode 0.	sigmall
SIGMA()		Individual variances, used in mode 1.	sigma[]
	YARRAY()	Data with random errors super- imposed. Returned in same array and destroys original data.	y[]

---

*M. Abramowitz and I.A. Stegun, *Handbook of Mathematical Functions*, 9th ed. (Dover, New
York, 1972).

Although the BASICA/MBASIC random-number generator is easy to use, you should be aware of the limitations of the generator in practice. At the beginning of a BASIC program using the generator, it is desirable to *seed* the generator with the RANDOMIZE function. The following program segment illustrates this:

```
 5 SEED = 5
10 RANDOMIZE SEED
20 FOR I = 1 TO 10
30 PRINT RND
40 NEXT
```

If this program is run a number of times, we come up with the rather surprising result that the same sequence of random numbers will be generated. Although the individual numbers in the set are random with respect to each other, they are not random if two of the sets are compared, unless one seeds the generator with a different SEED number. The seed number can lie in the range −32768 to 32767.

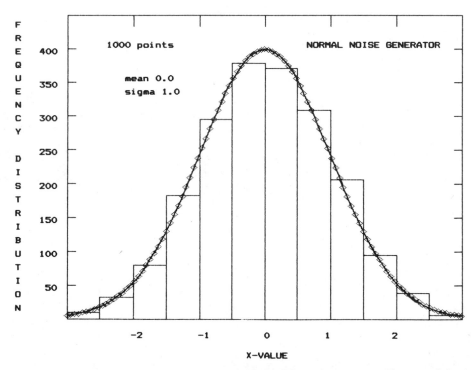

Figure 9.17. Normal distribution generated with BASICA noise generator library module.

The C data noise generator is based on the same algorithm and has the same I/O requirements as the BASIC routine. The C function requires the random number generator function ran ( ), which should be available in the C mathematical library. If this function is not available, a random number generator function may be written by using information provided in the *Handbook of Mathematical Functions** or another similar text.

The graphs in Figure 9.17 show a histogram distribution of 1000 generated points using the BASICA noise program with a bin width of 0.5, MODE=0, an array initially filled with zeros, and a value of SIGMALL(0) for the entire array of unity. Also shown on this figure is the normal curve about zero with unity variance.

9.9. SOLVING MODELS WITH TKSOLVER

Modeling is an important technique in many engineering or scientific applications. One of the most valuable commercial software packages available for mathematical model solving is TKSolver.[†] The software was developed by Software Arts, who were also responsible for the creation of VISICALC.[†] The program is available for the IBM-PC and also runs on most MS-DOS computer systems.

A complex mathematical model may involve a large number of highly coupled equations and related variable. The TKSolver program provides an environment in which the equations and related data may be organized and the model solved for the unknown variable or variables. The TKSolver software package virtually eliminates the necessity to develop solution algorithms and write software. An engineering model once created may be easily modified and expanded with a view to gaining further insight into the model behavior.

The TKSolver program is far too complex and has too many features for us to be able to do it justice in the space we have available. We will describe the program in the barest detail and also describe the method of setup and solution of an engineering model, chosen specifically for its numerical complexity, to demonstrate the versatility of the program.

9.9.1. Overview

The TKSolver software centers on a number of basic features that provide a unique working environment for problem solving. The program may be operated in one of two solution modes.

1. Direct solver.
2. Iterative solver.

*Abramowitz and Stegun, loc. cit.

[†]TKSolver is a trademark of Software Arts, Inc., 27 Mica Lane, Wellesley, MA 02181.

The *direct solver* works on a procedure of consecutive substitutions and may be used in cases where an explicit algebraic solution form is possible. It is not necessary for the user to find the explicit algebraic solution, since the program carries out the procedure automatically by a process of backsolving.

The *iterative solver* must be used for more complex problems in which variable or variables cannot be solved for explicitly. The program uses a modified Newton–Raphson iterative procedure to obtain a solution. It analyzes the set of equations at each point in the solution and tests how far the current set of values is away from the converged solution. It varies the unknowns and monitors the error behavior in arriving at a new set of guesses until convergence on a solution is reached.

Another extremely important feature of the program is the ability to keep track of unit conversions in a consistent manner. This is a particularly desirable feature from the standpoint of many of the complex models that may be carried out in engineering. The unit conversion feature is part of a larger environment of the I/O user interface. The I/O sheets described below are filled by the user using a simple screen editor provided as part of the programming package. An on-line help feature may be invoked from the editing environment where needed. Other worthwhile features of the TKSolver problem-solving environment are the ability to read and write data from DIF files, which allows data to be exchanged with the other powerful programs, such as VISICALC; and the ability to tabulate results and carry out simple graphing operations to demonstrate data trends.

The TKSolver program centers around the use of *sheets* that help organize the model solution in a structured fashion. There are eight sheets and three subsheets available in the program. A brief description of the sheets is given in Table 9.19. In most cases the sheet names are self-explanatory. The TKSolver RULE sheet brings a new concept to programming. Although the equations on a RULE sheet may look like the equations written down in any high-level computer language, in TKSolver the rules represent relationships between variables rather than language instructions. Thus, complex equation such as

$$3*Y^2 + 2*Y = COS(X)$$

would be illegal in C or BASIC or any other high-level language since in these languages the equals sign signifies "replace the contents of the variable with", which requires a single variable name on the lhs. Under TKSolver it is perfectly legal to ask the program to solve for the x value for a given value of y in the above equation by the backsolving method.

The TKSolver program will solve a complex series of connected equations for a single unknown variable that may be present in a number of the equations on the RULE sheet. The TKSolver package has two approaches to solving a set of equations. The direct solver is used in situations where an explicit form for the variable to be solved, in terms of all the other variables in the model, may be found. It is not necessary to enter the equations on the RULE sheet in an

Table 9.19. Sheets and Subsheets in the TKSolver Program

Variable Sheets	
RULE	Contains the equations that comprise the mathematical models that need to be solved. These rules must be typed in by the user or entered from disk.
VARIABLE	Contains the variables that are contained on the RULE sheet together with the values, units, and relevant comments. Much of this sheet is filled in automatically from the Rule sheet.
UNITS	Contains unit conversion information if one wishes to use alternative units to those specified on the RULE sheet.
GLOBAL	Contains information on the program's global default settings (machine dependent).
LIST	Contains a table of all the lists created in the program. A list of values might be created when one solves a set of equations for a dependent variable at a number of values of an independent variable.
USER FUNCTION	TKSolver has a large number of built-in functions. It is possible for the user to define other functions that are placed in the list on this sheet. The functions may be a set of numerical data related to a collection of names.
PLOT	Contains all information necessary to plot the data on the console in character graphics.
TABLE	Contains the information necessary to display a table of list values. It is used to organize the data to be printed out.
Variable Subsheets	
VARIABLE	The display of the complete information related to a single variable on the VARIABLE sheet.
LIST	Contains further information on a single variable on the list sheet.
USER FUNCTION	The subsheet may be used to display the data set or equation(s) that make up an individual function on the USER sheet.

explicit form, only that such a relationship is possible. The direct solver attempts to solve every equation in a model. As it satisfies the equality conditions, it uses the values it has determined in the solution process for one equation to satisfy other equations. Finally, the single unknown for which the solution needs to be determined will be found.

In many cases a model is too complex to be solved directly. The TKSolver program has an iterative option that may be invoked in such cases. This section of TKSolver may be used to solve for any intermediate and/or final variables that are not explicitly representable in terms of the already determined or specified variables. Initial guess values must be entered by the operator for all

Table 9.20.

TKSolver Mathematical Functions

ABS	ACOS	ACOSH	ASIN	ASINH
ATAN	ATANH	COS	COSH	EXP
LN	LOG	MOD	SIN	SINH
TAN	TANH			

Other TKSolver Functions

APPLY	ATAN2	COUNT	DOT	E
ELEMENT	GIVEN	INT	MAX	MIN
NPV	PI	POLY	SGN	SQRT
STEP	SUM			

variables that have to be determined with the iterative solver. The GLOBAL sheet contains the default values for some of the parameters that are required in an iterative solution, such as the maximum number of iterations to be attempted before abandoning the solution process. The program automatically invokes the direct solver for variables that can be solved for explicitly and solves the remainder by the iterative technique.

In the model solving, equations that are used often in a range of modeling applications may be defined as explicit functions. These supplement a set of mathematical functions that are available in TKSolver. The standard function list is more comprehensive than is available in the majority of high-level languages. These functions are listed in Table 9.20.

The contents of these lists are too long to describe in detail. The mathematical function operators are self-explanatory. The remaining TKSolver functions offer some extremely convenient operations that can make the task of model writing much easier. In particular, the MAX and MIN functions may be used to find the maximum and minimum of a list of numbers, and the COUNT function gives the number of elements in a list. The POLY(x,series) is used to calculate the value of a polynomial at x, where the series parameter contains the coefficients of the polynomial. A number of operations in the second list act on complete arrays of data.

The TKSolver package carries out arithmetic operations in double precision (11 to 12 significant digits). The package uses a modified Newton–Raphson iterative procedure for the model solution.

9.9.2.   A Modeling Test for TKSolver

To test the capabilities of TKSolver, we chose a highly coupled set of equations in which the same variable occurs in a number of complex-looking equations.

The problem chosen was taken from Miller's book,* a definitive work on engineering flow. We chose a problem that was not only difficult to solve manually but also had been thoroughly worked out, so that we would be able to compare the resulting solutions with those in the reference.

The problem is an interesting one that involves designing an orifice to meet a specific flow measurement application for a specified flow. In many industrial engineering applications it is necessary to measure liquid, gas, or vapor flows through a pipe. One of the more common methods is to place an orifice plate of a specified diameter in the flow stream, as is shown in Figure 9.18, and measure the pressure drop across the orifice plate with a differential pressure (D/P) cell. If we use different diameter orifice plates, different flow ranges may be accommodated with the same D/P cell and the same pipe diameter. The task of designing the system is one of obtaining the orifice diameter d for the specified flow. TKSolver is well matched to this kind of task in helping to organize the problem in a methodical manner and also in keeping track of the engineering units used in such calculations.

It is worth spending time discussing the equations that are to be solved in such a case. The major equation describing the mass flow rate q_m through the orifice is simply

$$q_M = N_{M\rho} K Y_I F_a' d^2 \sqrt{h_w \rho_{fl}}$$

We wish to solve for the variable d, which occurs explicitly on the rhs of the equation. Each of the other terms on the rhs also contain a dependence on d, which makes solving the equations nontrivial. In certain cases not specifically addressed here, the terms may also depend on q_M, h_w, and the properties associated with the fluid.

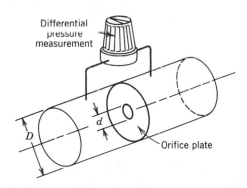

Figure 9.18. A schematic diagram of the differential pressure flow measurement.

*R.W. Miller, *Flow Measurement Engineering Handbook* (McGraw-Hill, New York, 1983).

The complete set of coupled equations containing all the information necessary to model the flow problem is shown in Figure 9.19. We cannot expect the reader to grasp the full significance of these equations without a careful study of Miller's book. What we do wish to bring to the attention of the reader is the form that the equations take and the steps that would be necessary to solve the equation set form first principles. The variable to be solved for, namely d, occurs in these equations in such a highly connected manner that a direct solution is obviously impossible. We show the RULE and VARIABLE sheets for this problem in Figures 9.20 and 9.21. We wish to solve the model for the variable d for a list of possible maximum flow rates q_M.

The basic flow equation
$$q_M = N_{M\rho}KY_1F_a'd^2 \sqrt{h_w\rho_{fl}}$$

Flow Coefficient
$$K = \frac{C}{\sqrt{1 - \beta^4}}$$

where $\beta = \dfrac{d}{D}$ and $C = C_\infty + \dfrac{b}{R_D^n}$

where $C_\infty = 0.5959 + 0.0312\beta^{2.1} - 0.184\beta^8$
$$+ 0.09 \frac{\beta^4}{D(1-\beta^4)} - 0.0337\frac{\beta^3}{D}$$

$$b = 91.71\beta^{2.5}$$

$$R_D = \left[2266.97 \frac{1}{\mu_{cD}DN_{M\rho}} \right] qM$$

Gas Expansion Factor
$$Y_1 = 1 - (0.41 + 0.35\beta^4) \frac{h_w}{27.73P_{f1}k}$$

with $k = \dfrac{(C_p)_i}{((C_p)_i - 1.986)}$

and $(C_p)_i = 19.86 - \dfrac{597}{\sqrt{T}} + \dfrac{7500}{T}$

$$F_a = 1 + 2\alpha_{PE}(T_R - 68)$$

Figure 9.19. The coupled set of flow equations describing the differential pressure flow measurement.

```
S  RULE
-------
*  qM = Nmrho * K * Y1 * Fa * d^2 * sqrt(hw * rho_fi)
*  K = C / sqrt(1-beta^4)
*  beta = d / D
*  C = Cinf + b/ RD^n
*  Cinf1 = 0.5959 + 0.0312 * beta^2.1 - 0.184 * beta^8
*  Cinf = Cinf1 + 0.09 * (beta^4 / (D*(1-beta^4))) - 0.0337 * beta^3 /D
*  RD = 2266.97 * qM / (mu_op * D * Nmrho)
*  Y1 = 1 - (0.41 + 0.35 * beta^4) * hw / (27.73 * Pf1 * k)
*  k = Cpi / (Cpi - 1.986)
*  Cpi = 19.86 - 597 / sqrt(T) + 7500 / T
*  T = 459.67 + TF
*  Fa = 1 + 2 * alphaPE * (TF -68)
*  b = 91.71 * beta^2.5
```

Figure 9.20. The TKSolver RULE sheet describing the flow measurement.

St Input	Name	Output	Unit	Comment
24000	qM		lb/hr	
358.93	Nmrho			
	K	.72151106		
	Y1	.99554357		
	Fa	1.0075264		
	d	4.2860840		
64	hw		in_H20	
.39524	rho_fi		lb/ft^3	
	C	.60090502		
	beta	.74398264		
5.761	D		in	
	Cinf	.59988659		
	b	43.701033		
	RD	1506109.2		
.75	n			
	Cinf1	.59539516		
.01747	mu_op		cP	
204	Pf1		psia	
	k	1.3130980		
	Cpi	8.3290610		
	T	919.67		
460	TF		oF	
.0000096	alphaPE		in/(in*oF)	

Figure 9.21. The TKSolver VARIABLE sheet.

First the RULE sheet must be filled out with all the pertinent equations for our model. As each equation (rule) is entered, the variables are automatically placed on the VARIABLE sheet. TKSolver tests to see if the variable is already on the sheet from a previously entered rule and, if not, includes the new information on the sheet. Next, all known numerical variable values are entered in the leftmost column of the variable sheet as input data. Units and

```
            Orifice diameter calculation
    Flow(lb/hr)                 Orif.Dia.(in)
       20000                    4.001216005
       21000                    4.07765725
       22000                    4.150483054
       23000                    4.219897516
       24000                    4.286083975
       25000                    4.349207905
       26000                    4.409419401
       27000                    4.466855338
       28000                    4.521641264
       29000                    4.573893063
       30000                    4.623718419
```

Figure 9.22.   The solution list for the TKSolver solution.

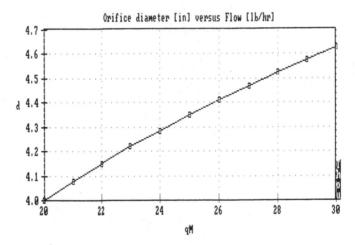

Figure 9.23.   A graphical presentation of the data with VISIPLOT.

comments may also be entered in the right columns. This is extremely useful, since the user does not have to continuously check for unit conversions because the program adapts to all units (United States and SI, for example).

We may now proceed with the solution. The direct solver solves the set of equations for as many variables as possible and lists the calculated values in the output column. Next, the iterative solver takes over and solves the system for the remaining variable(s). The iterative solution requires that a first guess be entered into the input column for all the variables to be determined by the iterative solver. The final answer, for d in this case, is put into the output column, as we show in Figure 9.21.

We wish to take our model further by solving for a complete list of maximum flow rates q_M and determining the corresponding orifice diameters d. The final LIST sheet is shown in Figure 9.22. The sheet had to be filled with the first-guess values for each entry. The solution data from the LIST sheet may be stored in a DIF file. We show the result of plotting this data with VISIPLOT in Figure 9.23.

10

Analysis of Experimental Data

Thus far we have discussed methods of acquiring experimental data in the laboratory, methods of storing the data efficiently, and methods of presenting the data graphically. There remains the subject of data analysis (data reduction), where in many cases the raw data must have some operation performed on it in order to obtain a meaningful interpretation.

We begin this chapter with a discussion of curve fitting to experimental data. Examples are given for the curve fitting of linear, polynomial, and nonlinear functional dependencies. We follow this with a generalized treatment of filtering and smoothing of experimental data, which is often encountered in spectroscopy and chromatography—that is, any data set acquired at equal increments along the x-axis. Finally, in Section 10.3, we introduce the important technique of Fourier analysis, a powerful tool for the treatment of experimental data.

In Table 10.1 we show the list of library routines that may be used to carry out some of the operations discussed in this chapter. The layout and nomenclature of these routines follows exactly what has been presented for the numerical analysis programs discussed in Chapter 9. Library routines are presented in both the BASICA and C languages for most of the operations. Program listings are given in the appendixes.

All the data analysis operations described in this chapter are assumed to be operations carried out on numerical data after the fact—that is, once the complete data set has been acquired and possibly stored on disk. In certain cases real-time software analysis of the data is necessary. In Chapter 11 we discuss an example of writing a real-time, boxcar average program in assembly language.

10.1. LINEAR REGRESSION ANALYSIS

Linear regression analysis involves fitting a best-fit straight line to a series of (x, y) data points. It is one of the simplest operations that may be applied to real data. We have a series of $1 \ldots N_p$ of data pairs (x_i, y_i), and we wish to find the constants a and b corresponding to the best-fit straight line $y = a + bx$. The

Table 10.1.   The Numerical Data Analysis Library

Description	BASICA			C
	File	Starting line	Option #	Function
Linear least squares module	LINRFIT.LIB			
solve for fitted constants		17000		linear_fit( )
Polynomial least squares fitting module				
	POLYFIT.LIB			
(a) Fitted constants to n degree polynomial		18000	1	poly_fit( )
(b) Calculation of probable error			2	
Nonlinear least squares fitting module				
	NONLNFIT.LIB			
(a) Fitted constants to function		19000	1	nonlnr_fit()
(b) Calculation of probable error			2	
Filtering Program	SMOOTH.LIB			
(a) Savitsky--Golay data filter		21000	—	—
Fast Fourier Transform	FFT.LIB			
(a) fft for N=2^m points		20000	1	fft( )
(b) Convolution f*g			2	fft_cnvl( )
Utility Function				
Weight function for fitting routines				weight( )

subject of linear regression has been covered many times in the literature.[*] The assumption usually made, and the one we follow, is that only one of the variables, usually y (labeled the dependent variable), has any error connected with it. The other variable, x, the independent variable, is assumed to be known to infinite precision. The reader is referred to the literature for a comprehensive discussion of linear regression analysis when both variables may have errors connected with them.[†]

We follow the notation given in the classical work on the subject of data fitting by Bevington. Our discussion will be limited to that which is required for the user to utilize the programs in MBASIC/BASICA and C listed in the appendixes.

A typical data distribution on which a linear regression has been applied is shown in Figure 10.1. The points y_i are the y-values of the experimental data points corresponding to the x data points x_i. The y-value of the best-fit straight

[*]P. R. Bevington, *Data Reduction and Error Analysis for the Physical Sciences* (McGraw-Hill, New York, 1969).

[†]M. T. Lybanon, in *Am. J. Phys.* **32**, 22 (1984).

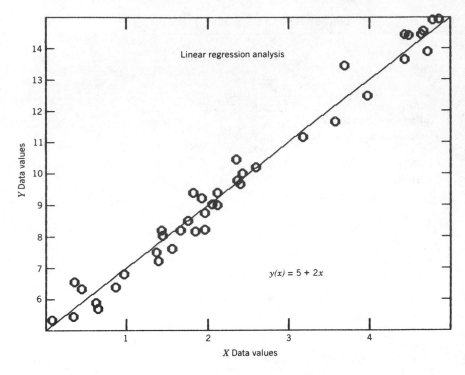

Figure 10.1.   A linear least squares fit example. Open circles are the data to be fit, generated from $y = 2x + 5$ with statistical noise superimposed. The line is the least squares fit straight line with constants found from the results of running the program in Figure 10.2.

line corresponding to this x_i is $y_L(x_i)$. The best-fit straight line is found by minimizing the χ^2 function:

$$\chi^2 = \sum_{i=1}^{N_p} w_i \; (y_i - y(x_i))^2$$

The weighting factor w_i is included so that the same formula may be applied to data that are governed by different statistical distributions. The three types of weighting factors included in all the least squares programs in this book are:

1.   Instrumental weight $w_i = 1/\sigma_i^2$.
2.   Equal weight $w_i = 1$.
3.   Statistical weight $w_i = 1/y_i$.

Instrumental weight is the most general. It applies to a situation in which each data point in the linear regression is itself the result of a number of measurements that have been averaged, so that we have prior knowledge of the standard deviation σ. Alternatively, the statistical noise distribution is known from the particular experiment where the data was collected. The *equal weight factor* is best used when no prior knowledge exists about the statistical noise distribution for a particular experiment. Finally, the *statistical weight factor* is used when the noise variance depends on the square root of the signal itself. This is the noise distribution expected in many counting experiments in physics, where the Poisson distribution approximates a normal distribution with the variance increasing with the square root of the signal itself.

It should be noted that it is only the relative distribution of the weighting factors between the points that is important. The same fitted parameters will be obtained by multiplying each weighting factor in the data series by a constant.

The best-fit straight line constants a and b are found from the solution of the matrix equation:

$$\left| \begin{matrix} \sum\limits_{i=1}^{N_p} w_i & \sum w_i x_i \\ \\ \sum w_i x_i & \sum w_i x_i^2 \end{matrix} \right| \left| \begin{matrix} a \\ \\ b \end{matrix} \right| = \left| \begin{matrix} \sum w_i y_i \\ \\ \sum w_i x_i y_i \end{matrix} \right|$$

This is a special case of the general polynomial fitting method described in the next subsection. The solution of the above equation for a and b is trivial in the case of a 2×2 matrix. The solution is carried out directly without using the matrix-equation solution technique presented in the last chapter. The summations are carried out over the complete data set.

In fitting such a set of data points, we are interested both in the optimum parameters a and b and some measure of the uncertainties in the fitted parameters based on the data being fitted. Uncertainties σ_a and σ_b may be determined from the data series corresponding to the 50% probability that the true values of a and b lie within the band $\pm \sigma_{a,b}$ of the mean.

The final important parameter in linear regression analysis is the correlation coefficient r between the (x, y) data points. This is a measure of the validity of using a linear least squares approximation for the data. Data which is perfectly represented by a linear least squares approximation will have a correlation coefficient of ± 1, depending on the sign of the gradient (slope) b. Uncorrelated data, however, has a correlation coefficient of zero.

The I/O list for the linear regression analysis library program is shown in Table 10.2. The interpretation of the BASIC and C parameters should be straightforward from this table and the above discussion. For the C implementation the fitted parameters and resulting errors are returned to the calling program in a C data structure lnr, the individual elements of which are represented by a dot extension, such as lnr.a, and so on. The structure is declared in

Table 10.2.   Linear Least Squares Fit

OPTION	MBASIC VARIABLES		DESCRIPTION	C variable
	Calling	Return		
			Linear Least Squares Fit to the Function $y = a + bx$	
		BASIC Call	GOSUB 15000	
		C Call	Linear_fit(npts,mode,&x,&y,&sigmay,&lnr)	
NPTS			Number N_p (x, y) data pairs to be fit.	npts
XARRAY()			x-values of (x, y) data pairs to be fitted XARRAY(1)...XARRAY(NPTS).	x[]
YARRAY()			Corresponding y-values to be fitted in YARRAY(1)...YARRAY(NPTS).	y[]
MODE			Weighing factor choice in fit = 0; instrumental weight. = 1; equal weights. = 2; statistical weights.	mode
SIGMAY()			Variance needed in weighing factor; only used for mode = 0.	sigmay[]
		AFIT	Fitted a value.	lnr.a
		BFIT	Fitted b value.	lnr.b
		AERROR	Probable error in a.	lnr.sigmaa
		BERROR	Probable error in b.	lnr.sigmab
		RCORRLN	Correlation coefficient r.	lnr.r
		CHISQ	Chi-squared valve of fit.	lnr.chi-sq

the header file b:nmrcl.h, which is declared at the beginning of the main and library programs. This file is listed in Appendix D.

The C program of Figure 10.2 shows the organization of a main program suitable for testing the linear-fit library function. First we generate a set of 40 data points. The x-values are randomly selected in the region $0 \rightarrow 5$. The y-values are generated for the curve $y = 5 + 2x$. Then we superimpose statistical noise corresponding to a single sigmall (mode=0) entered at the keyboard. Finally, the linear-fit function linear_fit() is used to find the best-fit parameters together with the computed probable errors and the correlation coefficient.

For an entered sigmall of 0.1, for the Noise generator, the following fitted parameters were determined:

```
     a = 5.006769 ± 0.039132
     b = 1.988880 ± 0.013191
     r = 0.999165
chi_sq = 1.29992e-02
```

This is the data presented in Figure 10.1.

```
#include "libc.h"
#include "math.h"
#include "b:numrcl.h"

#define N 41    /*  array dimension          */
#define A 5     /*  parameter definitions in */
#define B 2     /*    y = A + B x            *

main(){
     int i,mode,npts=40;
     double sigma11,x[N],y[N],sigmay[N],ran();
     struct linear_params prm1;
/*                  create (x,y) data pairs               */

     for(i=0;i<=npts;i++){
          x[i]=5 * ran();
          y[i]=A + B * x[i];
          prinlf("%4d      %6f       %6f\n",i,x[i],y[i];
     }
/*                  superimpose noise on y data            */

     printf("\n\nenter the sigma value for noise generator\n");
     scant("%fv,&sigma11);
     noise(npts,mode=0,&y,&sigma11);
     for(i=0;i<=npts;i++)
          printf("%4d     %6f      %6f\n",i,x[i],y[i]);

/*            carry out fit and print results             */
     linear_fit(npts,mode=1,&x,&y,&sigmay,&prm1);
     prinlf("\n\n          Fitted Data for y = a + bx\n");
     printf("    a        = %12.6c ±%12.6e\n",prm1.a,prm1.aerror);
     printf("    b        = %12.6e ±%12.6e\n",prm1.b,prm1.berror);
     printf("    r        = %12.6e\n",prm1.r);
     printf("chi_sq = %12.6e\n",prm1.chi_sq);
}
```

Figure 10.2. Example C program to test linear, least-square-fit function.

10.2. POLYNOMIAL DATA FITTING

Polynomial data fitting is a generalization of the fitting technique described for linear regression analysis in the last section. Much of the nomenclature described there is directly applicable to polynomial fitting. We consider, as before, that we have a series of N_p (x, y) data pairs to which we wish to fit the polynomial function

$$y_p(x) = a_0 + a_1 x + a_2 x^2 + \cdots + a_n x^n$$

We want to find a set of polynomial coefficients $a_0, a_1, \ldots, a_n$ that will minimize the χ^2 function

$$\chi^2 = \sum_{i=1}^{N_p} w_i (y_i - y_p(x_i))^2$$

This equation is very similar to the one used in the discussion on linear regression analysis, but now $y_p(x)$ is a polynomial function.

The best-fit parameters are the solution of the matrix equation

$$
\begin{vmatrix}
\displaystyle\sum_{i=1}^{N_p} 1 & \Sigma x_i & \cdots & \Sigma x_i^{\,n} \\[2ex]
\Sigma x & \Sigma x_i^2 & & \Sigma x_2^{\,h} \\[2ex]
\Sigma x_i^{\,2} & \Sigma x_i^{\,3} & \cdots & \Sigma x_i^{\,n+2} \\
\vdots & \vdots & \vdots & \vdots \\
\Sigma x_i^{\,n} & \Sigma x_i^{\,n+1} & \cdots & \Sigma x_i^{\,n+n}
\end{vmatrix}
\begin{vmatrix}
a_0 \\[2ex] a_2 \\[2ex] a_2 \\ \vdots \\ a_n
\end{vmatrix}
\begin{vmatrix}
\Sigma y_i \\[2ex] \Sigma x_i y_i \\[2ex] \Sigma x_i^{\,2} y_i \\ \vdots \\ \Sigma x_i^{\,n} y_i
\end{vmatrix}
$$

The library programming package POLYFIT.LIB may be used to find the best-fit parameters $a_0, a_1,\ldots,a_n$ to the series of (x, y) data points. The I/O parameter list for this library module is shown in Table 10.3 for both the

Table 10.3. Polynomial Fitting Module

OPTION	MBASIC VARIABLES Calling	Return	DESCRIPTION	C variable
1	Polynomial Fit to the Function $y = a_0 + a_1 x^1 + \cdots + a_n x^n$			
	BASIC Call		NPOLY%=1:GOSUB 15500	
	C Call		poly_fit(npts,&x,&y,mode,&sigmay,npoly,&pr)	
	NPTS		Number of data points N_p to be fitted	npts
	XARRAY()		x-values of (x, y) data points in XARRAY(1)...XARRAY(NPTS).	x[]
	YARRAY()		Corresponding y-values in array YARRAY(1)...YARRAY(NPTS).	y[]
	MODE		Weighting option in polynomial fit = 0; instrumental weights. = 1; equal weights. = 2; statistical weights.	mode
	SIGMAY()		Variance needed in weighting factor only used for mode = 0.	sigmay[]
	NPOLY		Degree of polynomial to be fit.	npoly
		APOLY( )	Fitted polynomial constants a0...,an APOLY(0)...APOLY(NPOLY).	pr.a[]
		CHISQ	Chi-squared value of fit.	pr. chi-sq
	Calculation of Probable Errors in Coefficients			
		AERRORY()	Probable error in coefficients AERRORY(0)...AERROR(NPOLY)	pr.error[]
	THE MATRIX MODULE IS CALLED BY THIS PROGRAM AUTOMATICALLY			

BASIC and C routines. The lists for both languages are almost identical and bear such similarity to the linear-fit routine that they are not further discussed. The one exception is the organization of the fitted and error arguments in the C program. The best-fit data is returned to the main routine in a data structure called pr in the parameter argument list. As is the case for the linear fit function, this structure is declared in the library header file "b:numrcl.h".

The polynomial-fit program requires another library program module to complete its work. The library program MATRIX.LIB described in Chapter 9 is used to solve the matrix equation for the fitted polynomial constants. All arrays necessary to communicate with this module are dimensioned internally to the POLYFIT.LIB module.

Option 1 of the library routine solves for the best-fit constant a. The second option in this polynomial-fit module calculates the errors in the polynomial coefficients directly. The probable errors $\sigma_0,\ldots,\sigma_n$ in the coefficients $a_0,\ldots,a_n$ are determined by using the diagonal elements of the inverse of the A matrix defined above at the position of minimum χ^2. The diagonal elements ϵ_{jj} in the inverse matrix $\epsilon = A^{-1}$ are related to each uncertainty by

$$\sigma_j{}^2 - s^2\epsilon_{jj}$$

where the inverse must be determined with a weighting factor of unity, and the variance s^2 is given by

$$s^2 = \frac{\Sigma_i (y_i - y_p(x_i))^2}{(N_p - n - 1)}$$

We illustrate the use of the polynomial-fit routine with a sample BASIC program (see Figure 10.3). We take the polynomial

$$y(x) = 2 + x + x^2 + 3x^3 - 4x^4 + x^5$$

As we have done previously for the linear fit, we generate random x-axis values in the range $0 \rightarrow 2$ using the noise generator, NOISE.LIB, and fill the corresponding y-array elements with the y-values calculated for the polynomial. We then add a degree of statistical noise on the y-values again using the noise generator, the amplitude of which is determined by the parameter SIGMALL corresponding to MODE=0. The value of SIGMALL is entered at the keyboard. Finally, we use the polynomial-fit routine to find the best-fit parameters. The data corresponding to this fitting exercise are shown in Table 10.4. We generate a fit for four different values of SIGMALL. The results of these fits are shown in the table. We see that, as SIGMALL is increased to 0.1, certain constants are fitted badly. We have included a fit with SIGMALL equal to zero to demonstrate that the fitting program itself is working properly.

In cases such as for SIGMALL equal to 0.1, where such bad fits are encountered, we must conclude that the degree of the fitting polynomial is over-

```
5    REM-------------- polynomial test program
10   DEFINT I-N : DEFDBL A-H,O-Z      :REM initialize system
20   REM-------------------------- polynomial fitting test
30        CHAIN MERGE"B:NOISE.LIB",40 :REM merge in library modules
40        CHAIN MERGE"B:POLYFIT.LIB'',50
50        CHAIN MERGE"B:MATRIX.LIB'',60
60        DIM XARRAY(50),YARRAY(50)    :REM arrays for initial data
70        DIM APOLY(10),AERROR(10)     :REM arrays for returned values
80        REM---------------------- create data set
90        RANDOMIZE 10                 :REM seed random number generator
100       NPTS=20                      :REM points in data set
110       FOR I=1 TO NPTS              :REM begin loop to generate data
120          X = 2 * RND : XARRAY(I) = X :REM generate random x values
130          YARRAY(I) = ( ( ( ( X - 4 ) * X + 3 ) * X + 1 ) * X + 1 ) * X + 2
140                                     :REM corresponding y value .
150       NEXT I
160       SIGMALL = .1                 :REM parameter for noise generator
170       MODE = 0 : GOSUB 12800       :REM superimpose noise on y data
180       REM------------------- polynomial fitting initialization
190       NDEGREE = 5 : MODE = 1       :REM polynomial degree; weighting
200       NPOLY% = 1 : GOSUB 18000     :REM call fitting option
210       NPOLY% = 2 : GOSUB 18000     :REM calculate errors
220       FOR I=0 TO NDEGREE           :REM display results on screen
230          PRINT "A(";I;") = ";APOLY(I),AERROR(I)
240       NEXT I
250  END                              :REM end of main routine
```

Figure 10.3. BASICA/MBASIC program demonstrating polynomial fit.

Table 10.4. Polynomial Fitted Constants

Term	Actual	0	SIGMALL 0.01	0.05	0.1
a_0	2	2.000	1.999 ± 0.011	1.995	1.989
a_1	1	1.000	1.002 ± 0.104	1.011	1.021
a_2	1	1.000	0.979 ± 0.309	0.895	0.791
a_3	3	3.000	3.079 ± 0.390	3.396	3.791
a_4	-4	-4.000	-4.073 ± 0.216	-4.364	-4.729
a_5	1	1.000	1.019 ± 0.043	1.079	1.194

specified for the quality of the data. For our example, the superposition of statistical noise on the data results in a corresponding loss of information, which makes it impossible to retrieve the original polynomial. The graphical form of the data in Figure 10.4 indicates that even with the introduction of a small amount of noise, which does not show up visually on the graph, we may still be very much in error in our polynomial fit.

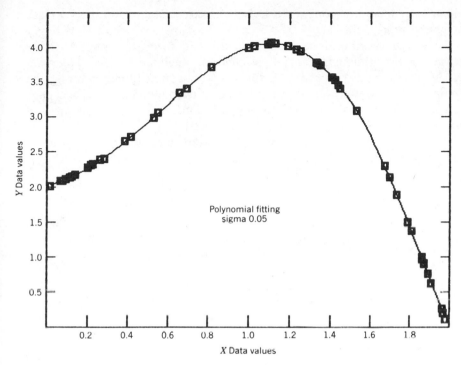

Figure 10.4. A polynomial fit programming example. The open squares are the data to be fitted starting from the polynomial curve $y = 2 + x + x^2 + 3x^3 - 4x^2 + x^5$ with statistical noise superimposed. The curve is the least squares polynomial fit.

10.3. NONLINEAR LEAST SQUARES FITTING

In many real-world scientific problems it is often necessary to fit a known functional dependence to some experimentally obtained numerical data. In such cases the fitting parameters may relate directly to some fundamental physical or chemical varible that must be systematically determined from the data. Polynomial fitting functions are inadequate in such cases, and it is desirable to fit the functions directly. In addition to a knowledge of the fitted parameters, we need a measure of the probable errors in the parameters as obtained from the data.

   In some cases seemingly complicated-looking equations may be reduced to a form linear in the coefficients over the data range of interest. In such cases a linear fitting approximization may be used. In many other cases, however, such a linearization cannot be achieved, and the functions (parameterizations) are said to be inherently nonlinear. It is necessary in these instances to use nonlinear fitting techniques.[*][†]

The fitting algorithm is very different from the form encountered for the polynomial fits. Although in the polynomial case obtaining the best-fit parameters involves only a single call to the matrix-equation library routine, the nonlinear case involves a step-by-step search for the minimum in χ^2 space, each step of which involves a matrix-equation solution. Thus, the nonlinear techniques are much more costly in system overhead.

Examples of some inherently nonlinear parameterizations to be fitted to some experimental data are

$$y_{nl}(x, \{a\}) = \frac{a_1 + a_2 x}{a_3 + a_4 x^2}$$

$$y_{nl}(x, \{a\}) = \exp\left(\sin\left(\frac{a_1 + a_2 x}{a_3 + a_4 x}\right)\right)$$

The first equation is a resonance form often found in many atomic and nuclear experiments. The second is a figment of the imagination with the object of creating an equation as unpleasant as possible. Both these and many more parameterizations may be fitted to a set of data by using the program of this subsection to obtain the best-fit values for the unknowns $a_1, \ldots, a_4, \ldots a_n$

Let us consider that we have a series of experimental data point pairs (x_i, y_i), where there are N_p data points $y_1, \ldots, y_N$. We wish to find the parameter set $\{a\}$ that will minimize the χ^2 function

$$\chi^2 = \sum w_i (y_i - y_{nl}(x_i, \{a\}))^2$$

Here w_i is the weight factor described for the other fitting methods earlier, and y_{nl} is the value of the parameterized equation at x_i.

The nonlinear least squares fitting technique used for the programs listed in the Appendixes, is based on the algorithm developed by Marquardt.[‡] Many nonlinear fitting techniques operate efficiently in certain areas of the χ^2 fitting space but fail completely in other regions. The Marquardt technique is extremely efficient in that it adjusts to its optimum in all areas of the fitting space.

Central to the minimization algorithm is the reduced curvature matrix α with the following elements:

$$\alpha_{jk} = \begin{cases} (1+\lambda) \sum w_i \dfrac{\partial y_{n1}}{\partial a_j} \dfrac{\partial y_{n1}}{\partial a_k} & \text{for } j=k \\[2ex] \sum w_i \dfrac{\partial y_{n1}}{\partial a_j} \dfrac{\partial y_{n1}}{\partial a_k} & \text{for } j \neq k \end{cases}$$

[*]P. R. Bevington, loc. cit.
[†]J. N. Demas, *Excited State Lifetime Measurements* (Academic Press, New York, 1983).
[‡]D. W. Marquardt, in *J. Soc. Ind. Appl. Math.* **11**, 431 (1963).

where j, $k = 1, 2,..., N_p$

The λ parameter in the curvature matrix is adjusted as part of the minimization process, guaranteeing movement towards the minimum of χ^2. The curvature matrix represents a linearization of the minimization process in the χ^2 space without having to explicitly linearize the equation being fitted. Far from the minimum of χ^2, λ will be increased to be much greater than unity, so that only the diagonal elements of the curvature matrix are used to calculate the increments in the parameters δa_j to move the system towards a minimum. As the minimum approaches, the value of λ will be decreased to a point where the complete matrix equation must be used;

$$\beta = \alpha \delta A$$

The probable errors in the parameters are given as in the case of the polynomial-fitting routine, as the diagonal elements of the inverse matrix $\epsilon = \alpha^{-1}$. Again the dependence is simply

$$\sigma_{aj} = s^2 \epsilon_{jj}$$

$$s^2 = \frac{\Sigma (y_i - y_{n1}(x_i))^2}{(N_p - n_t - 1)}$$

Note that in the event that a weighting function set $w_i = 1$ is chosen a priori in the reduced χ^2, then the χ^2 function should approximate $N_p - n_t$ so that $\sigma_a^2 - \epsilon_{jj}$.

The I/O parameter argument list for the BASIC and C library routines is shown in Table 10.5. Much of what is listed should be familiar from the linear and polynomial library routines. In addition to creating a main program to call the library routine, the user must provide a subroutine (or a function in C) at line 10600 containing the formula to be parameterized. The library program sends out an x-value to this subroutine and expects to get a corresponding y-value in return, using the latest values of the fitted parameters.

In the C implementation the name of the function is passed to the library function as a function argument. The incorporation of a function in the argument list represents a pointer. In the case of function argument pointers, the & pointer operator must not be used.

The fitted parameters and the corresponding errors are communicated between the main program and the library function by using the same data structure format as was used for the polynomial program. The structure is declared in the header file b:numrcl.h, which must be included at the beginning of the main routine. A major difference between the nonlinear fitting routine and the others discussed in this chapter is that initial (first guess) values must be provided to the nonlinear-fit routine when it is first called. The relative goodness of these initial-guess values determines how long the fitting routine will take to converge.

The following five parameters defined at the beginning of the library func-

Table 10.5.   Nonlinear Least Squares Fitting

OPTION	MBASIC VARIABLES Calling	Return	Description	C Variable
1	Fitting an Aribitrary Function $f(x,a1,...,an)$			
	BASIC Call		NONLNR%=1: GOSUB 19000	
	C Call		nonlnr_fit(fn,npts,&x,&y,mode,&sigmay,nterms,ps, nprint)	
	Y=f(X)		Function to be fit in subroutine at 10600. The variables X and APARAM() are passed, returning function value in Y.	fn()
	NPTS		Number of (x, y) data pairs $1...N_p$.	npts
	XARRAY()		Array containing x data points XARRAY(1),...,XARRAY(NPTS).	x[]
	YARRAY()		Array containing y data points YARRAY(1)...YARRAY(NPTS).	y[]
	MODE		Weighting functions mode = 0 instrumental weight. = 1 equal weight. = 2 statistical weight.	mode
	SIGMAY()		Variance used in weighting factor.	sigmay[]
	NTERMS		Number of free parameters to be fit $1...n_t$.	nterms
	APARAM()	APARAM()	Fitted parameters APARAM(1)...APARAM(NTERMS) (initial values needed).	
	NPRINT		Automatic screen print for each fit iterration for nprint = 1.	nprint
		CHISQ	Chi-squared value of fit.	ps. chi_sq

Calculation of Probable Errors

Must be called immediately after option 1 before the MATRIX routines are used for any other purpose in the BASICA routine. Calculated automatically in nonlnr_fit() in C and returned in data structure ps.

2		AERROR()	The probable error in the parameters	ps.error[]

tion, and which may be changed by the user (the library program in C will have to be recompiled), determine the rate and point of convergence:

```
#define   FLAMDA   0.001
#define   DELTA    0.001
#define   NMAX     10
#define   EPSLN1   1e-5
#define   EPSLN2   1e-5
```

FLAMDA is the initial value of the λ parameter described earlier. The DELTA parameter is used in the function that takes the derivatives dy_{nl}/da_j. If necessary, this derivative function may be rewritten by the user to be an analytical expression, obviating the need for the DELTA parameter.

The other three represent the cutoff parameters for the fitting-function operation. NMAX specifies the total number of cycles of the solution loop that will be carried out before the fitting exercise is abandoned. Reaching NMAX represents a failure of the routine to converge, and care must be taken in interpreting the resulting fitted constants.

EPSLN1 (ϵ_1) and EPSLN2 (ϵ_2) represent the following convergence conditions.

$$\text{Condition 1:} \quad |\ \chi_r^2 - \chi_{r-1}^2\ | < \epsilon_1 \chi_r^2$$
$$\text{Condition 2:} \quad |\ \chi_r^2 - \chi_{r-1}^2\ | < \epsilon_2$$

The fit is considered to have converged when either of these conditions is met. The parameters in this list are reasonable for many applications, but they may need to be changed in specific cases.

We illustrate the operation of the nonlinear, least-squares-fit, library program with a simple example. We generated a set of data from the Lorentzian function $\dfrac{a_1}{a_2^2 + (x - a_3)^2}$ with values of the constants set to $a_1 = 3.5$, $a_2 = 2$, and $a_3 = 100$.

The C main program to carry out the fitting exercise for this functional form is shown in Figure 10.5. First we generate the data and go on to prompt the user for initial values for the constants as if we were not aware of their actual values used to generate the data. With initial values of $a_1 - 2.1$, $a_2 = 1.5$, and $a_3 = 99$ the following data output is obtained.

Nonlinear Least Squares Fit Routine

Pass	λ	χ^2
Initial values	1e−03	—
1	1e−03	1.1977e−02
2	1e−04	3.2625e−03
3	1e−05	2.7235e−03
4	1e−06	2.7235e−03

Fitted Constants

$$a[0] = 3.468186 \pm 0.181153$$
$$a[1] = 1.974826 \pm 0.064475$$
$$a[2] = 1.000315 \pm 0.042014$$

```
/*    Program to generate Nonlinear least squares fit function        */
#include"libc.h"
#include"math.h"
#include"b:numrcl.h"

#define NUMPTS 101     /*    dimension of all arrays                   */
main()
{
    int k, npts=50, mode [NUMPTS], nterms=3, nprint;
    double xd,z,x[NUMPTS],y, sigmay[NUMPTS],sigmall;
    double ran(),functn();  /* C function defining function to be fit  */
    struct poly_params *ps; /* defintion of data structure for results */
/*                        generate x,y data pairs                      */
    for(k=1; k<=npts; k++){
        x[k]=95+10*ran();
        xd=x[k];
        y[k]=3.5/(4+(xd-100)*(xd-100));
    }
/*                   superimpose noise on y data                       */
    printf("\n\nnenter the sigma value for noise generator\n");
    scanf("%f",&sigmall);
    noise(npts,mode=0,&y,&sigmall);
/*          enter initial guesses for parameters                       */
    printf("enter initial values\n");
    for(k=1;k<=3;k++){
        scanf("%f",&z);
        ps->a[k]=z;
    }
/*            carry out non-linear fit                                 */
    nonlnr_fit(functn,npts,&x,&y,mode=1,&sigmay,nterms,ps,nprint=1);
/*                print out results of fit                             */
    for(k=1; k<=nterms; k++)
            printf("fitted parameter %12.6e ± %12.6e\n",
                                   ps->a[k],ps->error[k]);
            printf("\nchi squared = %12.6e\n",ps->chi_sq);
    }
}
/*            the function to be fit                                   */
functn(nterms,x,a)
/*
func
int nterms;
double x,a[NTWO];
{
    double y;
    y=a[1]/(a[2]*a[2]+(x-a[3])*(x-a[3]));
    return (y)
}
```

Figure 10.5. C program demonstrating a nonlinear least square fit exercise

For this particular example we entered 0.05 for the sigmall noise generator function, so that no data noise was superimposed. The first part of this output is derived from the nonlinear library function, the second must be programmed by the user in the main program.

After changing the initial value of a_3 to 90, the fitting routine experienced some difficulty in converging on the solution. The program only converged after 14 iterations and took at least four times as long, since numerous adjustments to λ were necessary. Interestingly the program converged on a value for

a_2 of -2, a quite acceptable alternative solution. Some attention should be given to the properties of each function being fit in order for optimum use to be made of the fitting function. In the above case, for example, the parameter a_3 represents the center of the Lorentzian profile. We chose an initial guess value so far from the true value that we were in a regime of the χ^2 space where the gradients necessary to move towards the minimum were not well characterized and could, in fact, even move one to a local minimum and not the true minimum.

10.4. FILTERING AND SMOOTHING

Every laboratory scientist has had to cope with noise and the resulting loss of valuable information from his or her experiment. The elimination of this noise is an experimental design consideration and becomes particularly important when one is working near the limit of detectability of the experimental apparatus. The process concerned with removing noise components from the signal is called *filtering*. The hardware implementation of filtering was introduced in Chapter 5. In this chapter, we discuss methods of software filtering. As mentioned previously all forms of filtering lead to some distortion of the data, and thus it is important for the experimentalist to understand the various forms of filtering and their smoothing effect on the experimental data.

10.4.1. Boxcar Averaging

This discussion will be confined to numerical methods of filtering, usually called *digital* filtering. The digital filter operates by modifying a given data point to some function of itself and the nearby points. It has an advantage over the analog *RC* filter discussed in Chapter 5 (which only uses past information) in that it *can use both past and future information* stored in the array of experimental data. The digital filter thus provides a smoother operation, without the phase shift present with an analog filter. This means that although digital filtering may lead to peak broadening, it does not change the fundamental shape of the signal form.

Filtering is basically a convolution operation. The results of the operation depend on the shape and width of the filter function convolved with the data. Convolution is illustrated graphically in Figure 10.6a.* The convolution or filter operation is depicted as a multiplication of data points by appropriate integers, *C*, and a sum and a division by the number of integers in the box. This gives a new center point that is the *weighted average* of a number of the original data points; it is entered in the column labeled "SMOOTHED." The box is shifted down one line, and the process repeated. This type of filtering

*R. Annino "Signal and Resolution Enhancement Techniques in Chromatography," in *Advances in Chromatography*, Vol 15, Giddings, Grushka, Cazes and Brown, eds., Marcel Dekker N.Y. (1977) p. 33.

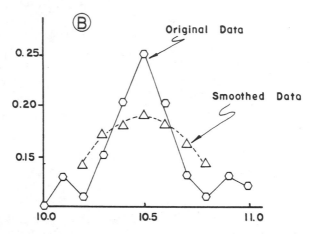

TIME			RAW mv	SMOOTHED mv
10.0			0.10	
10.1			0.13	
10.2	X_{-2}	C_{-2}	0.11	0.14
10.3	X_{-1}	C_{-1}	0.15	0.17
10.4	X_0	C_0	0.20	0.18
10.5	X_1	C_1	0.25	0.19
10.6	X_2	C_2	0.20	018
10.7			0.13	0.16
10.8			0.11	0.14
10.9			0.13	
11.0			0.12	

Figure 10.6. Convolution and signal degradation. (*a*) convolution or filter operation. (*b*) Signal degradation that accompanies the filtering. Reprinted from R. Annino, loc. cit *Advances in Chromatography*, Vol 15, by permission of Marcel Dekker, Inc.

is often called a *moving window average*. In Figure 10.6b, both the original and the smoothed values are plotted to show the signal degradation that accompanies the filtering.

The values of the raw data X_n are convoluted with a rectangular filter or a *box*; that is, each of the *convolution integers* C_n is set equal to 1. One calculates the smoothed value (0.18) of X_0 from its raw value (0.20) and the raw values of its neighbors (0.25, 0.20, 0.15, 0.11) in the following manner:

$$X(\text{smoothed}) = \frac{1}{5} \{ (X_{-2})(C_{-2}) + (X_{-1})(C_{-1}) + (X_0)(C_0) + (X_1)(C_1) + (X_2)(C_2) \}$$

$$X(\text{smoothed}) = \frac{1}{5} \begin{array}{l} \{(0.11) \ (1) + (0.15) \ (1) + (0.2) \ (1) \\ + (0.25) \ (1) + (0.20) \ (1) \ \} \end{array}$$

This filter is called a *boxcar filter* if it is moved five data points ahead for the calculation of each point. This is the type of crude filtering one might use in real-time data filtering. As long as the sampling rate is high compared to the frequency components of the signal waveform, minimum distortion is evident.

A more efficient use of the data is obtained if the box is moved each time by only one data point in the array and a new average point for the cluster is calculated. It is then called a *moving window boxcar filter* and yields a smoothed data array containing almost the same number of points as the original. The two procedures are illustrated in Figures 10.7 and 10.8.

We can thus write a more generalized form for the above filter equation where the *j*th point is modified by the $2m+1$ points of which it is the center:

$$Y_j^* = \sum_{i=-m}^{+m} \frac{C_i Y_{j+i}}{N_m}$$

where C_i (convolution integers) are the integers chosen to given the desired weighting function, Y and Y^* are the raw and smoothed data, respectively, and N_m is the normalization factor $2m+1$.

It is clear that the width of the filter, $2m+1$, can be set to any value. For normally distributed noise, the amount of noise remaining after a single pass of the filter is inversely proportional to the square root of the filter width.

10.4.2. The Method of Savitsky and Golay

Of course, a better way to smooth the data and avoid signal degradation is to fit a polynomial to a set of data points minimizing, in a least squares sense, the deviation of any point from the best fit. This polynomial would then be used to calculate a new best-fit data point as the center point to the selected cluster of points. The data set would then be moved one point (throw away the old value and add a new one), and the process repeated until a while new array of smoothed data was obtained. The process is illustrated in Figure 10.9. The circled central value within the box is the one obtained by solving the final optimized polynomial for the section of the curve within the box. The 7-point box is then moved (by dropping the last point and adding a new one) and a best-fit polynomial is found for the calculation of the central point of the new section.

As mentioned earlier, calculations using the usual least squares minimization procedure can be quite time consuming. However, as pointed out by Savitsky and Golay in their now-classic paper,* this procedure is analogous to con-

---

*A. Savitsky and M. J. E. Golay, in *Anal Chem.*, **36**, 1627 (1964).

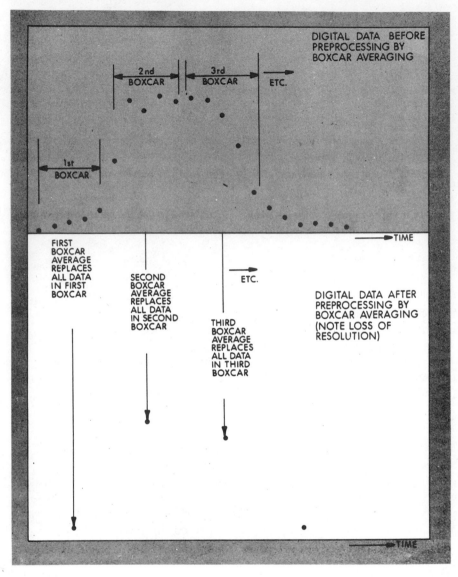

Figure 10.7. Digital data before and after preprocessing by boxcar averaging. Reprinted from G. Dulaney, *Anal. Chem.*, **47**, 24A–32A (1975) by permission of the American Chemical Society.

voluting the data with a moving average smoothing filter, provided that the correct weighting coefficients (the C's of our boxcar example) are used. Savitsky and Golay presented tables of these coefficients for the various filters (quadratic-cubic, quartic-quintic, derivatives, etc.). These tables have since been revised.* One is reproduced in Table 10.6.

---

*J. Steiner, Y. Termonia, and J. Deltour, in *Anal. Chem.*, **44**, 1906 (1972).

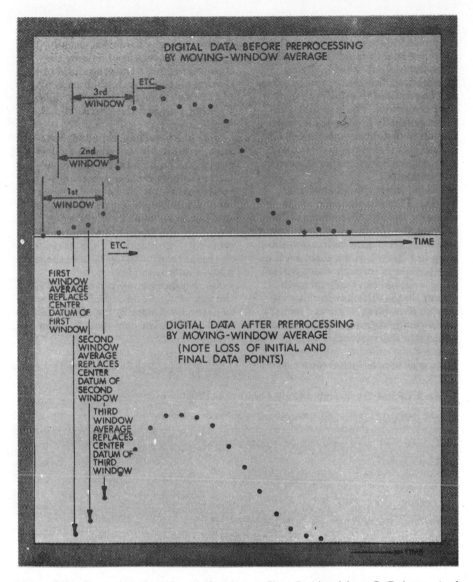

Figure 10.8. Illustration of moving window boxcar filter. Reprinted from G. Dulaney, *Anal. Chem.*, **47**, 24A–34A (1975) by permission of the American Chemical Society.

Thus, we can construct an extremely simple and versatile algorithm by using these previously calculated convoluting coefficients that can be used to smooth digital data.[†] However, the decisions as to which filter to use and the number of points to utilize in the cluster remain with the user.[‡,§,**]

[†]I. E. Bush, in *Anal. Chem.*, **55**, 2353 (1983).
[‡]C. G. Enke and T. A. Nieman, in *Anal. Chem.*, **48**, 705A (1976).
[§]P. Jans and J. B. Gill, in *Appl. Spectrosc.*, **37**, 515 (1983).
[**]P. Marchand and L. Marmet, in *Rev. Sci. Instrum.*, **54**, 1034 (1983).

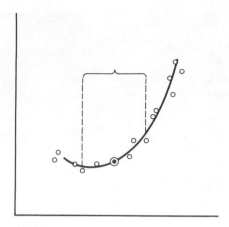

Figure 10.9.   Least square smoothing with a 7-point polynomial. Reprinted from R. Annino, loc. cit in *Advances in Chromatography*, Vol 15, by courtesy of Marcel Dekker, Inc.

As pointed out by Savitsky and Golay, polynomial filters only reproduce exact replicas of a polynomial function, but they have been found to perform extremely well with other functional dependencies, such as Gaussian peaks found in chromatography.[††]

10.4.3.   The First Derivative

A first-derivative calculation can be performed in much the same way as the smoothing technique just described, except that one uses a different set of convolution integers. A set of these integers is reproduced in Table 10.7.

If one desires higher-order derivatives, it is only necessary to make the appropriate number of passes (two for the second derivative, three for the third derivative, etc.) over the derivatized data. In fact, this is preferred to using single passes with higher-derivative convolution integers, because multiple passes provide better smoothing.

10.4.4.   A Filtering Example

We have included a simple program module written in BASICA/MBASIC in our program library to carry out a 7-point Savitsky–Golay smoothing operation. The I/O parameters are shown in Table 10.8. The program operates on data in an array YARRAY ( ) to produce a set of smoothed data and a smoothed first derivative. The central core of the program is extremely simple and follows the technique described above. The majority of the program is taken up with data I/O and data reorganization. It is left as an exercise to the

[††]I.E. Bush, loc. cit.

Table 10.6. Convolute Integers for Smoothing Using Quadratic Integers

POINTS	25	23	21	19	17	15	13	11	9	7	5
−12	−253										
−11	−138	−42									
−10	−33	−21	−171								
−09	62	−2	−76	−136							
−08	147	15	9	−51	−21						
−07	222	30	84	24	−6	−78					
−06	287	43	149	89	7	−13	−11				
−05	322	54	204	144	18	42	0	−36			
−04	387	63	249	189	27	87	9	9	−21		
−03	422	70	284	224	34	122	16	44	14	−2	
−02	447	75	309	249	39	147	21	69	39	3	−3
−01	462	78	324	264	42	162	24	84	54	6	12
00	467	79	329	269	43	167	25	89	59	7	17
01	462	78	324	264	42	162	24	84	54	6	12
02	447	75	309	249	39	147	21	69	39	3	−3
03	422	70	284	224	34	122	16	44	14	−2	
04	387	63	249	189	27	87	9	9	−21		
05	322	54	204	144	18	42	0	−36			
06	287	43	149	89	7	−13	−11				
07	222	30	84	24	−6	−78					
08	147	15	9	−51	−21						
09	62	−2	−76	−136							
10	−33	−21	−171								
11	138	−42									
12	−253										
Norm	5175	8059	3059	2261	323	1105	145	429	231	21	35

reader to derive an equivalent C implementation for the same operation. We have written the library module in a manner that will allow repeated smoothing and/or differentiation operations to be performed on the data. A single call to the library module produces data in two arrays. YSMTH( ) contains the smoothed data, and YDRV( ) the first derivative. On the first call to the module, the indices NFIRST, NLAST of the first and last data points in the data series must be specified. A control parameter NREPLC may be set so that the data in the array YARRAY( ) is replaced by either the smoothed data or the first derivative. The parameters NFIRST and NLAST are automatically updated to take into account the three numbers that must be truncated at each end of the data series. The addition of the replacement operation allows successive smoothing operations or nth-derivative determinations to be performed with ease.

To illustrate the details of the smoothing program, we operate on the set of experimental data shown in Figure 10.10a, which exhibits considerable data noise. The program in Figure 10.11 uses the data smoothing library module to

Table 10.7.   Convolute Integers for a First Derivative Quadratic

POINTS	15	13	11	9	7	5
−7	−7					
−6	−6	−6				
−5	−5	−5	−5			
−4	−4	−4	−4	−4		
−3	−3	−3	−3	−3	−3	
−2	−2	−2	−2	−2	−2	−2
−1	−1	−1	−1	−1	−1	−1
0	0	0	0	0	0	0
1	1	1	1	1	1	1
2	2	2	2	2	2	2
3	3	3	3	3	3	
4	4	4	4	4		
5	5	5	5			
6	6	6				
7	7					
Norm	280	182	110	60	28	10

Table 10.8.   Savitsky−Golay Data Smoothing

OPTION	MBASIC VARIABLES		DESCRIPTION
	Calling	Return	
	Savitsky−Golay Smoothing Operation on Data Array		
	BASIC Call		GOSUB 21000
	YARRAY()		Array containing function to be smoothed
	NFIRST		First array element to be used in next smooth
	NLAST		Last array element to be used in next smooth
	NREPLC		Determines final contents of YARRAY():
			= 0 : leave original data
			= 1 : replace by smoothed function
			= 2 : replace by first derivative
		YARRAY()	Final contents depend on NREPLC
		YSMTH()	Array containing smoothed data
		YDRV()	Array containing first derivative
		NFIRST	⎱ Numbers updated if NREPLC
		NLAST	⎰ set to 1 or 2

Figure 10.10.   (*a*) A sample set of noisy data showing a number of overlapping peaks from a spectroscopy experiment. (*b*) Results of carrying out a 7-point Savitsky−Golay smoothing on the data in (*a*). The first derivative is contained in array YSMTH( ) after execution of line 150 in Figure 10.11. (*c*) The first derivative calculated with program in Figure 10.11. The derivative is returned in array YDRV( ) after execution of line 150.

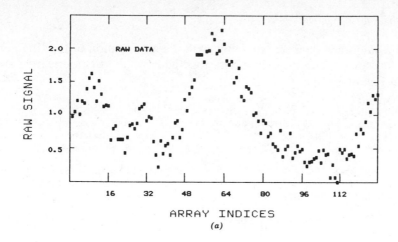

(a)

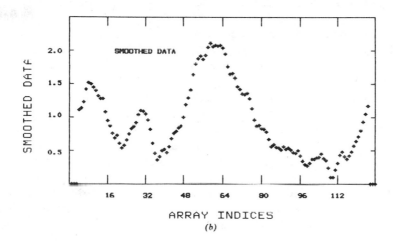

(b)

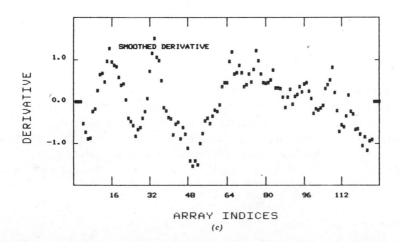

(c)

349

produce a smoothed data set, together with a determination of the first and second derivatives. The smoothed data together with the first derivative are shown in Figure 10.10*b, c.*

```
100 REM  A program to demonstrate the S-G Library module
110   DIM YARRAY(100),YSMTH(100),YDRV(100)  :REM global arrays
120   MERGE "SMOOTH.BAS"            :REM read in smoothing module
130   GOSUB 1000                    :REM read in data
140   NFIRST=1 : NLAST=100          :REM define parameters
150   NREPLC=2 : GOSUB 21000        :REM call module,derivative
                                         in YARRAY()
170   NREPLC=0 : GOSUB 21000        :REM take second derivative
180   FOR I=NFIRST TO NLAST
190       PRINT I,YARRAY(I),YDRV(I)  :REM list derivatives
200   NEXT I
210 END
1000 REM subroutine to read in experimental data
```

Figure 10.11. BASICA calling program for Savitsky–Golay smoothing.

The program ends with the smoothed first derivative in YARRAY( ) and the doubly smoothed second derivative in YDRV( ). The NFIRST and NLAST parameters refer to the first smoothing cycle, and the YDRV( ) array will shorten by three points on each end.

The operation of data smoothing is a controversial one in the sense that the operation results in no gain of information and possibly a net loss compared to the original data. Thus, if further operations, such as curve fitting, are to be carried out on the data then it is questionable whether the original data smoothing operation should be carried out. Possibly its major advantage is to provide a more visually acceptable form in which to graphically view the data. This may allow the user to make certain decisions with regard to operations, that is, should there be two or three peaks included in a data fit operation, using, say, the nonlinear least squares fit routine described earlier? Such fits should then be carried out on the original data. A major strength of the Savitsky–Golay technique is in providing a consistent manner in which to determine the first and higher derivatives of noisy data without tying up vast computer resources.

10.5. FOURIER METHODS

Fourier transform techniques are of general applicability in all branches of science and engineering. They may be used for such diverse tasks as spectral analysis, data smoothing, or autocorrelation analysis. The fast Fourier transform (fft) algorithm, developed by Cooley and Tukey in 1965,* made it possible to use the transform techniques on small computers. Even with the use of the fft algorithm, the time overhead for calculating an fft on a microcom-

---

*J. W. Cooley and J.W. Tuckey, in *Math. Comp.* **19**, 297 (1965).

puter is still large. Thus, without the addition of an 8087 coprocessor on the IBM−PC or a 68000 card on an Apple, the use of such techniques does not represent a viable alternative to the common data smoothing technique. The methods presented in this section are universal, however, and represent an excellent method of learning about the property of the operations when used with small data sets.

For a comprehensive discussion of the fast Fourier transform one should consult some of the classic references dealing with its underlying theory and operation.[*,†] The forward Fourier transform of a function $h(t)$ is defined by the integral

$$H(\nu) = \int_{-\infty}^{\infty} h(t) \exp(-i2\pi\nu t) \, dt$$

where $i = \sqrt{-1}$. The functions $h(t)$, $H(\nu)$ are Fourier transform pairs. The inverse transform to go from frequency space back to time space is given by

$$h(t) = \int_{-\infty}^{\infty} H(\nu) \exp(i2\pi\nu t) \, d\nu$$

The Fourier integral may be carried out analytically for a number of functions that occur regularly in science and engineering. Examples of two of these functions are shown in Table 10.9. The functions being operated on are both real. The first represents the Fourier transform of a Gaussian function symmetric about $t=0$, where the width of the curve at height $1/e$ is equal to 2a. It may be shown that the Fourier transform of a Gaussian is itself a Gaussian but with $1/e$ points at $\pm 1/a\pi$. A pictorial representation of this transform for the same equation written in slightly different form is shown in Figure 5.4.

Table 10.9. The Fourier Transforms of Some Well-Known Functions

TIME SPACE	$\longleftrightarrow$	FREQUENCY SPACE
(a) Gaussian function		
$h_r(t) = \exp(-t^2/a^2)$		$H_r(\nu) = a^2\pi^2\exp(-a^2\pi^2\nu^2)$
$h_i(t) = 0$		$H_i(\nu) = 0$
(b) Exponential function		
$h_r(t) = 0 \qquad t < 0$		$H_r(\nu) = 1/((2\pi\nu T)2 + 1)$
$\quad = 1/2 \qquad t = 0$		
$\quad = \exp(-t/T) \quad t > 0$		
$h_i = 0$		$H_i(\nu) = 2\pi\nu T/((2\pi\nu T)2 + 1)$

*E. O. Brigham, *The Fast Fourier Transform* (Prentice-Hall, Englewood Cliffs, N.J. 1974)
†R. N. Bracewell, *The Fourier Transform and Its Applications* (McGraw-Hill, New York, 1978).

The second function is an exponential that is zero until $t=0$, rises suddenly at this point, and decays with a functional dependence $\exp(-t/A)$ for all positive t. In this case the Fourier transform has real and imaginary parts. The real part is a symmetric Lorentzian curve, and the imaginary part is an antisymmetric function. One universal property of these functions is that a real symmetric function leads to a Fourier transform that is also real and symmetric. Any break in the symmetry of the function about $t=0$ results in an imaginary component being present.

Both these functions also exhibit the important universal property that as the characteristic width of the function to be Fourier transformed is increased, the width in the Fourier space decreases and vice versa.

In the limited space available for the topic in this book, we will take an experimentalist's approach to the Fourier transform. We have the tools available in the progams listed in the appendixes to carry out fft operations on real data. We illustrate some of the properties of the fft with discrete data by operating on the two functions presented in Table 10.9 under a variety of conditions.

10.5.1.   The Fast Fourier Transform

The analytical solution of the Fourier transform cannot be directly carried out on a computer. Two changes are necessary. First, the range of the integral must be made finite. Second, the integral must be calculated from the value of the function at a finite, discrete number of points. The standard representation* of the integral is as a data series, where the real and imaginary parts are given at a number of discrete points $h_r(mT)$, $h_i(mT)$, where $0 \leq m \leq N-1$, and T is the time increment between each point. The forward discrete Fourier transform may be written.

$$H\left(\frac{n}{NT}\right) = T \sum_{m=0}^{N-1} h(mT) \exp\left(\frac{-i2\pi nm}{N}\right)$$

The value of m can range from 0 to $N-1$. One should note that a shift has occurred in this series compared to the analytical integral that was centered at $t=0$. The summation is taken over positive time only. This is for convenience in dealing with positive indices in the summation. A one-to-one correspondence may be made with any analytically calculated transform if one is careful in setting up the problem and interpreting the resulting data. As we will discuss a bit later, the first half of the data series represents the positive half of the Fourier integral; the second half, the negative.

If one were to carry out the series transform given above in the obvious manner by straight multiplication of the entire series, then it would require approximately N^2 multiplications to obtain the complete transform. The major

*E. O. Brigham, loc. cit.

advance in Fourier analysis brought about by the now-classic Cooley–Tuckey* algorithm was to find a pattern in the calculation that could be exploited to dramatically increase the speed of the transform with no loss in accuracy. The Cooley–Tuckey algorithm takes approximately Ng multiplications for the same data set, where $N=2^g$. Thus, for a 1024-point calculation on a complex data set the saving is more than a factor of 200.

The inverse transform in the discrete Fourier transform case is

$$h(mT) = \frac{1}{NT}\sum_{n=0}^{N-1} H\left(\frac{n}{NT}\right) \exp\left(\frac{i2\pi nm}{N}\right)$$

where m can only lie in the range 0 to $N-1$. In reality, it is not necessary to have separate programs for the forward and inverse transforms. We may use the same basic fft program by exploiting the relationship shown below:

$$h(mT) = \frac{1}{NT}\sum_{n=0}^{N-1}\left[H*\left(\frac{n}{NT}\right) \exp\left(\frac{-i2\pi nk}{N}\right)\right]*$$

where $H^*=H_r-iH_i = H_r+i(-H_i)$, and the sign change operation must be carried out twice: once on the data to be inversely transformed, and once on the final transformed data. The inverse transform option in the library module carries out the procedure automatically. First, the sign of all the data in the imaginary array YIMAG( ) are all changed in sign, the fft is carried out with the forward fft algorithm, and all the resulting imaginary array components are again changed in sign to give the net inverse transform.

The I/O list for the fft library module is shown in Table 10.10. Listings for the programs are given in MBASIC/BASICA and C in the appendixes. The first option in this module deals with the calculation of the fft and its inverse. A Hanning function (see below) may be incorporated into the calculation to avoid anomalies due to the end points. The second option in the library module carries out the convolution between two functions.

Before proceeding with an fft calculation we explore the link between the Fourier integral and the fft summation. Let us refer to Figure 10.12, where in Figure 10.12a we show an analytical function to be transformed. The function must be truncated between $-T/2$ and $T/2$. The function that we actually transform is this truncated function replicated infinitely on both sides of the original function, as we show in Figure 10.12b. We could equally well have started with the function between 0 and T shown in Figure 10.12c and replicated it infinitely at each end to end up with the same cyclic function with periodicity T. This has the advantage that our basic function is over positive time only and may be approximated by a positive summation. The fft algorithm operates on a discrete number of points, as shown in Figure 10.12d. The most

*J. W. Cooley and J. W. Tuckey, loc. cit.

Table 10.10.   The Fast Fourier Transform

OPTION	MBASIC VARIABLES		DESCRIPTION	C variable
	Calling	Return		
1	Fast Fourier Transform Program (forward and inverse)			
	BASIC Call		NFFT%=1 : GOSUB 20000	
	C Call		fft(nu,sgn,hng,&yreal,&yimag)	
	NU		The number of points to be transformed must be 2^{ν} points.	nu
	YREAL()		The real and imaginary parts of function	yreal[]
	YIMAG()		to be transformed.	yimag[]
	ISIGN		=+1 forward fft time → frequency.	sgn
			−1 backward fft frequency → time.	
	IHNG		= 0 no Hanning filter.	hng
			1 Hanning filter included.	
		YREAL()	The resulting real and imaginary	
		YIMAG()	components of transformed data.	
2	Convolution Integral of Two Real Data Sets			
	BASIC Call		NFFT = 2 : GOSUB 20000	
	C Call		fft_cnvl(nu,hng,&yreal,&yimag)	
	YREAL()		Contains real part of first data set.	yreal[]
	YIMAG()		Contains real part of second data set.	yimag[]
	NU		See above.	nu
	IHNG		See above.	hng
		YREAL()	The convolved function returned.	

important fact to realize is that the data in Figure 10.12*d* is the most convenient data set that we can start with in attempting to Fourier transform the function originally shown in Figure 10.12*a*.

Another way to view the problem is that in our discrete data set running from 0 to $N-1$, we must interpret the points between 0 and $N/2-1$ as referring to the time axis between 0 and $T/2$, whereas the points between $N/2$ and N correspond to the time axis between $-T/2$ and T. Similarly, in the Fourier space the points between 0 and $N/2-1$ represent positive frequencies, whereas the points between $N/2$ and N represent negative frequencies. For the reasons discussed above we must sometimes shift both halves of the data sets about the center in order to end up with data that is easily interpreted as far as its Fourier transform is concerned.

Some examples should help to clarify the points we have discussed above. In all our calculations we will use a time increment of unity between data points; that is, the array indices represent time. We will study the fft characteristics of the Gaussian and exponential functions.

Consider first the Gaussian. We wish it to be centered about the $t=0$ axis; giving it a 1/*e* half-width at half-maximum of 2 [i.e., $\exp(-x*x/4)$], we start

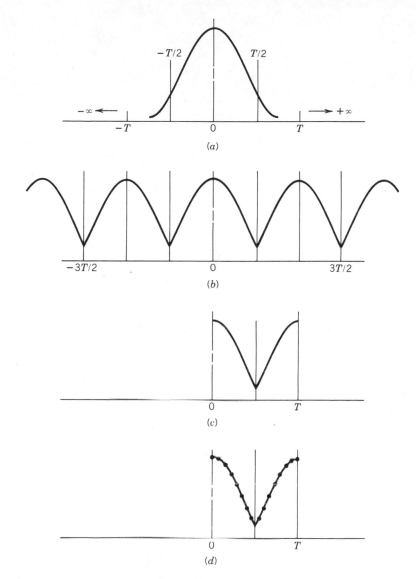

Figure 10.12. Illustration of fast Fourier transform (fft) procedure on a Gaussian data set showing the (*a*) original Gaussian curve, (*b*) the infinite periodic structure, (c) the alternative starting function, and (*d*) the sampled data set.

with the data series shown in Figure 10.13. Note that the data is entered in a way that puts the values of the Gaussian for positive x in the first half of the array, and the values for negative x in the second half. The reason for doing this should be clear from our earlier discussion.

The BASICA/MBASIC main program used to call the library program and carry out the fft calculation on the data is shown in Figure 10.14. We specify

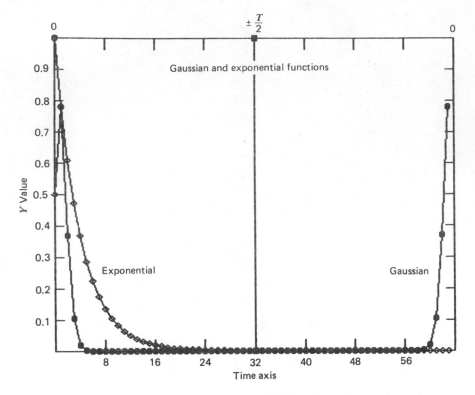

Figure 10.13. Starting Gaussian and exponential functions to be transformed.

```
100 DIM YREAL(64),YREAL(64)  :REM dimension global variables
110 FOR I = 0 TO 31          :REM create exponential centered
120 YREAL(I) = EXP(-I*I/4)   :REM            at zero
130 YREAL(I+32)=YREAL(I)     :REM pos. and neg. halves interchanged
140 YIMAG(I)=0 : YIMAG(64-I)=0 :REM imaginary part zero
150 NEXT I
160 IHNG=0 : ISGN=1          :REM no Hanning, forward fft calc.
170 NFFT=1 : GOSUB 20000     :REM call fft module
180 OPEN "I",#1,Z,"GAUS.DAT" :REM open file for storage
190 FOR I=0 TO 63:PRINT #1,I,YREAL(I):NEXT I:REM write real part
200 FOR I=0 TO 63:PRINT #1,I,YIMAG(I):NEXT I:REM write imaginary part
210 CLOSE #1                 :REM close file
220 END
```

Figure 10.14. Calculating the Fourier transform of a Gaussian.

356

that no Hanning filter is to be used in the transform calculation, and that we are calculating the fft in the forward direction. The final transformed data is returned to the main program in the arrays YREAL( ), YIMAG( ). These are stored in the file GAUS.DAT, the real data first followed by the imaginary array.

The calculated fft for the Gaussian function is shown in Figure 10.15. It is another Gaussian centered about zero in frequency space with a $1/e$ width of $64/2\pi$. The imaginary component is zero, since we started off with a symmetric real function.

We will also take the fft of an exponential function $\exp(-x/4)$, which is also shown in Figure 10.13. This is also sampled at unit intervals, giving 64 points in each series. Note that the negative part of the series (points 32 to 63) is not zero, as we had specified above, but is the dying part of the decay curve from the next exponential to the left in the periodic structure. Since the function has effectively reached zero by the time the midpoint is reached, no significant distortion will be introduced compared to the calculation of the fft that we originally specified.

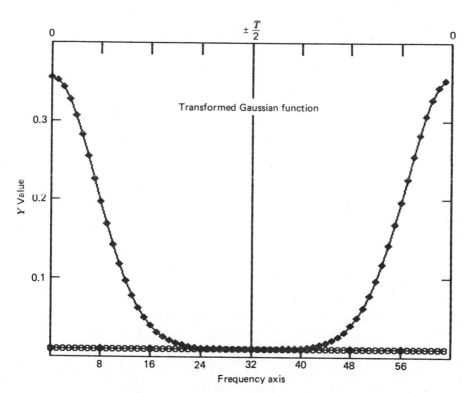

Figure 10.15. Calculated fft of Gaussian function showing real and imaginary parts of transform.

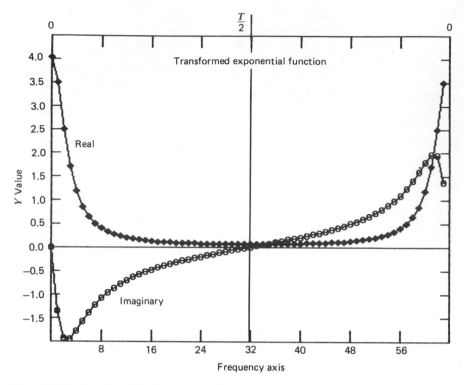

Figure 10.16.   Calculated fft of exponential function showing the real and imaginary transformed components.

The Fourier transform of the exponential function is shown in Figure 10.16. Since we began with a nonsymmetric function, we end up with a data set with an imaginary component. This particular calculation has been described in some detail in Brigham's book,* where the reader is referred for further information.

The scaling properties of the function and its transform are illuminating. The total "time" sampled by the function is from 0 to 63 in intervals of unity (we could be working in seconds, for example). In frequency space, on the other hand, the total range is 1 and the increment in frequency units between the data points is 1/64 frequency units. To generalize, when we have an increment of T between the data points of the original function and a total span of NT, the frequency range in the Fourier domain spans $1/T$ at frequency increments of $1/NT$.

*E.O. Brigham, loc. cit.

10.5.2.   Curve Distortions

A number of potential distortions may crop up in discrete Fourier analysis due to the discrete and bounded nature of the fft algorithm. A list of some of the more common distortions is given below:

1.   Leakage distortion.
2.   Noise distortion.
3.   Aliasing.

We discuss data smoothing from a convolution standpoint in the next subsection, where the result of data noise and leakage will be important.

Before we describe the Hanning function we should remind the reader of some background information. The formal definition of the Fourier transform has limits on the integral of plus and minus infinity. The discrete nature of the numerical transform, however, produces sharp discontinuities in the function at both ends of the summation range. This leads to a significant distortion of the higher-frequency components.

In actuality, the numerical evaluation of a Fourier integral introduces periodicity into both the function and its Fourier transform. That is, both the function and its transform may be thought of as an infinite sequence of similar discrete bounded functions stretching off in either direction to infinity. The boundaries between the periodic functions represent sharp discontinuities in the periodic function or its gradient, which lead to an enhancement of the higher-frequency components in the transformed space. The fact that there is a wraparound of the data about the ends means that if the data values have not dropped to zero at the ends, there will some leakage of the data across, especially during a convolution exercise.

One method to compensate for the discontinuities is to multiply the function whose Fourier transform is to be calculated by another function that drops to zero at both ends. The so-called Hanning function shown below conforms to this recipe:

$$X(t) \;=\; \frac{1}{2}(1 - \cos(2\pi t / T))$$

In terms of our discrete data representation necessary to carry out the fft calculation, a more convenient form of the Hanning function in BASICA notation is

```
YHNG(I) = (1 + COS(6.2831852*I/(2^NU))
```

This function is shown in Figure 10.17. It is centered at $t = 0$ and drops to zero at both ends, given that the point $N/2-1$ represents the dividing line between the two ends of the integral.

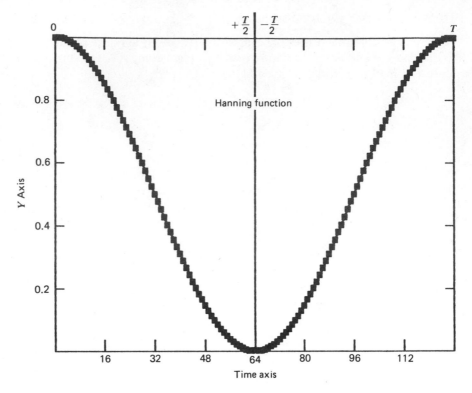

Figure 10.17. The Hanning function shown in positive index space.

If some noise is present on the data, there will be an enhancement of the higher-frequency components that can greatly distort the Fourier series, compared to that expected from a smoothed function. The operation of convolution described in the next subsection may be used to smooth out a noisy data set by effectively cutting down the higher-frequency components in the frequency space.

Aliasing is a phenomena that occurs when the sampling frequency is smaller than the highest-frequency component of the original signal. It leads to a loss in the high-frequency component of the original signal and the appearance of a spurious low-frequency component in the sampled data array. This problem can be verified easily. A 2-Hz signal is plotted in Figure 10.18. The signal is sampled every 0.375 s (i.e., sampling frequency 2.67 Hz), and the signal which results if this sampled data is plotted is shown below the original signal. Note that the original 2-Hz signal is no longer present. The data cycles every 1.5 s and thus represents a 0.677-Hz signal—a totally erroneous result, since this signal was not present originally. Also, as noted, we have lost the 2-Hz signal. As an exercise, the reader should decrease the sampling interval to 0.125 s (8-Hz sampling rate) and see what happens. As discussed in Chapter 5, according to

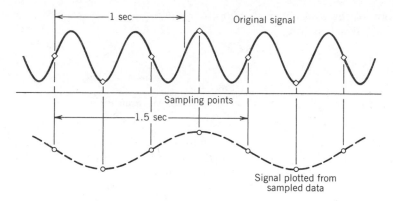

Figure 10.18.   An illustration of the effects of aliasing distortion arising from the sampling of data at too low a frequency. The original sinusoid of period 0.5 s is being sampled every 0.333 s. The resulting sampled data is misinterpreted as a sinusoid with period 1.5 s.

the Nyquist theorem, aliasing will occur if the sampling rate is not greater than twice the highest-frequency component of the signal.

A problem may arise when your signal contains frequency components much higher than the fastest possible data rate of your data acquisition system. To avoid the spurious low-frequency signals that can occur at the less-than-optimum sampling rate, you must filter out these high-frequency components with a hardware filter before you sample data. These filters are called *aliasing filters* for obvious reasons.

10.5.3.   Convolution and Data Smoothing

Data smoothing, which has been discussed in some detail from another stand-point in the last section, involves a convolution operation on a data series. The operation is most simply defined by the integral equation

$$ y(t) = \int_{-\infty}^{\infty} f(u)g(x-u)\ du = f(t) * g(t) $$

where we have two time-dependent functions, $f(t)$ and $g(t)$, that may be convolved through the above integral to form the function $y(t)$. The convolution operator symbol $*$ is sometimes used as a shorthand notation for the integral. The discrete form for this convolution follows similar notation lines to the discrete Fourier transform. Just as in the case of the definition of the Fourier integral itself, however, evaluating the convolution integral directly on two data series is extremely costly in terms of computer resources.

There is an important theorem that we can use to shorten the time for this calculation. The convolution of two functions is merely the inverse Fourier transform of the product of the Fourier transforms of the original functions. This is illustrated below.

$$
\begin{array}{cccc}
f(t) & * & g(t) & = & y(t) & \leftarrow \text{Convolution} \\
\text{fft} \downarrow & & \text{fft} \downarrow & & \uparrow \text{ fft}^{-1} \\
f(v) & \times & g(v) & \rightarrow & y(v) & \leftarrow \text{Multiplication}
\end{array}
$$

Let us presume that we have a noisy function $f(t)$ and that we wish to convolve it with a symmetric filter $g(t)$, where $g(t)$ is a Gaussian filter function. Thus, the convolution may be calculated from the following:

$$
y(t) = \mathscr{F}^{-1}[\mathscr{F}(f(t))\mathscr{F}(g(t))]
$$

where the operator $\mathscr{F}$ stands for the Fourier transform, and $\mathscr{F}^{-1}$ for the inverse Fourier transform.

To carry out the operation for the discrete data, the two data series must have the same number of points. In the event that this is not the case, one of the series may be filled with zeros to make them the same length. It is assumed that both $f(t)$ and $g(t)$ are real. The intermediate Fourier transform may be complex, but the resulting inverse transform should get us back to a real function.

Finally, we demonstrate the operation of convolution as used for data smoothing by operating on the same set of noisy data that we Savitsky–Golay-smoothed in the last section. The unsmoothed data is shown in Figure 10.10a. In Figure 10.19 we show the result of convolving this data with a Gaussian function with a width of the peak height at $1/e$ of ± 2 units. There are 128 points in the data sets, and the points are spaced by unity. Two curves are shown in Figure 10.19. One represents the convolution operation, with no Hanning filter, used in the forward fft calculations; the other has a Hanning filter. The final data should be divided by the Hanning filter function to restore the scaling of the smoothed data. The data calculated without a Hanning function is a successful smoothing operation, but we must be aware that some mixing of the data has occurred between the two ends of the series. Since the Gaussian function was relatively narrow, the mixing is not too great. Also since the y-values of the data at the two ends are comparable, no dramatic effect due to leakage is evidenced, even though it has occurred over the points lying within ± 4 units of the ends.

We show in Figure 10.20 the result of executing a convolution between the same noisy data set shown in Figure 10.10a and an exponential function $\exp(-i/4)$, where i are the array indices ranging from 0 to 127. The resulting data is much less acceptable as a representation of the original data, since the exponential function is not a symmetric function. This creates a large imaginary contribution in the Fourier transform and results in gross asymmetry being introduced into the data. In particular, it should be noted that there is a sizable

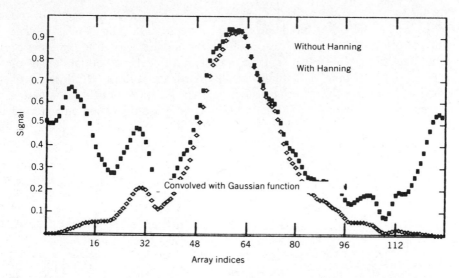

Figure 10.19. The results of carrying out a convolution smoothing operation on the noisy data shown in Figure 10.10 (*c*) with a Gaussian filter function with a 1/*e* width of 2 units. There is unity separation between each data point in the original spectrum.

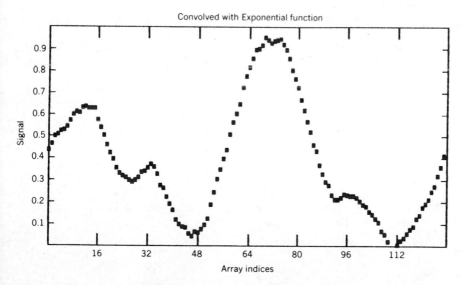

Figure 10.20. The result of carrying out the convolution smoothing operation on the noisy data shown in Figure 10.10*a* with an asymmetric exponential filter function.

shift in the data peaks from the original data. The symmetric shape of the Gaussian, on the other hand, produces no such shift. The data is a clear demonstration of the types of distortions that can occur with different types of smoothing filters. In particular, it is an indication of the potential danger of carrying out real-time data filtering with hardware filters (*RC* filters, for example) as regards the resulting distortion in the positions of peaks. Far better in many instances to software filter with a convolution operation on acquired data.

11

Assembly
Language
Programming

11.1. INTRODUCTION

Because so many high level laboratory language extensions are available, the only reason for attempting *assembly language* programming is to provide yourself with a program not already included in these extensions. Certainly it is not possible to teach assembly language programming in one chapter. We will only highlight some of the concepts so that the reader can better understand the examples provided herein. Some excellent assembly language programming books are now available and we recommend that you read these to get a better view of assembly language programming.*

Basically we are going to discuss programming the computer in a high-level *machine language*. A machine language consists of a set of binary coded instruction words that can be interpreted by the microprocessor. The instructions include various arithmetic and logical operations that the computer can execute.

Programming consists of storing a sequence of these instructions in memory. When directed to a specific memory location, the microprocessor will fetch and execute instructions sequentially in memory unless told otherwise by one of the instructions in the sequence.

It is quite tedious, however, to program directly in machine language. Imagine writing and entering into memory each instruction as a series of 0's and 1's that may be 3 or 4 bytes long.

Assembly programming uses certain *mnemonics* to designate specific instructions. These mnemonics are then translated to machine language by an *assembler program*. It is this machine language program that is loaded and executed by the microprocessor.

---

*R. Mottola, *Assembly Language Programming for the Apple II*, Osborne/McGraw-Hill, Berkeley, CA, 1982.

L. A. Leventhal, *6502 Assembly Language Programming*, Osborne/McGraw-Hill, Berkeley, CA, 1979.

D. C. Willen and J. I. Krantz, *8088 Assembler Language Programming: The IBM-PC*, Howard W. Sams, Indianapolis, IN, 1983.

11.2.   ELEMENTS OF ASSEMBLY LANGUAGE SOURCE CODE

A line of assembly language source code is broken up into a number of distinct parts called *fields*. There are specific fields designated for line number, label or pseudo-op, instruction mnemonic, operand, and comments. Not every line requires all of these but each line will have, minimally, both a line number and an instruction mnemonic, or alternatively, a pseudo-op, which is a directive to the assembler. The line numbers are assigned by the assembler and need not concern the user. They are only useful for editing and are eliminated when the program is stored.

11.2.1.   Label

Labels are useful in that they can be used as addresses in other instructions. For example, in line 12 of Table 11.1 the instruction JMP directs the program flow to the address where START is stored even though you, the programmer, in some cases may not know exactly where that is.

11.2.2.   Mnemonic

The field after the label is the operation or mnemonic field. This field may contain a specific computer instruction, such as the load and store (LDA,STA) instructions in lines 10 and 11, of Table 11.1 or it may contain a pseudo-op instruction, such as those in lines 8 and 9 (ORG,EQU). The pseudo-op mnemonics are not translated by the assembler to machine language instructions. Pseudo-ops are directives to the assembler to do certain things such as, assign the program to certain areas in memory, and define symbols. Thus, in the above program, the pseudo-op ORG directs the assembler to place the program at the address $1000 whereas, the psuedo-op EQU tells the assembler to assign an address of $0300 to the Label, STORE.

Table 11.1.   Typical Assembly Language Code

Line No. Field	Label Field	Mnemonic Field	Operand Field	Comment Field
8		ORG	$1000	PLACE THE PROGR HERE
9	STORE	EQU	$0300;	ADDRESS TO STORE NUM
10	START	LDA	$40 ;	GET THE NUMBER
11		STA	STORE;	SAVE IT
12		JMP	START;	DO IT AGAIN

11.2.3. Operand

The *operand or address* field may contain an address, some data, or it may be blank. Its contents will depend on the instruction. For example, a RETURN instruction such as RTS requires no operand.

11.2.4. Comments

Both the Comment and Label fields are optional. Comments are usually added to make the program easier to understand.

11.3. ASSEMBLERS

In practice one loads the *Editor* portion of the editor/assembler program from disk into memory. The user's assembly language program is then typed in following some simple rules (provided by the assembler instructions) with regard to the *fields* (line tabs) in which to place *labels, pseudo ops, addresses*, and so on. The editor program is available during this phase of program development to aid the user in making corrections. Upon completion, the program will resemble, in form, that shown on pages 373 and 374, except that the line numbers will also have been provided by the editor/assembler.

This program is then saved to disk under a user-selected name prior to loading the assembler. The assembler then loads the user's program and assembles it. The listing shown on pages 386 and 394 is an output from the Apple assembler in this next phase of program development. If errors have occurred during assembly, they are listed at this point. Corrections are made by the programmer, and the program is reassembled until a "successful assembly" message is received. The machine coded (binary) equivalent of the program is then stored on disk to be loaded for execution at the appropriate time.

Assemblers usually do not come with your microcomputer system, but they are readily available from your local computer store. Assemblers do a little more than just translate the mnemonic names of instructions into their binary equivalents. They allow the user to *assign names to memory locations and input and output devices* and *perform some arithmetic* during assembly. *All assemblers are not the same*. Some offer more features than others, and these may be a consideration when deciding which one to buy. The programs described herein were assembled with the fairly simple assembler available on the Apple "tool-kit' diskette (Version 1).

11.4. INTRODUCTION TO THE 6502 MICROPROCESSOR

The most commonly used instructions of the 6502 instruction set are shown in Table 11.2. Programming in assembly language involves only these rather

Table 11.2. Most Frequently Used 6502 Instructions

Instruction MNEMONIC	Meaning
ADC	Add the contents of the addressed memory location and the status of the carry bit to the accumulator. Leave the results in the accumulator.
AND	Conduct a logical AND operation with the contents of the addressed memory location and the contents of the accumulator. Leave the results in the accumulator: For each bit 1 *and* 1 = 1; 1 *and* 0 = 0; 0 *and* 0 = 0.
ASL	Shift the contents of the addressed memory location bit to the left. Shift the MSB into the carry and shift the carry out (original carry bit is lost). A zero is shifted into the LSB. The original contents are finally lost as eight shifts replace it with zeros.

```
+-----+        +------------------------+
|  C  | <----  |      7 <---- 0         | <----  0
+-----+        +------------------------+
```

BCC	Branch to addressed location if the carry bit is clear; that is, C = 0.
BCS	Branch if carry bit is set; that is, C = 1.
BEQ	Branch if zero status flag = 1 (branch if equal).
BNE	Branch if zero status flag = 0 (branch if not equal).
BMI	Branch if minus (S flag = 1). Branch occurs if bit 7 in the accumulator equals 1.
BPL	Branch if plus (S = 0). Branch occurs if bit 7 in the accumulator = 0.
CMP	Compare the contents of the memory location addressed with the contents of the accumulator. Do this by subtracting the memory contents from the accumulator and set the condition flags accordingly. If the accumulator contents were less than memory contents, C = 0. If the accumulator was larger and no borrow was required, C = 1. Nonzero result clears Z to 0. If bit 7 in the accumulator is 1, S = 1; if bit 7 is 0, S = 0.
DEC	Decrement the contents of the addressed location by 1.
DEX (DEY)	Decrement the X or Y register contents.
INC	Increment by one the contents of the addressed location.
INX (INY)	Increment the X or Y register by 1.
JMP	Jump to the address indicated.
JSR	Jump to subroutine.
LDA	Load the accumulator with contents of the addressed location. This is the most used of the 6502 instructions and is commonly called a "read" instruction. The accumulator can be loaded with

Table 11.2. (*Continued*)

Instruction MNEMONIC	Meaning
	a constant, from a variable, from a string, or indirectly through a pointer. Constants are specified by prefacing the number with pound (#) sign; for example LDA#45 says load the accumulator with the hex number 45. To load (or read) the low byte of the variable found at I, the instruction is LDA I (without the pound sign). To read the H. O. byte, we use LDA I+1.
LDX(LDY)	Load X or Y index register from the indicated address.
LSR	Shifts the contents of the accumulator 1 bit to the right. Shifts the l. o. bit into the carry and shifts a zero into the h.o. bit. It is the opposite instruction of ASL.

$$0 \longrightarrow \boxed{7 \longrightarrow 0} \longrightarrow \boxed{C}$$

PHA	Push (store) the contents of the accumulator on the top of the stack. This instruction is most frequently used to save the accumulator contents before servicing an interrupt or calling a subroutine.
PLA	Pull from the top of the stack and load the accumulator. Used to restore accumulator contents that have been saved on the stack—see PHA.
ROL	Rotat contents of location left through the carry bit. Carry bit is not lost as in ASL or LSR but is shifted onto the l. o. bit. The original

$$\boxed{C} \longleftarrow \boxed{7 \longleftarrow 0} \longleftarrow$$

contents of the memory location is restored after nine shifts.

ROR	Rotate right through carry; opposite of ROL. Similar to LSR except that the contents are never lost but restored after eight shifts.
RTS	Return from subroutine. Restores the program counter to the state it was in before the jump.
SBC	Subtract the contents of the addressed memory location from the accumulator with borrow. The carry bit is complemented if a borrow is required.
STA	Store (Write) the contents of the accumulator to the address indicated. This is probably the second most-used instruction in the set and is commonly called a "write" statement.
STX(STY)	Store contents of X or Y register in the selected memory location.

primitive commands. Arithmetic operations such as addition and subtraction are straightforward, but there are no simple commands for multiplication and division. To perform these tasks, we must construct routines from the basic instructions available. Alternatively, the monitor program may, in some cases contain machine language subroutines that can be called to perform these and other tasks.

The 6502 chip contains six rather special memory locations called *registers*, which have different properties than memory locations located outside the chip. The most important register is the *accumulator*. All arithmetic operations are performed with it. Also the movement of information from one place to another involves the accumulator during the transfer.

The 6502 register set is depicted in Figure 11.1. We will not be discussing in detail the use of the registers. Briefly, the X and Y registers are called *index registers* and are used to hold indexes, short offsets, or counters. Simple addition and subtraction commands can be used to increment or decrement by one the numbers held in them (e.g., DEX means decrement the value held in register X by 1).

The *processor status register* (PSR) is used by some commands for testing. The bits in the PSR are only set by operations affecting the contents of the accumulator. For example, the addition of 1 to the number 255 (the maximum value for one byte) produces an overflow or *carry*. To indicate that this has happened, the carry bit in the *status register* is set equal to 1. *Branching commands* use the carry or the zero bit of the status register to see if the condition is satisfied. For example, BNE is a branch instruction in which the

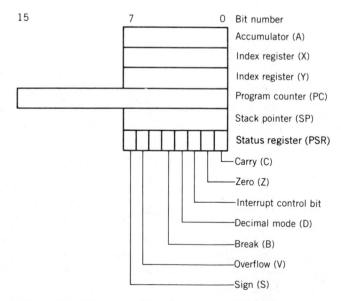

Figure 11.1. The 6502 register set and description of flag bits in status register.

branch is executed only if the *zero status bit is zero*, whereas with BCC the branch is executed only if the *carry bit is cleared* (zeroed).

Before proceeding further, we must point out again that the 6502 is an 8-bit microprocessor. That is, operations are carried out on 8-bit chunks. This will complicate most of our programming because it will be necessary to *divide numbers larger than 255 into 2 bytes*. These two bytes can then be used to *represent an unsigned integer* in the range of 0 to 65,535.

The 2-byte word is stored in sequential memory locations. The first byte is called the *low-order byte* (l.o. byte) and is stored at the lower address. The second byte, is called the *high-order byte* (h.o. byte).

A further complication occurs because a pure binary numbering system cannot be used to represent negative values. Most computers, including the Apple, use a two's complement numbering system that *divides the unsigned number range in half*. One-half of the values represent numbers in the range 0 to 32,767, and the other half of the available values represent numbers in the range $-32,768$ to -1. This can be confusing. For example, in assembly language 32,000 pluse 32,000 is equal to -1536. This can be converted to its positive value by adding 65,536. The two's complement system is illustrated in greater detail in Appendix G. The redesignation of the number line shown in Figure 11.2 illustrates the above-described allocation of number space.

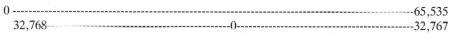

```
0 ----------------------------------------------------------------------------------65,535
  32,768---- ---------------------------------------0---------------------------------------32,767
```

Figure 11.2. Two representations of a line divided Into 65,536 equal parts.

11.5.   THE 6502 INSTRUCTION SET

Before proceeding to write some simple assembly language routines, let us examine in a little more detail the 6502 instructions shown in Table 11.2.

Certainly, the most-used instruction in the set is the *load accumulator* (LDA) instruction. It is referred to many times as a "read" command because it copies the contents of a memory location and places it into the accumulator. As indicated previously, this special memory location called the accumulator is located inside the 6502 processor within the logic of the CPU and is the most important register since it is involved in the execution of most instructions. The CPU operates on the contents of the accumulator in the execution of such instructions as additions, subtractions, logical operations, comparisons, and so on.

The LDA instruction is usually the first in a sequence. A value is loaded into the accumulator, and then this value is operated on by some arithmetic, logical, or transfer command. For example, LDA $9500 copies (reads) the contents of location $9500 into the accumulator. Recall that $ is an assembler notation for a hexadecimal number. If this instruction is followed by STA $9600, which is a command to store the contents of the accumulator (write to the addressed location), an effective transfer of the contents of $9500 to $9600 takes place (albeit through the accumulator).

A pound sign (#) is used to distinguish the just-demonstrated command, "read" the contents of an address, from a "read the value of the address"—that is, load the accumulator with a constant. For example, LDA#$9500 loads the accumulator with the *hex value* $9500, not the *contents of* $9500, as in the first example.

The next most-used instruction is the "write' or "store" command, STA. This instruction copies the contents of the accumulator and stores it at the memory location that is addressed. In the above example, STA $9600 stores the contents of the accumulator at location $9600.

The CMP instruction compares the contents of the accumulator with the contents of a memory location (or a constant). It does this by subtracting the contents of the selected byte from the contents of the accumulator. The results of this comparison affect the status of various bits (flags) in the process status register. Of interest to us at this point are the carry (C) flag (bit 0 of the PSR), the zero (Z) flag (bit 1 of the PSR), and the sign (S) flag (bit 7 of the PSR). The S flag is set by bit 7 of the accumulator: S = 1 if bit 7 of the accumulator = 1, and S = 0 if bit 7 of the accumulator = 0. The Z flag is set by the results in the accumulator. For a nonzero result, Z = 0, and for a zero result, Z = 1.

The branch instruction is used after the CMP instruction to test the results of the comparison. Using a BEQ (branch If equal) instruction after a CMP instruction will cause a branch to the address indicated if the comparison (subtraction) yielded a zero result in the accumulator, which sets Z = 1. The BNE (branch not equal) instruction causes a branch if the comparison indicates that the accumulator contents and selected byte are not equal (Z = 0).

Similarly, the BCC and BCS (branch if carry clear and branch if carry is set) instructions are used after a compare instruction to check if the accumulator contents are greater than or equal to the value addressed in the CMP instruction.

In contrast the BPL (branch if plus) and BMI (branch if minus) instructions usually follow an LDA instruction. For BPL the branch occurs if S = 0 in the PSR, which means that bit 7 of the accumulator is zero; for BMI the branch occurs if bit 7 of the accumulator is 1 (or S = 1 in the PSR).

11.6.   ASSEMBLY LANGUAGE ROUTINES

11.6.1.   Addition

A small assembly language routine for the addition of two 16-bit numbers is shown in Table 11.3 with appropriate explanation.

During the execution of this program whatever was previously present in

Table 11.3. Addition Routine

CLC		; CLEAR THE CARRY BIT.
LDA	FIRST	;LOAD THE ACCUMULATOR WITH THE CONTENTS ;OF THE MEMORY LOCATION CALLED "FIRST" ;THIS LOCATION CONTAINS THE L. O. ;BYTE OF THE FIRST NUMBER.
ADC	SECOND	;TO THE PRESENT CONTENTS OF THE ;ACCUMULATOR, ADD WITH CARRY THE CONTENTS ;OF MEMORY LOCATION CALLED "SECOND" ;SECOND CONTAINS THE L.O. BYTE ;OF THE SECOND NUMBER.
STA	TEMP	;STORE THE L.O. BYTE OF THE RESULTS IN ;MEMORY LOCATION TEMP.
LDA	FIRST+1	;LOAD THE H.O. BYTE OF THE FIRST NUMBER ;INTO THE ACCUMULATOR (THE LOAD COMMAND ;CLEARS THE ACCUMULATOR OF ITS PREVIOUS ;CONTENTS).
ADC	SECOND+1	;ADD WITH CARRY THE H.O. BYTE OF THE ;SECOND NUMBER TO THE CONTENTS OF THE ;ACCUMULATOR
STA	TEMP+1	;STORE THE H.O. BYTE OF THE RESULTS IN ;TEMP+1.

locations TEMP and TEMP+1 is lost as the contents are replaced by the L.O. byte and H.O. byte of the results.

The contents of FIRST,FIRST+1, SECOND, and SECOND+1 are not destroyed by the LDA and ADC instruction. Also, we would have placed the proper number in these locations by previous statements in assembly or BASIC language (the POKE commands).

Note that the carry bit was cleared before the addition, so that if a carry occurs as the result of the first addition (L.O. bytes), it will be added when the second ADC is executed.

We must define for the assembler the numeric addresses for the address symbols that we have used, such as TEMP, FIRST, and so on. We do this at the beginning of our assembly program with statements such as

```
FIRST   EQU $0300
SECOND  EQU $0302
TEMP    EQU $0304
```

As shown here, we have elected to use page 3 for the addresses. The lower part of this page ($0300 to $3CF) is usually a safe place for small machine programs and for storage. The upper part of the page is reserved for special linkage vectors. For example, $03F5 to $03F7 holds a "jump" instruction to the subroutine that handles Applesoft II "&" commands. This provides the linkage between Applesoft and Labsoft. Labsoft also uses some additional space on page three, and it is therefore wise to limit our usage to the area $0300 to $0380 (decimal 768 to 986).

You can elect to use any area below DOS for your programs. All that is required is that you set HIMEM at the beginning of your BASIC program, so that you don't step on your machine program during execution of the BASIC program. In our assembly language program for boxcarring, shown at the end of the chapter, we reserved the area $9500 to $9600 for the program, and we therefore set HIMEM to 38143 ($9449).

11.6.2.   Subtraction

Table 11.4 contains an assembly language subtraction routine.

Table 11.4.   Subtraction Routine

SEC		;SET THE CARRY BIT.
LDA	FIRST	;LOAD THE ACC. WITH THE CONTENTS OF FIRST. ;(L.O. BYTE).
SBC	SECOND	;SUBTRACT THE CONTENTS OF SECOND (L.O. BYTE ;OF SECOND NUMBER) FROM THE CONTENTS OF THE ACC.
STA	TEMP	;AND STORE THE DIFFERENCE INTO THE LOW BYTE ;OF TEMP.
LDA	FIRST+1	;LOAD THE ACC WITH THE H.O. BYTE OF THE FIRST ;NUMBER.
SBC	SECOND+1	;AND SUBTRACT THE H.O. BYTE OF THE SECOND NUMBER ;FROM IT
STA	TEMP+1	;AND STORE THE DIFFERENCE AT THE H.O. BYTE ;LOCATION OF TEMP

11.6.3.   Division

Since the 6502 instruction set does not directly support multiplication or division, we need to write a routine to do this, using what instructions we have available. Some assemblers provide these routines in their run-time support package, and the user need only program in JSR to the name of the routine. SPEED/ASM is such an assembler.* Alternatively, as illustrated further on, there are some Apple monitor routines that can be used.

The program we will write performs division in much the same way as you would do it with a pencil and paper.

For example, let us divide 10,312, by 72. We will do this in binary arithmetic. Decimal 72 = 01001000 binary and decimal 10,312 = 0010100001001000 binary.

*Sierra On-Line, Inc., 36575 Mudge Ranch Road, Coarsegold, CA 93614.

First try

```
                              1
         _____
01001000 | 0010100001001000
           01001000
```

The first thing we do is multiply the divisor by 1 and compare it to the most significant byte of the dividend. If it is larger, we place a 0 in the quotient rather than a 1 and shift the divisor right to try again. If the divisor is smaller, we subtract and again compare the difference with the divisor.

Shift and try again

```
                             01
         _____
01001000 | 0010100001001000
           01001000
           _____
            10001001
```

The completed division looks like this:

```
                        010001111
         _____
01001000 | 0010100001001000
           01001000
           _____
            10001001
            01001000
            _____
            10000010
             1001000
             _____
             01110100
             01001000
             _____
             01011000
              1001000
              _____
              10000  Remainder
```

Expressed in decimal form the answer is 143 Remainder 16.

In the following program it is easier to shift the dividend to the left rather than to keep shifting the divisor to the right. The effect is the same.

The program in Table 11.5 will divide a 16-bit number by an 8-bit number under the following conditions:

1.   The most significant bits of both dividend and divisor are equal to zero.
2.   The divisor is greater than the value of the H.O. Byte of the dividend.

This will produce an 8-bit quotient with a remainder. To understand exactly what is happening, it might be helpful for the reader to follow the program flow

Table 11.5. Divide Routine

1	LDX	#8	;LOAD THE X REGISTER WITH THE NUMBER ;EIGHT. THIS IS THE NUMBER OF BITS ;IN THE DIVISOR AND IS EQUAL TO THE ;NUMBER OF SHIFTS WE WILL MAKE.
2	LDA	DIVS	;LOAD THE ACCUMULATOR WITH THE ;CONTENTS OF LOCATION DIVS, WHICH ;IS THE DIVISOR.
3	STA	DIVS+1	;STORE IT IN DIVS+1.
4	LDA	FIRST	;LOAD THE ACCUMULATOR WITH L.O. ;BYTE OF THE DIVIDEND.
5	STA	DIVD	;AND STORE IT AT LOCATION DIVD.
6	LDA	FIRST+1	;LOAD THE ACCUMULATOR WITH THE H.O. ;BYTE OF THE DIVIDEND. FROM OUR ;HAND-EXECUTED EXAMPLE, THE ACCUMULATOR ;CONTAINS 00101000. WE ARE NOW READY ;TO BEGIN OUR DIVISION.
7 DIVIDE	ASL	DIVD	;THIS WILL SHIFT THE HIGHEST BIT OF ;THE L.O. BYTE FOUND AT DIVD INTO THE ;CARRY BIT. THIS INSTRUCTION, IN CONCERT ;WITH THE NEXT ONE, STARTS, THE PROCESS OF ;SHIFTING THE ENTIRE L.O. BYTE OF THE ;DIVIDEND INTO THE ACCUMULATOR.
8	ROL	A	;WHEN THE ACCUMULATOR BITS ARE SHIFTED, ;THE CARRY BIT IS SHIFTED INTO THE ;LOWEST BIT LOCATION IN THE ;ACCUMULATOR. FROM OUR HAND-EXECUTED ;EXAMPLE FOR THE NUMBERS, THE CONTENT OF ;THE ACCUMULATOR IS NOW 01010000.
9	CMP	DIVS+1	;COMPARE THE VALUE IN THE ACCUMULATOR WITH ;THE VALUE OF THE DIVISOR STORED AT ;DIVS+1. THE COMPARISON IS DONE BY ;SUBTRACTING THE CONTENTS OF DIVS+1 ;FROM THE ACCUMULATOR CONTENTS. IF THE ;DIVISOR IS GREATER THAN THE CONTENTS ;OF THE ACCUMULATOR, THE CARRY BIT IS ;CLEARED—THAT IS, CLEARED TO ZERO. IF ;IT IS LESS, THE CARRY BIT IS SET TO 1.
10	BCC	CNTR	;IF THE CARRY BIT = 0, BRANCH TO THE ;INSTRUCTION SET LABELED CNTR. ;OTHERWISE, CONTINUE TO THE NEXT ;INSTRUCTION.
11	SBC	DIVS+1	;SUBTRACT THE DIVISOR FROM THE CONTENTS ;OF THE ACCUMULATOR. THERE IS NO NEED

Table 11.5. (*Continued*)

			;TO SET THE CARRY BIT AS WE DID IN OUR ;PREVIOUS SUBTRACTION ROUTINE BECAUSE IT IS ;ALREADY SET IF YOU ARRIVE AT THIS ;INSTRUCTION.
12		INC DIVD	;INCREMENT THE CONTENTS OF DIVD. THIS ;INSTRUCTION IS EXECUTED ONLY IF WE ;HAVE MET THE BCC TEST (I.E., DIVISOR ;H.O. BYTE DIVD. THEREFORE, THIS ;QUOTIENT BIT IS 1). THE PREVIOUS ASL ;ON DIVD PUT A ZERO IN THE L. O. ;BIT OF DIVD. INCREMENTING DIVD THUS ;STORES THE QUOTIENT BIT IN THE L. O. ;BIT OF DIVD. AFTER EIGHT TIMES ;THROUGH THE LOOP ALL OF THE 8-BIT ;QUOTIENT WILL BE STORED HERE AT DIVD.
13	CNTR	DEX	;DECREMENT THE CONTENTS OF REGISTER X.
14		BNE DIVIDE	;IF THE CONTENT OF X IS NOT EQUAL TO ;ZERO, GO BACK TO THE PROGRAM LABEL ;"DIVIDE" AND GO THROUGH THE OPERATION ;ONCE MORE. IF THE CONTENT IS ZERO, ;WE HAVE SHIFTED EIGHT TIMES, AND THE ;DIVISION IS COMPLETE.
15		STA REMAIN	;STORE THE REMAINDER THAT IS LEFT IN THE ;ACCUMULATOR AT LOCATION REMAIN.
16		RTS	;RETURN TO THE ROUTINE THAT CALLED YOU.

in more detail by using our handworked example of 10,312 divided by 72. The first six instructions form the initialization section. After execution of these instructions the contents of the following locations are

Accumulator	00101000	;H.O. byte of dividend
Carry Bit	?	;
DIVD	01001000	;L.O. byte of dividend
DIVS	01001000	;Divisor
DIVS+1	01001000	;Divisor
X REGISTER	00001000	;Decimal 8 for # of shifts

The following section shows the contents of the designated locations after completion of the instruction.

Instruction

No.	Mnemonic			
7	ASL	Carry = 0	DIVD = 10010000	
8	ROL	Carry = 0	ACC = 01010000	
9	CMP	Carry = 1		;Compare instruction ;sets the carry = 1 ;if DIVS < ACC.
10	BCC	Carry = 1		;Branch only if ;carry is cleared, ;that is, carry = 0. ;Since carry = 1. ;continue.
11	SBC	Carry = 1	ACC = 00001000	;Result of subtraction ;left in accumulator.
12	INC	Carry = 1	DIVD = 10010001	;Quotient is beginning ;to appear here. See ;bit 0.
13	DEX			;X register = 00000111 ;(decimal 7).
14	BNE	Zero = 0		;Branch to 7 since the ;zero status flag is ;not set. X register ;does not contain a 0.
7	ASL	Carry = 1	DIVD = 00100010	
8	ROL	Carry = 0	ACC = 00010001	
9	CMP	Carry = 0		;Carry = 0, therefore, ;DIVS > ACC.
10	BCC	Carry = 0		;Branch to 13 since ;carry = 0.
13	DEX			;X register = 00000110.
14	BNE	Zero = 0		;Branch to 7 since ;X register ≠ 0.
7	ASL	Carry = 0	DIVD = 01000100	
8	ROL	Carry = 0	ACC = 00100010	
9	CMP	Carry = 0		;DIV > ACC.
10	BCC	Carry = 0		;Branch to 13 since ;carry = 0.
13	DEX			;X register = 00000101(5).
14	BNE	Zero = 0		;Branch back to 7:X ≠ 0.
7	ASL	Carry = 0	DIVD = 10001000	
8	ROL	Carry = 0	ACC = 01000100	
9	CMP	Carry = 1		;DIVS < ACC.
10	BCC	Carry = 1	ACC = 10001001	;Continue since carry = 1.
11	SBC	Carry = 1	ACC = 01000001	
12	INC	Carry = 1	DIVD = 00010001	
13	DEX			;X register = 00000011.
14	BNE	Zero = 0		;Branch to 7:X ≠ 0.

Instruction   (*Continued*)

No.	Mnemonic			
7	ASL	Carry = 0	DIVD = 00100010	
8	ROL	Carry = 0	ACC = 10000010	
9	CMP	Carry = 1		;Carry = 1, therefore, ;DIVS < ACC.
10	BCC	Carry = 1		;Carry = 1, continue.
11	SBC	Carry = 1	ACC = 00111010	
12	INC	Carry = 1	DIVD = 00100011	
13	DEX			;X register = 00000010.
14	BNE			;Branch to 7: X ≠ 0.
7	ASL	Carry = 0	DIVD = 01000110	
8	ROL	Carry = 0	ACC = 01110100	
9	CMP	Carry = 1		;Therefore, DIV < ACC.
10	BCC	Carry = 1		;Carry = 1, continue.
11	SBC	Carry = 1	ACC = 00101100	
12	INC	Carry = 1	DIVD = 01000111	
13	DEX			;X register = 00000001.
14	BNE			;Branch to 7: X ≠ 0.
7	ASL	Carry = 0	DIVD = 10001110	
8	ROL	Carry = 0	ACC = 01011000	
9	CMP	Carry = 1		;DIV < ACC.
10	BCC	Carry = 1		;Carry = 1, continue.
11	SBC	Carry = 1	ACC = 00010000	;This is our remainder.
12	INC	Carry = 1	DIVD 10001111	;This is our quotient.
13	DEX	Carry = 1	DIVD 10001111	;X register = 0000000.
14	BNE			;Continue since X = 0.
15	STA	Remain = 00010000		;Store remainder.
16	RTS			;Return.

11.6.4.   Multiplication

Similarly, we could write a multiply routine, but instead, we use this opportunity to call your attention to some very useful routines that are embedded in some versions of the Apple monitor program and are available at all times. This software is hidden from the casual user because it is written in machine language for use by the monitor, BASIC interpreter, or the DOS.

The complete guide to all of this software has been written by Luebbert.[*] This book is an absolute must for the serious Apple programmer.

For example, at location $F48C is a pointer to a floating point multiply routine that multiplies the multiplicand located at FP1 ($00F4 to $00F5) with the multiplier at FP2 ($00F6 to $00F7) and leaves the product in FP1. Of course,

[*]William F. Luebbert, *What's Where in the Apple*, (Micro Ink, Chelmsford, Mass. 1982).

we must place the desired multiplicand and multiplier into locations \$00F4 to \$00F5 and \$00F6 to \$00F7. This may be accomplished during the execution of the machine language routine, or it may be "poked" into place from a BASIC calling program, as illustrated in our "BASIC" boxcar program.

To execute the multiply instruction in assembly, you need only the line

```
JSR $F486.
```

From Applesoft BASIC it would be

```
CALL-2938 OR CALL 62598.
```

Recall the two's complement arithmetic that is used in the Apple. The integer number −2938 is obtained by subtracting 65,536 from 62,598.

There are also a number of divide routines. For instance, the one whose pointer is found at \$FB81 divides the 16 bit numbers found at \$0050 to \$0053 by the 8-bit number found at \$0054 to \$0055 and leaves the quotient in \$0050 to \$0051 with remainder in \$0053. Sounds familiar—didn't we just do that?

Unfortunately, after this buildup, the multiply and divide routines have been eliminated from the Apple II Plus and Apple IIe Autostart ROMs.

11.7.   ASSEMBLY LANGUAGE COMMUNICATION TO PERIPHERAL DEVICES

Before proceeding to a discussion of the boxcar program, which is placed near the end of this chapter, we should examine assembly language programming to access peripheral devices.

Recall from our Apple II Plus memory map that the 16 pages starting at 192 (\$C000) and ending at 207 (\$CFFF) make up a rather specialized area of memory. These locations are unique in their degree of specialization and are reserved for I/O hardware functions or activities associated with the Apple slots.

The page containing the locations \$C080 to \$C0FF is of particular interest, since it is this area that is assigned to slot peripheral card I/O space. Each of the eight slots has a block of 16 contiguous addresses assigned to it in this special area.

The total address space \$C080 to \$CFFF (2K memory) is reserved for common use by all the peripheral slots, but only one can share it with the central processor at any time.

Each peripheral card can determine if it is selected for operation by testing the condition of a special control line called the *device select*. The peripheral card contains a software flip-flop switch that is turned on when the device select line goes low. This alerts the peripheral that it must respond to a request for information from one of the 16 addresses it has assigned to it. Only when the central processor calls for an address in this area on another line, called the *strobe*, will full activation occur.

For example, our ISAAC card is plugged into slot 3 of our Apple. The 16 addresses assigned to this slot are $C0B0 to $C0BF. All communication with the ISAAC peripherals is done through this card by commands to consecutive memory locations $C0B8, $C0B9, $C0BA, and $C0BB.*

The first 2-byte location [called address low (AL) and address high (AH)] is used to select a particular ISAAC I/O device, and the second 2-byte location [data low (DL) and Data high (DH)] is used to pass data to or from the selected device.

One selects the appropriate ISSAC I/O device by writing the device number and a word to AL after first setting the contents of AH to zero.

For example, the device number for the ADC is 12 ($C). The ISAAC address byte is set up like so:

$$BYTE = (Device\# * \$10) + WORD\#$$

For the ADC with WORD# = 0 we send to AL:

$$(\$C * \$10) + 0 = \$C0$$

The word number designates how the bits of DH and DL will be used; for example, writing Word #0 as above designates the following information:

1. bit numbers to 0–3 of DH to hold the A/D channel #.
2. bits #0 of DL to be the convert line.
3. bit #1 of DL is for a short cycle (if set to 1, it will do an 8-bit conversion).

One reads data from DL and DH after the appropriate device number and word have been sent to AL. Reading the low byte first latches both bytes simultaneously.

There are also two words used with the read operation as follows:

1. Word #0 is used to check the status of the ADC to see if it's still busy. Its status is found in bit #0 of DL.
2. Word #2 is sent to read data from DL and DH. The full A/D value is found in all bits of DL and numbers 0 to 4 of DH (for a 12-bit A/D value).

These procedures are illustrated in the assembly program in Table 11.6 for reading an A/D channel.

Machine Language Access to the ISAAC 91A (Cyborg Corporation, 55 Chapel Street, Newton, MA 02158).

Table 11.6. Assembly Language Program for ISAAC AIN Command[a]

AIN	LDA	#$C0	;Device($C*10) + Word #0 = $C0.
	STA	$C0B8	;Writing device number plus word number to ;AL selects the ADC.
	LDA	CHAN	
	STA	$C0BB	;The channel number is written to DH.
	LDA	#0	
	STA	$C0BA	;This activates a strobe (a 10 μs ;pulse to a software switch). The ;multiplexer must connect the appropriate ;channel to the A/D. Depending on how ;many channels we are scanning, this may ;take as much as 150 μs, so we'll ;have to wait.
	LDA	#$4	
	JSR	$FCA8	;We can do this with a software timer ;found in the monitor at $FCA8. This ;routine takes approximately 107 μs ;when there is a 4 in the accumulator.
	LDA	#1	
	STA	$C0BA	;We request a conversion by writing a 1 ;to bit 0 of DL. Remember, we are still ;in a write Word #0 configuration.
	JSR	$FCA8	;An A/D conversion takes approximately ;25 μs with our system. This ;monitor routine takes 29 μs when ;there is a 1 in the accumulator.
AIN2	LDA	$C0BA	;We read the contents of DL because we ;wish to check bit #0 to see if a 1 or a 0 ;is present. This will tell us if the A/D ;is still busy.
	AND	#1	;We can accomplish this by conducting a ;logical AND operation on the contents ;of DL, which is now in the accumulator. ;Only if $C0BA still contains a 1 in ;bit 0 will this logical operation ;yield a 1 and thus clear the zero status ;flag in the PSR register to 0. Under ;these conditions the next instruction will ;execute a branch back to AIN2.
	BNE	AIN2	;If the A/D is still busy, we'll go back ;and check it again. The branch back to ;AIN2 occurs only if the zero ;status flag is cleared—that is, Z = 0.
	STA	$C0BA	;Clear the request line. To arrive at ;this instruction requires that the AND ;operation produce a 0 in the zero ;bit of the accumulator. This 0 is now ;written to $C0BA.

Table 11.6. (*Continued*)

LDA	#$C2	;If we wish to read data, we must first
		;change the status of DL and DH so that
		;it now contains the converted data value.
		;We must send a read device and Word #2.
STA	$C0B8	;Device ($C*10) + Word#2 = $C2.
LDA	$C0BA	;Now we can read the low data byte from DL
STA	DATAL	;and store it at a location we have selected.
LDA	$C0BB	;Similarly we read DH
STA	DATAL+1	;and store it at the next higher location.

[a]Courtesy of Cyborg Corporation.

11.8. BOXCAR FILTER

The next program will serve to illustrate a number of points to which we have already alluded. It consists of two parts: the calling program written in BASIC and the machine language program written in assembly language.

The problem that the program addresses is a real one and occurred in our laboratory when we wanted to digital filter the 5 to 10-ms points we were acquiring during our experiment. A crude way of doing this is to acquire a specific number of points during the 5 to 10-ms interval but use only the *averaged* number in the final data presentation. A common name for this type of filtering is *boxcar averaging* (see section 10.4.1).

The Labsoft language extension could not provide boxcarring on this sort of time scale so it was necessary to write our own routine. In outline form what was required in the routine was the following,

1. In order to provide as much data storage as possible, only integer arithmetic would be considered. Integer storage requires only 2 bytes per point vs. real number storage of 5 bytes per point.

2. In order to avoid overflow problems, the number of points boxcared would be limited to 15. The maximum binary number produced by a full-scale input to the 12-bit ADC we have is 4096, and the maximum number that can be handled by 2-byte storage (16-bit number) is 65,536. Thus 15*4096 = 61,450 would fall into a nonoverflow range.

3. The user would be allowed to input the final effective sampling interval. The program would sample as fast as possible to acquire the 15 points within this interval.

4. User input as to the total number of averaged points in the experiment would also be provided.

5. Some provision would have to be made so that the points gathered by the machine program would be stored at an address known to the BASIC calling program and could be retrieved from this BASIC program.

6. To speed the high-speed data acquisition process, the averaging arithmetic would be done on the 15-data point sum after the experiment was completed.

The BASIC program used to test the Boxcar routine is shown in Figure 11.3. The following points should be noted.

The ASCII character for CNTRL-D is CHR$(4). Line 90 sets the string D$ equal to CNTRL-D. The PRINT D$; command in the next line is a way of executing a DOS command from within a BASIC program. Line 91, then, tells the DOS to load from disk the binary file named "BOXCAR.OBJO". This is the machine program which was assembled and filed to disk under this name.

The next few statements solicit information from the user such as: What A/D channel is going to be sampled? What is the desired final sample interval? What is the total number of final data points to be taken (remember each final data point will be an average of 15 points gathered in a burst within the specified time interval)?

The reasoning behind line 123 is somewhat complicated and requires some explanation. The time interval will be obtained from the middle two bytes of two 16-bit timers that have been linked together to form a 32-bit one. The timer is run from the Apple processor clock, which has a frequency of 1.023 MHz. The lowest-order byte of this 4-byte timer runs at this frequency (or 0.97752 μs per count), so that it takes 250.244 μs for 256 bits to be counted. Examining the next higher-order byte then, we see that it takes 250.244 μs per/count within this byte, and it takes 64.0804 ms for this byte to overflow into the next-order byte. Similarly, the next byte takes 16.400 seconds to overflow. Obviously, for the time intervals in which we are interested (5 to 100 ms), only the two middle bytes of the timer are significant to us. This essentially gives us a timer with a resolution of 0.250 ms and a maximum range of 16.400 s.

Line 123 then breaks the user-inputted time interval into two appropriate numbers to be placed into the two bytes of the countdown timers.

The POKE commands in lines 124 and 132 constitute the procedure used to place the user inputs into the required location for the machine program's use. For example, POKE 769,TB% places the contents of the integer variable TB% in memory location 769 (hex $0301). As will be seen later, a page three location such as this will be defined to hold specific information for the assembled machine program.

Line 130 is an algorithm for taking a decimal number and splitting it into decimal parts that will be converted to the proper hexadecimal equivalents to be placed in the two byte locations by the POKE commands. The extra work arises because the POKE and PEEK commands demand *decimal* numbers. However, we know that numbers in machine code are interpreted in binary.

Line 130 dimensions an array to the user-selected number of points in the experiment. (Actually this statement will reserve A%(0) to A%(N) or N+1 elements for the array.)

Line 140 appears superfluous but is very important for putting the data in the right place once we have left the BASIC program for the machine program. Among the Apple monitor routines is one that keeps track of the address of the last variable used during the execution of a BASIC program. By executing the statement $A\%(0) = A\%(0)$ just before we enter our machine program, we assure ourselves that the variable pointer is pointing to the address for the beginning of the array. We will look at this pointer (called Varpntr) during our machine program execution to find out where to store the data we have gathered.

The CALL 38144 jumps to BOXCAR.OBJO, which starts at this address (hex $9500). At the end of the data-gathering portion of the experiment, control is again returned to the BASIC program at line 160.

Each data point stored in the array $A\%$ is the sum of 15 points. The routine at 175 to 178 divides each of these points by 15. It recognizes also that the integer number may have to be converted first to its positive equivalent. (Recall the two's complement arithmetic used by the computer.)

Line 220 is a machine routine that suspends the program until the user strikes a key. (Alternatively, we could have used Get A$). It allows time for user decisions before proceeding with the rest of the program. In our case the full program contains decisions that have to be made with regard to plotting and filing the data.

We now turn our attention to the assembly language program called BOXCAR.OBJO., shown in Table 11.7.

The first part of the listing is really not part of the program. It consists of a list of instructions to the assembler giving the exact addresses for the alphanumeric names used for them in the program. When the assembler encounters these names, it will substitute the appropriate numeric addresses. The proper numbers are "Poked" into these addresses before the machine program is called. (See BASIC calling program lines 124, 132.)

The listing indicates the memory locations and their machine language contents as well as the assembly language equivalents. For example, line 24 reading from left to right shows that location $9500 contains A9 (which is the machine language equivalent for LDA), location $9501 contains FB, and the assembly language instruction LDA #$FB follows. The next line starts with location $9502, which contains 8D, $9503 contains B8, and $9504 contains C0. The machine code for STA is 8D. Notice that the high byte (C0) of the address AL (C0B8) is stored at the higher location ($9504), and the low byte (B8) at the lower one ($9503).

The origin of the program is set to $9500 by statement 21. The next two statements link the two 16-bit timers together to form a 32-bit one. These instructions are dictated by the 6522 chip, which contains the timers.

Similarly, in the next section, communication with the timer is established in accordance with the ISAAC communication protocols with the 6522 peripheral interface chip. Thus LDA $F4 and STA AL establish communication with byte 1 of timer 1. The next two statements set this byte equal to zero. Communica-

```
80   PRINT "BOXCAR SAMPLING ROUTINE"
90   D$ = CHR$ (4)
91   PRINT D$;"BLOAD BOXCAR10.OBJO"
92   HIMEM: 38143
100  PRINT "BOXCAR SAMPLING ROUTINE"
101  PRINT "  "
110  INPUT "DATA ACQ CHANNEL # :";C%
111  PRINT "  "
120  INPUT "SAMPLE INTERVAL IN MSEC:";T%
121  PRINT "  "
122  IF T% < 5 THEN PRINT "THIS IS TOO SMALL AN INTERVAL":
     PRINT "  ": GOTO 120:REM THIS PROGRAM HAS BEEN TESTED AND
     FOUND TO BE ACCURATE ONLY DOWN TO 5 MS. IT CANNOT
     GATHER 15 POINTS WITHIN AN INTERVAL LESS THAN THIS.
123  TB% = INT (T% / 64.062):NX% = T% - (TB% * 64.080)
     :NB% = INT (NX%/.25024):PRINT INTERVAL IS: ";(TB% * 64.080)
     + (NB% * .25024):PRINT" "
124  POKE 769,TB%; POKE 768,NB%:POKE 770,C%:POKE 771,0
126  INPUT "NUMBER OF DATA POINTS: ";N%: PRINT "  "
128  IF N% = 6000 THEN PRINT "NUMBER MUST BE SMALLER THAN
     6000": PRINT "   ":GOTO 126
130  HB% = INT (N% / 256):LB% = N% - (HB% * 256)
132  POKE 773,HB%: POKE 772,LB%
135  DIM A%(N%)
140  A%(0) = A%(0)
150  CALL 38144
160  INPUT "TYPE 1 TO SEE THE AVERAGED DATA AND 2 FOR THE RAW";Y
170  IF Y = 2 GOTO 180
175  FOR I = 0 TO (N% - 1)
176  IF A%(I) > 0 THEN A%(I) = A%(I) / 15
177  IF A%(I) < 0 THEN A%(I) = (A%(I) + 65536) / 15
178  NEXT
179  GOTO 210
180  FOR I = 0 to N%
190  PRINT A%(I)
200  NEXT
205  GOTO 160
210  PRINT "STRIKE ANY KEY TO CONTINUE: "
220  WAIT - 16384,128
230  HOME : TEXT
240  END
```

Figure 11.3. BASIC boxcar sampling program   (Applesoft).

Table 11.7. Assembly Language Boxcar Program

SOURCE FILE:	BOXCAR	
0000:	1	;NAME: ;BOXCAR SAMPLER
0000:	2	;DEVICE ADDRESSES: ;AL,AH
0000:	3	;DATA FROM AND ;TO DEV:DL,DH
0000:	4	;POINTER TO ;ARRAY:VARPNTR
0000:	5	;LOC OF SAMPLING ;INT:TIMINT

Table 11.7. (*Continued*)

```
SOURCE FILE:      BOXCAR
0000:             6                                    ;LOC OF NUM OF
                                                       ;SAMP:NUMBER
0000:             7                                    ;LOC OF CHAN
                                                       ;DATA AQ:CHAN
0000:             8                                    ;
0000:             9                                    ;
0000:            10                                    ;BOXCAR:
C0B8:            11 AL:        EQU    $C0B8
C0B9:            12 AH:        EQU    $C0B9
C0BA:            13 DL:        EQU    $C0BA
C0BB:            14 DH:        EQU    $C0BB
0083:            15 VARPNTR:   EQU    $83
0300:            16 TIMINT:    EQU    $0300
0302:            17 CHAN:      EQU    $0302
0304:            18 NUMBER:    EQU    $0304
FCA8:            19 WAIT:      EQU    $FCA8
-----NEXT OBJECT FILE NAME IS BOXCAR.OBJ0
9500:            21            ORG    $9500
9500:            22 BOXCAR     EQU    *
9500:            23                                    ;LINK TWO 16-BIT
                                                       ;TIMERS TOGETHER TO
                                                       ;GET A 32-BIT ONE
                                                       ;TIMER 1 IS THE
                                                       ;FASTER TIMER
9500:A9 FB       24            LDA    #$FB             ;CONNECT TIMER 1&2
9502:8D B8 C0    25            STA    AL
9505:A9 E0       26            LDA    #$E0
9507:8D BA C0    27            STA    DL
950A:A5 F4       28 CLRTIM:    LDA    $F4              ;ADDRESS TIMER1.
950C:8D B8 C0    29            STA    AL               ;BYTE 1
950F:A9 00       30            LDA    #$0
9511:8D BA C0    31            STA    DL               ;SET BYTE 1, TIMER
                                                       ;1 EQUAL TO ZERO
9514:A9 F5       32            LDA    #$F5             ;ADDRESS TIMER 1,
9516:8D B8 C0    33            STA    AL               ;BYTE 2
9519:AD 00 03    34            LDA    TIMINT           ;SET BYTE 2, TIMER
                                                       ;1 TO THE VALUE
                                                       ;FOUND AT TIMINT
951C:8D BA C0    35            STA    DL
951F:A9 F8       36            LDA    #$F8             ;ADDRESS TIMER 2,
9521:8D B8 C0    37            STA    AL               ;BYTE 1
9524:AD 01 03    38            LDA    TIMINT+1
9527:8D BA C0    39            STA    DL               ;SET BYTE 1, TIMER
                                                       ;2 EQUAL TO ZERO
952A:A9 F9       40            LDA    #$F9             ;ADDRESS TIMER 2
952C:8D B8 C0    41            STA    AL               ;BYTE 2
```

Table 11.7. *(Continued)*

```
SOURCE  FILE:     BOXCAR
952F:A9 00       42              LDA    #$0
9531:8D BA C0    43              STA    DL              ;SET BYTE 2 EQUAL
                                                        ;TO ZERO

9534:20 5B 95    44              JSR    AIN
9537:18          45  CHKNUM:     CLC
9538:A9 02       46              LDA    #$2             ;INCREMENT THE
                                                        ;ADDRESS HELD AT
                                                        ;VARPNTR BY 2

953A:65 83       47              ADC    VARPNTR
953C:85 83       48              STA    VARPNTR
953E:A9 00       49              LDA    #$0
9540:65 84       50              ADC    VARPNTR+1
9542:85 84       51              STA    VARPNTR+1
9544:38          52              SEC
9545:AD 04 03    53              LDA    NUMBER          ;DECREMENT THE
                                                        ;VALUE HELD AT
                                                        ;NUMBER

9548:E9 01       54              SBC    #$1
954A:8D 04 03    55              STA    NUMBER
954D:AD 05 03    56              LDA    NUMBER+1
9550:E9 00       57              SBC    #$0
9552:8D 05 03    58              STA    NUMBER+1
9555:0D 04 03    59              ORA    NUMBER
9558:D0 B0       60              BNE    CLRTIM:         ;IF IT'S NOT ZERO
                                                        ;START AGAIN
955A:60          61              RTS                    ;RETURN TO BASIC
                                                        ;PROGRAM THAT
                                                        ;CALLED BOXCAR

955B:A2 0F       63  AIN:        LDX    #$F             ;SET BURST MODE CTR
955D:A9 C0       64  AIN2:       LDA    #$C0            ;DVICE NUM +WORD 0
955F:8D BB C0    65              STA    AL
9562:AD 02 03    66              LDA    CHAN
9565:8D BB C0    67              STA    DH              ;SELECT CHANNEL
9568:A9 00       68              LDA    #$0
956A:8D BA C0    69              STA    DL              ;STROBE IN THE
                                                        ;CHANNEL

956D:A9 05       70              LDA    #$5
956F:20 AB FC    71              JSR    WAIT            ;WAIT APPROX
                                                        ;150 MICROSEC

9572:A9 01       72              LDA    #$1
9574:8D BA C0    73              STA    DL              ;CONVERSION STARTS
                                                        ;WHEN BIT 0 IS SET
                                                        ;TO 1

9577:20 AB FC    74              JSR    WAIT            ;WAIT
957A:AD BA C0    75  AIN3:       LDA    DL
```

Table 11.7. (*Continued*)

```
SOURCE FILE:    BOXCAR
957D:29 01      76              AND    #$1              ;CHECK BIT 0 TO
                                                        ;SEE IF A/D IS
                                                        ;STILL BUSY
957F:D0 F9      77              BNE    AIN3             ;IF IT IS
                                                        ;CHECK AGAIN
9581:8D BA C0   78              STA    DL               ;CLEAR REQUEST
                                                        ;LINE BY WRITING
                                                        ;0 TO DL
9584:A9 C2      79              LDA    #$C2             ;REQUEST TO
                                                        ;READ (WORD 2)
9586:8D B8 C0   80              STA    AL
9589:18         81              CLC
958A:AD BA C0   82              LDA    DL               ;GET LOW BYTE
958D:A0 01      83              LDY    #$1
958F:71 83      84              ADC    (VARPNTR),Y      ;ADD TO IT THE
                                                        ;CONTENTS OF
                                                        ;LOW-BYTE MEM
9591:91 83      85              STA    (VARPNTR),Y      ;STORE IT BACK IN
                                                        ;THE SAME PLACE
9593:88         86              DEY
9594:AD BB C0   87              LDA    DH               ;GET HIGH-BYTE
9597:71 83      88              ADC    (VARPNTR),Y      ;AND DO THE
                                                        ;SAME THING
9599:91 83      89              STA    (VARPNTR),Y
959B:CA         90              DEX
959C:D0 BF      91              BNE    AIN2             ;DO THIS UNTIL
                                                        ;THE BURST COUNTER
                                                        ;READS 0
959E:18         92  CHKTIME:    CLC
959F:A9 FB      93              LDA    #$FB             ;ADDRESS TIMERS
95A1:8D B8 C0   94              STA    AL
95A4:A9 E0      95              LDA    #$E0
95A6:8D BA C0   96              STA    DL
95A9:A9 F9      97              LDA    #$F9             ;READ BYTE 2,
                                                        ;TIMER 2
95AB:8D B8 C0   98              STA    AL               ;HIGH BITS ARE 0
                                                        ;UNTIL TIME DOWN
                                                        ;THEN ALL BITS
                                                        ;ARE SET TO 1
95AE:AD BA C0   99  LDA         DL
95B1:0A         100             ASL    A
95B2:90 EA      101             BCC    CHKTIME          ;SHIFT LEFT SETS
                                                        ;CARRY WHEN BITS = 1
95B4:60         102             RTS                     ;RETURNS TO CHKNUM
**SUCCESSFUL ASSEMBLY: NO ERRORS
```

tions with the other bytes of the timers are established by writing the appropriate codes $F5, $F8, $F9.

The proper time interval values previously Poked into locations TIMINT and TIMINT+1 are loaded into byte 2 of timer 1 and byte 1 of timer 2. Zeros are loaded into the other bytes.

The last WRITE statement in this group starts the timer, and control is transferred to the subroutine AIN by the next JSR instruction. The AIN data acquisition routine first sets up a counter with the number 15 ($F), which is the number of samples to be taken.

The next set of instructions (64 to 82) constitutes the data acquisition routine and has already been discussed in detail.

The instructions immediately following do, however, require some further explanation. In the first place a somewhat different method of addressing than previously encountered, called *indirect addressing*, is used in 84, 85, 88, and 89. In this form of indirect addressing, the instruction ADC (VARPNTR), Y is a request to add to the accumulator (with carry) the contents of the byte addressed by adding the contents of the Y register to the address found at VARPNTR. Second, notice that the high byte is stored at VARPNTR and the low byte is stored at the higher address VARPNTR+1. This is just opposite of how the processor accesses and stores information (L.O. byte at AL and H.O. byte at AH. However, Applesoft BASIC stores integer data the opposite way, and since we wish to retrieve the data from the BASIC program, we must follow this convention.

After the addition of the newest data point has been made to the previous sum of data points and stored in the same place, a test is made to see if the counter is zero (91). If it is not, the routine is repeated until the counter reads zero.

The next loop, named CHKTIME, is used to wait until the required time interval has elapsed before taking the next data burst. The timer is a countdown type. At the final count the counter contains 0 in all bits. The very next count sets every bit to 1. Thus, the test that is used to check if timeout has occurred is to load the accumulator with byte 2 of timer 2 (which was originally loaded with zeroes; see line 43) and test for MSB set to 1 by ASL and test the carry bit with the BCC instruction. A jump to CHKNUM only occurs when the carry bit is set. The routine increments the address held at VARPNTR and stores it back at VARPNTR. The counter holding the total number of data points is also decremented and tested to see if it is zero. If it is not, control is again given to CLRTIM. If it is, a return to the BASIC program is executed.

11.9.   INTERRUPTS

This section is devoted to *interrupts*. This is a very powerful concept of operation that allows us to share the processor among a number of tasks. The processor performs these tasks at times dictated by external events, whose order may not be predictable—that is, asynchronous operation.

Suppose, for example, that we wished to integrate an analog input signal. This could be accomplished by sampling the signal at a fixed time interval and summing these values over the desired time period. In addition, let us assume that it is necessary to find the maximum in the analog signal and at that time, to signal for a valve closure by sending out a 5-V signal on one of the binary channels. An algorithm could be written to aid in making this decision. For example, we might examine each digitized value of the analog signal and compare it to the previous value. On the basis of this comparison (whether the last value was greater than the present one), a decision could be made as to whether the binary signal should be sent out to the valve driver.

How can we accomplish both of the above tasks and still keep track of the time? If we don't sample at equal intervals, the summation will not be an accurate representation of the integral. One solution is to acquire data by an "interrupt-driven" process.

An *interrupt* is a hardware mechanism that forces the processor to stop what it's doing, go to a specific place in memory, and start executing the routine placed at that address. An analogy to this behavior can be found in answering a telephone or a door bell. These are unexpected events that require you to stop what you are doing and answer. Presumably you will remember what you were doing before you were interrupted and will return to complete the job. We assure this in the computer version of this situation by saving the contents of the program counter and the registers before we jump to service the interrupt.

In our present example, taking samples at finite time intervals is a priority task. After this is accomplished, the processor can return to the job of comparing data points to determine if a maximum has been reached. If so, it will follow with the appropriate action dictated by the program algorithm.

A real-time clock could provide the fixed sample-time interval signal. On receiving the signal it would be necessary for the processor to interrupt what it was doing and branch to a new location in memory where the priority program (called the *interrupt handler* or *interrupt service routine*) was stored. The contents of the registers in use prior to the interrupt would have to be saved before this jump occurred. It would also be necessary for the processor to return to the location from whence it came before the interruption.

The 6502 checks the status of the interrupt system after each instruction. If an interrupt has occurred, the CPU saves the contents of the program counter and the status register in the stack. It first disables the maskable interrupt by setting bit 2 of the status register. The RTI instruction at the end of the interrupt service routine automatically restores the status register with the original value of bit 2 and the program counter. The interrupted program then continues.

The CPU then fetches an address from locations $FFFF and $FFFE. The address found at these locations in the Apple is $03FE, which contains the pointer to the interrupt service routine.

In our case we have loaded the pointer address $9300 into locations $03FE to $03FF, since $9300 is where our service routine begins.

Both the ISAAC and the ADLAB boards contains a 6522 versatile interface adaptor (VIA) chip (actually the ADLAB board contains two of these chips). This integrated circuit functions as the interface between peripheral devices and the I/O bus.

The 6522 support chip shown schematically in Figure 11.4 is compatible with the 6502 microprocessor family and is designed for connection to the data and address buses. It contains two 16-bit timers, two bidirectional 8-bit I/O ports (where the data direction of each bit is programmable), four I/O control lines, and an 8-bit serial-to-parallel/parallel-to-serial shift register. Most important, the 6522 fully supports the 6502 interrupt structure and allows you to fully utilize the Apple interrupts.

Full details concerning programming this chip can be found in the manufacturers' literature and in Levanthal's book.* We are concerned here only with those details necessary to implement the interrupt-driven data acquisition program shown on the following pages.

There are two 6522 *control lines* that are always inputs. We use one of these inputs, called CA1, connected to an external oscillator (see Figure 11.5 for a description of the Statek oscillator we used) to generate the interrupts. The VIA is configured so that these interrupts occur on the negative edge of the voltage transition from the oscillator. With the ISAAC system the oscillator

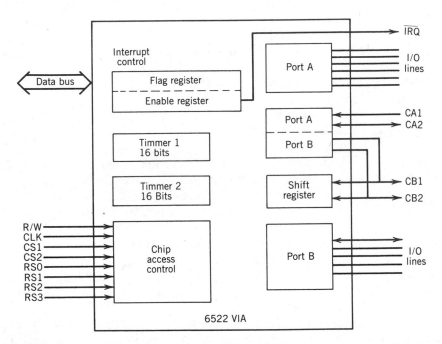

Figure 11.4.   Functional schematic of the 6522 versatile interface adapter chip (VIA).

*Lance A. Leventhal. *6502 Assembly Language Programming* (Osborne/McGraw-Hill, Berkeley, Calif. 1979).

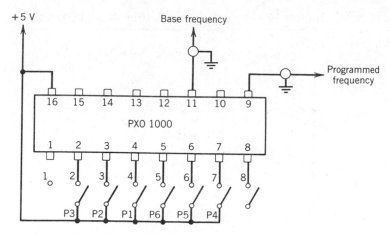

Figure 11.5a. Programmable clock. Schematic of PXO 1000 circuit.

Switch**	S7		0	0	0	0	1	1	1	1
Settings	S6		0	0	1	1	0	0	1	1
	S5		0	1	0	1	0	1	0	1
S4	S3	S2								
0	0	0	1M	100K	10K	1K	100	10	1	0.1
0	0	1	100K	10K	1K	100	10	1	0.1	0.01
0	1	0	500K	50K	5K	500	50	5	0.5	0.05
0	1	1	333.3K	33.3K	3.3K	333.3	33.3	3.3	0.33	0.033
1	0	0	250K	25K	2.5K	250	25	2.5	0.25	0.025
1	0	1	200K	20K	2K	200	20	2	0.2	0.02
1	1	0	166.6K	16.6K	1.6K	166.6	16.6	1.66	0.16	0.016
1	1	1	83.3K	8.3K	833.3	83.3	8.3	0.83	0.083	0.0083

Figure 11.5b. Programmable Clock. Output frequencies of model PXO-1000 (0.0083 Hz– 1 MHz). The PXO Series of Programmable Oscillator is a low-power device contianing a quartz crystal and a CMOS IC, both packaged in a standard 16-pin DIP. It is available from STATEK Corp., 512 N. Main Orange, CA 92668. The switch settings are settings of the miniature switches positioned on top of the DIP.

(external clock) is connected to pin 1 of connector strip J4 located on the ISAAC interface board in slot 3 of the Apple, and switch 2 of S2 is also turned on.

Let us turn our attention to the assembly language program in Table 11.8, which is an interrupt-driven data acquisition routine that is usable up to sampling rates of 4 kHz.

The question marks in the symbol table that follows the assembled program are used by the assembler to indicate that those particular symbols were never referenced.

Table 11.8. Assembly Language Program Listing of INTDDATAQ2

```
SOURCE FILE:  INTDATAQ2
03FE:            1 USRINT    EQU   $03FE          ;POINTER TO
                                                 ;INTERRUPT HANDLER

FCA8:            2 WAIT:     EQU   $FCA8
C0B8:            3 AL:       EQU   $C0B8
C0B9:            4 AH:       EQU   $C0B9
C0BA:            5 DL:       EQU   $C0BA
C0BB:            6 DH:       EQU   $C0BB
0300:            7 NUMBER:   EQU   $0300
0302:            8 FLAG:     EQU   $0302
0303:            9 DATAL     EQU   $0303
0305:           10 CHAN:     EQU   $0305
0083:           11 VARPNTR:  EQU   $83
-----NEXT OBJECT FILE NAME IS INTDDATAQ2.OBJO
9300:           12           ORG   $9300
9300:48         13 INTHDLER:PHA                  ;BEGIN INTERRUPT
                                                 ;SERVICE ROUTINE
9301:A9 FD      14           LDA   #$FD          ;VIAIFR SELECT
9303:8D BB C0   15           STA   AL
9306:A9 82      16           LDA   #$82          ;CLEAR CA1 FLAG
9308:8D BA C0   17           STA   DL
930B:A9 C0      18           LDA   #$C0          ;DEVICE SELECT,
                                                 ;ADC
930D:8D B8 C0   19           STA   AL
9310:AD 05 03   20           LDA   CHAN          ;SELECT CHANNEL
9313:8D BB C0   21           STA   DH
9316:A9 00      22           LDA   #$0
9318:8D BA C0   23           STA   DL
931B:A9 04      24           LDA   #$4
931D:20 AB FC   25           JSR   WAIT          ;WAIT FOR THE
                                                 ;MULTIPLEX TO
                                                 ;SETTLE (APPROX.
                                                 ;150 MICRO SEC)

9320:A9 01      26           LDA   #$1
9322:8D BA C0   27           STA   DL            ;REQUEST A
                                                 ;CONVERSION
9325:20 A8 FC   28           JSR   WAIT          ;WAIT FOR APPROX.
                                                 ;30 MICROSEC
9328:AD BA C0   29 AIN2:     LDA   DL            ;CHECK TO SEE
                                                 ;IF THE
932B:29 01      30           AND   #$1           :ADC IS STILL BUSY
932D:D0 F9      31           BNE   AIN2          ;IF IT IS GO BACK
                                                 ;AND WAIT
932F:8D BA C0   32           STA   DL
9332:A9 C2      33           LDA   #$C2          ;CHANGE STATUS
                                                 ;OF DL AND DH
9334:8D B8 C0   34           STA   AL
```

Table 11.8. *(Continued)*

SOURCE FILE:	INTDATAQ2				
9337:AD BA C0	35		LDA	DL	;GET THE LOW ;DATA BYTE
933A:8D 03 03	36		STA	DATAL	;AND STORE IT IN ;A TEMPORARY ;LOCATION
933D:AD BB C0	37		LDA	DH	;DO THE SAME FOR ;THE HIGH DATA ;BYTE
9340:8D 04 03	38		STA	DATAL+1	
9343:EE 02 03	39		INC	FLAG	
9346:68	40		PLA		
9347:40	41		RTI		
9348:78	42	SETUP:	SEI		;DISABLE ;INTERRUPT ;REQUEST LINE
9349:A9 00	43		LDA	#$0	;SET UP ;INTERRUPT POINTER
934B:8D B9 C0	44		STA	AH	
934E:8D FE 03	45		STA	USRINT	
9351:A9 93	46		LDA	#$93	
9353:8D FF 03	47		STA	USRINT+1	
9356:A9 FE	48		LDA	#$FE	;VIAIER SELECT
9358:8D B8 C0	49		STA	AL	
935B:A9 7D	50		LDA	#$7D	;DISABLE ALL
935D:8D BA C0	51		STA	DL	;INTERRUPTS
9360:A9 FD	52		LDA	#$FD	;VIAIFR SELECT
9362:8D BB C0	53		STA	AL	
9365:A9 82	54		LDA	#$82	;CLEAR CA1 FLAG1
9367:8D BA C0	55		STA	DL	
936A:A9 FE	56		LDA	#$FE	;SELECT VIAIER
936C:8D B8 C0	57		STA	AL	
936F:A9 82	58		LDA	#$82	;ENABLE CA1
9371:8D BA C0	59		STA	DL	;INTERRUPT FLAG
9374:A9 D2	60	BOUT:	LDA	#$D2	;CREATE OUTPUT ;PULSE FOR SCOPE
9376:8D B8 C0	61		STA	AL	
9379:A9 FF	62		LDA	#$FF	
937B:8D BB C0	63		STA	DH	
937E:8D BA C0	64		STA	DL	
9381:A9 00	65		LDA	#$0	
9383:8D BB C0	66		STA	DH	
9386:8D BA C0	67		STA	DL	
9389:A9 00	68		LDA	#$0	;CLEAR FLAG
938B:8D 02 03	69		STA	FLAG	

(Continued)

Table 11.8. *(Continued)*

```
SOURCE FILE:   INTDATAQ2
938E:58        70         CLI                      ;ENABLE CPU
                                                   ;INTERRUPTS

938F:AD 02 03  71 PAUSE:  LDA    FLAG
9392:F0 FB     72         BEQ    PAUSE             ;WAIT HERE
                                                   ;FOR INTERRUPT

9394:A0 01     73 LDY     #$1
9396:AD 03 03  74         LDA    DATAL             ;GET LOW BYTE
                                                   ;FROM TEMP
9399:91 83     75         STA    (VARPNTR).Y       ;AND STORE IT
                                                   ;IN THE ARRAY

939B:88        76         DEY
939D:AD 04 03  77         LDA    DATAL+1
939F:91 83     78         STA    (VARPNTR).Y       ;DO THE SAME
                                                   ;FOR THE HIGH BYTE

93A1:18        79         CLC
93A2:A9 02     80         LDA    #$2
93A4:65 83     81         ADC    VARPNTR           ;INCREMENT
                                                   ;THE POINTER

93A6:85 83     82         STA    VARPNTR
93A8:A9 00     83         LDA    #$0
93AA:65 84     84         ADC    VARPNTR+1
93AC:85 84     85         STA    VARPNTR+1
93AE:38        86         SEC
93AF:AD 00 03  87         LDA    NUMBER
93B2:E9 01     88         SBC    #$1               ;DECREMENT THE
                                                   ;VALUE HELD AT
                                                   ;NUMBER

93B4:8D 00 03  89         STA    NUMBER
93B7:AD 01 03  90         LDA    NUMBER+1
93BA: E9 00    91         SBC    #$0
93BC:8D 01 03  92         STA    NUMBER+1

93BF:0D 00 03  93         ORA    NUMBER
93C2:D0 B0     94         BNE    BOUT
93C4:78        95         SEI                      ;DISABLE
                                                   ;INTERRUPTS

93C5:A9 FE     96         LDA    #$FE              ;VIAIER SELECT
93C7:8D B8 C0  97         STA    AL
93CA:A9 7D     98         LDA    #$7D              ;DISABLE ALL
                                                   ;INTERRUPTS

93CC:8D BA C0  99         STA    DL
93CF:60        100        RTS
***SUCCESSFUL ASSEMBLY: NO ERRORS
```

COB9 AH	9328 AIN2	COBB AL	9374 BOUT
0305 CHAN	?9389 CLRFLAG	0303 DATAL	COBB DH

Table 11.8. *(Continued)*

SOURCE FILE:	INTDATAQ2						
COBA DL		0302 FLAG		?9300 INTHDLER		0300 NUMBER	
938F PAUSE		?9348 SETUP		03FE USRINT		83 VARPNTR	
FCAB WAIT							
83 VARPNTR		0300 NUMBER		0302 FLAG		0303 DATAL	
0305 CHAN		03FE USRINT		?9300 INTHDLER		9328 AIN2	
?9348 SETUP		9374 BOUT		?9389 CLRFLAG		938F PAUSE	
COBB AL		COB9 AH		COBA DL		COBB DH	
FCAB WAIT							

The entry point to the program is at location $9348 (37704 decimal). This is a routine to set up the 6522 (VIA) interrupt flag and interrupt enable registers (VIAIFR and VIAIER) before beginning actual data acquisition (instructions 48 to 59). Also the address of the interrupt service routine is loaded into the Apple pointer address locations $03FE and $03FF (instructions 43 to 47).

The next set of instructions (60 to 67), labeled BOUT, would be eliminated in the final program. It was used here to produce a 5-V output pulse to time the interrupt service and array storage routines. Both the clock signals and this timing pulse signal were displayed on an oscilloscope during testing of this program.

The following instructions clear the location called FLAG by writing a zero to it. As you will see further on, this location is incremented when an interrupt occurs. Instructions 71 and 72 constitute a continuous loop that will be executed as long as the contents of FLAG is zero.

Note that, instead of the PAUSE loop, one can substitute any of the other tasks required of the CPU (e.g., the decision algorithm and valve closure commands alluded to earlier). In order to simplify the explanation we have eliminated this section of the program.

Returning to our program, recall that we are in a loop at PAUSE waiting for something to happen. Remember, the CPU checks on every instruction cycle to see if an interrupt flag has been set.

An interrupt occurs. The CPU examine $FFFE and $FFFF, follows the pointer to $03FE, and finds the address $9300 to the interrupt routine. It goes to $9300 and starts to execute the instructions from $9300 on.

Notice that the first instruction is PHA, which stores the contents of the accumulator on top of the stack. The next set of instructions clears the interrupt flag. The by-now-familiar data acquisition routine follows (18 to 38) with the digitized value being stored in temporary locations DATAL and DATAL+1.

The interrupt routine ends by incrementing the value at FLAG and finally restoring to the accumulator whatever was in it before it was interrupted (PLA). The RTI instruction returns the processor to exactly the same instruction it was executing before it was interrupted. In our case this is the PAUSE loop.

However, the value at FLAG is now 1. Therefore the branch does not occur, and instructions 73 to 94 are executed. The first part of this routine is also familiar to the reader. It involves merely transferring the data from temporary storage (DATAL and DATAL+1) to the array defined in the BASIC program.

A test is also made to determine if the required number of data points has been taken (87 to 93). If not, the branch (94) to BOUT is executed. BOUT generates our timing pulse for the scope and then we are back at PAUSE, waiting for the next interrupt.

The lag between the beginning of the interrupt routine (negative clock transition) and when the BOUT pulse appears is 400 μs. A large portion of this is the 150 μs waiting for the multiplexer poll. Eliminating this (since we are taking data from only one channel) decreases the time to 250 μs (or a 4-Hz data rate). This is much faster than we originally thought would be possible with the Apple interrupt structure.

For slow data applications, such as normal speed gas chromatography, a data rate of 20 samples per second is more than adequate. This is a sample interval of 50 ms or 50,000 μs. Even if we subtract the larger 400-μs time needed for interrupt servicing, this still leaves us 49,600 μs to do whatever else we have to do before we have to worry about another interrupt. At an average of 4 clock cycles per instructions, we can execute a great number of instructions in 49,600 μs.

The simple BASIC calling program that was used to check this assembly language routine is shown below. It calls for a collection of 1600 points (POKE 768,0:POKE 769,16) on channel 7 (POKE 773,7). The array is dimensioned to 2000, and the assembly program is called (entered) at 37704 ($9348 hex). On return, the points are printed out to the monitor screen.

```
 5 D$ = CHR$ (4)
10 PRINT D$;"BLOAD INTDATAQ2.OBJ0"
20 POKE 768,0:POKE 769,16:POKE 770,0:POKE 773,7
30 DIM A%(2000)
40 A%(0) = A%(0)
50 CALL 37704
60 FOR N = 0 to 1600
70 PRINT A%(N): PRINT " ": NEXT
80 END
```

11.9.1. Interrupt-Driven Boxcar Routine

The interrupt-driven procedure should also be a more accurate way of running our boxcar program. The reader should be able to combine these programs to yield an interrupt-driven boxcar sampling routine.

The boxcar acquisition routine, labeled AIN (lines 63 to 91), would replace

Table 11.9.   Interrupt Handler Code

	Old Code		New Code
INTHHDLR:	PHA	INTHDLR:	PHA
	·		TXA
	·		PHA
	·		·
	·		·
	PLA		PLA
	RTI		TAX
			PLA
			RTI

the single data point acquisition program in the interrupt service routine (lines 18 to 38). Since you will now be using the X register (for the burst counter) in the handler routine, you will also have to save its contents along with the accumulator. Follow your PHA instruction with TXA and then PHA again to accomplish this. Remember to restore its contents before you exit with a PLA followed by a TAX instruction. See Table 11.9.

Eliminate instructions 73 to 91 from the original interrupt program and substitute the routine CHKNUM (instructions 45 to 61) from the original boxcar program (first change #60 to read BNE CLRFLAG). That should do it.

11.9.2.   Subroutine Interrupts in BASICA

A very useful and unusual feature of IBM BASICA is the ability to set up and service external interrupts from BASICA. The interrupt handler is not a machine language but a BASIC subroutine within the BASIC program. The interrupting events can be a keypress, incoming information from the IBM asynchronous communication card, activation of the light pen, or a trigger from a joystick.

The form of the statement is

```
ON event GOSUB line
```

where event is COMn, KEY(n), PEN, or STRING, and line is the beginning line number of the BASIC subroutine.

11.10.   MODIFYING THE APPLESOFT CALL INSTRUCTION TO PASS ARGUMENTS

In contrast to a BASICA CALL statement, the Applesoft CALL statement in its original form is quite limited. It can be modified, however, so that it can also pass parameters to a machine language program. The procedure is much like that for a pass-parameter ampersand statement.

A short machine language utility program is written to interpret the rest of the CALL statement. The modified CALL transfers control to this utility package, which loads the parameters into the A, X, and Y registers and finally passes control to the desired machine language routine.

The syntax of the new CALL is shown below.

```
CALL origin, Z-expr, X-expr, y-expr, location
```

where

origin = Decimal address of the utility program.
A-expr = A single byte integer (0 to 255) or any variable or expression. This parameter will be loaded into the accumulator.
X-expr = Same as above except that the X register will be loaded with the parameter.
y-expr = Same, but the Y register will be loaded with the parameter.
location = Decimal address of the entry point to the machine language program to be called that will use the above parameters.

The literature is replete with routines to accomplish the above modification in CALL. The following was taken from *What's Where in the Apple** and is a variant of one published by C. K. Mesztemyi[†]. The machine language routine is entered as Applesoft program lines in the BASIC program. The monitor program is "tricked" into reading the program and storing it at location $300 (decimal 768).

```
702 A$ = "300:20 F5 E6 8A 48 20 F5 E6 8A 48
          20 F5 E6 8A 48 20 BE DE 20 67 DD 20
          52 E7 68 A8 68 AA 68 6C 50 00 20 "
703 REM LINE 704 ADDS MONITOR COMMANDS FOR RETURN TO
    APPLESOFT; LINE 705 COPIES A$ INTO THE KEYBOARD BUFFER,
    RESETS STATUS
704 A$ = A$+"ND823G"
705 FOR I = 1 to LEN(A$):POKE 511+I, ASC(MID$(A$,I,1))
    +128:NEXT:POKE 72,0:CALL-144
```

The machine language utility program is written as a string, A$, in line 702. Line 705 enters this program beginning at location 512 decimal (POKE 511+I). These locations (512 to 767) define the buffer area in which inputs from the keyboard are stored. The CALL−144 transfers control to a monitor routine that reads the contents of this input buffer and stores it starting at $300 (decimal

*W. F. Luebbert, loc. cit.
†C. K. Mesztemyi *Passing Argument Values to Machine Language Subroutines in Applesoft, Apple Orchard* (Spring, 1981).

768). This machine language routine very cleverly uses the Applesoft interpreter subroutines (already present in memory) to read parameters and then transfer control to the user's machine language routine, which was the original CALL destination.

Alternatively, the machine language program could have been entered with individual POKE statements. As a matter of choice, the authors much prefer to use the mini-assembler that is part of the integer BASIC ROM package to enter the program and then file it as a binary file by using the BSAVE instruction. This is illustrated below, where the above machine language routine is rewritten in assembly language.

Normally, the mini-assembler is not available on the Apple II Plus. However, if you have the language card in place, you're in luck because the mini-assembler program is loaded into RAM on the language card, along with integer BASIC, when the system is booted. You must *access it from the monitor program via integer BASIC*. You can do this by typing INT and then RETURN. The Applesoft prompt], will be replaced by the integer BASIC prompt, >. Typing CALL−151 <RETURN> gets you into the Apple system monitor program (a * appears on the screen as a prompt) and if this is followed by typing F666G, the ! prompt will appear, signifying that you are now in the mini-assembler program.

The mini-assembler cannot understand symbolic labels. Therefore, it is necessary to use actual addresses of the subroutines we will be calling, rather than symbolic labels like GETBYTC, CHKCOM, and so on, that we normally define with EQU statements at the beginning of the program.

To set the program counter to the beginning of our program (0300), we type the beginning hexadecimal address, a colon, and then our first instruction:

```
!  300:JSR   $E6F5
```

When we press <RETURN>, the mini-assembler converts this program line into hexadecimal, stores it, starting at hex 300, and then disassembles it and displays it on top of our original input line. Thus, when we hit <RETURN>, the above line reappears as

```
0300 − 20 F5 E6   JSR $E6F5
```

where 20 F5 E6 is the machine language equivalent for JSR $E6F5 (note again the low-byte/high-byte storage convention).

The prompt, !, appears below this line. It is not necessary to type in any more instruction addresses. The instruction,

```
!  TXA
```

for example, becomes, on pressing <RETURN>

```
0303−    8A    TXA
```

Presuming we have entered our program, we can return to the system monitor program by typing

!$FF69G <RETURN>

You may list the program from the monitor by typing the starting address, followed by L; for example,

*300L <RETURN>

The listing in Table 11.10 will appear on your screen minus the comments, which we have added for explanatory purposes.

To save our routine, we can return to Applesoft by typing 3DOG <RETURN>. From Applesoft, typing

BSAVE EXTND, A$0300, L001F <RETURN>

saves this machine language program (1F bytes in length) under the name EXTND.

It should be noted that although we created this program using addresses $0300 to $031F, we can load it anywhere in memory we wish. For example, the instruction

BLOAD EXTND, A$95E1

will load the program just below DOS.

Returning to the explanation of our machine language program, note that GETBYTE is an Applesoft interpreter routine that gobbles the comma, evaluates the following byte (which happens to be a parameter), and places it in the X register. This number is then transferred to the system for temporary storage. This procedure is repeated three times, so that, finally, there are three parameters stored on the stack.

The fourth parameter is actually the address of the machine language program being called. After checking for a comma (with CHKCOM), the program uses FERNUM to evaluate the number as a 6-byte floating-point real number. The routine GETADR converts this number to a 2-byte address and stores it at location $0050 (called LINNUM). The parameters are now pulled off the stack one at a time (PLA) and transferred to the Y register (TAY), X-register (TAX), or left in the accumulator. Now all of the registers are full. Your machine program should contain instructions to obtain these parameters from the registers and perhaps store them before they are lost.

The last instruction is an *indirect address jump*. It says to go to location LINNUM ($0050) to find the address of the routine and then jump to that address. (Recall that the machine language address was stored in LINNUM by GETADR.)

Table 11.10. Mini-Assembler Listing of Extended CALL Utility Program

```
*300L
0300-20 F5 E6    JSR $E6F5    ;THIS IS THE ADDRESS OF THE
                              ;SUBROUTINE GETBYTE. THIS
                              ;ROUTINE GETS THE FIRST
                              ;PARAMETER, EVALUATES IT,
                              ;PLACES IT IN THE X
                              ;REGISTER.
0303-8A          TXA          ;TRANSFER IT TO THE
                              ;ACCUMULATOR.
0304-48          PHA          ;STORE IT TEMPORARILY ON
                              ;THE SYSTEM STACK.
0305-20 F5 E6    JSR $E6F5    ;REPEAT THE ABOVE STEPS
                              ;FOR THE SECOND PARAMETER.
0308-8A          TXA
0309-48          PHA
030A-20 F5 E6    JSR $E6F5    ;REPEAT FOR THIRD PARAMETER.
030D-8A          TXA
030E-48          PHA.
030F-20 BE DE    JSR $DEBE    ;JUMP TO THE ADDRESS OF
                              ;ANOTHER ROUTINE CALLED
                              ;CHKCOM, WHICH CHECKS FOR A
                              ;COMMA AND GETS READY FOR
                              ;THE FOURTH PARAMETER (WHICH
                              ;IS THE ADDRESS OF THE MACHINE
                              ;LANGUAGE ROUTINE THAT CALL
                              ;REQUESTED).
0312-20 67 DD    JSR $DD67    ;JUMP TO ANOTHER ROUTINE
                              ;(FRNUM) THAT WILL EVALUATE
                              ;THE NUMBER.
0315-20 52 E7    JSR $E752    ;THE ROUTINE GETADR STORED AT
                              ;$E752 CONVERTS THE NUMBER TO
                              ;ADDRESS BYTES AND STORES IT
                              ;AT LINNUM (0050).
0318-68          PLA          ;PULL THE THIRD PARAMETER OFF
                              ;THE STACK AND PUT IT IN THE
                              ;ACCUMULATOR.
0319-A8          TAY          ;TRANSFER IT TO THE Y REGISTER.
031A-68          PLA          ;PULL THE SECOND PARAMETER OFF
                              ;THE STACK.
031B-AA          TAX          ;TRANSFER IT TO THE X REGISTER.
031C-68          PLA          ;PULL THE FIRST PARAMETER.
031D-6C 50 00    JMP $0050    ;JUMP TO THE MACHINE LANGUAGE
                              ;ROUTINE SPECIFIED BY CALL VIA
                              ;ITS ADDRESS STORED AT 0050.
```

We have limited ourselves to a three-parameter pass in this example. If one wished to pass more than this, each could be stored at a specific memory location for retrieval later by the machine language program. The PHA instructions would then be replaced by STA $XXXX. Likewise, all the PLA and TAX, TAY instructions would be eliminated.

11.11.   ASSEMBLY LANGUAGE PROGRAMMING THE ADLAB HARDWARE

Addressing the ADLAB in assembly language is well documented in the *ADLAB Hardware Manual,** from which the following information has been extracted. Only the interrupt-driven A/D conversion is reviewed here.

There are two 6522 chips on each ADLAB interface card. The ADC is controlled by the so-called dedicated 6522 chip. The other chip is called the "user" 6522 and is completely under the control of the user. Each chip has 16 successive memory addresses. The dedicated 6522 addresses begin at $C000+N*$100 (where N is the slot number of the ADLAB card), and the user chip addresses begin at $C030+N*$100. The starting addresses are labeled BASE1 and BASE2, respectively, in the following programs.

The "dedicated" 6522 addresses and their functions are shown in Table 11.11.

To initialize the dedicated 6522 chip then, one writes

```
LDA #$0F          ;SET HIGH-BYTE DATA DIRECTION
STA BASE1+$02
LDA #$FF          ;SET LOW-BYTE DATA DIRECTION
STA BASE1+$03
LDA #$BE          ;SET LOW-BYTE TIMER 0
STA BASE1+$06
LDA #$C7          ;SET HIGH-BYTE TIMER 0
STA BASE1+$07
LDA #$E0          ;INITIALIZE AUXILIARY
STA BASE1+0B      ;CONTROL REGISTER
LDA #$8A          ;INITIALIZE PERIPHERAL CONTROL
STA BASE1+$0C     ;REGISTER
```

Writing to BASE1+0 starts the ADC. At the end of conversion an interrupt flag is set in the interrupt flag register found at BASE1+$0D. Bit 4 in this register is zero during the conversion and set to 1 on its conclusion. Testing this bit will determine if the conversion is completed. Such a routine is illustrated below.

---

*Paul K. Warme, *ADLAB Hardware Manual* (Interactive Microware Inc. P.O. Box 771, State College, Pa 1680).

Table 11.11. "Dedicated" 6522 Addresses

Address	Function
BASE1+0	High byte of D/A digital value; writing to this address also triggers ADC. This doesn't interfere with D/A, since D/A does not latch until the low byte of D/A is written to BASE 1+1.
BASE1+1	Low byte of D/A value: Reading or writing to this address latches the high-byte D/A.
BASE1+2	Data Direction Register B: Initialized to $0F.
BASE1+3	Data Direction Register A: Initialized to $FF.
BASE1+4	Timer 0 Low-byte data.
BASE1+5	Timer 0 High-byte data.
BASE1+6	Timer 0 Low-byte latched to preset value: initialized to $BE.
BASE1+7	Timer 0 High-byte latched to preset value: initialized to $C7.
BASE1+8	Timer 1 low byte.
BASE1+9	Timer 1 high byte.
BASE1+A	Shift register.
BASE1+B	Auxiliary Control Register: initialized to $E0.
BASE1+C	Peripheral Control Register: initialized to $BA.
BASE1+D	Interrupt Flag Register.
BASE1+E	Interrupt Enable Register.
BASE1+F	Low byte of D/A digital value.

```
        STA BASE1              ; START ADC
WAIT    LDA  BASE1+$0D         ; READ INTERRUPT FLAG REGISTER
        AND #$10               ; CHECK BIT #4
        BEQ WAIT               ; GO BACK TO WAIT IF IT IS NOT SET
```

The above routine only checks to see if the conversion is done. To enable this "conversion done" program to interrupt your main program, you must set bit 4 of the interrupt enable register found at BASE1+$0E. Writing $90 to this address enables the A/D interrupt, and writing $10 to this address disables the A/D interrupt.

Putting this all together with the necessary interrupt handler routine discussed in the preceding section yields the interrupt-driven program in Table 11.12. The interrupt is generated in this case by the "conversion done" routine, not by a timer, as illustrated previously.

The routine of Table 11.12 will acquire data at the fastest rate allowed by the ADC.

Four handshaking lines are available via the 6522 chip: CA1, CA2, CB1, and CB2. The CA1 and CB1 lines can be set to recognize either a negative or a positive transition, and each transition can be used to set a bit in the interrupt

Table 11.12. Interrupt-Driven Data Aquisition Routine for ADLAB
Hardware

SETUP	SEI	;DISABLE INTERRUPTS
	LDA #<INTADR	;LOAD THE LOW-BYTE ADDRESS ;OF THE INTERRUPT ;HANDLER INTHDLER
	STA $03FE	;AND STORE IT AT THE APPLE ;POINTER ADDRESS
	LDA #>INTADR+1	;LOAD THE HIGH-BYTE ADDRESS ;OF THE INTERRUPT HANDLER
	STA $03FF	;AND STORE IT AT THE HIGH- ;BYTE ADDRESS OF THE APPLE ;POINTER
	CLI	;REENABLES INTERRUPTS
	RTS	
INTHDLER	LDA BASE1+$0D	;LOAD THE CONTENTS OF THE ;INTERRUPT FLAG REGISTER
	AND #$10	;TO SEE IF BIT 4 HAS BEEN SET
	BEQ OTHER	;IF BIT 4 = 0, IT IS NOT AN ;A/D INTERRUPT
	AND BASE1+$0E	;IF BIT 4 OF THE INT. FLAG ;REGISTER SET = 1, IS BIT 4 ;OF THE ENABLE INT. FLAG ;REGISTER ALSO SET = 1
	BNE READ	;IF IT IS, BRANCH TO THE ;ROUTINE LABELLED READ TO
OTHER		;OTHER INTERRUPTS ARE ;HANDLED HERE
READ	LDA BASE1+$10	;READ THE LOW-BYTE A/D ;VALUE FROM THIS ADDRESS
	STA DATAL	;AND STORE IT AT MEMORY ;LOCATION DATAL
	LDA BASE1+$20	;READ THE HIGH A/D BYTE ;FROM THIS ADDRESS
	STA DATAL+$1	;AND STORE IT AT THE HIGH- ;BYTE MEMORY LOCATION
	PLA	;RESTORE THE ORIGINAL ;CONTENTS (BEFORE INTERRUPT) ;TO THE ACCUMULATOR
	RTI	;RETURN FROM INTERRUPT

flag register. Provided that the *corresponding* bit is set in the interrupt enable register, a transition on CA1 or CB1 will generate an interrupt. We have just demonstrated this with the assembly language, timed, interrupt-driven routine for the ISAAC 91A. Similarly, with ADLAB, we can enable interrupts when CA1 is triggered.

To enable interrupts on CA1 of the user 6522 chip, use the commands

```
LDA #$82              ;SET BIT 7 = 1 TO ENABLE
                      ;AND BIT 2 = 1 to
                      ;SELECT CA1
STA BASE2+$0E         ;ENABLE BY STORING AT THE
                      ;INTERRUPT ENABLE REGISTER
```

To disable interrupts we would store $02 in the same place. The setup routine to utilize a clock pulse on CA1 to generate interrupts would be:

```
SETUP        SEI                    ;DISABLE INTERRUPTS
             LDA #INTADR            ;LOAD LOW-BYTE ADDRESS OF
                                    ;INTERRUPT HANDLER
             STA $03FC              ;APPLE POINTER ADDRESS,
                                    ;LOW BYTE
             LDA #INTADR+1          ;LOAD HIGH-BYTE ADDRESS
                                    ;OF INTERRUPT HANDLER
             STA $03FF              ;HIGH-BYTE APPLE POINTER
                                    ;ADDRESS
             LDA #$82               ;ALLOW CA1 INTERRUPTS
             STA BASE2+$0E          ;INTERRUPT ENABLE REGISTER
             CLI                    ;RE-ENABLE INTERRUPTS
             RTS
```

Some Final Comments

The ISAAC was not designed around an interrupt system, and it takes some effort by the user to convert it to that type of operation. The ADLAB, however, is an interrupt driven system, albeit a rather slow one (20 cps maximum). This slow speed is due to the dual-slope integrator, which provides some smoothing of the data. A special fast A/D card is also available from Interactive Microware. The ADC on the ADLAB card is controlled by a dedicated 6522 chip. The *ADLAB Hardware Manual* contains all the necessary information for addressing the 6522 chips and some sample assembly language routines that should help the user design his own routine.

The Keithley DAS data acquisition system is also an interrupt-driven architecture. Programming with this system is discussed fully in Chapter 6.

Conclusions

Although many of the scientific language extensions will probably answer most needs, it may be necessary to write small routines to solve your unique problems. Despite the horror stories you may have heard, assembly language programming is not that difficult. Indeed, for some, the challenge can lead to addiction.

12

Standard Communications Interfaces

The remainder of this book is taken up with a discussion of some of the standard methods of interfacing in the computer industry. We describe some of the ways that computers may be configured to communicate with the outside world.

In this chapter we consider the following interfaces.

Computer bus interfaces
The RS-232 interface
The HP-IL interface
The parallel interface
The BCD parallel interface
The centronics interface

Most of these interfaces are available on all personal computers. Each of these interfaces or "communications paths" is standard enough that much commercial hardware is available that has been configured to be compatible. Together with the GPIB interface, described in the next chapter, these interfaces represent the vast majority of methods that are used for microcomputers to communicate with peripheral equipment or to establish a link with other microcomputers. We include a discussion of computer buses as a natural part of this chapter. The buses of the Apple and the IBM-PC have reached a stage of standardization where they may be considered as a communications path, if only over extremely short distances.

The GPIB interface provides such a critically important method of laboratory communication that it deserved a chapter of its own. It is discussed in detail in Chapter 13, where we have departed from the customary formal discussion of its design and concentrated instead on practical examples of its use in the laboratory.

12.1.   BUS INTERFACING

The configuration of a typical laboratory bus-based computer system is shown in Figure 12.1. The basic computer system consists of four interface cards. One card contains a single board computer including the CPU (central processing unit) and a minimum of memory; another contains additional RAM memory; a third board controls a hard-disk, mass-storage device; the fourth controls high-resolution screen graphics. The additional boards on the computer bus are used for laboratory interfacing. One of the boards contains a bus–GPIB interface converter that allows the computer to communicate with standardized laboratory equipment.

Before proceeding to a discussion of interfaces, it is helpful to review some of the concepts introduced in Chapters 1 and 2 regarding the communication path between CPU, memory, and peripheral equipment.*

12.1.1.   Bus Structure For Memory-Mapped I/O

One such system, illustrated in Figure 1.10, shows three bundles of conductors, called *buses*, to which various components are connected. These three buses

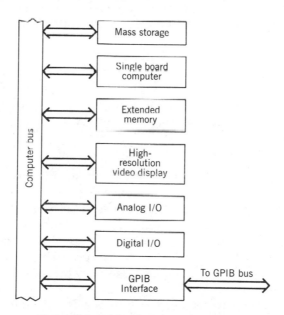

Figure 12.1.   A bus-based computer system.

---

*For the reader who wishes to pursue this subject further, a series of articles entitled *"The Input Output Primer,"* by Steve Liebson, appeared in the February to July 1982 issues of *Byte*. (Byte Publications, Inc., 70 Main Street, Peterborough, N.H.)

are called collectively, a *memory bus*. The particular architecture illustrated in this figure is called *memory-mapped I/O* because the peripherals are attached directly to the memory bus and assigned locations just as if they were memory.

As explained in Chapter 2, this is the system used in the Apple, where a special set of memory locations ($C000 to $CFFF) is reserved for I/O functions. The advantage of this architecture is that the same set of instructions used to access memory can be used to access the peripherals. The disadvantage is that the maximum memory size available to the CPU is reduced by the number of addresses assigned to the peripherals.

12.1.2.   I/O Bus Structure

The alternative to the above-discussed method of attaching peripheral devices is to create a new bus and attach the peripherals to it. This new bus is called an I/O bus and is quite similar to the memory bus in that it contains a peripheral data bus, a peripheral address bus, and a peripheral control bus.

The advantage of using an I/O bus is that the full memory capacity to the computer is retained. On the other hand, a new set of instructions must be created for the microprocessor. These are called *I/O instructions* to distinguish them from the normal *memory-referenced* instructions. In common with the memory-referenced instructions, though, they are usually written in machine language.

Writing an I/O instruction set is not a trivial task. The computer manufacturer therefore supplies the necessary machine language routines as part of the OS software, accessible to the user through a high-level language. One measure, then, of the strength of an OS is the ease with which new peripherals can be installed and supported by the system.

12.1.3.   The Interface

It would certainly be convenient if every computer I/O bus were the same, and/or every piece of peripheral equipment came with circuitry that could be connected directly to the I/O bus. Unfortunately, life is not that simple. Some peripherals have an 8-data line bus; others, 16; some present their data one bit at a time in a serial fashion, and others use parallel transmission. What is required then, is some specialized circuitry to be placed between the peripheral device and the I/O bus to adapt the signals used by the computer to that of the peripheral, or vice versa.

This specialized circuitry is called an *interface*. It is the interface that plugs into the I/O bus and is connected to the device. It acts as an intermediary and translates signals, voltage levels, and whatever else is necessary to establish communication between the computer and the device.

If every peripheral required a different interface, it would be extremely difficult, if not impossible, to connect more than a few specific devices to our system. Fortunately, most peripherals can be interfaced with one of four interfaces: *serial I/O, parallel I/O, GPIB* (also called IEEE-488 and HP-IB), and *BCD* (binary coded decimal). All of these interfaces will be discussed in more detail in this and the next chapters. However, before proceeding to these topics, let us explore our communication problem in a little more detail.

12.1.4.   Device Drivers

An interface describes only the hardware necessary to attach a device to the computer. It provides the necessary electronics to allow communication between the device and the computer. In itself this is not enough. What is also required to complete the communications picture is *software* that can translate the processor requests into language that the device can understand. These software interfaces are called *device drivers*.

One of the main tasks of the OS is to supply and support these device drivers. When an application program requests any DOS operation on a given device by a DOS I/O function call, the DOS determines which device driver is required and invokes it to perform the requested task.

One of the most significant features of Microsoft's PC-DOS 2.0 for the IBM-PC is its support for newly installed device drivers. To remember all of its device drivers, PC-DOS uses a linked list. At system start-up, as DOS installs a new device driver that has been specified in the CONFIG.SYS file, it adds that driver to the top of the list. When it later receives a request for a device I/O function, it starts at the top of the list and reads down for a name to match the requested device. It then invokes the first device driver that matches that name. This technique allows you to replace any existing character device by giving your device driver the same name as the device to be replaced.

12.1.5.   The Basic I/O System (BIOS) For the IBM-PC

PC BIOS is the name given to a set of device drivers for the IBM-PC. They are part of the operating system and are stored on ROM. Each BIOS subroutine can be activated by a user interrupt. Each of these BIOS subroutines can perform several operations that are selected by placing the appropriate values in the 8088's registers. The BIOS is well documented in the IBM-PC manuals and should present no problem for the user.

12.1.6.   Bus-Based Microcomputers

The simplest microcomputers are often built on one circuit board. These micros may be useful for simple dedicated tasks, but they lack the flexibility required for laboratory usage, where the problems and solutions are normally in a constant state of flux.

A *bus-based* microcomputer, on the other hand, overcomes these difficulties, because the overall system configuration has not been frozen. Certainly one reason for the success of the Apple and IBM-PC in the laboratory can be attributed to their bus structure, which provides a flexible environment for building a custom system. The computer is built of individual boards that plug

Table 12.1.   A Table of Bus Standards

| Bus | IEEE Standard | Lines | | | Typical | | |
		Total	Data	Addr.	Processor	Computers	Operating Systems
IBM-PC	—	62	8	24	8086,8088	IBM-PC	PC-DOS MS-DOS
Apple	—	50	8	16	6502,Z80	II+/IIe	DOS3.3 PRODOS
S100	IEEE-696	100	16	24	Z80,68000	Morrow	CP/M,MS-DOS
STD	IEEE-961	56	8	20	Z80,8086	Pro-Log	CP/M,MS-DOS
MULTIBUS	IEEE-796	86	16	24	8086,8088	Intel 310	RMX,XENIX
Q-BUS		72	16	22	J-11	DEC LSI-11 micro-VAX	UNIX micro-VMS
VME-BUS	IEEE-1014	96	32	32	68000	Motorola VME/10	VERSADOS

into a common circuit board called a *backplane* or *motherboard*. This motherboard contains all the computer buses. The system can be easily expanded by adding new interface boards, more memory, and so on.

A list of some of the more popular computer buses in the micro and minicomputer world is shown in Table 12.1. Where applicable we list the IEEE (Institute of Electrical and Electronics Engineers) standard designations of these buses. Note especially the total number of lines specified on each bus and how they are divided between data and address lines. The number of data lines determines the rate at which data may be moved along the interface. The address lines determine the total amount of memory which may be addressed directly by the processor.

12.2.   THE RS-232C STANDARD AND SERIAL COMMUNICATIONS

12.2.1.   Overview of the RS-232 Link

The RS-232 standard was created by the Electronics Industries Association* as a standard for connecting data terminals to telephone modems. Any device, such as a computer or terminal, requires an RS-232 interface to transform the computer's 8- or 16-bit parallel data signal into serial form. This is usually done with a *universal asynchronous receiver transmitter* (UART), as shown in Figure 12.2.

A brief list of the major features of the RS-232C standard is shown in Table

*Electronic Industries Association, 2001 Eye Street N.W., Washington, D.C. 20006.

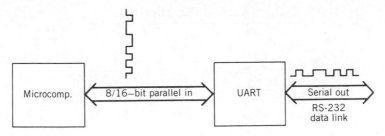

Figure 12.2. The universal asynchronous receiver transmitter (UART) transforming the parallel data of a computer bus to the serial data of the RS-232 link.

12.2. Much of the confusion with the RS-232 standard has developed because it has been used for applications for which it was not originally intended. These include attaching keyboards to computers and any other communications tasks in which there is not a modem present in the system.

The RS-232 standard was developed to accommodate a number of earlier communications standards. The definition of the logic levels in terms of the interface voltages had to be extremely flexible and accept anything between -5 and -25 V as logic .TRUE. and anything between $+5$ and $+25$ V as logic .FALSE. .

When you attempt to communicate between two devices by using the RS-232 interface, you must check four aspects of the system for compatibility.

1. The functional designations of the devices (DTE or DCE).
2. The rate of data transfer (baud rate).
3. The agreed data format regarding parity start bit, and stop bits.
4. Which of the control lines are used by both devices.

Each of these points is discussed in the following pages.

The RS-232 standard is a hardware standard that sets the protocol for data transfer along an RS-232 line one character at a time. Only a few lines on the RS-232 link are used for data transfer. Some of the other lines are used to establish communications between the two devices being connected. The standard does not have a provision for data handshaking for each individual bit, and one should therefore be alert to the possibility of data loss. The subject of protocol and error checking is dealt with at the end of this section.

The standard connector used for an RS-232 hookup has many more data lines than are designated by the RS-232 standard. Thus, each user has been free to designate their utilization. This has led to some confusion among users as to what is meant by the RS-232 standard.

Table 12.2. The RS-232C Interface

Data	
Format	Serial
Timing	Asynchronous
Rate	110–19,200 baud
Connector	
Type	DB–25
Number Lines	25
Data Lines	2
Signal Levels	
Negative logic	Pins 2 & 3
Positive logic	All other pins
High level	5 to 25 V
Low level	−5 to −25V
Line Naming Convention	
Lines named with respect to DTE	
Connector Gender	
DTE	Male
DCE	Female
This convention is not adhered to in practice	

The configuration of a standard communications system using a serial data link is shown in Figure 12.3. In this figure two devices are connected through serial interfaces and modems by means of a standard telephone link. At each end of the telephone line the RS-232 link is used as the channel of communications between two terminals or microcomputers. One of these terminals is commonly a small computer and is designated a *data terminal device* (DTE). On the other end, a modem is designated as a *data communications device* (DCE).

The DTE and DCE devices view the RS-232 lines from different perspectives. This is where much of the confusion arises in connecting to the RS-232 interface. When one is interfacing two devices directly to each other without a modem link being present, then it is important to know whether the devices are acting as DCEs or DTEs. This is shown in Figure 12.4. Either hookup is possible, as will be shown later. The connecting RS-232 cable varies from implementation to implementation.

12.2.2.   Serial Data Format

Although the basic idea of parallel-to-serial data transformation, which is necessary to go from the parallel 8- or 16-bit world of most microcomputer

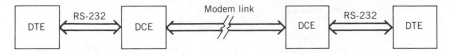

Figure 12.3. Standard serial communications link with UARTs and modem link.

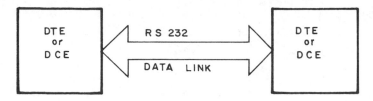

Figure 12.4. Direct serial communications data link with no modem present.

buses, is not particularly difficult to comprehend, there are some subtleties in its implementation that should be recognized. In this subsection we describe serial data communications without regard for the protocol or physical configuration necessary to reduce it to practice. These subjects are reserved until later.

Throughout, our discussion is limited to *asynchronous* serial data format. In this form of data transfer there is no absolute time standard to oversee the timing between the two devices. Rather, each character that is transmitted along the interface is time-referenced to the first bit of data transferred—the start bit. Thus, the internal time standards for both devices only have to remain in synchronization for the 10 bits or so of the character transferred, and the clocks are resynchronized at the beginning of the next data character that is transferred.

There is a considerable degree of flexibility in the data format that may be used in an RS-232 data link. A data stream for the transfer of a single data byte along the interface is shown in Figure 12.5. This data stream is the ASCII representation of a single character together with a predefined number of start, stop, and parity bits. Only if the device sending the data and the device receiving the data have been configured similarly will the data be interpreted properly by the receiving device.

This particular example sends a single start bit, a 7-bit representation of the character, and a parity bit followed by a single stop bit. This would usually be written as 7 + EVEN + 1. The other data formats commonly used for communications along an RS-232 data link are shown in Table 12.3. The start bit is taken for granted and is not explicitly shown in the table. Referring again to Figure 12.5, we see that the start bit is a logic 0, and the stop bit(s) is logic 1. This is always the case and results in guaranteed voltage change occurring at the beginning of the start bit with which to reference the timing of the two devices. We should note that the signal levels on the RS-232 interface are negative true, and the quantity shown in Figure 12.5 reflects this.

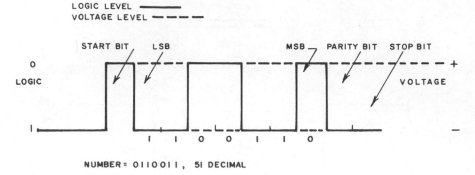

Figure 12.5.   Data stream for serial data format showing start bit, data bits, parity bit, and stop bits(s). Note that logic level 0 is positive and logic level 1 is negative.

Table 12.3.   Examples of Data Formats in Serial Data Transfer

Bits Per Character	Parity Bit	Stop Bits
7	+EVEN	+1
7	+ODD	+1
8	NONE	+2
8	NONE	+1
8	+EVEN	+1
8	+ODD	+1
7	+EVEN	+2
7	+ODD	+2

It should be emphasized that the RS-232 standard is a hardware standard only, and is only intended to oversee the transfer of data bytes between the two devices. The contents and interpretation of the 7 or 8 bits of data making up each character are the subjects of other data standards.

The only data standard used in computer applications is the ASCII (American Standard Code for Information Interchange) code. This is a 7-bit code that can represent up to 128 separate characters. There are 96 printable characters and 32 control characters in the standard code. A complete listing of these is given in Appendix I.

Although 7 bits are all that is normally necessary to represent an ASCII character, 8 bits are commonly used. The eighth bit is designated as a parity bit and is used to check for errors that may occur between the creation of a character and the reading of it. It is set to 1 or 0 so that the total number of 1 bits is even or odd. If for example, even parity were selected and an odd number of 1 bits were detected in the transmitted character byte, that byte must have been in error. The parity sense of the data stream includes the parity bit also.

The addition of the parity bit to a data stream is an extremely simple but powerful mechanism of increasing the inherent accuracy of the data transfer. The parity bit is generated by the asynchronous controller and is checked by the receiver, which should have been configured for a similar data format. Parity checking is not part of the RS-232 standard and must be part of the software development. The possible parity settings that are used in serial data transfer are listed below.

NONE   Parity bit is not included in data stream.

EVEN   Parity bit is set to make the complete data stream for single character, including the start, stop, data, and parity bits, even.

ODD   Parity bit is set to make complete data stream odd.

ONE   Parity bit is set to 1 for all characters and checked for each character transferred.

ZERO   Parity bit is always set to 0 for all characters and checked.

The parity check will not detect a double error that results when two data bits in a data character stream have been transmitted incorrectly. However, if the probability of losing any one data bit is not connected to the probability of losing another, then the probability of a data error occurring undetected will be the square of losing a single bit on the interface. Thus, if one bit in 10,000 is transmitted incorrectly then only one wrong character in 100,000,000 will slip through undetected.

12.2.3. Serial Data Transmission Rate

One of the most important parameters that must be set correctly between the two devices communicating on an interface is the *baud rate* (bits per second), or the speed of data transfer along the link. A list of some of the baud rates used in data communications is shown below.

Typical Baud Rates			
50	150	1200	4800
75	200	1800	7200
110	300	2400	9600
135	600	3600	19,200

The most popular baud rates in computer communications links are the 300 and 1200 baud, which are used for modem telephone communications, and the 9600 and 19,200 baud, which are used for internal networking between computer systems.

As a rule of thumb, the number of characters per second that can be transferred between two devices is approximately the baud rate divided by 10. The exact transfer rate will depend on the data format parameters set. In our example of a 7 + EVEN + 1 data format, the addition of the start bit makes 10 bits transferred per character. At 1200 baud this represents a character transmission rate of 120 per second.

The rate of data transfer chosen for communications between two devices is limited not only by the peak data transfer rate that may be sent between the two devices but also by the ability of the interfaces at both ends to handle large quantities of data. The UARTs on both ends usually communicate with their respective devices, such as a microcomputer, through a data buffer. The data buffer on an Apple computer, for example, can hold up to 256 bytes. If the transfer of data from the buffer is slower than the rate along the interface, a loss in the data transferred is possible. To avoid this error, breaks in the data streams are inserted at convenient points. This is part of the communications protocol to be discussed later.

12.2.4.   The RS-232 Signal and Control Lines

The discussion in the previous section was limited to data transfer along a single data line of the RS-232 link. We shall now consider some of the other lines on the RS-232 data link. The configuration of the interface as it was originally intended for the connection of a DTE to a DCE (in particular, a telephone modem) is described.

A schematic diagram of the standard RS-232 DB-25 connector is shown in Figure 12.6. It is somewhat surprising at first to learn that only two of the RS-232 lines on this connector (pins 2 and 3) are used to carry data. These are

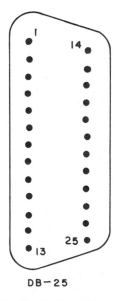

DB-25

Figure 12.6.   The DB-25 RS-232 connector showing pin layout.

also the only two lines that use negative true logic. All other lines, including all handshaking lines, use positive true logic. A third line on the interface (pin 1) represents signal ground.

What of the other 22 lines on the connector that do not carry serial data? A list of the pin assignments for the RS-232 data link is shown in Table 12.4. In reality, for asynchronous serial communications most of these lines are not used.

The RS-232 lines are all named with respect to the DTE. A schematic diagram of the wiring convention for connecting a DTE to a DCE is shown in Figure 12.7. The physical connection of the two devices is straightforward, there being a one-to-one correspondence between the lines on the DTE and DCE in this case.

In Figure 12.7 we have included arrows to denote the directional sense of the data and handshake lines on the connector of a particular device. An arrow out denotes that the device in question sets that particular line, whereas an arrow in the opposite direction indicates that the other device sets the line. Serial data is transmitted by a DTE to a DCE along line 2 and receives in the opposite direction along line 3.

A typical handshaking sequence on the RS-232 data link between the DTE and DCE is shown below, where the particular DTE is sending data through a modem and along a telephone line to another device waiting to receive it.*

The DTE sets the DTR and RTS lines to indicate that it is ready to send data.
The DCE responds and sets the DSR and CTS lines to indicate that the modem is ready to receive data.

Table 12.4. Pin Designation of the RS-232 Connector

CONNECTOR PIN	SIGNAL	MNEMONIC
Primary RS-232C Connections		
1	Frame (earth) ground	
2	Transmitt data	TxD
3	Receive data	RxD
4	Request to send	RTS
5	Clear to send	CTS
6	Data set ready	DSR
7	Signal Ground	
20	Data terminal ready	DTR
Secondary Connections		
8	Data carrier detect	DCD

*BASIC Interfacing Technique with Extensions 2.0 for the HP Series 200 Computers, Part No. 09826−90025, 1982.

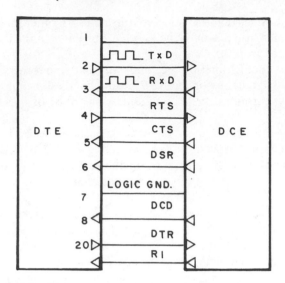

Figure 12.7.   Line connections for the serial DTE−DCE direct link.

When the above lines have been set, the data is transmitted (TxD) from the DTE to DCE and on down the modem.

Once all the data has been transmitted, the DTE clears the RTS and DTR lines.

There is an important limitation of the RS-232 interface that must be recognized when dealing with these control lines. The lines DTR, DSR, RTS, and CTS do not handshake data through the interface character by character as other communications interfaces described in this book do. These lines perform handshaking only at the *beginning and end of data transmission* to indicate that the data link has been established or interrupted. The DCE cannot clear the CTS line to inhibit the data flow unless the DTR line is first cleared. Some software protocols for data flow control have been established and will be described in the section on the Apple RS-232 Super Serial Card.

The sequence of events as seen by a modem terminal combination receiving data is somewhat different.

The DTE must set the DTR line but leave the RTS line clear.

The DTE checks that the DSR and DCD are SET.

If they are, data will be sent by the other system.

After all the data has been transferred, the DTR is cleared.

This somewhat complicated series of events may not be followed exactly in every case. The general pattern, however, will be similar in most terminal modem links. A full description of the many variables with this interface is beyond the scope of this book. As mentioned previously, one must be extremely wary of the term "standard" RS-232 link when dealing with this interface.

12.2.5. Direct RS-232 Connections

In this section we describe the use of serial communications in direct links between devices in the absence of modems. Since such connections represent the vast majority of RS-232 utilizations, we are loathe to refer to these as nonstandard hookups. Such interfacing, however, is far from what the original standard was created for.

A typical direct RS-232 communication link commonly used today is between two microcomputers. More than likely, both these devices will have been configured as DTEs. A direct connection between these two devices with a standard interfacing cable would give us major problems, since both computers would be attempting to transmit data on line 2 and listen on line 3. The control lines would be in a state of total confusion.

The solution is to cross the lines in order to fool both DTEs into thinking that they are communicating with DCE devices. The configuration most often used is shown in Figure 12.8. The cross connections of lines 2 and 3 to carry data between devices DTE1 and DTE2 are obvious.

The control lines are more involved. The RTS lines are connected to the CTS line of the same device, effectively disabling that handshake function, and to the DCD line of the other device. Similarly, the lines are crossed with DTR lines of the opposite device. The net effect is that both devices set their

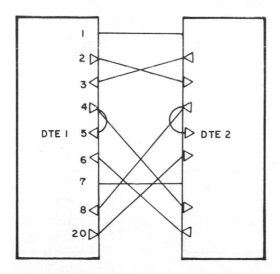

Figure 12.8. Line connections for the serial DTE−DTE direct link.

particular output lines, all input lines are satisfied, and data transmission can commence.

The handshaking role of the RS-232 DTE−DTE interface is just as inadequate as it was for the DTE−DCE links described in the previous section. Some implementations do use the DTR or DCD lines to inhibit transmission, but unless the transmitting device has been programmed correctly to respond to such a protocol, the result of such an action in unpredictable from device to device.

Some of the simpler RS-232 links only utilize three lines of the interface. These represent the two data lines and the signal ground line. These links for DTE−DTE and DTE−DCE communications are shown in Figure 12.9. These are typical of the short-distance links that are used to connect keyboards to computers or any implementation in which little flexibility is required.

The straight-through cable used for DTE−DCE interfacing is usually termed a DTE cable, and the crossed cable for DTE−DTE interfacing is, by obvious extension, the DCE Cable. Cabling is an area in which much confusion can occur, because for all the many "implementations" of the RS-232 interface that exist, there are custom-made cables to match. Finally, some of the more sophisticated RS-232 device communications interfaces may have provisions for configuring the output of the device to look like a DTE or DCE. Such a case is the Apple Super Serial Card, to be described later. This has the obvious advantage of making the card usable with a standard DTE cable in any circumstance.

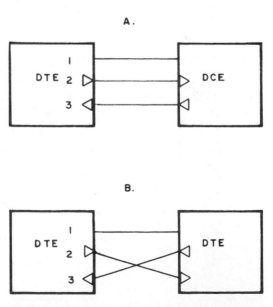

Figure 12.9.   The minimum RS-232 data link where no handshaking lines are connected. (*a*) The DTE−DCE link. (*b*) The DTE−DTE link.

12.2.6. Protocol in Serial Communications

The RS-232 standard is only concerned with the physical data and handshaking links. There is no universal software standard, however, for data handshaking on a byte or message basis. During manual operation the single and full-duplex modes of a serial interface may be used to diagnose a bad communications link, but, in general, a missed data character cannot be easily diagnosed. The term *duplex* is used to denote two-way communication. The simultaneous conversion of an incoming and outgoing serial data stream is called full duplex and requires two data carriers. Half-duplex is sometimes used. It allows two-way communication also, but only one direction is active at a time.

One protocol convention that has become accepted by the computer industry, but is still by no means a universal standard, is the XON/XOFF data inhibit protocol. The command XOFF when sent along an interface will inhibit the transmitter from sending any more data until an XON message is received. The accepted protocol is shown below.

COMMAND	IMBEDDED CHARACTER	CHARACTER
XOFF	CHR$(19)	CTRL-S
XON	CHR$(17)	CTRL-Q

The use of these commands presupposes that both devices on the serial interface recognize the standard.

Most computers have a serial buffer that is set up when establishing communications. On the IBM-PC the buffer has a default of 256 bytes but may be software set to some other value. It is necessary to include buffer size checking in the developed software. This is the case with communications on the IBM-PC. The Apple Super Serial Card, on the other hand, can be configured to automatically use XON/XOFF as needed, and since the checking does not cycle through the BASIC interpreter, the response time to prevent data overflow is fast. This is an important consideration at higher baud rates.

A communications protocol standard that includes error checking, that is fast becoming an accepted standard in computer communications between microcomputers, is the Ward Christensen protocol.* This protocol was developed for the CP/M OS but is now available on most microcomputers and on many mainframe systems, such as the VAX† UNIX‡ systems. The Christensen protocol is used on many public-domain programs, such as XMODEM, MODEM7, and MODEM711 for intercomputer communications. It may be used to trans-

---

Microsystems; The Journal for Advanced Microcomputing, June 1984, has an extensive discussion of communications protocols.

†VAX is a trademark of Digital Corporation.
‡UNIX is a trademark of AT&T Bell Laboratories.

mit any type of file structure between machines, including executable binary files.

The Christensen protocol divides the file to be transferred into blocks 128 bytes long. Each block is sent separately to the receiver buffer. A start of header (SOH) message is sent, followed by two sector number bytes, error checking bytes, and then the data bytes. Two conventions are in use for error checking. The simplest is the checksum test. The checksum number sent along before the data is compared with a similarly calculated number by the receiver. Agreement in these two numbers at the receiving end initiates an ACK (acknowledgment) character to be transmitted by the receiver, which ends the data cycle and allows a new data block to be transferred. Any discrepancy induces a NAK (negative acknowledge) signal to be transmitted that signals the sending computer to retransmit the data. The number of repeated transmission calls allowed before the transmission process is abandoned varies from system to system. A more complex and more accurate protocol convention is the cyclic redundancy check (CRC) protocol. This is the block transfer data mode that has become standardized on floppy disk controllers.

12.2.7.   The Modem

The final component that may be added to a serial communications link is the telephone (modem). Most, but not all, modems are linked to the computer by an RS-232 link. We have shown the action of a modem communications link in Figure 12.3. In the standard configuration the modem is configured as a DCE with the microcomputer RS-232 output configured as a DTE. Originally modems were developed as completely passive communications devices that converted the bit patterns coming along the RS-232 link into acoustical signals for transmission along the telephone wire. Of late, however, modems have been developed with built-in microprocessors (smart modems), allowing a certain degree of built-in intelligence that may be used to establish and control the communications flow along the data link.

The 1200-baud, modem data rates are being established as a standard for communications over large distances, superseding the slower 300-baud data rate. Many modem systems are of the 1200/300-baud rate type and are stand-alone, auto originate/answer devices for maximum flexibility. An added feature on many modern-day modem systems is the ability to autodial, which allows a completely software-driven communications system.

Smart modems may be placed in one of two modes. The *terminal mode* is used once communications have been established. All data placed on the RS-232 link, whether originating at the keyboard or in a disk file, is sent directly along the telephone link and is received by the receiving computer's modem. The *local mode* is used to program the operation of smart modems. Some smart modems are menu driven; other, for maximum flexibility, are command driven.

A modem command language that has become an accepted standard in computer communications is the Hayes modem convention. Many modem systems from various manufacturers allow the choice of the Hayes system or their own menu-driven system to be invoked. The advantage of the Hayes system is that much software has been developed to support the convention. We show a subset of the Hayes local mode commands in Table 12.5.

Each command must be preceded by the AT command to be understood. The complete Hayes instruction set allows complete software control of all the features of the modem interface. For example, the following command string may be used to dail a telephone number (pulse dial) and to pause for 2 s after dialing the first number.

$$\text{AT} \quad \text{D} \quad \text{P} \quad 9,5551212\text{<cr>}$$

where the <CR> is used to terminate the command.

12.2.8. The Apple Super Serial Card

Universal serial interface cards like the Apple Super Serial Card for the Apple II Plus and Apple IIe microcomputers are configured for wide flexibility and

Table 12.5. Subset of the Hayes Command Protocol

COMMAND	TITLE	PARAMETERS	DESCRIPTION
AT	Attention code	none	Command string must precede all command lines
A	Answer	none	Answer without waiting for ring
A/	Reexecute	none	Reexecute last command to modem
B	Select options	none	Allows changes in default options of modem operation
D###.	Dial number	# 0 to 9	Automatic dialing of keyboard entered telephone number
T	Tone	none	Tone-dialed telephone
P	pulse	none	Pulse-dialed telephone
En	Echo in command mode	n = 0	Do not echo character in command state
		n = 1	Echo character in command state
Hn	Hang up	n = 0	Causes modem to hang up
		n = 1	Places modem off-hook
O	Return to on-line	none	Returns to on-line after being in command state
, "comma"	Pause	none	Causes 2s wait in dialing procedure

ease of use. The card was developed by Apple Computer to supersede a number of earlier devices and to integrate all the functions provided by the earlier devices into a single communications interface. The documentation that comes with this card is extremely well prepared, and we shall only discuss some of the salient points of the interface, especially in relation to its use in the laboratory.

As with most other Apple interfaces, the card fits into one of the internal slots on the Apple computer. Any slot may be used and an internal cable connects the card to a standard RS-232 DB-25 connector.

The Super Serial Card has two major modes of operation:

1.   Printer mode, where the device is normally configured as a DCE.
2.   Communications mode, where the device is configured as a DTE.

There are two further modes of operation, in which the card can emulate the workings of the Apple SIC P8 and SIC P8A serial cards, two earlier Apple communications cards. A block diagram of the SSCs full operating capability is shown in Figure 12.10.

The mode of operation may be selected with two switches on the SSC main board. In addition to this a jumper block must also be positioned as a straight-through connector (TERMINAL) or as a modem eliminator (MODEM). The wiring diagram of the jumper block is shown in Figure 12.11. Referring to our

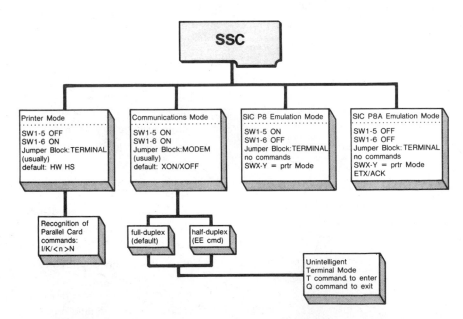

Figure 12.10.   The operating modes of the Apple super serial card. Reproduced by permission of Apple Computer.

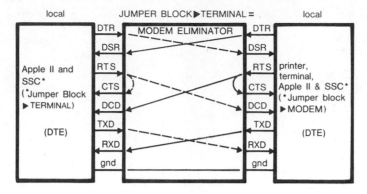

Figure 12.11. The jumper block for the super serial card used in modem elimination. Reproduced by permission of Apple Computer.

earlier discussion of RS-232 connections, we see that with the block in the modem position the RS-232 connector output at the back of the Apple acts as a DTE, whereas if the block is in the TERMINAL position, the output has the characteristics of a DCE.

In addition to the gross configuration of the system described above, there are a number of parameters that must be set before the card can communicate with another device. There are three ways in which the SSC parameters may be set:

1. By using the hardware switches on the card.
2. Through an Applesoft, C, or PASCAL program.
3. In immediate execution mode through the keyboard.

The second and third methods overide the default switch settings on the SSC. However, the switches that move the card between the communications and printer configurations or the other two emulation modes discussed previously are not software selectable. It is also not possible to software select the wiring output of the RS-232 connector.

The number of possible configurations of the SSC offered by the large number of selectable parameters is sufficient to satisfy almost every interfacing application. The default-switch setting capabilities closely parallels the software-selectable settings, apart from the exceptions discussed above, and we will concentrate on the software entirely from now on.

A partial listing of the parameters corresponding to both the printer and communications modes is shown in Table 12.6. There is a one-to-one correspondence between most of the commands related to these two modes, apart from the substitution of the control characters.

The simple program in Figure 12.12 sets the baud rate to 1200 when the card has been configured for the communications (DTE) mode.

Table 12.6. Apple Super Serial Card Commands

Communication mode (DTE)	Printer mode (DCE)	Command Name	<n> Value	Interpretation
CTRL-A<n>B	CTRL-I<n>B	Baud rate	1,2,3,4 5,6,7,8	50,75,110,135 150,300,600,1200
CTRL-A<n>D	CTRL-I<n>D	Data Format	0 1 4 5	8 DATA + 1 STOP 7 DATA + 1 STOP 8 DATA + 2 STOP 7 DATA + 2 STOP
CTRL-A<n>P	CTRL-A<n>P	Parity	0,2,4,6 1 3 5 7	NO PARITY ODD PARITY EVEN PARITY PARITY BIT 1 PARITY BIT 0
CTRL-A<n>C	CTRL-I<n>C	CR delay	0	no delay
CTRL-A<n>L	CTRL-I<n>L	LF delay	1	32 ms
CTRL-A<n>F	CTRL-I<n>F	FF delay	2	250 ms
			3	2 s
CTRL_A<n>S	—	Screen slot	0–7	chain SSC to slot n ↑
CTRL-A<n>T	CTRL-I<n>T	Case translation	0–3	see manual
(CTRL-A)B	—	Break		233 ms break
—	(CTRL-I)C	Column overflow		
(CTRL-A)R	(CTRL-I)R	Reset SSC		SW reset + PR#O,IN#O
(CTRL-A)T	—	Terminal mode		direct terminal mode
(CTRL-A)Z	(CTRL-I)Z	Zap <ctrl>		ignore ctrl characters
(CTRL-A)	(CTRL-I)			
(E_E/D)	(E_E/D)	Echo enable/disable		
(F_E/D)	(F_E/D)	Find/disable keyboard		
(L_E/D)	(L_E/D)	LF enabled/disabled		
(M_E/D)	(M_E/D)	Mask enabled/disable LF in		
(T_E/D)	(T_E/D)	enable/disable Tab in BASIC		
(X_E/D)	(X_E/D)	enable/disable XON/XOFF protocol		

```
 5 REM   SSC SET UP IN COMMUNICATIONS (DTE) MODE
10 D$ = CHR$(4): REM CTRL-D FOR DOS COMMANDS
20 A$ = CHR$(1): REM CTRL-A FOR COMMUNICATIONS MODE COMMANDS
30 PRINT D$;"PR#5" : REM SSC IN SLOT 5 FOR WRITING
40 PRINT A$;"8 BAUD": REM SET BAUD TO 1200
```

Figure 12.12.   Setting up the SSC in communications mode.
Language: Applesoft.

Much of the program should look familiar. Line 30 is the standard method of addressing a slot with a DOS command from within an Applesoft program. Once communications have been established with the SSC, line 40 sends the instruction to change the baud rate. The software implementation only recognizes the first letter of every word sent after a CTRL-A or CTRL-I character. However, one is allowed to write a descriptive word to better describe the command. For example, in line 40, only 8B, not 8 baud, is recognized by the software.

The CTRL-A character is sent to change the SSC parameters related to the communications mode, whereas the CTRL-I character deals with the printer mode parameters. As will be seen from Table 12.6, most of the parameters are identical for the communications and printer modes, but there are subtle differences within the SSC software that require one to differentiate between the parameters for these two modes.

With the SSC set in the printer (DCE) mode, there is an added parameter that allows the system to be configured as a dumb terminal. The simple program in Figure 12.13 sets the parameters on a card to communicate through a 300-baud modem with 7 + EVEN + 1 data format.

```
200 REM   SSC SET UP IN PRINTER (DCE) MODE
205 D$ = CHR$(4) : I$ = CHR$(9)
210 PRINT D$;"PR#4":REM          WRITE TO SSC IN SLOT 4
220 PRINT D$;"IN#4":REM          INPUT TO APPLE FROM SSC IN SLOT 4
230 PRINT I$;"6 BAUD"   :REM  SET 300 BAUD
240 PRINT I$;"1 DATA"   :REM  DATA 7 DATA + 1 STOP
250 PRINT I$;"3 PARITY" :REM  EVEN PARITY
260 PRINT I$;"T" :REM          TERMINAL MODE
270 END
```

Figure 12.13. Program to set up the SSC card in printer mode.
Language: Applesoft.

12.2.9. An SSC-Controlled Instrument

An example illustrating the operation of a remote instrument under the control of an Apple computer through the SSC serial interface is presented next. The instrument used in the example is the Princeton Applied Research (EG & G) Model 2100 Dyescan tunable dye laser. This interfacing exercise is typical of what one needs to carry out laboratory interfacing. The instrument has both RS-232 and GPIB interfaces. We describe the RS-232 implementation of the interfacing exercise.

The Dyescan system is a nitrogen-pumped dye laser that emits narrow and repetitive temporal pulses of laser light (typically 1 ns) in a narrow spectral bandwidth (typically 0.1 nm). To establish a successful RS-232 connection, we must be aware of the serial communications requirements for the Dyescan. The important RS-232 parameters for this instrument are shown in Table 12.7.

Table 12.7. RS-232 Interface on Model 2100

DESCRIPTION	VALUE
Configuration	DTE
Data	8 DATA + 1 STOP
Parity	NONE
Baud rate	50 to 9600 (switch selectable)
Echo	echo all characters
Line terminator from model L100	CR only (LF optional)
Line terminator from model L100	Next instruction

The Dyescan is configured as a DTE, which means that the SSC must be configured as a DCE for proper operation with a standard RS-232 cable.

The program segment to configure the interface correctly is shown in Figure 12.14.

```
300 REM   RS-232 SETUP FOR APPLE CONTROL OF DYESCAN
310 D$ = CHR$(4): REM              CTRL-D FOR DOS
320 I$ = CHR$(9): REM              CTRL-I FOR SSC
330 PRINT D$;"PR#4": REM           SSC IN SLOT 4 FOR WRITING
340 PRINT D$;"IN#4": REM           PROGRAM INPUT FROM SLOT 4
350 PRINT I$;"8 BAUD": REM         BAUD RATE TO 1200
360 PRINT I$;"0 DATA": REM         8 DATA + 1 STOP
370 PRINT I$;"0 PARITY": REM       NO PARITY
380 PRINT I$;"LF D": REM           LINEFEED DISABLE
390 PRINT I$;"ECHO E": REM       . ECHO ENABLE
```

Figure 12.14. The setup program for the Apple control of Dyescan.
Language: Applesoft.

The Dyescan has a limited vocabulary. The full instruction set is shown in Table 12.8. It can receive instructions over the RS-232 interface and respond either by operating the laser or, where instructed, by sending a response back along the interface to the computer.

Like many RS-232-interfaced instruments the internal communications language of the instrument is terse, and programming needs to be carried out with the aid of a table such as Table 12.8. This is the same instruction set used for the GPIB control of the instrument. In either communications mode the instrument must be placed in the *remote enabled* mode on the front panel of the instrument before computer control is active.

The language syntax of the Dyescan model 2100 instrument control language can have one of two forms.

```
<instruction>?
```

```
<instruction> <numerical value>
```

Table 12.8. Model 2100 Dyescan Command Set

CHARACTER	FUNCTION
A	Read or set wavelength1, wave number 1
B	Read or set wavelength2, wave number 2
C	Read or set pulses per second
D	Read or set pulses per step
E	Read or set scan rate
F	Read or set nm
G	Read or set cm-1
H	Read or set function
I	switch laser off
J	switch laser on
K	Scan on
L	Scan off
M	Scan fast
N	To blue
O	To red
P	To wavelength 1, wavenumber 1
Q	To wavelength 2, wavenumber 2
R	Calibrate
S	Read primary status
T	Read scan direction
U	Read status 1
V	Read status 2
0 -> 9	0 -> 9
: ; < = > @	space
?	inquire

Sensing an instruction from Table 12.8 followed by a question mark prompts the model 2100 to return the current value of the parameter controlled by that instruction. On the other hand, an instruction followed (possibly) by a numerical value requires that the instruction be executed. The protocol for instruction input has been configured so that no line terminator such as a <CR> or <LF> is required. The Dyescan system takes the beginning of the next instruction as its signal to execute an instruction. Thus, looking at Table 12.8, let us say that we wish to set the value of the pulse repetition rate to 25. We might send the command sequence

C25C?

where we sent the instruction C followed by 25 to set the pulse rate. Just sending this sequence will do nothing until we send the next instruction, the one to send us the set pulse rate. The sending of the second C activates the first instruction.

The model 2100 is typical of many RS-232 controlled instruments in that it will ignore instructions sent to it until it has completed the previous instruction. This can have disastrous consequences on the running of a program. In the GPIB implementation of Dyescan computer control, it is possible to do a serial poll (see Chapter 13) to test the status of the instrument, an operation that does not require the participation of the model 2100's internal processor. In the RS-232 implementation this is not possible, and a different approach is necessary.

The easiest approach, is to introduce a time delay into the read/write cycle of the RS-232 communications such that enough time has elapsed for all instructions to be carried out. A single subroutines be written to handle all I/O operations to the RS-232 interface. The programs should be written in a completely modular fashion to ease the process of program writing. The simple Applesoft program of Figure 12.15 is based on a single main routine and a single subroutine for input instructions to the Dyescan laser. The program assumes that the RS-232 interface setup program of Figure 12.14 has already been executed. The RS-232 interface card is assumed to be in slot number 4.

```
1000 REM      MAIN DYESCAN CONTROL ROUTINE
1010 AI$="J" : AI=-1   : GOSUB 2000 : REM    TURN LASER ON
1020 AI$="F" : AI=-1   : GOSUB 2000 : REM    WORK IN NM
1030 AI$="C" : AI=50   : GOSUB 2000 : REM  SET PPS TO 50
1040 AI$="D" : AI=0.1  : GOSUB 2000 : REM  SETS SCAN RATE 0.1 NM/SEC
1050 AI$="4A" : AI=588 : GOSUB 2000 : REM  SET L1 TO 588 NM
1060 AI$="B" : AI=592  : GOSUB 2000 : REM  SET L2 TO 592 NM
1070 AI$="K" : AI=-1   : GOSUB 2000 : REM  BEGIN SCAN
1080 END                            : REM  END OF MAIN ROUTINE
2000 REM      DYESCAN INSTRUCTION INPUT
2010 PRINT D$;"PR#4": PRINT D$;"IN#4"   : REM WRITE READ FROM SLOT 4
2020 IF AI=-1 THEN PRINT AI$;           : REM WRITE INSTRUCTION
2030 IF AI>=0 THEN PRINT AI$+STR$(AI);  : REM INSTRUCTION WITH PARAMETER
2035 PRINT AI$ + "2";                   : REM EXECUTE
2040 FOR I=1 TO 1000:NEXT I             : REM TIME DELAY
2050 PRINT D$;"PR#0": PRINT D$; "IN#0"
2060 RETURN
```

Figure 12.15. Program to control the Dyescan model 2100 system.

All input instructions to the Dyescan are passed in the variable AI$, parameters in the variable AI. Some instructions require a corresponding numerical variable, others do not. We pass the value -1 when the instruction to be passed without a variable, which indicates to the subroutine that it should be ignored. We have included this example only to illustrate some of the programming practices that tend to be a universal aspect of computer interfacing.

12.2.10. The Serial Interface on the IBM-PC

Serial communications on the IBM-PC are accomplished through an optional asynchronous communications adapter card placed in one of the five expansion slots on the PC. A number of such cards are available for the IBM-PC. The characteristics of the interface on the IBM-PC are shown in Table 12.9. A block diagram showing the major components of the asynchronous interface adapter on the IBM-PC is shown in Figure 12.16. The normal operation of the interface is with voltage inputs and outputs. A current loop output is available to run IBM printer devices.

Software implementation of serial communications on the IBM-PC is much easier than on the Apple. The BASICA language contains the OPEN "COM... statement, which is used to control all aspects of the serial interface. The full range of options that may be set with this statement is shown in Table 12.10.

Table 12.9.   Characteristics of the IBM-PC Serial Interface

DESCRIPTION	CHARACTERISTIC
Interface configuration	DTE
Baud Rates	75 to 9600
Buffer size (default)	256 bytes
Bits per character	5,6,7, or 8
Stop bits	1, 1½, or 2
Interrupt capability	prioritized transmit, receive, error line status and data set

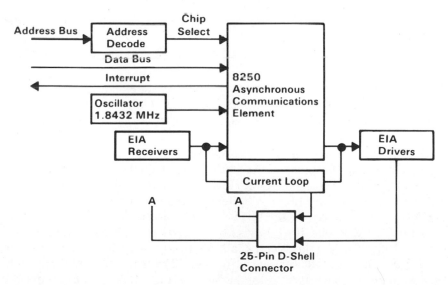

Figure 12.16.   The IBM-PC asynchronous interface adapter. Reproduced by permission of IBM Computers.

Table 12.10.   BASICA Serial Interface Commands

(a)   Setting the interface

OPEN "COMn:[speed] [,parity] [,data] [,stop] [,RS] [,CS[n]] [,DS[n]]
[,CD[n]] [,CD[n]] [,LF]" AS [#]filenum [LEN=number]

COMn	n	number of serial adaptors	speed	75−9600	baud rate
parity	S	SPACE (0 bit)	data	4−8	number data bytes
	O	ODD parity	stop	1,2	number stop bits
	M	MARK (1 bit)			
	E	EVEN parity			
	N	NO parity	filenum		can refer to linked file by number
RS		suppress RTS			
CS[n]		controls CTS			
DS[n]		control DSR	number		number of bytes which can be read by PUT or GET
CD[n]		controls CD (carrier detect)			
LF		send LF after CR			

(b) I/O Statements

Input statements	Output statements
INPUT#	PRINT#
LINE INPUT#	PRINT# USING
INPUT$	WRITE#

(c) Buffer checking statements

LOC(f)	returns number of characters in buffer to be read
LOF(f)	returns amount of free space in input buffer
EOF(f)	returns −1 if buffer empty, 0 if data to be read

Also included in this table are the other BASICA statements that are used in one form or another in serial interfacing. The BASICA serial interfacing commands are extremely powerful and allow easy access and control of the serial interface.

The BASICA program in Figure 12.17 uses some of the commands in Table 12.10 to establish a file dump of the data coming in on the serial interface. The data is placed in a file named DUMP.DAT on disk drive B. Buffer 1 is opened for the serial interface buffering; buffer 2 is the file buffer.

The XON(CTRL-S) and XOFF (CTRL-Q) characters for serial protocol control are defined in line 1010. Lines 1020 and 1030 open the serial and file buffers. Line 1040 is a time delay that may need to be adjusted for different baud rates. The delay allows serial buffer 1 to fill with data from the serial link. We test in line 1050 whether or not the buffer is more than half full. If not, we

```
1000 '    serial interface file dump
1010 XON$=CHR$(17) : XOFF$=CHR$(19)        'protocol variable
1020 OPEN "COM1:300,E,7,1" AS #1           'open serial link
1030 OPEN "B:DUMP.DAT" AS #2 FOR INPUT     'open file
1040 FOR I=1 TO 100:NEXT I                 'time delay
1050 IF LOC(1)<128 THEN GOTO 1040          'if buffer not half full
                                           'collect more data
1060 PRINT #1,XOFF$;                        'if more than half full
                                           'send CTRL-Q
1070 B$=INPUT$(LOC(1),#1)                   'read buffer into string
1080 PRINT #2,B$;                           'write to file buffer
1090 PRINT #1,XON$;                         'send CTRL-S
1100 GOTO 1040                              'begin over again
```

Figure 12.17. Serial interface to file dump.
Language: BASICA.

go through the delay loop again before testing. If more than 128 characters have been received, an XOFF signal is sent to the buffer, and the complete buffer is read in with the INPUT$ command into the variable B$. The position LOC(1) contains the number of characters to be read out of the buffer. The contents of the variable B$ are then written into the file buffer (2).

12.3. THE HP-IL INTERFACE

The recent development of the Hewlett-Packard interface loop (HP-IL) allows one to interconnect a large number of laboratory devices, from a simple hand-held calculator to the most sophisticated of laboratory devices, in a single unified measurement system. In terms of its software implementation it has borrowed somewhat from the software philosophy developed for the GPIB interface. The hardware implementation is totally different. It is a single, two-wire, loop system, as shown in Figure 12.18. Each device, which is HP-IL compatible, has a single input connector and a single output connector, and for communications to take place between the devices they must be chained together in a continuous loop, where the output from one device is connected to the input connector of the next device. Information is passed along the loop from one device to the next. Each device takes a more active role in data communications than the equivalent data transfer on a parallel communications system.

A table of the HP-IL loop specifications covering some of the more important hardware, software, and protocol specifications is shown in Table 12.11.

One extremely interesting facet of the interface is that it allows for *power-down* of all systems on the loop when not in use and makes provision for activating the system when needed.

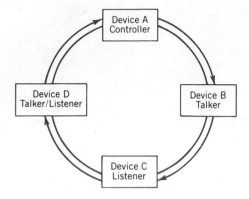

Figure 12.18.   Schematic of the HP-IL loop showing a single controller, talker, listener, and a talker/listener on the loop.

Table 12.11.   The HP-IL Specifications

Data Rate	2 K per second currently available
	20 K theoretical limitation
Number Devices	31 on single loop
	960 using extended addressing
Loop Structure	Two-wire balanced pair
Loop Length	maximum 10 meters (m) between devices
	using simple two wire configuration
	maximum 100 m using shielded twisted-
	pair wires
Signal Definition	Three-level system: -1.5, 0, $+1.5$ V
Loop Hierarchy	Calculator/microcomputer as controller:
	talkers and listeners
Power	Battery-powered systems
	Power-down mode when not in use

12.3.1.   Loop Hierarchy

The designation of devices on the HP-IL loop parallels that which is discussed for the GPIB interface in Chapter 13. Devices come in three different sets of clothing: *controllers, talkers,* and *listeners.* The four devices on the HP-IL loop in Figure 12.18 have been defined in this manner. *Controllers* are devices on the bus that oversee the traffic of data and commands along the loop. Only one device on the loop may be in active control at any one time. It is possible under the HP-IL convention for there to be other controllers on the bus, but they must play a passive role in loop communications under the supervision of the active controller. The active controller may relinquish overall command of the bus to another controller at any time.

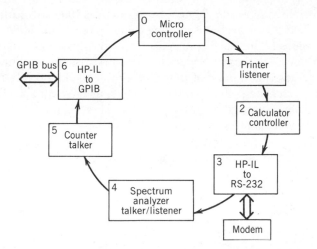

Figure 12.19. Configured HP-IL loop showing the possible layout of a complex laboratory setup using the loop.

Talkers and listeners perform self-explanatory roles. *Talkers* are devices that can be addressed to send data, and although there may be more than one functional talker on the loop, only one at a time may be instructed to begin talking under the supervision of the controller. *Listeners* are devices that may only receive data, and there may be more than one listener active at any one time. Devices may have the combined role of talker and listener. The designation of these roles depends on the internal software functions possessed by the particular device's HP-IL interface electronics. Each device on the interface loop, regardless of its functional designation, must play an active role in receiving data and retransmitting it along the loop.

A typical example of a configured HP-IL loop is shown in Figure 12.19. On the loop we have two controllers: a microcomputer and a hand-held calculator. This might allow one to control an experiment from either the microcomputer or a remote location. Various other instruments on the loop have talker and listener functional designations. Of special interest are the interface converter modules. An HP-IL to the RS-232 interface module connects the loop directly to a modem for communications to a host computer. An HP-IL to GPIB converter connects the loop to a GPIB bus with a full range of GPIB-compatible instruments. The software compatibility of the HP-IL and GPIB interfaces allows the instruments to communicate across the interface converter as if it were transparent.

12.3.2. Loop Structure

The electrical configuration of the HP-IL loop has been designed to minimize electrical interference from external noise, and with a shielded, twisted-pair cable it is possible to space the devices by as much as 100 yards without loss of information. The electrical circuit relating to signal reception and transmission is shown in Figure 12.20. Each connection between devices is a balanced-pair transmission line. Pulse transformers at both ends isolate the line from the device voltage levels and prevent potential problems due to ground loops.

The voltage and logic levels are somewhat unconventional. The system operates on a three-voltage-level convention. There is no direct correspondence between voltage levels and logic levels as there is in other communications interfaces. The voltage sequence for logic 0 and logical 1 is shown in Figure 12.21. Zero voltage is, in fact, the idle state, whereas a logical 1 requires

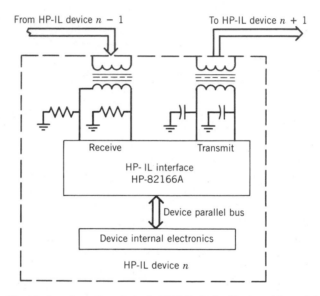

Figure 12.20. Electrical configuration of a typical HP-IL device (device address n) showing the use of the HP-82166A chip for interface control.

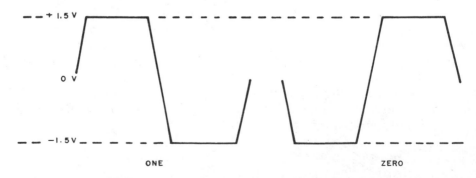

Figure 12.21. Voltage sequence of HP-IL signals showing the logical 1 and 0 signal shapes.

a $+1.5V$ transition followed closely by a $-1.5V$ transition, then back to 0; the reverse is true for a logic 0.

Data itself is composed of 11-bit message units sent out sequentially along the loop one bit at a time. The first 3 bits of the message contain control information. This is followed by 8 bits (D7 to D0) of data information. Each device on the loop must contain sufficient intelligence to interpret the content of these message units. The built-in checking that takes place on the loop requires that a message must travel the whole loop and be received back at the transmitting device before any more messages are sent. One exception to this is when a device other than the controller has been in active charge of the loop. The controller can interrupt a message traveling the loop and reestablish control of the system.

Devices are assigned addresses on the loop under the guidance of the system controller. This is quite different from what happens in the GPIB case, where device addressing is a hard-wired (switch-selectable) procedure. Using an autoaddress option the controller can send a message around the loop that informs each device that it is to assign a sequential address to itself and pass that information on to the next device in the sequence. The last device in the loop thus transmits its address back to the controller so that the controller then knows the address of each device. GPIB addresses may be incorporated into the addressing system.

12.3.3. Interface Loop Commands

The HP-IL command set bears a striking resemblance to the GPIB command set, which is discussed in the next chapter, both in terms of the categories of available commands and, more importantly, in the sequences in which they are used. The interface loop commands and related messages may be divided into a number of convenient categories that describe their relative hierarchy in the loop communications. These categories are listed in Table 12.12.

Commands can only be sourced by the active controller on the loop, whereas the ready messages, which can have the same imperative nature as commands, may originate from either the controller or the active talker on the loop.

The most important category of commands in HP-IL communications is the universal command group (UCG), which acts on all the devices in the loop system. These commands are given priority, and each device immediately passes on the command to the next device before acting on the command itself. The TAG commands are those that may be used to command one of the devices with talker function to begin talking. Similarly, one or a number of devices in the LAG group may be commanded to listen. For a device to respond to the TAG or LAG group commands it must have the functional intelligence to understand that command category, or a loop error will occur. The SAG category of commands must be used to assign 2-byte addresses to the devices when more than 30 devices are to be placed on the loop. For a full

Table 12.12.   The HP-IL Interface Message Subgroups

MNEMONIC	DESCRIPTION	TYPE
Message Subgroups		
UCG	Universal Command Group	commands
TAG	Talk Address Group	commands
LAG	Listen Address Group	commands
ACG	Addressed Command Group	commands
SAG	Secondary Address Group	commands
AAG	Autoaddress group	ready status
ARG	Addressed Ready Group	ready status

description of these command groups and a more complete description of the HP-IL interface, see Kane et al.*

12.3.4.   HP-IL Implementation on Personal Computers

The relative newness of the HP-IL interface means that little has been documented on the use of the interface on personal computers other than on Hewlett-Packard systems. We discuss two methods of utilizing the interface. One, an indirect method, has already been mentioned—namely, the use of an interface translation adapter that can be used to utilize the GPIB or RS-232 interface as a link to the HP-IL loop. The other loop implementation involves using an HP-IL controller card on the IBM-PC.

The indirect interfacing method we describe involves the use of a GPIB/HP-IL translator† (Hewlett-Packard HP-82169). To understand fully the implementation of the GPIB/HP-IL converter, we must be familiar with the HP-IL and GPIB (see Chapter 13) interfaces separately. Both interfaces are very similar in many of their organizational facets, especially in the hierarchy of controllers, talkers, and listeners, which may be designated on both the HP-IL loop and the GPIB bus. The autodressing capability of the HP-IL loop requires that care be taken in setting the device addresses so that a conflict does not arise.

The GPIB/HP-IL translator may be operated in one of three modes:

1.   Translator mode with controller on the GPIB bus.
2.   Translator mode with controller on the HP-IL loop.
3.   Translator mode with controllers on both the GPIB and HP-IL interfaces.

*G. Kane, S. Harper, and D. Ushijima, *The HP-IL System* (Osborne/McGraw-Hill, New York, 1982).

†*HP-IL/HP-IB Interface Owners Manual*, HP-82169A, Hewlett-Packard manual number 92169-90001/4.

In the first two modes the complete system is acting as a single communications pathway with a single controller and a single talker being allowed on the pathway at one time. In the third mode, called the *letter box* configuration, the HP-IL and GPIB interfaces are operating essentially independently, apart from the single HP-IL/GPIB translator node through which data may be exchanged between the two interfaces.

Hewlett-Packard has developed an HP-IL expansion card capable of turning the IBM-PC either into a device on the HP-IL loop or into a loop controller. The HP-IL expansion card (HP-82973A)* was developed to allow the IBM-PC to work in unison with a Hewlett-Packard model HP-110 portable computer and to share peripherals, such as disk drives, printers, and display devices.

As HP-IL-controlled instruments become available, the driving software will be developed to allow the HP-82973A card to act as the loop controller for these devices. The IBM/HP-110 link allows either of the devices to be configured as the loop controller. Software has been written to allow data to be transformed between two or more computers using the HPLINK software provided by Hewlett-Packard.

12.4. PARALLEL INTERFACES

The parallel interface is a general-purpose interface that has great flexibility in its I/O specifications. The interface may be used in communications between a computer and a peripheral device, or, in some circumstances, a direct communications link may be established for data transfer between two computers. Most parallel computer interfaces have 16 input lines and 16 output lines as well as a variable number of handshaking and grounding lines. There is no definitive parallel interface standard. The data representation is the same in almost all implementations. What varies is the protocol for data handshaking in I/O data transfer. In that regards the input and output data transfer on the ISAAC interface are handled completely separately and have separate data transfer handshaking lines for I/O. The Hewlett-Packard parallel interface (GPIO interface), on the other hand, has a single set of handshaking lines that handle data transfer in both directions. These are discussed later.

The popular data representation for parallel data is shown in Figure 12.22. Most parallel interfaces have 16 data lines that can handle the transfer of two

```
           :            high byte           :            low byte           :
bit r →    :   15   14   13   12   11   10    9    8 :   7    6    5    4    3    2    1    0 :
0 or 1 →   :  n15  n14  n13  n12  n11  n10   n9   n8 :  n7   n6   n5   n4   n3   n2   n1   n0 :
example →  :    0    1    1    0    0    0    1    1 :   0    0    1    1    0    1    0    1 :
```

Figure 12.22 The parallel interface data representation.

*HP 82973A HP-IL Interface for the IBM Personal Computer, Owner's Manual (Hewlett-Packard Company, 1984).

8-bit bytes through the interface. The interface is sometimes divided into a *low* byte and a *high* byte, and the protocol of data transfer may be handled separately for them.

Each bit on the interface may be set to 0 or 1. If a bit r is set it represents 2^r, so that the full number transferred across the interface may be reconstructed with the calculation.

$$(n15)2^{15} + (n14)2^{14} + \cdots + (n1)2^1 + (n0)2^0$$

where each of the numbers n15, n14,..., n1, n0 may take only the values 1 or 0, depending on whether or not the bit is set. It is left as an exercise to the reader to show that the 16 lines may represent any integer in the range 0 to 65,535, and this, in general, is what the software will return when the parallel interface is being read. In many cases the highest bit (15) is a sign bit that, if set, represents a negative number, so that the data range is then $-32,767$ to $32,767$.

In our particular example we have included a possible bit pattern at the bottom of the figure that represents the number 25,407.

12.4.1.   The ISAAC Parallel Interface

The binary I/O system of the ISAAC was introduced in Chapter 6 from a software standpoint. The appropriate commands to interrogate the interface are &BIN and &BOUT, and their matrix equivalents are &@BIN and &@BOUT. The matrix commands allow data to be moved across the interface directly into a data array in blocks without having to go through a BASIC software loop. The handshaking protocol becomes particularly important in such cases for the efficient transfer of data. We concentrate on the handshaking aspect of the interface in this chapter. Much of what we discuss in this section is equally as valid for the parallel BCD interface, which is discussed in the next section.

The general configuration of the ISAAC parallel interface is shown in Figure 12.23. There are two sets of 16 separate parallel binary lines:one set for input, one set for output. The high and low bytes for input and output have separate handshaking lines, making a total of 12 on this interface. In the default configuration of this interface, no handshaking of data across the interface is necessary, since all handshaking lines are pulled high unless constrained to go low with an external TTL signal.

Three handshaking lines—CLEAR TO SEND, STROBE, and HOLD—are provided on the ISAAC for the high and low lines of I/O. Data transfer is made with the following protocol, which is described for binary input only. The handshaking is shown graphically in Figure 12.24.

1. The CLEAR TO SEND line on the binary input port goes high to indicate to the external device that the system is ready to take data.
2. The external device is then free to put data on the data lines, set the STROBE line high, keep it high for at least 12 μs, and then bring it low

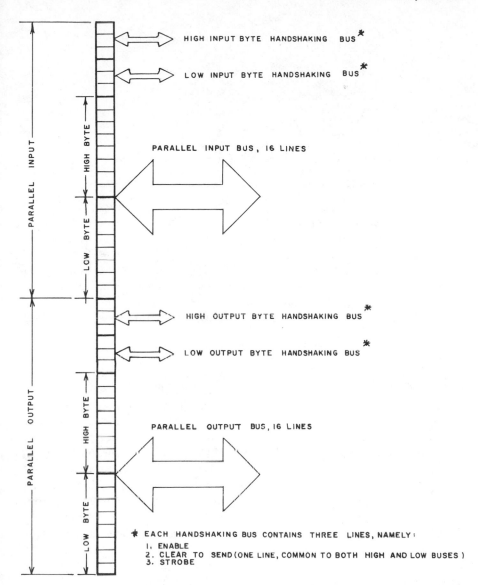

Figure 12.23. The ISAAC parallel interface for I/O showing the data and handshaking lines.

again. The binary data lines must be stable for at least 50 μs from the leading edge of the STROBE pulse.

3. ISSAC clears the binary port's CLEAR TO SEND line as soon as it detects a STROBE, thus telling the external device that ISAAC has received the data but is not ready yet for the next word.

4. The entire binary input bus may be held (latched) at any time by pulling the HOLD lines low. There are two HOLD lines for the binary input

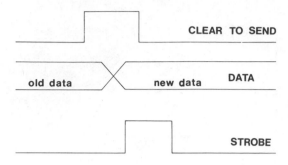

Figure 12.24.   Data input handshaking on the ISAAC interface.

subsystem: one for each byte of the input. They can be used separately or tied together to latch the entire bus.

The protocol has been developed to allow the interface to operate at the speed of the slowest instrument. Since operation of these commands includes waiting for a CLEAR TO SEND signal, the matrix instruction may be slowed if the specified sampling rate is faster than the transmit rate of the external device.

12.4.2.   The GPIO Parallel Interface

The general-purpose I/O (GPIO) bus is a widely used standard developed by Hewlett-Packard for parallel interfacing. Like the bus described in the last section it has 16 input and 16 output lines. The handshaking system is, however, more extensive, with four lines being able to handle data transfer in both directions across the interface, allowing much greater flexibility in interfacing to external equipment. The GPIO interface standard has been developed to allow either positive- or negative-true logic to be used.

In its most general implementation the GPIO interface has 50 lines with the designations shown in Figure 12.25. As before, there are 16 input and 16 output data lines. The four handshaking lines on this figure take the place of the 12 handshaking lines described for the ISAAC interface. The data transfer across this interface may be configured to be compatible with the ISAAC data transfer protocol. The interface also has a series of six user-definable lines that allow the interface to be adapted to a host of interfacing tasks.

All data transfer through the GPIO interface into an HP computer is carried out under the control of the four handshaking lines listed below. We describe briefly the configuration for an ENTER operation, as we have already discussed for the ISAAC interface in the last subsection.

1. An I/O line defines the direction of data transfer. The line being high defines an ENTER operation.
2. A peripheral control (PCTL) line is controlled by the HP device and is used to initiate data transfer. This is equivalent to the CLEAR TO SEND line.

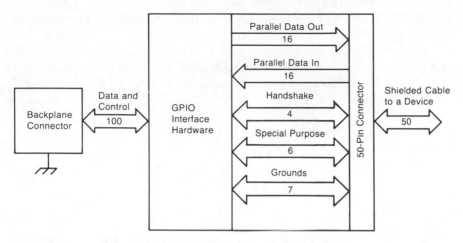

Figure 12.25. The GPIO interface. Reproduced by permission of Hewlett-Packard Company.

3. A peripheral flag (PFLG) line is controlled by the peripheral device and indicates that the peripheral is ready to continue data transfer. This is completely equivalent to the STROBE line.

4. Finally, an external interrupt line (EIR) allows interrupts to be serviced.

The logical sense of the PCTL and PFLG lines may be hardware defined for high-true or low-true logic. This allows almost any peripheral to be interfaced for data transfer. As far as data handshaking protocol is concerned, again a great deal of flexibility is available with the interface. Two modes are possible: the so-called *full mode*, and the *pulsed mode*, which can be used to synchronize data transfer. The full-mode transfer is equivalent to the ISAAC data transfer protocol already described. The pulsed-mode transfer protocol has the potential of higher data rate transfer, but since the PFGL line is not checked before initiating the transfer, the possibility of data loss is greater.

12.5. THE BCD INTERFACE

The first digital instruments that appeared in the laboratories coded binary information in a form that was easily decoded in hardware to yield a decimal display. This representation of binary information was called *binary coded decimal* (BCD). Initial attempts at laboratory automation involved interfacing these BCD instruments to computers. What does not follow is that you can directly connect a BCD instrument to a computer I/O or memory bus. An interface is required to reformat the BCD information, encode it as its ASCII representation, and synchronize machine and computer.

Only if an instrument is supplied with a BCD "interface" for your particular computer and the software to operate it (called device drivers) can the instrument be easily run by your computer. Interfacing older BCD instruments to your computer can be laborious.

One instrument vendor supplying a BCD interface is Hewlett Packard. This particular interface that we describe is the HP-98033 BCD interface input* used on the HP-9800. The interface connector consists of 50 lines divided in the following way:

Thirty-eight lines to represent a number
An overload line
a 4-line function code
Four lines for handshaking
Signal ground, shield ground, and +5-V reference

These are the minimum number of lines necessary to complete an interface connection. Other implementations of the interface, such as the HP-98623 interface, contain many more lines (64 in this case), but close inspection of the manuals shows that all the essential information is still contained in the 50 lines mentioned above.

The 98033A can be configured for either positive- or negative-true logic levels. Input signal voltages are constrained to TTL-compatible levels: that is, 0 to 0.7 V for low, and 2 to 5.5 V for high.

We first describe the BCD representation of a number, with special emphasis on the format used for BCD data transfer, and then we briefly discuss the method of data transfer.

12.5.1.   The BCD Representation

BCD is a method for coding decimal digits in binary form. Any decimal number in the range 0 to 9 requires at least four binary digits to represent it. Thus, the number 9, for example, may be divided as:

$$9 = 2^3*1 + 2^2*0 + 2^1*0 + 2^0*1 = 1001 \text{ (binary)}$$

The method of representing a number in BCD is to separately code each of the decimal digits in binary. An example is the number 96, which would end up as |1001| 0110 |, where we have used the vertical lines to sepate the binary parts corresponding to each digit. Since four bits can take up to 16 possibilities, the representation is inefficient in representing numbers in the range 0 to 9.

Some of this inefficiency is removed in the way that the representation is used for the BCD interface to transfer numbers in scientific notation. The notation in Table 12.13 is in common use for the BCD interface;

*HP Handbook No. 98033-90000, Hewlett-Packard Instruments.

Table 12.13. Full BCD Representation

BINARY PRESENTATION (of single character)	CHARACTER
0 0 0 0	0
0 0 0 1	1
0 0 1 0	2
0 0 1 1	4
0 1 0 0	5
0 1 0 1	6
0 1 1 0	7
0 1 1 1	8
1 0 0 1	9
1 0 1 0	line-feed
1 0 1 1	+ [plus]
1 1 0 0	, [comma]
1 1 0 1	− [minus]
1 1 1 0	E [exponent]
1 1 1 1	. [period]

12.5.2. The BCD Connection

A listing of the line designations on the HP 98033A BCD interface is shown in Table 12.14. As we see in the table, 38 of the lines connected to the BCD instrument generate at the interface a signed 8-digit BCD mantissa with a 1-digit exponent, also with sign. The number is represented as shown in Figure 12.26.

If the instrument has fewer digits to send, the unused inputs are grounded so as to read zero. The maximum number that can be accommodated by this interface is 99,999,999E9. Any number larger than this will set the overflow bit, OVLD. With instruments that have multiple ranges, the 4-bit function code is used to indicate the range setting for the data currently on the data lines.

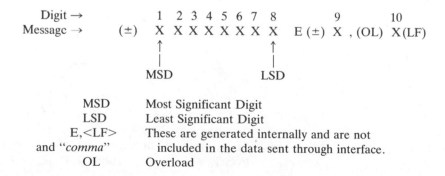

Figure 12.26. The BCD message format generated by the HP-98033A interface.

Table 12.14.   BCD Interface Message Format on HP 98033A

MNEMONIC	NUMBER LINES	DESCRIPTION
Standard Format Data Lines		
SGN1	1	Mantissa sign
D1	4	Mantissa digit 1
D2	4	Mantissa digit 2
D3	4	Mantissa digit 3
D4	4	Mantissa digit 4
D5	4	Mantissa digit 5
D6	4	Mantissa digit 6
D7	4	Mantissa digit 7
D8	4	Mantissa digit 8
SGN2	1	Exponent sign
D9	4	Exponent digit
O.L.	1	Overload indicator
D10	4	Function code
Control and Reference Lines		
CTLA	1	} Standard control lines
DFLGA	1	}
CTLB	1	} optional control lines
DFLGB	1	}
GND	1	}
+5 V	1	} reference signals
SHIELD GROUND	1	}
	50 lines	

Two handshaking lines, CTL and DFLG, are commonly used to insure that the instrument does not send data faster than the computer can read it. The CTL external trigger from the computer provides a timing pulse for data acquisition. The DFLG is the return handshake signal from the instrument, indicating that new data is available to be read on the input lines.

The function of the interface is to transcribe the data appearing at its input to a form that computer recognizes as I/O data. Thus, when the computer wants a reading, the interface scans each BCD digit and converts it to ASCII characters. It is these ASCII characters that are transmitted on the computer I/O bus.

The BCD interface message format is shown in Figure 12.26. Each message is composed of 16 ASCII characters. Eight of these comprise the mantissa. These are followed by an ASCII "E" to indicate an exponent, an exponent sign, the exponent, a comma, an overflow character, a function code, and a linefeed terminator.

The 10th, 13th, and 16th characters of the ASCII string sent by the interface are *generated within the interface itself*. These characters are used by the computer to aid in deciphering the meaning of the ASCII digit string coming from the interface. The E separates the mantissa from the exponent, and the comma separates the exponent from the function code. A linefeed, <LF>, informs the computer that the transmission is complete.

12.5.3.   BCD Computer Interfaces

There are no full implementations of the BCD interface for any of the popular personal computers that allow scientific data input. The only computer companies that support this interface on their computers are Hewlett-Packard and Tektronix.

What of the task of interfacing a personal computer to an instrument with a BCD output? There are two options:

1.   Design and build an interface between the computer bus and the BCD output of the instrument. As you can well appreciate after our discussion of the HP–BCD interface, this is no trivial task.

2.   Most laboratory microcomputer systems have provisions for binary I/O. Configuring these to accept BCD inputs is not difficult. You will probably have to be satisfied with only four significant decimal digits, however, since most of the systems have only 16 lines of binary as standard.

There are a number of software-addressable input BCD devices available on the IBM and Apple. The binary input lines on the ISAAC 91A interface may be addressed as a BCD input device. Since each BCD digit requires four lines, only four digits of a BCD device output may be addressed in this way. The requirement for further digits may be addressed only with the addition of more binary input lines to the 91A or, alternatively, by the fabrication of a multiplexing device to strobe various digits of a BCD output device onto the available input lines in turn.

The ISAAC system will handle 16 bits of binary I/O. Handshaking lines are also included for each I/O. Of interest to this discussion are the commands &BCDIN and &BCDOUT on the Apple. These commands read or output four digits of BCD from the input or output ports of the ISAAC 91A. It interprets the value at the binary port as four unsigned digits of BCD according to the following arrangement:

BIT#	15 14 13 12	11 10 9 8	7 6 5 4	3 2 1 0
BCD DIGIT	1000's	100's	10's	1's

The protocol for data transfer across the interface follows exactly that for the parallel implementation of the interface described in the last section.

The Rogers Laboratories* A32 I/O optoisolated interface board for the Apple comes with 32 I/O lines, all of which may be configured as a full BCD input device allowing the acquisition of eight BCD digits in parallel. The lines may be configured (in software) as full BCD or binary inputs. The system also contains four optoisolated interrupt lines that may be used for handshaking and data transfer. The interface may be addressed by the familiar & jump vector. Alternatively, for use in circumstances where the jump vector is needed for the Labsoft system running the ISAAC interface, the data lines may be addressed directly with a series of PEEK and POKE commands.

In the 32-pin BCD input configuration, the A32 board lines are divided into a series of four ports, each of eight lines. Each port contains the information for two decimal digits. A single one of the four ports is addressed with the extended Applesoft command

```
&BCDR, PORT, VALUE
```

where the variable PORT contains the address of the port (memory mapped I/O), and the variable VALUE returns the input BCD value for that port. With the BCD card in slot 4 the following are the port addresses:

PORT	ADDRESS
1	49344
2	49346
3	49348
4	49350

If, for example, we address port 4, which has the bit pattern 00110100 at its input, by using the program

```
100 PORT = 49350    :REM PORT 4
110 &BCDR, PORT, VL
120 PRINT VL
```

the value we should see printed is 34.

To read the complete set of 32 lines as an 8-digit number, we must read the four ports in turn and carry out a simple exercise to form the data into a single number. See Figure 12.27.

This program uses the fact that the complete number must be the sum

$$num4 * 10,000,000 + num3 * 10,000 + num2 * 100 + num1$$

where num1,...,num4 designate the results of the BCD values at each port.

*Rogers Laboratories, 2710 So. Croddy Way, Santa Ana, CA 92704.

```
200 PORT   = 49344 : VL = 0
210 FOR I = 0 TO 3
220 PORT   = PORT + 2*I
230 &BCDR, PORT, NUM
240 VL = VL + NUM * 100^I
250 NEXT I
260 PRINT "BCD INPUT VALUE ";VL
270 END
```

Figure 12.27.   Program for running a BCD interface.
Language: Applesoft + Roger's Lab. Software.

If we are interfacing the BCD lines to, for example, a Hewlett-Packard instrument which is returning full scientific notation numbers, then one of these numbers may be the exponent. The position of the decimal point is also important. If the number is of the form X.XXXXXEXX, where the decimal point and exponent are implied, we may have

$$(num4/10 + num3/1000 + num2/100,000)*10^{(num1)}$$

The sign of the number and the exponent may have to be read in on other BCD lines.

12.6.   THE CENTRONICS INTERFACE

The Centronics parallel bus interface has become the standard parallel interface for connecting computers to printers. It sends standard ASCII characters

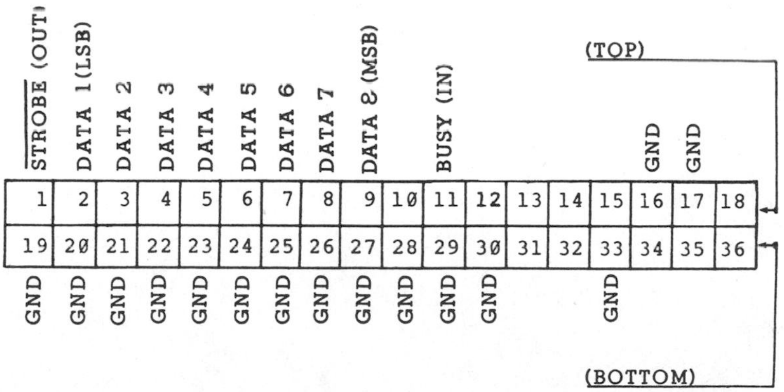

Figure 12.28.   Line designation for Centronics interface. Reproduced by permission of Kaypro Corporation, who makes no claim as to the accuracy of reproduction.

through the interface in 8-bit bytes. Although the connector has 36 lines, most are not used. The handshaking capability is extremely straightforward, and in the future it is likely that this interface may be used in place of the RS-232 interface when higher data rates are required.

A typical pin assignment for the interface is shown in Figure 12.28. Unfortunately, there is as yet no standard connector that is being used for this interface, since many computer manufacturers custom design the cables and connectors to their own particular applications.

13

The GPIB Interface

The GPIB (general–purpose interface bus), often referred to by its IEEE standard designation IEEE 488-1978* is a generalization of the HP–IB developed by the Hewlett-Packard company more than a decade ago. Using the interface, the user can monitor and control a number of measuring instruments from a single computer interface. Once the interface has been mastered a sizable increase in productivity may be realized in laboratory data acquisition and control.†

Although it is quite popular in scientific and engineering applications, there are few explanations of this interface available to the nonspecialist. Hardware books do not deal with it because they feel it is a software standard. Likewise the software literature neglects it because of its hardware aspects. Some of the articles that have been written on the standard are for the professional engineer who may be designing an instrument to be compatible with GPIB. Because of its generality, it is not an easy interface to learn and use. One must be familiar with the software characteristics of the host controller or computer, the interface bus, and the device or devices with which it is communicating. This can be a confusing state of affairs, to say the least.

What we have attempted to do in this chapter is to present the minimum amount of material necessary to give one the ability to get two systems talking to each other without getting bogged down in the detailed aspects of the standard, which is guaranteed only to confuse. We try and balance the general aspects of the interfacing task with examples taken from particular laboratory situations. Our method of discussion of the interface differs in a major way from the published literature of GPIB, which usually begins with a lengthy explanation of the detailed bus communications before describing the software necessary to control the interface. We postpone all but a brief description of the bus aspects until later in the chapter in order to simplify the discussion. Information on detailed bus communications is only required if one is attempting to troubleshoot a particularly difficult interfacing problem.

At a minimum, this chapter should alert the novice to the fact that a statement concerning an instrument's IEEE-488 or GPIB compatibility does not necessarily mean plug-in compatibility, especially for older instruments.

---

*ANSI/IEEE Standard 488-1978; *Standard Digital Interface for Programmable Instrumentation.* (IEEE, Inc., 345 E. 47th St., New York, NY 10017).
†G.C. Stanley, m *ISA Trans.*, **21**, 9 (1982).

How much programming effort will be required by the user will depend both on the implementation and on the devices to be interfaced. Readers who wish to understand the workings of the interface in more detail are advised to consult the literature.*[†]

13.1. SIMPLE OVERVIEW OF THE GPIB INTERFACE

In this section we present a simple overview of the whole GPIB concept for those who are completely new to it.

We emphasize general concepts rather than detailed descriptive explanations, and we concentrate on the following topics:

1. The GPIB bus.
2. Device addressing.
3. The role of controllers, talkers, and listeners.
4. The GPIB functions.

A typical configuration for the GPIB bus with a number of GPIB interfaced instruments is shown in Figure 13.1. Each device has a different address PA. The general characteristics of the GPIB interface system are presented in Table 13.1. Many of the aspects of the interface will be new and are discussed in this section; others are obvious from the table and do not need further explanation. The GPIB standard covers the operation of the bus hardware, the device functions, and the GPIB bus commands.

13.1.1. Bus Hardware

Interconnecting devices on a bus to the host computer controller is a trivial matter. The hardware interconnection aspect of the GPIB standard is straightforward. A single, well-designed GPIB connector is used for all interfacing. The connector, shown in Figure 13.2, has both male and female joining connections at each end of the interconnecting cable. The connector cable design has the advantage that one may accomplish a multitude of interconnecting patterns, ranging from a daisy chain to a star-connected configuration, with no degradation of performance as long as one is careful to keep within the overall specifications of the system.

Each connector and the adjoining cables have a total of 24 lines, eight of which are command lines, eight are data lines, and the remaining eight are grounding lines. The GPIB standard uses negative true TTL logic, where TTL

---

*IEEE-488 Home Study Course (Measurement and Data Corporation, 2994 W. Liberty Avenue, Pittsburg, PA 15216).
[†]*Tutorial Description on the Hewlett-Packard Interface Bus* (Hewlett-Packard Corporation, 1820 Embacadero Road, Palo Alto, CA 94303).

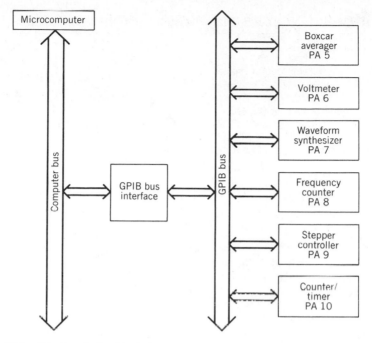

Figure 13.1. The interfacing block diagram of a typical GPIB bus-controlled experiment.

low (0 V) represents logic. TRUE., and TTL high (5 V) represents logic. FALSE..

13.1.2. Device Addressing

To insure communications between instruments and a GPIB controller requires one further hardware task to be performed prior to powering up the devices and developing the software. The device addresses of each instrument on the bus must be set. Under the GPIB standard each instrument on the bus must have a unique address so that direct communications with each instrument may be made without interference from any of the other instruments on the interface. No two devices on the bus may have the same device address.

On the backpanel, or at some other convenient location within a GPIB-compatible instrument, there should be an area clearly labeled IEEE 488-1978 on which there will be a row of switches. Some of these switches are used to set the device principal address PA. The particular example shown in Figure 13.3 is from a Wavetek spectrum analyzer and is representative of many other IEEE-488-compatible devices. The switches marked device address (binary) are the ones in which we are interested. The method of interpreting the numbers using a binary on/off (1 or 0) conversion to decimal or some other numbering

Table 13.1.   General Characteristics and GPIB Specifications

Data Rates

    250 K per second typical
    1 M per second maximum

Number of Devices on Bus

    15 devices maximum (electrical limit)
    8 devices typical (parallel poll limit)

Bus Length

    20 m maximum
    2 m per device typical

Bus Structure

    Byte oriented 24 line bus
    8 bits for commands
    8 bits for data
    8 bits for grounding

Interrupt Driven

    Serial poll (slower response)
    Parallel poll(fast response)

Bus Hierarchy

    Microcomputer/controller
    Talkers and listeners
    Only single active controller or talker allowed
    System may consist of talker and listeners only

Communications

    At any time only one talker may be active
    Multiple listeners are allowed

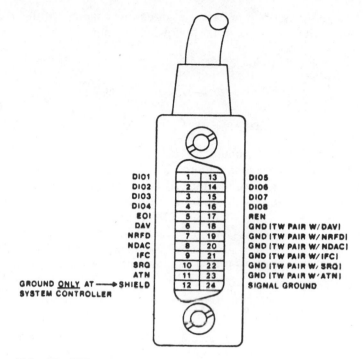

DIO1	1	13	DIO5
DIO2	2	14	DIO6
DIO3	3	15	DIO7
DIO4	4	16	DIO8
EOI	5	17	REN
DAV	6	18	GND (TW PAIR W/DAV)
NRFD	7	19	GND (TW PAIR W/NRFD)
NDAC	8	20	GND (TW PAIR W/ NDAC)
IFC	9	21	GND (TW PAIR W/IFC)
SRQ	10	22	GND (TW PAIR W/ SRQ)
ATN	11	23	GND (TW PAIR W/ ATN)
GROUND ONLY AT ──► SHIELD	12	24	SIGNAL GROUND
SYSTEM CONTROLLER			

Figure 13.2. The GPIB connector. Reproduced by permission of National Instruments.

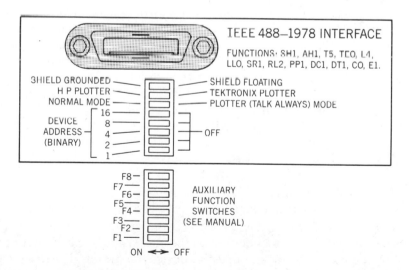

IEEE 488–1978 INTERFACE

FUNCTIONS: SH1, AH1, T5, TEO, L4, LLO, SR1, RL2, PP1, DC1, DT1, CO, E1.

SHIELD GROUNDED ———
H P PLOTTER ———
NORMAL MODE ———

SHIELD FLOATING
TEKTRONIX PLOTTER
PLOTTER (TALK ALWAYS) MODE

DEVICE ADDRESS (BINARY) — 16, 8, 4, 2, 1

OFF

F8, F7, F6, F5, F4, F3, F2, F1

AUXILIARY FUNCTION SWITCHES (SEE MANUAL)

ON ◄─► OFF

Figure 13.3. Typical GPIB instrument configuration showing the address switches and functional designation. This example is for a Wavetek Spectrum Analyzer.

system has been described in detail in an earlier chapter. In this particular example the switches are set in the following positions:

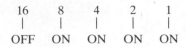

Figure 13.4.   The GPIB switch settings

which represent the binary number 01111, the decimal number 15, the octal number 17, and the hexagonal number F.

In a later section we show how the GPIB bus commands have to be configured to address a device with this or any other device address. A common mistake made when configuring the GPIB interface is in device addressing. The confusion occurs because it is not the actual device addresses that are used in the program but rather a derivative of them. Furthermore, this coded address changes in a program depending on whether one is reading from or writing to a particular device.

13.1.3.   Controllers, Talkers, and Listeners

In any situation where there is a need for communication between a number of separate entities such as the devices on a communications bus, some form of order must prevail. Two criteria must be met for the communications to be successful. First, the devices on the bus must be speaking and understanding the same language, and, second, some form of hierarchy must be established to control the flow of communications along the bus.

This section is concerned with the establishment of a hierarchy on the bus. The GPIB standard allows for the designation of three classes of devices on the bus. These are the controller, talkers, and listeners. Although the device designations are descriptive of their operation, a more detailed definition is helpful in establishing their relationship to each other.

1. *Controller.*   The controller is the device, usually a microcomputer, that oversees all other devices on the GPIB bus. It controls the flow of commands and data along the bus and regulates the roles of the talkers and the listeners. In the implementation that we describe in this book, only one controller is allowed on each GPIB bus.

2. *Talker.*   Talkers transmit data to the controller or possibly one or more of the listeners. Only one talker on the bus may be in the active state at one time.

3. *Listener.*   Listeners are devices whose primary function it is to receive commands or data from other devices on the bus. Within the hierarchy of the GPIB standard they are the most passive devices on the bus. Devices such as printers and plotters fall into this category. More than one listener may be in the active state at one time.

The above designation for a given device within the GPIB standard is determined by the GPIB functions that are implemented within that device. These functions will be discussed later.

Controllers have the obvious characteristic of being able to operate both as talkers and listeners in addition to satisfying their primary function of control. Many devices have this dual property. An example of such a device is the Wavetek spectrum analyzer that we introduced in the last section. Referring to Figure 13.3, this device may be hardware set to be either a talker/listener in the normal mode or merely a talker. In the normal setting of switch 6 on this device, the spectrum analyzer will have a designation of a talker/listener and may be controlled by a higher-level controller device, such as a microcomputer, as we show in Figure 13.5*a*. If switch 6 is set to the other position, the plotter (talk only), it can now only operate as a talker and can only feed data to one or the other of two possible listener devices defined by the position of switch 7. The bus configuration in this case is shown in Figure 13.5*b*.

13.1.4. Bus Communications

The topic of device communications along the bus is a complex one. Each device along the bus must be able to monitor the states of the control and data lines. Each device along the bus must be able to interpret commands sent to it from any other device and to then execute the designated task. Since each device may have its own language, there must be an interface at each end of the link that will act as an interpreter to translate the commands either from the device language to communications language—that is, the GPIB command language, or from the communications language to the device language. When we consider the number of possible permutations that can occur in the re-

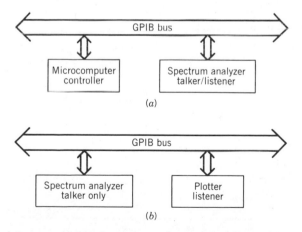

Figure 13.5. The possible configurations of a two-instrument bus. (*a*) Configuration as a talker/listener. (*b*) Configuration as a controller/talker.

sponses of the devices to a command, even when there are as few as eight devices on the bus, we see that the communications task is not a trivial matter.

Let us consider, for example, communications between a controller microcomputer and any other single device on the bus. A schematic representation of the microcomputer—peripheral device linkup is shown in Figure 13.6. As mentioned above, for the microcomputer to talk successfully to the device, there must be interfaces at both ends that interpret between the internal languages of the devices and the GPIB command language set. A software eye view of the GPIB communications between a microcomputer controller and a peripheral device is shown in Figure 13.7. We have the following levels of language interpretation that need to be considered:

1. The microcomputer high-level language.
2. The microcomputer—GPIB interface language syntax.

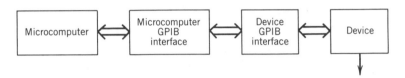

Figure 13.6. A simple GPIB linkup showing the layers of control translators needed in a two-instrument bus configuration.

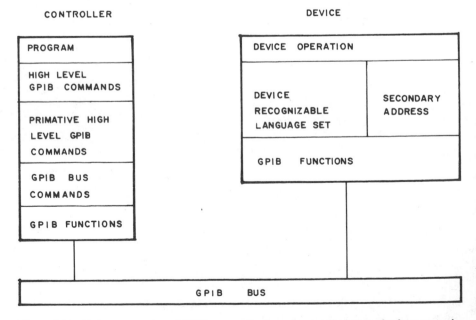

Figure 13.7. Software eye view of GPIB communications showing the layers of software translators needed for communications.

3. The GPIB bus command language set.
4. The peripheral device language set.

These divisions are somewhat arbitrary, but they do highlight all of the essential aspects of the GPIB communication. Points 1 and 2 on this list are microcomputer dependent, the last point is wholly dependent on the device being interfaced, and the third point, the GPIB language set, is universal. It must be chosen, however, so that all of the instructions in each device instruction set can be sent between the devices.

Brief examples illustrating the different levels of language that must be used are listed below. A short program, written in Applesoft BASIC, is given in Figure 13.8a. This sends a simple message between an Apple computer and the Wavetek spectrum analyzer previously discussed.

```
10 D$ = CHR$(4) : REM CTRL-D          :REM DEFINE CONTROL CHARACTERS
15 Z$ = CHR$(26): REM CTRL-Z
20 PRINTD$; "PR#3": PRINT D$;"IN#3":REM GPIB CARD IN SLOT 3
30 PRINT "WT4"; Z$; "SET FR R";        :REM SEND MESSAGE TO DEVICE 20
40 PRINT D$; "PR#0": PRINT D$; "IN#0"
50 END
```

Figure 13.8a. Program to control Wavetek through Apple GPIB card.
Language: Applesoft.

In this example the Apple GPIB interface card is in slot 3 of the Apple computer. Line 20 transfers control to this card as an output interface device. The device code 10100 (decimal 20) has been previously set on the back address switches of the Wavetek. Line 30 may be interpreted as an instruction to send the message SET FR R to the device with primary address 20 along the GPIB bus. Why WT4 is interpreted as device 20 will become clear in the following sections. The Wavetek recognizes the command SET FR R as an instruction to disable its front-panel manual inputs and accept all further instructions only from the GPIB bus. It should be emphasized that this instruction is exclusively a device-dependent instruction that would not be recognized by any other GPIB-compatible instrument along the bus. Finally, line 40 disconnects the GPIB interface card and reconnects the monitor.

Line 30 of this program contains a number of language levels, we discussed above. We can make the following language breakdown according to our earlier discussion.

```
A microcomputer high-level language [Basic];
30 PRINT "   "; character; "   "
A microcomputer-GPIB language syntax;
WT4 followed by control-Z followed by message
A GPIB bus command;
OUTPUT message to device 20
A peripheral device language set instruction;
SET FR R
```

The same program run on a California Computer System Apple GPIB card would be slightly different. See Figure 13.8*b*.

```
10  D$ = CHR$ (4)          :REM   CTRL-D
20  PRINT D$; "PR#3"       :REM   CONNECT SLOT 3
30  PRINT @4; "SET FR R"   :REM   SEND MESSAGE
40  PRINT D$; "PR#0"       :REM   RECONNECT MONITOR
50  END
```

Figure 13.8b.   Program to control Wavetek through CCS card.
Language: Applesoft.

Now line 30 is quite a bit different, there being no CTRL-Z character used to designate a GPIB command, and the write instruction WT has been replaced by @.

Finally, the same instruction communicated on an HP-9826 microcomputer would look totally different. See Figure 13.8*c*.

```
10  ASSIGN @WAVETEK TO 720
20  OUTPUT @WAVETEK: "SET FR R"
30  END
```

In this case the GPIB (HP-IB) interface has an interface select code of 7, equivalent in some ways to instruction 20 in the previous program, indicating that we had an Apple GPIB in a designated slot. The spectrum analyzer is device 20 on the GPIB bus as before, and once we have defined the path 720 as belonging to the Wavetek, all subsequent communication with this device could be made using this path name, which would make the job of program documentation much easier.

These three examples for sending the same message from three different controllers to the same device illustrates the difficulty in describing bus communications.

13.1.5.   GPIB Functions

Not every device on the GPIB interface is able to respond to every instruction sent out along the interface. We have alluded to this earlier when we mentioned the difference between controllers, talkers, and listeners. The ability of a certain device to operate and interact on the interface depends on the GPIB functions that are implemented within its instruction set. The relationship of the functions to the device and GPIB bus is shown in Figure 13.9. Thus, each device that is GPIB compatible recognizes and responds only to a subset of all the GPIB commands that are sent along the interface. For example, a listener has none of the talker functions and so will not be able to respond to a talk command from the controller.

A device that is GPIB compatible can recognize and respond to a subset of the GPIB command set. The response of each device is constructed from the

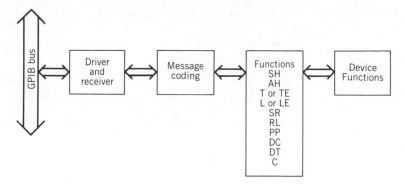

Figure 13.9. Relationship between GPIB functions and bus layout.

set of GPIB functions with which that device has been endowed. When it receives a GPIB command, the device responds through a complex series of procedures, utilizing this GPIB function set. In the language of structured programming, these functions are the primitives needed by a particular device if it is to operate as desired.

For example, our Wavetek analyzer (see Figure 13.3) implements the following GPIB functions.

```
WAVETEK SPECTRUM ANALYZER GPIB FUNCTIONS
    SH1,AH1,T5,TE0,L$,LE0,SR1,RL2,PP1,DC1,DT1,C0,E1
```

This list as it stands is extremely confusing to the first-time user. If we now write a similar list taken for the Apple II GPIB interface card, the confusion is compounded.

```
APPLE COMPUTERS GPIB CARD
    SH1,AH1,T3,L1,C4,C3,C25,DC,C2,DT,C1
```

From the user's standpoint there is no simple way of telling whether two devices with such apparently diverse lists of functions will be able to talk to each other. The exact meanings of these function lists are buried deep within the documentation of the GPIB standard and are meant for the designer rather than the user of GPIB-compatible instrumentation. It is, however, possible to draw some fairly general conclusions from these function lists, as we see by referring to Table 13.2.

The numbers following the function designations, such as in C4, indicate the subset of the GPIB function standard to which the device responds. A zero following function reference letter(s) indicates that the function is *not* implemented on that particular device. In particular, the Wavetek has C0 among its function designation, indicating that it cannot operate as a bus controller. Examining the same list in more detail, we note the designations TE0 and LE0. These indicate that the instrument cannot respond to secondary addressing

Table 13.2.   GPIB Function
Interpretation

T	Basic Talker
TE	Extended Talker
L	Listener
LE	Extended Listener
SR	Service Request
RL	Remote Local
PP	Parallel Poll
DC	Device Clear
DT	Device Trigger
C	Controller

commands—that is, they cannot operate as extended talkers or extended listeners by responding to secondary addressing.

13.2.   A PROCEDURAL APPROACH TO GPIB SOFTWARE

In this section we develop a procedural or algorithmic approach to the establishment of communications along the GPIB interface from a controller's standpoint without discussing the exact methods used to program an individual microcomputer or the details of the GPIB bus traffic. The procedures that we define represent the typical tasks that a user needs to implement in order to communicate with and control a nework of instruments. Although these procedures do not conform exactly to any of the GPIB commands in use on microcomputers, they do bear a more than passing resemblance, both in syntax and operation, to the macro commands used on systems like the HP-9826 when programmed in BASIC.

So that there will be no confusion we just mention the different types of control commands that we discuss in this chapter.

1. *GPIB Bus commands.*   These are a series of commands at the bus level that are covered by the GPIB IEEE 488-1978 standard. Any task that needs to be accomplished can be executed by sending a combination of these commands along the interface.

2. *GPIB Macro instructions.*   These are convenient macro commands in a language such as BASIC or C that accomplish a single task on the interface. They may have the same name as the most important bus command that they use, but they are not covered by the GPIB standard and are a combination of GPIB bus commands. The macro instructions are a high-level programming convenience that are available on the better computers of GPIB interfaces and are machine and manufacturer dependent. They make the task of programming through the GPIB interface much easier.

3. *GPIB Macro procedures.*   These are a set of language independant macro commands that we have constructed to simplify explaining and illustrating the capabilities of the interface. They are machine independent and will eliminate the confusing device language details we have already come across at the beginning of this chapter.

4. *GPIB Device commands.*   These are data sent along the interface to a device that, internally to that device, need to be recognized as commands. They are completely device dependent and are not covered by the IEEE-488 standard.

   To avoid confusion we adopt the convention that GPIB *MACRO PROCE-DURES*, which are device independent, will be written in uppercase italics. As before the remainder of all *device-independent algorithms* are written in lowercase italics.

13.2.1.   Procedure Definitions

In the following section we expand on our procedure definitions and demonstrate, with the set of procedures shown in Table 13.3, how we may accomplish communications with GPIB-compatible devices to fulfill all requirements for data acquisition and control.

Two types of activity—data transfer and command activity—can take place along the bus. Both data and bus commands are communicated through the *OUTPUT* procedure as "data." Most of the procedures defined in this section transfer a combination of bus level commands and data along the bus.

Table 13.3.   GPIB Macro Procedures

Data Transfer Procedures
   OUTPUT data to listed devices
   ENTER data from listed devices
   TRANSFER data from specified device to listed devices
Bus Management Procedures
   ABORT all bus activity
   CLEAR listed devices to predefined device-dependent state
   LOCAL enable of listed devices' front-panel controls
   LOCAL LOCKOUT, disable of listed devices' front-panel controls
   PARALLEL POLL of all devices on the bus
   PARALLEL POLL CONFIGURE, enable setup of devices' poll response
   PARALLEL POLL UNCONFIGURE; disable of listed devices' poll response
   REMOTE, enable listed devices in device-dependent mode
   SEND series of GPIB bus commands and data along the bus
   SERIAL POLL of listed devices
   TRIGGER listed devices

In the language of the GPIB interface, *Data is any set of alphanumeric characters that are to be transferred between two or more devices on the bus*. The data may be a collection of numbers that represent the result of a particular set of measurements being transferred to the control computer or some peripheral listener by a measuring instrument. It may be the address code of a device on the bus, or it may even represent a device-dependent command, such as 'SET FR R', used as an example in the last section. These device commands should not be confused with GPIB bus commands and are treated as data when they are transferred along the bus.

More detailed explanations of the GPIB macro procedures are given below. Following each procedure, where applicable, are the arguments that need to be satisfied each time the procedures are used.

1. *OUTPUT (listener list, "data")*.   The *OUTPUT* procedure covers any transfer of data from the host computer to a peripheral device(s). It contains all necessary commands to accomplish the complete transfer of data.

2. *ENTER (talker, "data")*.   This is the command procedure for reading data into the microcomputer on the GPIB interface. As part of the *ENTER* procedure a device on the interface must be identified to talk.

3. *TRANSFER (talker, listener list)*.   This controls the transfer of data from an identified talker to a group of identified listeners. At the end of this procedure the controller must regain control of the bus.

4. *ABORT*.   This macro procedure resets each device on the interface bus to their internal known start-up states and clears the GPIB interface bus. It should be used only at program start-up or to abort the existing bus traffic.

5. *CLEAR (listener list)*.   The *CLEAR* macro procedure is used to to clear all the specified devices on the bus to their predefined initial state. The action of this procedure is device dependent.

6. *LOCAL (listener list)*.   Many intelligent devices have the ability to be controlled via the front-panel controls or the GPIB interface. This macro procedure returns the listed devices on the bus to front-panel operation.

7. *LOCAL LOCKOUT*.   This single macro procedure sets all devices on the bus to GPIB bus control and disables their front-panel controls.

8. *PARALLEL POLL ("status byte")*.   The essence of this macro procedure is its speed. Devices on the GPIB bus can indicate that they require service from the controller by means of a single service request line on the command lines of the bus. The controller is able to sense from monitoring this line that a device on the bus requires attention, but it does not know which one. By issuing a *PARALLEL POLL* all the devices on the bus are asked to put out their status bits on a different line of the bus, so that in a single GPIB interface cycle the requesting device can be identified.

9. *PARALLEL POLL CONFIGURE (listener list).* A macro procedure in which each device on the bus is assigned a particular data bit that it must set in response to a parallel poll.

10. *PARALLEL POLL UNCONFIGURE (listener list).* This macro procedure informs the listed devices that they are not to respond to the parallel poll command.

11. *REMOTE (listener list).* This macro procedure puts the listed devices on the bus in their device-dependent remote mode.

12. *SEND (listener list, "data").* In the event that the high-level macro procedures listed here do not provide sufficient flexibility to communicate with some of the interfaced devices on the bus, it is necessary to work at the bus level. The individual GPIB bus commands may be sent with this procedure.

13. *SERIAL POLL (talker, "status byte").* This macro procedure is used when only a single device on the bus needs to be polled to see if it needs attention.

14. *TRIGGER (listener list).* This macro procedure triggers the listed devices simultaneously. In general, the individual devices on the bus will need to have been configured to expect the trigger command.

15. *UNTALK.* This macro procedure is usually sent along the bus at the beginning of each of the other procedure commands described here. It is a universal command that effects every device on the bus and establishes the supremacy of the controller.

16. *SERVICE REQUEST ("status byte").* A simple macro procedure that determines whether the 'service request' flag has been set on the bus.

The high-level GPIB macro instructions and procedures shown in Table 13.4 are not generally covered by the IEEE-488 standard. What is covered by the standard are the lower-level bus functions and GPIB commands. If one is fortunate enough to be working in a programming environment where these high-level command procedures have been developed, the task of programming the interface is fairly trivial. There will be times, however, when a device on a bus does not respond to these high-level commands as expected; it will then be necessary to have a good understanding of the bus, as described in the following sections, so that "bus-level" programming can be effectively accomplished.

Figure 13.10 is a short algorithm, using the macro procedures defined above, that describes a sequence of operations along the GPIB bus. The program sets up all the instruments with their device settings and then begins the data-taking loop. For each trip around the loop a stepping motor is reset to a new position, following the triggering of a waveform synthesizer. Then a parallel poll is taken of the bus, and all instruments that have data to provide are read out. Finally, the data is stored and the sequence repeated.

Table 13.4. GPIB Macro Procedures and the Corresponding BASIC Macro Instructions

	MACRO COMMANDS	
PROCEDURE	HP-9826	Apple II+,IIe
DATA TRANSFER COMMANDS		
OUTPUT	**OUTPUT** @devices,\<data>	**WT**\<listen list>Z$\<data>
ENTER	**ENTER** @devices,\<data>	**WC**\<listen list>Z$\<count>\<data>
TRANSFER	**ENTER** @device;\<data>	**RD**\<talker>Z$\<count>\<data>
BUS MANAGEMENT COMMANDS		
ABORT	**ABORT** @Hpib	**AB**
CLEAR	**CLEAR** @devices	**CL**\<listen list>
		CA
LOCAL	**LOCAL**	**LO**\<listen list>
		LA
LOCAL LOCKOUT	**LOCAL LOCKOUT**	**LL**
PARALLEL POLL	**PPOLL**	**PP**\<status word>
PARALLEL POLL CONFIGURE	**PPOLL CONFIGURE**	**PE**\<neable list>
PARALLEL POLL UNCONFIGURE	**PPOLL UNCONFIGURE**	**PE**\<listen list>
		PU
REMOTE	**REMOTE**	**RM**\<listen list>
		RA
SEND	**SEND**	
SERIAL POLL	**SPOLL**	**SP**\<talker>Z$\<status>
TRIGGER	**TRIGGER**	**TG**\<listen list>
UNTALK		**UT**

```
main program
begin
  ABORT bus
  CLEAR (devices 5-9)
  LOCAL LOCKOUT
  PARALLEL POLL CONFIGURE (devices 5-9)
  for k = 5 to 9
     OUTPUT (device k, "device settings")
  end_for
  for j = first to last stepping motor setting
     OUTPUT (stepping motor, "new device setting")
  TRIGGER (waveform synthesizer)
  PARALLEL POLL
  if (device 8) then ENTER (frequency counter, "data")
  if (device 9) then ENTER (counter timer, "data")
  if (device 7) then ENTER (waveform synthesizer, "data")
  if (device 5) then ENTER (boxcar averager, "data")
  store data in permanent file
  end_for
end
```

Figure 13.10. Algorithm showing sequence of operations carried out under GPIB control.

13.3. THE GPIB BUS

In this section a brief overview of the GPIB bus is presented. Although it is not generally necessary to have a detailed knowledge of what is going on at the bus level in order to communicate with many devices on the bus, there are some features of bus communication that are most easily explained with reference to the bus. Also, with even a minimal knowledge of the bus, it may be possible for a user to troubleshoot some of the simpler communication problems by observing the system at the bus level.

A schematic diagram of the bus is shown in Figure 13.11. The signal levels on the bus correspond to negative-level TTL logic. There are eight data lines and eight control lines. The role of each bus line is described in Table 13.5. Five of these control lines are for general GPIB management, and the other three are for data handshaking. These three 'transfer control lines' (alternatively called handshake lines) are overseen by the source handshake (SH1) and acceptor handshake (AH1) functions. The handshaking capability of the bus is the most standardized part of the GPIB standard, since it is close to the hardware implementation of the bus. The five management control lines can implement a multitude of control management tasks along the bus, depending on the specific applications. We now describe each of the control lines in more detail.

The Management Control Lines

ATN   The attention line is possibly the most important control line on the whole GPIB bus. The state of the ATN line defines whether the signals placed on the data bus lines are to be interpreted as data or a bus-level command. When the ATN line is true a bus-level command is placed on the line; when false, data is. When the ATN and EOI lines are simultaneously true, a parallel poll is being executed.

EOI   Setting the EOI line true is used primarily to indicate the end of a data string. Most talkers are able to set this line true at the end of a data string, but some use a special predefined character sent along the bus. This lack of standardization can be a problem. One should be particularly diligent in reading the manuals for each device on the bus to determine what convention is being used for this line.

SRQ   This line is set true by any device on the bus that requires service or attention by the controller. The proper response from the controller will be to carry out either a parallel poll or a serial poll to determine which device on the bus produced the service request. The controller must be specifically programmed to carry out the polling process. Some of the more advanced GPIB controllers may be configured to sense the SRQ line in an interrupt mode.

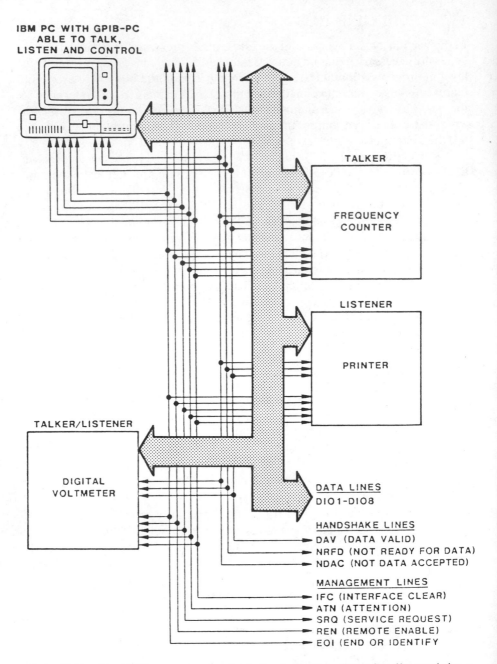

Figure 13.11. The GPIB bus structure showing the line designations. Reproduced by permission of National Instruments.

Table 13.5. The GPIB Bus Lines

Line Mnemonic	Description	Pin
Management Control Lines		
ATN	Attention	11
EOI	End or identify	5
SRQ	Service request	10
IFC	Interface clear	9
REN	Remote enable	17
Transfer Control Lines		
NRFD	Not ready for data	7
NDAC	Not data accepted	8
DAV	Data valid	6
Data Lines		
DIO1	Bit 0 (LSB)	1
DIO2	Bit 1	2
DIO3	Bit 2	3
DIO4	Bit 3	4
DIO5	Bit 4	13
DIO6	Bit 5	14
DIO7	Bit 6	15
DIO8	Bit 7 (MSB)	16

IFC   This line is only used with an *ABORT* command. When this line goes true, all device interfaces are set to their initial start-up state and the bus is cleared.

REN   This line in combination with the ATN line will disable the front-panel controls of the listed devices and put the devices under GPIB bus control.

The Transfer Control Lines

The three transfer control lines NRFD, NDAC, and DAV are at the heart of the GPIB data transfer handshaking capability. The data transfer is carried out asynchronously, so that the bus is slowed down to the speed of the slowest talker or listener. A talker may only put data on the lines if the NRFD line is true and the NDAC line false. The design of bus electronics is such that a single device wishing to set a line true will override all the other devices on the bus. When the talker is satisfied that the NRFD line is false (high), it sets the DAV line true and puts the data on the line. As the devices that have previously been designated as listeners accept the data, they will attempt to set the NDAC line false. When the last device on the bus has accepted the data, the line will finally be allowed to go false. The controller of talker will now set the DAV device line false. As long as no device on the bus sets the NRFD true to inhibit further data transmission, the sequence may be repeated with new data.

13.3.1. GPIB Bus Commands

A knowledge of the GPIB bus commands is vitally important for a proper understanding of the GPIB bus operation. As indicated previously, in the eventuality that the higher-level GPIB macro instructions do not exist for a particular GPIB computer interface, the bus interface may be directly programmed through these bus commands.

A complete listing of the GPIB bus commands is shown in Table 13.6. Any higher-level command procedures may be broken down into a sequence of these bus commands. Many of the procedures have the same name as the bus commands, the difference being that the procedures have all the software necessary to complete the task, whereas the bus commands after which they are named require supporting software to operate.

The bus commands are divided into four categories: the primary command group, the listen address group, the talk address group, and the secondary

Table 13.6. GPIB Bus Commands and Codes

Interface Message	Description	Decimal Value
PCG	*Primary Command Group*	
GTL	Go to Local	1
SDC	Selected Device Clear	4
PPC	Parallel Poll Configure	5
GET	Group Execute Trigger	8
TCT	Take Control	9
LLO	Local Lockout	17
DCL	Device Clear	20
PPU	Parallel Poll Unconfigure	21
SPE	Serial Poll Enable	24
SPD	Serial Poll Disable	25
LAG	*Listen Address Group*	
	Listen Address 0 through 30	32−62
	Unlisten	63
TAG	*Talk Address Group*	
	Talk Address 0 through 30	64−94
	Untalk	95
SCG	*Secondary Address Command Group*	
	Secondary Commands 0 through 30	96−126

address group. Each of these bus commands is sent along the data lines with the ATN line high.

The primary command group should be somewhat self-explanatory, given our previous discussions on the corresponding procedures. The only command that has not been encountered before is the **TCT** (take control) bus command. This enables a controller to pass control to another controller on the bus. It is an advanced GPIB programming command and will not be further discussed here. Most of the primary command group commands have to be implemented in combination with listen address group commands that define which devices on the bus are to respond with the correct handshake to these commands.

A number of listen address group commands may be sent down the bus in sequence. In contrast, only a single talk address group bus command may be sent, or there will be untold confusion on the bus.

Finally, the secondary address group will only be sent to devices that have an extended listening capability (LE1). A device with this capability, once addressed, expects a secondary address byte to be placed on the data bus in sequence with the first. This second address byte is used by the device in its internal program mode. For example, some devices may use the secondary address byte as a menu-select option to choose between a number of possible options. The documentation for each device must be consulted for the exact implementation in each case.

A different decimal value is assigned to each of the different bus commands, including the complete range of primary and secondary addressing commands in Table 13.6. All decimal numbers below 31 represent the primary command group, and numbers in the range 32 to 126 are concerned with addressing.

There are some subtleties about device addressing for talking or for listening that are somewhat confusing when first encountered. As discussed earlier, the device primary addresses that are set by hardware switches on the body of each instrument can only be in the decimal range 0 to 30. These addresses, however, have already been assigned to the primary command group. Confusion is avoided by adding an offset to the hardware device address, as explained below.

Devices are commanded to listen or talk by using listen addresses and talk addresses. The IEEE-488 has stipulated the following convention.

```
LISTEN ADDRESS =  32 + PRIMARY ADDRESS decimal
       UNLISTEN =  32 + 31 = 63
  TALK ADDRESS  =  64 + PRIMARY ADDRESS decimal
         UNTALK =  64 + 31 = 95
```

The unlisten and untalk commands are universal, acting on every device on the bus. All other address commands act only on the devices addressed, the address being determined by the primary address.

What further confuses the novice is that the decimal value of the calculated address is encoded, and it is this value that is used in programming. Table 13.7

Table 13.7.   Primary and Secondary Address Commands

Device Primary Address	Listen Commands char.	Listen Commands dec.	Talk Commands char.	Talk Commands dec.	Secondary Address char.	Secondary Address dec.
0	space	32	@	64	`	96
1	!	33	A	65	a	97
2	"	34	B	66	b	98
3	#	35	C	67	c	99
4	$	36	D	68	d	100
5	%	37	E	69	e	101
6	&	38	F	70	f	102
7	'	39	G	71	g	103
8	(	40	H	72	h	104
9	)	41	I	73	i	105
10	*	42	J	74	j	106
11	+	43	K	75	k	107
12	,	44	L	76	l	108
13	−	45	M	77	m	109
14	.	46	N	78	n	110
15	/	47	O	79	o	111
16	0	48	P	80	p	112
17	1	49	Q	81	q	113
18	2	50	R	82	r	114
19	3	51	S	83	s	115
20	4	52	T	84	t	116
21	5	53	U	85	u	117
22	6	54	V	86	v	118
23	7	55	W	87	w	119
24	8	56	X	88	x	120
25	9	57	Y	89	y	121
26	:	58	Z	90	z	122
27	;	59	[	91	{	125
28	<	60	\	92	¦	124
29	=	61	]	93	}	125
30	>	62	^	94	~	126
31	?	63	−	95		

lists the primary address codes along with the corresponding addresses and encoded address commands for talking and listening. The table is arranged so that the listen and talk addresses are read horizontally starting from the primary address. For example, the device with a primary address 20 will have an encoded listen address of 4 (decimal 52) and an encoded talk address T (decimal 84). The convention for the secondary address group is also shown in the table.

13.3.2. Synthesis of GPIB Macro Procedures from Primitive Bus Commands

The construction of the high-level GPIB Macro procedures that we are using in this chapter is illustrated here. A macro procedure is broken down into its more primitive components, which involve the actual bus commands and the status of the GPIB control lines. The first high-level procedure that we describe is the transfer of data from the controller to a listener via an *OUTPUT* macro procedure.

The breakdown of the *OUTPUT* procedure necessary to accomplish the transfer of data is shown in Figure 13.12. By our convention, statements enclosed in curly brackets describe action on the five management control lines. Depending on the GPIB interface controller which is in use, these control lines may have to be specifically set by the controller software. In other cases the vendor may have taken care of these chores within the high-level commands, and the user may not be aware of the sequence that is initiated when the macro command is executed.

```
procedure OUTPUT (device 1, device 2,   ,"data")
begin
  {set attention line true}
  My (Controller) Talk Address
  Unlisten
  Listen Address 1
      .
      .
  Listen Address n
  {set attention line false}
  while not EOS (end of string) do
       Put next data character on the bus
  end_while
  Set EOI line true
end
```

Figure 13.12. A typical bus sequence for an *OUTPUT* procedure. Language: Algorithmic.

The corresponding procedure for a typical *ENTER* sequence is shown in Figure 13.13

Finally, outlined in Table 13.8 is the bus sequence for the *OUTPUT* procedure, assuming that we are outputting the data sequence **SET FR R** to the Wavetek analyzer designated as primary address 20, as described previously in this chapter.

```
procedure ENTER (Talk address, "data")
begin
   Primary Talk Address
   Unlisten
   My(Controller) Listen Address
   {set attention line false}
   while not EOI(end or identify) do
       get next data character from bus
       concatenate character to string
   end_while
   set attention line true
end
```

Figure 13.13.   A typical bus Sequence for an *ENTER* procedure.
Language: Algorithmic.

Table 13.8.   A Typical GPIB Bus Sequence for an
OUTPUT Procedure
Language: GPIB Bus Commands

DOI Mnemonic	ASCII	Management Lines	Handshake Lines
MTA		ATN	LSTN
UNL		ATN	
S		ATN	
E			
T			
space			
F			
R			
space			
R			
{EOS}		EOI	
idle		ATN	

13.4.   GPIB ON HEWLETT-PACKARD COMPUTERS

It should be obvious to the reader by now that GPIB-compatible devices come
in many forms, and the designation by itself does not sufficiently characterize
the power of the interface. The problem is traceable to the original design
philosophy adopted by each manufacturer. In a great many cases the GPIB
interface is an "add on" to an instrument. The manufacturer has not committed
much time to its development, and most of the work of establishing communications is left to the user. This is especially true on older GPIB-compatible

instruments. In other cases, we have already discussed, the instruments have been developed and standardized to recognize the macro commands to aid the user in the interfacing task.

As an example of the latter case, Hewlett-Packard's implementation of the GPIB interface is discussed in this section. We have already mentioned some of the general aspects of the HP implementation in an earlier section, and we shall expand on this, detailing the strength and flexibility of the HP interfacing philosophy. This section should be viewed as a benchmark of what well-thought-out, GPIB-compatible communications software should be able to provide.

Interfacing to the GPIB bus is an anticipated function with most HP instruments. The HP extended BASIC language contains a number of statements that operate on the data interfaces directly. All data is transferred to and from the computer by the ENTER and OUTPUT extended BASIC statements. These statements are the ones used for data transfer from all the interfaces on the HP computer's bus. They are not in themselves detailed in the IEEE-488 standard, but they use a combination of bus-level commands that are. In HP BASIC each I/O interface is designated an interface select code. Typical, default, interface select codes for some of the standard I/O interfaces are shown in Table 13.9.

Each device connected to an HP computer is uniquely determined with reference to that instrument's device select code, which is formed by concatenating the interface select code for the interface with the primary address code for the particular device on, say, the GPIB bus.

For example, sending the message SET FR R over the GPIB bus (interface select code 7) to an instrument with primary address 20 may be written thus:

```
10 MESSAGE$ = "SET FR R"
20 OUTPUT 720; MESSAGE$
```

Table 13.9. Default Interface Select Codes used in HP BASIC

Fixed interfaces	
CRT display	1
Keyboard	2
HP-IB	7
Switch Selectable Defaults	
HP-IB	8
RS-232	9
GPIO	12
Data communications	20

where the variable MESSAGE$ contains the string to be sent along the bus, and 720 is the device select code. Notice that we do not have to be involved in the intricacies of the talk and listen addresses under this implementation. This is taken care of within the macro *OUTPUT* command of line 20.

Using numbers to designate devices can become confusing and tedious in a long program written to collect data and control many peripheral devices. The ASSIGN statement on some HP computers allows one to name I/O paths at the beginning of a program. Thus we might wish to assign the name WAVETEK to the device select code 710, giving us an alternative program segment.

```
10 MESSAGE$ = "SET FR R"
20 ASSIGN @WAVETEK TO 710
30 OUTPUT @WAVETEK; MESSAGE$
```

In certain circumstances we might want to assign a single path identifier, so that we could communicate with a number of devices simultaneously. In the unlikely event that we had three spectrum analyzers on the bus with primary device addresses 20, 22, and 23, we could make the assignment

```
ASSIGN @WAVETEKS TO 720,722,723
```

The incredible flexibility of the Hewlett-Packard interfacing philosophy should be apparent where the language statements take on the attributes of the procedural language that we discussed earlier.

The bus-management, high-level commands for the HP GPIB have been presented in Table 13.4. These may all be used with the assigned path names to give some extremely simple-looking software. For example, we might want to *ABORT* the bus activity.

```
30 ABORT 7 ' Universal command abort on 7
```

This same result could be achieved with the statements

```
30 ASSIGN @GPIB TO 7
40 ABORT @GPIB
```

Line 30 only has to be executed once at the front of the program, and thereafter all universal GPIB commands follow the @GPIB path name.

13.5.   GPIB INTERFACING ON THE APPLE

There are a number of GPIB cards available for the Apple II plus and Apple IIe computers. We describe two examples with varying degrees of sophistication as far as the end user is concerned.

13.5.1. The Apple GPIB Card

The Apple GPIB card is an advanced GPIB interface suitable for laboratory use. The GPIB function capability of the interface is

$$SH1, AH1, T3, L1, C4, C3, C25, DC, C2, DT, C1$$

These are almost all the functional capabilities required for device control in many common laboratory situations. An exception is the absence of a function to transfer and receive control from another controller on the bus. This capability is not often found on GPIB interfaces of most microcomputers, the IBM-PC, which is described in the next section, has such a capability.

The Apple GPIB card can be placed in any one of the internal slots of the Apple computer in the usual manner. The card contains 2K of ROM with software to control the GPIB bus and to act as a link between the Apple and the GPIB buses. The DOS PR#n command may be used from within Applesoft to access the interface card. Command strings are sent to and received from the card by using the normal Applesoft PRINT and INPUT commands.

The standard format of the Apple GPIB interface command string is

$$\langle command \rangle \quad \langle control\ characters \rangle \quad \langle data \rangle$$

which are usually included in quotes in a PRINT statement.

The commands are represented by two-letter mnemonics. These high-level macro commands are not in themselves covered by the IEEE-488 standard. A list of some of the GPIB high-level commands for this card have already been given in Table 13.4, where their relationship to our ideal set of GPIB macro procedures was noted.

A comprehensive listing of the Apple GPIB card, high-level commands together with the corresponding arguments is shown in Table 13.10. The first half of the table shows data transfer commands and the second half shows the bus management high-level commands. All these commands should be easily understandable from our earlier discussions of the GPIB interface.

For example, the simple, four-line program of Figure 13.14 inputs data from a device with primary address 17 and subaddress 6 and puts it into the variable C$.

We have assumed in this example that the Apple GPIB card is contained in slot 3 of the Apple bus. The control character CTRL-Z is used to separate bus commands from data. Unlike the HP interface software described in the last section, where each device on the bus may be referred to by its primary address, the Apple card requires the encoded talk of listen address commands to be used, depending on the sense of the data flow. This makes software writing for this interface somewhat more complicated than on an HP computer.

If one wishes to work with the interface without having to be bothered with the talk and listen addresses, then one could develop a programming approach

Table 13.10. Apple GPIB Card High-Level Commands

APPLE GPIB COMMAND	DESCRIPTION
Data Transfer Commands	
WR <listen list><ctrl><data>	*OUTPUT* data to the listed devices
WC <listen list><ctrl><count><ctrl><data>	*OUTPUT* specified character count [count] to listed devices
RD <talker><ctrl><data><term>	*ENTER* data from listed talker until <term>
RC <talker><ctrl><count><ctrl><data><term>	*ENTER* specified count from talker
XF <talker><ctrl><talker><listen list><ctrl>	*TRANSFER* data from talker to listed devices
Bus Management Commands	
AB	*ABORT* all bus traffic
CA	*CLEAR* all devices on bus
CL <listen list>	*CLEAR* listed devices
LA	*LOCAL* mode for all devices
LO <listen list>	*LOCAL* mode for listed devices
LL	*LOCAL LOCKOUT* all devices
PE <listen list>	*PARALLEL POLL ENABLE* of listen list
PD <listen list	*PARALLEL POLL DISABLE* of listen list
PP	*PARALLEL POLL* of bus
PU	*PARALLEL POLL UNCONFIGURE*
SP <talker><ctrl><status>	*SERIAL POLL* status of bus
SR <srq status>	*SERVICE REQUEST* status of bus
TG <listen list>	*TRIGGER* devices of listen list
DV <device number>	Set device number of controller

```
 5 D$ = CHR$(4)
10 PRINT D$; "PR#3" :PRINT D$; " IN#3"
20 PRINT "RCQf";Z$;"7";Z$;
30 INPUT C$
```

Figure 13.14. Receiving data from a device with the Apple GPIB card.
Language: Applesoft.

to work directly with the primary addresses. In the example shown in Figure 13.15 we can specify any number of listening devices by their primary addresses and send them a message defined by the user.

```
100 REM-----Program to send message to devices on GPIB bus
105 D$ = CHR$(4) : Z$ = CHR$(26)    :REM CTRL-D, CTRL-Z
110 LA$ = "" : ID = 0 : TEXT:HOME:VTAB(4):REM initialization
115 PRINT "ENTER ADDRESSES OF LISTENERS"
120 PRINT "ENTER NEGATIVE NUMBER TO END LIST"
125 ID = ID + 1: PRINT "DEVICE";ID
130 INPUT "ENTER PRIMARY ADDRESS";PA%
135 IF PA% < 0 THEN GOTO 150
140 LA$ = LA$ + CHR$(32 + PA%): GOTO 125
150 PRINT; INPUT "ENTER MESSAGE";MS$
155 PRINT D$;"PR#3"
160 PRINT "WT" + LA$ + Z$ + MS$
165 PRINT D$; "PR#0: END
```

Figure 13.15. Program to send message to devices on GPIB bus.
Language: Applesoft.

In this example the primary addresses of the devices are entered by the user one at a time in an infinite loop from lines 130 and 140. The program will sit in this loop and for more data until a negative number is entered, at which point it jumps to line 150 and requests the operator to enter the message to be sent to all the listening devices. Up to this point no communications have taken place with the interface. The GPIB card is assumed to be in slot 3 on the Apple bus. Line 160 contains the actual information to be communicated with the interface. We are assuming that the correct end-of-string character will be sent at the end of this data stream. If we need to use the WC command instead of the WT command, we would substitute the following line for line 160.

```
160 PRINT "WC" + LA$ + Z$ + STR$(LEN(MS$)) + Z$ + MS$
```

The extra few terms in this command provide information on the length of the data string.

This extension of this approach to all the other GPIB commands listed in Table 13.10 is straightforward.

Before leaving the Apple GPIB card, we will describe Parallel polling on the bus by using this card. Let us assume that we have five devices on the bus with primary addresses 20 to 25 and that we wish to configure the interfaces to respond to a *PARALLEL POLL*.

Our first task is to configure each interface so that it can flag a different line of the GPIB data lines if it needs attention. The number that will be read on that line by a *PARALLEL POLL* is called the status byte. Let us set up the bits on the line in the order shown in Figure 13.16*a*. The correspondence between bits and device addresses does not necessarily have to be in any particular order.

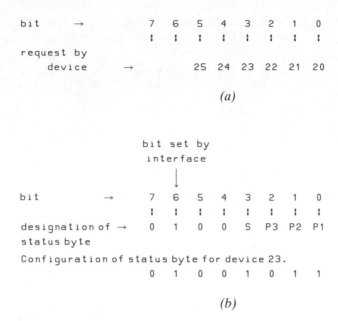

(a)

(b)

Figure 13.16.   Desired configurations of status bit and enable byte. (*a*) Status bit. (*b*) Enable byte.

We need to use the *PARALLEL POLL ENABLE* command **PE** of the GPIB interface to set up the status byte configuration. The enable list is made up of an alphanumeric string of which each element sets a different bit and corresponds to a different device. There are two elements of the string corresponding to each status bit, the device listen address and an enable byte that gives the bit information. Each enable byte takes on the form given in Figure 13.16*b*.

The three lowest bits—P1, P2, P3—of this number can describe any number in the range 0 to 7. This is the bit number of the status bit corresponding to the addressed device to be configured. The S line specifies the TTL logic sense of the request for assistance. A 1 here tells the interface to expect a logic 1 on the line when it needs assistance.

A careful study of the bit pattern in Figure 13.16*b* will show that the enable byte may always be given by the expression

```
decimal value of status byte = 64 + NS%*8 + NB%
```

where NS% = 0 for S = 0 and NS% = 1 for S = 1, and NB% is the bit to be designated to the particular device addressed as a listener. In the case of a device with primary address 23, for example, NB% = 3 from Figure 13.16, and, assuming S = 1, we have a decimal value of 75 for the status bit, which corresponds to the character K in the ASCII code. Since the listen address corresponding to the primary address 23 is 7, we would send the combination 7K to set the status bit of this device.

The devices with addresses in the range 20 to 25 and bit patterns set as in Figure 13.16*a* would be configured with the program elements

```
10 PRINT D$;"PR#3"
20 print "PE";"4HFI6J7K8L9M"
    .
    .
    .
```

or

```
10 PRINT D$;"PR#3"
20 print "PE"
20 FOR I = 0 TO 5
30 PRINT CHR$(64 + 20 + I)CHR$(64 + 8 + I);
40 NEXT I
```

The interpretation of this program should clearly follow from the previous contents of this chapter.

13.5.2. The CCS-7490{Apple} GPIB Card

The California Computers System (CCS) model 7490 GPIB interface card is a much more primitive interfacing device with respect to the degree of user programming required for its operation. With this card you are essentially working at all times at the bus command level and must be well versed in the idiosyncracies of the IEEE-488 standard. Using the CCS card instead of the Apple GPIB card is essentially a trade-off between cost and programming convenience. The documentation on the CCS-7490 is not that complete, but if one is knowledgeable about the GPIB standard, this will not restrict its use.

The following potential limitations should be kept in mind when using this card:

1. It is difficult to adapt the interface to the needs of different devices on the interface, such as sending nonstandard EOS characters.
2. With the method of data transfer recommended in the CCS-7490 manual, one cannot read commas and colons in the data input strings from the external devices when using the Applesoft INPUT command.
3. Parallel polling of the bus is not possible using this interface.
4. There are no high-level commands that parallel the procedural macro commands described at the beginning of this chapter.
5. One must be aware of the timing constraints of the GPIB when using this interface. For example, using the interface *CLEAR* command as

the bus command does not automatically hold the interface lines in the clear state for the time period recommended for the GPIB bus (100 ms). *The delay must be provided by the user.*

These points aside, the interface can be used to communicate with a host of GPIB-compatible equipment.

The CCS-7490 is placed in one of the Apple expansion ports in the standard manner. The DOS command PR#n in combination with the Applesoft PRINT and INPUT commands is used for data and command transfers to and from the interface. It is also possible to use the GET command to pick data off the bus character by character.

The instruction set of the CCS-7490 interface may be divided into two classes:

1. Standard GPIB bus commands corresponding to the GPIB talk and listen commands (see Table 13.7).
2. A special CCS-7490 control command set used specifically to set the control lines to particular states.

The complete command set for the CCS-7490 is shown in Table 13.11. Remember that the GPIB bus commands described in Section 13.3 are sent along the GPIB bus in ASCII code with the ATN line high. As we later show, these commands may be imbedded in our PRINT statements and, apart from the handshaking protocol provided by the interface, are passed through the interface as if the CCS-7490 were essentially transparent. The special control commands shown at the beginning of this table operate mostly on the control lines, and the second group of bus commands set both the data and control lines.

All the interface commands with this card must be represented by a single ASCII character, because the interface does not have a higher-level command language. We have already encountered this as far as the talk and listen addresses are concerned on the Apple card, but we must extend this to all commands on the bus.

The syntax of a typical series of commands and data capable of being formed into one of the procedures discussed earlier in this chapter has the form.

```
PRINT "<control command ><@> <GPIB bus commands><:><'><data><'>"
```

The three characters {@, ', : } are also control commands. The others are shown in Table 13.11.

The following convention is recognized by the CCS-7490:

1. Characters representing control commands, GPIB bus commands, or data are all sent by the PRINT statement and imbedded as a string between quotes. Alternatively, a character may be sent by using the CHR$(..) function without quotes.

Table 13.11. CCS-7490 Apple GPIB Interface Command Set

COMMAND	DESCRIPTION	DECIMAL	MNEMONIC
Control Commands			
%	Set the IFC line to clear interface must be true for 100 m	37	
&	Turn off IFC line	38	
#	Clear REN. Used to go to local	35	
'	Delimits data when address mode enabled	39	
@	Enables address mode; sets ATN and REN line true	64	
:	Disables address mode. Clears ATN	58	
Standard GPIB Commands (must have address mode enabled)			
	Primary Command Group		
^@	Parallel poll configure	0	**PPC**
^A	Go to local	1	**GTL**
^D	Selected device clear	4	**SDC**
^H	Group execute trigger	8	**GET**
^Q	Local lockout	17	**LLO**
^T	Device clear	20	**DCL**
^U	Parallel poll unconfigure	21	**PPU**
^X	Serial poll enable	24	**SPE**
^Y	Serial poll disable	25	**SPD**
	Listen Address Group		
space	Listen address 0 through 30	32−62	
to >	Unlisten	63	
	Talk Address Group		
@ to ^	Talk address 0 through 30	64−94	
	Untalk	95	

2. The control commands { @ } and { : } enclose all GPIB bus commands. The character @ is recognized by the interface as an instruction to set the ATN line. At the end of the bus command string, the : character turns off the ATN line. Note that characters outside the quotes would not be sent to the interface; a { : } at the end of a line, for example, is interpreted by Applesoft as an end of line.

Data for the bus must be imbedded between single quotes { ' } in addition to being within the double quotes. For example, let's say that we want to send the simple message SET FR R to a device with primary address 20. Here's that simple example again in a simple procedural form:

```
OUTPUT to device 20 the message "SET FR R"
```

From Table 13.4 we remember that device 20 has a listen address of 4 (decimal 52), so the command takes the form

```
10 PRINT CHR$(4);"PR#3"
20 PRINT "@?4:'SET FR R'"
```

There are a multitude of ways of writing this simple program, all of which look different but which end up producing the same bit sequence on the GPIB bus. Here are a couple of other ways to write line 20:

```
20 PRINT "@?";CHR$(52);":'SET FR R'"
```

or

```
20 PRINT "@?4:";
30 PRINT "'SET FR R'"
```

The semicolon at the end of line 20 in the last example suppresses the <CR> and allows the data string to be continued.

The standard, GPIB, bus-level commands used on the CCS-7490 and given in Table 13.11 are represented under IEEE-488 by control characters. For example, device clear (**DCL**) is represented by CTRL-T (usually written ˆT). If we wanted to send the message

```
CLEAR devices 20,22,23
```

By the CCS card, the Applesoft program would be

```
20 PRINT "@?467:"
```

where we typed CTRL-T in typing in the program line between 7 and :. The CTRL-T or any other control characters do not show up in an Applesoft listing. The alternative would be to write

```
20 PRINT "@?467";CHR$(20);":"
```

Although this provides better documentation than the earlier example, it is still a difficult syntax to debug.

13.6.   GPIB INTERFACING ON THE IBM-PC AND IBM-XT

We have chosen to restrict our discussion of GPIB interfacing on the IBM to National Instruments' GPIB-PC interface card. This is available for both the IBM-PC and the IBM-XT. It is an extremely powerful implementation of the GPIB interface for a microcomputer and has many of the features found only with interfaces for much larger systems.

In particular, it supports the following features:

> DMA (direct memory access) or non-DMA operation
> Programmed wait mode for any of 12 selected events
> Adjustable wait times to prevent hangups
> PC-DOS error reporting

The DMA feature, in particular, is a very powerful capability not found on most IBM-PC interfaces. It allows the transfer of data between systems at the rate of 300 K per second. This capability may be used to set up a powerful network between the IBM-PC and larger systems, such as the DEC UNIBUS or Q-bus systems.

Two aspects of the GPIB-PC interface give it flexibility: the *hardware configuration* and the *software drivers* that have been developed to communicate with the interface from the IBM-PC.

13.6.1. Hardware Overview of the System

The National Instruments GPIB interface card fits into any one of the expansion slots of the IBM-PC (or IBM-XT). It may be addressed as a series of I/O ports on the PC bus by using 10 of the bus address lines. Information on the register designation of the eight configured I/O port addresses contained on the interface is shown in Table 13.12. The addresses of these registers may be reconfigured with jumpers on the interface card.

A block diagram of the GPIB-PC card showing the functional relationships between the important sections is shown in Figure 13.17. The card is seen to have a block that controls the DMA capability of the interface. There is also an interrupt capability on the card indicated by the interrupt arbitration block. In theory this will allow foreground/background operation, which permits the IBM to be used simultaneously for data acquisition and manipulation. At

Table 13.12. Addresses on the GPIB-PC

Register Address	Read Register Content	Write Register Content
$2B8	Data in	Command/data out
$2B9	Interrupt status 1	Interrupt mask 1
$2BA	Interrupt status 2	Interrupt mask 2
$2BB	Serial poll status	Serial poll mode
$2BC	Address status	Address mode
$2BD	Command pass through	Auxiliary mode
$2BE	Address 0	Address 0/1
$2BF	Address 1	End of string

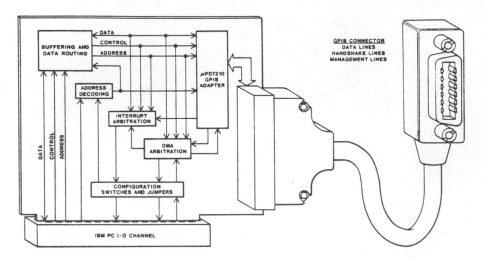

Figure 13.17.   Block diagram of the GPIB-PC. Reproduced by permission of National Instruments.

present, however, the software to drive the interface is not fully capable of using this interrupt feature. Custom software would have to be written by the user to utilize this capability, using the registers 2B9 and 2BA listed above.

13.6.2.   GPIB functions on the GPIB-PC

The GPIB-PC interface allows the IMB-PC to be operated as either a controller, talker, or listener. The complete functional specifications of this particular GPIB interface are

SH1,AH1,T5,TE5,L3,LE3,SR1,RL1,PP1,PP2,DC1,DT1,C1-5,E1/2

A brief discussion of the meanings of these mnemonics has already been made at the beginning of this chapter. Briefly the GPIB-PC has complete source and handshaking capabilities. It can operate as a basic or extended talker and can respond to a serial poll. It may be placed in a talk−only mode, and it will be unaddressed to talk when it receives its listen address. The interface can operate as a basic or extended listener. It may be placed in a listen-only mode, and it will be unaddressed to listen when it receives its talk address. More information may be found in the GPIB-PC user manual* or the IEEE 488-1978 standard.†

The GPIB-PC has full capabilities to request service from another control-

---

The GPIB-PC Interface Handbook (National Instruments, 12109 Technology Boulevard, Austin, TX 78759).
†IEEE 488-1978 Standard, loc. cit.

ler. The interface may, under some circumstances, be placed in a local mode. Full parallel poll capability is included in the interface. The implementation of this is software dependent.

All controller functions specified under the IEEE-488 standard (C1 to C5) are included in the GPIB-PC. These include the following capabilities:

1. Can be programmed by the active system controller for the purpose of initializing the GPIB interfaces of other devices and placing these devices in remote or local program modes.
2. Can send multiline interface messages or commands to other devices.
3. Can detect other devices as requesting service and conduct serial or parallel polls.
4. Can pass control to other controllers and receive control from them.
5. Can be set to standby to allow an addressed talker to send data to the addressed listeners and to take control again after the transfer has been completed.

In particular, the last two points are of vital importance when one is attempting to configure a flexible measurement system. Passing control successfully between a number of controllers on a bus is central to networking using the GPIB bus.

13.6.3. The GPIB-PS Software Handler

The software to control the GPIB-PC is installed by the user as part of IBM's OS. The software is designated the handler and becomes one of the systems resources on the IBM-PC.

The system user may communicate with the GPIB-PC interface in one of two ways.

1. Through subroutine calls to subroutine procedures provided as part of the user library software.
2. Through an interactive control program that may be loaded into the IBM-PC and used as a troubleshooting diagnostic tool.

The subroutines provided as part of the user library software are available for a number of popular languages in use on the IBM. It is possible to use DOS interface object code files for BASICA, FORTRAN, C, PASCAL, and 8088 assembly language. The DOS interface object codes are contained in a series of files listed below.

BIB.M	interface to BASIC
CIB.OBJ	interface to C
FIB.OBJ	interface to FORTRAN
PIB.OBJ	interface to PASCAL
MIB.OBJ	Interface to 8088 assembly language

The mechanism for linking these files to the program is different for BASICA, being an interpreted language, than for the other languages. For the complied languages the linking process is straightforward, as we demonstrate in Figure 13.18. In the standard manner for a compiled language the source code is compiled (or in the case of assembly language, assembled), and then all the compiled object files, including the interface object file for the GPIB, are linked with the system linker. The resulting file FINAL.EXE can be executed directly.

13.6.4.   Using the GPIB-PC from BASICA

In this subsection we discuss the method for controlling the interface from within a BASICA Program. First, a method of linking the interface software to the control programs written by the user is illustrated. The program segment in Figure 13.18, which accomplishes the linking, must be included at the beginning of every program that interfaces with the GPIB-PC.

```
 5 REM ----------- organize memory for GPIB interface.
10 MLOC=              ' highest address location entered here
11 CLEAR ,MLOC        ' sets highest location of mbasic prog.
12 IBINIT = MLOC      ' program goes below this address
13 BLOAD "BIB.M", IBINIT  ' load in GPIB-PC interface
                                        above location IBINIT
14 REM initialize operation codes
15 IBSTA% = 0    ' status word giving status if GPIB-PC
16 IBERR% = 0    ' returns error code if error occurs.
17 IBCNT% = 0    ' count of bytes transferred in operations
18 CALL IBINIT(IBRD%,IBWRT%,IBCMD%,IBWAIT%,IBRPP%,IBONL%,
          IBRSC%,IBSIC%,IBSRE%,IBRTL%,IBRSV%,IBLPE%,IBPAD%,
          IBSAD%,IBIST%,IBDMA%,IBEDOS%,IBTMO%,IBEOT%,IBGTS%
                         IBCAC%,IBDIAG%,IBSTA%,IBERR%,IBCNTS%)
19 ' Arguments in IBINIT(.. ) are GPIB function names
          called from BASIC program to communicate with IBM-PC
```

Figure 13.18.   The BASICA initialization program for a GPIB card. Language: BASICA.

This program segment summarizes many of the elements of the GPIB-PC interface software. Lines 11 to 13 allocate the IBM-PC memory. The binary file BIB.M is loaded in below DOS, and the highest memory location for the BASICA Program, contained in the variable IBINIT, is set to protect the binary program from being overwritten. The binary program contains the various CALL subroutines needed to drive the GPIB interface. Lines 15 to 17 initialize the three most important condition variables used by the interface. As an example, we list the interpretation of the status word variable in Table 13.13. Each bit of the 16-bit word has a different meaning. The word can be read at any time during program execution and yields the exact status of the system.

Table 13.13. Status Word IBSTAT% Interpretation

Mnemonic	Bit Position	Description
ERR	15	GPIB or DOS error
TIMO	14	Timeout exceeded
END	13	GPIB detected END or EOS
SRQI	12	Service requested (SRQ) detected
CMPL	8	I/O completed
LOK	7	GPIC-PC is in local lockout state
REM	6	GPIB-PC is in remote state
CIC	5	GPIB-PC is controller in charge
ATN	4	Attention is asserted
TACS	3	GPIB-PC is talker
LACS	2	GPIB-PC is listener
DTAS	1	GPIB-PC is in device trigger state
DCAS	0	GPIB-PC is in device clear state

Finally, line 18 is used to CALL the function IBINIT, which initializes the interface. Most of the arguments in this function are themselves high-level function commands used to communicate with the interface. These high-level function commands were developed by National Instruments to allow easy user programming of the interface and are equivalent to our command procedures discussed at the beginning of this chapter. They are not covered by the GPIB standard, but each is a combination of bus-level commands and communication software necessary to complete the relevant task.

The complete list of the National Instruments, intermediate, high-level, GPIB-PC, calling functions usable under BASICA program control is shown in Table 13.14. We call these commands "intermediate high-level commands" because although they take care of much of the interface control traffic, thus releasing the user from appreciable programming, each command only carries out a single task. There are higher-level functions available for the GPIB-PC that carry out more complex operations, such as taking data off the bus directly into a buffer. These are described in our discussion of C GPIB-PC interface programming in the next subsection. The relationship of these functions to each other and to the software handler is shown in Table 13.14. Each function is shown with its necessary argument list. Also included in this table are the GPIB calling functions for three other widely used computer languages. The same format has been kept for the calling functions in all these languages, which eases software mobility between languages.

The single argument BD% identifies the GPIB interface being used. The other argument that occurs with frequency is V%, which is a function-dependent variable, the meaning of which is presented in the table.

The command function IBCMD% is the most widely used of the GPIB command functions. It is used to send GPIB bus-level commands directly down

Table 13.14. GPIB-PC Intermediate High-Level Function Syntax

Description	BASIC C/FORTRAN/PASCAL	Argument Description
Become active controller	IBCAC%(BD%,V%) ibcac(bd,v)	V%=0 synchronous control =1 immediate control
SEND commands	IBCMD%(BD%,CMD$) ibcmd(bd,cmd,cnt)	CM$ −bus commands(s)
Enable/disable DMA	IBDMA%(BD%,V%) ibdma(bd,v)	V%=0 disable DMA =1 enable DMA
Change/disable EOS message	IBEOS%(BD%,V%) ibeos(bd,v)	V% −selected EOS character
Enable/disable END message	IBEOT%(BD%,V%) ibeot(bd,v)	V%=0 disable END message 1 enable END message
Active controller to standby	IBGTS%(BD%,V%) ibgts(bd,v)	V%=1 listen in continuous mode
Set/clear individual status bit	IBIST%(BD%,V%) ibist(bd,v)	V%=0 clear bit 1 set bit
LOCAL PARRALLEL *CONFIGURE*	IBLEPE%(BD%,V%) iblpe(bd,v)	V% −configuration parameter
Place GPIB on-line or off-line.	IBONL%(BD%,V%) ibonl(bd,v)	V%=0 disable =1 enable/reset GPIB-PC
Change primary address	IBPAD%(BD%,V%) ibpad(bd,v)	V% −new primary address of GPIB-PC
ENTER (Read) data	IBRD%(BD%,RD$) ibrd(bd,rd,cnt)	RD$ −Identifies storage buffer with data
Conduct a *PARALLEL POLL*	IBRPP%(DB%,PPR%) ibrpp(bd,ppr) ibrpp(bd,&ppr)	PPR% −variable containing PP response byte PASCAL only
Request/release system controller	IBRSCH%(BD%,V%) ibrsc(bd,v)	V%=1 allow functions requiring control capability
Request service	IBRSV%(BD%,V%) ibrsv(bd,v)	V% −specifies response or status byte
Go from *REMOTE* to local	IBRTL%(BD%) ibrtl(bd)	
Change secondary address	IBSAD%(BD%,V%) ibsad(bd,v)	V% −secondary address
Send interface *CLEAR*	IBSIC%(BD%) ibsic (bd)	
Set/clear remote enable line	IBSRE%(BD%,V%) ibsre(bd,v)	V%=0 REN line unasserted =1 REN line asserted
Change/disable timeout limit	IBTMO%(BD%,V%) ibtmo(bd,v)	V% −timeout limit in seconds
Wait for selected event	IBWAIT%(BD%,MASK%) ibwait(bd,mask)	MASK% −bit mask for status word
OUTPUT (Write) data	IBWRT%(BD%,WRT$) ibwrt(bd,wrt,cnt)	WRT$ −variable containing data sent over GPIB

the bus. For example, if we wished to command two devices with primary addresses 6 and 8 to listen and device 3 to talk by using the listen and talk addresses in Table 13.4, we would write the simple program

```
30 CM$ = "?&(C" 'UNL LAD[6] LAD[8] TAD[3]
40 CALL IBCMD%(BD%,CM$)
```

where we have sent the universal unlisten command ? first follow by the listen and talk addresses. The single quote is an alternative method used in BASICA for placing a comment at the end of a program line.

13.6.5.   Using the GPIB-PC from C

The intermediate high-level driver functions described for BASICA in the last section are also available for C as well as for some other high-level languages. These C functions are listed in Table 13.14. There are also a series of higher-level functions available in C that parallel the procedures defined at the beginning of this chapter. Some of these high-level C functions are listed in Table 13.15. They are listed with their procedure equivalents that allow a comparison to be made with the GPIB high-level commands for other languages and interfaces.

In particular, the final two functions on this list require a buffer array buf[] of dimension cnt to be initialized prior to the function call. These high-level command functions have been developed so that all parameters and addresses that need to be invoked are hidden in the function software, allowing far clearer computer code to be written. In this way also the high-level aspects of C allow code to be self-documenting. Using the C define command, for example, one can use device names and not numbers in a very similar manner to the HP implementation of device communications. The simple program in Figure 3.19 is used to send a large body of data along the GPIB bus to an interfaced computer known as LSI__11, which has primary device address 20.

Table 13.15.   High-Level GPIB-PC C Functions

Description	C Function
CLEAR listed devices	**clear**(dev, . . .)
TRIGGER listed devices	**trig**(dev, ...)
REMOTE enable listed devices	**remote**(dev, . . .)
LOCAL enable listed devices	**local**(dev, . . .)
SERIAL POLL of device	**spoll**(dev)
OUTPUT data from	char buf[cnt];
buffer onto GPIB interface	**send**(dev,buf,cnt,seoi)
ENTER (receive) data from GPIB	char buf[cnt];
interface into buffer	**rev**(dev,but,cnt,eos)

```
#define LSI_11 20
#define N      10000

main(){
   char buf[N],seoi;
   int cnt,dev;
   data_in(cnt=N,buf);                      \*  read in data from file *\
   send(dev=LSI_11,buf,cnt = N,seoi); \*  send data out on GPIB  *\
}
```

Figure 13.19.   A simple C main program for GPIB interface.
Language: C.

The send( ) function is device dependent, but, in general, it may hide all the software necessary to carry out DMA data transfer at high speed (300 K) along the interface.

Appendix A
Operating Systems

From the standpoint of computers in scientific and engineering applications the choice of an OS must be made from a number of considerations.

Software mobility, such as library programs, from one computer system to another, which is determined by language and, ultimately, by the OS.

System flexibility, such as the redirection of data among the peripherals of a computer system, which is possible with the UNIX OS.

The need for *multitasking*, such as in the parallel acquisition of data and data evaluation of another data set.

OS mobility from one computer to another is an important question that is the focus of much creative energy in the computer industry. The original OS's were written in assembly language, and since much of the OS consists of I/O procedures that are usually systems dependent, there has traditionally been little mobility of OS's from one system to another. Recently there has been a change in philosophy in this regard. Some of the newer OS's are being written in a high-level language that makes them quite easily moved from one system to the other. Some new code must be written for the system-dependent features, but this is a much easier task because a high-level language is being used rather than the processor-dependent assembly language. Examples of these new breeds of OS's are the UNIX system, programmed in C and the p-system, written in PASCAL.

Some of the more popular OS's that may be run in one form or another on laboratory microcomputers are listed in Table A.1. This is by no means an exhaustive list, but it does give an overview of what is available.

MS-DOS,* developed by Microsoft, appears under different names, according to the brand of computer. Its copy on the IBM PC is called PC-DOS, and all IBM look-alikes use some version of MS-DOS. It has become accepted as the standard for the 8088 and related processors. The OS supports both hard and floppy disks and the addition of new device drivers.

The Apple DOS 3.3† was originally designed as an OS for small floppy disks, it does not easily support 8-in floppies or the popular Winchester hard-disk

---

*MS-DOS is a trademark of Microsoft Corporation, 10700 Northrup Way, Bellevue, WA 98004.

†DOS 3.3 and Prodos are trademarks of Apple Computer, Inc., Cupertino, CA 95014.

Table A.1. Some Popular Operating Systems on Microcomputers

Operating System	Typical Processors	Bits	Typical Memory	Computers
PC-DOS	8088	16	640K	IBM-PC, IBM-XT
MS-DOS	8088	16	640K	PC-compatible systems
DOS 3.3	6502	8	64K(128K)	Apple II+, (IIe)
PRODOS	6502	8	128K	
CP/M 2.2	Z80	8	64K	All Z80
CP/M 3.0	Z80	8	128K	All Z80
CP/M-86	8086	16	256K	IBM-PC compatible
Concurr. CP/M	8086	16	256K	IBM-PC compatible
TRSDOS 6.0	Z80	8	128K	TRS-80 Model 4
UCSD	Z80	8	64K	CP/M compatible
p-system	6502	8	128K	Apple II systems
	8088	16	640K	IBM-PC compatible
	68000	32	bus dependent	
	LSI-11, PDP-11	32	"	
UNIX and its derivatives[a]				
UNIX v5	80286, 68000	32	bus dependent	
	16032, Z8000	32	"	
XENIX[b]	8086, 68000	32	"	Apple Lisa, TRS-80m16
VENIX[c]	8086, LSI-11/2	32,16	"	DEC LSI11/2, IBM-PC
IDRIS[d]	8086	16	256K	IBM-PC compatible
COHERENT[e]	8086	16	256K	IBM-PC compatible
MICROSHELL	Z80	8	64K	CP/M compatible

[a]UNIX is a trademark of Bell Laboratories; For further information on UNIX, see *Byte*, **8**, No. 10 (1983).

[b]XENIX is a trademark of Microsoft Corporation, 10700 Northrup Way, Bellevue, WA 98004.

[c]VENIX is a trademark of Venturcom, 139 Main Street, Cambridge, MA 02142.

[d]IDRIS is a trademark of Whitesmiths, Ltd, 97 Lowell Road, Concord, MA 01742.

[e]COHERENT is a trademark of Mark Williams Company, 1430 West Wrightwood, Chicago, IL 60614.

drives. It also does not support large files or interrupts. The new PRODOS for Apple II and IIe developed more recently by Apple is meant to overcome these limitations, but it is not clear at this time whether the laboratory interface vendors will adapt their software to this new OS.

We have included just one of the many Radio Shack computer OS's in this table: the TRSDOS 6.0. The Radio Shack OS's share with Apple the distinction of being dedicated to a particular brand of computers.† However, in contrast to Apple, Radio Shack has treated its code as proprietary and has not made it easily available to users and software houses. Thus, there is not nearly

†TRSDOS is a trademark of Radio Shack, One Tandy Center, Fort Worth, TX 76102.

the software available for this computer as for the Apple.

The CP/M OS* was developed by Digital Research System for the Z80 and related processors. It has become a widely accepted industry standard for 8-bit systems and has been used on a number of computer buses. In its most popular version, CP/M 2.2, it can only address 64K of memory, but an enhanced version—CP/M 3.0—allows access to more memory. A version called CP/M-86 has been developed for 16-bit computers to compete with MS-DOS.

The UCSD p-system[†], developed originally by the University of California, San Diego, has the distinction of not being the primary OS on any computer. This is a reflection of its extreme portability between different systems, which makes it rather slow in comparison to the more widely used DOS systems. It is, however, widely used as an alternative OS by many users who require programs to be mobile between some 8-bit and 16-bit systems.

The final OS in our list, UNIX was not developed for microcomputers but for minicomputers, such as Digital's VAX systems. It has, however, been implemented on smaller systems and has produced a number of interesting UNIX look-alikes, some of which are included in our table. The central core of UNIX is the shell command interpreter that acts as an interface between the user and the OS. The shell may be accessed by the user from a terminal or via a group of commands contained in a file. The file within the UNIX structure may be named and accessed in a way that is indistinguishable from the system commands. This allows the command language structure to be easily extended.

The file system environment is an extremely important feature of the UNIX system. The simplest possible file system is used where a file, whether a text file or a binary executable file, is stored as a series of ASCII characters. Thus the operations on the file and not the file structure become the important aspect of file implementation. Directories and subdirectories are included within the file structure and may be written to but not written as ordinary files. In the same way, I/O devices are designated as special files that may be used by the I/O redirection structure of UNIX to move data easily in and out of peripheral devices.

As an illustration of the I/O redirection structure, we consider the following simple example. The command line

ls -l > filedump

creates a file directory with the **ls** command, adds the time and date stamp with the **-l** extension, and redirects the output from the default screen to the file named **filedump**. A sequence of programs may be chained with such a tech-

---

*CP/M is a trademark of Digital Research, P.O. Box 579, Pacific Grove, CA 93950.

†UCSD p-system is a trademark of the Regents of the University of California; distributed by Softech Microsystems, Inc., 16885 West Bernardo Drive, San Diego, CA 92127.

nique where the output of one program may be stored in a file which is chained as the input to the next command.

A simpler technique using the pipe operator: allows the output of one command to be automatically passed to the input of the next command. As an example, if we have created three UNIX commands **voigt, noise, nonlinear**— where **voigt** creates a data set, **noise** superimposes statistical noise on the data, and **nonlinear** fits a non-linear function to the noisy data (see Chapter 10)— under UNIX we might write the operation using the pipe operator as

voigt : noise : nonlinear > finalfile

where the commands are executed from left to right and the final data produced by nonlinear is placed in the file finalfile.

The flexibility and portability of UNIX stems in part from the intimate connection between UNIX and the C language. C has an extremely compact core which needs to be rewritten for each new computer system. Once this is done the rest of C described by the function libraries and the creation of the UNIX operating system itself can be fairly straightforward. Finally a further feature of UNIX that enhances its universality involves the standardization of a set of software tools for text editing (using **ed** or **vi**), communications (using **mail** and **write**), and C program debugging (using **lint**). These software tools are again written in C which makes them easily portable.

An alternative answer to software mobility has recently gained wide acceptance. This is the concept of coprocessing, in which a computer system may be configured to run with a number of alternative processors and OS's. The Apple IIe computer, for example, may now be configured with one of several alternative processors and corresponding OS's. There are a number of Z80 cards available that allow CP/M software to be run, and recently a 68000-based UNIX system has been developed. One of the facets of the Apple computer that make coprocessing simple to implement is the availability of expansion slots on the Apple bus. In general, computers that are bus oriented are more easily adapted for coprocessing, but with a little effort most microcomputers may be configured to accept coprocessors.

There are several MS-DOS and CP/M dual systems available at this time that use both 8088 and Z80 processors. With the availability of software from Microsoft to run Apple IIe programs on an 8088 processor, it is now possible to have an extremely flexible computer system for a reasonable investment.

As far as scientific and engineering applications are concerned, the choice of OS and processor may be determined by reasons other than speed or memory size, even though these play an extremely important role. The classic example of this is the availability of the laboratory language extensions that make the Apple, even with its slow BASIC and limited DOS 3.3, a remarkably powerful laboratory tool for data acquisition. The IBM-based laboratory systems do have the advantage here, since they can run with the 8087 coprocessor, which imparts a very powerful number-crunching ability to the system.

Appendix B
Computer
Languages

A multitude of computer languages are available for the more popular micro-computers used in scientific and engineering applications. The relative merits and disadvantages of each language are not only a function of the language itself but also of the task that one wishes to program in that language. There are, in general, a number of versions of the same language available for each computer system, each varying in its interpretation of the language standards if such a standard is available. For example, there are at least four versions of the C language for the CP/M OS, and six for MS-DOS.*

A list of some of the more popular computer languages that are used in laboratory applications is given. We have attempted not to distinguish between various interpretations of the language, but rather to place them in the context of their relative strengths and weaknesses. If more than one version of a language is in common use (i.e., what we consider to be major revisions of the language, not simple different interpretations of the standard, as is the case with FORTRAN IV and FORTRAN 77), we have included them as separate items.

Computer Languages on Microcomputers

MBASIC (Microsoft).   A general-purpose, simple-to-use BASIC.[†] This is the most popular version of the BASIC language on the market today. A brief description of its salient features is given in Chapter 2. It runs under CP/M and MS-DOS and requires 32K of memory. It is usually considered an interpreted language but compilers are available.

Applesoft.   A general-purpose BASIC used only on Apple Computers.[‡] The language was developed by Microsoft and has many features in common with Microsoft BASIC, but it is much simpler, taking only 8K of memory. It runs under DOS 3.3 and is an interpreted language with available compilers. The language was written in a form that allows it to be easily extended.

CBASIC.   A fast, simple, structured BASIC language developed by Digital Research and available for CP/M and MS-DOS. CBASIC[‡] is an interpreted language; a compiled version, CB-80, is available.

---

*MS-DOS is a trademark of Microsoft Corporation.

[†]Microsoft or MBASIC is a trademark of Microsoft, Corporation.

[‡]APPLESOFT is a trademark of Apple Computer.

[‡]CBASIC is a trademark of Digital Research.

C.   A wide ranging structured language being used for tasks such as writing OS's that are normally written in Assembly language. The basic structure of the language is fairly small, with the body made up of a library of routines on each computer system. A large number of C compilers are available for most of the popular microcomputers.*

FORTH.   A language well suited for I/O interfacing requirements and used extensively in robotics.† The user builds up his/her own language syntax as the program develops. A description of FORTH is given in Chapter 4.

FORTRAN IV.   The most popular and universally used computer language until a few years ago, especially for scientific purposes or applications where much number crunching is required. A large body of library and public domain software is available in this language. Compilers of varying degrees of conformity with the standard are available for FORTRAN IV on most of the popular microcomputers, such as the IBM-PC and Apple II. The variable passing syntax for compiled modules is identical to that required by Microsoft BASIC, which makes it ideal for interfacing fast program elements to an interpreted main program body.

FORTRAN 77.   A major revision of FORTRAN IV with many structured programming commands. It especially improves on many of the character handling aspects of the language that made FORTRAN IV difficult to use.‡

PASCAL.   An extremely popular language used especially in colleges for teaching purposes because of its classic structured aspects. Compilers are available for most computers, including all microcomputers referred to in this book. It is a language that has suffered many revisions with unfortunate consequences for software mobility between various compilers and computer systems.**

Modula-2.   A new structured language developed by Niclaus Wirth who originally developed Pascal. Modula-2 includes and extends the philosophy of structured languages that was first implemented in Pascal.***

---

*B. W. Kernighan and D. M. Ritchie, *The C Programming Language*, Prentice-Hall, N. J. (1978).
   J. J. Purdum, T. C. Leslie, and A. L. Stegemoller, *C Programmer's Library*, Que Corporation, Indianapolis (1984).
   M. I. Bolsky, *The C Programmer's Handbook*, A. T. & T. Bell Laboratories/Prentice-Hall, (1985).

†W. P. Salman, O. Tissorand, and B. Tolout, *Forth*, Springer-Verlag, N. Y. (1984).

‡N. K. Lehmkuhl, *Fortran 77, A Top Down Approach*, Macmilian, N. Y. (1983).

**G. M. Schnider, S. W. Weingart, and D. M. Perlman, *Programming and Problem Solving with Pascal, An Introduction*, Wiley, N. Y. (1982).
   K. Jensen and N. Wirth, *Pascal, User's Manual and Report*, Springer-Verlag, N. Y. (1984).

***N. Wirth, *Modula-2*, Springer-Verlag, N. Y. (1983).

APL.   A symbolic mathematical language with extremely concise syntax. It is well suited for tasks such as matrix or array manipulation and recursive operations encountered in differential equation solution algorithms.

ADA.   A new language developed by the US Department of Defence to replace all languages that they are currently using.‡

Our earlier observation that the efficiency of a programming language depends to a considerable extent on the application in which it is being used has an important corollary. In the future it is quite likely that users will become familiar with a number of computer languages, each of which will bring a degree of flexibility to the work environment not provided by the other languages. This is especially true in laboratory computing. Some languages will have to be used because they will have been adapted for communications with laboratory equipment. Such is the case for FORTH, C, Applesoft BASIC or Microsoft BASIC with suitable laboratory language extensions. The user will have more choices when the language is to be used for calculations.

We have come to the conclusion that in the laboratory environment it is vitally necessary to become familiar with one interpreted language and one compiled language. The interpreted languages are especially useful for data acquisition purposes. A programming sequence can be tested line by line in real-time—an almost impossible task with a compiled language.

On the other hand, any attempts to perform a great deal of number crunching for data reduction exposes one of the major defects of interpreted languages: their extreme slowness. For data reduction it is imperative to have available compiled routines for fast manipulation of data. Interestingly, some of the interpreted languages, an example being Microsoft BASIC, have the capability of calling compiled subroutines written in, say, FORTRAN. Alternatively a language such as FORTH may be run as an interpreted or a compiled language.

---

‡S. H. Saib and R. E. Fritz, *The ADA Programming Language*, Computer Society of the Institute of Electrical and Electronic Engineers, P.O. Box 80542, Worldway Postal Center, Los Angeles, CA 90080.

Appendix C

The BASICA Numerical Analysis Program Library

This appendix contains the complete set of BASICA/MBASIC library modules that make up the numerical analysis library. The library was developed in the BASICA* version of BASIC running on the IBM-PC. We have used a subset of BASICA that corresponds to the Microsoft MBASIC† version of BASIC running on all CP/M computers. With a CP/M card the program may also be run on Apple computers.

The programs may be run in double precision arithmetic. The main program should include the following header.

```
10 DEFDBL A-H,O-Z
20 DEFINT I-M
```

The trigonometric functions in BASICA/MBASIC are returned in single precision.

Note that we have specified that externally referenced functions which need to be written by the user need to be entered as subroutines and not as BASIC functions. This was done to accommodate more complex functions than could otherwise be defined as a single BASIC function. We have indented the program listings to conform to structured programming practice. In some instances we have used multiple lines for the program statements connected with a single numbered line for ease in reading the program. These statements should be entered on a single line when typing the program. A description on how to use these programs is given in Chapter 9.

---

*BASICA is a trademark of IBM Computers, Inc.
†MBASIC is a trademark of Microsoft, Inc.

C.1.   THE ERROR FUNCTION

```
11000 REM******************** ERROR FUNCTION *************************
11002 REM external in : X
11004 REM external out: ERF
11006    ON ERROR GOTO 11034              :REM  error pointer
11008    DIM A.A(5)                       :REM  dimension local variables
11010    RESTORE 11040                    :REM  pointer to data statements
11012    FOR K.A=0 TO 5:READ A.A(K.A):NEXT K.A :REM  read in data
11014    READ P.A                         :REM  read in parameter
11016    T.A=1#/(1#+P.A*X)                :REM  the calculation proper
11018    TMP.A=A.A(5)
11020    FOR K.A=4 TO 0 STEP -1
11022        TMP.A=T.A*TMP.A+A.A(K.A)
11024    NEXT K.A
11026    ERF=1#-TMP.A*EXP(-X*X)
11028    ON ERROR GOTO 0                  :REM  restore error pointer
11030 RETURN
11032 REM----------------------------- error trap
11034    IF(ERR=10) AND (ERL=11008) THEN RESUME 11016
11036    PRINT "ERROR #"ERR" IN ERROR FUNCTION MODULE AT LINE "ERL
11038 REM-------------------------data
11040 DATA 0,0.254829592,-0.284496736,1.421413741,-1.453152027,1.061405429
11042 DATA 0.3275911
11044 END
11046 REM********** END OF ERROR FUNCTION MODULE ***********************
```

C.2.   THE GAMMA FUNCTION

```
11100 REM**************** GAMMA FUNCTION *************************
11102 REM external in : X
11104 REM external out: GAMMA
11106    ON ERROR GOTO 11170              :REM  set error trap
11108    DIM B.A(8)                       :REM  dimension internal arrays
11110    RESTORE 11176                    :REM  pointer to data
11112    FOR K.A=0 TO 8:READ B.A(K.A):NEXT K.A:REM read in data
11114    FACT.A=1#
11116    X.A=X
11118    IF X>2 THEN GOSUB 11130          :REM  decision point
11120    IF X<1 THEN GOSUB 11142
11122    GOSUB 11154
11124    GAMMA=GAMMA*FACT.A
11126    ON ERROR GOTO 0                  :REM reset error trap before leaving
11128 RETURN                             :REM return to main program
11130 REM----------------------calculation for x > 2
11132    WHILE X.A>2
11134        X.A=X.A-1#
11136        FACT.A=FACT.A*X.A
11138    WEND
11140 RETURN
11142 REM----------------------calculation for x < 1
11144    WHILE X.A<1
11146        X.A=X.A+1#
11147        IF X.A=1 THEN PRINT "gamma("X") = infinity":GOTO 11150
11148        FACT.A=FACT.A/(X.A-1#)
11150    WEND
11152 RETURN
```

```
11154 REM------------------------- calculate gamma for 1 < x < 2
11156    Y.A=X.A-1#
11158    GAMMA=B.A(8)
11160    FOR K.A=7 TO 0 STEP -1
11162       GAMMA=GAMMA*Y.A+B.A(K.A)
11164    NEXT K.A
11166 RETURN
11168 REM------------------------- error trap
11170    IF (ERR=10) AND (ERL=11108) THEN RESUME 11114
11172    PRINT "ERROR # "ERR" IN GAMMA FUNCTION MODULE AT LINE "ERL
11174 REM------------------------- data statements
11176 DATA 1.0
11178 DATA -0.577191652,0.988205891,-0.897056937,0.918206857
11180 DATA -0.756704078,0.482199394,-0.193527818,0.035868343
11182 END
11184 REM************* END OF GAMMA FUNCTION MODULE ******************
```

C.3.   THE BESSEL FUNCTION OF THE FIRST KIND

```
11300 REM***************** BESSEL FUNCTIONS ***************************
11302 REM external in : X,JN%
11304 REM external out: BESSEL
11306    IF X<-3 THEN PRINT "APPROXIMATION IS NOT VALID ":RETURN
11308    ON ERROR GOTO 11402        :REM   error trap
11310    DIM BSL.A(5,6)             :REM   dimension internal variables
11312    RESTORE 11410              :REM   pointer to data statements
11314    READ PI                    :REM   read in all data
11316    FOR I.A=0 TO 5:FOR J.A=0 TO 6:READ BSL.A(I.A,J.A):NEXT J.A:NEXT I.A
11318    IF JN%>1 THEN GOSUB 11322
                ELSE IF JN%=1 THEN GOSUB 11368
                ELSE IF JN%=0 THEN GOSUB 11346
11320 RETURN                       :REM   return to calling program
11322 REM------------------------- calculation of any jn
11324    JDUM.A=JN%:JN%=0:GOSUB 11346
11326    BNMO.A=BESSEL
11328    JN%=1:GOSUB 11368
11330    BN.A=BESSEL
11332    FOR K.A=2 TO JDUM.A
11334       BNPO.A=2#*(K.A-1#)*BN.A/X-BNMO.A
11336       BNMO.A=BN.A:BN.A=BNPO.A
11338    NEXT K.A
11340    BESSEL=BNPO.A
11342    JN%=JDUM.A
11344 RETURN
11346 REM------------------------- calculation of j0
11348    IF X>=-3 AND X <3 THEN Y.A=(X/3#)*(X/3#):I.A=0
                           :GOSUB 11390 ELSE GOTO 11356
11350    BESSEL=ANS.A
11352 RETURN
11354 REM-------------------- j0 for x<3
11356    IF X>=3 THEN Y.A=3#/X:I.A=1:GOSUB 11390
11358    FZERO.A = ANS.A
11360    I.A=2:GOSUB 11390
11362    THETAZ.A=X+ANS.A
11364    BESSEL=FZERO.A*COS(THETAZ.A)/SQR(X)
11366 RETURN
11368 REM------------------------------ calculation of j1
```

```
11370    IF X>=-3 AND X<3 THEN I.A=3:Y.A=X*X/9#
                          :GOSUB 11390   ELSE GOTO 11376
11372    BESSEL=ANS.A*X
11374 RETURN
11376 REM-------------- approximation for x>3 for j1
11378    Y.A=3#/X:I.A=4#:GOSUB 11390
11380    FSMALL.A = ANS.A
11382    Y.A=3#/X:I.A=5#:GOSUB 11390
11384    THETA.A=X+ANS.A
11386    BESSEL=FSMALL.A*COS(THETA.A)/SQR(X)
11388 RETURN
11390 REM--------------approximation for x<3 for j1
11392    ANS.A=BSL.A(I.A,6)
11394    FOR J.A=5 TO 0 STEP -1
11396        ANS.A=ANS.A*Y.A+BSL.A(I.A,J.A)
11398    NEXT J.A
11400 RETURN
11402 REM--------------------------------- error trapping
11404    IF (ERR=10) AND (ERL=11310) THEN RESUME 11318
11406    PRINT "ERROR # "ERR" IN BESSEL FUNCTION MODULE AT LINE "ERL
11408 REM--------------------------------- data statements
11410 DATA 3.1415926
11412 DATA 1.0,-2.2499997,1.2656208,-0.3163866,0.044479,-0.0039444,0.0002100
11414 DATA 0.79788456,-0.00000077,-0.00552740,-0.00009512
11416 DATA 0.00137237,-0.00072805,0.00014476
11418 DATA -0.78539816,-0.04166397,-0.00003954,0.00262573,-0.00054125
11420 DATA -0.00029333,0.00013558
11422 DATA 0.5,-0.56249985,0.21093573,-0.03954289,0.00443319
11424 DATA -0.00031761,0.00001109
11426 DATA 0.79788456,0.00000156,0.01659667,0.00017105,-0.00249511
11428 DATA 0.00113653,-0.00020033
11430 DATA -2.35619449,0.12499612,0.00005650,-0.00637879,0.00074348
11432 DATA 0.00079824,-0.00029166
11434 END
11436 REM*************** END OF BESSEL FUNCTION MODULE *******************
```

C.4. THE VOIGT FUNCTION

```
11500 REM**************** VOIGT FUNCTION ***************************
11505 REM external in : P , D
11510 REM external out: VOIGT
11515    ON ERROR GOTO 11580
11520    DIM ALPHA.A(4),BETA.A(4),GAMA.A(4),DELTA.A(4)
11525    RESTORE 11595
11530    FOR I.A=1 TO 4
11532        READ ALPHA.A(I.A),BETA.A(I.A),GAMA.A(I.A),DELTA.A(I.A)
11533    NEXT I.A
11535    SUM.A=0
11540    FOR J.A=1 TO 4
11545        ANUM.A = GAMA.A(J.A)*(P-ALPHA.A(J.A))+DELTA.A(J.A)*(D-BETA.A(J.A))
11550        DEN.A= (P-ALPHA.A(J.A))*(P-ALPHA.A(J.A))
                              + (D-BETA.A(J.A))*(D-BETA.A(J.A))
11555        SUM.A=SUM.A +ANUM.A/DEN.A
11560    NEXT J.A
11565    VOIGT = SUM.A
11570 RETURN
11575 REM--------------------------------- error trap
```

```
11580     IF (ERR=10) AND (ERL-11520) THEN RESUME 11535
11585     PRINT "ERROR # "ERR" IN VOIGT FUNCTION MODULE AT LINE "ERL:END
11590 REM-------------------------------- data
11595 DATA -1.2150,1.2359,-0.3085,0.0210
11600 DATA -1.3509,0.3786,0.5906,-1.1858
11605 DATA -1.2150,-1.2359,-0.3085,-0.0210
11610 DATA -1.3509,-0.3786,0.5906,1.1858
11615 END
11620 REM********************************************************************
```

C.5. DIFFERENTIATION OF A KNOWN FUNCTION

```
10500 REM--------------------- function to be differentiated
10590 REM--------------------- end of differentiation function
12500 REM******************** DIFFERENTIATION ************************
12505 REM external in : Y = f(X) at 10500 , MODE% , NDEGREE%, H
12510 REM external out: DERIVX
12515     ON ERROR GOTO 12690
12520     ON MODE% GOSUB 12570,12530
12525 RETURN
12530 REM----------------------- extrapolation to limit, differentiation
12540     HINPUT.B=H
12545     H=H*2:GOSUB 12570
12550     DH2.B=DERIVX
12555     H=HINPUT.B:GOSUB 12570
12560     IF NDEGREE%=1 THEN DERIVX=(4#*DERIVX-DH2.B)/3#
                          ELSE IF NDEGREE%=3 THEN DERIVX=(16#*DERIVX-DH2.B)/15#
12565 RETURN
12570 REM----------------------------- standard differentiation
12575     IF NDEGREE%=1 THEN GOSUB 12585 ELSE IF NDEGREE%=3 THEN GOSUB 12625
12580     RETURN
12585 REM----------------------------- first degree derivative
12590     XCENTER.B=X:DERIVX  =0#
12595     X=XCENTER.B-H:GOSUB 10500
12600     DERIVX-Y
12605     X=XCENTER.B+H:GOSUB 10500
12610     DERIVX=(Y-DERIVX)/(2#*H)
12615     X=XCENTER.B
12620 RETURN
12625 REM----------------------------- third degree derivative
12630     XCENTER.B=X:DERIVX=0#
12635     X=XCENTER.B-2*H:GOSUB 10500
12640     DERIVX=Y
12645     X=XCENTER.B-H:GOSUB 10500
12650     DERIVX=DERIVX-8*Y
12655     X=XCENTER.B+H:GOSUB 10500
12660     DERIVX=DERIVX+8*Y
12665     X=XCENTER.B+2#*H:GOSUB 10500
12670     DERIVX=DERIVX-Y
12675     DERIVX=DERIVX/(12#*H)
12680     X=XCENTER.B
12685 RETURN
12690 REM----------------------------- error trap
12695 PRINT "ERROR # "ERR" IN DIFFERENTIATION MODULE AT LINE "ERL
12700 END
12705 REM**************** END OF DIFFERENTIATION MODULE ********************
```

C.6.   INTEGRATION OF A KNOWN FUNCTION

```
10200 REM------------------------- function Y = f(X)
10290 REM------------------------- end of integration function
12000 REM********************* INTEGRATION *****************************
12005 REM option 1 - Newton-Coates : option 2 - Gauss-Legendre
12010 REM external in: NINTGL% , NFORM , MODE , A , B , Y
12015 REM external out: AINTGL , X
12020     ON ERROR GOTO 12280
12025     ON NINTGL% GOSUB 12035,12220
12030 RETURN
12035 REM------------------------- Newton-Coates Integration (option 1)
12040     ON NFORM GOSUB 12080,12140
12045     DH.B=AINTGL
12050     IF MODE=1 THEN RETURN ELSE IF MODE>2 THEN PRINT "MODE UNDEFINED"
12055     N=N*2
12060     ON NFORM GOSUB 12080,12140
12065     IF NFORM=1 THEN AINTGL=(4#*AINTGL-DH.B)/3#
12070     IF NFORM=2 THEN AINTGL=(16#*AINTGL-DH.B)/15#
12075 RETURN
12080 REM------------------------- Trapezoidal Integral
12085     H.B=(B-A)/N
12090     AINTGL=0#
12095     FOR K.B=1 TO N-1
12100         X=A+H.B*K.B:GOSUB 10200
12105         AINTGL=AINTGL+Y*H.B
12110     NEXT K.B
12115     X=A:GOSUB 10200
12120     AINTGL=AINTGL+Y*H.B/2#
12125     X=B:GOSUB 10200
12130     AINTGL=AINTGL+Y*H.B/2
12135 RETURN
12140 REM------------------------- Simpson integral of known function
12145     N.B=N/2
12147     IF ABS(2*N.B) <> N THEN PRINT "The number N must be even":RETURN
12150     H.B=(B-A)/N
12155     X=B:GOSUB 10200
12160     AINTGL=Y
12165     X=A:GOSUB 10200
12170     AINTGL=AINTGL-Y
12175     FOR K.B=1 TO N.B
12180         FOR M.B=1 TO 2
12185             X=A+(2*K.B+M.B-3)*H.B
12190             GOSUB 10200
12195             AINTGL=AINTGL+2*M.B*Y
12200         NEXT M.B
12205     NEXT K.B
12210     AINTGL=AINTGL*H.B/3#
12215 RETURN
12220 REM------------------------- Gauss-Legendre integration (option 2)
12225     C.B=(B-A)/2#:D.B=(B+A)/2#
12230     W.B=5#/9#:V.B=8#/9#
12235     Z.B=.77459666692000011#
12240     X=C.B*Z.B+D.B:GOSUB 10200
12245     AINTGL=W.B*Y
12250     X=-C.B*Z.B+D.B:GOSUB 10200
12255     AINTGL=AINTGL+Y*W.B
12260     X=D.B:GOSUB 10200
12265     AINTGL=AINTGL+V.B*Y
```

```
12270      AINTGL=C.B*AINTGL
12275 RETURN
12280 REM-------------------------------- Error Trap
12285 PRINT "ERROR # "ERR" IN INTEGRAL MODULE AT LINE "ERL
12290 END
12295 REM************* END OF INTEGRATION MODULE *********************
```

C.7. SPLINE OPERATIONS

```
13000 REM***************CUBIC SPLINE INTERPOLATION ********************
13001 REM option 1 - parameter calculation : option 2 - interpolated value
13003 REM external in : NSPLINE%,XARRAY(),YARRAY(),NPTS,XVAL,SPLDRV%,A,B
13004 REM external out: S,SDERIV,SCNDRV
13005 REM------------------------------- header
13010     ON ERROR GOTO 13385
13015     ON NSPLINE% GOSUB 13025,13165
13017     ON ERROR GOTO 0
13020 RETURN
13025 REM---------------- calculate spline parameters  (option 1)
13030     DIM A.C(50),D.C(50),C.C(50),B.C(50),SDP.C(50),H.C(50)
13035     NPM.C = NPTS-1 : NPT.C = NPTS-2
13040     FOR K.C=1 TO NPM.C : H.C(K.C)=XARRAY(K.C+1)-XARRAY(K.C) : NEXT K.C
13045 REM--------------- compute A
13050     A.C(2) = 2#*(H.C(1)+H.C(2))
13055     FOR K.C = 3 TO NPM.C
13060        A.C(K.C)=2#*(H.C(K.C-1)+H.C(K.C))
                            - H.C(K.C-1)*H.C(K.C-1)/A.C(K.C-1)
13065     NEXT K.C
13070 REM---------------compute D
13075     FOR K.C=2 TO NPTS
13080        C.C(K.C) = (YARRAY(K.C)-YARRAY(K.C-1))/H.C(K.C-1)
13085     NEXT K.C
13090     FOR K.C=2 TO NPM.C
13095        D.C(K.C) = 6#*(C.C(K.C+1)-C.C(K.C))
13100     NEXT K.C
13105 REM--------------- compute B
13110     B.C(2)=D.C(2)
13115     FOR K.C = 3 TO NPM.C
13120        B.C(K.C) = D.C(K.C)-H.C(K.C-1)*B.C(K.C-1)/A.C(K.C-1)
13125     NEXT K.C
13130 REM--------------- solve for SDP
13135     SDP.C(NPTS-1) = B.C(NPTS-1)/A.C(NPTS-1)
13140     FOR K.C=NPT.C TO 2 STEP -1
13145        SDP.C(K.C) = (B.C(K.C)-H.C(K.C)*SDP.C(K.C+1))/A.C(K.C)
13150     NEXT K.C
13155     SDP.C(1) = 0 : SDP.C(NPTS) = 0
13160 RETURN
13165 REM---------------- calculate interpolated value (option 2)
13170     GOSUB 13345    :REM find position of XVAL
13175     PRINT KP.C:K.C=KP.C
13180     SPRIM = C.C(K.C+1)-SDP.C(K.C+1)*H.C(K.C)/6#
                            - SDP.C(K.C)*H.C(K.C)/3#
13185     XX.C=XVAL-XARRAY(K.C)
13190     S = YARRAY(K.C)+SPRIM*XX.C+SDP.C(K.C)*XX.C*XX.C/2#
13195     S = S+(SDP.C(K.C+1)-SDP.C(K.C))*XX.C*XX.C*XX.C/(6#*H.C(K.C))
13200     IF SPLDRV% = 0 THEN RETURN
```

```
13205      SDERIV =SPRIM+SDP.C(K.C)*XX.C
                       + XX.C*XX.C*(SDP.C(K.C+1)-SDP.C(K.C))/(2#*H.C(K.C))
13210      SCNDRV = SDP.C(K.C)+XX.C*(SDP.C(K.C+1)-SDP.C(K.C))/H.C(K.C)
13215 RETURN
13345 REM-------------------------- find nearest knot
13350      X0.C = XARRAY(1)+H.C(1)
13355      IFLAG.C = 0
13360      FOR K.C=1 TO NPM.C
13365          IF XVAL<=X0.C THEN IFLAG.C=1:KP.C=K.C:K.C=NPM.C:GOTO 13375
13370          X0.C = X0.C+H.C(K.C+1)
13375      NEXT K.C
13380 RETURN
13385 REM------------------------------- error trap
13390 IF (ERR=10) AND (ERL=13030) THEN RESUME 13035
13395 PRINT "ERROR # "ERR" IN SPLINE MODULE AT LINE "ERL
13400 END
13405 REM************** END OF SPLINE MODULE ************************
```

C.8.   MATRIX OPERATIONS

```
14000 REM****************** MATRIX MODULE ****************************
14005 REM options    1) solve Ax=b : 2) upper triangle matrix : 3) inverse
14010 REM external in : NMATRIX%,MDEGREE,SMTRX(,),BCLM()
14015 REM external out: SMTRX(,),DET,XCLM()
14020      ON ERROR GOTO 14310
14025      DIM AM.D(20,20),JSUB.D(20)
14027      NEWA.D = NEWA
14030      ON NMATRIX% GOSUB 14165,14045,14240
14035      ON ERROR GOTO 0
14040 RETURN
14045 REM------------------------ Option 2    Create upper triangle matrix
14050      NINTR.D = 0
14055      FOR I.D = 1 TO MDEGREE : JSUB.D(I.D) = I.D : NEXT I.D
14060      FOR K.D=1 TO MDEGREE-1
14065          AMAX.D=0
14070          FOR I.D = K.D TO MDEGREE
14075              ABSA.D = ABS(SMTRX(JSUB.D(I.D),K.D))
14080              IF AMAX.D<ABSA.D THEN 9MAX.D = ABSA.D : INDX.D = I.D
14085              NINTR.D = NINTR.D + 1
14090          NEXT I.D
14095          IF AMAX.D = 0 THEN PRINT "ERROR EXIT" : END
14100          J.D=JSUB.D(K.D):JSUB.D(K.D)=JSUB.D(INDX.D):JSUB.D(INDX.D)=J.D
14105          PIVOT.D = SMTRX(JSUB.D(K.D),K.D)
14110          FOR I.D = K.D+1 TO MDEGREE
14115              AM.D(JSUB.D(I.D),K.D) = -SMTRX(JSUB.D(I.D),K.D)/PIVOT.D
14120              FOR J.D=K.D+1 TO MDEGREE
14125                  SMTRX(JSUB.D(I.D),J.D)=SMTRX(JSUB.D(I.D),J.D)
                           + AM.D(JSUB.D(I.D),K.D)*SMTRX(JSUB.D(K.D),J.D)
14130              NEXT J.D
14135          NEXT I.D
14140      NEXT K.D
14145      DET = (-1)^NINTR.D
14150      FOR K.D=1 TO MDEGREE : DET = DET * SMTRX(K.D,K.D) : NEXT K.D
14155      IF DET=0 THEN PRINT "WARNING ZERO DETERMINANT"
14160 RETURN
14165 REM------------------ Option 1    Solve the matrix equation Ax = b
14167      IF NEWA.D = 1 THEN GOSUB 14045          :REM   new A matrix calcn.
```

```
14170        FOR K.D=1 TO MDEGREE-1
14175           FOR I.D = K.D+1 TO MDEGREE
14180              BCLM(JSUB.D(I.D))=BCLM(JSUB.D(I.D))
                              + AM.D(JSUB.D(I.D),K.D)*BCLM(JSUB.D(K.D))
14185           NEXT I.D
14190        NEXT K.D
14195        XCLM(MDEGREE) =
                       BCLM(JSUB.D(MDEGREE)) / SMTRX(JSUB.D(MDEGREE),MDEGREE)
14200        FOR K.D = MDEGREE-1 TO 1 STEP -1
14205           XCLM(K.D) = BCLM(JSUB.D(K.D))
14210           FOR I.D = K.D+1 TO MDEGREE
14215              XCLM(K.D) = XCLM(K.D)-SMTRX(JSUB.D(K.D),I.D)*XCLM(I.D)
14220           NEXT I.D
14225           XCLM(K.D) = XCLM(K.D) / SMTRX(JSUB.D(K.D),K.D)
14230        NEXT K.D
14235 RETURN
14240 REM---------------- Option 3      Calculate inverse matrix
14245        DIM TEMP.D(20,20)
14247        IF NEWA.D = 1 THEN GOSUB 14045
14248        NEWA.D = 0
14250        FOR II.D = 1 TO MDEGREE
14255           FOR KK.D = 1 TO MDEGREE:BCLM(KK.D) = 0# : NEXT KK.D
14260           BCLM(II.D)=1#
14265           GOSUB 14165
14270           FOR KK.D=1 TO MDEGREE:TEMP.D(KK.D,II.D)=XCLM(KK.D):NEXT KK.D
14275        NEXT II.D
14280        FOR II.D=1 TO MDEGREE
14285           FOR KK.D = 1 TO MDEGREE
14290              SMTRX(II.D,KK.D) = TEMP.D(II.D,KK.D)
14295           NEXT KK.D
14300        NEXT II.D
14305 RETURN
14310 REM----------------------------------------------- error trap
14315        IF (ERR=10) AND (ERL=14025) THEN RESUME 14027
14320        IF (ERR=10) AND (ERL=14245) THEN RESUME 14247
14325        PRINT "ERROR # "ERR" IN MATRIX MODULE AT LINE "ERL
14330 END
14335 REM************** END OF MATRIX MODULE *****************************
```

C.9. ROOTS OF KNOWN FUNCTIONS

```
10500 REM----------------------- function for root module
10510 REM    function Y = f(X) used in root module
10590 REM----------------------- end of root function
15000 REM************** ROOTS OF EQUATIONS ***********************
15001 REM options 1) Secant Method   2) Decker-Brent Method
15002 REM external in : NROOT%,X0,X1, Y=f(X) at 10500
15003 REM external out: X1
15005        ON ERROR GOTO 15220
15010        RESTORE 15230
15015        IF NMAX=0 THEN READ NMAX,EPSILON1,EPSILON2
15020        ON NROOT% GOSUB 15030,15135
15025 RETURN
15030 REM------------------------- secant method (option 1)
15035        RESTORE 15230
15040        IF NMAX=0 THEN READ NMAX,EPSILON1,EPSILON2
```

```
15045      X=X0:GOSUB 10500
15050      FZERO.E=Y
15055      X=X1:GOSUB 10500
15060      FONE.E=Y
15065      IF ABS(FONE.E)>ABS(FZERO.E) THEN SWAP X1,X0:SWAP FONE.E,FZERO.E
15070      FOR K.E=0 TO NMAX
15075          IF ABS(FONE.E)<EPSILON2 THEN
                   PRINT "CONVERGENCE °f(x)°<epsilon2":XSOLN=X1:NCONVRG=1
                   : RETURN
15080          S.E=FONE.E/FZERO.E
15085          P.E=(X0-X1)*S.E
15090          Q.E=1#-S.E
15095          XTWO.E=X1-P.E/Q.E
15100          IF ABS(X1-XTWO.E)<(EPSILON1*ABS(XTWO.E))
                       THEN PRINT "CONVERGENCE ":XSOLN=XTWO.E:NCONVRG=1
                       :RETURN
15105          X=XTWO.E:GOSUB 10500
15110          FTWO.E=Y
15115          IF ABS(FTWO.E)>ABS(FONE.E) THEN X0=XTWO.E:FZERO.E=FTWO.E
                   : ELSE X0=X1:FZERO.E=FONE.E:X1=XTWO.E:FONE.E=FTWO.E
15120      NEXT K.E
15125      PRINT "FINISHED AFTER NMAX= ";NMAX
15130 RETURN
15135 REM----------------------- decker-brent method (option 2)
15140      YONE.E=X0:YZERO.E=YONE.E+1#:YMN.E=YZERO.E
15145      X=X0:GOSUB 10500
15150      F0=Y
15155      X=X1:GOSUB 10500
15160      F1=Y
15165      IF (F0*F1)>0 THEN
               PRINT "Initial values do not satisfy criterion f1 f0 < 0":RETURN
15170      WHILE(ABS(X1-YONE.E)>EPSILON1*ABS(X1)) AND (ABS(F1)>EPSILON2)
                                                    OR (K.E>NMAX)
15175          IF (YONE.E<>YMN.E) THEN D.E=F1*(X1-X0)/(F1-F0)
                   :IF SGN(D.E)<>SGN(X1-YONE.E) OR ABS(D.E)>ABS(X1-YONE.E)
                   THEN D.E=.5#*(X1-YONE.E)
15180          IF (YONE.E=YMN.E) THEN D.E=.5#*(X1-YONE.E)
15185          X0=X1:F0=F1
15190          X1=X1-D.E:X=X1:GOSUB 10500
15195          F1=Y
15200          YMN.E=YZERO.E:YZERO.E=YONE.E
15205          IF (F0*F1)<0 THEN YONE.E=X0
15210      WEND
15212      XSOLN=X1
15215 RETURN
15220 REM----------------------------- error trap and data
15225 PRINT "ERROR # "ERR" IN ROOT FINDING MODULE LINE "ERL
15230 DATA 50,0.00001,0.00001
15235 END
15240 REM**************** END OF ROOT FINDING MODULE *********************
```

C.10.   SOLUTIONS OF DIFFERENTIAL EQUATIONS

```
10900 REM------------- The functions F=f(X,Y) or F=f(X,Y,Z),G=g(X,Y,Z)
10999 RETURN
16000 REM*************** SOLUTION OF DIFFERENTIAL EQUATIONS ****************
16005 REM options: 1) P-C single equation : 2) P-C two coupled equations
```

```
16010 REM external in : NDIFFEQ%,A,B,NDIV,ETA,F=f(X,Y,Z),G=g(X,Y,Z),PSI
16015 REM external out: XARRAY(),YARRAY(),ZARRAY(),ERROR()
16020     ON ERROR GOTO 16325
16022   H=(B-A)/NDIV
16025     ON NDIFFEQ% GOSUB 16035,16170
16030 RETURN
16035 REM------------ Predictor Corrector - single eqn. (option 1)
16040     X=A:YZERO.F=ETA
16045     Y=YZERO.F:GOSUB 10900
16050     FZERO.F=F
16055     X=X+H
16060     Y=YZERO.F+H*FZERO.F
16065     GOSUB 10900
16070     FONE.F=F
16075     YONE.F=YZERO.F+.5*H*(FZERO.F+FONE.F)
16080     XARRAY(0)=A:YARRAY(0)=ETA
16085     XARRAY(1)=X:YARRAY(1)=YONE.F
16090     K.F=2
16095     WHILE X<=B
16100         Y=YONE.F:X=X:GOSUB 10900
16105         FONE.F=F
16110         Y1P.F=YONE.F+.5*H*(3#*FONE.F-FZERO.F)
16115         X=X+H
16120         X=X:Y=Y1P.F:GOSUB 10900
16125         F1P=F
16130         YONE.F=YONE.F+.5#*H*(F1P+FONE.F)
16135         EST.F=ABS(Y1P.F-YONE.F)/6
16140         XARRAY(K.F)=X:YARRAY(K.F)=YONE.F:ERRORY(K.F)=EST.F
16145         IF NPRINT=1 THEN PRINT USING "##.########   ";K.F,X,YONE.F,EST.F
16150         NARRAY=K.F:K.F=K.F+1
16155         FZERO.F=FONE.F
16160     WEND
16165 RETURN
16170 REM----------------- Predictor Corrector - two eqns (option 2)
16175     X=A:YZERO.F=ETA:ZZERO.F=PSI
16180 REM external functions F=f(x,y,z) and G=g(x,y,z) calculated at 10900
16185     Y=YZERO.F:Z=ZZERO.F:GOSUB 10900:REM CALCULATE F,G
16190     FZERO.F=F:GZERO.F=G
16195     X=X+H:Y=YZERO.F+H*FZERO.F:Z=ZZERO.F+H*GZERO.F
16200     GOSUB 10900
16205     FONE.F=F:GONE.F=G
16210     YONE.F=YZERO.F+.5#*H*(FZERO.F+FONE.F)
16215     ZONE.F=ZZERO.F+.5#*H*(GZERO.F+GONE.F)
16220     XARRAY(0)=A:YARRAY(0)=ETA:ZARRAY(0)=PSI
16225     XARRAY(1)=X:YARRAY(1)=YONE.F:ZARRAY(1)=ZONE.F
16230     K.F=2
16235 REM-------------Predictor Corrector Loop
16240     WHILE X<=B
16245         Y=YONE.F:Z=ZONE.F:X=X:GOSUB 10900
16250         FONE.F=F:GONE.F=G
16255         Y1P.F=YONE.F+.5#*H*(3#*FONE.F-FZERO.F)
16260         Z1P.F=ZONE.F+.5#*H*(3#*GONE.F-GZERO.F)
16265         X=X+H
16270         XARRAY(K.F)=X
16275         Y=Y1P.F:Z=Z1P.F:GOSUB 10900
16280         F1P.F=F:G1P.F=G
16285         YONE.F=YONE.F+.5#*H*(F1P.F+FONE.F)
16290         ZONE.F=ZONE.F+.5#*H*(G1P.F+GONE.F)
16295         YARRAY(K.F)=YONE.F:ZARRAY(K.F)=ZONE.F
16300         IF NPRINT=1 THEN PRINT USING "##.########   ";K.F,X,YONE.F,ZONE.F
```

```
16305          NARRAY=K.F:K.F=K.F+1
16310          FZERO.F=FONE.F:GZERO.F=GONE.F
16315      WEND
16320 RETURN
16325 REM--------------------------------------- error trap
16330 PRINT "ERROR # "ERR" IN DIFFERENTIAL EQN. MODULE AT LINE "ERL
16335 END
16340 REM**************** END OF DIFFERENTIAL EQUATION MODULE *************
```

C.11.   A DATA NOISE GENERATOR

```
12800 REM**************** NOISE GENERATOR ********************************
12802      RANDOMIZE 10           :REM              seed generator
12805 REM    INPUT NPTS,YARRAY(),MODE,SIGMALL,SIGMA()
12810 REM    OUTPUT   YARRAY()
12812      PI=3.1415926#
12815      FOR I.A=1 TO NPTS
12820          IF MODE=2 AND YARRAY(I.A)=0 THEN SIGMA.A=1#
12825          IF MODE=2 AND YARRAY(I.A)<>0 THEN SIGMA.A=SQR(YARRAY(I.A))
12830          IF MODE=1 THEN SIGMA.A=SIGMA(I.A)
12832          IF MODE=0 THEN SIGMA.A =SIGMALL
12835          IF MODE>3 OR MODE <0 THEN PRINT "MODE outside acceptable range"
                                    : RETURN
12845          U1.A=RND:U2.A=RND
12850          X.A=SQR(-2#*LOG(U1.A))*COS(2#*PI*U2.A)
12860          YARRAY(I.A)=YARRAY(I.A)+SIGMA.A*X.A
12865      NEXT I.A
12870 RETURN
12875 REM***************** END OF NOISE MODULE *********************
```

Appendix D

The C Numerical Analysis Program Library

This appendix contains the complete set of C functions that make up our numerical analysis library. The library was developed in the Aztek version of C.* The program should compile without modifications under all versions of the Aztek C compiler on the IBM-PC and IBM compatibles, all CP/M computer systems, and the Apple II plus and IIe. Some modification to the language syntax may be necessary with other C compilers. All functions are written to run under double precision arithmetic. We have attempted at all times to use standard Kernighan and Ritchie† syntax in all C code. However, we cannot accept any liability if errors are found in these programs. A discussion on how to use these functions is given in Chapter 9.

D.1.   THE ERROR FUNCTION

```
/*
*      Reference.   Handbook of Mathematical Functions (9th Edition),
*    M. Abramowitz and I.A. Stegun (Dover, N.Y., 1972), p. 299.
*
*/

#include "libc.h"
#include "math.h"

#define   A1    0.254829592
#define   A2   -0.284496736
#define   A3    1.421413741
#define   A4   -1.453152027
#define   A5    1.061405429
#define   P     0.3275911
```

*Aztek C is a trademark of Manx Software Systems, P.O. Box 55, Shrewsbury, NJ 07701.

†B. W. Kernighan, and D. M. Ritchie, *The C Programming Language*, (Prentice-Hall, Englewood Cliffs, N.J., 1978).

```
double erf(x)
double x;


{
    double t, y;
    t = 1.0 / ( 1 + P * x );
    y = t * ( t * ( t * ( t * ( t * A5 + A4 ) + A3 ) + A2 )+A1);
    return 1.0 - y * exp(- x * x );
}
```

D.2.   THE GAMMA FUNCTION

```
/*
*     Reference.   Handbook of Mathematical Functions (9th Edition),
*     M. Abramowitz and I.A. Stegun, (Dover, N.Y.1972), p. 257.
*/
#include "libc.h"
#include "math.h"

#define    B1    -.577191652
#define    B2     .988205891
#define    B3    -.897056937
#define    B4     .918206857
#define    B5    -.756704078
#define    B6     .482199394
#define    B7    -.193527818
#define    B8     .035868343
#define    B(y)   (((((((B8*y+B7)*y+B6)*y+B5)*y+B4)*y+B3)*y+B2)*y+B1)*y

double gamma(x)
double x;
{
          double y,gma;
          y=x-1;
          if(x>2) gma=(x-1)*gamma(x-1);
          else if(x<1) gma=gamma(x+1)/x;
          else if(x>=1 && x<=2)gma=1+B(y);
          return gma;
}
```

D.3.   THE BESSEL FUNCTION OF THE FIRST KIND

```
/*
*   Reference.  Handbook of Mathematical Functions (9th Edition),
*   M. Abramowitz and I. A. Stegun (Dover, N.Y., 1972), p. 369.
*
*   bessel(n,x)        Bessel function of first kind.
*            n         Order of bessel function 0,1,2.....NMAX where NMAX
*                          is a function of the computer system.
*            x         Argument of Bessel function.
*/
```

```
#include "libc.h"
#include "math.h"

#define     A1      -2.2499997    /*   these constants are defined  */
#define     A2       1.2656208    /*      in the above reference     */
#define     A3      -0.3163866
#define     A4       0.0444479
#define     A5      -0.0039444
#define     A6       0.0002100
#define     A(d)    (((((A6*d+A5)*d+A4)*d+A3)*d+A2)*d+A1)*d
#define     F0       0.79788456
#define     F1      -0.00000077
#define     F2      -0.00552740
#define     F3      -0.00009512
#define     F4       0.00137237
#define     F5      -0.00072805
#define     F6       0.00014476
#define     F(d)    ((((((F6*d+F5)*d+F4)*d+F3)*d+F2)*d+F1)*d+F0)
#define     T0      -0.78539816
#define     T1      -0.04166397
#define     T2      -0.00003954
#define     T3       0.00262573
#define     T4      -0.00054125
#define     T5      -0.00029333
#define     T6       0.00013558
#define     T(d)    ((((((T6*d+T5)*d+T4)*d+T3)*d+T2)*d+T1)*d+T0)
#define     B1      -0.56249985
#define     B2       0.21093573
#define     B3      -0.03954289
#define     B4       0.00443319
#define     B5      -0.00031761
#define     B6       0.00001109
#define     B(d)    (((((B6*d+B5)*d+B4)*d+B3)*d+B2)*d+B1)*d
#define     G0       0.79788456
#define     G1       0.00000156
#define     G2       0.01659667
#define     G3       0.00017105
#define     G4      -0.00249511
#define     G5       0.00113653
#define     G6      -0.0002033
#define     G(d)    ((((((G6*d+G5)*d+G4)*d+G3)*d+G2)*d+G1)*d+G0)
#define     U0      -2.35619449
#define     U1       0.12499612
#define     U2       0.00005650
#define     U3      -0.00637879
#define     U4       0.00074348
#define     U5       0.00079824
#define     U6      -0.00029166
#define     U(d)    ((((((U6*d+U5)*d+U4)*d+U3)*d+U2)*d+U1)*d+U0)

double bessel(n,x)
int n;
double x;

{
    double d,bsl,f0,t0,f1,t1;

/*                  Calculation for order zero                     */
```

```
            if(n==0 && x>=-3 && x<=3){
                    d=x*x/9;
                    bsl = 1+A(d);
            }
            else if(n==0 && x>3){
                    d=3/x;
                    f0=F(d);
                    t0=x+T(d);
                    bsl=f0*cos(t0)/sqrt(x);
            }

/*              Calculation for order one                    */

            else if(n==1 && x>=-3 && x<=3){
                    d=x*x/9;
                    bsl=(0.5+B(d))*x;
            }
            else if(n==1 && x>3){
                    d=3/x;
                    f1=G(d);
                    t1=x+U(d);
                    bsl=f1*cos(t1)/sqrt(x);
            }

/*          recursion calculation for higher orders          */

            else if(n>=2 && x>-3){
                    bsl=2*(n-1)*bessel(n-1,x)/x-bessel(n-2,x);
            }
            else if(x<-3){
                    printf("approximation out of range \n");
                    return;
            }
            else if(n>=2 && x>-3){
                    bsl=2*(n-1)*bessel(n-1,x)/x-bessel(n-2,x);
            }
            else if(x<-3){
                    printf("approximation out of range \n");
                    return;
            }
            return bsl;
}
```

D.4.   THE VOIGT FUNCTION

```
/*
*   Reference.   "Three and four generalized Lorentzian approximations
*                for the Voigt lineshape." P. Martin and J. Puerta,
*                Applied Optics 20, p. 3923 (1981).
*                There are some typographical errors in this article.
*
*   voigt(p,d)          Voigt function; double precision arithmetic.
*        p              Lineshape collisional width factor.
*        d              Detuning factor.
*/
```

```
#include "libc.h"
#include "math.h"

double voigt(p,d)
double p,d;
{
      int i;
      double vgt,pal,deb;
      static double alpha[]={-1.2150,-1.3509,-1.2150,-1.3509};
      static double beta[]= {1.2359,.3786,-1.2359,-.3786};
      static double gamma[]={-.3085,.5906,-.3085,.5906};
      static double delta[]={.0210,-1.1858,-.0210,1.1858};

      vgt=0;
      for (i=0;i<=3;i++){
             pal=p-alpha[i];
             deb=d-beta[i];
             vgt += (gamma[i]*pal+delta[i]*deb)/
                                     (pal*pal+deb*deb);
      }
      return vgt;
}
```

D.5. DIFFERENTIATION OF A KNOWN FUNCTION

```
/*                                                                    *
*    Reference;     Introduction to Numerical Computations; Second Edition;  *
*                   J. L. Vandergraft, Academic Press NY (1983).      *
*                                                                     *
*    diff_f()       Returns differential to known function.           *
*      degree       Degree of approximation; 1 and 3 supported.       *
*      mode         =1   Standard approximation.                      *
*                   =2   Extrapolation to Limit procedure.            *
*      h            Increment used in approximation.                  *
*      x            x-value at which dy/dx to be calculated.          *
*      f            C function containing the known function to be    *
*                                             differentiated          *
*/

#include "libc.h"
#include "math.h"

/*              gradient calculation driver for standard       *
*               and Extrapolation to the Limit calculation     */

double diff_f(degree,mode,h,x,f)
int degree,mode;
double h,x,(*f)();
{
      double diff_etl(),diff_d();

      if(mode==1)return diff_d(degree,h,x,f);
      else if(mode==2)return diff_etl(degree,h,x,f);
}

/*     Extrapolation to the Limit gradient calculation        */
```

```
double diff_et1(degree,h,x,f)
int degree;
double h,x,(*f)();
{
    double dg,diff_d();

    if(degree==3)dg=(16*diff_d(degree,h/2.,x,f)-diff_d(degree,h,x,f))/15;
    else if(degree==1)dg=(4*diff_d(degree,h/2,x,f)-diff_d(degree,h,x,f))/3;
    else if(degree != 1 && degree != 3)printf("degree not supported \n");
    return (dg);
}

/*          standard gradient calculation                    */

double diff_d(degree,h,x,f)
int degree;
double h,x,(*f)();
{
    double g;
    if (degree == 3)g=((*f)(x-2*h)-8*(*f)(x-h)+8*(*f)(x+h)-(*f)(x+2*h))/(12*h
    else if(degree == 1)g=((*f)(x+h)-(*f)(x-h))/(2*h);
    else if(degree != 1 && degree != 3)printf("degree not supported \n");
    return g;
}
```

D.6.   INTEGRATION OF A KNOWN FUNCTION

```
/*
*   Reference.     Introduction to Numerical Compuations; Second Edition,
*                  J. L. Vandergraft, Academic Press NY (1983).
*
*   intgl_f()      Calculate the numerical integral of known function.
*        n         Number of elements to be used in integration.
*      nform       = 1   Trapezoidal integration.
*                    2   Simpson integration.
*      mode        = 1   Standard integration.
*                    2   Extrapolation to Limit integration.
*      a,b         Upper and lower limits of integration.
*      f()         Name of the C function containing the function to
*                  be integrated - single argument f(x) only.
*/

#include "libc.h"
#include "math.h"

#define   D1(N)   intgl_t(N,a,b,f)    /*    Trapezoidal macro      */
#define   D2(N)   intgl_s(N,a,b,f)    /*    Simpson macro          */

/* General integral driver for Simpson and Trapezoidal          *
 *   with Extrapolation to the Limit option                     */

double intgl_f(n,nform,mode,a,b,f)
int n,nform,mode;
double a,b,(*f)();
{
        double integral,intgl_t(),intgl_s();;

        if(nform == 1 && mode == 1)
                    integral =  D1(n);
```

```
        else if(nform -= 1 && mode == 2)
                  integral = (4*D1(2*n)-D1(n))/3;
        else if(nform == 2 && mode == 1)
                  integral = D2(n);
        else if(nform == 2 && mode == 2 )
                  integral = (16 * D2(2*n) - D2(n))/15;
        return integral;
}

double intgl_s(n,a,b,f)    /*    Simpson approximation           */
int n;
double a,b,(*f)();
{
    int k,m;
    double n2,h,integral;

    n2 = n / 2;
    if(n%2 != 0)printf("Simpson integration must have n even\n");
    h=(b-a)/n;
    integral=((*f)(b)-(*f)(a));
    for(k=1;k<=n2;k++){
         for(m=1;m<=2;m++)integral += 2*m*(*f)(a+(2*k+m-3)*h);
    }
    return integral*h/3;
}


double intgl_t(n,a,b,f)    /*    Trapezoidal approximation        */
int n;
double a,b,(*f)();
{
     double h,integral;
     int k;

     h=(b-a)/n;
     integral=((*f)(a)+(*f)(b))*h/2;
     for(k=1;k<=n-1;k++) integral += ((*f)(a+h*k))*h;
     return integral;
}

/*
*    Reference.    Introduction to Numerical Compuations, Second Edition,
*                  J. L. Vandergraft (Academic, N.Y. 1983).
*
*    intgl_gl()    Gauss-Legendre integration.
*      a,b         Upper and lower limits of integration.
*      f()         Name of the C function containing the function to
*                  be integrated; single argument f(x) only.
*/
#define   C    (b-a)/2
#define   D    (b+a)/2
#define   A1   (5*C/9)
#define   A2   (8*C/9)
#define   A3   (5*C/9)
#define   Z    0.7745966692

double intgl_gl(a,b,f)
double a,b,(*f)();
{
    return  A1 * ((*f)(D+C*Z)) + A2 * ((*f)(D)) + A3 * ((*f)(D-C*Z));
}
```

D.7.   SPLINE INTERPOLATION

```
/*
*   Reference.      Introduction to Numerical Compuations, Second Edition,
*                   J. L. Vandergraft (Academic, N.Y. 1983).
*
*   spline_prm()  Finds Spline coefficients corresponding to inputted data.
*     spline_y()  Find interpolated y value corresponding to given x.
*                   spline-prm() muse have been run first for data set.
*       n           Number of points in data set   1...... n
*       x[]         Array containing x values of points to be interpolated.
*       f[]         Array containing y points to be interpolated between.
*       xval        x value at which interpolated value is to be determined.
*       pdx         First derivative of interpolated curve at xval.
*       pddx        Second derivative of interpolated curve at xval.
*/

#include "libc.h"
#include "math.h"

#define  NS   100

static double a[NS],d[NS],b[NS],spp[NS],sp[NS],h[NS],c[NS],aa,bb;

/*                  Calculation of Spline parameters               */

spline_prm(n,px,pf)
int n;
double *px,*pf;
{
      int i,k;

/*                      Compute H                                  */

      for(i=1;i<=n-1;i++)h[i]=*(px+i+1)-*(px+i);
      aa=*(px+1);
      bb=*(px+n);

/*                      Compute A                                  */

      a[2]=2*(h[1]+h[2]);
      for(k=3;k<=n-1;k++)a[k]=2*(h[k-1]+h[k])-h[k-1]*h[k-1]/a[k-1];

/*                      Compute D                                  */

      for(k=2;k<=n;k++)c[k]=(*(pf+k)-*(pf+k-1))/h[k-1];
      for(k=2;k<=n-1;k++)d[k]=6*(c[k+1]-c[k]);

/*                      Compute B                                  */

      b[2]=d[2];
      for(k=3;k<=n-1;k++)b[k]=d[k]-h[k-1]*b[k-1]/a[k-1];
      spp[n-1]=b[n-1]/a[n-1];
      for(k=n-2;k>=2;k--)spp[k]=(b[k]-h[k]*spp[k+1])/a[k];
      spp[1]=spp[n]=0;
      for(k=1;k<=n-1;k++)sp[k]=c[k+1]-spp[k+1]*h[k]/6-spp[k]*h[k]/3;
}

/*          Interpolated value for a given x-value                 */
```

```
double spline_y(n,xval,px,pf,pdx,pddx)
int n;
double xval,*px,*pf,*pdx,*pddx;
{
    int k,nknot();
    double s,xm;
    if(xval<aa || xval >bb){
          printf("x value out of range\n");
          return;
    }
    k=nknot(n,xval);
    xm=xval-*(px+k);
    s=*(pf+k)+sp[k]*xm+spp[k]*xm*xm/2+(spp[k+1]-spp[k])*xm*xm*xm/(6*h[k]);
    *pdx=sp[k]+spp[k]*xm+(spp[k+1]-spp[k])*xm*xm/(2*h[k]);
    *pddx=spp[k]+(spp[k+1]-spp[k])*xm/h[k];
    return s;
}

int nknot(n,xval)
double xval;
{
    int k;
    double x0;

    x0=aa+h[1];
    if(xval>=aa && xval<=bb){
            for(k=1;k<=n-1;k++){
                    if(xval<=x0) break;
                    x0 += h[k+1];
            }
    }
    else if(xval < aa || xval > bb){
            printf("x value out of range \n");
    }
    return k;
}
```

D.8. MATRIX OPERATIONS

```
/*                                                                  *
*    Reference.    Introduction to Numerical Compuations, Second Edition,  *
*                  J. L. Vandergraft (Academic, N.Y. 1983).        *
*                                                                  *
*    mtrx_sln()    Solve the matrix equation Ax=b for x[]          *
*        n         Specifies an n X n matrix in array elements 1....n. *
*        newa      If newa=1 then upper triangle routine mtrx_tri() *
*                                    automatically calculated.     *
*        a[][]     The matrix A whose upper trianlge form to be determined.*
*        x[]       The solution of the matrix equation Ax=b.       *
*        b[]       Array for which a new solution is to be found.  *
*        det       The value of the determinant of the matrix.     *
*/

#include "libc.h"
#include "math.h"
#include "b:numrcl.h"
```

```
static int sub[NTWO];
static double m[NTWO][NTWO];

mtrx_sln(n,newa,pa,px,pb,pdet)
int n,newa;
double (*pa)[NTWO],*px,*pb,*pdet;
{
      int k,i;

      if(newa == 1)mtrx_tri(n,pa,pdet);
      for(k=1;k<=n-1;k++){
              for(i=k+1;i<=n;i++)(*(pb+sub[i])+=m[sub[i]][k]*(*(pb+sub[k])))
      }
      *(px+n)=(*(pb+sub[n]))/(*(pa+sub[n]))[n];
      for(k=n-1;k>=1;k--){
              *(px+k)=*(pb+sub[k]);
              for(i=k+1;i<=n;i++)(*(px+k))-=(*(pa+sub[k]))[i]*(*(px+i));
              *(px+k)/=(*(pa+sub[k]))[k];
      }
}


/*    mtrx_tri()    Create upper triangle matrix of inputted matrix.      */

mtrx_tri(n,pa,pdet)
int n;
double (*pa)[NTWO],*pdet;
{
      int i,k,indx,j,nintr;
      double max,ab,f,pivot;

      for(i=1;i<=n;i++)sub[i]=i;
      for(k=1;k<=n-1;k++){
            max=0;
            nintr=0;
            for(i=k;i<=n;i++){
                  f=(*(pa+sub[i]))[k];
                  ab=fabs(f);
                  if(max<ab){
                          max=ab;
                          indx=i;
                      }
            }
            if(max==0)printf("error exit/n");
            if(indx != k)nintr+=1;
            j=sub[k];
            sub[k]=sub[indx];
            sub[indx]=j;
            pivot=(*(pa+sub[k]))[k];
            for(i=k+1;i<=n;i++){
                  m[sub[i]][k]=-(*(pa+sub[i]))[k]/pivot;
                  for(j=k+1;j<=n;j++)
                          (*(pa+sub[i]))[j]+=m[sub[i]][k]*(*(pa+sub[k]))[j];
            }
      }
      *pdet=1;
      if(nintr!=0)for(k=1;k<=nintr;k++)(*pdet)*=(-1);
      for(k=1;k<=n;k++)(*pdet)*=(*(pa+k))[k];
}
```

```
/*      mtrx_inv()      Operation of finding inverse matrix.          *
 *        inv[]         Array containing inverse matrix.             */

mtrx_inv(n,pa,pinv)
int n;
double (*pa)[NTWO],(*pinv)[NTWO];
{
    int i,j,k,newa=0;
    double x[NTWO],e[NTWO],det;

        for(i=1;i<=n;i++){
                for(k=1;k<=n;k++)e[k]=0;
                e[i]=1;
                mtrx_sln(n,newa,pa,&x,&e,&det);
                for(k=1;k<=n;k++) (*(pinv+k))[i]=x[k];
        }

}
```

D.9.   ROOTS OF KNOWN FUNCTIONS

```
/*                                                                    *
 *   Reference.     Introduction to Numerical Compuations, Second Edition,  *
 *                  J. L. Vandergraft (Academic, N.Y. 1983).          *
 *                                                                    *
 *   root_sec()     Finds root of given function by the Secant method. *
 *   root_dbr()     Finds root of given function by the Decker-Brent Method. *
 *     x0 ,x1       Two initial guesses must be provided.             *
 *      fcn         C function name whose root is to be found.        *
 *                                                                    *
 *          For Decker-Brent method we must have fcn(x0) to be opposite  *
 *                       sign to fcn(x1).                             *
 */
#include "libc.h"
#include "math.h"

#define NMAX     20
#define EPSLN1   0.000001
#define EPSLN2   0.000001

double root_sec(x0,x1,fcn)
double x0,x1;
double (*fcn)();
{
    int k;
    double f0,f1,s,p,q,x2,f2;

    f0=(*fcn)(x0);
    f1=(*fcn)(x1);
    if(fabs(f1)>fabs(f0)){
        swap(&x0,&x1);
        swap(&f0,&f1);
    }
    for(k=0;k<=NMAX;k++){
        if(fabs(f1)<EPSLN2){
                printf("convergence |f(x)| < EPSILON2\n");
                return x1;
```

```
            }
            s=f1/f0;
            p=(x0-x1)*s;
            q=1-s;
            x2=x1-p/q;
            if(fabs(x1-x2)<EPSLN1*fabs(x2)){
                    printf("convergence |deltax| < EPSLN1*|x|\n");
                    return x2;
            }
            f2=(*fcn)(x2);
            if(fabs(f2)>fabs(f1)){
                    x0=x2;
                    f0=f2;
            }
            else{
                    x0=x1;
                    f0=f1;
                    x1=x2;
                    f1=f2;
            }
    }
    printf("no convergence after NMAX = %d iterations\n",NMAX);
}


double root_dbr(x0,x1,fcn)
double x0,x1;
double (*fcn)();
{
    int k;
    double y1,ym1,y0,f0,f1,d;
    int sign();

    y1=x0;
    ym1=y0=y1+1;
    f0=(*fcn)(x0);
    f1=(*fcn)(x1);
    while((fabs(x1-y1)>EPSLN1*fabs(x1)) && (fabs((*fcn)(x1))>EPSLN2)){
        if(y1 != ym1){
            d=f1*(x1-x0)/(f1-f0);
            if((sign(d) != sign(x1-y1)) || (fabs(d) > (x1-y1))) d=0.5*(x1-y1);
        }
        else if(y1 == ym1)d = 0.5*(x1-y1);
        x0=x1;
        f0=f1;
        x1=x1-d;
        f1=(*fcn)(x1);
        ym1=y0;
        y0=y1;
        if(f0*f1 < 0)y1=x0;
    }
    return x1;
}

int sign(x)
double x;
{
        return (x/fabs(x));
}
```

```
swap(px,py)        /*      interchange *px and *py      */
int *px,*py;
{
      int temp;

      temp=*px;
      *px=*py;
      *py=temp;
}
```

D.10. SOLUTIONS OF DIFFERENTIAL EQUATIONS

```
/*
 *   Reference.      Introduction to Numerical Compuations, Second Edition,
 *                   J. L. Vandergraft (Academic, N.Y. 1983).
 *
 *   diff_pc1()      Solve one first order differential equation numerically.   *
 *       f           The C function containing f in dy/dx = f(x,y).             *
 *       n           The number of steps to be used in the solution.           *
 *       a,b         The initial and final x value to be used in the solution. *
 *       eta         The boundary condition y(a).                              *
 *       psi         The boundary condition z(a).                              *
 *       x[]         The x values at which the solution y(x) is calculated.    *
 *       y[]         The solution y(x).                                        *
 *       e[]         The best estimate of the errors in the single solution case*
 *       nprnt       The screen print parameter                                *
 */
#include "libc.h"
#include "math.h"

diff_pc1(f,a,b,n,eta,px,py,pe,nprnt)
int n,nprnt;
double a,b,eta,*px,*py,*pe;
double (*f)();
{
    int k;
    double x,h,x0,x1,y0,y1,f0,f1,y1p,f1p,est;

    h=(b-a)/n;
    f0=(*f)(x=a,y0=eta);
    f1=(*f)(x+h,y0+h*f0);
    y1=y0 + 0.5*h*(f0+f1);
    *px=a;
    *py=eta;
    *(px+1)=a+h;
    *(py+1)=y1;
    *pe=0;
    if(nprnt==1){
        printf("%d      %10.4e      %10.4e\n",k=0,*px,*py);
        printf("%d      %10.4e      %10.4e\n",k=1,*(px+1),*(py+1));
    }
    x+=h;
    for(k=2;k<=n;k++){
        f1=(*f)(x,y1);
        y1p=y1+0.5*h*(3*f1-f0);
        x+=h;
```

```
      f1p=(*f)(x,y1p);
      y1+=0.5*h*(f1p+f1);
      est=fabs(y1p-y1)/6;
      *(px+k)=x;
      *(py+k)=y1;
      *(pe+k)=est;
      if(nprnt==1)
            printf("%d    %10.4e      %10.4e\n",k,*(px+k),*(py+k));
      f0=f1;
   }
}


/*
*  diff_pc2()  Solve two coupled first order differential equations; this *
*              is used indirectly to solve a second order equation.       *
*     f        The C function containing f in dy/dx = f(x,y,z).           *
*     g        The C function containing g in dz/dx = g(x,y,z).           *
*     psi      The boundary condition z(a).                               *
*     z[]      The z(x,y) solution in the coupled equations case.         *
*/

diff_pc2(f,g,a,b,n,eta,psi,px,py,pz,nprnt)
double (*f)(),(*g)();
double a,b,eta,psi,*px,*py,*pz;
int n,nprnt;
{
   int k;
   double x,h,x0,x1,y0,y1,z0,z1,f0,f1,g0,g1,y1p,z1p,f1p,g1p;

      h=(b-a)/n;
      x=a;
      y0=eta;
      z0=psi;
      f0=(*f)(x,y0,z0);
      g0=(*g)(x,y0,z0);
      f1=(*f)(x+h,y0+h*f0,z0+h*g0);
      g1=(*g)(x+h,y0+h*f0,z0+h*g0);
      y1 = y0 + 0.5*h*(f0+f1);
      z1 = z0 + 0.5*h*(g0+g1);
      *px=a;
      *py=eta;
      *pz=psi;
      *(px+1)=a+h;
      *(py+1)=y1;
      *(pz+1)=z1;
      if(nprnt==1){
          printf("%d %10.4e   %10.4e  %10.4e\n",k=0,*px,*py,*pz);
          printf("%d %10.4e   %10.4e  %10.4e\n",k=1,*(px+1),*(py+1),*(pz+1));
      }
      x+=h;

      for(k=2;k<=n;k++){
            f1 = (*f)(x,y1,z1);
            g1 = (*g)(x,y1,z1);
            y1p = y1 + 0.5*h*(3*f1-f0);
            z1p = z1 + 0.5*h*(3*g1-g0);
            x+=h;
            f1p = (*f)(x,y1p,z1p);
            g1p = (*g)(x,y1p,z1p);
```

```
            y1 += 0.5*h*(f1p+f1);
            z1 += 0.5*h*(g1p+g1);
            *(px+k)=x;
            *(py+k)=y1;
            *(pz+k)=z1;
            if(nprnt==1)
                    printf("%d  %12.6e  %12.6e  %12.6e\n",
                                k,*(px+k),*(py+k),*(pz+k));
            f0=f1;
            g0=g1;
    }
}
```

D.11.   DATA NOISE GENERATOR

```
/*                                                                          *
 *    Reference.    Handbook of Mathematical Functions (9th Edition),        *
 * M. Abramowitz and I. A. Stegun (Dover, N.Y. 1972), p. 299.                *
 *                                                                          *
 *    noise()         Returns y with random deviation of Gaussean probability *
 *                    superimposed.                                          *
 *    sigmay          Width of gaussean probability distribution.            *
 *      y             Argument containing number to be operated on.          *
 *                                                                          *
 *    The C library of functions should contain ran(), a random number      *
 *       generator for a uniform distribution over the domain (0,1)          *
 */

#include "libc.h"
#include "math.h"

#define  PI   3.1415926

double noise(n,mode,py,psigmay)
double *py,*psigmay;
int n,mode;
{
    double u1,u2,x,sigmall,ran();
    int i;
    for(i=1;i<=n;i++){
        if(mode==2)sigmall=sqrt(*(py+i));
        else if(mode==1)sigmall=*(psigmay+i);
        else if(mode==0)sigmall=*psigmay;
        u1=ran();
        u2=ran();
        x=sqrt(-2*log(u1))*cos(2*PI*u2);
        *(py+i)+=x*sigmall;
    }
}
```

D.12.   THE LIBRARY HEADER FILE B:NUMRCL.H

The following is a header file that is placed at the begining of each library
function program. It declares each function in the library as well as the data
structures that are used for the linear, polynomial and nonlinear least squares
fitting functions.

```
/*                 mathematical function library              */
double erf(),gamma(),bessel(),voigt();
double noise(),weight();
double intgl_f(),intgl_gl(),diff_f();
double spline_y();
double root_sec(),root_dbt();

/*            dimension of two dimensionsal arrays            */
#define     NTWO       21

/*                structure for linear parameters            */
     struct linear_params{
            double a;
            double b;
            double aerror;
            double berror;
            double r;
            double chi_sq;
     };

/*     structure for polynomial and nonlinear parameters      */
     struct poly_params{
            double a[NTWO];
            double error[NTWO];
            double chi_sq;
     };
```

The BASICA Data Reduction Program Library

This appendix contains the complete set of BASICA/MBASIC library modules that make up the data reduction library. The library was developed in the BASICA* version of BASIC running on the IBM-PC. We have used a subset of BASICA corresponding to the Microsoft MBASIC† version of BASIC running on all CP/M computers. With a CP/M card the programs may also be run on Apple computers. A description of how to use these programs is given in Chapter 10.

The programs may be run in double precision arithmetic. The main program should include the header

```
10 DEFDBL A-H,O-Z
20 DEFINT I-M
```

The trigonometric functions in BASICA/MBASIC are returned in single precision.

E.1. LINEAR LEAST SQUARES FITTING

```
17000 REM**************** LINEAR LEAST SQUARES FIT ********************
17005 REM external in :   XARRAY(),YARRAY(),SIGMAY(),NPTS
17010 REM external out:   AFIT,BFIT,AERROR,BERROR,RCORRLN
17015     ON ERROR GOTO 17140
17020     SUM.G=0#:SUMX.G=0#:SUMY.G=0#:SUMX2.G=0#:SUMXY.G=0#:SUMY2.G=0#
17025     FOR I.G=1 TO NPTS
17030         XI.G=XARRAY(I.G):YI.G=YARRAY(I.G)
17035         IF MODE=0 THEN GOSUB 17125
                  ELSE IF MODE =1 THEN WEIGHT.G=1#
                  ELSE IF MODE =2 THEN WEIGHT.G =1#/(SIGMAY(I.G)*SIGMAY(I.G))
17040         SUM.G=SUM.G+WEIGHT.G
17045         SUMX.G=SUMX.G+WEIGHT.G*XI.G
17050         SUMY.G=SUMY.G+WEIGHT.G*YI.G
```

---

*BASICA is a trademark of IBM Computers, Inc.

†MBASIC is a trademark of Microsoft, Inc., 10700 Northrup Way, Bellevue, WA 98004.

```
17055        SUMX2.G=SUMX2.G+WEIGHT.G*XI.G*XI.G
17060        SUMXY.G=SUMXY.G+WEIGHT.G*XI.G*YI.G
17065        SUMY2.G=SUMY2.G+WEIGHT.G*YI.G*YI.G
17070     NEXT I.G
17075 REM----------------- calculate cofficients etc.
17080     DELTA.G=SUM.G*SUMX2.G-SUMX.G*SUMX.G
17085     AFIT=(SUMX2.G*SUMY.G-SUMX.G*SUMXY.G)/DELTA.G
17090     BFIT=(SUMXY.G*SUM.G-SUMX.G*SUMY.G)/DELTA.G
17095     CHISQ=1#
17100     IF MODE=1 THEN CHISQ=(SUMY2.G+AFIT*AFIT*SUM.G
                + BFIT*BFIT*SUMX2.G-2#*(AFIT*SUMY.G+BFIT*SUMXY.G
                - AFIT*BFIT*SUMX.G))/(NPTS-2)
17105     AERROR=SQR(CHISQ*SUMX2.G/DELTA.G)
17110     BERROR=SQR(CHISQ*SUM.G/DELTA.G)
17115     RCORRLN=(SUM.G*SUMXY.G-SUMX.G*SUMY.G) / (SQR(DELTA.G*(SUM.G*SUMY2.G-
SUMY.G*SUMY.G)))
17120 RETURN
17125 REM-------------------------------------- calculate weights
17130     IF YI.G>0 THEN WEIGHT.G=1/YI.G  ELSE IF YI.G<0 THEN WEIGHT.G =-1/YI.G
ELSE IF YI.G=0 THEN WEIGHT.G =1#
17135 RETURN
17140 REM------------------------------- error trap
17145     PRINT "ERROR # "ERR" IN LINEAR LEAST-SQUARES MODULE AT LINE "ERL
17150 END
17155 REM*************** END OF LINEAR FIT ******************************
```

E.2. POLYNOMIAL LEAST SQUARES FITTING

```
18000 REM********** POLYNOMIAL FITTING ROUTINE *************************
18005 REM options : 1) calculate fitted coefficients  2) error calculation
18010 REM external in :  XARRAY(),YARRAY(),SIGMAY(),NPTS,NDEGREE,MODE
18015 REM external out:  APOLY(0),APOLY(1)....APOLY(NDEGREE)
18020     ON ERROR GOTO 18460
18025     ON NPOLY% GOSUB 18035,18280
18030 RETURN
18035 REM----------------- fitting routine (option 1)
18040     DIM SUMX.H(19),SUMY.H(10)
18045     DIM SMTRX(10,10),BCLM(10),XCLM(10)
18050     NTERMS.H=NDEGREE+1:NMAX.H=2*NTERMS.H-1
18055     FOR K.H=1 TO NMAX.H:SUMX.H(K.H)=0#:NEXT K.H
18060     FOR J.H=0 TO NTERMS.H:SUMY.H(J.H)=0#:NEXT J.H
18070     FOR I.H=1 TO NPTS
18075        XI.H=XARRAY(I.H):YI.H=YARRAY(I.H)
18080        IF MODE=0 THEN GOSUB 18420
                    ELSE IF MODE =1 THEN WEIGHT.H=1#
                    ELSE IF MODE=2 THEN WEIGHT.H=1#/(SIGMA(I.H)*SIGMA(I.H))
18085        XTERM.H=WEIGHT.H
18090        FOR K.H=1 TO NMAX.H
18095           SUMX.H(K.H)=SUMX.H(K.H)+XTERM.H
18100           XTERM.H=XTERM.H*XI.H
18105        NEXT K.H
18110        YTERM.H=WEIGHT.H*YI.H
18115        FOR K.H=1 TO NTERMS.H
18120           SUMY.H(K.H)=SUMY.H(K.H)+YTERM.H
18125           YTERM.H=YTERM.H*XI.H
18130        NEXT K.H
18135        SUMY.H(0)=SUMY.H(0)+WEIGHT.H*YI.H*YI.H
18140     NEXT I.H
```

```
18145 REM------- -------------------- construct matrices
18150     FOR J.H=1 TO NTERMS.H
18155         FOR K.H=1 TO NTERMS.H
18160             N.H=J.H+K.H-1
18165             SMTRX(J.H,K.H)=SUMX.H(N.H)
18170         NEXT K.H
18175     NEXT J.H
18180     FOR K.H=1 TO NTERMS.H
18185         BCLM(K.H)=SUMY.H(K.H)
18190     NEXT K.H
18195     MDEGREE=NTERMS.H
18200     NEWA=1
18205     NMATRIX% = 1 : GOSUB 14000
18210     FOR K.H=0 TO NDEGREE:APOLY(K.H)=XCLM(K.H+1):NEXT K.H
18220      REM------------- calculate chisqr
18230     CHISQ=SUMY.H(0)
18235     FOR J.H=1 TO NTERMS.H
18240         CHISQ=CHISQ-2#*APOLY(J.H)*SUMY.H(J.H)
18245         FOR K.H=1 TO NTERMS
18250             N.H=J.H+K.H-1
18255             CHISQ=CHISQ+APOLY(J.H)*APOLY(K.H)*SUMX.H(N.H)
18260         NEXT K.H
18265     NEXT J.H
18270     CHISQ=CHISQ/(NPTS-NTERMS.H)
18275 RETURN
18280 REM--------------------- error calculation (option 2)
18290     SSQR.H=0
18300     FOR I.H=1 TO NPTS
18310        YI.H=APOLY(NDEGREE)
18320        FOR J.H = NDEGREE-1 TO 0 STEP -1
18330            YI.H=YI.H*XARRAY(I.H)+APOLY(J.H)
18340        NEXT J.H
18350        SSQR.H=SSQR.H+(YI.H-YARRAY(I.H))^2
18360     NEXT I.H
18365     NEWA=0
18370     NMATRIX%=3:GOSUB 14000
18375     SSQR.H=SSQR.H/(NPTS-NTERMS.H)
18380     FOR J.H=0 TO NDEGREE
18390        AERROR(J.H)=SQR(SSQR.H*SMTRX(J.H+1,J.H+1))
18400     NEXT J.H
18410 RETURN
18420 REM--------------------------- statistical weight
18430     IF YI.H>0 THEN WEIGHT.H=1/YI.H ELSE IF YI.H<0 THEN WEIGHT.H =-1/YI.H
ELSE IF YI.H=0 THEN WEIGHT.H=1
18440 RETURN
18450 REM--------------------------- error trap
18460     IF (ERR=10) AND (ERL=18040) THEN RESUME 18045
18470     IF (ERR=10) AND (ERL=18045) THEN RESUME 18050
18480     PRINT "error number "ERR" in polyfit module at line "ERL
18490 END
18500 REM**************************************************************
```

E.3. NON-LINEAR LEAST SQUARES FITTING

```
10600 REM-------------- FUNCTION Y = F( X , APARAM() ) FOR NON-LINEAR FIT
10695 RETURN
19000 REM************* NONLINEAR LEAST SQUARES FIT ********************
```

```
19005 REM Marquard algorithm for least-squares fitting
19010 REM options:  1) fitted parameter calculation : 2) error calculation
19015 REM external in : XARRAY(),YARRAY(),SIGMAY(),NPTS,NTERMS,function with
19020 REM                parameters APARAM() at 10600,DELTAA(),NDERIV
19025 REM external out:  CHISQ,APARAM()
19030      ON ERROR GOTO 19520                    :REM error trap
19031      ON NONLNFIT% GOSUB 19034,19330         :REM choose option
19032      ON ERROR GOTO 0                        :REM reset error trap
19033 RETURN                                      :REM return to main program
19034 REM----------------Option 1         non-linear fit
19035      DIM ALPHA.I(10,10),BETA.I(10),DERIV.I(10),BDUM.I(10),WEIGHT.I(100)
19040      DIM SMTRX(10,10),BCLM(10),XCLM(10)    :REM global for matrix module
19042 .    RESTORE 19534
19043      READ FLAMDA.I,DELTA.I,NMAX.I,EPSLN1.I,EPSLN2.I :REM convergence pr.
19045      NFREE.I = NPTS-NTERMS : IF NFREE.I<=0 THEN RETURN
19050      MODE.I = MODE                         :REM internal weight parameter
19060      GOSUB 19495                           :REM weighting function calcn.
19062      REM---------------------- Solution loop
19064      FOR NPASS.I=1 TO NMAX.I
19070        REM-----------------evaluate alpha and beta matrices
19075        FOR JJ.I=1 TO NTERMS
19080           FOR KK.I=1 TO NTERMS
19085              ALPHA.I(JJ.I,KK.I)=0#
19090           NEXT KK.I
19095           BETA.I(JJ.I)=0#
19100        NEXT JJ.I
19105        FOR I.I=1 TO NPTS
19110           X=XARRAY(I.I)
19115           IF NDERIV=0 THEN GOSUB 19440 ELSE IF NDERIV=1 THEN GOSUB 10650
19120           X=XARRAY(I.I) : GOSUB 10600               :REM calculate function
19125           FOR J.I=1 TO NTERMS
19130              BETA.I(J.I) = BETA.I(J.I)
19130                        + WEIGHT.I(I.I)*(YARRAY(I.I)-Y)*DERIV.I(J.I)
19135              FOR K.I=1 TO J.I
19140                 ALPHA.I(J.I,K.I)=ALPHA.I(J.I,K.I)
19140                           + WEIGHT.I(I.I)*DERIV.I(J.I)*DERIV.I(K.I)
19145              NEXT K.I
19150           NEXT J.I
19155        NEXT I.I
19160        FOR J.I=1 TO NTERMS
19165           FOR K.I=1 TO J.I
19170              ALPHA.I(K.I,J.I)=ALPHA.I(J.I,K.I)
19175           NEXT K.I
19180        NEXT J.I
19185        GOSUB 19400
19190        CHISQR1.I=CHISQR2.I
19195        REM----------------------------find solution
19200        FOR J.I=1 TO NTERMS
19205           FOR K.I=1 TO NTERMS
19210              SMTRX(J.I,K.I)=ALPHA.I(J.I,K.I)
19215           NEXT K.I
19220           SMTRX(J.I,J.I)=(1+FLAMDA.I)*ALPHA.I(J.I,J.I)
19225           BCLM(J.I)=BETA.I(J.I)
19230        NEXT J.I
19235        MDEGREE=NTERMS
19240        NMATRIX%=1 : NEWA = 1 : GOSUB 14000   :REM  Solve Ax = b
19250        FOR JJ.I=1 TO NTERMS
19255           XCLM(JJ.I) = APARAM(JJ.I) + XCLM(JJ.I)
19260           SWAP XCLM(JJ.I),APARAM(JJ.I)  :REM  new parameters in APARAM()
19270        NEXT JJ.I                        :REM  old in XCLM()
```

```
19275        GOSUB 19400
19290        DELTACHI.I=CHISQR2.I-CHISQR1.I
19295        IF DELTACHI.I<=0 THEN FLAMDA.I=FLAMDA.I/10:GOTO 19315
19300        FOR I.I=1 TO NTERMS:SWAP APARAM(I.I),XCLM(I.I):NEXT I.I
19305        FLAMDA.I=10#*FLAMDA.I          :REM  old back in APARAM()
19310        GOTO 19195
19315        REM----------------- a new solution found
19320        CHISQ = CHISQR2.I
19321        IF NPRINT=1 THEN GOSUB 19516
19322        IF NPASS.I=NMAX.I
                  THEN PRINT "FIT DID NOT CONVERGE AFTER "NMAX.I" PASSES"
                  :GOTO 19326
19324        IF ABS(DELTACHI.I) < (EPSLN1.I*CHISQR1.I)
                  THEN PRINT "CONVERGENCE CONDITION 1 SATISFIED":NPASS.I=NMAX.I
19325        IF ABS(DELTACHI.I) < EPSLN2.I
                  THEN PRINT "CONVERGENCE CONDITION 2 SATISFIED":NPASS.I=NMAX.I
19326     NEXT NPASS.I
19328 RETURN
19330 REM-------------------Option 2         error calculation
19335     MODE.I = 1 : GOSUB 19495          :REM weighting function calcn.
19337     NEWA = 0                          :REM keep same matrix A
19340     MDGREE = NTERMS
19345     NMATRIX% = 3 : GOSUB 14000        :REM inverse matrix calcn.
19350     FOR J.I=1 TO NTERMS
19355        AERROR(J.I) = SQR( CHISQ * SMTRX(J.I,J.I) )
19360     NEXT J.I
19395 RETURN
19400 REM----------- -----------------------------evaluate chisquared
19405     CHISQR2.I=0
19410     FOR I.I=1 TO NPTS
19415        X=XARRAY(I.I):GOSUB 10600
19420        CHISQR2.I=CHISQR2.I+WEIGHT.I(I.I)*(Y-YARRAY(I.I))^2
19425     NEXT I.I
19430     CHISQR2.I=CHISQR2.I/NFREE.I
19435 RETURN
19440 REM----------- --------------------------derivative calculation
19445     FOR JJ.I=1 TO NTERMS
19450        AJJ.I=APARAM(JJ.I)
19455        IF DELTA.I=0# THEN DERIV.I(JJ.I)=0#:GOTO 19485
19460        APARAM(JJ.I)=AJJ.I+DELTA.I:GOSUB 10600.REM CALCULATE POINT
19465        YLST.I=Y
19470        APARAM(JJ.I)=AJJ.I-DELTA.I:GOSUB 10600
19475        DERIV.I(JJ.I)=(YLST.I-Y)/(2#*DELTA.I)
19480        APARAM(JJ.I)=AJJ.I
19485     NEXT JJ.I
19490 RETURN
19495 REM-==================================weighting function
19500     FOR I.I=1 TO NPTS
19505        IF MODE.I=0 THEN WEIGHT.I(I.I) = 1#/(SIGMAY(I.I)*SIGMAY(I.I))
                  ELSE IF MODE.I =1 THEN WEIGHT.I(I.I)=1#
                  ELSE IF MODE.I =2 THEN WEIGHT.I(I.I)=1#/SQR(ABS(YARRAY(I.I)))
19510     NEXT I.I
19515 RETURN
19516 REM--------------------------------------- printing
19517     PRINT "PASS ";NPASS.I;" SOLUTION":PRINT "CHIS_SQUARE = "CHISQ
19518     FOR JJ.I=1 TO NTERMS
              :PRINT "PARAMETER ";JJ.I" = ";APARAM(JJ.I): NEXT JJ.I
19519 RETURN
19520 REM--------------------------------------------------error trap
19525     IF (ERR=10) AND (ERL=19035) THEN RESUME 19040
```

```
19530      IF (ERR=10) AND (ERL=19040) THEN RESUME 19055
19533      PRINT "ERROR # "ERR" IN NON-LINEAR FIT MODULE AT LINE "ERL
19534      DATA 0.001,0.001,10,1.0E-5,1.0E-5
19535 END
19540 REM****************** END OF NON-LINEAR FIT *********************
```

E.4.   SAVITSKY-GOLAY DATA SMOOTHING

```
21000 REM***************** SAVITSKY-GOLAY SMOOTHING ********************
21005 REM external in :   NPTS,YARRAY()
21010 REM external out:   YSMTH(),YDRV()
21020      ON ERROR GOTO 21500
21040      DIM SMTH.K(7),DSMTH.K(7)
21060      RESTORE 21520
21080      FOR J.K=0 TO 7:READ SMTH.K(J.K):NEXT J.K
21100      FOR J.K=0 TO 7:READ DSMTH.K(J.K):NEXT J.K
21110 REM--------------------------------- smoothing routine
21120      FOR I.K=4 TO NPTS-3
21125          YSMTH(I.K)=0:YDRV(I.K)=0
21130          FOR J.K=1 TO 7
21140              YSMTH(I.K)=YSMTH(I.K)+YARRAY(I.K-J.K+4)*SMTH.K(J.K)/SMTH.K(0)
21150              YDRV(I.K)=YDRV(I.K)+YARRAY(I.K-J.K+4)*DSMTH.K(J.K)/DSMTH.K(0)
21160          NEXT J.K
21190      NEXT I.K
21195      ON ERROR GOTO 0
21300 RETURN
21500 REM--------------------------------- error trap
21510 IF (ERR=10) AND (ERL=21040) THEN RESUME 21110
21515 REM--------------------------------- data
21520 DATA 21,-2,3,6,7,6,3,-2
21530 DATA 28,-3,-2,-1,0,1,2,3
21540 REM****************** END OF S-G ROUTINE ********************
```

E.5.   THE FAST FOURIER TRANSFORM

```
20000 REM****************** FAST FOURIER TRANSFORM MODULE ***********
20002 REM options: 1) fft or inverse  : 2) convolution
20004 REM external in : NFFT%,NU,YREAL(),YIMAG(),ISIGN,IHNG
20006 REM external out: YREAL(),YIMAG()
20010      N=2^NU
20015      PI=3.1415926#
20020      ON NFFT% GOSUB 20030,20670
20025 RETURN
20030 REM----------------- the fft calculation (option 1)
20040      IF IHNG=1 THEN GOSUB 20590
20050      IF ISIGN=1 THEN GOSUB 20150
20060      IF ISIGN=-1 THEN GOTO 20070 ELSE PRINT"ISIGN UNDEFINED":RETURN
20070      FOR K.J=0 TO N-1
20080          YIMAG(K.J)=-YIMAG(K.J)
20090      NEXT K.J
20100      GOSUB 20150
20110      FOR K.J=0 TO N-1
20120          YIMAG(K.J)=-YIMAG(K.J)/N
20130      NEXT K.J
20140 RETURN
```

```
20150 REM -------------------------- basic fft subroutine
20155     N2.J=N/2
20160     NU1.J=NU-1
20170     K.J=0
20180     FOR L.J=1 TO NU
20190         FOR I.J=1 TO N2.J
20200             IALPHA=INT(K.J/(2^NU1.J)):GOSUB 20490
20210             P.J=IBITR
20220             ARG.J=6.28319*P.J/CDBL(N)
20230             C.J=COS(ARG.J)
20240             S.J=SIN(ARG.J)
20250             K1N2.J=K.J+N2.J
20260             TREAL.J=YREAL(K1N2.J)*C.J+YIMAG(K1N2.J)*S.J
20270             TIMAG.J=YIMAG(K1N2.J)*C.J-YREAL(K1N2.J)*S.J
20280             YREAL(K1N2.J)=YREAL(K.J)-TREAL.J
20290             YIMAG(K1N2.J)=YIMAG(K.J)-TIMAG.J
20300             YREAL(K.J)=YREAL(K.J)+TREAL.J
20310             YIMAG(K.J)=YIMAG(K.J)+TIMAG.J
20320             K.J=K.J+1
20330         NEXT I.J
20340         K.J=K.J+N2.J
20350         IF K.J<N-1 THEN GOTO 20190
20360         K.J=0
20370         NU1.J=NU1.J-1
20380         N2.J=N2.J/2
20390     NEXT L.J
20400     FOR K.J=0 TO N-1
20410         IALPHA.J=K.J:GOSUB 20490
20420         I.J=IBITR.J
20430         IF I.J<=K.J THEN GOTO 20460
20440         SWAP YREAL(I.J),YREAL(K.J)
20450         SWAP YIMAG(I.J),YIMAG(K.J)
20460     NEXT K.J
20470 RETURN
20480 END
20490 REM-------------------------- calculate function ibitr(ialpha)
20500     IALPHA1.J=IALPHA.J
20510     IBITR.J=0
20520     FOR II.J=1 TO NU
20530         IALPHA2.J=INT(IALPHA1.J/2)
20540         IBITR.J=IBITR.J*2+(IALPHA1.J-2*IALPHA2.J)
20550         IALPHA1.J=IALPHA2.J
20560     NEXT II.J
20570 RETURN
20590 REM-------------------------------------- hanning function
20610     FOR K.J=0 TO N-1
20620         HN.J=(1+COS(2*PI*K.J/N))/2
20630         YREAL(K.J)=YREAL(K.J)*HN.J:YIMAG(K.J)=YIMAG(K.J)*HN.J
20640         PRINT "HANNING",K.J,YREAL(K.J),YIMAG(K.J)
20650     NEXT K.J
20660 RETURN
20670 REM-------------------------- convolution calculation (option 2)
20680     DIM YTMPR.J(128),YTMPI.J(128)
20685     ISIGN=1
20690     FOR I.J=0 TO N-1
20695         YTMPR.J(I.J)=0:YTMPI.J(I.J)=0
20700         SWAP YTMPR.J(I.J),YIMAG(I.J)
20705         PRINT "ARRAYS", YREAL(I.J),YIMAG(I.J),YTMPR.J(I.J),YTMPI.J(I.J)
20710     NEXT I.J
20720     GOSUB 20030
```

```
20730     FOR I.J=0 TO N-1
20740         SWAP YREAL(I.J),YTMPR.J(I.J)
20750         SWAP YIMAG(I.J),YTMPI.J(I.J)
20755         PRINT "FIRST",I.J,YTMPR.J(I.J),YTMPI.J(I.J)
20760     NEXT I.J
20770     GOSUB 20030
20772     FOR I.J=0 TO N-1
20773         PRINT "SECOND",I.J,YREAL(I.J),YIMAG(I.J)
20774     NEXT I.J
20780     FOR I.J=0 TO N-1
20790         YREAL(I.J)=YREAL(I.J)*YTMPR.J(I.J)-YIMAG(I.J)*YTMPI.J(I.J)
20800         YIMAG(I.J)=YREAL(I.J)*YTMPI.J(I.J)+YIMAG(I.J)*YTMPR.J(I.J)
20805         PRINT "MULTIPLIED",I.J,YREAL(I.J),YIMAG(I.J)
20810     NEXT I.J
20815     IHNG=0
20820     ISIGN=-1:GOSUB 20030
20825     FOR I.J=0 TO N-1
20826         PRINT "SMOOTHED DATA",I.J,YREAL(I.J),YIMAG(I.J)
20827     NEXT I.J
20830 RETURN
20840 REM**************** END OF FFT MODULE ***************************
```

Appendix F

The C Data Reduction Program Library

This appendix contains the complete set of C functions that make up the data reduction library. The library was developed in the Aztek version of C.* The program should compile without modifications under all versions of the Aztek C compiler on the IBM-PC and IBM compatibles, all CP/M computer systems, and the Apple II plus and IIe. Some modification to the language syntax may be necessary with other C compilers. All functions are written to run under double precision arithmetic. We have attempted at all times to use standard Kernighan and Ritchie† syntax in all C code. However, we cannot accept any liability if errors are found in these programs. A description on how to run these functions is given in Chapter 10.

F.1. LINEAR LEAST SQUARES FITTING

```
*/
*   Reference: Data Reduction and Error Analysis for the Physical Sciences.   *
*                P. H. Bevington, McGraw Hill, N.Y. (1969).                   *
*                                                                             *
*    linear_fit()     Operator that carries out the linear fit.              *
*        npts          Number of Data Points                                 *
*        mode          Defines weighting function.                           *
*        x[],y[]       x,y data pairs                                        *
*        psigmay[]     Statistical factor used for mode=2;                    *
*           pl         Pointer to data structure containing fitted constants. *
*/

#include "libc.h"
#include "math.h"
#include "b:numrcl.h"

linear_fit(npts,mode,px,py,psigmay,pl)
int npts,mode;
double *px,*py,*psigmay;
struct linear_params *pl;
{
```

---

*Aztek C is a trademark of Manx Software Systems.

†*The C Programming Language*, B. W. Kernighan and D. M. Ritchie, (Prentice-Hall, Englewood Cliffs, N.J., 1978).

```
int i;
double sum,sumx,sumy,sumx2,sumxy,sumy2;
double wght,delta,v;

sum=sumx=sumy=sumx2=sumxy=sumy2=0;
for(i=0;i<=npts;i++){
        wght=weight(i,mode,psigmay,py);
        sum += wght;
        sumx += *(px+i)*wght;
        sumy += *(py+i)*wght;
        sumx2 += *(px+i)*(*(px+i))*wght;
        sumxy += *(px+i)*(*(py+i))*wght;
        sumy2 += *(py+i)*(*(py+i))*wght;
    }
delta = sum*sumx2-sumx*sumx;
pl->a = (sumx2*sumy-sumx*sumxy)/delta;
pl->b= (sumxy*sum-sumx*sumy)/delta;
v = (sumy2+(pl->a)*(pl->a)*sum + (pl->b)*(pl->b)*sumx2
    -2*((pl->a)*sumy+(pl->b)*sumxy-(pl->a)*(pl->b)*sumx))/(npts-2);
pl->aerror = sqrt(v*sumx2/delta);
pl->berror = sqrt(v*sum/delta);
pl->r = (sum*sumxy-sumx*sumy)/sqrt(delta*(sum*sumy2-sumy*sumy));
pl->chi_sq = v;
}
```

F.2.   POLYNOMIAL LEAST SQUARES FITTING FUNCTION

```
/*                                                                      *
*   Reference. Data Reduction and Error Analysis for the Physical Sciences.  *
*              P. H. Bevington, McGraw Hill, N.Y. (1969).              *
*                                                                      *
*   linear_fit()    Operator that carries out the linear fit.          *
*      npts         Number of Data Points.                             *
*      mode         Treatment of weighting.                            *
*      x[],y[]      x,y data pairs                                      *
*      psigmay[]    Statistical factor used for mode=2;                *
*      npoly        Degree of Polynomial to be fitted                  *
*       p           Pointer to data structure containing fitted constants.  *
*/

#include    "libc.h"
#include    "math.h"
#include    "b:numrcl.h"

poly_fit(npts,px,py,mode,psigmay,ndegree,p)
int npts,mode,ndegree;
double *px,*py,*psigmay;
struct poly_params   *p;
{
    int nmax,nterms,n,newa,i,k,j;
    double sumx[2*NTWO-1],sumy[NTWO],array[NTWO][NTWO];
    double b[NTWO],x[NTWO],epsln[NTWO][NTWO],wght,xterm,yterm,det;

    nterms = ndegree+1;
    nmax = 2*nterms-1;
/*                        accumilate weights                    */
```

```
    *sumy=0;
    for(k=1;k<=nmax;k++)*(sumx+k)=0;
    for(k=1;k<=nterms;k++)*(sumy+k)=0;
    for(i=1;i<=npts;i++){
        wght = weight(i,mode,psigmay,py);
        xterm = wght;
        for(n=1;n<=nmax;n++){
            *(sumx+n)+=xterm;
            xterm*=(*(px+i));
        }
        yterm = wght*(*(py+i));
        for(n=1;n<=nterms;n++){
            *(sumy+n)+=yterm;
            yterm *=(*(px+i));
        }

        *sumy += wght*(*(py+i))*(*(py+i));
    }
    for(j=1;j<=nterms;j++){
        for(k=1;k<=nterms;k++)
            array[j][k] =*(sumx+(j+k-1));
        b[j] = *(sumy+j);
    }
    mtrx_sln(nterms,newa=1,&array,&x,&b,&det);
    for(k=0;k<=ndegree;k++)p->a[k] = x[k+1];

/*          calculate chisquared                              */

    p->chi_sq = *sumy;
    for(j=1;j<=nterms;j++){
        p->chi_sq -= 2*x[j]*(*(sumy+j));
        for(k=1;k<=nterms;k++)
            p->chi_sq += x[j]*x[k]*(*(sumx+(j+k-1)));
    }
    p->chi_sq /= (npts-nterms);

/*          calculate errors                                  */

    if(mode==1){
        mtrx_inv(nterms,&array,&epsln);
        for(k=0;k<=ndegree;k++)
            p->error[k] = sqrt(p->chi_sq*epsln[k+1][k+1]);
    }
    else printf("Warning!\n Calculate errors with mode=1");
}
```

F.3. NON-LINEAR LEAST SQUARES FITTING FUNCTIONS

```
p/*
 *   Reference. Data Reduction and Error Analysis for the Physical Sciences.
 *                P. H. Bevington, McGraw Hill Book, N.Y. (1969).
 *
 *   nonlnr_fit()   Operator that carries out the non-linear fit.
 *     fnctn()      Function to be fit to the data
 *      npts        Number of Data Points.
 *     x[],y[]      x,y data pairs.
```

```
*         mode             Treatment of weighting factor.                    *
*         psigmay[]        Statistical factor used for mode=2.               *
*         nterms           Number of free parameters  1 .... nterms to be fit. *
*         ps               Pointer to data structure containing fitted constants. *
*         nprint           screen print parameter.                          *
*/

#include "libc.h"
#include "math.h"
#include "b:numrcl.h"

#define NUMPTS 200
#define NMAX 20
#define DELTA 0.001
#define EPSLN1 0.000001
#define EPSLN2 0.000001
#define FLAMDA 0.001

static double alpha[NTWO][NTWO],beta[NTWO],deriv[NTWO];
static double array[NTWO][NTWO],epsln[NTWO][NTWO],prmts[NTWO];
static double wght[NUMPTS];

nonlnr_fit(fnctn,npts,px,py,mode,psigmay,nterms,ps,nprint)
int npts,mode,nterms,nprint;
double (*fnctn)(),*px,*py,*psigmay;
struct poly_params *ps;
{
    int i,j,k,npass,newa,nconvrg = 0;
    double idbl,dlta,chisqr,chsq1,lamda,det;
    double xclm[NTWO],bclm[NTWO];
    double chisq();

/*            initialization                            */
    for(i=1;i<=npts;i++)
            *(wght+i)=weight(i,mode,psigmay,py);
    lamda=FLAMDA;

/*            solution loop                             */
    for(npass=1;npass<=NMAX;npass++){

/*            evaluate alpha and beta matrices          */
        for(j=1;j<=nterms;j++){
                *(beta+j)=0;
                for(k=1;k<=j;k++)alpha[j][k]=0;
        }
        for(i=1;i<=npts;i++){
            for(j=1;j<=nterms;j++)*(prmts+j)=ps->a[j];
            grad(fnctn,px,i,nterms);
            for(j=1;j<=nterms;j++){
                dlta=*(py+i)-(*fnctn)(nterms,*(px+i),prmts);
                *(beta+j)+=wght[i]*dlta*(*(deriv+j));
                for(k=1;k<=j;k++){
                        alpha[j][k]+= (*(wght+i))*(*(deriv+j))*(*(deriv+k));
                }
            }
        }
        for(j=1;j<=nterms;j++){
                for(k=1;k<=j;k++)alpha[k][j]=alpha[j][k];
        }
```

```
/*           evaluate chi square at starting point          */
      chsq1=chisq(fnctn,npts,px,py,nterms);

/*           create alphaprime matrix and invert            */
        do{
            for(j=1;j<=nterms;j++){
                for(k=1;k<=nterms;k++){
                    array[j][k]=alpha[j][k];
                }
                bclm[j]=beta[j];
                array[j][j]=alpha[j][j]*(1+lamda);
            }

            mtrx_sln(nterms,newa=1,&array,&xclm,&bclm,&det);

            for(j=1;j<=nterms;j++){
                prmts[j]=xclm[j]+(ps->a[j]);
            }
            chisqr=chisq(fnctn,npts,px,py,nterms);
            if(chisqr>chsq1)lamda*=10;
            if(nprint==1){
                printf("\n\nINTERMEDIATE RESULTS:\n");
                printf("npass = %4d     lamda = %10.4e\n",npass,lamda);
                printf("chi_squared = %10.4e\n",chisqr);
                for(j=1;j<=nterms;j++)
                        printf("parameter %4d - %12.6e\n",j,prmts[j]);
            }
        }while(chisqr > chsq1);

        for(j=1;j<=nterms;j++)(ps->a[j])+=(*(xclm+j));
        if(fabs(chisqr-chsq1)<EPSLN2){
            printf("convergence 2 after %4d iterations \n",npass);
            nconvrg = 2;
        }
        if(fabs(chisqr-chsq1)<EPSLN1*chisqr){
            printf("convergence 1 after %4d iterations \n",npass);
            nconvrg = 1;
        }
        if(nconvrg > 0){
            mtrx_tri(nterms,&alpha,&det);
            mtrx_inv(nterms,&alpha,&epsln);
            for(j=1;j<=nterms;j++)
                    ps->error[j]=sqrt(chisqr*epsln[j][j]);
            ps->chi_sq = chisqr;
            return;
        }
        lamda/=10;
        chsq1=chisqr;
    }
    printf("Fit did not converge after NMAX\n");
}

/*           partial derivative calculation              */

grad(fnctn,px,i,nterms)
int i,nterms;
double (*fnctn)(),*px;
{
```

```
    int j;
    double yfit,yfit2,aj;

    for(j=1;j<=nterms;j++){
        aj=*(prmts+j);
        *(prmts+j)=aj+DELTA;
        yfit = (*fnctn)(nterms,*(px+i),prmts);
        *(prmts+j)=aj-DELTA;
        yfit2 = (*fnctn)(nterms,*(px+i),prmts);
        deriv[j]=(yfit-yfit2)/(2*DELTA);
        *(prmts+j)=aj;
    }
}


chisq(fnctn,npts,px,py,nterms)
int npts,nterms;
double (*fnctn)(),*px,*py;
{
    int nfree,i;
    double ch,dlta;

    ch=0;
    for(i=1;i<=npts;i++){
        dlta=(*(py+i)-(*fnctn)(nterms,*(px+i),prmts));
        ch+=*(wght+i)*dlta*dlta;
    }
    nfree=npts-nterms;
    ch/=nfree;
    return ch;
}
```

F.4.   FAST FOURIER TRANSFORM OPERATIONS

```
/*
*   Reference. The Fast Fourier Transform:   E. Oran Brigham
*                   (Prentice-Hall, Englewood Cliffs, N.J.1974), p. 161.
*/

#include "libc.h"
#include "math.h"

#define NFFT 1024
#define PI 3.1415926
#define hanning(K) (1+cos((2*PI*K)/n))

fft_cnvl(nu,hng,pareal,pbreal)
int nu,hng;
double *pareal,*pbreal;
{
    int k,n,sgn;
    double aimag[NFFT],bimag[NFFT],tempa,tempb;

    n = pwr2(nu);
    for(k=0;k<=n;k++)bimag[k]=aimag[k]=0;
    fft(nu,sgn=1,hng,pareal,&aimag);
    fft(nu,sgn=1,hng,pbreal,&bimag);
    for(k=0;k<=n-1;k++){
        tempa=*(pareal+k);
```

```
            tempb=*(pbreal+k);
            printf("%4d    %12.6e       %12.6e\n",k,tempa,tempb);
            *(pareal+k)=tempa*tempb-aimag[k]*bimag[k];
            *(pbreal+k)=aimag[k]*tempb+tempa*bimag[k];
    }
    fft(nu,sgn=-1,hng,pareal,pbreal);
}


fft(nu,sgn,hng,pyreal,pyimag)
int nu,sgn,hng;
double *pyreal,*pyimag;
{
    int pwr2(),n,k;

    n=pwr2(nu);
    if(hng==1){
        for(k=0;k<=n-1;k++){
            *(pyreal+k) *= hanning(k);
            *(pyimag+k) *= hanning(k);
        }
    }
    if(sgn==1)           fft_prm(nu,pyreal,pyimag);
    else if(sgn==-1){
        for(k=0;k<=n-1;k++)*(pyimag+k)*=-1;
        fft_prm(nu,pyreal,pyimag);
        for(k=0;k<=n-1;k++)*(pyimag+k)/=(-n);
    }
}



fft_prm(nu,pyreal,pyimag)
int nu;
double *pyreal,*pyimag;
{
    double treal,timag,p,arg,c,s;
    int n,n2,nu1,i,l,k;
    int pwr2(),bitrev();

    n=pwr2(nu);
    printf("passed parameter n= %6d nu= %6d\n",n,nu);
    n2 = n / 2;
    nu1 = nu-1;
    k = 0;
    for (l = 1; l <= nu; l++)
    {
        do {
            for (i = 1; i<=n2 ; i++)
            {
                p = bitrev(k/pwr2(nu1),nu);
                arg = 2 * PI * p / n;
                c = cos(arg);
                s = sin(arg);
                treal = *(pyreal+k+n2) * c + *(pyimag+k+n2) * s;
                timag = *(pyimag+k+n2) * c - *(pyreal+k+n2) * s;
                *(pyreal+k+n2) = *(pyreal+k) - treal;
                *(pyimag+k+n2) = *(pyimag+k) - timag;
                *(pyreal+k) += treal;
                *(pyimag+k) += timag;
                k=k+1;
            }
```

```
                k=k + n2;
         } while( k <n-1);
         k=0;
         nu1 = nu1-1;
         n2 = n2 / 2;
      }
   for (k=0;k<=n-1;k++){
            i=bitrev(k,nu);
            if (i > k) {
                  treal = *(pyreal+k);
                  timag = *(pyimag+k);
                  *(pyreal+k) = *(pyreal+i);
                  *(pyimag+k) = *(pyimag+i);
                  *(pyreal+i) = treal;
                  *(pyimag+i) = timag;
            }
      }

}


int bitrev(j,nu)
int j,nu;
{
   int i,j1,j2,k;

   j1 = j;
   k = 0;
   for (i = 1; i<= nu; i++) {
      j2 = j1 / 2;
      k = 2 * k + (j1 - 2*j2);
      j1 = j2;
   }
   return (k);
}

int pwr2(n)
int n;
{
    int p,i;

    p=1;
    for(i=1;i<=n; ++i) p = p*2;
    return(p);
}
```

F.5. THE WEIGHING FUNCTION FOR FITTING ROUTINES

```
/*                                                                   *
 *    Reference    "Data reduction and Error Analysis for the Physical
 *                 Sciences", P. R. Bevington, McGraw-Hill. N.Y. (1969).
 *    weight()     Returns weight factor for point i in data series
 *    mode         =0   Individual statistical weights for each data point.*
 *                 =1   Equal weights of unity for each point.            *
 *                 =2   Poisson weighting distribution.                   *
 *    psigmay      Individual statistical weights; Used for mode=0 only.  *
 *    y[]          Array of y data points; Pass the address &y.           *
 */
```

```
#include "libc.h"
#include "math.h"
#include "b:numrcl.h"

#define ONE 1

double weight(i,mode,psigmay,py)
int i,mode;
double *psigmay,*py;
{
    double sg;
    if(mode==0){
        sg=*(psigmay+i);
        return (1/(sg*sg));
    }
    else if(mode==1)
            return (ONE);
    else if(mode==2)
            return (1/(*(py+i)));
    else
            printf("mode out of range\n");
}
```

Appendix **G**
Binary
Arithmetic

As indicated previously a computer understands only two states: on or off, high or low, and so on. Complex instructions can be written as a combination of these two states. To represent these two conditions mathematically, we can use the digits 1 and 0. We already have described how numbers can be represented in both the binary and hexadecimal systems. Some simple mathematical operations, such as direct binary addition and subtraction, as well as the two's complement subtraction procedure used by most computers, will be reviewed here.

DIRECT BINARY ADDITION

In binary arithmetic if one adds 1 and 1 the answer is 10. The answer is not decimal 10. It is *one zero*. There are only two digits in the binary system. Therefore, when one adds 1 and 1, one gets 0 and a carry of 1 to give 10. Similarly, in the decimal system, $5 + 5$ is equal to zero with a carry of 1. Here are some examples of binary addition.

```
column  4 3 2 1
          0 1 1 1
        + 0 1 1 1
          1 1 1 0
```

In column 1, $1 + 1 = 0$ and a carry of 1. Column 2 now contains $1 + 1 + 1$. This addition, $1 + 1 = 0$ carry 1 and $0 + 1 = 1$, is entered in the sum. Column 3 now also contains $1 + 1 + 1$, which gives a 1 with a carry of 1 to column 4. The answer to the next example is found in a similar manner.

```
  1 0 0 1 1 0 1 1
+ 0 0 1 1 1 1 1 1
  1 1 0 1 1 0 1 0
```

DIRECT BINARY SUBTRACTION

Although binary numbers may be subtracted directly from each other, it is easier from a computer-design standpoint to use another method of subtraction, called *two's complement* subtraction. This will be illustrated next. However, to enable the reader to follow the hand-division example in Chapter 9, direct binary subtraction will be discussed also.

Direct binary subtraction is similar to decimal subtraction, except that when a borrow occurs, it complements the value of the number. Remember also that the value of the number 1 depends on the column in which it is situated. The values increase according to the power series of 2: that is, $2^0, 2^1, 2^2$, and so on, in columns 1, 2, 3, and so on. Thus, if you borrow from column 3 you are borrowing a decimal 4.

In the example

$$
\begin{array}{r}
\text{column } 3\ 2\ 1 \\ \hline
1\ 1\ 0 \\
-\ 1\ 0\ 1 \\ \hline
0\ 0\ 1 \\
\end{array}
$$

a borrow had to be made from column 2, which changed its value to 0 while putting decimal 2 (or binary 11) in column 1. Thus, after the borrow the subtraction in column 1 involved $2 - 1 = 1$; in column 2 we had $0 - 0 = 0$; and finally in column 3 we had $1 - 1 = 0$.

What happens if the next column contains a 0 instead of a 1? You must then proceed to the next column until you find one with 1 from which you can borrow,

For example,

$$
\begin{array}{r}
1\ 0\ 0\ 0 \\
-\ 0\ 1\ 0\ 1 \\ \hline
\end{array}
$$

After the borrow from column 4,

$$
\begin{array}{r}
0\ 1\ 1\ (11) \\
-\ 0\ 1\ 0\ \ 1 \\ \hline
0\ 0\ 1\ \ 1 \\
\end{array}
$$

Notice that a borrow from column 4 yields an 8 (2^3). Changing column 3 to a 1 uses a 4, and column 2 uses a 2, thus leaving 2 of the 8 you borrowed to put in column 1.

A final example:

$$
\begin{array}{r}
0\ 1\ 1\ 0\ 0\ 0\ 1\ 0 \\
-\ 0\ 0\ 0\ 1\ 0\ 1\ 1\ 1 \\ \hline
\end{array}
$$

After the first borrow:

$$
\begin{array}{ccccccc}
0 & 1 & 1 & 0 & 0 & 0 & 0 & (11) \\
- & 0 & 0 & 0 & 1 & 0 & 1 & 1 & 1 \\
\hline
\end{array}
$$

After the second borrow (from column 6):

$$
\begin{array}{ccccccc}
0 & 1 & 0 & 1 & 1 & 1 & (11) & (11) \\
- & 0 & 0 & 0 & 1 & 0 & 1 & 1 & & 1 \\
\hline
0 & 1 & 0 & 0 & 1 & 0 & 1 & & 1
\end{array}
$$

TWO'S COMPLEMENT SUBTRACTION

The above example illustrates that the process of direct binary subtraction involves converting one of the numbers to its negative equivalent and then adding the two. The question then arises as to how a negative number is represented by the computer since the hardware has no provision for recognizing + and −.

The easiest way to visualize the rationale for how a computer is designed to recognize negative numbers is to consider what happens when we rotate a car's mileage indicator backward. As we pass through zero all the digits are set to their highest value, from which they decrease as we continue to rotate the register.

$$
\begin{array}{c}
0000004 \\
0000003 \\
0000002 \\
0000001 \\
0000000 \\
9999999 \\
9999998 \\
9999997
\end{array}
$$

Clearly, the number 9999999 corresponds to −1, 9999998 to −2, and so on. Thus, if we add

$$
\begin{array}{c}
0000004 \\
9999997 \\
\hline
1\ 0000001
\end{array}
$$

and ignore the carry, we have performed a subtraction of 4 − 3 = 1. The number 9999997 is described as the *10's complement of 3*. This example illustrates that subtraction in the decimal system can be performed by adding the 10's complement of the number to be subtracted to the other number. Therefore, if a system of complements were used for representing negative numbers, the minus sign could be omitted. Subtraction could be performed by complementing the appropriate number and adding.

It is necessary, however, to establish some sort of convention as to what is a negative number. For example, in the above illustration what does 4,000,000 represent? Is it 4,000,000 or −6,000,000? In order to have as many negative numbers as positive, one might say that 0 to 4,999,999 should be regarded as positive and 5,000,000 to 9,999,999 as negative. This is exactly what is done in the 16-bit word machines such as the Apple and IBM-PC. In this case the maximum value that can be represented by a 16-bit word is 65,535. Zero is taken as the center of the scale, and therefore the maximum positive value is taken as 32,767, and the maximum negative value as −32,767. One must recognize the conversions that can occur because of this convention. For example, Applesoft will return an error message if an integer addition produces an answer that is greater than 32,767. Also, when using Labsoft commands such as & ASUM with integers, the sum is represented as a negative number when its value exceeds 32,767. It will be necessary to add 65,536 to these numbers to convert them to their positive equivalent. (See line 177 of the BASIC calling program for the Boxcar Sampling routine in Chapter 11 for an example of this.)

For our binary subtraction problem, the computer does subtraction by a procedure called *two's complement* subtraction. The two's complement of a number is defined as the number that gives a value of unity when added to the original number.

The easiest way to find the two's complement is to add 1 to the one's complement of the number. The one's complement in turn is found by setting each digit of the number to the opposite value. For example,

```
1110  0111   Number
0001  1000   One's complement
         1   Add 1
_____
0001  1001   Two's complement
```

and

```
1010  0000   Number
0101  1111   One's complement
         1   Add one
_____
0110  0000   Two's complement
```

Subtraction is performed by taking the two's complement of one number and adding it to the other. For example, to subtract 01110000 (112 decimal) from 11111111 (255 decimal):

```
01110000   Number (112 decimal)
10001111   One's complement
       1   Add                                          1
_____
10010000   Two's complement
11111111   Add the other number (255 decimal)
_____
1 10001111   255-112=143
```

The answer does not include the *carry*. The carry is used to ascertain whether the subtraction resulted in a negative number or a positive number. Our example gives a positive number (carry = 1). Suppose we had reversed the order of subtraction.

```
11111111   Number (255)
00000000   One's complement
       1   Add 1
_____
00000001   Two's complement
01110000   Add 112
_____
01110001   Negative answer in two's
           complement form
10001110   One's complement of this number
       1   Add  1
_____
− 10001111   The final answer converted to its
             common form with a minus sign
             assigned because the original
             subtraction did not produce a
             carry.
```

Appendix H

Decimal to Hexadecimal Conversion Table

Decimal	Hex	Decimal	Hex
1	1	256	100
2	2	512	200
3	3	768	300
4	4	1024	400
5	5	1280	500
6	6	1536	600
7	7	1792	700
8	8	2048	800
9	9	2304	900
10	A	2560	A00
11	B	2816	B00
12	C	3072	C00
13	D	3328	D00
14	E	3584	E00
15	F	3840	F00
16	10	4096	1000
32	20	8192	2000
48	30	12288	3000
64	40	16384	4000
80	50	20480	5000
96	60	24576	6000
112	70	28672	7000
128	80	32768	8000
144	90	36864	9000
160	A0	40960	A000
176	B0	45056	B000
192	C0	49152	C000
208	D0	53248	D000
224	E0	57344	E000
240	F0	61440	F000

Appendix I

ASCII Character Codes

Character	ASCII Decimal Code	ASCII Hexadecimal Code
NULL	0	00
SOH	1	01
STX	2	02
ETX	3	03
ET	4	04
ENQ	5	05
ACK	6	06
BEL	7	07
BS	8	08
HT	9	09
LF	10	OA
VT	11	OB
FF	12	OC
CR	13	OD
SO	14	OE
SI	15	OF
DLE	16	10
DC1	17	11
DC2	18	12
DC3	19	13
DC4	20	14
NAK	21	15
SYN	22	16
ETB	23	17
CAN	24	18
EM	25	19
SUB	26	1A
ESCAPE	27	1B
FS	28	1C
GS	29	1D
RS	30	1E
US	31	1F
SPACE	32	20
!	33	21
"	34	22

Appendix I *(Continued)*

#	35	23
$	36	24
%	37	25
&	38	26
'	39	27
(	40	28
)	41	29
*	42	2A
+	43	2B
,	44	2C
−	45	2D
.	46	2E
/	47	2F
0	48	30
1	49	31
2	50	32
3	51	33
4	52	34
5	53	35
6	54	36
7	55	37
8	56	38
9	57	39
:	58	3A
;	59	3B
<	60	3C
=	61	3D
>	62	3E
?	63	3F
	64	40
A	65	41
B	66	42
C	67	43
D	68	44
E	69	45
F	70	46
G	71	47
H	72	48
I	73	49
J	74	4A
K	75	4B
L	76	4C
M	77	4D
N	78	4E
O	79	4F
P	80	50
Q	81	51
R	82	52

Appendix I   *(Continued)*

S	83	53
T	84	54
U	85	55
V	86	56
W	87	57
X	88	58
Y	89	59
Z	90	5A
[	91	5B
\	92	5C
]	93	5D
^	94	5E
—	95	5F
`	96	60
a	97	61
b	98	62
c	99	63
d	100	64
e	101	65
f	102	66
g	103	67
h	104	68
i	105	69
j	106	6A
k	107	6B
l	108	6C
m	109	6D
n	110	6E
o	111	6F
p	112	70
q	113	71
r	114	72
s	115	73
t	116	74
u	117	75
v	118	76
w	119	77
x	120	78
y	121	79
z	122	7A
{	123	7B
1	124	7C
}	125	7D
~	126	7E
DEL	127	7F

Appendix J

Glossary of Computer Terms

ACCURACY: The deviation or error by which an actual output varies from the expected or absolute value.

ADDRESS: The label or number identifying the memory location where a unit of information is stored.

ACCUMULATOR: A register in the CPU where data fetched from memory is stored. The CPU acts on data stored in its accumulator rather than directly on data stored in memory.

A/D (ADC): Analog-to-Digital converter. A device or circuit that outputs a binary number corresponding to an analog voltage level at that input.

ALU: Arithmetic Logic Unit. The part of the CPU where binary data is acted upon with mathematical operations. The accumulator is part of the ALU.

ASCII: American Standard Code for Information Interchange. A 7-bit code used to represent alphanumeric characters. It is used for sending information between a computer and a peripheral and from one computer to another. See Appendix I for ASCII character codes.

ASSEMBLER: A program that translates assembly language instructions into machine language instructions.

ASYNCHRONOUS: A communication method where data is sent when it is ready rather than waiting until the receiver signals that it is ready to receive (see HANDSHAKE).

BASIC: Beginner's All-purpose Symbolic Instruction Code. A high-level programming language designed at Dartmouth College as a learning tool. It includes simple English words such as RUN, STOP, GOTO, LIST, and so on. There are several versions of this language available. Most can be simply translated from one to the other.

BAUD: A unit of data transmission speed usually meaning bits per second: that is, 300 baud = 300 bits per second.

BINARY: Refers to the base 2 number system in which the only allowable digits are 0 and 1.

BCD: Binary Coded Decimal. The representation of a decimal number (0 through 9) by means of a 4-bit binary "nibble."

BIT:　Binary digit. The smallest unit of computer information, it is either a binary 0 or 1.

BUFFER:　A temporary storage area for data when transmitted from one area to another to compensate for a speed difference.

BUS:　Parallel lines used to transfer signals between devices or components. Computers are often described by their bus structure: for example, an S-100 bus computer.

BYTE:　A group of eight bits.

CLEAR:　To restore a device to a prescribed initial state, usually the zero state.

CLOCK:　The timing signal for a microprocessor. It can be defined as a real-time clock or as a run-time clock.

COMPILER:　A program that translates a high-level language, such as BASIC or FORTRAN into machine language.

CP/M:　Control Program for Microprocessors. It is an operating system for microcomputers that is widely used by a number of computer manufacturers.

CPU:　Central Processing Unit. The part of the computer containing the circuits that control and perform the execution of computer instructions. A microprocessor is described by a specific set of electronic logic that is equivalent to a CPU.

CRASH:　A hardware or software fault that causes the computer to cease operating, usually requiring a CLEAR or RESET operation.

D/A (DAC):　Digital-to-Analog Converter. A device or circuit to convert a digital value to an analog voltage level.

DATABASE:　A large amount of data stored in a well-organized manner. A database management system is a program that allows access to the information by using certain matrix options.

DEDICATED:　Refers to programs, procedures, specific I/O ports, hardware, and so on. Devoted to a single task or, at the most, a small number of tasks.

DISKETTE:　An off-line data storage medium consisting of a thin platter coated with magnetic material in which the digital data is stored for later retrieval. It may be single- or double-sided, single- or double-density, and soft- or hard-sectored (see page 8).

DMA:　Direct Memory Access provides a rapid way of moving data between I/0 ports and memory. It bypasses the usual "transfer through the accumulator register operation"and transfers data directly to a memory location. There is no impact on the program logic or microprocessor operation, except that these operations are slowed down by the number of clock periods "stolen" by the DMA logic. A hardware device called a DMA controller is required to manage the DMA process.

DOS:　Disk Operating System. The program used to control the transfer of information to and from a disk.

DOT-MATRIX PRINTER: A printer that forms characters from a two-dimensional array of dots. Increasing the number of dots in a given space produces more legible characters. Available with thermal head, impact, and ink jet types.

DRIVER: Describes both hardware and software. In hardware it is a circuit that, when activated, supplies enough energy to run a particular device, such as relay, solenoid, and so on. In software it refers to the software needed to complete the computer–device interface, so that computer instructions can operate the device. This software is often called a "device driver."

EIA: Electronic Industries Association. A standards organization specializing in the electrical and functional characteristics of interface equipment.

EPROM: Erasable Programmable Read-Only Memory. A PROM which can be erased by a user usually by exposing it to ultraviolet radiation.

FILE: A collection of data that is treated as a unit.

FIRMWARE: Software that is made a permanent part of the system by storing it in ROM.

FLOPPY DISK: (see Diskette) A small flexible disk carrying a magnetic medium in which digital data is stored for later retrieval and use. They normally come in 8" and 5¼" sizes. These disks are exposed to the environment and can be corrupted by magnetic fields, solvents, heat, grease, dust, dirt, and physical mutilation. They also have a useful life expectancy of 50 hours.

FORMATTED: Refers to floppy diskettes that have been prepared for recording data by recording the necessary track and sector "information" on the diskette required by the particular DOS with which the diskette is to be used.

FORTRAN: FORmula TRANslation. A widely used high-level programming language well suited to problems that can be expressed in terms of algebraic formulas. It is generally used in scientific applicatiions.

FULL DUPLEX: Two way communication, where both sides are transmitting and receiving at the same time.

F/V: A device which converts frequency to voltage.

GBYTE: Gigbyte or 1000 million bytes.

GPIB: General Purpose-Interface Bus. A bus over which a variety of peripherals may be connected to each other and the computer.

HALF-DUPLEX: One-way communication at a time. Both sides can send and retrieve data, but only one at a time.

HANDSHAKE: An interface procedure that is based on status/data signals that assure orderly data transfer, as opposed to asynchronous exchange.

HARD COPY: Output in a permanent form (paper or tape) as opposed to a temporary visual display like a CRT.

HARDWARE: The electrical, mechanical, and electromechanical equipment and parts associated with a computing system, as opposed to firmware (ROM) or software (programs).

HEXADECIMAL: Refers to a base 16 number using the characters 0 through 9 and the letters A through F to represent the values. Machine language programs are often written in hexadecimal notation.

HPIB: Hewlett-Packard Interface Bus. Hewlett-Packard's general-purpose interface bus conforming to IEEE-488 specification.

Hz—Hertz: Relates to number of data points per second that is acquired—that is 5 Hz = 5 data points per second. Not to be confused with line-voltage cycle, which is 60 Hz in the United States.

IEEE-488:   A standard for a general-purpose interface bus, created by the Institute of Electrical and Electronics Engineers. Defines a parallel format for the interface that accommodates a variety of signal types.

INITIALIZE: To prepare a floppy disk for storing data.

INTERFACE: The means by which two systems or a system and a peripheral are connected and interact with each other.

INTERPRETER: A program that converts each instructiion in a high-level language program into machine code as it runs. Programs that use interpreters run much slower than an assembled (compiled) program.

I/O: Input/Output port.

K: Kilobyte = 1024 bytes.

KEYBOARD: The set of keys found on a terminal for the entering of characters into the computer. It is the interface between operator and computer.

LANGUAGE: A defined set of characters that are used to form symbols, words, commands, and so on. It also contains the rules for combining these characters into meaningful communicatiions. High-level languages are those that allow the user to write the program by using familiar English-like terms (see BASIC, FORTRAN, etc.). Low-level languages are closer to the computer's machine language.

LSI: Large-Scale Integration. The combining of about 1000 to 10,000 circuits on a single chip. Typical examples of LSI circuits are memory chips, microprocessors, calculator and watch chips.

LETTER QUALITY PRINTER: The printer used to produce final copies of documents. It produces typing comparable to quality typewriters.

L.I.M.S.:   Laboratory Information Management System. A databased multi-matrix system designed to keep track of sample status and their analysis for storage and collation.

MACHINE LANGUAGE: Instructions that are written in binary form that a computer can execute directly. Also called object code and object language.

MAGNETIC TAPE: A magnetic storage media for permanent storage of computer data on reels of tape. Sometimes referred to as magtape.

MASS STORAGE: A device like a disk or magtape that can store large amounts of data readily accessible to the central processing unit.

M or Mbyte: Megabyte or 1,000,000 bytes.

MICROCOMPUTER: A computer that is physically very small in size with a microprocessor as its CPU.

MICROPROCESSOR: The brain of a microcomputer on a single integrated circuit chip (see CPU).

MINICOMPUTER: A computer smaller in size than a mainframe computer but larger in size than a micro. Its CPU is not integrated on one chip and thus can take on many forms, depending on the computer vendor's design philosophy.

MODEM: MOdulator/DEModulator. A device that transforms digital signals into audio tones for transmission over telephone lines and does the reverse for reception.

MONITOR, CRT: A television-like unit for display of computer input and output text and graphics. Usually refers specifically to devices designed for computer display.

MONITOR PROGRAM: A simple control program (written in machine language) residing in ROM which serves as a link between a high-level language, like BASIC, and the various low-level machine functions such as plotting a line, printing a character etc.

MOTHERBOARD: In a multiboard system, the board that contains the bus lines and edge connectors to accommodate the other boards in the system.

NETWORK: A group of computers that are connected to each other by communications lines to share information and resources.

NIBBLE: One half of a byte (usually four bits).

OPERATING SYSTEM: A collection of computer programs that controls the overall operation of a computer and performs such tasks as assigning places in memory to programs and data, process interrupts, scheduling jobs, and controlling the overall I/O of the system.

PARALLEL TRANSMISSION: Sending all data bits simultaneously; one wire is needed for each bit. It requires a parallel interface (see serial).

PARITY: A one-extra-bit code used to detect recording or transmission errors by making the total number of "1" bits in a unit of data, including the parity bit itself, odd or even.

PEAK THRESHOLD: The microvolt set point at which a peak begins and ends.

PERIPHERAL: A device external to the CPU and main memory—that is, printer, modem, terminals—but connected to it with appropriate electrical connections.

PIXELS: Picture Elements. Definable locations on a display screen that are used to form images on the screen. For graphic displays, screens with more pixels generally provide higher resolution.

PORT: A signal input or output point on a computer. A place on the exterior of the computer where peripheral devices are connected.

PROGRAM: A list of instructions that a computer follows to perform a task.

PROM: Programmable Read-Only Memory. A semiconductor memory chip whose contents cannot be changed by the computer after it has been programmed.

PROTOCOL: A formal definition that describes how data is to be exchanged.

RAM: Random Access Memory. A semiconductor memory chip that can both be read and changed during computer operation. If power to the RAM is cut off, all data stored in the device will be lost.

READ: To obtain information from a memory location or device.

REMOTE: A peripheral device usually located away from the CPU, that is, printer.

RESOLUTION: The smallest detectable increment of measurement. Resolution is usually limited by the number of bits used to quantize the input signal; that is, a 12-bit A/D can resolve to one part in 4096.

REVERSE VIDEO: A feature on a display unit that produces the opposite combination of characters and background from that usually employed.

ROM: Read-Only Memory. A semiconductor memory chip containing fixed data. The computer can read the data but cannot change it in any way.

RS-232C: A serial interface standard developed originally for data transmission over telephone lines. It has also been adopted by many manufacturers of laboratory equipment, printers, and other peripherals as a simple, reliable interface.

SERIAL TRANSMISSION: Sending one bit at a time on a single transmission line.

SOFTWARE: Generally, programs loaded into a computer from external devices; it can include operating systems and documentation.

SOURCE CODE: A nonexecutable program written in a high-level language. A compiler or assembler must translate the source code into object code (machine language) that the the computer can understand.

SYNCHRONOUS: Data transmission in which there is a constant time interval between successive bits, characters, or events.

TAPE: A recording media for data or computer programs. Tape can be in permanent form, such as perforated paper tape. Generally, tape is used as a mass-storage medium, in magnetic form, and has a far higher storage capacity than disk storage, but it takes much longer to write or recover data from tape than from a disk.

TERMINAL: An I/O device is used to enter data into a computer and record the output. Terminals are divided into two categories: hard copy (printers) and soft copy (CRT).

TRANSDUCER: A device that converts something measurable into another form. Also referred to as a sensor; e.g., a flow transducer may send out an electrical signal related to the flow.

TRANSMITTER: A device that translates the low-level output of a sensor to a higher-level signal suitable for transmission to a site for further processing.

V/F: Voltage to Frequency. A device or circuit that converts a voltage to a frequency.

WINCHESTER DRIVE: Large mass-storage device utilizing a nonremovable hard disk.

WORD: Number of bits treated as a single unit by the CPU. In an 8-bit machine, the word length is 8 bits.

WRITE: To put information into a storage location or device.

Index